Introduction to Organisational Behaviour

Edited by Michael Butler and Ed Rose

The Chartered Institute of Personnel and Development is
the leading publisher of books and reports for personnel and
training professionals, students, and all those concerned
with the effective management and development of people
at work. For details of all our titles, please contact the
publishing department:

tel: 020 8612 6204

e-mail: publish@cipd.co.uk

The catalogue of all CIPD titles can be viewed on the CIPD
website:

www.cipd.co.uk/bookstore

Introduction
to Organisational Behaviour

Edited by Michael Butler and Ed Rose

Chartered Institute of Personnel and Development

Published by the Chartered Institute of Personnel and Development,

151, The Broadway, London, SW19 1JQ

© Chartered Institute of Personnel and Development, 2011

Typeset by and printed by Charlesworth

British Library Cataloguing in Publication Data

A catalogue of this publication is available from the British Library

ISBN 978 1 84398 247 0

The views expressed in this publication are the authors' own and may not necessarily reflect those of the CIPD.

The CIPD has made every effort to trace and acknowledge copyright holders. If any source has been overlooked, CIPD Enterprises would be pleased to redress this in future editions.

Chartered Institute of Personnel and Development, CIPD House,

151, The Broadway, London, SW19 1JQ

Tel: 020 8612 6200

Email: cipd@cipd.co.uk

Website: www.cipd.co.uk

Incorporated by Royal Charter. Registered Charity No. 1079797

Dedication

"To Gabi"

Michael Butler

Brief contents

Detailed contents

List of figures and tables

Author biographies

Dr Michael Butler is a Senior Lecturer in Management, Aston Business School, UK. He researches change management, adapting promising management practices to enhance performance, contributing to receptivity for change, knowledge exchange and project-based organisations. The research wins funding from national competitions (eg the ESRC for The TRANSFORMATION Project which has project partners from all sectors and is being extended into Twinings and Saudi Aramco, see www.thetransformationproject.co.uk). His research and teaching has won awards and nominations for prizes. He features in international media (for instance, the BBC). He consults on organisation development and policy processes (eg General Motors and the Cabinet Office) and is a Non Executive Director of Beyond Engagement. He is on the Editorial Board of the *Asia-Pacific Journal of Business Administration*. His work has appeared or is forthcoming in 27 peer reviewed articles (including *Organization Science*). He has published three books: *Language, Power and Identity* (Hodder and Stoughton, 1999, selling 10,000 copies), *The Social Cognitive Neuroscience of Organizations* (Blackwell, 2007) and *Introduction to Organisational Behaviour* (CIPD, 2011). He received his Ph.D. from Warwick Business School (UK) in 2000.

Dr Ed Rose is a Senior Lecturer at Liverpool John Moores University Business School and teaches both organisational behaviour and employment relations on a wide variety of undergraduate and postgraduate courses. His research interests range from Nuffield-Foundation-funded research into the effects of pay upon productivity within the automotive industry to more recent research examining the links between satisfaction, alienation, commitment and control in a variety of call centres. The latter research has yielded a number of publications in highly rated journals such as the *International Journal of Human Resource Management*. Ed's other publications include a very successful text *Employment Relations*, published by Pearson, which is now in its third edition. His other roles have included membership of the editorial board of the journal *Employee Relations* and various consultancy assignments for organisations in both the private and public sectors.

Dr Emma Jeanes works at the University of Exeter Business School, and is a visiting academic at Queensland University of Technology, Australia, and Lund University, Sweden. Emma was previously Head of Section and Head of Taught Programmes at Exeter. She is Associate Editor for *Gender Work and Organization* and co-editor of a companion handbook, and was series editor for *Gender and Organization Theory* for Ashgate Publishing. She publishes in the field of organisation theory and organisation behaviour, and draws on political theory and philosophy to inform her research. Emma's research has been supported by the ESRC, the Housing Corporation, Defra and the British Academy.

Dr Steven A. Woods is Director for Master's courses in Work and Organisational Psychology at Aston Business School, and a chartered occupational psychologist. He received his PhD in 2004 from the University of Surrey. He is known for his research on personality trait assessment, and recruitment and selection, which he publishes in scientific and professional journals, scholarly books, and at national and international conferences. Steve has taught work and organisational psychology to professionals, graduates and students in the UK and internationally, and presents regularly at universities in the UK on his research, and on contemporary challenges and issues in organisational assessment. Steve has also worked extensively as a consultant psychologist with organisational clients in selection and development, and is co-founder of Aston Business Assessments Ltd, a spin-out company of Aston University.

Claire Hardy is an Applied Psychology Doctoral Researcher at the University of Nottingham and Teaching Fellow in Distance Learning with Technologies at the University of Leicester. Claire was awarded a Psychology BSc (Hons) from the University of York in 2004 and an MSc in Occupational Psychology from the Institute of Work, Health, and Organisations, University of Nottingham, in 2005. Claire then began her doctoral research within the field of expatriation under the supervision of Dr Steve Woods. Claire and Steve have worked together on a number of research projects and publications within the areas of selection and assessment.

Dr Jenna Ward is a Lecturer in Organisation Studies at the Bristol Business and Law School at the University of the West of England. Her research focuses on emotion management and narrative storytelling with a particular interest in the work of cabin crew and front-line public sector workers.

Dr Robert McMurray is Senior Lecturer in Management at the Durham University Business School, England. His research focuses on processual accounts of change, professional identity, gender, emotions, culture and health care. His work has been published in journals including *Organization*, *Human Relations*, *Culture and Organization*, and *Public Administration*.

Tricia Harrison is Programme Leader for MA International HRM and for MA Change Management (with Anglesey County Council) at Liverpool John Moores University, and has specific Organisational Behaviour module responsibilities. Her research areas are the development of professional practice, questioning in deep learning and action learning. Previously she worked at Webster University, Geneva, Kingston University and Bournemouth University as Senior Lecturer. She also has extensive HR consultancy experience and previous employment with Siemens.

Dr Crystal Ling Zhang is Senior Lecturer in Human Resource Management and Organisational Behaviour at Leeds Business School, Leeds Metropolitan University. She received her PhD and Master's in HRM/OB from the University of Leeds. Her current research interests focus on cognitive style, processes of acculturation for expatriates, ethnic minority groups' career development and internationalisation in the Higher Education sector. She acted as Chair of the thematic session on the topic of Acculturation at the 18th Congress of IACCP in Athens. She is the contributor of three chapters in Gold, J. *et al.* (eds) (2010) *Human Resource Development: Theory and practice* (Palgrave Macmillan).

Niki Kyriakidou is a Senior Lecturer in HRM/OB at Leeds Metropolitan University. She received her PhD and Master's in HRM from the University of Leeds, and her Bachelor degree in Political Science and Public Administration from Athens University. Current research work focuses on graduate employment and the skill needs of the knowledge-based economies of the Northern European countries. Her work has been published in international conferences, journals and books. Niki is a member of many professional and research associations both in the UK and in Europe. She is also an international reviewer of many journals and conferences.

Professor Michael West is Dean at Aston Business School. He is a Fellow of the British Psychological Society, the American Psychological Association (APA), the APA Society for Industrial/Organizational Psychology, the Higher Education Academy, the International Association of Applied Psychologists, and a Chartered Fellow of the CIPD. He is a member of the Board of the European Foundation for Management Development and an Academician of the Academy of Social Sciences. His areas of research interest are team and organisational innovation and effectiveness, particularly in relation to the organisation of health services. He lectures widely both nationally and internationally.

Dr Joanne Richardson is currently a Research Fellow in the Work and Organisational Psychology Group at Aston University. Her principal research interest is the nature and workings of teams in organisations. With a background in social and organisational psychology, Joanne recently completed her PhD on the development and validation of the real team scale. In relation to this, she is currently conducting research into the functioning of multi-professional mental healthcare teams in the National Health Service. She is also particularly interested in the antecedents of team innovation and the effectiveness of virtual teamworking.

Dr Alf Crossman is a Senior Lecturer in Industrial Relations and HRM at the University of Surrey. Alf is also a member of faculty at the TiasNimbas Business School in Utrecht and holds visiting appointments at the Moscow International Higher Business School (MIRBIS) and Linköping University in Sweden. Alf has a particular interest in industrial conflict/action and is a frequent contributor to national and regional television and radio in relation to developments in this area of industrial relations.

Dr Markus C. Hasel is Assistant Professor for Leadership and Organisational Behaviour at EMLyon Business School in France. He teaches MSc- and MBA-level students in leadership and OB, and provides consultancy, including training on communication, for organisations within and outside France. He is also a partner in HaNi Consulting, a consultancy firm providing consultancy for companies working across the European-African borders.

Dr Yves R. F. Guillaume is a lecturer in Organisational Behaviour at Aston Business School. His current research interests are in leadership and diversity management. His research has been published in outlets including *Human Relations*, the *Journal of Occupational and Organizational Psychology*, and the *Journal of Cross-Cultural Psychology*. In addition to his academic work, he has experience of consulting, training and coaching managers in leadership and diversity management in both profit and non-profit organisations.

Nils-Torge Telle received his Master's degree from Aston Business School in Organisational Psychology and Business. Currently, he is a doctoral student at the Institute of Experimental Industrial Psychology of Leuphana University of Lüneburg in Germany. His research interests include behavioural decision-making, emotional intelligence, empathy, and the theory of mind, with respective implications for social interaction in business-related contexts.

Keith Bezant-Niblett is Director of Executive Education, Michigan State University, USA. He is also Chairman of the Board of a fast-growing US National Home-Owners' Association services company, and a senior board member of a New-York-based international manufacturing and marketing company. Keith worked in the media industry for 20 years, holding senior executive and directorship positions in seven countries. He was Associate Vice-President at the Thunderbird School of Global Management, Executive Education Director at Cranfield University School of Management, and a Managing Consultant at P.A. Consulting.

Karen Caine has varied commercial experience, from being a senior manager in Capgemini (a major multinational business and IT consulting company) to working in the public sector, to founding her own small company. She is also a sessional Lecturer at Aston Business School, teaching the Creative Decisions for Effective Change MBA module.

Maureen Royce is Principal Lecturer in Human Resource Management at Liverpool John Moores University. Maureen leads a range of HR programmes which are CIPD-accredited in the UK and international market. Maureen has extensive private sector experience as an HR practitioner and specialises in the development of recruitment, selection, performance and reward strategy. Her current research and consultancy interests are in equality and diversity, including the responses of organisational structures to a more diverse workforce, the role of Higher Education in social inclusion and the culture of managing people in the social enterprise sector. Maureen is involved in the voluntary sector as a Trustee with HR responsibility and is working with the British Red Cross in building sustainability into inclusive training.

Scott A. Hurrell is a lecturer in Work and Employment Studies in the Stirling Institute for Socio-Management, University of Stirling. Scott teaches a number of topics related to work and employment, from a critical perspective, including HRM, Employment Relations and wider organisational and labour market issues. Scott's research interests include contemporary changes to the labour market, skills and work organisation, recruitment and selection and women's experience of work, especially within service and non-profit sectors. Scott is currently Stirling Management School's undergraduate Programme Director for HRM.

Dr Vincenza Priola is a Lecturer in Organisation Studies at Aston University. Her research interests and publications are in the general field of management processes and practices, with a particular focus on gendered processes in organisations. She is interested in managerial identities and how these are constructed within organisations, therefore looking at the role of organisational culture and HRM. She has also done research into Higher Education and teamwork. Her book (co-edited with Matthew Brannan and Elisabeth Parsons) *Branded Lives: The production and consumption of identity at work*, will be published in 2011 by Edward Elgar.

Dr Michel Ehrenhard is an Assistant Professor in Strategy and Entrepreneurship at the School of Management and Governance, University of Twente. His research focuses on the management of strategic change – in particular the role of decision-making and leadership – and is mostly conducted in professional service settings, both in the public and private sector. In relation to technology and work organisation he has published papers on enterprise systems implementation and cross-cultural aspects of enterprise portals. His PhD thesis was awarded the 'best dissertation' award from the Public and Non-profit Divison of the Academy of Management.

Tanya Bondarouk is Associate Professor of Human Resource Management at the University of Twente. Since 2002 she has been busy with the emerging research area of Electronic HRM. Her main publications concern an integration of human resource management and social aspects of Information Technology implementations. Her research covers both private and public sectors and deals with a variety of areas such as the implementation of e-HRM, the management of HR-IT change, HRM contribution to IT projects, the role of line managers in e-HRM, and the implementation of HR shared service centres. She has conducted research projects with the Dutch Ministry of Interior and National Relations, the Dow Chemical Company, Ford, IBM, and Shell. Among her current research projects are the implementation of HR shared service centres at the Dutch Ministry of Defence and the Belgian Federal Public Health Service. Since 2006 she has been involved in organising European academic workshops on e-HRM, and international workshops on HRIS.

Dr Huub Ruel is Assistant Professor International (HR) Management at the University of Twente. He has also held positions at the Utrecht School of Governance, Utrecht University, Kuwait-Maastricht Business School and the Olayan S. School of Business, American University of Beirut. Huub has written a large number of national and international journal articles and books. His research is focused around web-based HRM/ e-HRM, (e-)HRM in an international context, HRM in the Middle East, networked HRM and HRM in global companies and commercial diplomacy.

Dr Rory Donnelly is a Lecturer in Human Resource Management and Organisational Behaviour and Director of the HRM MSc programme at Birmingham Business School in the UK. He is a chartered member of the CIPD and his research interests include the management of the employment relationship and careers and flexibility in knowledge-intensive firms.

Praise for the book

'This is the outstanding organisation behaviour textbook of the decade. It neatly combines information and new thinking with a subtle and sensitive approach to teaching – a must buy.'
Andrew Kakabadse, Professor of International Management Development, Cranfield School of Management

'Organisational behaviour has for too long been understood in narrow terms. This book changes the mould. It links scholarly understanding to the real world of using organisational skills and communication in a global environment.'
Brian Head, University of Queensland, Australia

'This text will definitely be on my bookshelf and I commend it to you. The innovative and timely focus on employability applied to the UK and elsewhere, supported by its rich online resources, will make a major contribution to your learning and teaching, specifically your development as leaders and managers, whatever your background, because of its practical but rigorous approach.'
Chris Alexander CMgr MCMI, ANPR Manager, Warwickshire Police

'At last, a comprehensive coverage of organisational behaviour that will help students apply theory to practice. It is accessible and interesting to read, and also evaluates in an ongoing manner – making it easier to encourage students to do the same.'
Stephanie J. Morgan, Kingston Business School

'This book brings together three things that are important for those seeking to make a difference in organisations, public or private: rigorous thinking, practical skills and international insight. Each of these is important in its own right. The power of this book is that they are woven together to excellent effect.'
Quintin Heath, Human Resources Director, British Sugar Group

'The key message of this book is crystal clear: it is vital to get highly educated students with employability skills into the international marketplace. Globalisation is offering unlimited opportunities for young talents with the right skills and education. "The world is my oyster" – and this book is providing the ideal practical tools for students to open this oyster and find the pearl!'
Jan Urlings, Secretary General, West Midlands European Centre

Foreword

Employability is not just a 'buzz word' for today but a continuing and future reality for us all. Students of any age entering or re-entering the workforce in the twenty-first century are likely to find themselves with a series of careers in the future, rather than the past idea of a job for life. A further reality is that we are increasingly working in a multicultural and international workplace, where all of us must seek to become more globally aware and competent. 'Preparing learners to work effectively across cultures in a context of global employability is something that cannot be ignored' (Shiel 2008), and the challenge of global citizenship is our willingness to be open-minded and develop some understanding of and empathy with the beliefs, values, attitudes and languages of others.

A key to understanding organisational behaviour is understanding those same beliefs, values and attitudes of the individuals that make up that organisation, whatever their role. Having worked at all levels in a complex multicultural organisation (the NHS) for many years, I know the opportunities for unintentionally putting your foot in it are many! But a willingness to be open to others, to learn and to consider issues one person at a time makes a big difference because it is those in the front line who actually deliver the organisation's strategy and purpose day by day.

This book is both a textbook and a gateway to a range of resources for both teachers and students. The blending of text, activities and online resources offers a comprehensive and attractive approach to developing an understanding of organisational behaviour. The chapters follow a logical progression which supports Biggs' (1999) constructive alignment ideas of designing a curriculum with learning activities and assessments through which students can construct meaning from what they do to learn aligned with the intended learning outcomes. The practical focus of each chapter and the associated activities and case studies provide a solid basis for students to develop a sound undrstanding of this topic.

Richard Atfield, Assistant Director,
Higher Education Subject Centre for Business, Management, Accountancy and
Finance www.heacademy.ac.uk/business

Biggs, J. (1999) *Teaching for Quality Learning at University*. Buckingham: Open University Press.

Shiel, C. (2008) 'Introduction', in Atfield, R. and Kemp, P. (eds) (2008) *Enhancing the International Learning Experience in Business and Management, Hospitality, Leisure, Sport, Tourism*. Oxford: Threshold Press.

Acknowledgements

Writing textbooks is a very labour-intensive endeavour and requires the participation of all those involved. The editors would like to thank all the chapter authors for their unswerving commitment to the project. Thanks are also due to the numerous practitioners who gave up their time to be interviewed. The editors would also like to thank the technicians and AV specialists at both Aston and Liverpool John Moores Universities for providing the AV facilities and ensuring that the practitioner interviews were dealt with in a sensitive and professional manner. Last, but not least, the editors are deeply indebted to the CIPD staff for advice and encouragement. Special thanks go to Ruth Anderson for her unwavering enthusiasm for the project, and to her successor, Kirsty Smy.

This is the first truly integrated print and electronic learning package for introductory OB modules. The following walk-throughs demonstrate how the textbook and the online resources can be used together to provide a more creative, interactive and visual learning and teaching experience.

Walk-through of textbook features

CHAPTER-OPENING FEATURES

Contents

CHAPTER CONTENTS

The chapter contents lists outline the key topics covered and the key learning features within each chapter and are designed to help you navigate the book. Skip straight to the information or feature you need or read the chapter from start to finish.

Key Learning Outcomes

By the end of this chapter you should be able to:

- describe commonsense views of personality, and understand how they differ from scientific theories
- describe and understand theories of personality:
  - Psychodynamic
  - Behaviourist
  - Social cognitive
  - Trait
- understand the importance of trait theory for organisational behaviour
- describe the Big Five model of personality, and understand its importance in organisational behaviour
- discern how important work outcomes are related to personality traits
- understand how personality is related to other kinds of individual difference attributes.

KEY LEARNING OUTCOMES

At the beginning of each chapter, a set of key learning outcomes summarises what you can expect to learn from the chapter and will help you to track your progress.

PRACTITIONER INSIGHT

E.ON UK

E.ON UK is one of the leading energy suppliers in the UK, supplying around 8 million gas and electricity customers, including domestic and corporate customers. E.ON UK is part of the larger E.ON group, of which the headquarters is in Germany. E.ON is the world's largest investor-owned power and gas company. E.ON UK stemmed from the privatisation of the UK energy industry in February of 1988, and strives to meet the energy challenge trilemma – energy efficiency, energy security, and climate. We speak to **Fran Pestana, Learning and Development Business Partner**, about a learning development intervention that was developed at the company to enable middle managers to increase their level of competence.

E.ON employs over 80,000 employees worldwide and approximately 17,000 of these are in the UK. These employees work under E.ON's functional structure that comprises Energy generation, Distribution, and Retail. The Retail division is responsible for E.ON UK's marketing, sales and customer service strategy and operations. Following the arrival of a new Customer Service Director, a new management methodology was developed the new management methodology, the Customer Service Director worked with the HR team to define areas of behavioural competence required to apply the management method effectively.

Assessment centres were used to determine current levels of competence in the middle managment populaion. The results of the assessment centres highlighted the need for middle managers to develop their self-awareness, leadership, ability to manage performance, hold difficult conversations, deal with conflict, lead change, and work more effectively in teams. The Learning and Development Team were brought in to consult further and create a learning and development intervention to address these needs. They considered personality to be a key issue to focus on.

How could you apply knowledge of personality to build self-awareness, leadership and team development for this management population?

What techniques could be used to integrate personality into strategies for developing middle managerial competence?

PRACTITIONER INSIGHT

Each chapter opens with a practitioner insight box. These contain descriptions of real-life organisational challenges faced by practitioners from a variety of settings. Consider the challenges as you work through each chapter and then have a go at solving the problems presented.

Introduction

Think for a moment about your perception of an ideal work colleague – or perhaps an ideal employee working in administration, sales, or customer service. Describe them. Write down your description on a scrap of paper, keeping it to about five or six sentences. Do it now, perhaps while getting a tea or coffee. Then read on.

Look at the description you've written, and highlight all those aspects that you think refer to aspects of individual **personality**. Our bet is that most of them do. If you have used words like 'organised', 'courteous', 'friendly', 'talkative', 'reliable', 'dependable', 'calm under pressure', 'flexible', 'creative', 'positive', 'sociable', 'confident' and 'understanding', then you have presumed that personality attributes are important determinants of people's behaviour, and of effectiveness at work. And the really important thing is: you are correct. Personality is one of the most crucial aspects of **individual differences** that determines how people respond to different situations at work, how they typically interact and behave with other people, and in respect of their work tasks. How do we know this? Because over the past 100 years or so, psychologists – and in particular, work and organisational psychologists – have accumulated a vast array of theory, knowledge, and evidence that personality matters at work. This chapter is a journey through that knowledge, and its applied implications for organisational behaviour.

INTRODUCTION

Concise introductions will set each chapter firmly in the context of OB and the rest of the book, engaging you with the subject matter and helping you to make connections.

IN-CHAPTER FEATURES

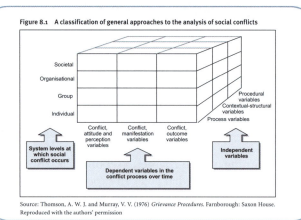

Figure 8.1   A classification of general approaches to the analysis of social conflicts

Source: Thomson, A. W. J. and Murray, V. V. (1976) *Grievance Procedures.* Farnborough: Saxon House. Reproduced with the authors' permission

TABLES AND FIGURES

Where possible, ideas are illustrated by tables and figures to appeal to all learning styles.

Taking your learning further: The nature and nurture of personality

Do you perceive your parents' personality traits in your own behaviour? It's probably reasonable if you do. The genes we inherit influence not only our physical appearance but are also proposed to play a key role in the development of our mental characteristics too. For example, as well as sharing physical similarities in appearance, family members typically share common elements of their personality. Psychological experiments involving monozygotic (identical) twins have also revealed that such family similarities are stronger between these kinds of siblings that share their genetic make-up. In fact, on average, around 40% of population variation on the Big Five personality dimensions is attributable to inherited genetic factors (Bouchard, 1994).

The flip side of this finding is, of course, that we are able to dismiss the

values that are acceptable within a society or sub-set of society. These cultural factors provide individuals with the necessary information about how to behave appropriately within a certain society. This is important because cultural rules vary considerable between cultures. For example, in Western societies value is placed on individualism and achieving personal success. For Eastern societies, however, such values are frowned upon and instead a more collectivist culture is present, which emphasises a more cohesive and team-driven success approach. As a result, the personalities of individuals from each category of culture reflect the goals that culture has. For individualistic cultures, a 'need to achieve' personality disposition is common (McClelland, 1967), whereas for collectivist cultures, being a 'good team player' is more evident in personalities (Hofstede, 1980).

TAKING YOUR LEARNING FURTHER

These boxes signpost seminal journal articles and books that have defined the subject. Read these to broaden your understanding of the topics covered in each chapter.

Applying theory to practice: Personality across cultures

Are personality traits the same the world over? It really depends on your perspective. One philosophy is that personality traits are descriptive representations of patterns or regularities in behaviour, which develop in part because of the influences of tradition, custom and language. There is plenty of evidence that different personality traits are more or less important in different cultures, or are completely culture-specific (eg Saucier, Hampson and Goldberg, 2000).

An alternative perspective suggests that the Big Five is a universal for humans (McCrae and Costa, 1997), suggesting that the five dimensions reflect some underlying biological system. In this perspective, culture plays a part in determining average levels of

trait behaviour in different countries (eg people from the USA and other Western countries typically have higher levels of assertiveness than those from, for example, East Asia).

Regardless of which perspective is adopted, there are obvious implications for cross-cultural working. If we are used to understanding people's traits in our own culture, we are inevitably likely to misperceive or completely ignore aspects of personality that are salient in other cultures. We might also fall into the trap of relying on our own value system, in which certain traits are valued in our own country but might be considered socially undesirable in another. These points are important to bear in mind when interacting with people from different cultures.

APPLYING THEORY TO PRACTICE

This feature links theory with up-to-date examples of company practice, helping you to place theory within a real-world context and understand the practical implications.

BEST PRACTICE

Jan's early career in sales had been difficult. Slightly shy, hesitant, and very thoughtful, she had struggled to compete in a sector dominated by men, many of whom were not afraid to be aggressive in their dealings with clients and each other. Warned by her team leader that she would have to look for work elsewhere unless she shaped up, Jan re-evaluated her approach to sales and working.

Seven years on, and Jan had engineered a meteoric rise to the position of sales director. She had a reputation for being smarter, harder-working and more aggressive than just about anyone else in the organisation. She made decisions quickly, eschewed consultation, never admitted mistakes and directed others with absolute authority. These were all learned characteristics that had served her well as she climbed the corporate ladder.

As part of the senior management team she quickly became aware that this model of working was not always as successful as it had been. Aggression was often ignored or attributed to emotional instability by senior colleges, while her failure to consult on new plans was frequently met with a denial of interdepartmental collaboration. On reflection, Jan was aware that the model of working she had developed needed to change. This did not mean that strong decisions and robust assertion were to be abandoned – rather, they were to be tempered according to context. Tailoring her performances for particular audiences was soon found to be an effective method of managing how she was perceived in different contexts, thus increasing the likelihood that her goals met with success.

BEST PRACTICE

An example of best practice is included in each chapter to inform and inspire you.

WORST PRACTICE

The worst practice in this area is a general one, and refers to the behaviour of some consultants and test companies. There are some really poor examples of tests available for purchase, and you should always be sceptical about sales claims that one new test is vastly better than all the others. Always insist on seeing the evidence. The very worst practice, though, is the positioning of 'type' instruments (usually purporting to be based on the theories of Carl Jung) as scientific. The difference between trait and type is simple. In a trait perspective we can identify different degrees of extraversion (eg highly extraverted, a little

extraverted, and so on). In a type model, a person is either extraverted or introverted, and there is no room for determining *how* extraverted or introverted they are. For a variety of reasons (see Woods and West, 2010, Chapter 3 for a brief review of these) personality type theory is flawed, unscientific, incomplete, and provides only limited information about individual differences. In your practice, accept that personality is complex – that's why it's so interesting – and that personality type theories, and assessments of types, simply fail to capture its intricacies.

WORST PRACTICE

An example of worst practice is included in each chapter to act as a warning.

END-OF-CHAPTER FEATURES

Conclusion

Personality is a major determinant of important aspects of organisational behaviour. Indeed, an understanding of people management and organisational behaviour is incomplete without a grasp of the influences of personality.

When we discuss personality, we are really talking about people's characteristic patterns of behaviour, thought and emotion, alongside the internal mechanisms and processes that give rise to those patterns. There are numerous theories that explain how best to conceptualise and model personality, and there are important organisational implications of behaviourist and social cognitive theories. However, by far the most influential in organisational behaviour is trait theory, consolidated in recent research by the emergence of the Big Five model of personality, consisting of extraversion, agreeableness, conscientiousness, emotional stability, and openness.

CONCLUSION

At the end of each chapter, conclusions bring together the main themes and arguments discussed.

End notes

1 See also Chapter 6.

2 See also Chapter 6.

3 See also Chapter 10.

4 See also Chapters 5 and 17.

5 See also Chapter 5.

6 See also Chapter 6.

END NOTES

Some topics are covered in more than one chapter. Where a heading is marked with a number, an end note at the end of the chapter will direct you to other chapters covering that topic.

REVIEW AND DISCUSSION QUESTIONS

REVIEW QUESTIONS

1 Describe three different personality theories. What does each tell us about personality?

2 In what ways do personality traits relate to important work and organisational behaviour outcomes?

3 What are the Big Five personality dimensions? What are the kinds of traits and characteristics associated with each?

4 How does personality relate to cognitive ability/intelligence?

5 Identify two common applications of personality assessment in organisations.

DISCUSSION QUESTIONS

1 How would knowledge of theory and research on personality at work help a manager to manage his or her team?

2 How have you experienced the influence of personality in groupwork or teamwork?

3 Rate yourself on the short measure of personality in the box entitled *Rate yourself on the Big Five traits*. Discuss with others the extent to which they agree with your ratings.

4 How could information about personality traits be used to help manage individual job performance in organisations?

5 What traits do you think are important for specific kinds of jobs? (Choose one – eg university lecturer – and discuss.)

REVIEW QUESTIONS

Review questions are designed to test your understanding of the chapter's key themes.

DISCUSSION QUESTIONS

Discussion questions should be approached as a group and will help develop your analytical, debating and team-working skills.

FURTHER READING

Woods, S. A. and West, M. A. (2010) *The Psychology of Work and Organizations*. London: CENGAGE. Chapter 3 on 'Individual differences at work' is key reading, but there is lots of discussion of personality at work and in HRM in other chapters too. Practical and accessible throughout.

Furnham, A. (2008) *Personality and Intelligence at Work*. Sussex: Routledge. A book that specifically focuses on these two aspects of individual differences at work.

Barrick, M. R., Mount, M. K. and Judge, T. A. (2001) 'Personality and performance at the beginning of the new millennium: what do we know and where do we go next?', *International Journal of Selection and Assessment, Vol.9*: 9–30. A technical review of the evidence that personality predicts job performance, accumulated over a 10-year period.

John, O. P., Robins, R. W. and Pervin, L. A. (eds) (2008) *Handbook of Personality: Theory and research*. New York: Guildford Press. Plenty of further reading in this edited book on theories and approaches to personality, including the Big Five model.

Holland, J. L. (1996) 'Exploring careers with a typology: what we have learned and some new directions', *American Psychologist, Vol.51*: 397–406. John Holland explores his theory of vocational types and vocational interests in this review article.

Ozer, D. and Benet-Martinez, V. (2006) 'Personality and the prediction of consequential outcomes', *Annual Review of Psychology, Vol.57*: 401–21. In this article, the authors explore some of the main associations between personality and outcomes at work and beyond. Fascinating reading, and very informative.

And finally, if all of this too heavy, read about personality in non-human animals, and personality and music preferences!

Gosling, S. D. (2001) 'From mice to men: what can we learn about personality from animal research?', *Psychological Bulletin, Vol.127*: 45–86.

Rentfrow, P. J. and Gosling, S. D. (2003) 'The do-re-mi's of everyday life: the structure and personality correlates of music preferences', *Journal of Personality and Social Psychology, Vol.84*: 1236–56.

FURTHER READING

Annotated lists of useful sources of information will enable you to read about an area of particular interest in more depth.

KEY SKILLS

Knowledge about personality and its influence at work has important implications for the development of key skills. Here they are discussed based on three perspectives:

AWARENESS OF YOUR OWN PERSONALITY TRAITS

Personal development planning

Insights into you own personality traits enable you to identify where they may represent personal development needs. A good way to apply this thinking is to complete a self-report personality questionnaire and get some feedback on it (try the IPIP NEO five-factor model recommended in this chapter). Critically review your personality profile and decide where it is really well suited to your chosen job, and where it is less so. Then try to find some ways to develop in the areas that are less well suited to your job.

Time management

Conscientiousness is a key individual difference dimension that relates to time management. People high on conscientiousness typically get down to work quickly, like making plans, and take deadlines seriously. The limitation of this approach is lower flexibility when it comes to changing schedules and demands. If you are low on conscientiousness, then be aware that at times you are

others, manage them, or interact with them, it is worth thinking about their personality traits, and how they are likely to influence their behaviour.

Professional judgement about the causes of behaviour is another area to think about. One mistake we often make is to over-emphasise the importance of personality as a cause of behaviour (eg a person did not submit the report on time because they are unreliable). It is much more likely that situation had an equal influence (workload, interruptions, etc).

WORKING WITH OTHERS

Leadership, coaching and mentoring

As highlighted above, leadership decision-making should account for individual differences in order to be effective. This applies very clearly in coaching and mentoring, where people's personality traits represent important strengths, development areas, and preferred styles of learning and responding to development interventions.

In respect of leadership style, dominance is a key personality trait. If you are high on dominance or assertiveness, you are likely to emerge as a leader in groups of people with less social confidence and presence. But you must also beware not to allow this to cause

KEY SKILLS

In order to appeal to employers and be able to tackle the issues raised within each chapter, you will need a number of key skills. Refer to this feature for more information on each of those key skills.

Ethical implications: What is ethical behaviour?

In the current high-tech society, people regularly comment that business is much faster-paced. For example, technology means that emails can be read from many mobile phones and that Internet access to respond is easily available. Autonomy and responsibility have been passed down the command chain in many organisations as technology provides the platform for easier communication. Behaving ethically in a world of downsizing, de-layering of organisations, greater expectations of employee loyalty and responsibility, and increasing worker productivity and accountability can be challenging. There are many views of what constitutes ethical behaviour. For example, some people believe that the end justifies the means; others believe that as long as a decision provides the

for staff to have autonomy? For some individuals it can feel that they are being 'dumped on', and that autonomy means that if something goes wrong, there is somebody to blame. For others, it can cause a strain that could possibly result in pressure and stress – particularly when tasks are combined, as suggested in Hackman's job design model.

Discuss the issue of autonomy raised in this chapter. Do you have any personal experience that you can share about the positive or negative benefits of employee autonomy?

Managers are interested in motivation because they want to

ETHICAL IMPLICATIONS

It is important to understand the ethical implications of any decisions you might make. These boxes identify the ethical implications arising from each chapter.

END-OF-BOOK FEATURES

Glossary

Agency the capacity of an individual to act and have an impact on their surroundings (as opposed to merely being affected by their surroundings)

Contingency theory theory that argues that there is no 'one best way' to organise because the optimal solution is contingent on the context, and thus the appropriate mode of organising is that which aligns most effectively with these contingent factors

Deconstruction form of analysis that seeks the meaning of a text and in doing so demonstrates that the 'foundations' of the text are irreducibly complex and unstable (and thus unknowable). It demonstrates that there isn't a meaning of text, but meanings which are irreconcilable and often contradictory. Text therefore has more than one interpretation, and interpretation of text can only go so far but never grasp the 'true' meaning

nature of gender inequality through understanding women's experiences and role in society. It seeks to expose the systematic nature of discrimination and promote women's rights and interests

Globalisation the way in which economies and societies worldwide have become integrated. The driver for this is primarily economic (international trade, cross-border investment, worker migration) but there are also cultural, political, technological drivers, amongst others. Changes in patterns and ease of communication have assisted in the pace of globalisation

Grand narratives Lyotard's expression for narratives that reflect a legitimised knowledge that becomes dominant. The Enlightenment project of modernism argued that reason would produce universal knowledge

GLOSSARY

Key terms are highlighted in bold the first time they are used in the text. Definitions of these key terms can be found in the glossary at the end of the book.

References

Chapter 1

BIS (Department for Business Innovation and Skills) (2009) *Higher Ambitions – The future of universities in a knowledge economy*. London: BIS.

Boyer, E. L. (1997) *Scholarship Reconsidered: Priorities of the professoriate*. San Francisco: Jossey-Bass/Carnegie Foundation for the Advancement of Teaching.

Butler, M. J. R. (2008) 'Inquiring how a lecturer keeps learning about their teaching – a personal case history on reflective imagination', *International Journal of Quality and Standards*, Vol.2, No.1: 1–39.

Butler, M. J. R. (2010) 'Innovative management education through work-based assessment – the case of "strategy for future leaders"', *Learning and Teaching in Higher Education*, Special issue on work-based learning.

Butler, M. and Gheorghiu, L. (2010) 'Evaluating the skills strategy through a graduate certificate in management – an experiential learning theory approach', *Education and Training*, Vol.52. No.6-7: 450–62.

Butler, M. J. R. and Reddy, P. (2010) 'Developing critical understanding in HRM students – innovative teaching methods encourage deep approaches to study', *Journal of European Industrial Training*, Vol.34, No.8-9: 772–89.

REFERENCES

Where key ideas need recognition or where you might want to use a quote, we have included chapter-by-chapter references at the end of the book.

Walk-through of online resources

Visit www.cipd.co.uk/olr or capture the QR code with your smartphone to access the following online resources which are an integral part of this textbook.

ONLINE STUDENT RESOURCES

WEB-LINKS

A suite of annotated web-links has been provided to help you develop your understanding of each chapter.

Click through to a wealth of seminar papers, YouTube video clips, podcasts, tools and useful websites.

ONLINE TUTOR RESOURCES

We recognise that tutors have different needs.

Some of you have taught OB many times before. You will have designed your own resources to use in class and may only need a few additional resources. Others of you will be new to teaching this subject. You will need to design your resources from scratch in a limited amount of time.

We have taken this into account and broken our online resources into two areas – Area 1 includes the majority of resources that could be used by any tutor using the book and Area 2 includes additional materials. All tutors will have access to both areas.

ONLINE TUTOR RESOURCES - AREA 1

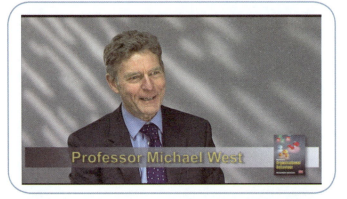

Professor Michael West

PRACTITIONER INTERVIEWS

For each practitioner insight box in the text, there is an accompanying practitioner video clip online. Once students have finished reading the chapter and have considered how they would approach the challenge presented, as a tutorial activity, show them the corresponding video clip. In these clips the practitioners describe how they overcame the challenges presented. The interviews have been produced to a high standard and last approximately ten minutes each.

KEY SKILLS VIDEO CLIPS

For many of the skills outlined in the key skills boxes in the text, there are accompanying video clips online in which the skills discussed are demonstrated through role play. Show the clips in class to bring these skills to life. Featuring professional actors and filmed in HD.

TEST-BANK

20 multiple choice, multiple-response, true and false or matching questions are available in our online Test-Bank. Use these to test students' understanding of specific OB concepts.

Nature and definition

- **Equality and diversity** is concerned with the unequal and inequitable treatment of some employees irrespective of their ability to perform their jobs.
- **Equality** itself is seen as being focused on the nature of the disadvantage in terms of the collective categories of gender, ethnicity, disability and age.

Chapter 13 – Tutorial activities

1. **Role play**

   Adopt a role for a particular power position. This can be from either the French and Raven or Morgan typology of power positions. In pairs, one person acts the power position role while the other person guesses which position of power the actor is playing out. Reverse the roles for another position of power.

2. **Group discussion**

   Compare and contrast the power and control structure of a large organisation such as a metropolitan local authority with a small organisation or business such as an independent restaurant or bar. In preparation for this activity you should choose a 'real life' example which would entail some preparation a week in advance. Explain and justify any differences between the organisations you have selected.

LECTURE SLIDES

Save yourself a lot of time and structure your lectures around these ready-made PowerPoint presentations that link closely to the chapters and include tables and figures from the book.

TUTORIAL ACTIVITIES

For each chapter, there are three additional tutorial activities online including, for example, topics for group discussions, case study analysis, role-plays and site visits to relevant organisations.

ANSWERS TO DISCUSSION QUESTIONS

Get the author's perspective on how the discussion questions in the book could be answered.

FIGURES AND TABLES FROM THE BOOK

Where possible, tables and figures from the book have been made available online as JPEGs.

ONLINE TUTOR RESOURCES - AREA 2

Short case study: Local knowledge

James had worked for a large insurance company in the US for 20 years. Over this time he had been extremely successful, working his way up the career ladder until finally making regional director at just 40 years old. His knowledge of US insurance law and his fantastic people skills had made him popular with the Executive Board. When the company decided to open a new branch in Athens, James was their first choice to head-up the operation.

After relocating his family to Europe, it was time for James to begin the good work the board expected of him. At 9am he gathered his predominantly Greek team together for a pep-talk in which explained his five point plan for success. As James raised his hand to metaphorically depict the points on his five fingers, all of the Greek employees drew breath

Assignment questions

1. Critically analyse the role of new communication media. What issues might arise when introducing new media in an organisation and how might these be overcome? Use examples and evidence to support your answer.

2. Compare and contrast two types of communication such as face-to-face and letters. Critically evaluate the advantages and disadvantages of each communication type regarding aspects such as information richness. How might one increase the effectiveness of the chosen communication?

ADDITIONAL SHORT CASE STUDIES

Each chapter is accompanied by one short case study online including questions. These can be used as a classroom activity or for personal reflection and individual learning.

ADDITIONAL LONG CASE STUDIES

Each chapter is accompanied by one long case study online including questions or tasks and tutor notes. These can be used as the basis for assignments.

ADDITIONAL ASSIGNMENT QUESTIONS

There are three additional assignment questions for each chapter online. Use these to test your students' understanding of the links between the different chapters and broader OB issues.

Chapter 1
Introduction: A New Model of Learning Blending Employability Skills, International Focus and Multimedia Elements

Michael Butler and Ed Rose

Contents

Key Learning Outcomes

By the end of this chapter you should be able to:

- state the benefits of reading this textbook and introduce a new model of learning, blending employability skills, international focus and multimedia elements
- understand why we have focused on employability skills
- relate employability skills to an international focus
- utilise the multimedia elements of the chapters
- be ready and energised to read the book.

Introduction: a new model of learning

Confronted with a crowded selection of organisational behaviour textbooks, you may wonder why you should choose this one. The editors believe that this book addresses a significant gap in the market. Today's undergraduates face tremendous competition for jobs and need to set themselves apart from their rivals who, in today's marketplace, could be from anywhere in the world. A new organisational behaviour textbook must be relevant to the modern generation of students. This book focuses on three unique selling points which will help students to transition into the workplace and to improve their learning:

- It improves students' prospects for employability in a competitive work environment by emphasising the development of key skills.

- It relates employability skills to an international focus, given the mobility within the global workplace.

- It enhances the learning experience by integrating the textbook with a wide range of innovative online materials to help modern and sophisticated students to learn in a way that suits their approach to study.

The three unique selling points lie at the heart of the publication strategy of the Chartered Institute of Personnel and Development (CIPD). This is why the editors saw a unique opportunity and synergy between our aspirations and their practical achievement through the CIPD and this book. The partnership also brings a more creative, interactive and visual approach to the presentation of ideas about organisational behaviour.

Blending improving employability skills with adopting an international focus and integrating multimedia elements is a new learning model, which clearly differentiates this textbook from rival books (Figure 1.1). It is important to be aware that Coffield (2000) points out that there are a range of learning models – Coffield (2000) identifies 10. The focus is on employability skills because of the growing consensus that the issue has to be addressed within higher education, especially its interconnections with global ideas about how to manage and lead, all underpinned by recent research on pedagogy in learning and teaching. All these issues are discussed in the following sections.

Because organisational behaviour is core to virtually all undergraduate business degrees, there are a number of topics that must be included as standard, and the textbook reflects this. Nevertheless, we are enhancing the reader experience by introducing contemporary real-world issues – the new learning model. In tackling core topics and up-to-date issues, we assume that students have no prior knowledge of organisational behaviour. Authors use clear explanations to get students started, although they do engage with critical debates in order to get students thinking analytically.

To expand on the intended approach and level of the book: it moves student discussion from A-level standard – or the international equivalent – to provide a balance between a managerialist approach and an employee perspective. Both approaches are subject to critical evaluation – that is to say, a weighing up of the strengths and weaknesses of the approaches and how they might privilege certain world views which should not necessarily be taken for granted. 'Bottom-up' analysis is included in the relevant chapters. One example is how the managerialist approach might disenfranchise certain social groups – for instance, women senior managers. A further example would relate to conflict as perceived by both employer and worker.

Figure 1.1   A new model of learning, blending employability skills, international focus and multimedia elements

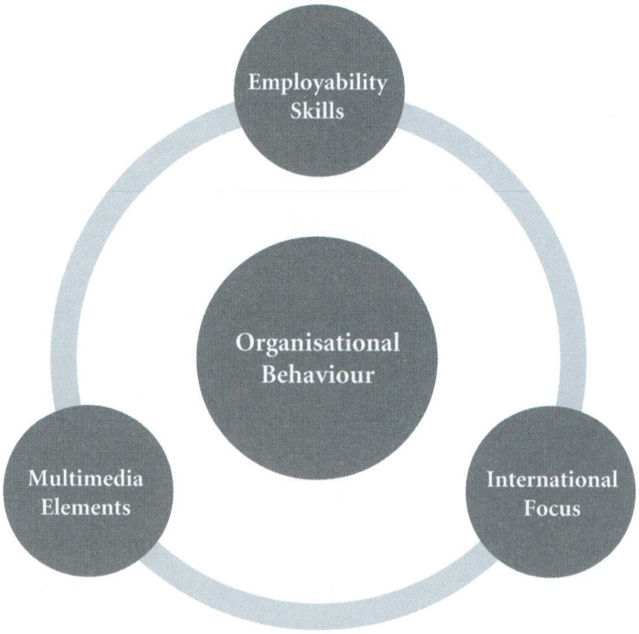

The book does not include separate chapters on human resource management (HRM). However, the obvious links between organisational behaviour and HRM are highlighted as appropriate throughout the text.

The issues of employability skills, international focus and multimedia integration are discussed in more detail below.

EMPLOYABILITY SKILLS

Employability is a hot topic from all points of view – the teachers', the students', the employers' and recent government policy, whether devised by parties on the right or the left of politics. In 2009, the Department for Business, Innovation and Skills (BIS) – one of the UK's government departments – issued a policy document titled *Higher Ambitions*, which seeks to clarify the future of universities in a knowledge economy and is already being widely implemented in higher education (Butler, 2010). *Higher Ambitions*' clear aim is on improving employability skills (BIS, 2009: 4):

> In order to attract a greater diversity of students, more part-time study, more vocationally-based foundation degrees, more work-based study and more study whilst living at home must be made available. This is a core aim of these proposals, and our wider skills strategy.

Employers believe that universities ought to develop the employability skills of students (Cassidy, 2006). This is because they perceive that future graduates will overcome the relative lack of managerial and technical skills in the workplace (Wilton, 2008). Students also target skills development, expecting the teaching of professional skills to enhance their employability (Connor and Shaw, 2008). Such unified activity has contributed to 'institutional improvement that enhanced student learning and involved faculty development' (Hurtado, 2009: 28).

The underpinning philosophy of our book is to focus on employability skills, defined as the development of future managers and leaders who realise that managing is about getting things done through other people. More specifically, managing and leading people involves understanding individual needs, integrating people in effective teams, so that they achieve organisational goals. Leading and managing change takes place in all types of organisations, whether private, public or in the third sector – for example, non-government organisations (NGOs) – or UK- or globally based.

The book endeavours to develop future managers and leaders who may often operate within environmentally challenging contexts and who therefore require a secure foundation of relevant knowledge that can be used as they build their career. The knowledge provided by the book and acquired by the student can be deployed though the development of relevant skills and practice. Established theory is linked to emerging research, and the practical implications of this for organisational behaviour are explored.

Employability skills are specifically addressed through exploring the textbook's learning features and by linking organisational behaviour to key skills. Through these features we seek to improve students' prospects for employability by making them more competitive, when compared with other students.

Textbook learning features

Each chapter includes the following learning features:

- Case problem boxes – Each chapter starts with a case problem ('Practitioner insight') box, in which a practitioner describes a real-life organisational challenge. Students are invited to read the chapter and then go back and decide how they would approach this situation themselves, utilising the ideas they have learned during the chapter.

- Review questions – These are designed for students to assess their understanding of the central themes, including employability skills, within a chapter.

- Discussion questions – In order to consolidate critical thinking skills, authors ask review and discussion questions: these are for students to respond to on their own or as part of a team because the capacity to move between individual and teamworking is a central business and organisational competence in modern workplaces.

- Identifying ethical implications boxes – In light of the growth of corporate governance as a central concern for organisations and business schools, especially in the wake of the contemporary financial crisis and retrenchment management, each author addresses ethics in the context of the chapter content.

- Applying theory to practice boxes – These are up-to-date examples of organisational practice to illustrate the link between theory and practice.

- Taking your learning further boxes – Authors suggest seminal papers and books to extend students' reading (with links to the seminal papers on the website); these include examples related to employability.

- Best and worst organisational practice boxes.

Linking organisational behaviour and key skills

An essential part of delivering the new learning model is to link organisational behaviour and key skills. Cotton (2001) argues that although employers are in general pleased with the technical skills of new graduates, they are less persuaded that the non-technical skills are at high standards – for example, teamworking, problem-solving, communication and attitude to work (Connor and Shaw, 2008).

Practitioners like David Farnham (Farnham and Smith, 2005), a CIPD Chief Examiner, echo Cotton's (2001) academic argument. Farnham notes that CIPD professional standards require students both to have knowledge of the subject and to demonstrate a critical understanding of what they have learned, revealed through explanation, analysis and evaluation. Indeed, nurturing critical minds is part of a high-quality higher education (HE) experience (Malcolm, 2009) because 'higher skills are keys to social mobility ... as well as one of competitiveness' (Lord Mandelson, 2009). Critical understanding is used by HR managers to deliver business performance, as expressed by Sacha Romanovitch, Head of People and Culture, Grant Thornton (2009: 39):

> In an increasingly service-oriented economy the differentiation for a business usually comes down to its people. To provide an outstanding service to its clients any business needs to recruit and retain the best people – promoting and creating an effective working environment.

The focus in this textbook is on generic and transferable skills.

Drawing on this work, the editors selected the key skills in the list below to be addressed by the contributing authors:

- creative skills
- developing critical thinking skills
- emotional intelligence, empathy, sympathy and listening
- leadership, coaching and mentoring
- making presentations
- negotiating, arbitration and conflict resolution skills
- personal development planning
- professional judgement, decision-making and problem-solving
- reflective learning
- social responsibility
- teamworking
- time management.

Each chapter ends with some tips on how the topic could be linked to the skills, outlining why each skill is important, and giving some advice on how to develop this skill. The website includes activities for these skills. Not every chapter relates to every skill, but by the end of the book, all the skills have been discussed. The list is not exhaustive, but does help students in their quest to manage and lead people effectively, as individuals, in teams, or in an organisation.

INTERNATIONAL FOCUS

We have made a deliberate choice to have an international focus because of the mobility within the global workplace. Mintzberg and Gosling (2002) argue that in educating future managers and leaders, it is important to break down borders. For them, education goes beyond globalisation. They say: 'To broaden people beyond geographic borders means not only to teach about globalisation, but also to provide a truly balanced international experience' (Mintzberg and Gosling, 2002: 67). This is part of the reason why a Master's programme they run operates in five different business schools. The International Master's Programme in Practising Management (IMPM) (www.ipm.org) operates in the Indian Institute of Management, INSEAD, Lancaster University School of Management, McGill and a collaboration of faculties from Japan and Korea.

Mintzberg and Gosling (2002) also break down borders in a way that supports the previous arguments about employability skills. Educating managers and leaders goes beyond teaching: 'Learning occurs where concepts meet experiences through reflection' (Mintzberg and Gosling

2002: 66). This is a blended strategy in which formalised knowledge is linked to personal experience by confronting old beliefs with new ideas – a process enhanced by collaboration.

One of the editors, Butler (2008), developed the ideas of Mintzberg and Gosling (2002) by writing a personal case history of a visit to Harvard Business School in which he enquired how a lecturer keeps learning about teaching as a quality assurance process to improve learning and teaching. He proposed 'six activities of reflective imagination' as a means of keeping learning:

- Question educational processes.

- Review the international dimension (as a means to critique the educational process by looking for alternative and world-class good practice).

- Link concepts and experiences.

- Know yourself by changing routines.

- Return to how educational processes can be improved.

- Use imagination to create and convey insights.

In this book there are examples of multinational organisations and organisations that operate in other countries. There are also discussions of established Western economies and developing emerging countries.

Examples of how we achieve an international focus are:

- drawing on international authors who are experts in their field

- using international case studies – this is a direct consequence of having a wide range of authors

- highlighting the need for cultural sensitivity to avoid miscommunication in interpersonal interactions.

A good example is Chapter 11 on *Decision-making*. One of the co-authors, Keith Bezant-Niblett, is an Assistant Director at the James B. Henry Center for Executive Development, the Eli Broad Graduate School of Management, Michigan State University, USA. He was able to source a case study about Nathan M. Bisk, Chairman of Bisk Education, who built up an organisation in the USA that has become a world leader in online education. Because of this international perspective within the chapter, the chapter goes on to consider the cultural context of decision-making. The authors are a product of European and North American traditions, and as a consequence the concepts selected for the chapter reflect those traditions, although their application is global.

MULTIMEDIA INTEGRATION

The editors are aware of the changing needs of students, and our ability to improve their international employability can only be nurtured by helping modern and sophisticated students to learn in a way which suits their approach to study. Together with the CIPD, the editors decided that the best way to share contemporary ideas about organisational behaviour is through both the standard textbook format and by integrating it with digital media, thus creating a multimedia approach – a blended strategy. In doing so we are joining a growing international trend (Senior, Butler, Wood and Reddy, 2009).

In 1998, the Carnegie Foundation for the Advancement of Teaching in the USA commissioned an investigation into the current state of undergraduate teaching in the United States, headed up by the then President of the Carnegie Foundation, Professor Ernest Boyer. In terms of this textbook, the five-year investigation advocated using information technology creatively, arguing that undergraduate students should use (and also be exposed to the creative use of) technological advancements – competent graduates need more than just a working knowledge of standard software packages (Boyer, 1997: 5). The Boyer Report met with mixed success. It has 'done a lot of interesting things' but the agenda for change had not become 'part of the real value system of research universities, and it's really time to do something about it' (Wilson, 1998: 13).

Similar issues are facing the UK. Many undergraduate students embrace information technology to such an extent that they are described as 'digital natives', compared to their teachers who are termed 'digital immigrants' (Prensky, 2001). At the Technologies in Learning and Teaching Conference (TILT 2008), Sir David Watson (Director, Institute of Education) stressed that the need for the digital natives to develop a broad collection of skills that had employment value was probably the single biggest factor affecting the higher education sector.

The digital native student enters the higher education sector with an 'information-age mindset' (Frand, 2000: 15) and has distinctive characteristics. Workstations are no longer libraries, although they are used, but also mobile phones because they have the ability to access the Internet from any place on Earth. As with computer games, many students want to learn by constant trial and error, by testing out their learning online as often as they want. This approach is anathema to the digital immigrant, who is used to poring over books and instruction manuals before starting a task. Multitasking is a way of life and may occur at every level of the students' day. For example, they may text questions regarding a lecture or coursework to their peers while at work, and they use social networking sites to create study groups – the singular mode of information transfer is simply inefficient.

We view learning and teaching as a symbiotic relationship between the teacher and the learner, and the book – with its supplementary resources – underpins this relationship by addressing the needs of the digital native student. The book includes a number of innovative learning features that will engage students. We note below the teacher and student resources which accompany each chapter, and highlight the videoed practitioner interviews and access to CIPD resources.

Teacher resources

Each chapter is supported by a range of online teacher resources, although the specific numbers of each item might vary according to the learning needs identified by individual authors:

- 10 PowerPoint lecture slides including figures and tables from the book

- 20 test bank questions

- 3 tutorial activities

- answers to the discussion questions in each chapter

- 2 additional case studies – one long, one short – each accompanied by questions and solutions

- 3 additional assignment questions.

The editors are aware that different teachers have different needs. Teachers who have just started teaching organisational behaviour and who would like as much support as possible could use the lecture slides, the test bank questions, the tutorial activities and the answers to the discussion questions. In other words, the website offers resources to help to teach an organisational behaviour module from scratch.

Teachers who have taught organisational behaviour before and have already developed a range of their own teaching resources might find additional resources that they can add to their own. The additional case studies and assignment questions help in these circumstances.

Student resources

Within and at the end of each chapter, in order to consolidate student learning, there are a range of student resources, taking a multimedia approach. Again, the specific numbers of each item might vary to match the different learning aims and objectives of the chapters:

- 5 review questions

- 5 discussion questions

- between 5 and 10 annotated suggestions for further reading (books or articles)

- 1,000 words on how the topic relates to different key skills

- an Ethical implications box

- Applying theory to practice boxes

- Taking your learning further boxes

- Best and worse practice boxes – one of each

- 3 to 4 web links to seminal papers

- 3 to 4 other web links, including to YouTube.

At the end of the book, listed by chapter, are glossary terms relevant to each chapter, and references for students' assignment writing and further reading.

Videoed practitioner interviews

Perhaps the most innovative feature is the videoed practitioner interviews which can be accessed online to make teaching more interactive and experiential. It has already been noted that each chapter starts with a case problem ('Practitioner insight') box, in which a practitioner describes a real-life organisational challenge. Not only can students read the chapter and then go back and decide how they would approach the described situation themselves, but during a lecture or tutorial activity, the teacher can ask the students for ideas and solutions and then show them a short 10-minute video linked to each chapter. These videos are interviews with the practitioners featured in the chapter. The practitioner explains how he or she actually did deal with the organisational challenge. The video interviews are also available as Word files.

The interviews connect students directly with the world of work because they are examples taken from real organisational life. By 'practitioner' we mean anyone participating in organisational activities. They can be from any function, at any level, and comprise any stakeholders within and between organisations, including customers, service users or people browsing the websites of organisations they might buy from.

The interviews connect with a student's current experience. Examples are from organisations, products, services and brands that they can relate to. There are also examples from outside organisational settings.

Because the textbook is published by the CIPD, in addition to the videoed practitioner interviews, we have had access to the CIPD's research publications and recent issues of *People Management* so that they can be incorporated without the usual permissions fees into the chapters. We have also had access to key skills video clips.

Conclusion: the next steps

This chapter has focused on the three unique selling points of the textbook – blending employability skills, international focus and multimedia integration – to propose a new model of learning. These benefits will help students to transition into the workplace and to improve their learning.

By adopting employability skills and its associated strategies as a learning model, it is anticipated that student conceptions of learning will move more quickly to being a sophisticated approach to study (Butler and Reddy, 2010; Butler, 2010). Drawing on ideas about deep and surface learning (Entwistle, 1990; Martin and Saljo, 1976), if students have a sophisticated conception of learning, knowledge and evidence, they adopt a deep approach in order to reach their own understanding of material and ideas. If students have an unsophisticated conception, they adopt a superficial approach and memorise or acquire facts in order to merely meet course requirements or to respond to external influences.

We hope that you are now ready and energised to read more chapters.

Chapter 2
Approaches to Organisational Behaviour

Emma Jeanes

Contents

Key Learning Outcomes

By the end of this chapter you should be able to:

- understand the context and interdisciplinary nature of organisational behaviour, drawing on organisation theory
- demonstrate an awareness of the importance of organisation as both a structure which frames activity and as a process which creates structure, and of how this has implications for understanding organisational behaviour
- more confidently be critical of the field of study, and more reflexive of your own ways of knowing and conceptual development
- understand the disciplining effects of knowledge, and how it shapes the way in which you think (and get better at seeing where and when it happens) and be mindful of the ethical implications
- relate to your own knowledge and experience of organisational behaviour in a more reflective manner
- be more creative in your thinking and in the ways in which you approach the topic of organisational behaviour.

 PRACTITIONER INSIGHT

LG Electronics

LG Electronics, a $50 billion multinational company, is one of the world's largest manufacturers of electronic goods. However, even in a large multinational company, past success does not guarantee future performance. How can LG Electronics cope with falling sales during the global economic downturn? We speak to **Reg Bull, former Global Chief HR Officer**, to find out more.

LG Electronics is a brand that is familiar to many, with its extensive range of televisions and mobile phones, and more than 112 operations including 81 subsidiaries around the world. LGE promotes its vision of *jeong-do* management (management by principle), which involves creating value for customers and respecting human dignity. LG Electronics' ambition is to achieve the position of market leader as a result of its ethical management.

In October 2008, like all of its competitors, LG Electronics faced a dramatic overnight double-digit reduction in its year-on-year sales as a result of the global economic downturn. Such a significant decline in sales was all the more of a contrast for LGE, having been enjoying a period of rapid growth over the previous ten years. LGE was facing challenging times and needed to rethink its operations and make quick tactical changes to address volume decline through assessing the product portfolio and determining whether there were too many over-engineered

products that people didn't want or couldn't afford; whether changes could be made to the product range (and prices); and if not, what otherwise could be done to help the bottom line. The tactics employed included reducing labour, but also redeploying labour to ensure that LGE was in the best position to improve its sales position.

For Reg, these times were particularly interesting because the LGE organisation culture contrasted with more familiar Western ways of working. When radical change is required, such wide-scale change projects often involve extensive periods of consultation, and even employee participation, at all levels of the organisation. As the Global Human Resource Officer, Reg might have been expecting to have been part of the extended consultation team working on planning the response. However, LGE took a more authoritarian approach to managing the problem at the very start, with limited initial discussion and a clear direction already in place. Implementation of this strategy was swift – in effect, over a four-week period.

How would you imagine Reg felt about this approach to managing change given his previous experiences? What would be the advantages and risks in such an approach?

Once you have read this chapter, return to these questions and think about how you could answer them.

Introduction

The study of organisational behaviour usually involves taking a step back from day-to-day activities, many of which we take for granted and go unnoticed, to try to make sense of such behaviour in a more systematic fashion. Studies may focus on the ways in which people are motivated to work (or not), why employees may resist change initiatives, and so on. Underlying these behavioural questions are fundamental understandings of the meanings and values that shape work and organisation. Organisation is not just about the workplace but about organisation (and organising) more broadly – which affects all aspects of everyday life. Organisation is typically thought of in terms of organisations as entities (businesses, institutions and the like) rather than 'organising', the latter being fundamental to interaction in all aspects of life. Family routines are modes of organising, just as arranging a night out with your friends requires some organisation. Despite this being the case, organisational behaviour is usually studied in the context of organisations (as entities) and is focused on the formal rather than informal dynamics within organisations. This means that our understanding of organisational behaviour is often limited in its scope. This partial account is at the same time partisan – focusing on the view of behaviour from the perspective of management and how other employees can be managed more effectively to achieve goals such as profitability. Even though, as has been the case in more recent years, the informal aspect of organising has received more attention, many texts on organisational behaviour still give more attention to managing and achieving 'good behaviour' while neglecting the everyday lived experience of organisation and the nature and reasons behind so-called 'misbehaviour' (Ackroyd and Thompson, 1999). Furthermore the context of organisation is usually limited to that of legitimised paid employment (Wilson, 2010). Thinking about organisational behaviour in relation to processes of organis*ing* opens us to think about organisational behaviour in broader terms – and will also enable those with little or no work experience to draw on knowledge and life experience to understand these concepts.

It is common to differentiate between 'levels' of interaction in organisational behaviour. Usually this is divided into the behaviours of 'individuals', 'groups', and the effects of 'structure and processes'. But of course these are inherently intertwined and need to be understood as mutually constituting. Divisions between levels or topics (culture, group, personality, and so on) are artificial divisions. They allow us to break down and make sense of work, organisation, and management. Trying to say everything about all things at all times becomes an impossible exercise. However, we do need to keep in mind that the divisions we make are just devices for organising our knowledge into manageable proportions. The same can be said for our ways of 'interpreting' organisations and organisational behaviour. Different perspectives open us up to a new way of seeing, questioning, and thinking. But the way we evaluate is, in practice, only ever partial, and partisan.

The complexity of the interrelationships between the various foci of our interest cannot be overplayed. We must also keep in mind the dynamic nature of these interrelationships. The context in which we exist frames how we behave, but it is also constituted by this activity: human activity (or **agency**) is structured by its context, but at the same time this structural context is the outcome of the actions of humans (we create the structure). This means that not only do we need to keep in mind context when discussing action, and action as that which creates structure, but also how these two co-evolve – often referred to as 'structure-agency' or Structuration Theory (Giddens, 1984). Although the focus of organisational behaviour is often, unsurprisingly, on 'people', we need to keep in mind context (such as the structure, culture, systems and technologies of operation) both as the environment in which people act, and also as an outcome of their action (which in turn frames their actions, and so on). Even when focusing on the management of people, structure remains of central importance (see Chapters 14 and 16). Indeed, much of management is focused on developing systems of control and working practices, rather than responding to individual needs and concerns, and an understanding of organisational behaviour is used to assist in the design and implementation. However, if we think about the different ways in which we organise our lives, it will become apparent that the principles of organisation are not only that which might be seen as 'rational', but also *embodied* and emotional. Furthermore, we need to understand organisational behaviour in the context of **globalisation**. It is these organising principles that often receive limited attention in texts on organisational behaviour.

This chapter seeks to achieve two things. Firstly, it aims to put the study of organisational behaviour in some historical context. Secondly, it introduces students to the different perspectives that assist in the analysis of behaviour and organisation. The different lenses which can be applied to organisations not only help explain the development of management knowledge (and some of the fads and fashions in thought) but also provide us with some means with which to critique it. This chapter should hopefully help you navigate your way around the diversity of theories and perspectives in organisational behaviour.

PERSPECTIVES IN ORGANISATION BEHAVIOUR/THEORY

Organisation theory is characterised by a multiplicity of theories and perspectives. It draws on a wide range of disciplines in the social sciences, particularly psychology, sociology, social psychology, anthropology, economics, philosophy and politics, and engineering from the sciences. It is the subject of study rather than the discipline which is the focal point of interest in organisation theory. Organisational theory is not a theorem – a single, integrated way of explaining – but an umbrella term for a range of theories that are often unrelated, contested and even conflictual, which leads to ambiguity in knowing how 'best' to manage behaviour. It is unsurprising, therefore, that organisational behaviour is a subject replete with diversity in its perspectives and approaches. For some this is a sign that this is a young, developing field in need of development (Pfeffer, 1993); for others it is a sign of its rich diversity (Van Maanen, 1995; De Cock and Jeanes, 2006). For example, from psychology we draw on research that explores the nature of individuals and their differences (such as personality, ways in which individuals learn); from sociology we gain understanding of how behaviour is influenced by and influences the social, political and economic dynamics in society. No one aspect is sufficient to understand behaviour – hence the need for the study of organisational behaviour to be understood as multidisciplinary. Approaching a question from one discipline alone will only give a partial view. To focus on personality to understand an individual's motivation would ignore the contextual factors such as the dynamics within the work group, the policies of the organisation, the politics of decision-making, and the economic circumstances in which one is working. Furthermore, the experience of the workplace is also intertwined with experiences 'outside', such as relations with family, social networks, and the broader cultural and historical conditioning factors. All of these factors are implicated in the decisions, actions and behaviours exhibited in the organisation, and relate not only to the immediate circumstances but also to people's sense of **identity**, their personal projects and career ambitions, and their desire to retain security, amongst many other motivations. Organisational behaviour relates not only to the behaviours that we may desire or strive for in organisations but also to the behaviours that we may try to suppress (*mis*behaviour) and behaviours that might ordinarily be seen as private, but once undertaken within the context of an organisation become relevant to study because they have an impact – such as, for example, a personal relationship between work colleagues. Organisational behaviour relates to behaviours in the context of, informed by or related to organisation (Jackson and Carter, 2000: 2). The perspectives will be reviewed in a loosely structured temporal order.

TRADITIONAL MODERNIST PERSPECTIVES

As will become apparent, any kind of labelling can be problematic and will not be agreed upon. However, for the sake of some sense of order, 'traditional' will predominantly be associated with an earlier period of management theory and focus on how to manage from the perspective of management. This is not to suggest that such perspectives (also referred to as 'mainstream') are 'all in the past' – far from it – but that these perspectives emerged at an early stage in management thought. Despite subsequent developments in theorising, many of the earlier ideas can be seen, or their traces identified, in current theories (see Hatch and Cunliffe, 2006: 6 for a timeline of organisation theory and its sources of inspiration). Interest in organising practices can be traced back through many centuries, but the focus here will be on the modern period, post-industrialisation.

Taylorism and scientific management [1]

Many of the early approaches in organisation theory were developed with a focus on efficiency in working practice. This can be seen as early as the eighteenth century, when Adam Smith noted the efficiency to be found in the **division of labour** (Smith, 1776). Frederick Winslow Taylor, working in the late nineteenth and early twentieth century, was similarly interested in efficiency. Taylor worked in a steel company and conducted experiments to improve the efficiency of the workers. His approach involved detailed examination and experimentation with different ways of working from which he developed standard practices – an approach subsequently described as **scientific management**. From this 'scientific' approach, Taylor (1911) was able to set work targets, standardise the working methods, and develop the appropriate skills in the workforce. These 'efficient' ways of working were designed to increase productivity and profitability, but have been criticised for being highly mechanised and dehumanising. An incentive-based means of reward was designed to ensure that it was in the workers' best interest to cooperate. Taylor's work and the principles of efficiency spawned considerable interest (and criticism) at the time. One of the best-known applications of 'Taylorism' at the time was Henry Ford's mass-production line ('Fordism'). Charlie Chaplin's *Modern Times* (1936) is a classic film that captures the realities of Taylorism (and Fordism), offering a humorous critique reflecting the contemporary attitude towards these methods. But we can also recognise Taylorism in today's organisation. How many jobs do you know of which apply standard work routines and targets? These are not just found in the manufacturing production line but also in service delivery: call centres are a good example (see Chapter 13).

Max Weber and bureaucracy [2]

Another key figure around this time was Max Weber, a German sociologist with an interest in the changing nature of society. Weber's focus was on different forms of authority structures in society – namely, charismatic, traditional or rational-legal (Weber, 1978). In contrast to traditional authority (that which is vested by virtue of inheritance) and charismatic authority (that which is achieved through the charisma of, or power of attraction towards, a particular individual), rational-legal authority was **legitimised** through its legal rationality. Weber believed this form of authority to be the result of developments in society at that time – in particular, the development of modern means of organisation – the system of bureaucracy. This rational-legal authority was, for Weber, a superior form of authority because of its rational underpinnings. Who had power in this system, and the nature of that power, was determined rationally, through laws and guiding norms of society rather than by chance of inheritance or charisma. The holders of the positions of authority were chosen for their qualities, but were also required to operate within the confines of their position and the rules of operation, limiting their power to that which was given to the holder of that position. Weber's ideas often appear within the lexicon of management ideas in relation to organisational structure (see Chapter 14) and to authority, and issues of power (see Chapter 13). Arguably, almost all organisations have elements of bureaucracy, but some organisations – particularly large organisations operating in comparatively stable markets, or where accountability is paramount (such as the public sector) – come closer to Weber's 'ideal type'.

Rationality

Both Taylor and Weber consider organisation through the lens of rationality and striving for efficiency. In Weber's bureaucracy we can see why its apparent technical superiority may have had much to commend it (Du Gay, 2000). Unlike the partiality of traditional/charismatic forms of authority (we need only think back to history and the tendency of monarchs to dispense with their enemies as it suited them, often without recourse to independent judicial review), the bureaucratic form of authority – through its legal-rationality – sought a fairer, more judicious mode of operation. In bureaucracy we would expect to find rules applied fairly and equitably, promotion to be based on ability, and so on. This mode of organising appears to be 'neutral' or free from any partial values through its basis in 'technical' rationality. In fact, bureaucracy is influenced by values like any other mode of organising. In replacing traditional modes of authority including religious doctrine as a guide for human behaviour with scientific, reasoned understandings as a basis for 'rational' control, what has often gone unnoticed is that science has its own values and **ideology**. The key distinction is between the instrumental (or formal) rationality and substantive rationality. Instrumental rationality refers to the means-end relationship: the technicalities of efficiency in achieving the end goal. Substantive rationality refers to the nature of the desired ends. In short, we may be efficient in how we achieve our goal, but is the end goal the right one?

It is easy to overstate the focus on managerial or technical efficiency. Weber, for example, was concerned with the social effects of authority structures, and warned of the dangers of an unreflective focus on instrumental rationality ahead of substantive rationality – what he referred to as the 'iron cage' of instrumental rationality (see Ritzer, 1996 for a review of this in the context of today's society – what he terms the 'McDonaldization' of society). Weber was interested in how we avoided becoming trapped in these machine-like practices (a metaphor we will return to later). Terry Gilliam's *Brazil* (1985) is a film that combines comedy and fantasy that demonstrates what can go wrong with bureaucracy when it is an all-encompassing system of control. Bauman's *Modernity and the Holocaust* (1989) provides a more serious review of the technical efficiency of bureaucracy in pursuit of a tragic end result – namely, the extermination of the Jewish people. We can find similar concerns for society in the writing of Karl Marx. Marx was interested in the social consequences of capitalism and examined the effect of the division between those who owned capital (the means of production) and those who laboured, and the fairness of the 'sharing' of the surplus value (profit) from the production process. The profit earned can either be paid to labourers through higher wages or be taken as interest on the capital invested by the owner. Consequently, Marx argued, there was an inherent conflict between the two parties (see Chapter 8). To maximise profit the capitalists have an incentive to control the labour costs, and these means of control increasingly lead to the alienation of the workers from the product of their efforts. Workers are increasingly treated as instrumental components to the production process subject to 'technical control' (Bottomore and Rubel, 1963; Edwards, 1979). This approach laid emphasis on the 'resource' of human resource management – treating labour much like any other material input into the process. The resource view of labour fails to grasp the need of individuals to find meaning in their work. Marx's *Das Kapital* (first volume published in 1867) was interested in the dynamic of capital, but also gave attention to its social consequences (see Bottomore and Rubel, 1963).

There were many others who contributed to the formative years of management theory, including academics, practising managers and management consultants – such as Mary Parker Follett (also notable for being a women in what was, and arguably still is, a male-dominated field), Henri Fayol (1949) and Chester Barnard (1938). What their ideas shared in common was the aim of developing rational principles of management. The knowledge gained from the study of behaviour and organisation was seen as the means for improvement in management practice. The work of the early management theorists (or those contributing to this body of knowledge) has received much criticism. Despite this, we can also find evidence of their ideas in current theory and practice. (Follett's ideas of 'self-governing groups', 1924, is often a term used to describe recent developments in teamwork!) We must also contextualise these ideas in terms of when they were written. Many of these studies were grappling with the challenges of society at that time. Taylor, for example, was coping with a diverse mix of immigrant workers (and their inability to communicate), had an interest in fairness between workers (no longer reliant on patronage), and desired a safer controlled workplace (Grey, 2005: 38). The ostensibly rational approach helps explain their endurance in today's management. Imagine you were faced with the task of reorganising the production process. How would you attempt to understand, evaluate and respond to the challenge? Do you think you would view this as a technical problem?

Human Relations

The Human Relations movement, which emerged from the Hawthorne Studies of the 1920s and 1930s, led by Elton Mayo, was particularly interested in the nature of groups, and individual behaviours within groups (Roethlisberger and Dickson, 1939). What Mayo and colleagues observed, after the failure of traditional experimentation methods exploring the effect of variables such as illumination on performance, was the lack of a clear linear relationship between the changing of these variables and the productivity of the workforce. Indeed, some quite bizarre results emerged. Even when illumination was reduced to very low levels (clearly not optimal working conditions), productivity increased. The initial reaction to this 'failed' experiment was to bring in new researchers to develop a more controlled experiment. However, what transpired from the follow-up experiment (the relay assembly test room) was the impact on performance of the social needs of humans. The attention they received as a consequence of being part of an experiment and the nature of the dynamics of the group affected the performance of the individuals (all women). These experiments had a significant impact on the development of the field of management research, and in particular theories of group behaviour (see Chapter 7). Whereas earlier approaches attempted to neutralise the human effect, the Human Relations approach put more emphasis on the effect of human nature such as the emotional needs of members and other 'non-rational' aspects of behaviour (see Chapter 4). However, these studies have also been criticised (Bendix, 1956; Landsberger, 1958). In particular, the Hawthorne studies have been challenged for the lack of contextual sensitivity given to the interpretation of the data, such as the economic (employment) conditions at the time, and the effect of having an all-female study (Acker and Van Houten, 1974).

The Human Relations School was built on through the work of the Tavistock Institute in the UK, where the interrelationship between technology and humans was researched. **Socio-technical theory** explored the effect of technology on workers and was first developed by Eric Trist and Ken Bamforth (1951). As with the Hawthorne Studies, Trist and Bamforth observed counter-intuitive shifts in performance as a result of social dynamics, with less efficient technical systems enabling higher levels of performance due to the social aspects of work organisation (higher levels of work group autonomy). Focusing on the technology of working practices in isolation failed to predict the better performance. Instead, an understanding of the relationship between the working methods, both technical and social, was required. From this body of work we have developed our understanding of teamwork, work group autonomy, and the importance of meaningful work in job design, as well as the effect of technology on work (see Chapters 7 and 16). Think about your own behaviour and how you behave differently in the company of others. Even having another person in the room makes us adjust our behaviour, so it's easy to understand how working in a group can affect us. The technical or technological aspects also affect us in everyday life. Reflect on how communication between friends has changed over time, with the growing prevalence of mobile telecommunications. How has that changed the way we live our lives? What ways of organising are now optimal, when compared with a decade ago?

Systems theory

Systems theory, largely drawing on the work of Ludwig von Bertalanffy (1968), developed the principle of scientific exploration in order to find a way of explaining the complex interrelationships in systems, whether natural or social. This 'science of systems' included individuals, groups and societies – from the atomic level to the broadest category of system. To develop a 'general theory of systems', Bertalanffy sought to demonstrate general laws or principles that could be used as a framework for analysis. What is important about Bertalanffy's work is the recognition that an organisation is a complex entity comprising interrelating parts, and that breaking the organisation down into its component parts ignores the complex interplay between these components and how this interdependence produces a unique system. One cannot deduce the whole from its parts, or the parts from the whole: it is the system that must be understood. Systems theory, although interdisciplinary in nature, has been influential in developing organisation theory – not least for the way in which it counters the classical approaches such as Taylor and Weber, for their more fragmented partial accounts, and for challenging reductionist approaches in favour of a more holistic approach. The cybernetic model of control, for example, draws heavily on systems theory. To adopt this approach, researchers need to define their level of analysis (whether they are focusing on the individual, group, or organisation, for example) and engage with the complex whole at this level. The challenge of such a grand project may be readily apparent, but there are deeper challenges within this system, which we will return to later when we explore postmodern approaches to the study of organisation. What difficulties can you envisage for a time-pressured manager attempting a systematic analysis?

Contingency theory [3]

What emerges from the studies explored so far is the use of science and rationality as a means to achieving a better understanding of behaviour, resulting in prescriptive approaches to 'managing better'. Not all approaches insisted on a 'one best way' approach, and the idea that 'it depends' emerged in the form of **contingency theory**. In essence, contingency theorists argue that what practice is 'best fit' in a context will depend on a number of factors, such as technology (Woodward, 1965) or the size of the organisation (Pugh *et al*, 1969). Factors that are key variables (or contingencies) in a particular situation need to be analysed to determine what is best practice for that context. Although contingency approaches do not prescribe one best way, they do argue along the lines of '*if*' certain specified variables are the case, '*then*' this particular approach is best (see Chapter 10). And in this way contingent approaches are still prescriptive. These theories have had a substantial impact on organisation theory, and in particular on designing organisation structures to achieve structure-environment fit (see Chapter 14).

Take a moment to return to the Practitioner insight box at the beginning of the chapter, and to Reg's experience in LGE. Do you think there are a set of culturally contingent management practices for dealing with a global downturn?

Rethinking modernist perspectives

The modernist theories seek to create and build on existing management knowledge with the aim of improving our understanding of behaviour so we can manage more effectively. **Modernism** is associated with the Enlightenment (typically assumed to start around the mid-seventeenth or eighteenth centuries, although with origins that can be traced back further) whereby traditional, often religious, orthodoxy was questioned and scientific inquiry and empiricism were employed to find reason. This involved calling into question matters and opinions traditionally taken for granted and ways of working in what might be termed pre-modern times. The contribution of modernism, and the Enlightenment (or 'Age of Reason'), is the act of questioning, and seeking reason and justification behind what is believed (or serving to overturn these facts when they are disproved) and thus explaining phenomena. The search for knowledge allowed society to progress. Knowledge is then codified through the creation of concepts so that it can be communicated. These concepts must be differentiated from the 'everyday' concepts, which tend to be more generalised and simplified. The comparatively rigorous 'academic' concepts, and the interrelationships between these concepts, form the basis of our theories and frameworks of understanding. However, once these concepts are created and shared, they become abstracted from the particular circumstances under which they were formed. (Think of the way Taylor is too readily criticised for the creation of dehumanising work routines without reflecting on many of the organisational challenges he faced at the time.) Over time, we add experience to these abstracted concepts – which adds richness to them of one kind. But of course it also means that these concepts are no longer connected to their origin, and unreflective abstraction can result in concepts that become meaningless as they are divorced from their context, and – through being sufficiently abstract to apply to more than one thing – apply directly to no *particular* circumstance, because no circumstance is 'general' (it always has unique features). This knowledge, developed through rigorous research and analysis, is then used to develop the frameworks we use to order our knowledge. These frameworks help us manage the knowledge we have and also influence our way of processing the information. As we categorise our knowledge, so we build in assumptions regarding similarities between the various parcels of knowledge we place in each category (while ignoring or underplaying the differences). The assumptions are then reflected in the way in which we organise and manage behaviour. These modernist frameworks help simplify or formalise the expectations we have of behaviour. To summarise, modernism is characterised by:

- rationality,
  - based in scientific reason (promoted by experts, and difficult to argue against),
    - which assumes that greater knowledge can be achieved, discovering
      - predictability and stability in patterns of behaviour
        - that can be used to control/organise society better (in the name of 'progress')
          - with a tendency towards prescription towards the 'best way'
            - from the perspective of management.

Ultimately, it is argued here, these approaches fail to deliver consistent results for a multitude of reasons. For one, we are inherently limited by our inability to address all of these factors. What might seem like the perfect solution to a problem – on paper – often doesn't work out in practice because our ability to think through all the variables, interactions and consequences of actions is beyond our bounded capacity. We do not have all the information, and even if we did, we would never be able to think it all through. In addition to the failure to grasp all relevant factors or think them through, both independently and as variables that are intertwined, there is also the individuality of the people being managed (see Chapter 3). Just because, for example, theories of motivation suggest that we are motivated by meaningful work doesn't mean that that applies to everyone (the theories don't make this claim either – see Chapter 5) and simplified, often linear, models almost certainly do not reflect experience. People are unpredictable and different. Models that seek to provide generalised accounts tend towards treating everyone as the same. As we will explore in the box below (see also Chapter 12), this assumption of sameness ignores the difference of individuals and, from a more political stance, can ignore important differences that enable people to live a life truer to their sense of self. However, most students (and managers) rely on modernist thinking in their decision-making. Why might that be the case?

Ethical implications: Levinas and the ethical relation between two parties

One of the great challenges in life is in how we manage sameness and difference (or 'otherness'). Take the work of Emmanuel Levinas (1969), when he says (p.39): 'The collectivity in which I say "you" or "we" is not a plural of the "I". I, you – these are not individuals of a common concept.' What Levinas means, in simple terms, is that we are all different. To reduce (simplify) another person to someone we can understand means that we have reduced them to someone like us, or what we understand of people – because that is the limit to our understanding, but in doing so we lose the nature of the other person, imposing a 'sameness' upon them, and failing to recognise the way in which they are – and must be – different. This is a matter of no small importance to Levinas because his primary concern is the ethical relation between the two parties. Levinas argues that we are in an ethical relation to another (and all others) whether we like it or not. (Of course, what we choose to do with that responsibility is another matter.) How do we respond to them without making assumptions along the lines of what we know about ourselves and others? This challenge lies at the heart of the managing of equality and diversity in organisations. Do we treat everyone the same and thus ignore their differences, or treat everyone differently, and thus not equally?

CRITICAL MANAGEMENT STUDIES

Critical management studies denotes the field of studies that challenges the traditional modernist perspectives for their focus on the **managerial** viewpoint of organising and organisation (Parker, 2002). Let's return to the Introduction, where we considered the approach to organisational behaviour, and in particular the tendency for texts to focus on 'OB' as a body of work that enables a manager to manage more effectively. Or, to put it another way, management knowledge is not so much 'of' management but 'for' management. For example, the Human Relations studies were interested in human behaviour inasmuch as it improved productivity (rather than responded to workers' social needs *per se*). This managerial perspective is criticised by those working in the Critical School for being too interested in how to manage from the point of view of achieving improvements in productivity, or profit, and in doing so failing to consider the 'view from below' (Wilson, 2010). This latter approach is interested in the experience of work, but also in exposing the unequal power relations and inequities within the workplace – those individuals or groups who are (often systematically) disadvantaged within the organisation. Critical perspectives seek to expose these dynamics, and in doing so demonstrate that managing behaviour is not a neutral activity. The 'rationality' of the modernist theories are thus not value-free but exhibit a managerial rationality.

Theorists working within this tradition are therefore confronting what they would describe as the dominant *ideology* of management that pervades our approach to organisational behaviour, where management practices that often exploit individuals (or the environment) have been taken for granted as normal or necessary for 'progress' within society. Critical management studies is noted for its interest in the 'local' experiences of individuals in a particular context, but also, unlike many non-critical studies, in exploring management studies at a macro level, such as the effects of capitalism and globalisation in society (Hardt and Negri, 2001).

Taking your learning further: Manufacturing the Employee

Roy Jacques' *Manufacturing the Employee* (1996) is an excellent book for debunking the myths of management knowledge, and the dominance of managerial discourse. Focus on the Preface and Chapter 1.

Critical theory

Critical theory is not simply a theoretical position or perspective on work and organisation, it is also inherently political in its intentions. By exposing the politics in management and organising practices, critical theorists seek to enable the emancipation of those who have been disadvantaged. They argue that if we are able to understand the nature of these practices through a critical lens, we are better placed to make choices and find ways of working that empower those in the organisation who have traditionally been disempowered – seeking equity in the balance of power. Critical theorists are interested not only in the structure of the organisation, such as the hierarchy of power, but also in the practices and processes that sustain the power relations and are infused in both the formal and informal dynamics of the organisation.

Similarly, they are interested not only in the deliberate acts that seek to maintain advantage (or the status quo) but also in the unintentional, unconscious acts that have the effect of achieving the same end. For example, a job that required someone to be at work by 9 am every morning would systematically discriminate against a single parent who had sole responsibility for taking and collecting the children from school (see Chapter 12).

Critical theorists have an interest in organising beyond the boundary of the workplace, including the 'second' economy of housework (typically unremunerated, mostly undertaken by women and undervalued), cash-in-hand work which is not declared as income, or work that is deemed illegal, such as drug-dealing or, in some countries, prostitution.

Studies within this tradition are usually seeking transformations of practice at a structural level – that is, for example, for all women. This has its own problems because it treats issues of disadvantage in a categorical manner – as if all women, or working mothers, are affected by these dynamics in the same way and a 'universal' response is applicable. As we have noted, critical theory seeks to be political in that it aims to redress the imbalance in society – but in doing so it often looks to find solutions that operate at the level of society, categorising the experiences of disadvantaged 'groups' (women/ethnic minorities/those with a disability, and so on) and seeking ways of empowering these groups with solutions that operate at the structural level (Alvesson and Willmott, 1991). There is also, therefore, a tendency in critical theory towards prescription through its assumptions about the nature of categories of people. It assumes that the majority of people accept the inequalities of the status quo through **false consciousness**, which misleads them into rationalising and accepting society as it is (a form of ideological control) so that they fail to understand the true nature of social processes and how these processes operate at a personal cost to them. Think about a situation in which you felt you were treated unjustly. On reflection, do you think unfair discrimination might have been an underlying cause of your treatment? Have you ever discriminated against someone without realising it at the time? Critical theory challenges us to question our actions more carefully.

Critical theory challenges the modernist project for failing to identify the underlying values within it and for allowing inequalities, but it does not challenge the principle of modernism itself – namely, that through improvements in understanding we can improve society (Alvesson and Willmott, 1991: 435). Critical theory seeks to expose these inequalities and find new and fairer ways of organising. It also highlights the different meanings and experiences of organising.

Symbolic interaction, social construction and sense-making [4]

In contrast to the systemic approaches desired by those working within the modernist tradition which seek to find solutions at the structural or systems level (consider the 'big ideas' in management thinking, such as business process re-engineering and total quality management), an alternative approach is to focus on the relational, or processual, aspect of organising. This approach to understanding organising and organisation treats organisation as the 'outcome' of processes of meaning-making and negotiation of meaning. The negotiated order does not lead to a static outcome but is in a constant process of flux as the 'order' is negotiated and renegotiated. (Think back to 'structure-agency' in the Introduction.)

Underpinning the way in which we make sense of the world is the importance of symbols and signifiers which are implicated in the process of our meaning-making through our interpretations of these symbols and our interactions with others. The work of George Herbert Mead (1934) and then Herbert Blumer were key to developing this understanding. Blumer (1969) developed the idea of 'symbolic interactionism' (SI), stating (p.2) that:

- Human beings act toward things on the basis of the meanings they ascribe to those things.

- The meaning of such things is derived from, or arises out of, the social interaction that one has with others and the society.

- These meanings are handled in, and modified through, an interpretative process used by the person in dealing with the things he/she encounters.

What becomes clear under SI is that 'reality' in organisation is not an independent reality that exists 'outside' of the human perceiving it, but is the reality that is produced through the interactions and negotiations and processes of **sense-making** (Weick, 1969; 1995) in which individuals engage. Contrast this with the modernist approach to understanding human behaviour through 'objective' analysis. Of course, individuals in this process of meaning-making will interpret things differently, and thus the meanings we make will be different (see Chapter 4). At the same time, with some shared social history and context, it is likely that the negotiation of meaning (in simpler terms, what we do when we try to communicate) will result in shared meanings being created that have some corresponding features such that communication is possible (see Chapter 9). The way in which we negotiate our worlds is thus not achieved in isolation but through a process of **intersubjectivity** via shared experiences, and their communication.

One area of organisation study that has benefited most from this field of study is organisational culture (see Chapter 15). Culture is not a 'thing' that can exist independently of the meanings that we make and communicate. A culture's existence and significance is constructed by the members of that organisation, communicated through language in which they express and share, make sense of and negotiate the meaning of the organisation's culture and subculture(s). This communication often involves the use of symbols that reflect the nature of the organisational culture. We only need to discuss an issue with someone else – a news item, or a film, perhaps – to realise that people interpret things differently, so the idea of people interpreting the world differently probably comes as no surprise. However, we tend to treat these subjective world views as if they were 'real' – that is, as if they existed independently. Returning to culture, we find evidence of discussing culture 'as if' it existed 'outside' of the interpretations of its members: it takes on what appears to be an objective reality.

The same can be said for the way in which we understand/create the organisation (Berger and Luckmann, 1966: 54). Berger and Luckmann (1966) argue that what occurs is a process of **objectification** – by which *subjective* phenomena are constructed and negotiated such that they appear and are treated *as if* **objective**/real. The process of negotiation demonstrates how these constructions remain open to continuous change, yet such changes tend to be gradual and minimal – giving the constructs a degree of stability without which they would never achieve an apparently objective status. Once objectified, these constructions (concepts, ideas, and so on) are then the basis for future communication, which explains why constructs are often sustained, comparatively unchanged over time. Indeed, it is the tendency of many constructions not to change easily that is often the cause for concern.

Returning to critical theory, we can see how false consciousness is maintained because certain constructions are socialised and sustained over generations. **Feminist theory** in particular grapples with the challenges of embedded sexed/gendered social stereotypes, and the difficulties in overturning assumptions of what women 'should' do which are not based in biology but sustained social constructions that are, in turn, embedded in the socialisation of future generations (see Chapter 12). This process of taking on the (socially constructed) norms of society is important for understanding the nature of power and the ways in which groups socialise new members (see Chapter 7).

These constructions not only affect the way in which we understand particular concepts but also frame our thinking, which in turn influences our actions. Karl Weick's (1969) theory of sense-making explored how organisational realities are enacted and given an appearance of objective reality (p.243): 'Managers construct, rearrange, single out, and demolish many "objective" features of their surroundings. When people act they unrandomize variables, insert vestiges of orderliness, and literally create their own constraints.' We assume the environment is real, but it is actually the way in which we make sense of it that 'creates' the features to which we then respond.

We can see this in everyday behaviour. Imagine that someone makes a joke at our expense. If we sense this as an insult, we behave very differently from the way we do if we understand it as part and parcel of everyday banter. By reacting in this (or that) way, we *create the environment* (hostile, or friendly). We can also see here how sense-making 'frames' our decisions and actions. Weick argues (1995: 127) that we think in narratives, and that for things to make sense we favour coherence and plausibility over accuracy – tending to 'tidy up' conflicting accounts so that they appear to 'make more sense'. These narratives are not only managerial or authoritative but are also found in gossip and workplace humour.

Return to the LGE Practitioner insight case study at the beginning of this chapter. Consider how the organisation's interpretation of the global economic environment (as a sustained downturn rather than a 'blip' in the market) shaped its actions.

POSTMODERNISM

Perhaps one of the most challenging views that we face when exploring theories of organisation can be found within the postmodern tradition, not least because – by its very nature – it precludes simple definition. **Postmodernism** forces us to consider *why* it is that we understand organisations in the way that we do, and in particular exposes the issues that have tended to be marginalised such as gender, power, and ethics. (In this sense it has much in common with critical theory.)

Although any 'definition' can be challenged, a few points of orientation are nonetheless useful (see Cooper and Burrell, 1988). Firstly, postmodernism has its origins outside of organisational theory, is influenced by philosophy and literary theory, and can be seen in fields of practice such as architecture. Those not schooled in philosophy may therefore find the concepts more challenging. Secondly, postmodernism is often contrasted with post-modernism, the latter typically interpreting 'post-' as meaning 'after' modernism. Critical theory can be seen as post-modernist in that it critiques the modernist project of Enlightenment for failing to achieve fairness and equality in its project – its critique thus comes 'after', even though both are currently in usage. But as we have already seen, these temporal categorisations are problematic, as elements of all these perspectives coexist. Alternatively, postmodernism (without the hyphen) usually refers to a movement in which there are shared concerns and challenges to the modernist project of Enlightenment. The labelling of what is postmodernism is further confused by the fact that even those who are identified with this movement eschew the label because the idea of labelling represents a containment that the postmodernist would reject (Parker, 2002).

Postmodernism as a 'perspective' tends to demonstrate concern for claimed 'truths' in society that shape knowledge and frame thinking. Postmodernism shares many parallels with critical theory and understands reality as socially constructed, but unlike critical theory, postmodernism does not view modernism as a project in need of fixing but as an impossible, pointless project that can never be fulfilled. To explain this it is best to return to the ambitions of the modernist project – namely, to produce increasingly refined knowledge with which to organise society more effectively. Because of the use of 'reason' and scientific inquiry to develop new knowledge, these developments have given the impression of being value-neutral – but as we have already seen, there is always an underlying substantive rationality: a set of values deemed to be 'progressive'. These are often framed in terms that are hard to challenge, such as 'freedom', 'equality' or 'human rights'. However, the nature or content of these values (or their interpretation) demonstrates their partiality. For example, as *postcolonial* theorists will point out, many of these values are in fact 'Western' and 'imposed' as 'good practice' through supranational institutions on other nation states in the name of progress. What the West understands as 'freedom', for example, may not be recognised as freedom by other societies with markedly different religious and cultural traditions (Prasad, 2003).

Lyotard (1979) drew attention to what he referred to as the myth of progress and its failure to respond to human needs. What we can take from this is not only that developments (even those based on 'science') may not always be for the best, but also that we should question the premise of what is deemed to be 'progress'. Let us take organisational change (see Chapter 14). Typically, we assume that change is good, and usually worry about those who resist change (and how we can persuade them to change). But what if there are good reasons why change is resisted – are we sometimes changing for change's sake? What are the criteria for judging 'progress' – or, to put it another way, towards what end goal is progress being made: personal wealth, happiness, a better global environment, more money for the shareholder?

What is brought into question here is the unreflective assumptions behind the creation of a better society – what Lyotard referred to as the **grand narrative** of progress. Furthermore, these unreflective assumptions are not neutral in their impact but have powerful effects in society. Most of us accept the idea that 'progress' is good, and do not challenge the dominant view (or ideology) of what is considered progressive. For example, it is only comparatively recently that concerns about the environmental impact of our activities and our modes of organising production and consumption (from industrialisation into the modern age) have received widespread and sustained criticism (see Chapter 18). This shift in thinking forces us to question what has previously been encapsulated in the term 'progress'. Postmodernism seeks to expose that myth, and in doing so to enable different viewpoints to emerge and new actions to be taken. As Lyotard put it (1979: xxiv), postmodernism is about an incredulity toward meta-narratives.

Narratives and discourse

Our theories – particularly those within the modernist tradition – claim to give us the means to manage better by employing reason and rationality to overcome the pre-modern approach which relied upon the religious orthodoxy of superstition for its guiding structures. By and large we have been convinced by the modernist project through its use of science, and the implication of expert knowledge. We are convinced that these ideas are right not only because of what is said but also because of who said it (the experts). The voice of experts carries greater legitimacy, and their **discourse** – or their (grand) narrative – becomes dominant in society (see O'Connor, 1996). Challenges to these narratives are limited in part because of the truth claims they make, which are accepted in society (until another dominant narrative, from a competing expert community, 'takes over': we are currently experiencing the battle for dominance between the environmentalists and the sceptics in the debate over climate change, for instance).

The ability to create and sustain these dominant narratives reflects the distribution of power in society. Those who shape knowledge in society are clearly in a more powerful position partly because they influence the way people think but also – through their perceived expertise in making their truth claims – because it is hard to resist the effects of this knowledge. Those who challenge dominant 'truths' in society are marginalised as 'ignorant' or 'subversive', and their views are consequently discounted. Postmodernism exposes what it sees as the fallacy of this assumption, and argues for the validity of all voices – including the voices of those typically silenced by their being discounted. The climate change debate, and the implications for the way in which we live our lives, is challenging the dominant pro-business lobby which has enjoyed a privileged position in shaping political discourse. After all, how do you disagree with a sector that seeks to give people employment, create wealth, and so on?

The role of language – of *discourse* – is important to the postmodernist. Languages used in everyday communication are often referred to as 'living languages'. Any such language is not simply 'used' but also (re)created through its use. New words are formed and new meanings are created. Postmodernism highlights the arbitrary nature of the language of modernism. It exposes the way the knowledge or common sense of modernism institutionalises certain ways of seeing the world. It can be said to 'do the thinking for us' or close off the range of possibilities of thinking. The language of rational-neutrality, science and management efficiency are discourses that we have come to take for granted. These discourses are partial and incomplete. For the postmodernist knowledge cannot be made complete. No amount of scientific endeavour (the modernist project) can enable us to 'capture' all knowledge. Instead, it remains reductive and *representational* of reality – our concepts inevitably remain inadequate when attempting to grasp the nature of things. A postmodernist exposes these failings, and their irresolvable nature, but also requires us to consider the impact of this state of affairs. In short, if our structures of knowledge are flawed, what does this mean for the knowledge we are constructing, which in turn is being used to govern society? What are our 'rules' for generating and evaluating our theories? What does this mean in terms of what can be said, and be recognised as meaningful and valid as opposed to rejected as spurious and without a claim to validity?

Knowledge is thus inextricably linked with power (see Chapter 13) both in the way it creates, produces and reproduces knowledge (what can be said) and in the way it recognises only those voices which conform to, or reproduce, this knowledge (who can speak and be taken seriously). These norms of society both shape our thinking and are implicated in regulating us – trying to ensure that we remain 'normal' or *normalized* (Foucault, 1980). The arbitrary nature of discourse is obscured by the perceived legitimacy (acceptability, normality) of the dominant narrative in society at the time.

In Weir's film (1989) *Dead Poets Society*, Mr Keating (played by Robin Williams) is the new English teacher in a conservative boy's boarding school who encourages his students to stretch their minds and challenge the 'authoritative' texts on how to read poetry. Symbolically, he asks the students to tear out the pages that prescribe the way students are asked to read the poems. Mr Keating teaches his students to think for themselves, to reject the pressure to conform, and to express themselves freely. Do you think another teacher would give high marks to essays that did not conform to the traditional and recognised way of reading poetry?

Management discourse frames our thinking in particular ways and remains largely unchallenged – treated as a taken-for-granted 'common sense' (Jacques, 1996). As Clegg and Palmer (1996: 2) remind us, most of what managers do is about discourse:

> discussion, ordering, pleading, condensing, summarizing, synthesizing, presenting, reporting – all activities that take place through the media of various texts and representations.

HRM specialists are key for framing what is considered fair and ethical, how to manage equality, and provide support (Deetz, 2003). As Townley (1993: 526) argues, HRM is

> a discipline and a discourse ... HRM serves to render organizations and their participants calculable arenas, offering, through a variety of technologies, the means by which activities and individuals become knowable and governable.

HRM specialists are the *experts* with the *legitimised knowledge* who *frame acceptable ways* of managing. Consider how psychological approaches to understanding people are both a contribution and limitation to understanding behaviour in the way that they define how people are knowable (see Chapter 17).

Taking your learning further: Power/knowledge and HRM

Barbara Townley's paper (1993) is a good way to work through the implications of power/knowledge in the context of HRM.

The perceived 'expertise' and legitimacy of managers, academics and management consultants in framing problems and offering solutions means that they play a crucial role in the production of knowledge (note the use of the word 'production', and not 'discovery' – see Alvesson, 2004). Some of these discourses become dominant and receive widespread acclaim. Peters and Waterman's *In Search of Excellence* (1982), incorporating eight themes for success, received widespread attention. The subsequent failures of some of its 'excellent' companies a few years after the book's publication have led to criticism, but the millions of copies sold demonstrate how 'formulas for success' can be persuasive and pervasive. Not only does it seem common sense to adopt the 'latest management thinking' but those who do not do so might appear to be less competent (Abrahamson, 1996).

Metaphors [5]

The way in which we make sense of organisations and behaviour is often through the use of metaphors as a rhetorical device. The key text exploring this is Gareth Morgan's book *Images of Organization*, which (Morgan, 1997: 4):

> explores and develops the art of reading and understanding organizational life. It is based on a very simple premise: that all theories of organization and management are based on implicit images or metaphors that lead us to see, understand, and manage organizations in distinctive yet partial ways ... The use of metaphor implies *a way of thinking* and *a way of seeing* that pervade how we understand our world generally.

We might, for example, refer to an organisation operating like a machine or in military style. These images are powerful tools of communication, and draw on aspects of something which is seen to be comparable with another. It brings to the fore certain aspects of something, but not of other things. A business organisation operating 'in military style' might be characterised by clear lines of authority and discipline, but is unlikely to involve killing people, even though it might involve expanding into another country. The use of a metaphor also means that attention is drawn to certain aspects of the organisation, but – consequently – not others. Using metaphors *frames* the way in which we see the organisation. Morgan takes this argument further (1997: 5):

> When we approach metaphor in this way we see that our simple premise *that all theory is metaphor* has far-reaching consequences. We have to accept that any theory or perspective that we bring to the study of organization and management, while capable of creating valuable insights, is also incomplete, and potentially misleading ... Metaphor is inherently paradoxical. It can create powerful insights that also become distortions, as the way of seeing created through a metaphor becomes a way of *not* seeing.

Morgan argues that management has been dominated by a reliance on the 'mechanistic' metaphor, and has managed accordingly (at this point you might be thinking 'Taylorism!'). Held by the dominant metaphor (read 'narrative' or 'discourse'), we have become trapped into one way of managing and find it difficult to conceptualise and manage differently. This metaphor also links with the bureaucratic mode of organising (Morgan, 1997: 6). Mechanistic approaches are seductive because they are relatively simple, and relate to recognised ideas such as rational organisation and efficiency, but result in our seeing everything through what becomes a commonsensical or 'obvious' lens. Unfortunately, this includes the tendency to treat humans as 'mechanical' components.

Meaning and deconstruction [6]

Postmodernism has excited strong views within the field, resulting in a new turn in theorising, but has also been criticised. In particular, it is accused of being a 'fatal distraction' from the proper role of organisation studies (Thompson, 1995; Linstead, 2004). In organisation theory, postmodernism suffers from a tendency towards a simplification of its tenets to enable its communication – which this text is equally guilty of.

There are many challenges facing the scholar who wishes to delve deeper into this field of study. One such issue worthy of a brief mention here is the difference between postmodernism and post(-)structuralism (written with or without the hyphen). Poststructuralism is often used as an interchangeable term with postmodernism, but is also seen as distinct from, or an 'aspect' of, postmodernism. Poststructuralism emerged as a response to the criticisms of structuralism in language, and is associated with the work of Jacques Derrida and his method of '**deconstruction**' (Derrida, 1976). In particular, poststructuralists are keen to dissociate words with fixed meaning, insisting instead that language and its meaning is unstable and plural. The links between the two are such that to treat them 'together' is broadly accepted within organisational behaviour.

Why does language matter so much? As we have already seen, discourse communicates knowledge that is invested with power (Foucault referred to knowledge/power). Derrida argues that language has no fixed meaning – indeed, it already has multiple interpretations. (Just think about the meaning of words taken out of context, or placed in different contexts.) In deconstructing the text, Derrida attempted to expose the foundations upon which the text was developed, but at the same time demonstrate its irreducible nature and complexity. If multiple interpretations are possible, and the nature of language is fundamentally unstable, one cannot ascribe meaning to text – meaning always escapes us. If the meaning of language is unknowable, then so must be the 'knowledge' we communicate. Derrida was interested in how language is structured, and the genesis of this structure – but not from the point of an origin (an original meaning) but from its original complexity (it never had 'a' meaning). Deconstruction of the text (spoken or written) is not to demonstrate the 'true' or 'alternative' meaning (for there isn't one), but to reveal the nature of the text as based on assumptions, contradictions and exclusions.

In particular, Derrida argued that language tended to be structured in binary terms – good/ evil, man/woman, master/slave – with a corresponding tendency to privilege certain terms or categories. We can see here how Derrida's work is important for feminism. Women are not only contrasted with men (with ascribed values attached as to what it means to be a woman/man) but they are also viewed as 'second'. Similar inequalities can be found in other categories, such as race, (dis)ability, class, and so on. These categories form the basis of anti-discrimination legislation. The nature of language is very important. Because language enables the construction of reality, the way in which we order this language (or the way in which it is ordered) shapes our reality and thus our ways of thinking and acting: it has a disciplining effect. The fact that language is not based on a pure origin fundamentally destabilises the notion of truth claims as to what text means. It challenges the claims of experts to be able to 'explain' and find truth. There are, and always will be, multiple meanings. All these meanings are valid. We should not treat the meaning of concepts as 'fixed' but understand them as contested and fluid (Kilduff, 1993; Linstead, 1993).

Postmodernism 'in practice'

One of the challenges faced by organisation theorists in working through the implications of postmodernism for organisational behaviour is in responding to the 'So what?' question. Postmodernism clearly rejects the replacement of current structures of knowledge with a revised structure (as found in critical theory). Its challenge is instead to expose us to the ordering devices of such structures. Its project is that of destabilising, exposing, and giving voice – refusing any totalising account and always keeping open space for difference. This creative possibility remains, however, unstructured. Even the idea of 'method' is, strictly speaking, beyond what can be said as a postmodernist. So how can we try to be postmodernist?

1 *Contextualise*

   We may not be able to ascertain one true meaning, but we can at least take time to consider meaning in its context. What is the genesis of this meaning? Or, to put it another way, how did we get to this way of understanding what this word means? How does the context shape its meaning?

2 *Challenge*

   If there is no 'truth', what is it that we are currently taking for granted and, moreover, upon which we are making future decisions? Whose expertise or authority are we taking for granted? Learn to be sceptical of others, but also question your own motives and interpretations (see the box below). Avoid what is called 'discursive closure' (where a meta-narrative takes over).

3 *Be creative*

   Learn to see the world differently – disrupt your usual way of thinking. Be creative with your concepts and see where this takes you.

4 *Allow for change*

There's no point in creating a new meta-narrative, or 'grand narrative' – the object is not to totalise but to recognise the fundamental instability of knowledge and possibilities: meaning is always beyond our grasp. Remain curious!

5 *Take a chance.*

There are risks in challenging the status quo: we may be marginalised and ignored. Refusing to conform to the norms can result in a crisis of identity as we are no longer recognised as doing things the 'normal' way.

Applying theory to practice: Reflexivity

When we interpret and order our understanding we inevitably impose our own interests (knowingly or otherwise) in this process. Reflexivity demands that we apply the critical lens with which we are investigating a phenomenon to ourselves in that process. If, for example, we are challenging a body of knowledge and the way in which it employs ways of ordering knowledge and thus, perhaps, giving priority to certain aspects of knowledge over others, then we must apply the same principle of questioning to our own ordering of knowledge and prioritisation. For example, you may ask yourself 'Why do I think the management consultant's report on our market position is more credible than views from our workforce? With what criteria have I developed my own account of a particular dispute between colleagues?' See Gergen and Gergen (1991) for a discussion of reflexivity, and on the impact we have on the phenomenon being studied.

Theory or common sense?

The types of problems we face in organisations often parallel problems we may face in other contexts that we approach with what we might call 'common sense'. This way of understanding relies on beliefs and assumptions that are taken for granted. It contrasts with what we might consider to be a more reflective common sense – common sense that comes from critical thinking. It may confirm the everyday assumptions that we usually make, or it may demonstrate that a more nuanced position has to be taken, informed by theory and experience. We wouldn't expect research findings to be consistently in stark contrast with common sense, after all, because research explores the experiences of people in organisations. We must also, as we have already seen, understand the difference between the everyday use of language and concepts, and more precise and detailed, rigorous understandings. The danger of common sense is that everyday common sense can turn into an unquestioned state of affairs, treated as self-evident – turned into 'ideas' and 'concepts'. Being lulled into a state where we no longer ask questions that may on the surface appear unnecessary, perhaps even silly questions to ask, risks the perpetuation of systematic problems and limits our understanding.

Applying theory to practice: How do we know?

These perspectives raise questions of the truth claims that we can make, of what we can know, and how we can know (see Burrell and Morgan, 1979). In technical terms, these are questions of epistemology (how we can know the world) and ontology (what we know). Ontology relates to what we understand as 'real'. Essentially, we either view the world *subjectively*, which argues that things exist when we experience them and give them meaning, or *objectively*, by which things exist independently of their being experienced and attributed meaning. Epistemology relates closely to ontology in that it looks at how people develop knowledge (and decide what is true or not). Subjectivists would seek knowledge through accounts of experience, seeking to understand people's interpretations of their experiences (and of course in turn 'interpret' these interpretations which experienced researchers seek to manage through reflective practice). If we think about the example of culture, we can understand how culture is socially constructed by its members – through processes of interpretation, negotiation and communication. It also means that if an observer external to the organisation attempts to understand or interpret this culture, they will not only have their own, differing interpretation, but as an outsider they risk imposing an interpretation that lacks insight. **Postcolonialism** would challenge the ability of the Western researcher to provide a meaningful account of the organisational culture of an institution based in a developing economy of which they had no prior experience. In contrast, objectivists would seek to understand the world as independent of these interpretations, and thus observe and measure people's behaviour, seeking to make it more predictable. Understanding ontology and epistemology enables us to think through questions of the validity of truth claims.

Conclusion

In the light of what has been said, you might be wondering what studying organisational behaviour can achieve, since studying behaviour doesn't give any clear answers to the question of what to do, or how to manage. However, the subject gives us insight into behaviours, and, through the various perspectives, provides us with alternative ways of thinking through problems. Greater understanding of the motivations and behaviours of individuals enables us to make more informed decisions and to reflect more carefully on our own practice (whether as managers or employees at any level of the organisation). The multiplicity of perspectives and 'ways of seeing' may, for some, appear to be leading towards unnecessary confusion. Instead, we argue here that this position is not only inevitable (no two situations are identical, and there is always ambiguity, so unreflective application of off-the-shelf universal solutions are at best naïve, at worst dangerous) but that there is also an ethical imperative to see each situation for what it is – to understand its particularities, contextualised, and with competing understandings. In this way we have the best chance of applying our theories of motivation and behaviour in a useful and fair way. To treat these theories as prescriptive guidelines risks poor decisions, and undermines the responsibilities of the decision-maker to 'think for themselves' (Jeanes and Muhr, 2010). To that end the more recent approaches do not replace the earlier studies but can all play a part in informing understanding and practice.

The challenge for many within organisations (rather than those working in a theoretical tradition, such as organisation theorists) is how to balance the critical perspectives with the need to apply management knowledge to improve the effectiveness of activities. Writing on organisational behaviour, as well as our own way of seeing the world which we bring into the organisation, is not value-neutral. We must therefore be reflective and reflexive in the way we think and practise. Awareness of the multiple lenses available to us that help us understand behaviour in organisations enables us to be more politically aware and ethical in our choices. In this way these critical, more esoteric perspectives are inherently practical. You may not remember every study you learn about, but developing the practice of reflexive thinking is a skill that is highly desirable.

This ambiguity may be frustrating or liberating for a student of organisational behaviour. We hope that it is what makes this field exciting. It does not undermine the value in exploring studies, but requires us to keep open the space for alternative views, and explains why the generic solutions to managing behaviour often do not work. Imagine what might have happened if Reg Bull – who was introduced at the start of this chapter – had insisted on sticking to his Western, consultative approach to management!

End notes

[1] See also Chapter 14.

[2] See also Chapters 13 and 14.

[3] See also Chapter 10.

[4] See also Chapters 9 and 12.

[5] See also Chapter 9.

[6] See also Chapter 16.

REVIEW AND DISCUSSION QUESTIONS

REVIEW QUESTIONS

1 How does the terminology of management affect the way in which we think about organisational behaviour?

2 Why are traditional approaches to management (those which would be deemed as 'modernist') so compelling?

3 Why is discourse so important to the study of organisations?

4 What are the similarities and differences between critical theory and postmodernism?

5 What role does rationality play in helping us to understand organisational behaviour?

DISCUSSION QUESTIONS

1 How practical are the critical and postmodern perspectives for a manager?

2 How would you go about trying to be an ethical manager?

3 How important are 'big events' like the collapse of Enron (and the revelations about the corporation's working practices) and the banking crisis in shaping the way in which we talk about and think about organisations and organisational behaviour?

4 How do these various perspectives help us understand organisational behaviour, and become more effective managers and colleagues? How could an understanding of these perspectives make you more attractive to an employer?

5 What metaphor would you use to describe the institution in which you work or study? How does this help you explain the organisation? How does it not help?

FURTHER READING

Grey, C. (2005) *A Very Short, Fairly Interesting and Reasonably Cheap Book about Studying Organization.* London: Sage. This text explores a range of management perspectives: it contextualises and critiques some of the standard interpretations through which these accounts are presented.

Alvesson, M. and Willmott, H. (2003) *Studying Management Critically.* London: Sage. This follows a more critical tradition and relates the different perspectives to different areas of management, such as HRM, and business ethics.

Parker, M. (2000) 'Postmodernizing organizational behaviour: new organizations or new organizational theory?', in Barry *et al*, *Organization and Management: A critical text.* London: Thomson Learning. This chapter is an updated and revised version of a paper first published in *Organization Studies* (1992). The paper gives a sense of history behind the influence of postmodernism in studies of organisational behaviour.

Hardy, C., Clegg, S.R. and Nord, W. (1996) *Handbook of Organization Studies.* London: Sage. This covers just about everything, including comprehensive chapters on the different perspectives.

Morgan, G. (1997) *Images of Organization.* London: Sage. Morgan's 'images' enable you to delve deeper into the use and consequences of metaphors.

Gabriel, Y. (2008) *Organizing Words.* Oxford: Oxford University Press. This is a useful thesaurus (extended glossary) of the key terms used in the field of organisation studies.

KEY SKILLS

DEVELOPING CRITICAL THINKING SKILLS AND REFLECTIVE LEARNING

In this chapter there has been an emphasis on the need to reflect on the ways in which knowledge is produced and the capacity of knowledge to then regulate further knowledge creation. One of the challenges we face with management knowledge is the separation between our management concepts and everyday experience. By its very nature our codified knowledge must abstract itself from the nature of the thing itself. However, this poses challenges for the ways in which we work. Derrida, with others, reminds us that we need to be aware of the genesis of our concepts, and the dangers that underlie the tendency to build on knowledge/concepts that have become accepted, uncritically. Organisation, even management, is a construction – a concept that we have created rather than a pre-given 'fact' (see the section on sense-making). The problem with labelling a thing is that we lose sight of its origin, and often then transfer this label too readily to 'similar' things – and in doing so lose the thing itself, and its meaning, or forget that this relates to our own construction. Management education has been described as a 'violence' to the mind because it means people stop *thinking*. This is not to suggest that the theories of organisational behaviour have no value, but that they are not a substitute for thinking, and must be used reflectively and reflexively. This also poses challenges to teachers of organisational behaviour. Do we fill students with theorems and ideas that are posed as absolute knowledge, or do we undermine this knowledge in an endeavour to encourage students to 'think for themselves'? The consequences of education can be seen in the LGE Practitioner insight case study – in which (culturally specific) education was implicated in how the problem was posed, and the solution found. As Reg put it: 'Socrates versus Confucius!'

We have commented on the partiality of theories and perspectives, but of course it is also our own partiality that is important and of which we must remain reflective when thinking through problems. Remember – how you frame the problem then affects how you think it through.

CREATIVE SKILLS

The great thing about challenging traditional ways of working and thinking is that it actually demands that we be creative in the way we think and act – to rip up the book of instructions, as they did in *Dead Poets Society*. This sounds difficult – and it should do, because it is! To be a creator you must be grabbed by the impossibilities of a situation and create your own possibilities as a consequence. If each challenging situation is novel (no two situations are ever alike in all ways), then you cannot reach for an off-the-shelf solution, you must *create* it. Of course, this doesn't stop you thinking with the help of previous ideas – and

organisational behaviour has a wealth of material to help you – it just means that you should not rely on them to give you 'the answer': that's for you to create. And it's not just in your ways of thinking that you are creative, but also in the way you live your life. The act of living is about creating new ways of life. If you think about some of the people we most admire, it is often because they have lived their life differently – created new possibilities. The global environmental challenges we face will soon require all of us to create new ways of living.

PROFESSIONAL JUDGEMENT, DECISION-MAKING, PROBLEM-SOLVING AND SOCIAL RESPONSIBILITY

Management education is not about providing all the answers but sensitising students to their own particular way of sense-making, and ordering of the world, and how management knowledge is not 'fact' but is produced and legitimised (Chia and Morgan, 1996). Students of organisational behaviour (and by students, one can also include managers and other employees – anyone who needs to understand behaviour – which pretty much includes everyone) therefore need to keep an open mind to different ways of seeing the world, reflecting on why things are organised in the way they are, and how things could be organised differently. Unlike many of the early approaches to understanding behaviour, such as those employing experimental methods, decisions on how to manage or behave must be made in time and space, in the context of an immediate situation. We need to remain reflective of what is going on, but also reflexive about our own self in this process. Decision-making is **embodied**: a particular person, with a particular identity (or identities), *feeling* in a particular way, is making the decision. How is that shaping the way in which they think and decide? We must consider:

- the intertwined nature of work-life: non-work life affects behaviour at work, and work life affects life 'outside' – organising doesn't stop at the factory gates
- the everyday realities of work (see Noon and Blyton, 2007) – what people experience in the workplace, and how this is influenced by (and influences) their class status, gender, and so on
- difference in people: we need to be sensitive to their individual sense of identity, needs, and so on
- complexity and ambiguity – keeping this in mind enables you to think through the particularities of circumstances, rather than assume that some 'off-the-shelf' solution can be applied; it also reminds you that your decision is not legitimised by taking the packaged solution, and that you will never be able to make sense of everything
- power: there will always be alternative accounts – the dominant narrative isn't the only narrative that is important.

BEST PRACTICE

The reflexive manager who is mindful of the way in which language frames thinking, and seeks to disrupt and challenge these ways of seeing the world, keeping an open mind and remaining aware that there are always alternative perspectives. Such managers won't be stuck with a sense of 'unknowability' even though they recognise the imperfections of their knowledge: they will act and make decisions after reflection. An awareness of people's inherent differences will make such a manager a more ethical manager.

WORST PRACTICE

The unreflective manager, who follows the latest (or oldest!) fads and fashions in management without thinking about the context and the nature of the problem. A manager who focuses only on the managerial problem, and forgets the perspective of those working in the organisation – that is, treating people as resources in a system rather than as humans with needs and differences that may not be captured in our traditional ways of understanding.

PART ONE

Individuals

Chapter 3
Personality

Steven A. Woods and Claire Hardy

Contents

Key Learning Outcomes

By the end of this chapter you should be able to:

- describe common-sense views of personality, and understand how they differ from scientific theories
- describe and understand theories of personality:
  - Psychodynamic
  - Behaviourist
  - Social cognitive
  - Trait
- understand the importance of trait theory for organisational behaviour
- describe the Big Five model of personality, and understand its importance in organisational behaviour
- discern how important work outcomes are related to personality traits
- understand how personality is related to other kinds of individual difference attributes.

 PRACTITIONER INSIGHT

E.ON UK

E.ON UK is one of the leading energy suppliers in the UK, supplying around 8 million gas and electricity customers, including domestic and corporate customers. E.ON UK is part of the larger E.ON group, of which the headquarters is in Germany. E.ON is the world's largest investor-owned power and gas company. E.ON UK stemmed from the privatisation of the UK energy industry in February of 1988, and strives to meet the energy challenge trilemma – energy efficiency, energy security, and climate. We speak to **Fran Pestana, Learning and Development Business Partner**, about a learning development intervention that was developed at the company to enable middle managers to increase their level of competence.

E.ON employs over 80,000 employees worldwide and approximately 17,000 of these are in the UK. These employees work under E.ON's functional structure that comprises Energy generation, Distribution, and Retail. The Retail division is responsible for E.ON UK's marketing, sales and customer service strategy and operations. Following the arrival of a new Customer Service Director, a new management methodology was introduced throughout the customer service function. The aim was to develop consistency in management style and approach from senior manager through to front-line manager. Having

developed the new management methodology, the Customer Service Director worked with the HR team to define areas of behavioural competence required to apply the management method effectively.

Assessment centres were used to determine current levels of competence in the middle managment popluation. The results of the assessment centres highlighted the need for middle managers to develop their self-awareness, leadership, ability to manage performance, hold difficult conversations, deal with conflict, lead change, and work more effectively in teams. The Learning and Development Team were brought in to consult further and create a learning and development intervention to address these needs. They considered personality to be a key issue to focus on.

How could you apply knowledge of personality to build self-awareness, leadership and team development for this management population?

What techniques could be used to integrate personality into strategies for developing middle managerial competence?

Once you have read this chapter, return to these questions and think about how you could answer them.

Introduction

Think for a moment about your perception of an ideal work colleague – or perhaps an ideal employee working in administration, sales, or customer service. Describe them. Write down your description on a scrap of paper, keeping it to about five or six sentences. Do it now, perhaps while getting a tea or coffee. Then read on.

Look at the description you've written, and highlight all those aspects that you think refer to aspects of individual **personality**. Our bet is that most of them do. If you have used words like 'organised', 'courteous', 'friendly', 'talkative', 'reliable', 'dependable', 'calm under pressure', 'flexible', 'creative', 'positive', 'sociable', 'confident' and 'understanding', then you have presumed that personality attributes are important determinants of people's behaviour, and of effectiveness at work. And the really important thing is, you are correct. Personality is one of the most crucial aspects of **individual differences** that determines how people respond to different situations at work, how they typically interact and behave with other people, and in respect of their work tasks. How do we know this? Because over the past 100 years or so, psychologists – and in particular, work and organisational psychologists – have accumulated a vast array of theory, knowledge, and evidence that personality matters at work. This chapter is a journey through that knowledge, and its applied implications for organisational behaviour.

If you think that personality is important at work, then we hope to confirm it, but we will probably also challenge some of your assumptions about the relationship between personality and behaviour. If you are not sure, we hope instead to present enough evidence to convince you that an understanding of organisational behaviour is incomplete without an understanding of personality.

The following chapter presents an overview of the field of personality. The chapter begins by briefly presenting factors that are believed to determine an individual's personality (including genetic factors, social factors, situational factors and cultural factors). The main theories of personality are then discussed before we explore evidence that illustrates important personality attributes which influence various organisational behaviours, including job performance, leadership, teamwork, job attitudes, ability, motivation and vocational interest. By the end of the chapter you should have a clearer understanding about the area of personality and appreciate its significant role in business and organisations.

IMPLICIT VERSUS SCIENTIFIC IDEAS ABOUT PERSONALITY

Just as individuals differ in their physical appearance, people also differ psychologically in terms of their temperament and character. We regularly make assumptions about people we meet and about the 'kind of person they are'. You most likely do this with people you meet at work, whether they are clients, colleagues, supervisors or subordinates. If you are a student, you probably make assumptions about the personalities of your course colleagues or university teachers.

Everyday theorising about personality and individual traits is referred to as '**implicit personality theory**'. It is our common-sense, often stereotypical and evidence-free judgement about the kinds of characteristics that we like, and that we perceive in others. Such theories help us to make sense of the social world around us. Our perceptions are biased and simple, but if they were more complex, we would find it very difficult to be productive and to get on in our lives. Our own judgements and perceptions are no basis for a scientific approach to understanding individuals, however, and this is where theory helps.

Psychologists have studied personality for more than a century, and this has led to a diversity of theories and ideas about how best to conceptualise it. We will review these theories in the chapter, but first it is important to think about some background to them. First, it is essential to understand that each theory presents a representation of personality. Theory aims to describe and explain the antecedents, processes and mechanisms underlying regularities and patterns in people's behaviour, and their thoughts and feelings. Second, the theories should not be seen as competing in a true sense. Different theories provide unique insights into personality and its consequences, such that they are complementary. Moreover, the ideas can be integrated, which is evident in Funder's (2001: 198) definition of personality:

> an individual's characteristic pattern of thought, emotion, and behavior, together with the psychological mechanisms – hidden or not – behind those patterns.

This is a good working definition, which captures the main essence of personality. It consists of regularities and patterns in characteristics, behaviour, thought and emotion, and the mechanisms and processes that give rise to them. In the next section, we review the major theories of personality.

THEORIES OF PERSONALITY

Psychodynamic theory

Psychodynamic, or psychoanalytic, theory will forever be associated with the work of Sigmund Freud. A Viennese physician by training, Freud has made one of the most influential contributions of any psychologist, despite his theorising having serious weaknesses and limitations. Freud's revolutionary theory challenged the view that behaviour was a consequence of rational, conscious thought processes. He believed rather that behaviour resulted from unconscious conflicts nurtured and developed through experience in childhood. His theories are undoubtedly interesting, and do have some implications for the way we understand personality at work.

Freud proposed that personality is developed by individuals passing through four psychosexual stages of development. Freud claimed that although normal personality development involves passing through each stage successfully, most individuals experience some degree of fixation at some point during their development. This can occur when there is some problem with adjustment or development at a particular psychosexual stage. In psychoanalytic theory, such fixations manifest themselves in adult behaviour and personality.

Another important area of Freud's work was his proposed structure of the mind, and of unconscious conflict. Freud divided the mind into three structures, which he called the id, the ego, and the superego. According to Freud, each of these structures is responsible for different operations and influences on individuals' behaviour and personality.

- The unconscious part of the mind is called the *id*, containing the primary source of all instinctual motivation.

- The *superego* is divided into two substructures – the conscious, and the ego-ideal. The conscious part contains the rules of society and determines which behaviours are acceptable, and punishes unacceptable behaviours with feelings of guilt.

- Mediating between the desire of the id and the morals of the superego is the *ego*, reflecting the self, and controlling behaviour. It is driven by the reality principle, negotiating and facilitating a compromise between competing pressures of the id and the superego.

Freud said that these competing structures created conflicts, to refer to which he used the term *psychodynamic*. The results or outcomes of these conflicts are observed in the subsequent behaviour. Patterns in conflict processes and outcomes lead to regularities in behaviour, and thereby to personality.

The major criticism of psychodynamic theory is that it is not testable, and therefore cannot be considered scientific. The theory also lacks applied value – but there are some important implications of Freudian thinking for how we understand behaviour:

1   Childhood development has an important influence on later-life personality. This influence might not work in the ways that Freud assumed, but childhood experience and learning is critical to personality.

2   People's behaviour is not divorced from societal considerations and social contexts. Behavioural drives are controlled and managed according to people's perceptions of the world around them, and how behaviour is deemed acceptable or unacceptable. A similar argument could be made about behaviour in organisations. People may be driven, or prefer to behave, in one way, but be constrained by the accepted norms of an organisation.

3   Some of the processes that drive our thoughts, emotions, and behaviour are unconscious, although the unconscious processing probably does not affect personality in the way that Freud suggested.

Behaviourist theory [1]

A reaction to the focus on unseen, unconscious process in Freudian theory was an equally staunch focus on only that which could be observed: behaviour. **Behaviourism** was a dominant paradigm in the USA between the 1920s and the 1950s. The essence of behaviourism was that all behaviour represented learned responses to elements of the environment. Anything else was considered unimportant.

Behaviourist theory adopted key ideas of classical conditioning, associated with Ivan Pavlov and his famous experiments with dogs. Pavlov observed that the dogs could be taught how to respond to people and objects in certain ways. For example, when dogs are presented with food (a stimulus) they naturally salivate (a response). But when food was regularly presented at the same time as a bell rang or a light went on, over time the dogs began to salivate when the bell was rung or when the light was turned on even in the absence of food. Pavlov believed that the environmental stimulus (the light or bell) had 'conditioned' the behavioural response (salivation), and the stimulus-response (S-R) association process has ever since then been referred to as classical conditioning (see Figure 3.1 for a summary of the process).

Impressed by Pavlov's work, the American psychologist Watson (1878–1958) used Pavlov's observational techniques in his own research and replicated the studies in the USA. Watson and Rayner (1920) conducted a famous study with a young baby known as 'Little Albert'. The study

Figure 3.1   A summary of classical conditioning

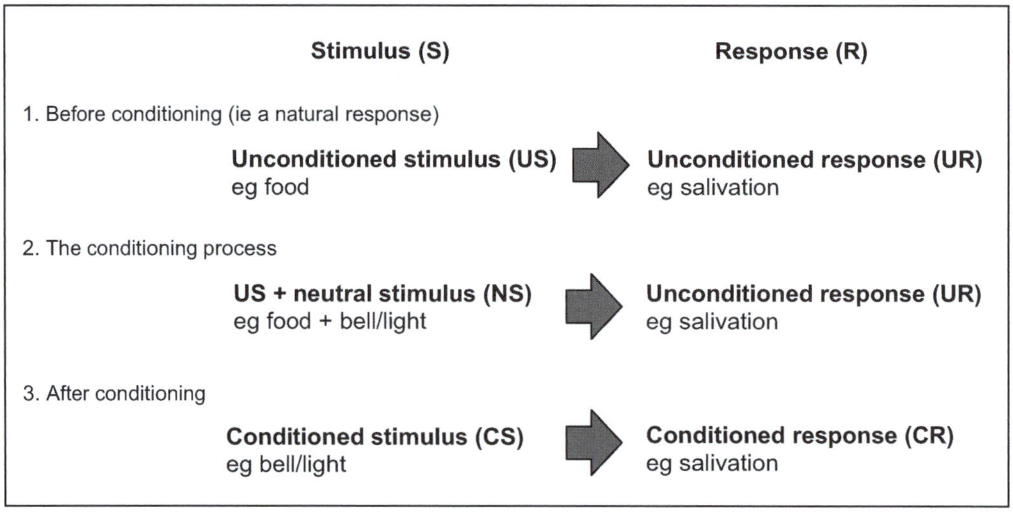

was designed to show that human emotional reactions could be conditioned. Albert was shown a white rat, and he exhibited no signs of fear or anxiety at the experience. However, whenever Albert reached for the rat, the researchers produced a loud, startling noise in order to invoke anxiety and fear. Repeated experience of this led Albert to develop a fear of the white rat itself, a fear that even generalised to other white furry objects, including a mask of Father Christmas and Watson's own hair. The study had shown that at this early age, emotional reactions are shaped by experience.

Behaviourism was developed further by B.F. Skinner, who accepted the principles of classical conditioning but argued that the S-R learning was too simplistic for humans, and could be applied only to a limited range of learning situations. Skinner argued that it is instead the consequences of the response that is crucial to determining whether it will be demonstrated. For example, if a negative consequence occurs after a response (for example, a punishment or the removal of a reward), that response is likely to be inhibited. A positive consequence from behaviour (for example, a reward or an absence of punishment) is likely to promote the response. Skinner referred to these types of consequences as positive and negative **reinforcements**, respectively, and called this learning process 'operant conditioning'.

Through the work conducted under the behaviourist approach, Skinner and colleagues showed that behaviour could be moderated or shaped through the influences of the environment. These behaviourists did not claim that internal states or unconscious processes did not exist, but they felt that they were unscientific ways to explain behaviour. They believed that observable processes and objects should be the focus of research because behaviour is a direct result of learned responses to environmental stimuli. The theory implies that behaviours result not from some internal predisposition but rather from previously learned associations. When a person gets nervous about presentations, the theory proposes that the cause is not a nervous disposition but rather a learned association of presenting with emotions of anxiety and nervousness.

Behaviourism is a very neat perspective on the determinants of behaviour, but it is criticised for being too simplistic in respect of the human mind. Nevertheless, some of the basic concepts are regularly applied in management through processes of reinforcement. One need look no further than the bestselling book by Kenneth Blanchard and Spencer Johnson, *The One Minute Manager*. In the book, Blanchard and Johnson (1983) describe how employee performance can be managed by carefully praising and rewarding (reinforcing) positive behaviour, and reprimanding (punishing) negative behaviour. The effect is to shape employee behaviour to fit the needs of the manager or organisation.

The founding principles of behaviourism fell by the wayside somewhat as psychology developed more sophisticated models and techniques, and the tradition morphed during the 1960s to become what is today known as **social learning** or social cognition.

Social learning theory [2]

Social learning theory integrates the influences of internal processes and external environment in determining personality characteristics, and regularities in behaviour. The approach is most often associated with the work of Albert Bandura. He suggested (1978) that personality and behaviour were regulated through the process of reciprocal determinism (see Figure 3.2). The model suggests that all three components (person, environment, and behaviour) are constantly affecting one another. A person perceives stimuli or situational cues in their environment, and the way that they perceive it is unique to them. They decide how to respond, and behave accordingly. That behaviour has an impact on the environment, and invokes an outcome. This information is perceived and integrated into decision-making about future situations or behaviours.

Imagine that a colleague asks you to help them with their assignment (environmental stimuli). You weigh up whether you think this person deserves your help. Perhaps you have helped them before, and you assess the desirability of that outcome in the past (person processes). You decide

Figure 3.2   Bandura's model of reciprocal determinism

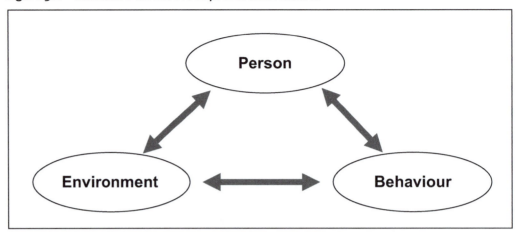

to help them (behaviour), but later learn that they copied a lot of your work and claimed it as their own (further environmental stimuli). This makes you feel bad (person process), and will figure in your decision-making if they ask you again.

A central component of social learning is expectancy, which refers to the individual's belief that a certain outcome will happen as a result of behaviour. Expectancy develops in part through the process of observational learning. Bandura proposed that children learn to behave in particular ways by observing the behaviour of role models. The child observes the situation, the behavioural response, and the outcome, using all three to decide whether they should behave in the same way. One can hypothesise how this observational learning process might apply in organisations, underlining the importance of leader behaviour in influencing employee behaviour. The final piece of the puzzle is **self-efficacy**, which refers to the extent of our belief that we can achieve something or successfully behave or perform in a particular way. Self-efficacy is important for people at work, especially in relation to goal-setting or objective-setting. People feel more committed to their goals if they believe that they can achieve them. At a basic level, people are more likely to perform at work if they expect the outcome to be positive, and believe that they can achieve the necessary standard. Such ideas are consistent with the expectancy theory of motivation (see Chapter 5).

Social cognitive theory is an important theory of personality to grasp, although it is complex, and represents behaviour and cognitive processes in complicated ways. This has proved a barrier to their widespread application. Nevertheless, the broad ideas are influential in our thinking about organisational behaviour.

Trait theory [3]

The final, and most dominant, theory of personality is **trait theory**. In personality psychology, the idea of 'traits' is inevitable (Hofstee, 1984), because trait theory taps into our intuitions about personality characteristics, which tell us that people are orderly and predictable. If a group of people with no knowledge of psychology worked together for a few hours on developing a theory of personality, they would probably arrive at a position that was similar to trait theory. When we observe the behaviour of others, we try to find order and regularity in it. You probably have your own expectations about the behaviour of people you know and the people you work with, and feel that you can predict how they will respond to you, and how they will respond to particular situations. These stable patterns of behaviour can be described as dispositional or trait-like. This person is organised, so he will work through this task methodically. That person is somewhat disorganised, so she may not develop a plan or schedule for completing the task.

Personality traits are typically conceptualised as internal dispositions that remain generally stable over time (Chamorro-Premuzic, 2007). Example traits are 'friendly', 'talkative', 'organised', 'calm'. Trait theory suggests that individual differences in behaviour, thought, and emotions can be described and explained by personality traits (McCrae and Costa, 1995). Although this is a fairly simple idea, psychologists have grappled with the definition over the past 50 years. The original consensus about personality traits was captured by Hampson (1988), who described assumptions that personality traits were internal, stable (unchanged over time), consistent (apply across different situations) and different. These features, and some of the challenges to them, give a feel for what trait theory is in contemporary applied psychology:

- *internal*

   Although traits are considered internal by some (eg Costa and McCrae, 1992), others (eg Goldberg, 1990) believe that there is not sufficient evidence to suggest that the origins of traits are internal. The debate on the nature and nurture of personality (see the box below) helps to understand the distinction. A parsimonious way to view traits is as part internal (in the sense that our genetic make-up does indeed contribute to our personality traits) and part developed through our unique experiences. In organisations, this means that it is best to see traits as a means of describing regularities in behaviour, thought and emotion.

Taking your learning further: The nature and nurture of personality

Do you perceive your parents' personality traits in your own behaviour? It's probably reasonable if you do. The genes we inherit influence not only our physical appearance but are also proposed to play a key role in the development of our mental characteristics too. For example, as well as sharing physical similarities in appearance, family members typically share common elements of their personality. Psychological experiments involving monozygotic (identical) twins have also revealed that such family similarities are stronger between these kinds of siblings that share their genetic make-up. In fact, on average, around 40% of population variation on the Big Five personality dimensions is attributable to inherited genetic factors (Bouchard, 1994).

The flip side of this finding is, of course, that we are able to dismiss the view that personality is solely determined by genes (Pervin, 1980; Plomin, 1994). Other non-hereditary factors are also accepted as being influential on an individual's personality. Personality is also believed to be a reflection of an individual's interactions with other human beings. In particular, early socialisation by parents, siblings and peers that teach children how to behave in social situations are thought to be quite significant in influencing personality and behaviour later in an individual's life (Wanous *et al*, 1984).

Similarly, cultural factors are also proposed to influence an individual's behaviour. Culture provides a wider set of social beliefs, motives and values that are acceptable within a society or sub-set of society. These cultural factors provide individuals with the necessary information about how to behave appropriately within a certain society. This is important because cultural rules vary considerably between cultures. For example, in Western societies value is placed on individualism and achieving personal success. For Eastern societies, however, such values are frowned upon and instead a more collectivist culture is present, which emphasises a more cohesive and team-driven success approach. As a result, the personalities of individuals from each category of culture reflect the goals that culture has. For individualistic cultures, a 'need to achieve' personality disposition is common (McClelland, 1967), whereas for collectivist cultures, being a 'good team player' is more evident in personalities (Hofstede, 1980).

Situational factors are also believed to bear some relation to a person's personality. Every person has experienced unique, individual situations throughout their life. Such experiences – for example, the traumatic loss of a loved one – can bring about a change in a person's personality and behaviour. Likewise, certain situations can bring about uncharacteristic patterns of behaviour in a person that may stem from repressed experiences in earlier life. Although personality characteristics are influenced strongly through predispositions to behave in certain ways, such characteristics can be overwhelmed by situational factors (Epstein, 1980). It is important to keep these effects in mind in the day-to-day management of people in organisations.

- *stable*

   Personality traits have shown evidence of stability over time, particularly through adulthood (Caspi and Roberts, 1999). However, this does not negate the possibility of change. Provided that people's lives remain stable, their personality is also likely to, but change can happen to characteristic patterns of behaviour as a result of life events, or through conscious behaviour management.

- *consistent*

   Trait theory implies that behaviour should be consistent in different situations. However, this is clearly a false assumption. People's behaviour varies according to context or situation. The 'you' that you know at home is likely to be different in important ways from the 'you' that you know at work. Situational inconsistency was the observation of Walter Mischel (1968), who published a powerful critique of trait theory suggesting that situations should be the object of

Figure 3.3   Behaviour as a product of personality traits interacting with situations

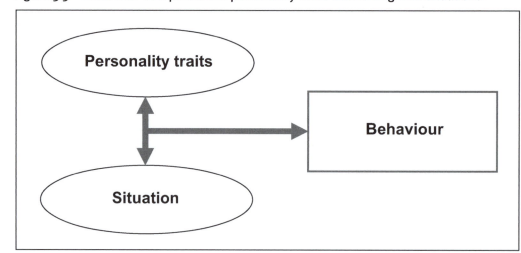

focus in understanding personality, rather than internal traits. His focus solely on situations did not pervade, but the integration of situations into our understanding of traits is important. Traits are best thought of as characteristic ways of responding to particular situations (see Figure 3.3).

- *different*

The real applied value of traits is that they differ between people. This means that they offer a way to understand and describe how people differ in terms of their personality, and their characteristic patterns of behaviour, thought and emotion. This has numerous applications in organisations, notably in selection, diagnosing development needs and understanding organisational behaviour such as leadership and teamwork.

The Big Five personality dimensions

An ongoing question in personality research and practice is how to best represent and organise the multitude of personality traits that we observe in people's behaviour. The winning answer to this problem is undoubtedly five (Hampson, 1999). The consensus has emerged because independent sources have reported similar findings, particularly when examining personality traits in North American and north-west European populations. In the early 1960s, three separate sources reported that factor analyses of personality traits revealed five major personality dimensions (Tupes and Cristal, 1961; Norman, 1963; Borgatta, 1964). The study of traits was advanced by Goldberg and Digman in the early 1980s. The result of their work was the clear identification and description of five broad dimensions of personality, collectively termed the Big Five or the five-factor model. The **Big Five model** suggests that the most adequate representation of personality traits is to group them into five broad bipolar dimensions. These are:

- *extraversion*: the extent to which a person is outgoing and sociable, as opposed to quiet and reserved

- *agreeableness*: the extent to which a person is warm and trusting, as opposed to cold and unfriendly

- *conscientiousness*: the extent to which a person is organised and dependable, as opposed to impulsive and disorganised

- *emotional stability*: the extent to which a person is calm and stable, as opposed to neurotic and anxious

Figure 3.4   Extraversion and its six associated facets

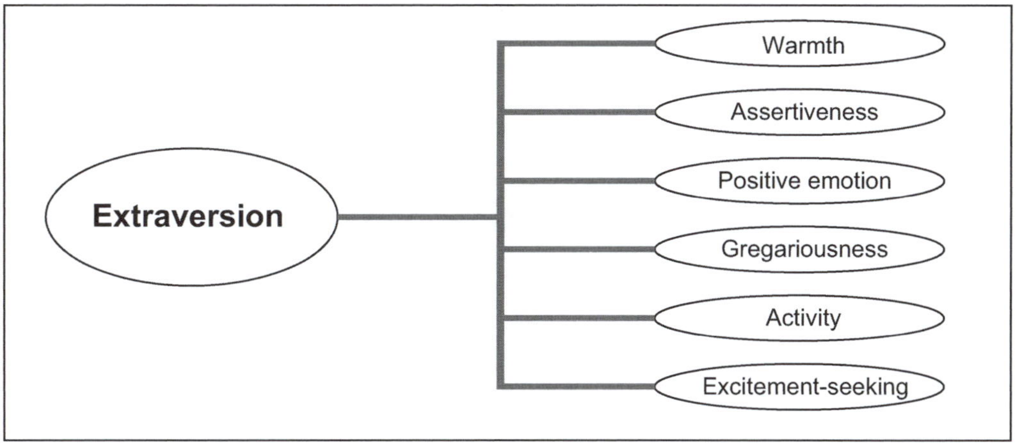

- *openness/intellect*: the extent to which a person is imaginative and open to new experiences, as opposed to narrow-minded and unimaginative.

The work of Costa and McCrae (eg Costa and McCrae, 1992) has helped to consolidate the Big Five model. Their work on personality measurement has revealed a five-factor structure in numerous different cultures (McCrae and Costa, 1995). They also explore the nature of the five factors by dividing them into narrower facets. Their model of personality, like others, is hierarchical. The Big Five represent broad factors, under which are organised narrower personality dimensions. An example is shown in Figure 3.4, which shows extraversion, and six facets.

The Big Five model has become the largely agreed classification of personality traits, permitting the accumulation of a huge literature on their effects at work and in life. The implication of the model is that individual differences in personality traits can be described and understood effectively by determining how people differ on these five personality dimensions. Importantly, the dimensions are theoretically independent or unrelated to one another (ie a person's level of extraversion is theoretically unrelated to their level of conscientiousness). There still remains some debate about the labelling of the factors, and some have criticised the trait theory as being too descriptive and not explaining the reasons for differences. However, trait theorists argue that before it is possible to explain we must be able to measure, and traits provide an effective way to measure personality. You can rate yourself on the Big Five model in the box overleaf.

Applying theory to practice: Measure your own Big Five traits

Below are five pairs of descriptions representing the Big Five personality traits. They are presented in the order: extraversion, agreeableness, emotional stability, conscientiousness, openness/intellect. Read each pair of descriptions carefully and place yourself somewhere on the scale between the opposing descriptions. Do this honestly – rate yourself as you think you really are, not as you would ideally like to be.

The single-item measures of personality

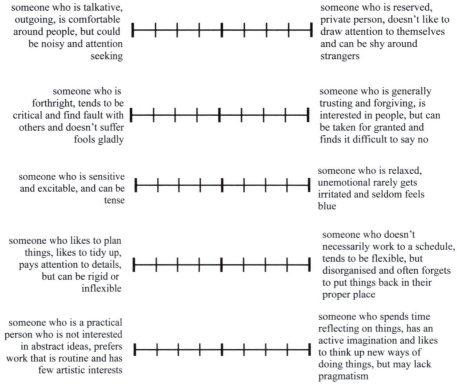

someone who is talkative, outgoing, is comfortable around people, but could be noisy and attention seeking

someone who is reserved, private person, doesn't like to draw attention to themselves and can be shy around strangers

someone who is forthright, tends to be critical and find fault with others and doesn't suffer fools gladly

someone who is generally trusting and forgiving, is interested in people, but can be taken for granted and finds it difficult to say no

someone who is sensitive and excitable, and can be tense

someone who is relaxed, unemotional rarely gets irritated and seldom feels blue

someone who likes to plan things, likes to tidy up, pays attention to details, but can be rigid or inflexible

someone who doesn't necessarily work to a schedule, tends to be flexible, but disorganised and often forgets to put things back in their proper place

someone who is a practical person who is not interested in abstract ideas, prefers work that is routine and has few artistic interests

someone who spends time reflecting on things, has an active imagination and likes to think up new ways of doing things, but may lack pragmatism

Source: Woods and Hampson (2005)

Taking your learning further: Personality types

Theories of personality traits usually strike a chord with our intuitive ideas about personality, but ironically, the first encounter that most people have with personality theory in organisations is **personality type theory,** usually peddled ably by consultants and practitioners using the Myers-Briggs Type Inventory (MBTI). The MBTI is one of the most widely used personality questionnaires in organisations, drawing on an aspect of Carl Jung's theory which posits that personality should be represented as a typology rather than as dimensional traits like those of the Big Five model.

For example, in the Big Five model, extraversion is a dimension, so people can be described as having varying degrees of extraversion (ie very introverted, slightly introverted, neither introverted nor extraverted, slightly extraverted, very extraverted). On the MBTI typological model, extraversion-introversion is represented as a dichotomy, so that a person is either introverted (labelled I) or extraverted (labelled E). The MBTI contains four such dichotomies, and the combinations of the various letter codes for each gives a total of 16 personality types.

The model behind the MBTI is a simple one to grasp and that makes it popular. Indeed, as a way of having managers explore the idea of individual differences, anecdotal reports suggest it is useful. One often hears people reeling off their four-letter codes like membership cards of some exclusive learned club. However, human personality is not a simple concept, and it is lazy to assume it to be so. There are also some very serious problems reported in the research literature concerning typological theory, the MBTI, and by extension, all such questionnaires and assessments that represent personality as typologies (Woods and West, 2010).

Users of the MBTI will bat away such criticisms with much talk of practical utility, of the exploratory, non-definitive nature of the MBTI, and the in-depth discussion process that typically follows assessment using the questionnaire. However, only the uninformed would be convinced by these weak arguments. All of the advantages could equally apply to the use of trait assessments, with the added confidence that comes from using an approach endorsed by the scientific evidence in the field.

Applying theory to practice: Personality across cultures

Are personality traits the same the world over? It really depends on your perspective. One philosophy is that personality traits are descriptive representations of patterns or regularities in behaviour, which develop in part because of the influences of tradition, custom and language. There is plenty of evidence that different personality traits are more or less important in different cultures, or are completely culture-specific (eg Saucier, Hampson and Goldberg, 2000).

An alternative perspective suggests that the Big Five is universal for humans (McCrae and Costa, 1995), suggesting that the five dimensions reflect some underlying biological system. In this perspective, culture plays a part in determining average levels of

trait behaviour in different countries (eg people from the USA and other Western countries typically have higher levels of assertiveness than those from, for example, East Asia).

Regardless of which perspective is adopted, there are obvious implications for cross-cultural working. If we are used to understanding people's traits in our own culture, we are inevitably likely to misperceive or completely ignore aspects of personality that are salient in other cultures. We might also fall into the trap of relying on our own value system, in which certain traits are valued in our own country but might be considered socially undesirable in another. These points are important to bear in mind when interacting with people from different cultures.

PERSONALITY AT WORK

The perceived importance of personality in the workplace has varied over the decades. During the 1960s, personality traits were discredited by Guion and Gottier (1965) and Mischel (1968), who declared its use as ineffective for predicting workplace outcomes. Their conclusions had a significant negative impact on the use of personality assessment for applications of management. However, a couple of decades later, limitations in their research and conclusions were acknowledged. With better research and the availability of more advanced statistical techniques, a wealth of empirical evidence accumulated to support the importance of personality in the world of work. Figure 3.5 shows the kinds of work outcomes that personality traits are associated with.

Much of this empirical support has stemmed from the use of the Big Five framework, which provided a platform to understanding personality in a more credible and practical way (Ones and Viswesvaran, 1997). Research has since explored personality's relationship with various workplace behaviours and found tremendous consistency in its patterns of influence. In this section we explore the evidence of the associations between personality traits and work outcomes, and consider some of the mechanisms that give rise to these associations. We start with arguably the most important: job performance.

Job performance [4]

Job performance is generally regarded as the behaviours individuals engage in or produce that are in line with and contribute to an organisation's goals (Viswesvaran and Ones, 2000). In

Figure 3.5 Some work outcomes influenced by personality traits

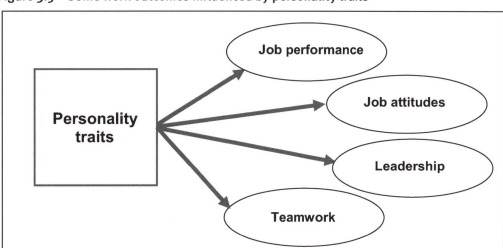

other words, for organisations to succeed, employees are required to carry out the necessary behaviours for that role and perform them well. Knowing what we do about personality, we understand that certain people are more likely to carry out certain behaviours than others. Unsurprisingly, the five-factor model of personality has been applied in many areas of research and has accrued convincing evidence for helping us to understand the relationship between personality and job performance (Hough and Oswald, 2000; Salgado, 2003).

Several meta-analyses (see the box below) have been carried out over the past two decades exploring the relationships between personality measures and job performance outcomes. The overall results from these show that general job performance is significantly related to personality across various occupations and cultural groups, including managers, the police, sales positions, customer service workers and professional roles, as well as skilled and semi-skilled jobs, both in the USA and Europe (eg Barrick, Mount and Judge, 2001; Barrick and Mount, 1991; Hurtz and Donovan, 2000; Salgado, 1997). The job performance of employees who are sent across cultures in expatriate assignments have also been shown to relate to their personality (Mol *et al*, 2005).

Taking your learning further: Meta-analysis

Meta-analysis is a technique which allows researchers to integrate the findings of past studies and to arrive at an overall result. It is generally considered to provide the strongest form of evidence in applied research. This is because it allows people to determine whether a research finding is robust enough to apply in multiple studies and research contexts.

Job performance itself can also be broken down into different forms. For example, a commonly used distinction is between **task performance** and **organisational citizenship behaviour** (Figure 3.6). Task performance refers to the actual proficiency of the job itself (ie the acts specifically related to the technicalities of the job). Meta-analyses that have focused on task performance specifically show that personality predicts this kind of performance, but less effectively than **cognitive ability** (intelligence: eg Hurtz and Donovan, 2000; Organ and Ryan, 1995). Organisational citizenship behaviour (OCB) refers to behaviours that extend beyond the technical aspects of the role. They contribute to the organisation's effectiveness through helping the social and psychological contexts for the job, and are not typically formally included in a job role (Borman and Motowidlo, 1997). Such behaviours include volunteering to help with tasks not directly associated with the employee's own job. Personality is a key predictor of these aspects of performance, and influences behaviour related to co-operation, altruism, initiative and compliance (Borman, Penner, Allen and Motowidlo, 2001).

Figure 3.6   The relationship between individual differences and job performance

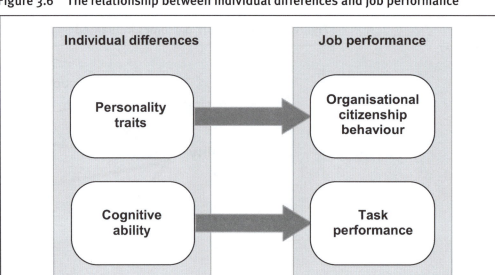

Which of the Big Five are the most consistent predictors of performance? A consensual finding from the research is that *conscientiousness* and *emotional stability* have superior relationships with employee job performance over the others (Salgado, 2003). Specifically, individuals who are high in conscientiousness and high in emotional stability generally have better performance in most occupations.

According to Barrick and Mount (2005), conscientiousness and emotional stability refer to 'the willingness to follow rules and to exert effort', and the 'capacity to allocate resources to accomplish tasks'. They are said to appear to affect job performance across all jobs because of their 'will do' motivational components. Of these two, however, conscientiousness has been shown to be the more important or influential factor on job performance, and such findings have sparked increased research focus on this trait (eg Dudley, Orvis, Lebiecki and Cortina, 2006).

With such findings, does this mean that it is always more desirable or beneficial for employees to be higher on conscientiousness and emotional stability? The answer is: not necessarily.

Although *openness*, *agreeableness*, and *extraversion* have received less empirical support as predictors of job performance, they emerge as important traits for specific or niche occupations, or with specific performance criteria (Barrick, Mount and Judge 2001; Barrick and Mount, 2005). Ones, Dilchert, Viswesvaran and Judge (2007), for example, showed that extraversion is related to job performance in occupations such as management and police officers. In these kinds of jobs, being assertive, energetic and outgoing is important because social interaction and influencing are necessary for performance. Agreeableness has also been shown to be important in certain jobs that require social interaction and teamwork, but especially where the nature of these social relationships are more nurturing and require the employee to be helpful and co-operative.

In jobs that require a high degree of creativity and flexibility, openness deals more specifically with behaviours such as these and therefore, unsurprisingly, has shown significant relationships with job performance in such roles (George and Zhou, 2001). These occupations would include designers, artists, and jobs where tasks are quickly changed, such as managers. Interestingly, some research has shown facets of conscientiousness to be negatively related to jobs that entail creativity, highlighting the importance of understanding the specifics of job performance in any given occupation.

Hogan and Holland (2003) provide a good illustration of the importance of matching specific personality traits to specific outcome criteria. In their study they explored the relationships between personality traits and two different but related job performance criteria: 'getting along' and 'getting ahead'. Their study found that for the jobs requiring people to principally 'get along with others', the best predictors were agreeableness, emotional stability and conscientiousness. When performance depended on people being driven to get ahead, the best predictors were shown to be a facet of extraversion (ambition), conscientiousness and emotional stability. The implication is that given the diversity of jobs and their associated job performance criteria, some behaviours will be more important than others. It is important to consider the job and criteria in question before dismissing the importance of some traits.

Hogan and Holland's (2003) study highlighted another important element to understanding personality and its influence on job performance. The key predictor of performance in jobs that required people to be driven or to get ahead of others was *ambition*, a facet of extraversion. This turned out to be a better predictor of performance than the broad extraversion dimension. In fact, numerous studies have shown that these lower-level more specific traits can outperform the broader traits in predicting job performance (eg Ashton *et al*, 1995; Dudley, Orvis, Lebiecki and Cortina, 2006; Hastings and O'Neil, 2009). The reason for this is quite clear. When the performance or outcome of interest is quite specific, the lower-level narrow trait is likely to match the outcome more closely.

Researchers over the last few decades have debated whether it is better to use broader traits or narrow traits in HRM activities such as recruitment and development. This debate has been referred to as the *fidelity-bandwidth debate*. Early debaters originally favoured the use of the broad personality dimensions (eg Ones and Viswesvaran, 1996; Barrick and Mount, 1994). However, today the debate appears to favour the narrow traits because of the stronger relationships that are exhibited with performance.

Overall, the empirical evidence for supporting the importance of personality in job performance is overwhelming, demonstrating a clear, significant role across occupations, job settings and cultures. The traits conscientiousness and emotional ability are typically found to be important for performance in most occupations, but for more specific niche occupations the other three traits may play more of a role. It is unsurprising that the most-used application of personality in organisations is for the purposes of selection. Being able to assess an applicant's personality provides considerable information about the potential behaviours of individuals in organisations. If the requirements of the job match these underlying preferences, higher job performance is likely to occur.

Applying theory to practice: The use of personality assessment in recruitment and selection

Personality traits are assessed in a number of different ways during **recruitment and selection** processes. Selectors often make informal judgements about personality traits during interviews and observational assessments. However, the assessment of traits is formally operationalised in personality trait inventories or questionnaires (self-report inventories that require candidates to respond to questions or statements, rating their agreement with them).

There are a huge number of different personality tests available for practitioners to use, of variable quality. Organisational assessment, in particular for selection, has been a driving force in promoting the development of new personality inventories, and there are a number of measures available that are designed to specifically assess job-relevant personality traits. Well-designed tests can be highly useful in selection, but poorly designed tests are at best useless and at worst potentially damaging to the well-being of job candidates. Without knowledge of testing theory and practice, it can be difficult for users to distinguish good from poor tests, and so training in the use of personality testing is essential for those using assessments in organisations.

When deciding how to use personality assessments for selection, HR practitioners should draw on **job analysis** information (a systematic analysis of the requirements of the job and the essential and desirable qualities of the employee). The most prevalent approach to using personality assessment for selection is to undertake a profile-matching exercise. This usually draws on the practitioner's detailed knowledge of a specific personality instrument and the different traits that it assesses. Relevant traits are matched to aspects of the person specification, and an overall 'ideal' or 'desirable' personality profile constructed. For example, if a systematic, organised approach is needed, then high conscientiousness is desirable in job candidates. If social confidence is essential in a job, then employees with high extraversion are likely to be well suited.

Candidates are then evaluated in terms of how well their profile fits with the ideal profile. In making these judgements, assessors may draw on interview data as well as the self-report data from a **personality inventory**.

Try it for yourself. Use the definitions of the Big Five to decide what kinds of traits would be desirable for your own job, or for a job that you are familiar with.

Personality and organisational behaviour

According to Judge, Klinger, Simon and Yang (2008), there is hardly an area of organisational behaviour that has not been influenced through personality research. In addition to job performance, some of the most notable behaviours include leadership, teamwork, and organisational attitudes such as **job satisfaction** and **organisational commitment**. In this section we consider each of them.

Leadership

The interest in discovering a dispositional basis for leadership behaviour has spanned several decades and resulted in thousands of studies on the topic. The search, however, was almost terminated prematurely because of early research providing inconsistent and disappointing results. Several of the early reviews were criticised for producing 'a myriad characteristics, few of which reoccurred consistently across studies' (Anderson and Schneider, 1978: 690). Even when the same traits were included, they were often assumed to be different because of the different labels often used. This meant it was almost impossible to find true consistent relationships. It led many scholars to the conclusion that 'the search for universal traits was futile' (House and Aditya, 1997: 410).

However, since the emergence of the Big Five model of personality, more convincing evidence has emerged for the significance of personality in leadership. One of the most complete studies on the area is from Judge, Bono, Ilies and Gerhardt (2002). They conducted a **meta-analysis** involving over 300 pieces of research that examined the relationships between the five personality traits and leadership (perceived and effectiveness). Overall, they found that personality was significantly (and consistently) related to leadership. In particular, extraversion was shown to be the strongest trait, followed by conscientiousness and openness.

According to Hogan *et al* (1994), leadership can be conceptualised in different ways. For example, Judge and colleagues above separated leadership into two broad areas called 'perceived leadership' and 'leadership effectiveness'. More recently it has been broken down into another two forms, referred to as transactional and transformational leadership (see Chapter 10). As with the two earlier conceptualisations, meta-analyses using the five-factor model have shown personality traits to be important in both transactional and transformational leadership (Bono and Judge, 2004). Overall, though, the evidence still provides a strong demonstration that early pessimism regarding the importance of personality traits in leadership behaviour was premature, and that personality does have a significant relationship to leadership in its various forms.

Teamwork

Teams are extensively used in organisations and allow tasks that require more than one person to be fulfilled. The performance of these teams is therefore an important organisational behaviour and an area in OB research (see Chapter 7). Research on teams has included looking at the influences of personality on team member performance and the performance of the team as a whole. For example, individual team member performance has been shown to be related to personality traits – specifically, agreeableness and conscientiousness (Neuman and Wright, 1999). A team's viability or capability has also been shown to relate to personality, teams higher in group extraversion and emotional stability receiving the greatest ratings for potential by supervisors (Barrick *et al*, 1998).

The 'team personality' or composition is another important aspect of a team, and out of all the team research is probably the area that has received the most attention. Team composition refers to the configuration of team members' attributes (Levine and Morland, 1990), including personality, and is considered highly instrumental in effective team outcomes and performance. An influential meta-analysis conducted by Bell (2007) showed that each of the Big Five traits was significantly related to team effectiveness. Other important work outcomes are accuracy and work completed, and similar results have been shown here too. For example, Neuman and Wright (1999) explored the relationship between personality traits and objective measures of work team accuracy and work completed, and found that agreeableness and conscientiousness were related to these other team outcomes.

Overall, the research on this topic suggests that teamwork (and its related outcomes) is influenced by the personality of the members. Noting this, Bell (2007) suggested that this is of interest to both researchers and practitioners because through appropriate action (eg selection of team members or re-structuring of jobs) team performance may be enhanced by improving the team composition.

Job attitudes – job satisfaction and organisational commitment

Closely related to work behaviours are the job attitudes that are believed to influence them. Two of the most commonly studied are job satisfaction and organisational commitment. Job satisfaction is generally defined as the positive emotional state that results from the individual's job experience (Locke, 1976). Job satisfaction is regarded as important because evidence has shown that 'a happy worker tends to be a more productive worker' (eg Judge *et al*, 2001: 262).

A key question in understanding the antecedents of job satisfaction is the extent to which dispositions play a part. Are some people simply more likely than others to be satisfied at work? Recently, there has been accumulating evidence exploring this relationship, which suggests that dispositions can indeed play a large role in the level of job satisfaction people experience.

Judge, Heller and Mount (2002) reported a meta-analysis that demonstrated a significant relationship between personality and job satisfaction. In particular, the traits extraversion and emotional stability showed the most convincing and consistent relationship with satisfaction. The findings suggest that individuals who are more emotionally stable and more extraverted are more likely to be happy in their jobs.

In comparison, however, organisational commitment has received much less attention in research. As a result, it has had much less empirical support for the influence of personality. Organisational commitment is defined as the strength of involvement and identification an employee has with their organisation (Mowday *et al*, 1979: 265). It is viewed as a multidimensional construct (Allen and Meyer, 1990), typically comprising the following three forms: affective commitment (the employee's emotional attachment to the organisation), continuance commitment (the employee's perceived costs and risks in relation to leaving the organisation) and normative commitment (the employee's feeling of obligation to the organisation). A substantial amount of research has been carried out on the attitude since the 1980s, yet comparatively less research has explored the relationship between personality and organisational commitment than the previous organisational attitude (Judge *et al*, 2008).

One of the notable exceptions, however, is Erdheim, Wang and Zickar (2006), who found personality to relate to this organisational attitude also. In particular, they found that extraversion was significantly related to all three forms of commitment (affective, continuance, and normative). Moreover, the traits neuroticism, conscientiousness and openness were related to continuance commitment, and agreeableness was related to normative commitment. This research provides support for the role of personality disposition in this organisational attitude, meaning that certain people are just more likely to be committed to organisations than others.

None of the evidence of the associations of personality and positive work attitudes should be overplayed, though. The findings suggest that personality influences job satisfaction and commitment, but that these influences are limited. As we will see in other chapters of this book, work environments, job characteristics, work design, managerial behaviour and support, and work conditions all play an important role in promoting and fostering positive attitudes at work. The role of personality is best viewed alongside these other factors (see Figure 3.7). In other words, when two people have the same kinds of general life satisfaction, and work in the same kinds of job and organisation, differences in their attitudes are most likely down to personality influences.

Personality and work: summary

Over the past two decades there has been substantial improvement in the research conducted to explore the relationship between personality and various important work behaviours – namely, the emergence of the Big Five model of personality and the advanced statistical technique of meta-analysis. Overall, the evidence is clear that personality plays a significant part in job performance, leadership, teamwork, and job attitudes (satisfaction and commitment). Although more research is still needed, both researchers and organisations are becoming increasingly aware of the significance that employee personality plays in organisational behaviour.

PERSONALITY AND OTHER INDIVIDUAL ATTRIBUTES

Personality is just one aspect of a person's unique character. There are many other attributes to consider as we build up a picture of individuals. The interaction of personality and some of these other attributes is important to consider in doing so.

Figure 3.7 The interaction between personality traits and organisation factors in predicting satisfaction and commitment

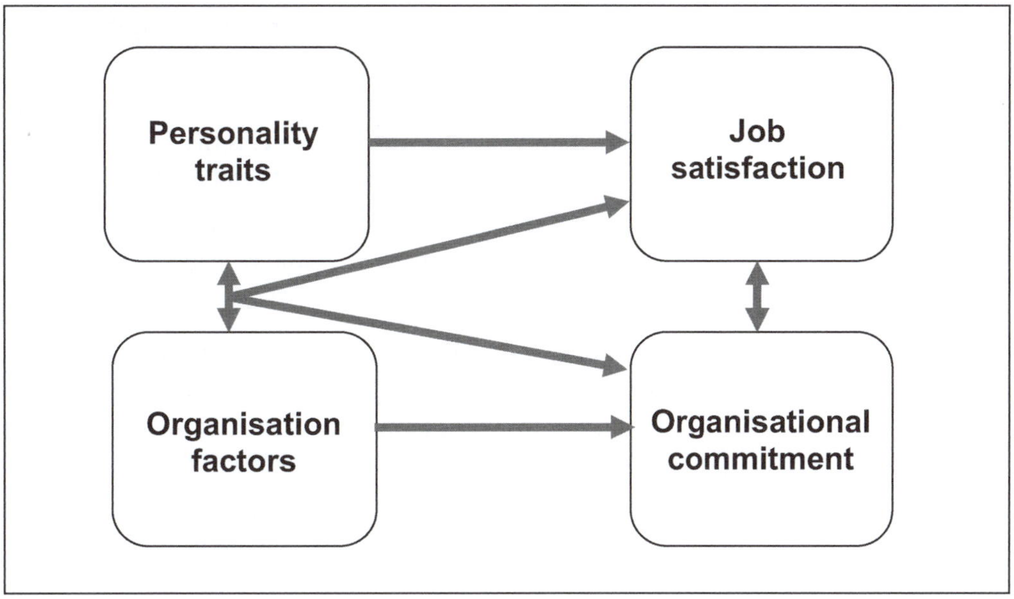

Motivation [5]

Motivation can be quickly defined as 'the processes that account for an individual's intensity, direction, and persistence of effort toward attaining a goal' (Robbins and Judge, 2009: 209). In other words, it comprises three elements: direction, effort, and persistence. Multiple theories of motivation have been proposed (see Chapter 5), and the lack of an accepted framework for studying motivational constructs (Barrick *et al*, 2001) makes it difficult to clearly ascertain whether personality is related to motivation. Despite personality being considered in numerous motivation studies, there is still an incomplete understanding of how personality relates to the construct (Parks and Guay, 2009).

According to Judge and colleagues (2008), prior to the Big Five model a wealth of personality traits had been related to work motivation, but the empirical results were relatively disappointing. Locke, Shaw, Saari and Latham (1981) at the time noted that 'the only consistent thing about studies of individual differences in goal-setting is their inconsistency' (p.142). However, the development of the five-factor model of personality allowed more consistent and comparable research to be conducted, and results provided evidence that personality was in fact related to work motivation. The most convincing evidence came from the meta-analysis by Judge and Iles (2002) who examined the relationship between the Big Five traits and various motivation concepts, including goal-setting, self-efficacy and expectancy. The results of the meta-analysis showed that personality was associated with motivation, with the traits emotional stability and conscientiousness having particularly strong positive correlations, respectively, with the three work motivation variables.

The mechanisms for these associations could be around commitment to goals, optimism in respect of achieving goals, and in confidence in one's capability. People who are more emotionally stable are more likely to be confident in their potential to succeed, and people higher on conscientiousness are more likely to take assigned goals seriously.

Cognitive ability/intelligence [6]

The term 'cognitive ability' is used to describe an individual's capacity for processing information and using it to carry out an appropriate behaviour. It is an area of psychology that has attracted much interest and debate over the decades. Several models have been proposed for its structure, including the most commonly used hierarchical model of cognitive ability, which proposes that we can think about different aspects of ability arranged in a hierarchy:

- General ability refers to general reasoning capability and problem-solving – being able to figure out what to do in different situations.

- Specific abilities, sitting underneath general ability, reflect reasoning and problem-solving of particular kinds (eg solving problems that require thinking about words, numbers, spatial arrangement, abstract information, and so on).

Since then there has been an extensive body of literature exploring the correlations between personality and ability. For example, a meta-analysis was carried out by Ackerman and Heggestad (1997) which summarised many of these studies and revealed that personality and ability were related, but only weakly. In particular, openness, extraversion and emotional stability were found to have weak but significant positive correlations with ability. There is also some inconsistency in reported associations of personality and intelligence, some studies finding positive relationships between traits and certain cognitive abilities (eg Pearson, 1993), and others showing the opposite relationship (eg Jorm et al, 1993).

The conclusion that can be drawn from these and other studies is that cognitive ability is largely independent of personality traits, and this has important implications for how the two kinds of attribute combine to influence organisational behaviour and job success.

Most people have worked with those who have high levels of intellectual ability, evidenced in their obvious technical skills (in engineering, for example) and in their problem-solving. However, some may lack key interpersonal competencies, drive or confidence. Having high levels of ability does not go hand in hand with having the right personality traits for one's job. The opposite can also occur. People who are interpersonally warm and skilled, organised and responsible may nonetheless struggle with some tasks or some kinds of jobs because of lower ability.

The independence of personality and ability in part gives us the rich diversity of people in the world, and in our organisations. Occasionally, people do emerge with exceptional cognitive abilities, combined with desirable or charismatic traits, and they normally rise quickly in organisations. Consider top CEOs, for example. These people are rare, and most generally have strengths in their attributes alongside weaknesses.

Vocational interests

In contemporary approaches to people management, organisations and individuals are paying increasingly more attention to managing and planning careers. As economies grow and globalisation expands, careers are in turn becoming more varied and difficult to manage. The following questions are frequently asked. How does someone decide what career they wish to pursue? Why do some careers interest some people and seem boring to others? According to one of the most prominent figures in the field of **vocational interest**, John Holland, the answers to these questions are due to personality.

Holland developed one of the most influential theories of career choice. He proposed that there are six vocational personality types, and these types can be mapped onto different occupations and job environments. Holland labelled these types Realistic, Investigative, Artistic, Social, Enterprising and Conventional (see Table 3.1). Individuals are said to fall into a type and accordingly demonstrate the behaviours associated with that type. Holland proposed that individuals will be attracted to and most satisfied with environments that are congruent with their behavioural patterns. These environments can be described using the same six types (**Holland's RIASEC model**), and it is believed that vocational interest is developed from this congruence and the resultant positive experiences that reinforce the interest.

Preferences for the occupation types shown in Table 3.1 are related to personality traits. Results have shown that relationships do exist between the types and traits that closely resemble each

Table 3.1: Holland's vocational personality and environment typology

Personality-environment type	Description
Realistic	A realistic person likes activities that involve physical and hands-on action. He/she is practical and enjoys the outdoors and using tools. Examples of occupations may include carpenters, builders and farmers.
Investigative	An investigative person is quite intellectual, enjoys analytical thinking, solving problems, and may be often interested in the physical sciences. Examples of occupations may include scientists, researchers and philosophers.
Artistic	An artistic person is creative and enjoys using his/her imagination. He/she enjoys activities where he/she is free to express ideas and feelings, and doesn't like rules and regulations. Examples of occupations may include designers, musicians and actors.
Social	A social person enjoys helping and teaching people, and is very supportive, caring and nurturing. Examples of occupations may include nurses, aid workers, and teachers.
Enterprising	An enterprising person thrives in competitive environments and prefers doing rather than thinking. He/she enjoys the company of others, usually in a more dominant role or to persuade them. Examples of occupations may include managers, entrepreneurs and officers in the armed forces.
Conventional	A conventional person prefers structure and order. He/she prefers to be organised and enjoys clerical activities. Examples of occupations may include receptionists, clerks and accountants.

other. For example, Tokar and Swanson (1995) found that those who scored highly on artistic and investigative interests were typically high on openness, and those who scored high on social and enterprising interests were higher on extraversion.

Holland's personality types and the Big Five have also been shown to predict future vocational choices. For example, De Fruyt and Mervielde (1999) found that Holland's types were able to moderately predict the type of occupation that new graduates entered into after leaving university. Interestingly, however, when personality traits of the Big Five model were also examined, the accuracy of the prediction improved. This suggests that personality traits can measure aspects of an individual career choice that Holland's could not. Prediction of later-life occupations have also been reported over long periods of time, between adolescence and adulthood by Judge *et al* (1999), and most extraordinarily from childhood (age 6 to 12) personality traits and jobs held in middle age (Woods and Hampson, 2010).

Other recent research has been conducted that specifically explores the relationship between the Big Five traits and career decision-making. For example, Lounsbury, Hutchens and Loveland (2005) explored career choice in adolescent children in the USA. They found personality to be related to students' decidedness about a career, and more specifically, conscientiousness and emotional stability showed significant relationships. Fabio and Palezzeschi (2009) found that extraversion was negatively related to career-decision difficulty and neuroticism was positively related to that difficulty. Career-searching behaviours also appears to be related to personality, in particular, extraversion (Caldwell and Burger, 1998). Overall, then, the role played by personality in vocational choice is generally well recognised (Borges and Savickas, 2002; Tokar, Fischer and Subich, 1998).

Conclusion

Personality is a major determinant of important aspects of organisational behaviour. Indeed, an understanding of people management and organisational behaviour is incomplete without a grasp of the influences of personality.

When we discuss personality, we are really talking about people's characteristic patterns of behaviour, thought and emotion, alongside the internal mechanisms and processes that give rise to those patterns. There are numerous theories that explain how best to conceptualise and model personality, and there are important organisational implications of behaviourist and social cognitive theories. However, by far the most influential in organisational behaviour is trait theory, consolidated in recent research by the emergence of the Big Five model of personality, consisting of extraversion, agreeableness, conscientiousness, emotional stability, and openness.

Each of the Big Five has shown importance in some aspect of organisational behaviour, and over the last two decades developments in research and perspectives have allowed us to develop a fuller understanding of the relations of personality and work outcomes. Personality traits have been identified as influential in:

- promoting more effective individual job performance
- promoting organisational citizenship behaviour
- determining leadership effectiveness
- building effective teams
- predisposing people to be more satisfied and committed at work
- promoting key aspects of motivation
- people's career interests, choices, and decisions.

The combination of personality and cognitive ability (intelligence) gives a particularly powerful combination of attributes for understanding individual differences at work, and their influences on organisational behaviour and job success. However, all of the influences of personality must be viewed in context, and a focus on individual differences is always only half of the story when it comes to organisational behaviour. Personality exerts its influence on behaviour that is nested or located in particular organisations and particular contexts and situations. So when you wrote down the characteristics of your ideal colleague or employee, keep in mind that the right traits are crucial – but also that the way those traits are expressed in behaviour is about the way people are managed, and, of course, the way in which *you* interact with them.

End notes

[1] See also Chapter 6.

[2] See also Chapter 6.

[3] See also Chapter 10.

[4] See also Chapters 5 and 17.

[5] See also Chapter 5.

[6] See also Chapter 6.

REVIEW AND DISCUSSION QUESTIONS

REVIEW QUESTIONS

1 Describe three different personality theories. What does each tell us about personality?

2 In what ways do personality traits relate to important work and organisational behaviour outcomes?

3 What are the Big Five personality dimensions? What are the kinds of traits and characteristics associated with each?

4 How does personality relate to cognitive ability/intelligence?

5 Identify two common applications of personality assessment in organisations.

DISCUSSION QUESTIONS

1 How would knowledge of theory and research on personality at work help a manager to manage his or her team?

2 How have you experienced the influence of personality in groupwork or teamwork?

3 Rate yourself on the short measure of personality in the box entitled *Rate yourself on the Big Five traits*. Discuss with others the extent to which they agree with your ratings.

4 How could information about personality traits be used to help manage individual job performance in organisations?

5 What traits do you think are important for specific kinds of jobs? (Choose one – eg university lecturer – and discuss.)

FURTHER READING

Woods, S. A. and West, M. A. (2010) *The Psychology of Work and Organizations.* London: CENGAGE. Chapter 3 on 'Individual differences at work' is key reading, but there is lots of discussion of personality at work and in HRM in other chapters too. Practical and accessible throughout.

Furnham, A. (2008) *Personality and Intelligence at Work.* Sussex: Routledge. A book that specifically focuses on these two aspects of individual differences at work.

Barrick, M. R., Mount, M. K. and Judge, T. A. (2001) 'Personality and performance at the beginning of the new millennium: what do we know and where do we go next?', *International Journal of Selection and Assessment,* Vol.9: 9–30. A technical review of the evidence that personality predicts job performance, accumulated over a 10-year period.

John, O. P., Robins, R. W. and Pervin, L. A. (eds) (2008) *Handbook of Personality: Theory and research.* New York: Guildford Press. Plenty of further reading in this edited book on theories and approaches to personality, including the Big Five model.

Holland, J. L. (1996) 'Exploring careers with a typology: what we have learned and some new directions', *American Psychologist,* Vol.51: 397–406. John Holland explores his theory of vocational types and vocational interests in this review article.

Ozer, D. and Benet-Martínez, V. (2006) 'Personality and the prediction of consequential outcomes', *Annual Review of Psychology*, Vol.57: 401–21. In this article, the authors explore some of the main associations between personality and outcomes at work and beyond. Fascinating reading, and very informative.

And finally, if all of this too heavy, read about personality in non-human animals, and personality and music preferences!

Gosling, S. D. (2001) 'From mice to men: what can we learn about personality from animal research?', *Psychological Bulletin*, Vol.127: 45–86.

Rentfrow, P. J. and Gosling, S. D. (2003) 'The do-re-mi's of everyday life: the structure and personality correlates of music preferences', *Journal of Personality and Social Psychology*, Vol.84: 1236–56.

KEY SKILLS

Knowledge about personality and its influence at work has important implications for the development of key skills. Here they are discussed based on three perspectives:

AWARENESS OF YOUR OWN PERSONALITY TRAITS

Personal development planning

Insights into your own personality traits enable you to identify where they may represent personal development needs. A good way to apply this thinking is to complete a self-report personality questionnaire and get some feedback on it (try the IPIP NEO five-factor model recommended in this chapter). Critically review your personality profile and decide where it is really well suited to your chosen job, and where it is less so. Then try to find some ways to develop in the areas that are less well suited to your job.

Time management

Conscientiousness is a key individual difference dimension that relates to time management. People high on conscientiousness typically get down to work quickly, like making plans, and take deadlines seriously. The limitation of this approach is lower flexibility when it comes to changing schedules and demands. If you are low on conscientiousness, then be aware that at times you are probably seen as somewhat disorganised or unreliable by others – amend your style if needed to counter this possibility.

Making presentations

Social confidence, represented in the Big Five model as part of extraversion and to lesser degree emotional stability, is an important determinant of how comfortable you feel about giving presentations to others. People who are extraverted are much more able to rely on their gregariousness and enthusiasm when giving presentations, and are consequently rated as more effective speakers by others. If you are low on extraversion, it's probably worth learning some strategies to help you give engaging and lively presentations – by emulating some of the traits associated with high extraversion.

APPLYING KNOWLEDGE IN MANAGERIAL THINKING

Professional judgement, decision-making, problem-solving and social responsibility

Decisions about people that do not account for individual differences, including differences in personality traits, are generally poor decisions. If you are making decisions about how to respond to others, manage them, or interact with them, it is worth thinking about their personality traits, and how they are likely to influence their behaviour.

Professional judgement about the causes of behaviour is another area to think about. One mistake we often make is to over-emphasise the importance of personality as a cause of behaviour (eg a person did not submit the report on time because they are unreliable). It is much more likely that situation had an equal influence (workload, interruptions, etc).

WORKING WITH OTHERS

Leadership, coaching and mentoring

As highlighted above, leadership decision-making should account for individual differences in order to be effective. This applies very clearly in coaching and mentoring, where people's personality traits represent important strengths, development areas, and preferred styles of learning and responding to development interventions.

In respect of leadership style, dominance is a key personality trait. If you are high on dominance or assertiveness, you are likely to emerge as a leader in groups of people with less social confidence and presence. But you must also beware not to allow this to cause you to miss the contributions or ideas of others who may feel occasionally bulldozed by your style.

Negotiating, arbitration and conflict resolution skills

Personality clashes are an important source of conflict in organisations, and conflict resolution and negotiation in such cases often involves careful consideration and unpicking of the ways in which working styles have been expressed and applied, and caused friction. By understanding personality and how it affects different work behaviours, it is possible to improve on the way we make sense of such issues.

Teamworking

Teams are made up of different personalities. We're sure you have examples of people whose personalities you have found very easy to work with, and those who were more difficult. The literature on personality and teams is fascinating and indicates that in some cases diversity in personality is important in teams, and in other cases homogeneity is better. The message is to not automatically assume that different personalities will tend not to work well together – there are situations where traits of different people complement one another and lead to effective teamworking.

Applying theory to practice

1 Personality and recruitment

The biggest area of application of trait theory in organisations is in the assessment of personality traits for recruitment and selection (see box in the chapter). The evidence of the associations between personality traits and job performance give confidence in this practice, and many organisations find that personality assessment provides important information for selection decision-making. One concern of managers about the use of personality assessment is the potential for faking or socially desirable responding (where people attempt to make themselves seem more suitable for a job than they really are). There is some evidence that the concerns are warranted, although the effects of faking are probably less important than people think (Hogan, Hogan and Roberts, 1996). With careful management of test systems, potential faking can be discouraged. Overall, then, personality assessment has a key role to play in the assessment of candidates applying for employment. The versatility of trait theory also means that it is possible to specify different profiles of characteristics for people working in different jobs.

2 Personality and development

When one appreciates the influence of personality on organisational behaviour, it is possible to use the information to help develop people at work. This could be approached from a number of perspectives. First, there is the area of career guidance. Personality traits have been shown to be important determinants of career interests, and when people work in jobs they find interesting and worthwhile, they tend to be happier in them. Information about personality could help people to explore potential career choices that match their traits.

In respect of leadership, we know that certain traits are important for effective performance. Personality measurement enables people to understand that where their traits are inconsistent with the requirements of leadership roles, it could be possible for them to undertake development and learn new behavioural strategies to address those areas.

Finally, personality measurement can help teams to understand how to work more effectively together. Once people understand the unique traits of team members, they can appreciate others' approaches more clearly and be more accommodating of different work styles. A team could also identify where they may need to develop in order to meet team goals and targets.

Ethical implications: Decision-making about work performance

People have a tendency to over-attribute the cause of people's behaviour to personality traits. We assume that a person is late because they are tardy by nature, not because their lateness was unavoidable due to situations. This raises an ethical issue for the management of individuals. Managers could potentially be hasty in deciding that poor performance was due mainly to a person's not having the right characteristics or abilities, when really the reason is equally likely to be due to the management of that person, their development, and so forth.

The point here is that in organisations we have a responsibility to keep our minds open to the causes of organisational behaviour. These are in part to do with individual factors, but also job and management factors. Integrating knowledge of personality into management systems is not a reason to assume that management behaviour is of less importance. Over-attributing the cause of behaviour as personality, or some other individual difference, is a risk in the management of people in organisations, and one that has implications for ethical decision-making about people's performance at work.

Taking your learning further

1 A really clear and up-to-date introduction to contemporary theories of personality and individual differences is provided by Chamorro-Premuzic (2007):
Chamorro-Premuzic, T. (2007) *Personality and Individual Differences*. Oxford: Blackwell.

2 A very clear exploration of the use of personality assessments in organisations is covered in an accessible way in the article by Hogan, Hogan and Roberts (1996):
Hogan, R., Hogan, J. and Roberts, B. W. (1996) 'Personality measurement and employment decisions', *American Psychologist*, Vol.51: 469–77.

The best and worst practices in this area are concerned with the application of personality assessment in organisations.

BEST PRACTICE

One example of very good practice in the use of personality information for management was experienced by the author while working as a consultant for a UK health company. They planned to introduce personality measurement as part of their systems for identifying future top leaders. Rather than simply opting for the nearest assessment tool to hand, they considered very carefully the kinds of traits they wanted to identify, and undertook a careful review of all of the available tools, concentrating on the research and evaluation evidence underpinning all of them. This was exactly the right thing to do.

WORST PRACTICE

The worst practice in this area is a general one, and refers to the behaviour of some consultants and test companies. There are some really poor examples of tests available for purchase, and you should always be sceptical about sales claims that one new test is vastly better than all the others. Always insist on seeing the evidence. The very worst practice, though, is the positioning of 'type' instruments (usually purporting to be based on the theories of Carl Jung) as scientific. The difference between trait and type is simple. In a trait perspective we can identify different degrees of extraversion (eg highly extraverted, a little extraverted, and so on). In a type model, a person is either extraverted or introverted, and there is no room for determining *how* extraverted or introverted they are. For a variety of reasons (see Woods and West, 2010, Chapter 3 for a brief review of these) personality type theory is flawed, unscientific, incomplete, and provides only limited information about individual differences. In your practice, accept that personality is complex – that's why it's so interesting – and that personality type theories, and assessments of types, simply fail to capture its intricacies.

Chapter 4
Perception and Managing Emotions

Jenna Ward and Robert McMurray

Contents

Key Learning Outcomes

By the end of this chapter you should be able to:

- benefit from a greater appreciation of theories of perception and their relation to managing

- consider the ways in which perceptions may be manipulated by others and changed by context

- understand the different ways in which we make sense of relationships in organising contexts

- have evaluated the use of stereotypes in organising and developing perceptions

- understand what is meant by 'emotion', 'emotion management' and 'emotional labour'

- create your own solutions to managing the emotions of self and others in challenging contexts.

 ## PRACTITIONER INSIGHT

Wycliffe

Wycliffe is a successful Peugeot dealership that has been a central part of the local community for over 40 years. The company prides itself on good customer service and a 'personal touch'. Its mission statement is 'to deliver high-quality service'. We speak to **Paul Ward, the After-Sales Manager** at Wycliffe, about how one of his colleagues dealt with a difficult customer.

Paul and his team have dealt with a number of emotionally charged situations. In one situation, a customer behaved aggressively towards Rebecca Smith, a customer sales adviser at Wycliffe. Rebecca could sense that the customer was unhappy,

and was concerned by his demeanour. She explained that his car had undertaken a routine first service which was free of charge and handed his keys back to him. The customer responded by shouting 'These are not my keys!' and throwing the keys at Rebecca.

If you were Rebecca how would you have felt in this situation?

If you were Paul, how would you manage the situation between the customer and Rebecca?

Once you have read this chapter, return to these questions and think about how you could answer them.

Introduction

The aim of this chapter is to consider how we perceive the world around us. Why is this important? Three reasons:

- Perception is the basis on which we come to understand organisations and the individuals we encounter within them (eg customers, recruits, staff, peers, shareholders, regulators). Understanding the different ways in which we and others perceive the world and make associated judgements can help us to be effective managers.

- As part of everyday sense-making we often employ or impose stereotypes and other 'commonsense' approaches to knowing. We need to be aware of how these are used and abused in organising contexts.

- Successful managers recognise the need to deal with feelings and emotions that inform perceptions. This requires an appreciation of the emotion experienced and enacted in different types of work. It requires emotional intelligence in managing our emotions, and in responding to those of clients, colleagues and other stakeholders. How we manage our own emotions and the emotions of others will inform our style of managing.

In tackling these issues we are going to cover 2,500 years of Western scholarship on perception and emotion, starting with Plato and ending with doctors' surgeries and call centres. We are going to touch on important theories related to intellect, our senses, psychology, sociology and organisation theory, but only to the extent that they help us understand what is required to be a better manager in the twenty-first century.

Be warned – we are not going to tell you what a good manager is. What it is to be a good manager at any given time varies according to where you are, what you are charged with doing, who you have to relate to, who you are employed by, what your personal goals are, and who is judging your performance and determining your rewards. Managing through and in relation to other people is by definition a contingent and ever-changing process.

What we will do is equip you with the necessary knowledge, tools and questions to make the right judgements in these varying contexts. We will help you understand how you and others perceive the world, and how this informs management decisions.

We will help you understand why your perceptions of people can be misguided by stereotypes and assumptions, and why not reconciling these inbuilt biases can reduce your effectiveness in selecting, directing and relating to other people.

Finally, we will introduce you to one of the hottest areas in organisational research and practice in advanced economies: emotion management. We will show you why managing your own emotions and the emotions of others impacts on how you are perceived as a manager, and why developing your emotional intelligence could be key to developing successful careers in the twenty-first century.

The key sections of the chapter are: Shaping perceptions, Deception and truth, The use of stereotypes, Emotions in organisations, Managing emotion, and Managing better.

SHAPING PERCEPTIONS

When we talk of perceptions we are referring to the processes used in sensing, interpreting and understanding the world around us. From the accent someone speaks with to the clothes they wear, the giving of eye contact, the language used in emails, the felt emotions of a customer, the grandeur of an office-building lobby, and the seating arrangements in a meeting-room – all have significance in terms of the sense we make of relations in organising contexts.

At its most basic, **perception** refers to sensory data – information received via the **senses**. In organisational behaviour this tends to mean an emphasis on seeing and hearing, although recent developments in organisation theory have also pointed to the value of accounting for smells, taste and touch (see, for example, Baxter and Ritchie, 2004). It refers to our ability to be aware of that which is around us through the complex processes by which we sense shapes, colours, attitudes and the flow of everyday life. It is an area of study that tends to be dominated by cognitive psychology and its concern with the ways in which the information is processed internally. While acknowledging the importance of cognitive research, our concern is with a more sociological understanding of perceptions as they relate to truth, deception, sense-making and emotions.

Making sense

Perception is more than the passive receipt of data from outside. It is a complex set of processes relating to the active project of sense-making. As mathematician and philosopher Alfred North Whitehead (1929: 131–3) observed:

> The world of present fact is more than a stream of sense-presentation. We find
> ourselves with emotions, volitions, imaginations, conceptions and judgements.
> No factor which enters into consciousness is by itself or even can exist in isolation . . .
> The material universe is largely a concept of the imagination which rests on a slender
> basis for direct sense presentation.

By this we take him to mean that the things we perceive are not simply out there, waiting as objective facts to be found. Rather, we construct our facts in choosing to pay attention to some things and not others. Our perceptions of objects, processes and experiences depend to a great extent on how we have been taught to look and interpret – they depend on how we relate things presented to our senses to each other. What matters for Whitehead are not the things we perceive but the connections we make between them. This concern with how things relate and change could be seen as one of the central preoccupations of managing. Consider for a moment the way Paul Ward's perception of the customer – and therefore the way he managed the situation – changed in the scenario described in the Practitioner insight box at the beginning of the chapter. The way in which we perceive situations will affect the way we manage them.

The importance of context

One way in which we can come to understand the importance of the relations we make and the things we perceive is to account for the issue of context. For example, focusing on the simple issue of 'dirt', anthropologist Mary Douglas (1966) sought to demonstrate how what counts as 'dirt' is highly dependent on the social and cultural context of the perceiver. To a gardener, mud or soil is perceived as the essential medium in which to grow things and, in the course of cultivation, to impose a desired order on nature. However, even the gardener is of the opinion that this same mud becomes unwanted dirt or 'matter out of place' (Douglas, 1966) when transferred onto the living-room carpet. This is because it disturbs the good order of the household. The physical properties of the mud are the same in each case, but its description as soil or dirt speaks of differences in perception based on changes in relation to contextual location.

How does this discussion of dirt relate to perception in organising and managing? Again, the same actions in alternative contexts may be perceived very differently. For an American footballer aggression, physical contact and tackling are part and parcel of the working day. They are necessary and accepted parts of the daily routine. Yet the same aggression in an office context would generally be regarded as highly inappropriate (see the Practitioner insight box at the beginning of the chapter). To physically tackle someone would be perceived as socially, culturally and legally wrong. The act of tackling has not changed, but the way we relate to it in different contexts has. Of course, it is precisely the act of blurring these social boundaries – of juxtaposing the physical violence of grid-iron tackling with the corporate context of office – that has made Reebok's *Terry Tate: Office Linebacker* commercials an online favourite. In these spoof commercials the use of Tate to dispense immediate physical justice to those who exhibit poor corporate citizenship is acknowledged as an innovative if unorthodox management practice – something we would ordinarily perceive to be out of place.

Perception is not a neutral thing. Returning to Douglas (1966: 36), we might suggest that:

> As perceivers we select from all the stimuli falling on our senses only those which interest us . . . In a chaos of shifting impressions, each of us constructs a stable world in which objects have recognisable shapes, are located in depth, and have permanence. In perceiving we are building, taking some cues and rejecting others. The most acceptable cues are those which fit most easily into the pattern that is being built up.

In other words, we have an active role in constructing and understanding the world around us. As we discuss in more depth below, our tendencies to select those issues that are of interest to us increases the danger of particular types of bias, while the desire to maintain the pictures we have already built up can make radical change difficult, particularly where others suggest that we are deceiving ourselves and denying the truth.

PERCEPTION, DECEPTION AND TRUTH

If we accept that perception is not a just a simple matter of seeing, and that apparent facts of the world are open to interpretation and change, then we also open up the possibility that our senses may deceive us. One of the earliest and best-known considerations of this problem is Plato's simile of the cave (*The Republic*, 375bc/1974, part 7, Bk VII).

Plato's simile of the cave

The simile constructs a conversation between Socrates and Glaucon, as told in Plato's *Republic*. The story begins with people chained to seats in a dark cave, unable to escape or even move their heads. Placed in this position since before they can remember, all they can do is look forward at a wall. Light from a fire casts shadows on the wall. The shadows are of people and things passing by. These images and the sounds that accompany them are the only things that the inhabitants of the cave ever perceive – like having always lived in a Japanese shadow theatre or a world viewed in silhouette (Figure 4.1). This theatre is for them the real and only world: 'In every way they would believe that the shadows of the objects mentioned were the whole truth' (Plato, 1974: 515a).

The story goes on to describe how one prisoner escapes his chair and makes it out of the cave into the light. At this point Socrates enquires, 'What do you think he would say if he was told that what he used to see was so much empty nonsense, and that he was now nearer reality and seeing more correctly? . . . Don't you think he would be at a loss, and think that what he used to see was far truer?' Thinking further, Socrates wonders whether would it not be the case that on looking into the light of the outside, 'it would hurt his eyes and he would turn back and retreat to the things which he could see properly' (Plato, 1974: 515d–e).

Plato suggests that on being forced back into the light, the person would in time begin to perceive that life outside the cave with its grass, birds, people and movement, all lit by the much more powerful sun, was a more authentic world. He would come to understand that this was the real world that had been kept from him up until now, the shadows describing not the world but rather the limits placed on his past life.

The person goes back to the cave to enlighten those left behind. Unaccustomed to the gloom of the cave, the man now struggles to see what those who are still tied to the chairs see. He does poorly at the old games of guessing what the shadows represent, and is ridiculed for his lack of perceptiveness as those still chained to their chairs all agree that the light of the outside has ruined his sight. Those in the cave struggle to understand or see what the returning person has to teach. They do not want to see the light, they do not think they are prisoners (for they have known nothing else), and they do not want to give up the expertise and status they have acquired

Figure 4.1 Shadow puppets

Reproduced by kind permission of Becky McMurray

in interpreting shadows (the games of shadow-guessing have evolved into a practice of ranking ability and attributing status).

The point of the story is to highlight the limits of our everyday perceptions, to get us to question what we know about our own taken-for-granted worlds. It is intended to get us to 'picture the enlightenment or ignorance of our human condition' (Plato, 1974: Bk VII) and point up the need for education if we are not to be deceived.

Plato is aware that the process of educating ourselves may also be painful, and that it may be necessary to drag us kicking and screaming from the comforting shadows of our false perceptions in order that we might get closer to the truth of living and life. It is this unpicking of worlds we once cherished that challenges our minds and causes us to shield our eyes from the blinding light.

Perceptual blindness [1]

A contemporary retelling of this story is to be found in the Wachowski brothers' film *The Matrix* (1999), in which the hero, Neo, discovers that his life as an office worker was an illusion: everything that he has done since the time of his birth has taken place in computer simulation designed to control his thoughts and limit his freedom. Just like the prisoners in Plato's cave, Neo's first reaction to seeing the light is painful denial. He does not want to engage with the possibility that his life has unwittingly been used in the service of others – others who have exploited his perceptions and stolen his individual power.

Marx and false consciousness

This is not a new theme in organisation theory. The notion that others more powerful than ourselves may deceive us and use our individual talents and powers for their own ends is an underlying theme of Marxist critiques on the functioning of capitalism. Broadly, Marx (*Capital*, 1976) argues that the working class are exploited by those who own capital through the unfair extraction of surplus value (profit) derived from their labour power – in other words, workers are not properly recompensed for their efforts. The problem is that workers do not perceive their own exploitation and thus fail to free themselves of it.

Their failure to perceive their exploitations is a consequence of their labouring under **'false consciousness'**, or an inability to see social relations as they really are (at least as Marxists suppose them to be). According to this model, those of us that think we are happy in our roles have been deceived into accepting a work life that is well below our potential. Rather than being free and creative workers who express our humanity through our production, we have been turned into imperfect cogs in a machine run by and for the benefit of others. As Georg Lukács (1923/1971) said in *History and Class Consciousness* (p.89):

> In consequence of the rationalisation of the work process, the human qualities and idiosyncrasies of the worker appear increasingly as mere sources of error when contrasted with these abstract special laws functioning according to rational predictions. Neither objectively nor in his relation to his work does man appear as the authentic master of the process; on the contrary, he is a mechanical part incorporated into a mechanical system. He finds it already pre-existing and self-sufficient; it functions independently of him and he has to conform to its laws whether he likes it or not.

Of course, not everyone feels that they are happy in their work. We all know people trapped in a job they hate – parents forced to work rather than care for their children, or students obliged to be full-time baristas to pay for their degree. For Marxists the only way out of this situation is intellectual enlightenment (similar to Plato) as prelude to revolutionary system change. That this does not occur is a consequence of people's perceiving that the status quo represents the natural order of things, and that all that can be done to ameliorate their present condition is to appeal to extrinsic work motivations and consumerism. The film *Confessions of a Shopaholic*

(2009) takes a light-hearted look at the negative effects of capitalism – eg debt and social isolation in a consumer society. This then is a necessarily bleak diagnosis with respect to perception and the human condition, with a highly radical prescription.

To this point we can see that there has long been a concern with perception and the manner in which we make sense of the world around us. From Plato through Marx, Whitehead and others we are warned that perceptions are not neutral but, rather, constructed and open to manipulation. It is up to us to question our sense presentations, acknowledging that how we perceive things, situations and processes depends on our experiences, culture, intentions and context. Perception is then an active process of **sense-making**.

Sense-making

'Sense-making' is a useful term for describing the daily processes by which we reach 'agreements as to what is real and illusory' (Colville 2008: 198, citing Weick, 1979). The notion of sense-making has been made popular by organisation theorist Karl Weick (1979, 1995, 1996) and his attempts to shed light on how we go about rendering the world sensible. Just like us, Weick notes that how we make sense of the world around us depends on issues such as the context we are in, our past experiences, the stories we hear and the things that we do. A very useful account of Weick's sense-making is provided by Hernes (2007), in which it is noted that as managers and workers we do not simply stumble on 'reality' but have an active role in making it. For example, how a meeting between managers goes depends on what we choose to say, how co-operative we are feeling, what sense we make of shared problems, the notes we take, the actions we agree to follow up on, and how we reflect upon it subsequently. It points to sense-making as a range of ongoing processes in which we negotiate the reality of a situation through talking, listening, observing, inference, doing and reflection. We are, in other words, involved in the ongoing enactment of daily life.

Routine sense

This is good news for managers because it emphasises our active role in making and changing things. According to this theory we are not merely buffeted by the world around us but have an active choice over what we do and the type of organisations we live in. The way we say, do and sell things has a fundamental impact on how others experience them. Of course, over time rules and roles may become more structured. New accountancy methods direct us to make sense of organisational throughputs in particular ways, and health and safety legislation guides our decisions about the working environment (whether from scaffolding on a building site or the position of the monitor on your desk). The point is that these rules are not just pre-existing facts that we respond to passively: rather, they are negotiated by people just like us who make them real in the ways we choose to abide, bend or ignore them. Equal opportunities laws state that people should not be discriminated against on the basis of their age, sex, race or religion. However, the realities of promotion and progression depend on the attitudes, actions, unspoken biases and alternative explanations that come from employers, executives and shareholders, not the law (see *The Economist*, 'Female power', January 2010).

Another useful contribution to our understanding of work and organising is Weick's (1995) account of routines. He notes that over time the spontaneity of organising and doing may be replaced by repetition and learned routines. To avoid learning how to do something as if from new each time, we settle on effective methods for dealing with similar situations. We impose a sense of orderliness on events through the application of set procedures and rules. We might think of attempts to rationalise the customer encounter in certain fast-food restaurants where it appears staff are working to a script, or the procedures to be gone through to obtain new office equipment, or the experience of going through automated telephone systems that seek to routinise and direct our personal enquiries. Often such routines and scripts are highly effective in organising terms, ensuring that processes are managed efficiently and that organisations outlast their individual members thanks to the persistence of plans, policies, budgets, organisation charts, mission statements, branding and other relics (Hernes, 2007).

Drop your tools

Such relics and routines tend to become thought of as facts of organising, and as such taken for granted and left largely unquestioned. It is this 'taken-for-granted' aspect that poses a danger. In a very powerful account of fire-fighters being overcome by wild fire, Weick (1996) notes that our tendency to stick to routines or the taken-for-granted facts rather than revert back to spontaneity can leave us in real danger. In his example, fire-fighters' adherence to the routine of never dropping their tools costs them their lives – the tools weighing them down as forest fires change direction and engulf them (the point being that they could have outrun the advancing fire had they discarded their heavy tools). The organisational equivalents are 'jobs-worths' or bureaucrats who stick with the rules even when they do not apply to a particular situation.

So 'sense-making is what it says it is – namely, making something sensible' (Weick, 1995: 16, cited in Colville, 2008: 198). As part of that ongoing process we often employ a range of models or routines to help us make sense of the world around us and impose a sense of stability. Management literature is replete with handy tools and grids that are intended to aid our attempts to render the world sensible – the SWOT (strengths, weaknesses, opportunities and threats) analysis being an enduring example. However, not all our models are so explicit. What is more, they are not necessarily sensible or benign. A discussion of stereotypes may help to illustrate the point.

THE USE OF STEREOTYPES

> There is nothing either good or bad, but thinking makes it so: to me it is a prison.
>
> (Shakespeare's *Hamlet*, Act II, Scene II)

Stereotyping refers to the assumption that some apparent features or characteristics apply to all members of a group. In the main, stereotyping is assumed to afford a narrow image of those involved, often in a pejorative sense: the receptionist as dragon, footballers as unintelligent, women as emotional, and 'all men are rapists' (Cochrane, 2005).

In one sense stereotyping is a form of simplified and routinised sense-making. It is ready shorthand for classifying individuals and behaviours based on an agreed set of assumptions about the groups to which they are judged to belong. As such they can be reassuring, their familiarity and ease of access serving to reduce the anxiety felt in managing new relations. Academic research on organisational cultures and behaviours can be said to feed into such sense-making. A good example is Hofstede's (2001) research on national and organisational cultures that encourages the broad categorisation of countries and groups in terms of individualism, masculinity or power-distance.

While some may deem such categorisations a useful first step in understanding and developing relations with those who are as yet unfamiliar, it also holds dangers. Poorly or maliciously constructed stereotypes can lead to discrimination or prejudice on the basis of gender, race, religion, physical ability, age and place of origin. For example, women may be preferred to men when it comes to employment in primary schools or kindergartens because the former group are presumed to be more empathetic or incapable of subjecting young children to abuse (the case of the Little Ted's nursery in England sadly refuting the stereotype). This draws attention to the other major limitation of stereotyping, the failure to perceive individual particularities and differences, assuming instead that those from outside groups are all the same (homogeneity bias). But not all bankers are greedy, not all medics are caring, not all English people display a stiff upper lip. What is more, no account is taken of context – something we have already established as an important component of perception. Even if someone does conform to the stereotypes we hold in one context, there is no guarantee that the typecasting will hold true in another. (When the English win sporting events, their stereotypical reserve is often in short supply.)

Common perceptual errors [2]

Stereotyping is just one form of sense-making shorthand that can be open to bias and error. Here are some more we should be aware of.

The halo effect

The '**halo effect**' describes situations in which a single positive characteristic, trait or action biases the assessment of the whole individual. For example, we may note that Geoff is always punctual when it comes to important meetings. On this basis we assume that Geoff is always well organised, well prepared and good at his job. The truth may be that Geoff is struggling to perform most of the duties assigned to him, but his parents' emphasis on the importance of good time-keeping when he was a child has made him very punctilious. Equally, it may be incorrectly assumed that Steve is a liability organisationally because he always arrives for meetings 10 minutes after the start. This negative extension of a single attribute proves to be incorrect, as Steve's ability to get things done means that he is often required in more than one place at a time. This type of negative assessment is sometimes known as the '**rusty halo**' or '**devil**' effect. Whether positive or negative, these effects speak to a bias in perception that can impact on how we relate to others in everyday encounters. Indeed, under specific circumstances performance appraisals may lead to unfair rewards or sanctions depending on the assessor's bias.

Selective perception

Selective perception occurs where we interpret events solely according to our own interests, experiences and background, or define people in very narrow terms. In failing to consider alternative perspectives we suffer a 'perceptual block' (Linstead and Linstead, 2005) because lack of attention to other information prevents us from seeing the full range of possibilities open to us when managing people or situations. Imagine a university teacher who believes that students whose first language is not English cannot excel in or cope with complex discursive subjects. This perception is based on past experience of teaching a course in which large numbers of non-native English speakers failed. The result is to dissuade such students from taking the course. What the teacher has failed to consider is that it may be his or her own teaching methods and pedagogy – not the students – that are at fault. Failure to perceive this possibility leads to continued poor teaching and unhappy students and teacher. Selective perception thus becomes a block to much needed change. As Douglas (1966: 38) notes:

> There are several ways of treating anomalies. Negatively, we can ignore, just not perceive them, or perceiving we can condemn; or more positively we can deliberately confront the anomaly and try to create a new pattern of reality in which it has a place.

We would suggest that effective management is likely to be found taking the latter approach.

Self-fulfilling prophecy (Merton, 1957)

This describes the tendency to make an initial judgement that may or may not be true, and then to allow that judgement to affect behaviour in order to obtain confirmation of that judgement. Say that, based on first impressions or rumours, we make an initial judgement that someone is going to be a good or poor colleague. In the former case we are welcoming and offer to help them as they settle into their new job. They learn the ropes and rules of the office quickly and are soon usefully assisting you in your own work. They are a good new colleague, just as you suspected they would be. Alternatively, suspecting the new person to be a poor or obstructive colleague, you are polite but aloof. You do not share information with the person, leaving them to make their own mistakes in terms of office policies and politics. Isolated and flailing, the new member of staff will not make eye contact with you, is of little help and, indeed, creates work because you are asked to cover the tasks they have not completed. As you expected, then, they have become a poor addition to the team. In each case our actions have served to validate our initial assessments and 'at the same time falsely improve our opinion of our ability to judge others' (Thompson and McHugh, 2009: 267).

Projection

Projection centres on the way in which we assume that others are the same as us in some essential way and treat them as we would want to be treated. This speaks of both a failure to reflect on our own preferential biases and a failure to communicate effectively with others. Professionals such as doctors and teachers often assume that their own perspective on issues is the same as their clients' – a perception that has long been found to be misplaced. Their opinions and wants may at times overlap, but they are rarely the same. In business, such a tendency may cause us to fail to recognise the needs of customers or misinterpret the motivations of those who work for us.

Attribution bias

Attribution bias is concerned with our tendency to externalise our failings and internalise our successes. Leaders such as Gordon Brown in Britain may be happy to claim credit for economic growth and at having 'broken the cycle of boom and bust'. However, when it comes to the development of the deepest recession since World War II, claims of responsibility appear thin on the ground. As students of managing and organising we need to be aware of these tendencies within ourselves and others.

Perceiving is, then, no simple matter. Our interactions with the world around us are mediated by our senses, selections, contexts, cultures and pragmatisms as part of the active construction of sense-making. We do not just receive the world as an essential fact but actively create it in the ways that we engage with it and process it. In organisations this is further complicated by the active sense-making of others who may work with us to construct accounts of the real and illusory, or more cynically seek to impose their accounts of the world upon us. We may thus be deceived by others, although it is just as likely that we will deceive ourselves if we are uncritical about our own methods for viewing organising and managing (the imposition of stereotypes being a case in point). It is, however, also possible that our attempts to manage the perceptions of others and the manner in which others perceive are not just a matter of clear deceit but rather of careful choreography for mutual benefit. A case in point is the management of emotions in organisations.

EMOTIONS IN ORGANISATIONS

Now that we have considered the way in which we come to make sense of ourselves, others, and the world around us through simplifications such as stereotypes, it is relevant to turn to a relatively new area of organisational behaviour: emotions in organisations. This section begins by making clear the conceptual differences between feelings and emotions, which highlights the requirement of individuals to be able to manage their emotions in order to be perceived as socially acceptable. We take a look back at how emotions were once relatively marginalised within the workplace, in comparison to now, when they have become the focus of the service industry but continue to be controlled and manipulated by organisations. In anticipation of introducing various conceptual forms of emotional labour in the following section, we conclude here with a critical discussion of how organisations are no longer only interested in manipulating the emotions of their workers but also how they seek to regulate the emotions of their customers too.

Feelings and emotions [3]

In everyday life emotions and feelings are often thought to be the same. However, when we discuss emotions in organisations it is often helpful to make a clear distinction between the two terms. **Feelings** are best thought of as what is going on inside, allowing us to understand how we are experiencing certain situations. Reflect on your first day at university: you most likely experienced feelings of sadness, anxiety, apprehension and excitement as the prospect of leaving the security and comfort of your family to begin a new life became a reality. Yet it is unlikely that you displayed all of these emotions to the people around you. As this simple example demonstrates, our feelings are sometimes conflicting, yet we regulate these internal experiences in order to make sense of, and to, the world around us. **Emotions** are the external presentation of our feelings. If you expressed your internal, conflicting feelings as emotions to your fellow freshers, it is unlikely that you would have made many friends. This is not to say that experiencing complex and conflicting feelings is wrong or a symptom of psychological illness, but the presentation of them, to the outside world, may be seen as an inability to 'manage your emotions' which particularly in Western societies is seen as socially unacceptable and often a symptom of psychological disturbance. The Academy Award-winning film *One Flew Over The Cuckoo's Nest* challenges our perception of 'sanity' and offers an interesting reflection on how our ability to manage our emotions is part of that. But why do we 'make sense of' emotional complexity in this way? Mr Winchester – the apparently enraged customer in the Practitioner insight box at the beginning of the chapter – could have been perceived as 'insane' or 'troubled' because he was unable to manage his emotions. However, as the perception literature suggests, our judgements are based on context.

No place for emotion?

So, surely emotions and feelings are a key part of being a manager and working within an organisation? Yet this has not always been perceived to be the case. The Industrial Revolution in the West was a time when science and reason became a new kind of religion. Advances in technology changed the nature of work and society and saw the birth of the **'modern organisation'**. By 'modern' we mean they were operated in the spirit of 'modernism'. Modernism is the term used to describe the way in which control and reason were applied to human behaviour for them to take control of their circumstances. **Principles of rationality** were applied to organisations and the people who worked within them. These principles of rationality are control, efficiency, calculability and predictability (Weber, 1948). Workers in the 'modern organisation' or **'bureaucracy'** were not seen as human beings but as part of the production line. While they were at work they were expected to behave like a machine with their inputs and outputs calculated and controlled by management. This process of rationalisation focused on eliminating risk and uncertainty for the capitalist. The owners and managers of the bureaucracies wanted calculable, predictable and increasing profit margins. They believed this could be achieved through rationalisation, which included the marginalisation of emotion within the workplace. In other words, emotions were perceived to be irrational and to hold the potential to negatively affect productivity.

Max Weber, a leading theorist in this area, pointed out (1948: 215–16) that:

> the more bureaucracy is dehumanised, the more completely it succeeds in eliminating from official business love, hatred, and all purely personal, irrational and emotional elements which escape calculation.

Bureaucratic organisations view emotions and feelings as dangerous, uncalculable and uncontrollable adages to the production process. 'The central ideology surrounding emotions in organisations is that they are irrational, idiosyncratic disturbances that are best controlled and kept undercover' (Gibson, 2006: 478). In modern organisations emotions were excluded from the boundaries of organisations in a modernist belief that 'efficiency should not be sullied by the irrationality of personal feelings' (Hancock and Tyler, 2001: 130).

As a consequence, emotions and feelings have been 'socially constructed' as irrational, unhelpful and often 'feminine' traits, and we therefore perceive the display of certain emotions as a sign of weakness or of being 'out of control'. The historical legacy of the way in which human emotion has been controlled by the capitalist system is still very much prevalent today both inside and outside the workplace. The way we control our emotions determines how we are perceived by others, and also how we perceive ourselves.

The place for emotion?

However, there have been some changes to the way emotions are perceived. The Industrial Revolution led to the rapid development of secondary sector or manufacturing industries. In more recent years service sector work has come to dominate Western society, in what has come to be known as the **'post-industrial'** era. Exponential growth of the service sector has meant that the ability to manage emotions has become increasingly important and so has become increasingly recognised as a field of study within organisational behaviour. Emotion plays a significant role within the service sector because jobs here are usually carried out either face-to-face or voice-to-voice. The immediacy of the interaction means that a service is produced and consumed at exactly the same point in time. Every service interaction is therefore uncontrollable, unpredictable and uncalculable in a 'modernist' sense. Emotions are no longer eliminated from the production process because they are a key part of what is being purchased and consumed. For example: when you go to a particularly nice restaurant for a meal, you are not just consuming the food that you order, you are also consuming the waitress's smile, the ambience of the room, the sound of the background music, the pictures hanging on the wall, and so on. In other words, going to a restaurant is not just about eating the food, it is a sensory experience – you are paying for the way it makes you feel.

Other people, usually the waiting staff, provide part of the service in a restaurant. Their knowledge of the menu, their ability to recommend a wine and their rapport with you as a customer are all important parts of the service being offered. Each of these elements requires the waitress to use her emotions to control the way you, as a customer, feel. This is known as **emotional labour**, which we cover in detail in the next section. For now, it is important to reflect on the way in which rationality is continuing to play a part in the way our emotions are managed.

'Have a nice day!'

Emotions are controlled and manipulated in a variety of ways. Some organisations make their front-line service staff use scripts when they interact with customers. This ensures that every customer has a similar and predictable experience. It also means that workers are not only required to suppress certain emotions – eg disguise the way they really feel – but they often have to induce, or pretend to feel, something they do not. The most famous example of the use of scripts is in McDonald's (Ritzer, 1996). McDonald's restaurants were one of the first organisations to adopt the principles of rationality into their services. Every element of working, and eating, at McDonald's is highly organised and controlled. Other organisations, however, take a more subtle approach to ensuring that customers receive standardised service, such as mystery shoppers and hidden cameras. One particular airline actually encourages their passengers to complain about their staff if they do not receive good service with the incentive of being entered into a prize draw for a free holiday.

Both of these examples show how emotions play a key part in the workplace while still being very much controlled through subtle forms of rationalisation. However, it is not only workers' emotions that organisations want to control. As a customer you consume these emotional performances, and in doing so this makes you feel a certain way. For example: you go into a store looking to buy a new game for your X-Box but you are unsure of which one to get. As you are looking around, considering your choices, a friendly shop assistant approaches you. You tell him you are unsure of which game to buy and he quickly recommends a particular new release. He talks enthusiastically and excitedly about the games and its features. After hearing him talk so positively about the game you take his advice and purchase it. Rushing home you invite your mates round to try it out. Meanwhile, the shop assistant stands exhausted at the till looking at his watch. He really feels the game you have just purchased – the one a moment ago he was enthusiastic about – is mediocre but he is being paid a commission on every copy he sells today.

This example illustrates how organisations can subtly manipulate their workers to manage their own emotions in order to influence the way customers feel.

Making customers believe they have freedom and control over their decision-making processes (see Chapter 11) is achieved through manipulating customer emotions. Korczynski and Ott (2004) call this 'the enchanting myth of consumer sovereignty'. In other words, organisations manipulate customer emotions to construct the perception that the customers are in control when in fact the organisation holds all the power. So 'the customer is always right' – as long as the customer wants what we want them to want!

The contentions described in this section between Western societies' desire for rationality and the acceptance of emotion into the organisational context has become more formally conceptualised as emotional labour.

MANAGING EMOTION

Emotions play a key role in the way that we communicate, interact and make sense of each other. We smile at an elderly neighbour, sigh at the barman who still has not served us and frown at our sporting rival. Each of these interactions is understood through the performance of our emotions and the emotional reactions of others. In everyday life the ability to manage and understand emotions is seen as a form of 'social glue' (Raz, 2002) because it binds society together.

The management of emotion in our private lives is known as **emotion work** (Hochschild, 1983). Yet when we manage our emotions as part of our job the emotion management is called **emotional labour** (Hochschild, 1983).

Emotion management

The concept of emotional labour was originally defined as the ability 'to induce or suppress feelings in order to sustain the outward countenance that produces the proper state of mind in others...' (Hochschild, 1983: 7). In other words, emotional labour requires the worker to manage their emotions in order to affect the way customers feel.

For example, Tim has a Saturday job working in a children's shoe shop. Last Friday his friends convinced him to go to the local pub for the evening. Tim goes into work the following morning feeling a little worse for wear. He was hoping for a nice quiet start to the day with an opportunity to sit in the back room for half an hour with a strong coffee. When he arrived Tim could see the shop was full of screaming children. His head throbbed and his tongue clung to the roof of his mouth – this was the last thing he needed! As he entered the shop and removed his coat, a flustered mum carrying a child with a mischievous look on his face approached him. 'Hi! My son seems to have his foot stuck in this shoe!' she grinned apologetically. Tim looked down at the child's foot that was wedged into a shoe three sizes too small. 'That's not a problem. Let's see if we can get that off for you!' and Tim smiled enthusiastically.

This short example demonstrates the way we manage our emotions within an organisational context despite how we are feeling on the inside. After all, Tim was not being paid to tell the woman she should have been watching her child, or that the shoe shop was not a dressing-up box. Instead, he was being paid to provide good customer service. A characteristic of emotional labour is that it is carried out in return for a wage. Organisations commodify, rationalise and routinise individual human emotion and subjectivity in order to increase profits. Just as the manual labourer on the production line is employed for his physical input, emotional labourers are employed for their emotional input.

Emotion management is the general term used for our ability to control the emotions we perform. Emotion work and emotional labour can be thought of as two forms of emotion management (Figure 4.2).

Figure 4.2 A typology of emotion management

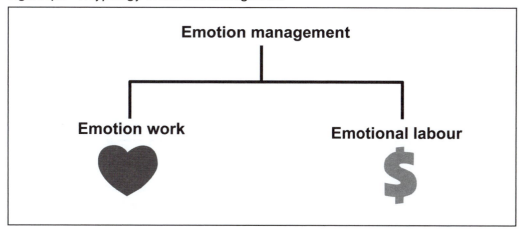

Emotional labour v emotion work

The distinction between emotional labour and emotion work should not just be made on where emotions are being managed, either in a public or private context. In fact, some scholars (Callahan and McCollum, 2002; Ward, 2009) have pointed to this distinction as causing confusion over the two terms, which has led to their being used interchangeably.

In *The Managed Heart*, Hochschild (1983) coined the term 'emotional labour' and developed her theoretical perspective. Emotional labour is based upon a Marxist perspective of labour. She argues that the regulation of emotion, in return for a wage, is fundamentally exploitative in its nature, just as Marx believed that labour exerted under capitalism was exploitative and alienating. Hochschild's emotion systems theory was in its most basic interpretation an extension to **labour process theory.** Upon this basis Hochschild (1983) felt there was a clear difference between what she called emotion work and emotional labour. The primary distinction between the concepts is that emotion work has **use value,** whereas emotional labour has **exchange value.** Use value is something that we can gain pleasure from but we could not sell, because it has no market value. Emotional labour, on the other hand, has exchange value and therefore has a market value, so it can be performed in exchange for a wage. See Table 4.1.

So hiding your feelings of horror at Christmas time when you open the present knitted by your Grandma is an example of emotion work, whereas a checkout operator telling customers to 'Have a nice day' accompanied by a beaming smile is emotional labour. Our ability to manage our emotions both as emotion work and emotional labour also affects the way we are perceived as individuals and within the job role we occupy.

Table 4.1:   Emotional labour *v* emotion work

Emotion work	Emotional labour
• has use value – ie it is possible to gain pleasure from it but it is not worth anything on the free market	• has exchange value
• is performed in a private context	• is performed in the public domain
• is performed for non-compensated benefit	• is performed in exchange for a wage
• involves the management of emotions by personal choice	• involves following organisationally prescribed display and feeling rules to manage emotions

Each job role comes with a different set of **'feeling rules'** (Hochschild, 1979) – for example, we expect a nurse to behave very differently from a clown or a bouncer. In order to make sense of ourselves and others and be perceived as good at our jobs we must comply with the specific set of feeling rules related to our job role. The following section looks at various types of emotional labour that are required by a range of different occupations.

Emotional labour

Every job requires a unique performance of emotional labour. A number of different emotional labour techniques have been suggested in the literature.

Surface and deep acting (Hochschild, 1983)

Hochschild's (1983) perspective on emotional labour was strongly influenced by the work of Erving Goffman (1959). Goffman was interested in the way individuals 'present' themselves, almost as if they are playing a part in a play. This is known as **dramaturgy.** Taking a dramaturgical approach, Hochschild (1983) identified two emotional labour techniques: surface acting and deep acting.

Surface acting involves managing outward appearances; pretending 'to feel what we do not, . . . we deceive others about what we really feel, but we do not deceive ourselves' (Hochschild, 1983: 33). In this case, the emotional labourer is aware of the difference between what they genuinely feel and the impression they are projecting. Put simply, surface acting is the art of impression management, which involves (Ashforth and Humphrey, 1993: 91):

> stimulating emotions that are not actually felt, which is accomplished by careful presentation of verbal and nonverbal cues, such as facial expression, gestures, and voice tone.

Research suggests that prolonged performances of surface acting can lead to negative consequences on well-being, such as burnout (Brotheridge and Grandey, 2002).

Deep acting, on the other hand, is the act of 'deceiving oneself as much as deceiving others . . . We make feigning easy by making it unnecessary' (Hochschild, 1983: 33). Deep acting is seen to require a 'successful transmutation of the private emotional system' – in other words, the emotional labourer begins to *feel* as if the aims of the organisation are his or her own. This emotional labour technique is thought to be the aim of most organisations, because it means that the worker is no longer having to consciously 'act' the part of the helpful shop assistant: he or she has *become* the helpful shop assistant.

Antipathetic and empathetic emotional labour (Korczynski, 2002)

Marek Korczynski (2002) considered emotional labour techniques from a different perspective. He looked at the type of emotions being performed and what the desired outcome of that performance was on others.

Empathetic emotional labour is often thought of as 'positive' emotional labour. This is because emotional labourers perform emotions that are empathetic or caring in order to make others feel welcomed, safe, happy and positive about the particular situation. Empathetic emotional labour is perhaps most commonly found in the work of cabin crew, shop assistants, nurses, entertainers, etc.

Conversely**, antipathetic emotional labour** performances are those that require the emotional labour to make others feel scared, insecure, upset or angry. This may at first seem like quite an unlikely request of any organisation, yet consider the work of traffic wardens, bailiffs, debt collectors and bouncers. All of the job roles require the performance of negative emotions.

Antecedent- and response-focused emotional labour (Grandey, 2000)

Grandey's (2000) work on emotional labour focuses on the way emotions are regulated by the emotional labourer. She identified two main ways by which emotions are regulated.

Antecedent-focused emotion regulation occurs when the individual 'modifies the situation or the perception of the situation in order to adjust emotions' (Grandey, 2000: 98). In other words, the individual must alter the way in which they *think of*, or *think in*, a situation in order to manage their emotions. Using an example from *The Managed Heart*, Hochschild describes how flight attendants are taught to think of disruptive passengers as young children in order to regulate their emotional reactions. Antecedent-focused emotion regulation is thought to be similar to Hochschild's deep acting in that 'the internal regulation [thoughts and feelings] is modified with the goal to make the expression more genuine' (Grandey, 2000: 99).

Response-focused emotion regulation is comparable to Hochschild's surface acting in that the emotional labourer modifies the way in which an emotional response is displayed, rather than trying to change the way they feel. For example, a flight attendant may feel exhausted after a long flight, but she will still smile politely as passengers disembark despite feeling antisocial.

Emotional intelligence

Emotion management is an important part of life. Not only is it influenced by the job we have and the social roles we occupy, but it also impacts on who we are and the way others see us. Success in a **post-industrial era** has been attributed to emotional intelligence, some theorists and consultants claiming that the ability to be emotionally intelligent can impact positively on organisational performance.

Emotional intelligence can be defined as 'the ability to sense, understand, and effectively apply the power and acumen of *emotions* as a source of human energy, information, connection, and influence' (Cooper and Sawaf, 1997: xiii; emphasis in original).

Goleman (1996) presents emotional intelligence as a process that will strip the 'irrationality' from emotionality, thereby enhancing 'managers' "intelligent", rational control' (Fineman, 2000: 105). Emotional intelligence assumes that we can somehow quantify our ability to manage our emotions. Those who do it well are said to have a higher EQ (emotional quotient) than those who do not. Some organisations ask their interview candidates to take emotional intelligence tests so they can calculate their EQ score. For some organisations EQ is more important than IQ, as the ability to successfully read and manage emotions has become a necessary component of the new 'working skills "toolkit"' (Hughes, 2005: 605).

Much of the critical literature questions whether it is possible to measure something that has always been an unpredictable, uncontrollable variable within the workplace. However, Fineman (2004) sees this as an example of the growing desire to commodify complex elements of private life. Being able to manage our emotions and make sense of the emotions of others within the bounds of our society and cultures is a key social skill, and one that is becoming increasingly valued by organisations.

Perceiving and managing emotions

Building on Fineman's critique of emotional intelligence, it is relevant to re-consider Hochschild's *The Managed Heart*. She presented emotional labour as the commodification, rationalisation and routinisation of individuals' private emotions. In other words, organisations were taking over areas of the self that were once seen to be private. In light of this presentation, for a long time performances of emotional labour were seen to be alienating and leading to negative consequences on well-being such as burnout, stress, strain and in some studies even physical illnesses (Frost, 2003). Yet despite all of the research into the consequences of emotional labour, the number of reported negative effects is minimal, given the number of emotional labourers there are in the service economy.

An alternative perspective might be that performances of emotional labour are much more complex ways of maintaining and constructing who we are and how we are perceived by others. By managing our emotions we are able to influence how we are seen by society (Ward, 2009). For example, if you were a qualified nurse you would be expected by both the hospital and your patients to be kind, caring and empathetic in your performances of emotional labour. Yet if you took a dislike to a particular patient who continually demanded your attention, you may 'feel' very differently from the emotional performance you were giving. However, if you let your feelings come to the surface – if, in other words, you were unable to perform emotional labour – your reputation as a nurse would be greatly affected, maybe even leading to disciplinary action, the loss of your job and the respect of your family and friends. Another example of the way emotional labour is used to manage perception is demonstrated in the Practitioner insight box at the beginning of the chapter. Thus, performances of emotional labour are not just about carrying out what is required of you by your organisation in return for a wage. Our ability to manage our emotions is closely intertwined with our identity, our social role and the way that we perceive ourselves and others perceive us.

Conclusion: managing better

This chapter began with a discussion of how perceptions are socially constructed phenomena that allow us to make sense of the world and people around us. Part of that sense-making process (Weick, 1995) involves the use of stereotypes. It was argued that the use of these simplified sense-making methods is often problematic, based as they are on narrow conceptions of groups of people that are often negative in character and inattentive to individual differences. There is a need therefore to be aware of the stereotypical ways that we may judge others and the implications this can have for our management of relations.

Following this line of argument it was also noted that emotions have been socially constructed in Western societies as irrational, dysfunctional and often 'feminine'. These 'stereotypes' or perceptions of emotion mean they were eliminated from the organisational context to prevent them hindering the production process and reducing profitability. The historical legacy of this particular perception of emotions continues to influence the way we behave, work and make sense of both ourselves and those around us.

In terms of the way emotions are used within organisational contexts we no longer expect emotions to be removed from the workplace, but in equal measure we do not expect to see a supermarket worker crying in the freezer aisle. Today, emotions are perceived to be a positive feature in organisational life – but only if they are kept under 'control'. For example, it would be perfectly acceptable to see the same supermarket worker smiling when she helped a customer locate the frozen peas.

Of course, we can also stereotype emotions and their role performance at work. We expect a nurse to be helpful and caring whereas we expect a bailiff to be intimidating and unforgiving. These expectations are based on stereotypes but they help society to function and shape our individual personalities. These are often referred to as 'feeling rules'.

Failure to comply with the 'feeling rules' that are associated with our roles in organisations leads us to be 'judged' or 'perceived' in a particular way by both ourselves and others. In this sense, emotion management techniques help us to remain a 'normal' member of society, while also upholding a stereotype. 'Feeling rules' often form the basis of stereotypical images, and so by complying with these prescribed norms we might also be simultaneously upholding a related stereotype. For example, cabin crew are taught to smile even in the case of an emergency. When they do this, their apparent calm and smiles may be perceived by others as a lack of intelligence or of awareness of the danger. This is usually not the case because cabin crews are highly aware of the dangers of flying – but are also aware of the acute danger caused by hysterical passengers. By conforming to the feeling rules prescribed by the organisation, cabin crew also therefore inadvertently uphold the negative stereotypes of 'trolley dolly'. If emotions were not so powerful and important to our society, and perceptions of ourselves, then there would be no need for us, or organisations, to manage them (Craib, 1995).

End notes

[1] See also Chapter 11.

[2] See also Chapter 12.

[3] See also Chapter 13.

REVIEW AND DISCUSSION QUESTIONS

REVIEW QUESTIONS

1 Is 'perceiving' an active or a passive process?

2 Describe three ways in which our perceptions may mislead us.

3 What is the difference between a feeling and an emotion?

4 What are the differences between emotion management, emotional labour and emotion work? Think of real-life examples to support your answer.

5 Identify four emotional labour techniques.

DISCUSSION QUESTIONS

1 Work in groups to identify circumstances in which the following behaviours would be a) appropriate, and b) inappropriate:

– shouting at a worker

– offering praise

– discriminating

– ignoring

What has changed in each circumstance?

2 Weick (1995) suggests there are times when we need to 'drop our tools' in order to respond to change. He is suggesting that our tendency to do some things 'the way we always have' can hinder us when flexibility and new thinking are called for. How might this apply to managers who face making changes within organisations?

3 Take a moment to consider the last time you used a stereotype to judge someone you had not met before . . .

– Why did you use the stereotype?

– Was the stereotype positive or negative?

– Did you have cause to re-evaluate the stereotype (perhaps because you got to know the person)?

– What were the positive and negative implications of using a stereotype in this case?

4 'Leave your personal life at the door!' Working in groups discuss this statement. Consider whether you feel there is a place for emotions and feelings within organisations.

5 Reflecting on your experiences, think of a time when you have had to manage your emotions. Consider the following:

– How did it make you feel?

– Why did you control your emotions in this way?

– What would have happened if you had shown how you had really felt?

FURTHER READING

Bolton, S. C. (2005) *Emotion Management in Service Work*. Basingstoke: Palgrave. This book offers a new way of considering emotion management within the workplace.

Frost, P. (2003) *Toxic Emotions at Work*. Boston: Harvard University Press. This important book raises the issues of what can happen if we do not recognise the power of negative emotions within the workplace.

Hernes, T. (2007) *Understanding Organization as Process: Theory for a tangled world*. Abingdon: Routledge. A fascinating guide to perceiving the world through a processual lens. A must for those interested in better understanding change.

Hochschild, A. R. (1983) *The Managed Heart: Commercialization of human feeling*. Berkeley/London: University of California Press. This is the seminal work on emotion management and emotional labour.

Korczynski, M. (2002) *Human Resource Management in Service Work*. Basingstoke: Palgrave. This book provides a good overview of some of the more complex issues surrounding the way emotions are managed within the workplace.

McMurray, R. (2010) 'Living with neophilia: case notes from the new NHS', *Culture and Organisation*, Vol.16, No.1: 55–71. For those interested in the work of Mary Douglas and how it can be applied to organising contexts. This paper focuses on her grid-group model of culture.

Payne, J. (2009) 'Emotional labour and skill', *Gender, Work and Organisation*, Vol.16, No.1: 348–67. This article questions the effect of perceiving emotional labour as a skill.

Plato (1974) *The Republic*. London: Penguin. Contains the simile of the cave – it is always worth going back to the source text.

Tressell, R. (1993) *The Ragged-Trousered Philanthropists*. London: Flamingo. A classic novel for those who are interested in a Marxist take on perception, deception, capitalism and power.

Weick, K. (1996) 'Drop your tools: an allegory for organizational studies', *Administrative Science Quarterly*, Vol.41, No.2: 301–13. This article helps us reflect on the causes and consequences of unquestioned action and routines in altered contexts.

KEY SKILLS

DEVELOPING CRITICAL THINKING SKILLS AND REFLECTIVE LEARNING

Having an awareness of the ways in which our perceptions and the way we make sense of the world we live in is an important way to develop critical thinking skills. Being aware of the way in which, often, taken-for-granted decisions are made helps us to better understand why we behave, speak and feel as we do. The topic of emotions and feelings is an important vehicle for facilitating reflective learning, because everyone – regardless of their age, gender, experience and culture – is able to reflect on their own emotional experiences. Doing so encourages and promotes the value of reflective learning.

By approaching the subject of perceiving and managing emotions from both a managerial and employee perspective we can question the often competing and conflicting demands of organising. In better understanding our own perspective and the perspectives of others we improve the chances that we will manage effectively.

LETTING GO OF OUTDATED PERCEPTIONS AND THEORIES

We all work hard to develop our understanding of behaviour in organisations as part of a commitment to a more enlightened approach to managing ourselves and others. Theory, practice and experience all combine to develop our personal models of how best to cope with situations. There is, however, the danger that over time aspects of the models we employ become outdated. The handy categories we have implicitly used to bracket different customers fail to account for changing demographics and tastes; our assumptions on what motivates colleagues become out of date; and our accounts of the nature and rate of change are found to be misplaced.

As we develop our skills as reflective manager practitioners it is important that we recognise that there is a need to change aspects of our personal models when we find them to be past their use-by date. The only good model or theory is the one that better helps us relate to the world around us. When aspects of such models no longer perform this function, we need to learn to let go of them, no matter how much time and emotion we have invested in their prior

development. This letting go allows space for the emergence of new and more effective models of working.

EMOTIONAL INTELLIGENCE, EMPATHY, SYMPATHY AND LISTENING

Being aware of the way perceptions and stereotypes occur, and of some of the advantages and disadvantages of these sense-making processes, means that through reflection students will think more critically of the generalisations they make on a regular basis. Understanding why people behave and feel the way they do is a key feature of what it means to be emotionally intelligent.

Conversely, having a critical understanding of how emotional intelligence is defined, measured and understood may also be useful for students when it comes to interpreting such data in recruitment and selection procedures.

Taking a reflexive approach to the topics covered will also encourage students to take a more empathetic and sympathetic approach to those around them. This will be perceived as a valuable skill in the management of both people and organisations by future employers and staff.

LEADERSHIP, COACHING AND MENTORING

Awareness and critical understanding of the importance of emotion management in shaping the way we perceive ourselves and others is a valuable skill when it comes to leading, coaching and mentoring. Having the ability to manage your own emotions and the emotions of others is a key part of what leadership is. Developing stable, long-lasting and effective relationships with followers is partly about recognising their relational needs while also managing them.

Perception and sense-making may also be a useful and powerful tool in shaping and framing realities in a coaching style of leadership by helping people see things in a way they may not have done before.

Ethical implications: The commodification of emotions

The historical legacy of the way in which emotions, along with other private areas of the self, have been perceived to be irrational, uncontrollable and unpredictable continues to influence the way in which organisations, and individual behaviour, is made sense of today. Emotions continue to be commodified, routinised and rationalised not only by organisations but also within the social rules that govern our society.

We label ourselves and others as 'normal' by making sense of behaviours in relation to social rules and norms. Yet by definition these rules and norms are 'social constructions': they are not pre-defined and predetermined – they are actively co-constructed and upheld by our desire to 'fit in'. It can be argued that we gain

'existential security' through performances of emotion management (Ward, 2009).

However, taking a Marxist view, organisations requiring their employees to perform 'emotional labour' through the use of prescribed scripts and emotional direction are in some way 'commodifying' individual parts of each worker's self.

What are the ethical implications of treating human emotions as a resource to increase profits?

What are the consequences on the individual and society as a whole?

Applying theory to practice: Emotional intelligence

Many management consultancy firms and a number of academics claim that it is important for organisations to acknowledge the emotional organisation. Part of this acknowledgement is seen to be achieved by calculating the 'emotional intelligence' of employees. Emotional intelligence (EI) is calculated and understood in a similar way to IQ, by responding to a questionnaire, after which the results are calculated. An individual's emotional quotient (EQ) is thought to represent how emotionally intelligent they are. The higher the EQ, the more responsive the individual will be to other people's emotions, and also the better the individual will be able to manage his or her own emotions. However, many theorists dispute the idea of emotional intelligence and our ability to calculate an emotional quotient (Fineman, 2004).

Fineman (2004) critically examines the use of emotion measurement in organisations' behaviour and discusses the problems related to 'boxing' emotion as being problematic and restrictive. EQ measurement and emotional intelligence is particularly problematic when the figures become associated with value judgements, power and organisational success. In other words, people are judged and therefore the way they are perceived and treated can be a consequence of a calculation. In addition, Fineman challenges the ability of 'experts' to use numbers to quantify a concept such as emotion.

Applying theory to practice: Emotional labour

One of the biggest areas of concern in terms of emotional labour has been the way in which organisations have moved the boundaries of their control. No longer are they interested solely in harnessing physical labour power for now their interests have moved to a part of the self that for a long time has been perceived as 'private'. The commodification of private areas of the self has been associated with negative effects on well-being such as burnout, physical illnesses, stress and exhaustion. Organisations are seen to coerce employees into being someone who they are not, and this in turn leads to emotional dissonance. Emotional dissonance is understood as the psychological feelings of discomfort that are aroused when you have to pretend to feel something that you do not. An example of this might be working in a fast-food restaurant and having to stick to a strict script which tells you what to say and when to smile. After some time this pretence is thought to become wearing and lead to negative effects on well-being.

Taking your learning further

1. Fineman, S. (2004) 'Getting the measure of emotion – and the cautionary tale of emotional intelligence', *Human Relations*, Vol.57: 719–40. This paper critically considers the concept of emotional intelligence from the perspective of the social sciences researcher, questioning whether it is possible to measure emotion.

2. Hochschild, A. R. (1983) *The Managed Heart: Commercialization of Human Feeling*. Berkeley/London, University of California Press. This seminal thesis introduces the terms 'emotional labour' and 'emotion management', drawing on empirical research from cabin crew and debt collectors.

3. Weick, K. (1996) 'Drop your tools: an allegory for organizational studies', *Administrative Science Quarterly*, Vol.41, No.2: 301–13. This paper questions to what extent we, as human beings, trap ourselves in perceptual webs of our own creation as we cling to set rules and routines.

BEST PRACTICE

Jan's early career in sales had been difficult. Slightly shy, hesitant, and very thoughtful, she had struggled to compete in a sector dominated by men, many of whom were not afraid to be aggressive in their dealings with clients and each other. Warned by her team leader that she would have to look for work elsewhere unless she shaped up, Jan re-evaluated her approach to sales and working.

Seven years on, and Jan had engineered a meteoric rise to the position of sales director. She had a reputation for being smarter, harder-working and more aggressive than just about anyone else in the organisation. She made decisions quickly, eschewed consultation, never admitted mistakes and directed others with absolute authority. These were all learned characteristics that had served her well as she climbed the corporate ladder.

As part of the senior management team she quickly became aware that this model of working was not always as successful as it had been. Aggression was often ignored or attributed to emotional instability by senior colleges, while her failure to consult on new plans was frequently met with a denial of interdepartmental collaboration. On reflection, Jan was aware that the model of working she had developed needed to change. This did not mean that strong decisions and robust assertion were to be abandoned – rather, they were to be tempered according to context. Tailoring her performances for particular audiences was soon found to be an effective method of managing how she was perceived in different contexts, thus increasing the likelihood that her goals met with success.

WORST PRACTICE

Throughout his career in management John had been subjected to psychometric testing whenever he applied for a job in a new company. He'd never liked the tests, as he considered the questions to be abstract simplifications of real-world challenges. He also felt that the results of the tests rarely described his character in a way he felt comfortable with. However, John quickly learned to spot what the questions were really asking and how desired responses would relate to the personal specifications for any advertised job. Consequently, John had become adept at completing the tests so that the results showed prospective employers what they probably wanted to hear (regardless of what John actually believed, felt or did).

Using this manipulation technique and his experience of psychometric testing he attained a senior position in a major insurance company. One of the first tasks John was charged with

was recruiting a new team of experienced workers capable of growing the company's market share of a new retail insurance market. Having short-listed the candidates for interview, he subjected them to a standard psychometric test. Despite John's awareness of the flaws in the process, and the unrepresentative nature of the results, he employed psychometric testing. His decision to do so was partly a consequence of the way psychometric testing was perceived by the insurance company. These recruitment and selection processes had a long and established history in the firm, and John was concerned about how he would be perceived by his colleagues if he moved away from them. In addition, he worried that if he made an argument against the validity of psychometric testing based on his own experiences of being able to shape the results, his own job might be called into question.

Chapter 5
Motivation and Satisfaction

Tricia Harrison

Contents

PART ONE

Key Learning Outcomes

By the end of this chapter you should be able to:

- define motivation and recognise the main characteristics of motivation
- understand the difference between content and process theories of motivation
- evaluate the main theoretical approaches pertaining to motivation
- describe and apply Hackman's job design model
- understand the link between satisfaction and well-being, skills and training, pay and performance
- identify the key characteristics of motivational interviewing (MI).

PRACTITIONER INSIGHT

Procter & Gamble

Procter and Gamble (P&G) is one of the largest global fast-moving consumable goods companies. It has sales in the region of $83.5 billion annually, operates in 64 countries, and has 23 billion-dollar brands (including Pampers, Ariel, Braun and Olay). We speak to **Karen Usher, Human Resource Manager**, about the challenges surrounding its 'promote from within' policy.

The company has nearly 140,000 employees globally, around 5,000 of them in the UK national head office and technical centres in the south-west and north-east, and in six manufacturing and distribution centres across the rest of the country.

The company has a long history. P&G was founded in 1837 by two brothers in Cincinnati, Ohio, USA, who started manufacturing candles. It grew from this humble beginning eventually to expand operations into Western Europe, the first such outpost being in the UK, through the acquisition of the Thomas Hedley Soap Company in 1937. Since then the organisation has expanded rapidly across the continents, in recent years primarily through the acquisition of other companies, including Gillette in 2004.

Key to the organisation's sustainability over time has been its ability to stay true to its stated purpose, values and principles. The company's vision is:

To be – and be recognised as – the best consumer products and services company in the world.

The company's purpose is:

We will provide branded products and services of superior quality and value that will improve the lives of the world's consumers. As a result, consumers will reward us with leadership sales, profit and value creation, allowing our people, our shareholders, and the communities in which we live and work, to prosper.

To underpin this vision and purpose, P&G has a number of core values and principles, which are seen in the way in which they operate on a day-to-day basis. A summary of the values is presented below:

P&G is its people and the values by which we live. We attract and recruit the finest people in the world. We build our organisation from within, promoting and rewarding people without regard to any difference unrelated to performance. We act on the conviction that the men and women of Procter & Gamble will always be our most important asset.

In keeping with the values of P&G the company operates a 'promote from within' policy, which is applied worldwide. This means that no external recruitment takes place for senior leadership roles in the company – any vacancies are filled with individuals who have joined the company at the entry-point level for management, typically as a graduate from university, either as a technician on one of the sites or in an administrative role within the head office and its divisions.

PRACTITIONER INSIGHT NEXT

In the light of the complexity of the business, the location of operations, and the challenges faced from the competition and from its own expanded brand portfolio over the past ten years, there have to be sound organisation structures and systems in place to ensure that the company is able to develop and grow talented and motivated individuals for future senior roles. Operating this policy is not an easy option – it provides significant challenges to ensure that employees are motivated and have the ability to meet their potential so that the company continues to fill the demanding senior-level leadership roles at country, regional and global levels.

Individuals recruited into the company are highly motivated and generally very ambitious and competitive, with a clear idea about what they expect, both in terms of financial reward and career fulfilment. The motivational needs of the individual, however, have to be aligned with the wide range of capabilities and requirements to run a business on a day-to-day basis. Unless systems are in place, this could lead to a very counterproductive competitive internal environment, in which everyone is out to climb the corporate ladder as quickly as possible, to the potential detriment of team-building and collaboration.

How do you think P&G maintain the motivation of staff, and what are the possible issues and practical considerations of its 'promote from within' policy?

Once you have read this chapter, return to these questions and think about how you could answer them.

Introduction

One of the most important goals of any organisation is to maximise employee performance in order to achieve organisational goals. In order to do this it needs highly motivated staff. It is necessary to maintain high levels of motivation wherever possible, not only to aid and increase productivity but also to assist the psychological well-being of individuals. In the 1920s the infamous 'Hawthorne effect' was discovered from research conducted at the Western Electric Company in the USA. A number of experiments were held on a control group of workers. One of the experiments concerned the effect of lighting on productivity and involved increasing and decreasing the lighting in the workplace. The result was surprising, because the researchers found that productivity increased in both circumstances. The researchers concluded that the increase in productivity was not specifically caused by changes to the lighting but was due to the fact that there had been intervention of any kind, because the workers felt involved in the process. Motivation intrigued people then, and it continues to do so now.

Initially, this chapter offers a definition of motivation, and the different theories on the subject are discussed. Both content and process theories are then introduced, following which the different topics of motivation and job design, individual change and rewards are examined.

UNDERSTANDING THE TERM 'MOTIVATION' [1]

Motivation is the cause of movement, the inspiration behind activity – it is the feeling within an individual that makes them want to achieve a personal need or expectation. The term 'motivation' suggests goal-oriented behaviour directed at achieving an individual goal or goals. Hence motivation is personal and comes from within – and may, therefore, be difficult to manage and control. This is possibly why no one universally applicable theory has been found, although long sought after.

Two categories that can help our understanding are intrinsic and extrinsic motivation.

- **Extrinsic motivation** is concerned with real, tangible rewards that are received by an individual – for example: salary, promotion and conditions of work. In general, these rewards are decided at an organisational level.

- **Intrinsic motivation** comes from within and is therefore psychological in nature – for example: feeling appreciated, being recognised and being treated in a respectful way. These rewards are derived from doing the job, and from the 'content' of the task (Mottaz, 1985).

Essentially, motivation in the workplace is concerned with three features of behaviour (Cooper, 1973):

- personal needs or wants

- rewards or outcomes of behaviour

- how individual needs are met.

This definition assumes that all individuals have an inherent set of needs that can be satisfied through their work. Through their performance in a job the individual will be rewarded and will, in the process of the reward, have their personal needs met. The important point is the individual's performance. In order for the individual's performance to be rewarded, the individual has also to meet organisational targets and needs. The responsibility of the organisation is to provide the appropriate rewards – for example, pay, promotion, autonomy – to meet different individuals' needs.

Content and process theories

There are a number of theories that contribute to our understanding of motivation and suggest ways to improve individual motivation. These theories help us to understand behaviour at different times. It is important to recognise that the different theories offer different insights to behaviour, and that far more benefit is derived from using the theories collectively than from using each in isolation.

As a rule most motivation theories can be classified as either content or process theories. **Content theories** focus on the essence and substance of what motivates an individual: what the needs are of the individual. Content theories are sometimes described as universal theories because they can be applied in the same way to all individuals in different cultures. **Process theories** are concerned with evolution and stages, and therefore focus on how motivation occurs. Process theories are not described as universal theories because they are not used in the same way in every situation since they can adapt and change depending upon individual circumstances. In the majority of cases the use of a number of theories from both process and content will be necessary to gain some understanding of a situation. Underpinning all the theories is the view that human beings have a set of needs that have to be met. These 'need theories' have been extensively explored because they are perceived as 'the most enduring ways to understand motivation' (Aram and Piraino, 1978: 79).

Table 5.1 summarises the key content and process theories that are discussed in this chapter.

Table 5.1:   Content and process theories

Content theories	Process theories
• Hierarchy of needs: Maslow	• Equity theory: Adams
• Modified hierarchy of needs: Alderfer	• Expectancy theory: Vroom
• Two-factor theory: Herzberg	• Goal-setting theory: Locke and Latham

CONTENT THEORIES

The hierarchy of needs

Maslow's theory of individual development and motivation, published originally in 1943, focused on the needs of the individual. Abraham Maslow was born in 1908 and described his childhood as 'isolated and unhappy'. In later life he changed profession from law to psychology (Shackle, 2010: 37). His aim as a psychologist was to understand differences in individuals. He is classed as the founding father of the school of thinking that is sometimes referred to as 'humanism'. At the time Maslow's work was ground-breaking and original because it introduced new ideas to understand motivation and used positive role-models, for example, with examples of self-actualisation. An example of this originality was how Maslow introduced the concept of love as a basic need – not the general thinking at the time. However, his work was not necessarily specifically intended for occupational psychology nor specifically the workplace. Nevertheless, this is where it has been applied most. His basic premise is that people have instinctual basic needs and desire those needs to be met. These needs, although initially strong, can appear to become weak and therefore be easily suppressed or ignored. They can be drowned out by learning, fear and expectations, and this makes them 'hard to know, not easy' (Maslow, 1998: 213). Maslow further argues that these needs, except in exceptional circumstances, are present in every human being.

As soon as a need is met, the desire for another need to be met will be stronger and take priority for the individual. The suggestion is also that once a need has been met, it will no longer be a source of motivation. Maslow's proposition is that there is an order – a hierarchy of importance – to the needs that people have. Maslow suggests that there are in all five needs. These are shown by level and displayed in Figure 5.1, from the lowest level, physiological needs, to the highest level, the need for self-actualisation.

The hierarchy was chosen by Maslow to illustrate the needs. The foundations of the hierarchy are the basic motives, with the higher human motives of love, justice and kindness at the top of the triangle. However, Maslow was very clear that the higher human motives were as important as the other 'lower-order' needs like hunger.

- *Physiological needs* – the basic needs of warmth, food and shelter: this category includes the basic needs to enable an individual to function (homeostasis) – for example, the need to sleep

Figure 5.1   Maslow's hierarchy of needs

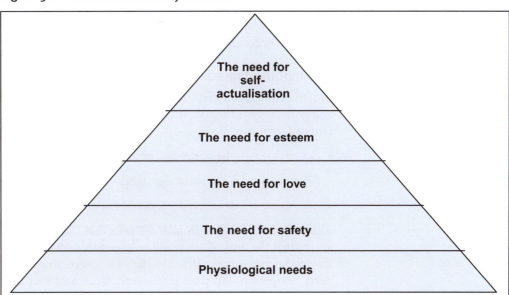

- *Safety needs* – the need to feel safe and secure; the need to feel safe from threat or pain and feel protected

- *Social needs* – the need for human relationships, for friendships, love and affection

- *Esteem needs* – the need for self-esteem and the respect of others

- *Self-actualisation needs* – the achieving of an individual's full potential . . .

Although Maslow's work is presented as a hierarchy that suggests an order to the meeting of the needs, he recognised – most importantly – that in reality this may not always be the case, that for some people the needs may be met in a different order. For example, some people may put social needs higher than esteem needs. For others, however – for example, creative people – self-actualisation may be more important than even basic needs.

Maslow spent a lot of time discussing the concept of self-actualisation and peak experience. Self-actualisation refers to the attaining of one's full potential. People who reach this stage enjoy life in general for every aspect. However, according to Maslow, self-actualisation is rare and enjoyed by less than 1% of adults (Maslow, 1998: 230). Maslow also argued that self-actualisers tend to make good choices. The theory stemmed from the free-choice behaviour of chickens. In an experiment where barnyard chickens were given freedom to choose their own diet, it was found that some chose well but others chose badly. The chickens that chose well were healthier than those that did not. Maslow compared this to the people he described as reaching self-actualisation and suggested that they choose well because they see 'reality more clearly and accordingly are more closely in touch with the realities of their own deeper inner natures' (Lowry, 1998). Maslow argued that some adults at some point will have 'peak experiences' that are similar in nature to that experienced more regularly by the individuals who have achieved self-actualisation, but this does not make these individuals the same as those who he defined as self-actualisers.

Maslow's work largely falls into the three areas of needs hierarchy, the self-actualisation concept and peak experience. The hierarchy, although criticised as described below, has been adopted more than the self-actualisation and peak experience concepts. Notwithstanding this, a number of theorists have failed to find empirical support for Maslow's view on needs theory (Korman *et al*, 1977; Rauschenberger *et al*, 1980). Instead, they contradict Maslow's argument. They have generally found little support for the view that need structures are 'organised along the dimensions proposed by Maslow' (Korman *et al*, 1977: 178). Another perhaps pragmatic argument is that some people meet their higher-order needs outside work – for example, social needs are met through friendships formed outside the workplace. Other issues highlighted are the ambiguity about the time that elapses between the achievement of lower-order needs and next higher-level needs. Finally, there is some criticism of the methodology used by Maslow, particularly regarding peak experiences (Lowry, 1998).

The modified needs hierarchy

Alderfer's model compresses Maslow's five levels of need into three levels of existence, relatedness and growth (ERG theory), with a specific aim related to workplace motivation (Alderfer, 1972; Luthans, 1998).

- *Existence needs* – basic survival needs, including physiological and safety ones

- *Relatedness needs* – relationships, including love, friendships and self-esteem

- *Growth needs* – developmental needs, including self-esteem and self-actualisation.

Alderfer's model differs from Maslow in that the emphasis is not on a hierarchy: instead, he argues that the three needs could be present simultaneously or individually. The needs do not have to be met sequentially. Alderfer also asserts that if an individual cannot attain a higher need, the person will then regress and focus on lower-level needs. This Alderfer called the frustration-regression effect. The point that the needs can be met in any order is relevant to managers in the workplace. For example, if it is difficult to meet growth needs for some workers in retail, the manager can place greater emphasis on existence and relatedness needs. One of the criticisms of this work is that the results of studies have not entirely agreed with Alderfer. The results have supported the suggestion that there will be greater desire to satisfy existence needs but not that the satisfaction of these needs prompts desire for relatedness needs.

The two-factor theory

The **two-factor theory**, which focuses on outcomes of satisfaction and dissatisfaction, was introduced by Frederick Herzberg (1959), who found that certain aspects of a job cause satisfaction and therefore motivation, but certain aspects caused dissatisfaction. However, in this model the two sets of outcomes of satisfaction and dissatisfaction are separate entities and not opposites. The 'opposite of job satisfaction is not job dissatisfaction but, rather, no satisfaction; and the opposite of job dissatisfaction is not job satisfaction but no dissatisfaction' (Herzberg, 2003: 91). Both are treated separately because Herzberg believed that the two constituted two different sets of needs. One set of needs is similar in description to Maslow's work, stemming from innate human nature – for example, the need for sleep. The second set of needs stems from the human desire to grow and develop. The factors that lead to satisfaction or to dissatisfaction are therefore different.

Factors that relate to job satisfaction have been called satisfiers or motivators. In the original research the following five factors stood out as 'strong determinants of job satisfaction' (Weir, 1976: 76):

- achievement
- recognition
- work itself
- responsibility
- opportunity for advancement or promotion.

Factors that relate to job dissatisfaction, known as dissatisfiers or hygiene factors, are:

- pay
- technical supervision
- working conditions
- company policies, administration and procedures
- interpersonal relationships with peers, supervisors and subordinates
- status
- security.

Factors that cause dissatisfaction, according to this research, must be fair and adequate or deemed to be fair. It is difficult to gauge this in some respects, and varies largely by industry and occupational area. For example, employees in medicine would have different expectations from those of employees in a call centre. It is useful here to consider average pay scales for occupational areas, providing relatively secure employment and maintaining healthy, balanced terms and conditions of employment – for example, holiday pay or sick pay. In order to motivate staff, the model suggests that the intrinsic aspects of work need to be considered separately. Research has been conducted into the use of the theory in relation to all levels of staff. On the other hand, some suggest that the theory does not apply equally to lower-level and higher-level staff. In research conducted by Arnolds and Boshoff (2002: 712), they found that top managers 'are primarily motivated by growth needs' and that front-line employees are motivated by relationships with peers, and pay had to be satisfactory in order to maintain motivation, as suggested by Herzberg's theory.

One of main criticisms of the original research concerns the methodology: that the research was conducted on accountants and engineers who are employed in the professions and are therefore not representative of the working population. However, as a counter-argument Herzberg has repeated the investigation on at least 16 occasions, with a wide variety of populations – albeit from a sample primarily of employees within different professions – since the original research, and obtained similar findings (Herzberg, 2003). It is argued that Herzberg assumed a relationship between job satisfaction and motivation or productivity. However, his research asked questions only about job satisfaction. Research into job satisfaction generally supports the view that satisfied employees are more productive, particularly for Western employees, yet this is not always the case and does not work across all cultures. On a pragmatic note, the theory is easy to understand and apply, although some would argue it is possibly too simplistic (Smerek and Peterson, 2007).

WORST PRACTICE

'You can go – as long as it does not affect your work'

This is an actual quote from a manager to his employee, taken from semi-structured interviews conducted as part of longitudinal research into professional practice (Harrison, 2007). The employee was working in Human Resources and was asking her manager if she could take the Professional Qualification Scheme (PQS) at a local university, attending one afternoon and one evening per week. The PQS is a necessary precursor to joining the Chartered Institute of Personnel and Development (CIPD). The response of the manager was as above – that is, he (and the company) would support the employee in taking the qualification, but on condition that it did not affect her work. The interesting point in this case is that, firstly, the employee was working in the Human Resources department; secondly, the CIPD is the professional body for the human resource profession; and thirdly, the content of the PQS is designed to develop the human resource professional. It is perhaps rather strange to understand the logic of a manager who does not want a staff member to use the information gained on a university qualification course in her work. The employee duly undertook the PQS and was thereafter dissatisfied and lacked motivation because she was not permitted to apply the learning to the workplace.

What is your view of the situation? Why do you think the manager responded in the way that he did? Have you (or do you know of someone who has) attended and learned from a training course but not been encouraged by a manager to use the new learning in the workplace?

PROCESS THEORIES

Equity theory

The notion of fairness and justice and comparing ourselves with others is highly plausible. For example, a brother and sister may compare the number of sweets they are given or the way they are treated with each other, resulting in the cry all too frequently heard by parents of 'That's not fair! She has more than me!' Or in the workplace, for example, staff may compare the workload of peers in similar positions and expect to have a similar workload. **Equity theory** suggests that individuals will compare the effort that they make against the efforts made by those around them. Individuals will compare themselves to others in similar circumstances to themselves (similar work, hours, study leave) and to the treatment that the others receive (pay, bonus, promotion) – and if there is similarity, the individual will sense a feeling of equity. However, if individuals believe that there is an input-outcome inequity (more work for less pay than others), they will sense a feeling of inequity. According to this theory, motivation is assessed by the perception of individuals that they are receiving a similar amount of reward as others when they make this comparison. If they feel that they are not, they will not be as highly motivated – and may go further and take action to redress the balance.

The theory suggests that when a person becomes aware of inequity it causes a reaction in them, potentially some form of tension that is 'proportional to the magnitude of inequity present' (Adams, 1963). Because of this tension, an individual might take any of a number of actions – as described in Table 5.2.

Table 5.2:   Possible actions to reduce inequity

Possible action to take	How
Increase outputs	Work more Attend training courses or education
Decrease inputs	Work less Do not take on as much responsibility or be so obliging to help others
Increase outcomes	Aim for extrinsic benefits such as more pay, extra holidays, promotion
Decrease outcomes	Aim to reduce extrinsic benefits (although this is less common) – for example, the bankers who did not take pay increases during the recession
Leave the field altogether	Resign from the job Absenteeism

Source: adapted from J. S. Adams (1963) 'Toward an understanding of inequity'.

The table provides practical examples and illustrates the individual nature of motivation and how beliefs and attitudes affect job performance. Equity theory is driven by the perception of individuals which can vary significantly depending upon the person's perceptual world.

Expectancy theory

One of the least criticised models of motivation is Victor Vroom's **expectancy theory** (Vroom, 1964). Vroom's theory suggests that motivation is driven by individuals' expectancy of the preferred outcome and the strength of the attractiveness of that outcome to the individual. Individuals will consider what they expect to gain from a given situation, what effort they will need to expend, and whether it is worth it to themselves, depending upon their personal goals. The individual will thus consider the following:

$$E \ (expectancy) \ = \ \text{Effort-performance relationship}$$

– whether the amount of effort that will have to be made will lead to the anticipated performance

$$I \ (instrumentality) \ = \ \text{Performance-reward relationship}$$

– whether by undertaking the task an expected outcome is likely to be achieved

$$V \ (valance) \ = \ \text{Rewards-personal goal relationship}$$

– whether the rewards are attractive to the individual and will satisfy the individual's personal goals.

According to expectancy theory:

$$\text{Effort} \ = \ E \ (expectancy) \ + \ I \ (instrumentality) \ \times \ V \ (valence)$$

The theory is based on the notion (Lawler, 1973) that:

> The strength of a tendency to act in a certain way depends on the strength of an expectancy that the act will be followed by a given consequence (or outcome) and on the value or attractiveness of that consequence (or outcome).

Underpinning expectancy theory is perception and the anticipation of the likely consequences of behaviour. Individuals will aim to predict what the consequences of their action may be. For example, the theory could be used to predict if an individual will undertake overtime, will work harder to achieve a promotion, will behave ethically. Vroom's theory suggests that individuals in their decision-making processes will calculate how much effort has to be made in order to achieve the anticipated or preferred output. An individual might, if asked to work overtime, calculate the amount of effort and therefore, in this case, how much time is needed to stay later at work – and how much reward will be forthcoming (in terms of pay *and* other benefits – for example, respect from the manager). A student will work out how much effort is required to achieve a higher grade in the final exam – and decide whether it is worthwhile and achievable in terms of that effort.

Mitchell (1974), in his comprehensive review of expectancy theory, suggests that the relationships suggested in the expectancy model are not clearly understood, and that greater understanding of the underlying theoretical components is required.

Goal-setting theory [2]

Goal-setting theory was introduced and developed by Locke (1968) and Locke and Latham (2002). Goal-setting theory was suggested at a time when behaviourist theory dominated the study of motivation. The underpinning thinking of goal theory is that an individual's goals or intentions affect their behaviour, because they influence the amount of effort, persistence and direction afforded by the individual. The authors of goal-setting theory clearly emphasised in their work the fact that their primary focus was on the workplace.

Goal-setting theory suggests that:

- Challenging, difficult goals are more rewarding to an individual than more simple, less difficult goals. Assuming that the goal is within an individual's capability, 'stretching' goals are important in the development of an individual. 'Stretching' goals are those that encourage the individual to use or develop existing or new skills and perhaps take on additional responsibilities. Preferably, these goals should link to the business context. Procter & Gamble, the company introduced at the beginning of this chapter, constantly uses this theory, expecting their staff to take on additional responsibilities and new tasks on a regular basis.

- Specific goals are better than vague goals such as 'Do better in the future'. The theory suggests that individuals will find it easier to adapt or change their behaviour if they have clarity about what is expected. This is because there is less ambiguity with specific goals. The acronym SMART – specific, measurable, attainable, realistic and time-related – is used by many companies to encourage managers to set specific, rather than vague, goals for their employees.

- The involvement of employees in the goal-setting process is preferable (although not always essential) in goal-setting. The primary benefit of involvement is that there is knowledge-sharing because individuals are working together to formulate strategies (Locke *et al*, 1997). However, goals set by a superior can be productive as long as they are explained clearly and justified.

- Knowledge of results or feedback for employees during the task is important, so that individuals know what is working well and not so well, and consequently can adjust their behaviour or other aspects in order to achieve the goal.

Locke and Latham (2002: 714) summarised key aspects of research undertaken over the history of goal-setting theory that involved '100 different tasks involving more than 40,000 participants in at least eight countries', and concluded that the effects of goal-setting theory are very reliable. Holman and Fernie (2000) highlighted the importance of management support in the process because they found that low levels of support from supervisors/team leaders and high levels of monitoring and target-setting had a largely negative impact upon satisfaction. Evidence of the generalisability of the theory was found in a Chinese sample of students (Fan *et al*, 2008).

In goal-setting theory the primary focus is on the study of conscious goals, with limited acknowledgement to the role of the subconscious. The understanding that action can be taken without the individual's being fully aware of what is motivating them or what stored information is affecting their decision-making is unclear. The lack of focus on the subconscious is, therefore, a limitation of goal-setting theory (Locke and Latham, 2002). For example, a colleague was extremely goal-oriented and highly driven but became unwell and suffered a partial mental breakdown. During therapy it emerged that the colleague at a young age had taken responsibility for the raising of a disabled younger sibling after his parents had divorced. He found that this experience had remained deep within his subconscious and he had not been aware of how it had affected his current goal-oriented behaviour. Binswanger (1991) found that there was a particularly strong alignment with the view that the theory affects performance and satisfaction with individuals who consciously choose to be purposeful and proactive.

THE PRACTICAL APPLICATION OF CONTENT AND PROCESS THEORIES

On a practical level the process and content theories inform our daily lives but also help us to understand the motives and needs of others. To take your learning further, one business and one personal example is provided below so as to evoke reaction and discussion. Why is it that some people appear to strive to earn so much more than others? To some degree it could be due to individual differences – although national cultures may have a strong influence. Take for example variations in pay differentials: the proportional difference between the chief executive's pay and that of front-line employees varies considerably. In the USA the difference can be as great as 500 times, but in Sweden it is more likely, on average, to be 50 times. There tends to be a greater differential in the USA and the UK than in continental Europe where the multiples are smaller. Data on international pay differentials can be found through Hay International or the US Department of Labor (Briscoe and Schuler, 2004). Do these differences affect the motivation of workers? Why is it that some people are motivated to achieve higher pay than others? One consideration is that the figures cited above suggest that where you live affects the payment for the job. For example, an administrator in Sweden will probably earn comparatively more than an administrator in the same or a similar job in the UK or the USA.

A headline in a newspaper in June 2010 asked 'Why did an ordinary taxi-driver turn mass killer?' The article, by Woods (2010: 15), told how the mass murderer Derrick Bird shot 12 people, including his twin brother who was also his solicitor. It went on to suggest that although on the surface Derrick Bird appeared fairly content, underneath this mask lay a number of insecurities. The final straw appeared to be that he was very concerned that he might go to prison because he owed money to the tax authorities. Derrick Bird had been due to have a formal meeting with his brother and solicitor on the afternoon of the murders. Perhaps content and process theories can help to provide some – albeit limited – understanding of what motivated Derrick Bird to commit these crimes. Taking Maslow's hierarchy of needs into account, certainly the basic need for warmth, shelter and security was, probably, in Derrick Bird's mind: he felt very much threatened. There also appear to have been issues with some of his personal relationships and possibly his self-esteem (he seems to have believed that his brother was regarded more favourably by his father). The article discusses other mass murderers and suggests that 'Most mass killers who are depressed and psychologically alone suffer one or more catastrophic losses before they open fire on their victims' (Levin, 2010). What do you think the content and process theories of motivation might contribute to an understanding of this situation? Maslow's hierarchy of needs has been mentioned as offering some understanding: what other content or process theories might be similarly enlightening?

THE JOB DESIGN MODEL [3]

One important further development of motivation theory was the practical job design model (Hackman and Lawler, 1971; Hackman and Oldham, 1979). This model takes motivation in the workplace a step further and suggests ways that jobs can be designed in order to improve their motivational content. It proposes that enriched jobs will encourage increased motivation, job satisfaction and work performance.

The job design model declares that a person's intrinsic motivation depends on the following three critical psychological states:

- the experience of meaningfulness in the work

- the experience of feeling responsibility for doing the job fully and well

- the satisfaction of seeing the results of having done the work.

The job design model suggests that individuals whose jobs are enriched through carefully planned job design will feel the psychological effects of the above and this will influence their behaviour at work. The suggestion is that individuals who feel this are more likely to enjoy internal work motivation, growth satisfaction, work effectiveness and low absenteeism. These critical states are integral to the model because it emphasises that it is the personal experiences of the person, which are not necessarily rational, objective states (Hackman and Lawler, 1971). The work outcomes are important to the practical aspects of managing people in the workplace. The model suggests that there are five core job characteristics that encourage the three psychological states (Hackman and Lawler, 1971; Hackman and Oldham, 1975):

1 skill variety – the extent to which a job involves a variety of different activities that use different skills and abilities

2 task identity – the extent to which a job involves the completion of a 'whole' meaningful piece of work

3 task significance – the degree to which a job is perceived by the worker as being important and having a significant impact on others

4 autonomy – the extent to which a job provides freedom and discretion

5 feedback – the extent to which performing a job results in the worker receiving clear feedback about his or her performance.

The more the job contains the five core job characteristics, the greater the motivation of the individual will be in the workplace. Hackman and Oldham in their research produced a formula that can be used to assess the motivational 'score' for an individual, and developed a means of assessing the core motivational dimensions called the Job Diagnostic Survey (JDS). The motivating potential score (MPS) is worked out using the following computation:

$$\text{MPS} = \frac{(\text{Skill variety} + \text{Task identity} + \text{Task significance})}{3} \times \text{Autonomy} \times \text{Feedback}$$

It should be noted that autonomy and feedback are given the same weighting as the combined effect of skill variety, task identity and task significance. Muraven *et al* (2007) supported this view but highlighted the importance of autonomy. They found that

> individuals who are forced to exert self-control perform more poorly on a subsequent test of self-control than individuals who feel more autonomous while exerting self-control.

The findings suggest that individuals perform better if they feel that that their decision-making is autonomous and that they have a degree of control in the decision-making process.

The job design model also shows how a job's motivational content can be improved through using one or a number of different methods that were termed 'implementing concepts'. These include:

- combining tasks – Employees can be given a number of different jobs to increase variety and involvement.

- forming natural work units – Encourage work that involves the employee in the whole process. For example, a recruitment manager could be involved in the whole process of producing a job advertisement, shortlisting and interviewing – as opposed to producing only the job advertisement.

- establishing client relationships – Encourage both internal and external contacts and the building of relationships.

- vertical loading – Give employees responsibilities that were traditionally allocated to supervisors – for example, authorising payment or quality control.

- opening feedback channels – Encourage wider formal and informal feedback, such as introducing 180-degree appraisal – a process that involves, for example, line managers obtaining feedback on their performance from both their manager and their staff.

Applying theory to practice: Woeful reception

A receptionist employed at a local leisure centre has complained that she feels bored. Currently, her work primarily includes answering the telephone and dealing with work associated with the reception area of the leisure centre. Using the job design model, evaluate her current work in order to improve its motivational content.

Procter & Gamble (P&G), introduced at the beginning of the chapter, provide a good example of the job design principles in practice. P&G emphasise the importance of organisation structures and systems in order to grow talent, including – during the interview that is on the website – the use of 360-degree appraisal, by which feedback is sought from the people with whom the job interacts – for example, customers, peers and subordinates. This fits entirely with the job design model, in which feedback is classed as one of the most important aspects to encourage motivation.

The job design model has been generally accepted. Nevertheless, there have been some criticisms made. Aldag *et al* (1981) suggested that there was not a clear and consistent link between the job characteristics and behavioural outcomes. Fried and Ferris (1987: 313) found that:

> the relationship between job characteristics and psychological outcomes are generally stronger and more consistent than the relationships between job characteristics and behavioural outcomes, although the latter do exist.

This means that there appears to be evidence that job characteristics can encourage people to feel more highly motivated – but that doesn't necessarily mean that people work harder as a result. There does not always appear to be a link between how people feel and how they act. This view is also supported by the work of Kelly (1992), who conducted a review of 31 case studies and experiments in **job redesign** and concluded that there was limited support for the job design model. Kelly (1992) suggested a twin-track model that showed how the determinants of performance are not the same as the determinants for job satisfaction.

On a cautionary note, enriched jobs with autonomy, responsibility, etc, can cause stress. A study on call centres by Holman and Fernie (2000) drew attention to work-based characteristics which contributed to stress and pressure and included lack of employee control over how calls are timed and handled, the use of scripts that limit what can be said to customers and the level and type of monitoring. They also found that the less control workers had over the job, the lower their satisfaction and mental health, and the higher the levels of anxiety.

Considerations for the world of work

From reviewing the literature on motivation, five key themes are highlighted in Table 5.3, which has been designed to illustrate the connections between the different theories and provide themes that an employer can use in job design or work patterning to encourage motivation.

The key themes have been developed from the different motivation theories. They are defined, in this context, as follows:

- self-respect – the self-belief that anything is possible

- social – the need to respect and be with other human beings

Table 5.3:   Theory and practice

	Self-respect	Social	Meaning	Feedback	Autonomy
Hierarchy of needs	X	X	X		
Modified needs hierarchy	X	X	X		
Two-factor theory	X	X		X	X
Equity theory		X		X	
Expectancy theory	X				X
Goal-setting theory			X	X	
Job design model		X		X	X
Motivational interviewing	X			X	X

- meaning – (to be interpreted in the broadest sense and found in) the knowledge and satisfaction of creating, doing, or experiencing or encountering others

- feedback – receiving information from others about the work that has been done

- autonomy – the freedom to make some decisions.

Applying theory to practice: Procter & Gamble under scrutiny

Working in groups of four and using the P&G case study outlined in the Practitioner insight box at the beginning of the chapter, respond to the following:

- Analyse the methods of motivation used.
- Identify examples of different methods.
- Explain the organisational constraints/considerations regarding motivation.

JOB SATISFACTION

In essence, **job satisfaction** refers to the attitudes and feelings that individuals have about their work. It is a hybrid concept that has attracted contributions from a number of related disciplinary perspectives mainly stemming from psychology or 'psychological humanism' and sociology (Watson, 2004). Of the psychological humanist contributions, that of Herzberg (1968) has informed subsequent research which seeks to validate the view that higher levels of employee productivity are an outcome of satisfaction with intrinsic or job-related factors, provided that extrinsic factors such as pay, job security and promotion prospects are acknowledged. This strand of research therefore brings to the fore the dialectic of the intrinsic and extrinsic. The observation of Mills (1956: 235), made some 55 years ago, is still highly relevant:

> Current managerial attempts to create job enthusiasm, to paraphrase Marx's comment on Proudhon, are attempts to conquer work alienation ... The overall formula for advice that the ideology of 'human relations in business' contains runs to this effect: to make the worker happy, efficient and co-operative, you must make the managers intelligent, rational, knowledgeable. It is the perspective of the managerial elite, disguised in the pseudo-objective language of engineers. It is the advice to the personnel manager to relax his authoritatative manner and widen his manipulative grip over the employees by understanding them better and countering their informal solidarities against management and exploiting these solidarities for smoother, less troublesome managerial efficiency.

Definitional issues and assumptions in relation to satisfaction

Traditional and classic interpretation of the satisfaction concept is provided by Locke (1976), who dates it back to the Taylorist assumptions concerning Scientific Management and fatigue reduction. Locke defines job satisfaction as 'a pleasurable or positive emotional state resulting from the appraisal of one's job or job experiences' (p.1300). The concept, as advanced by Locke, who examined around 3,000 published studies, refers to a variety of features in work and jobs that influence the workers' level of satisfaction. These normally include attitudes towards pay, working conditions, co-workers and team leaders, career prospects and intrinsic aspects of work.

To some extent, and following Locke, satisfaction is a measurement of job and work expectations rather than an overall or holistic attitudinal manifestation. However, certain seemingly contradictory issues arise which stem from the perspectives brought to bear upon the concept. For example, satisfaction may be regarded as a cluster of positive and negative dispositions, which are acquired and learned through experience (Griffin and Bateman, 1986). On the other hand, positive and negative satisfaction attitudes may be based at least partly upon a person's genetic inheritance. Satisfaction may also be regarded as the outcome of an individual's construction of his or her workplace reality, experience and mutuality of co-worker and worker-team leader evaluation. Finally, satisfaction may be linked to an individual's job characteristics and the extent to which an individual attempts to fit in with these characteristics according to what he or she requires from a job (Hackman and Oldham, 1979).

Locke's preferred formulation of satisfaction centres on the weighted sum of the discrepancies between how much of a certain valued aspect of working a job delivers and how much of this aspect an individual desires or expects. Hence the level of satisfaction is based on the outcome of certain 'weightings' or valuations of different facets of the job whereby, for example, higher satisfaction may arise from improvements in the job itself, from reduced expectations or desires concerning the job itself, or merely by a change, however induced, in an individual's valuation so that the perceived disagreeable or dissatisfying aspects of the job are de-emphasised, while those aspects that are more agreeable (and hence satisfying) are more positively evaluated.

Satisfaction may also be considered to be the balance of what is put into work in terms of, for example, effort, and what is derived from work in terms of reward, both intrinsically and extrinsically.

Approaches to the satisfaction concept

A number of contradictions within the satisfaction concept stem, at least in part, from the major social science perspectives brought to bear upon it. These perspectives include those drawn from labour economics, social psychology and sociology.

A labour economics approach

An approach drawn from labour market economics and the labour market itself, for example, would tend to elicit information from large-scale social surveys in order to identify those characteristics pertaining to individual personal circumstances and/or features of the workplace context which influence levels of satisfaction, as expressed by employees within a particular survey (Clark, 1996). Clark, for instance, argues that satisfaction is firstly a measure of individual well-being, and secondly, is a reflection of employees' perceptions and subjective evaluations of certain labour market attributes such as decisions concerning labour force participation, whether to remain in a job or quit, and how much effort should be expended in performing job-related tasks. Such an approach typically utilises statistical methods such as bivariate and regression techniques to examine measures of work satisfaction in national data sets. This approach, exemplified by Clark's research, gathers empirical results concerning satisfaction and relates them both to individual characteristics to include gender, age and education, and to work characteristics such as hours, pay, establishment size and promotion. Economists and labour market researchers, sceptical of the more widespread use of the satisfaction concept by psychologists and social psychologists, have tended to focus upon areas related to, for example, workers' 'utility from working' (Hamermesh, 2001) as based upon occupational choice, while nevertheless conceding (Freeman, 1978: 140) that:

> subjective variables like job satisfaction ... contain useful information for predicting and understanding behaviour but [can] also lead to complexities due to their dependency on psychological states.

A social psychological approach

A second approach to work satisfaction stems from the original Hawthorne studies of the 1930s mentioned at the beginning of the chapter, and further social psychological experiments on employee and occupational groups during the 1940s and 1950s (Roethlisberger and Dickson, 1964). The approach stresses that satisfaction 'should be viewed as a variable and possibly dynamic attribute of a workplace group, generated in, and by, a network of intense informal contacts' (Rose, 2000: 4), in which informal social relations would enable the researcher to understand job attitudes. Satisfaction, in this respect, was seen as a manifestation and outcome of the quality of informal working group relations. Notwithstanding certain methodological drawbacks, the association (however criticised) between satisfaction and informal social interaction has become established (Rose, 2000).

A sociological approach

A further perspective on satisfaction draws upon various sociological contributions reacting against the notion, made popular by Herzberg (1968), that satisfaction could be facilitated by the emphasis upon intrinsic factors ('motivators'), the outcome of which would be increased worker productivity once the extrinsic factors ('satisfiers') had been addressed. They argued that job satisfaction, or lack of it, was part of a broader human condition – that of employee alienation. The emphasis by this group of scholars focused on the effect of production technology, bureaucratic organisation or capitalist exploitation, or a combination of all three (Chinoy, 1955; Blauner, 1964). For example, textile workers were originally employed mainly in home working, with family and friends. However, factories were then built that included machines, managers and the encouragement of profit-making that some may argue has caused employee alienation. Other research, such as that of Goldthorpe *et al* (1968), considered satisfaction to be an outcome of an individual's 'orientation to work' which arose from and was embedded within the social, occupational and community milieux of the worker.

While numerous researchers concentrated upon blue-collar industrial contexts, a few considered white-collar groups such as female office workers (Mills, 1956). These early studies are significant since they raise issues which are continually occurring and recurring in contemporary workplaces and organisational settings, and which also have certain implications for assisting our understanding of satisfaction within occupational categories. Rose (2000) identifies two areas stemming from this concern that are advantageous in relation to job satisfaction. The first of these is *control of skill level* whereby individuals' degree of work experience, acquired skill, level of training and educational attainment are important factors in determining and estimating levels of satisfaction, and where skill levels prior to entering employment are equally as important as those acquired within employment. The second area of importance stressed by Rose concerns satisfaction within a particular occupation or group of occupations. Data is obtained from the British Household Panel Survey with satisfaction gradients defined for occupations and occupational groups known as occupational unit groups within the Standard Occupational Classification. The argument here is that occupational groups can offer contexts for comparing individual circumstances and well-being, especially for employees who are members of them for any length of time.

Satisfaction, skills and training [4]

Rose's (1994) research in connection with a significant study of social change and economic life (SCELI) conducted by Penn, Rose and Rubery (1994) considers job satisfaction to be related to skill, but not inevitably to characteristics such as management control, style and pay. In essence, it is argued that people are more likely to be satisfied in their jobs when skills acquired as part of the job and as a result of HR interventions, equate with the skills they actually have, or have brought to work (own-skill). This argument has gained credence now that a good deal of generic skill training takes place within the secondary and further education sectors. Three main categories of skill situation are identified, each having three subgroups, as identified in Table 5.4. The satisfaction levels in the table are described as units and range from –27 units (very low satisfaction) to +33 units (very high satisfaction).

This suggests that people who feel their talents are under-utilised at work are the unhappiest category, whereas those who work where talents both needed and possessed are equivalent are generally satisfied with their work.

Satisfaction, performance and pay [5]

The adage that 'the happy worker is a productive worker' has been subjected to a considerable amount of empirical analysis which has not revealed a particularly strong association between the two. This outcome was indeed predicted in the early 1950s by Mills (1956: 233):

> Management efforts to create job enthusiasm reflects the unhappy unwillingness of employees to work spontaneously at their routinised tasks.

American research by, for example, Iaffaldano and Muchinsky (1985), which reviewed a large number of studies dealing with the assumed link between productivity and satisfaction, suggests a positive but weak relationship. A number of explanations have been advanced for this. First, many workplaces provide little opportunity for performance and productivity variations. Some jobs are structured in such a way that employees are obliged to maintain minimum levels of performance with minimal fluctuation one way or the other. Moreover, the work output of employees – for example, within the call centre context – is often linked to those of co-workers via performance targets and, as such, performance and productivity may be, as a consequence, fairly uniform and will probably not be highly responsive to changes in employee attitudes.

A more critical view of the satisfaction/performance relationship is provided by Thompson and McHugh (2002), who argue that the relationship tends to ignore the operation of social, cultural, organisational and environmental factors 'which will intervene to make a simple more satisfaction, more performance relationship less likely' (p.297). Citing Argyle (1974), who examined the relations between satisfaction and productivity, absenteeism and turnover, and within the context of their argument, Thompson and McHugh argue that Argyle's conclusion

Table 5.4:   Types of skill matching and satisfaction levels

Skill situation of subgroup	Satisfaction levels (units)
Under-utilised:	
Low job skill, high own-skill	–27
Moderate job skill, high own-skill	–15
High job skill, low own-skill	–10
Matched:	
Low job skill, low own-skill	+1
Moderate job skill, moderate own-skill	+5
High job skill, high own-skill	+4
Under-qualified:	
Moderate job skill, high own-skill	+12
Moderate job skill, moderate own-skill	+13
High job skill, low own-skill	+33

Source: Rose (1994: 261)

that whereas absenteeism and turnover did have a direct relationship to levels of satisfaction, productivity only did so for highly skilled or intrinsically motivated workers – and even in these cases individual differences were highly significant. Moreover, the same research contends that effort, or 'working harder', had little impact upon satisfaction. Although some employees did work harder when satisfied, others worked harder when less satisfied – and some less hard when more satisfied.

Regarded as part of the extrinsic dimension of work, it could be argued that if work yields no value in itself, work becomes a means to an end, and that satisfaction and fulfilment is sought outside work. The link between satisfaction and extrinsics including pay is, therefore, a positive one – hence, the lower the pay, the lower the satisfaction (Watson, 2004). This assertion is supported by Porter and Lawler (1968), who conclude from their researches that higher-paid employees are more likely to be satisfied. Additional factors that may influence the pay/satisfaction relationship are concerned with whether individuals feel that their rate of pay has been determined fairly; whether rewards are commensurate with perceptions of employees about their ability, contribution and value to the organisation; and whether employees are satisfied with other aspects of their employment (intrinsic or extrinsic), such as status, promotion prospects, opportunity to use and develop skills, and relationships with managers and co-workers.

The final theory discussed in this chapter concerns the individual and change. Motivational interviewing (MI) is a tool that has been developed that focuses on intrinsic needs to encourage individuals to change.

BEST PRACTICE

Keystone Food

Motivated employees are likely to deliver higher productivity and influence others to work harder. However – as mentioned at the beginning of the chapter – motivation is not a simple concept and different approaches motivate different employees. If a group of people is asked what would motivate them to work hard and asked to choose four from a list of 25 items, it is rare to find many people who will choose four that are the same. This is because people have different needs and expectations. Consequently, it is important that an organisation that wishes to take motivation seriously will use a range of approaches that will encourage intrinsic and extrinsic motivation.

Keystone Food is a fast-food supplier and a good example of how to motivate employees. According to the HR manager, Keystone has a 'strong belief in engaging employees in everything that they do'. This belief underpins the many systems and strategies that it has to encourage a motivated workforce. Consequently, the majority of management are developed from within. The Manchester plant has a lifelong learning centre which staff are encouraged to use for all types of learning. For example, staff on

the shop floor may choose to learn a language or computer skills – something that is not necessarily directly related to their work but will encourage a learning culture.

Keystone Food is involved in the local community in that the HR manager is part of 'Heart for Heywood', which includes HR managers from different companies who encourage activities in the local community. For example, some staff have been involved in a literacy mentoring scheme in which they go to local primary schools and listen to kids read for one hour per week. Keystone Food encourages health awareness days and blood donation, and runs campaigns like Respect at Work, which encourages staff to value each other.

The company clearly does its best to create a motivated workforce. Not surprisingly, the activities at Keystone have been recognised in that it has won the award for people development from the Chartered Institute for Logistics and Transport.

What are the potential advantages and disadvantages of Keystone Food's development policy described above? Using the theory discussed in this chapter, describe the practice adopted by Keystone Food.

MOTIVATIONAL INTERVIEWING [6]

Motivational interviewing (MI) is a client-centred directive method for enhancing intrinsic motivation to change by exploring and resolving ambivalence. MI is intended to focus on motivational problems that an individual has with change, who is either unwilling or not ready to make change. Introduced two decades ago, it has been supported in a series of clinical trials as effective in enhancing behaviour change through relatively brief intervention (Rollnick *et al*, 2008). MI is a relatively new concept, the origins of which are in addictions, although this is changing and the method is becoming popular in different settings. The focus of motivational interviewing is intrinsic motivation, in that the desire and ability to change comes from within the individual.

Integral to MI is the spirit of MI which is collaborative in nature – ie the individual who wishes to change and the person supporting the change should be working together. A positive atmosphere is therefore important, with the implicit understanding that the individual who wants to make the change is fully responsible and able to do it. The overall goal is to increase the intrinsic motivation of the individual to change, so that change comes from within rather than being imposed. Ambivalence is when there are opposed and conflicting emotions – for example, individuals who would like to give up smoking because they know it is affecting their health but who enjoy smoking. Or individuals who work long hours and know that it is affecting their health but enjoy the benefits and status that they receive as a result.

The spirit of MI is characterised by:

- collaboration – a key component of the spirit of MI is its collaborative nature: the relationship is collaborative, not antagonistic, 'conducive rather than coercive to change' (Rollnick *et al*, 2008: 35)

- evocation – the resource and motivation for change is within the individual who wishes to make the change: they are the expert and need the information to be drawn out of them

- autonomy – the responsibility for change in MI is left with the individual.

The process of MI

The spirit of motivational interviewing described above is essential.

- OARS is an acronym to describe four key methods of MI.

  - **O**pen-ended questions: clients, particularly at the beginning, are encouraged to do most of the talking through the use of open-ended questions

  - **A**ffirmation: affirmation – for example, including compliments – is important to build trust and reinforce understanding

  - **R**eflection: reflective listening is essential. This means that the listener 'will make a guess as to what the speaker means' (Rollnick *et al*, 2008: 69)

  - **S**ummarising: summarise regularly to reinforce what has been said and link information.

- recognising, eliciting, strengthening and reinforcing change talk

- rolling with resistance

- developing a change plan

- consolidating client commitment

- switching between MI and other methods.

The communication style used by a person expresses the attitude of that person towards the person being spoken to. A fundamental aspect of MI is that the communication style adopted is easy and non-confrontational. For Rollnick *et al* (2008: 12), the term they use for the communication style is 'guiding'. For example, in the guiding approach, if a friend had a problem and asked for advice, you would listen carefully to understand the problem, and ask them about the different options exploring the pros and cons. You might offer some of your experiences that are relevant to the situation but with the full awareness that the decision is up to your friend. Finally, as the solution unfolds, you will help them in line with their chosen wishes. Other communication methods are appropriate – but with MI the idea is to support and keep the communication moving forward but in the full knowledge that the individual with the problem is making the decision and has the power and knowledge to do this.

At the moment there is little evidence of MI being used in management because it is a relatively new concept primarily developed in psychology to encourage change in individuals with addictions. However, a common theme of the motivation chapter is the need for individuals to be involved in their work and be given autonomy in decision-making. The key focus of MI is to encourage this autonomy. Managers who understand and learn how to impart this important skill are more likely to encourage higher motivational levels in the workplace. Also, specifically, MI could be used in the appraisal process to understand and encourage poor performers.

Conclusion

In this chapter a selection of the literature dealing with the concepts of motivation and satisfaction has been explored. The content theories of motivation refer to the importance of security, self-esteem and loving relationships that foster kindness and sensitivity to others. But this is different from the description developed by Nietzsche who claimed (Campolo, 2009: 14) that 'people have a craving to control their own destinies and to be free to realize their individualistic potential without restraints from anyone.' Although Herzberg suggested that individuals are striving for self-actualisation, this was set in the context of self and respect for others that is slightly different from that suggested by Nietzsche. The process theories of motivation consider how humans compare the way that they are treated to the way others are, are goal-oriented, and how expectations are created about what it is possible for them to achieve.

How jobs are designed is of importance in motivation. The practical use of different skills, autonomy and feedback is an important aspect of job design. There is the suggestion that if jobs are designed with the key objective of motivation in mind, the individual will experience 'meaningfulness' in his or her work (Hackman and Oldham, 1979). Viktor Frankl's (2004: 79) research into meaning is as a 'direct result of his experience as an inmate in Nazi death camps'. During his time in Auschwitz he decided to study what made some people live and some die. He considered a number of variables including religious beliefs. What he concluded was that it was man's quest for meaning in life that made him more able to live. Those that could look to the future and find meaning in their lives were more likely to live than others who could not. He further considered that if a person can find meaning in their lives, they can be happy and capable of enduring suffering. Frankl (1978) suggested that meaning can be found in any activity through creating, doing and experiencing, or through encountering others. This striving for meaning can fit with a number of aspects of the motivation theories discussed. It has been suggested that some employees want to work for organisations that will allow them to do good (Grant, 2008).

Nevertheless, the evidence for the humanist aspects of motivation and needs as described in this chapter is often contradictory, confusing and inconsistent. For example, there is evidence that lower-level workers can take an instrumental orientation to their work and show greater evidence of determining their work satisfaction from pay, fringe benefits and general extrinsic reward, but that higher-level workers place greater importance on intrinsic rewards and thus place emphasis on meeting their higher-order needs of growth, advancement and recognition (Mottaz, 1985). However, there is also evidence that both groups place importance on intrinsic reward.

At the beginning of the chapter it was emphasised that motivation theories cannot be utilised in isolation, and this is the final reiteration of this chapter. In addition, it is important to recognise that the different theories are not successful in all cultures. In order to gain from theory in this important subject area, the use of the different theories can provide insight and support to practising managers, particularly in the Western world, where motivation theories have been more extensively tested, when used holistically rather than in isolation.

End notes

[1] See also Chapter 3.

[2] See also Chapter 10.

[3] See also Chapter 16.

[4] See also Chapter 6.

[5] See also Chapter 3.

[6] See also Chapter 9.

Ethical implications: What is ethical behaviour?

In the current high-tech society, people regularly comment that business is much faster-paced. For example, technology means that emails can be read from many mobile phones and that Internet access to respond is easily available. Autonomy and responsibility have been passed down the command chain in many organisations as technology provides the platform for easier communication. Behaving ethically in a world of downsizing, de-layering of organisations, greater expectations of employee loyalty and responsibility, and increasing worker productivity and accountability can be challenging. There are many views of what constitutes ethical behaviour. For example, some people believe that the end justifies the means; others believe that as long as a decision provides the greatest gain for the majority, it is ethically sound. Consequently, the application of ethics can be challenging.

Just as ethical behaviour is fairly difficult to draw precise conclusions about, so is motivation, which comes from within and is not tangible. For instance, a person can appear motivated by how hard they work – but this does not mean that they are motivated, necessarily. They may be coerced into completing a task rather than be motivated. A common theme of motivation is the importance of autonomy for individuals and that this will motivate staff to work harder. But how much autonomy should an individual be given? Is it always the right thing for staff to have autonomy? For some individuals it can feel like they are being 'dumped on', and that autonomy means that if something goes wrong, there is somebody to blame. For others, it can cause a strain that could possibly result in pressure and stress – particularly when tasks are combined, as suggested in Hackman's job design model.

Discuss the issue of autonomy raised in this chapter. Do you have any personal experience that you can share about the positive or negative benefits of employee autonomy?

Managers are interested in motivation because they want to increase productivity. They want their employees to achieve the targets and goals. But who sets the goals? How much say does the employee have in the goal-setting process? An employee is often promised bonus, promotion or other rewards for the achievement of goals. However, it is not always possible for employees to achieve individual goals, through no fault of their own. A salesman is dependent upon the production or distribution of a product or on the system to deliver what they have promised. A waitress is dependent upon the chef to produce good-quality food in a restaurant so that she will gain good customer feedback on her performance.

REVIEW AND DISCUSSION QUESTIONS

REVIEW QUESTIONS

1 How would you explain the importance of motivation as a concept in relation to management and organisational behaviour?

2 Explain the difference between content and process theories of motivation.

3 Identify and describe one content theory and one process theory of motivation.

4 What, in your opinion, is the importance of Hackman's job design model?

5 Identify the key characteristics of motivational interviewing (MI).

DISCUSSION QUESTIONS

1 With reference to Maslow's hierarchy of needs, identify your current motivation level, and consider what has influenced it.

2 To what extent do you think that pay is a motivator in the workplace? If possible, interview a number of students – preferably including international students – and ask them about their view of pay as a motivator.

3 Discuss the reality of applying Hackman's job design model in the workplace. What contextual factors would have to be considered to enable the model to be put into practice?

4 Discuss the advantages and disadvantages of motivational interviewing and how it could be used in the workplace.

FURTHER READING

Herzberg, F., Mausner, B. and Snyderman, B. (1959) *The Motivation to Work*. New York: John Wiley & Sons. This book shows in detail the methodological approach, including semi-structured interview questions and the survey used to collect the data to understand the work of Herzberg's infamous two-factor theory. The book is not only useful to understand this theory but also provides a step-by-step illustration of a mixed-method research approach.

Rollnick, S., Miller, W. R. and Butler, C. (2008) *Motivational Interviewing in Health Care: Helping patients change behavior*. New York: Guilford Press. This book is a hands-on practical handbook which deals with the skills that can be learned and used to advantage by managers and others. Some of the basic concepts, even if not used in their entirety, are beneficial to an understanding of motivation.

Locke, E. A. and Latham, G. P. (2002) 'Building a practically useful theory of goal-setting and task motivation', *American Psychologist*, Vol.57: 705–17. This paper is the summary of 35 years of work by Locke and Latham about understanding and using goal theory. The article offers useful practical illustrations, including evidence of how goal theory can be used in the workplace.

Grant, A. M. (2008) 'Designing jobs to do good: dimensions and psychological consequences of prosocial job characteristics', *Journal of Positive Psychology*, Vol.3: 19–39. Generation Y and other employees are particularly interested in employment that has a social conscience and work that benefits others. This paper aims to discover the psychological benefits of prosocial job characteristics.

Herzberg, F. (2003) 'One more time: how do you motivate employees?', *Harvard Business Review*, Vol.81: 86–96. Herzberg is one of the founding fathers of motivation and has been writing on the subject since the 1950s. The following quote summarises his view on how to motivate employees to work harder: 'Forget praise. Forget punishment. Forget cash. You need to make their jobs more interesting.'

Mitchell, T. R. (1974) 'Expectancy models of job satisfaction, occupational preference and effort', *Psychological Bulletin*, Vol.81: 1053–77. The author evaluates the research into expectancy theory, providing an interesting overview of the different ideas in this area.

KEY SKILLS

UNDERSTANDING THE WHOLE PERSON

Maslow was set apart from his contemporaries to some extent due to his belief in human nature. By elevating love and self-esteem as a need of every human being and highlighting the importance of self-actualisation over all these areas, his emphasis was on having regard for the whole person and retaining a positive belief in human nature. Lewis (*Five Families: Mexican case studies*, 1959), introducing the notion of a 'culture of poverty', states that low self-esteem/low confidence keeps people stuck and unable to change. However, according to Maslow's theory a lack of confidence or low self-esteem will affect motivation. The importance of Maslow's work is to highlight the integrated, whole nature of the individual. It is therefore critical for a manager who wishes to motivate that he or she understands the whole person. Every individual is unique, with a different perceptual world and background, and may therefore be motivated in a different way. The starting point and the first skill of any manager is thus to understand the whole person. An example can be taken from as far back as biblical times. Moses in the book of *Exodus* was asked by God to lead his people out of slavery. Moses offered many reasons why he was not the right person to take on this challenge. One of the main reasons he gave was that he felt that his public speaking skills were not good enough. God, after listening to Moses, suggested that Moses' brother could do the speaking and Moses should complete the rest of the task (Exodus 3:9–4:17). This suggests that even in very ancient times the importance of listening and of understanding the whole person was perceived. To motivate an individual, the starting point is therefore to aim to understand the whole person, as much as is possible in the workplace, in order to be able to work out what will motivate that unique individual.

COMMUNICATION STYLE

According to Rollnick *et al* (2008: 12) there are three communication styles:

- *direct* – Tell someone what they should do.
- *follow* – Listen to someone.
- *guide* – Listen and help someone to make up their own mind.

The context of the situation will influence the communication style that should be adopted. For example, *direct* may be appropriate when there is a correct answer or one way to do something. In general, particularly in the development of individuals, the most appropriate communication style is *guide*. In the guiding approach it is important to listen carefully to understand the issue or problem. The listener should use open questions as described below to encourage the talker to consider different options. The listener is able to offer suggestions but, most importantly, is not responsible for finding the right solution, let alone resolving the problem. The responsibility for that remains with the talker. This does not mean that the listener abdicates all responsibility because his or her role is to support and help the individual to be motivated to move forward.

QUESTIONING SKILLS

Questioning is a process that may change the listener as well as the person being questioned and, ideally, should consist of short, insightful questions that build on a line of argument. Low-level questions require learners to recall information presented or to retrieve information from the long-term memory. High-level questions require learners to make connections and to engage in application, analysis, interpretation or evaluation of ideas (Vogt and Brown, 2004). Typically, questions begin with 'What', 'Why', 'When', 'How', 'Where' and 'Who', but according to Marshall and Rowland (1998) the question 'Why?' is one of the most important questions you can ask, especially if it enables the identification of assumptions that may be hidden. Vogt *et al* (2003) argue that the quality of learning depends on an individual's skill in questioning. Questioning may be regarded as a dialectical process: 'Thus, from the very beginning of a person's experience of being human, questions and statements together form the very fabric of conversation' (Goldberg, 1998: 28). One reason given by Vogt for the lack of questioning, in their research in the USA, is a culture of wanting to know the 'right answer' rather than discovering the 'right question' – with the possible emphasis on *one* correct answer. Finding the right questions rather than the right answers is important because it focuses on what people do not know as well as what they do know (Mumford, 1995). Moreover, more time is needed to find the right question and not just focus on the right answer. Harrison (2006) offered some suggestions on how to improve questioning:

- Monitor the type and range of questions used. What results are gained from the different types of questions? Are these appropriate to your field of knowledge? Are there other types of questions that the learner needs to know and should be using?

- Encourage learners to question each other and to use a range of questions in their activities. Observers within an action learning set could be used to focus on the development of this skill.

- Teach staff about the different types of questions, or teach a 'system of inquiry' (Revans, 1983). Allow time for individuals to practise questioning skills.

Chapter 6
Learning Theories and Practices

Crystal Zhang and Niki Kyriakidou

Contents

Key Learning Outcomes

By the end of this chapter you should be able to:

- differentiate between learning and training
- evaluate the different approaches of learning theories
- recognise the variety of learning styles and their instruments
- understand training needs analysis and training delivery
- identify and explain formal and informal learning and training methods.

PRACTITIONER INSIGHT

Merlin

Merlin is the only specialist UK charity that specialises in health, saving lives in times of crisis and helping to rebuild shattered health services. Each year, Merlin helps more than 15 million people in up to 20 countries. We speak to **Michele Dennison, the HR consultant of MD Management Development** (MDMD), to find out how she helped Merlin to build a stronger and more effective management culture through developing individual training modules targeted at different management levels. Michele worked alongside Merlin's Learning and Development Manager and Jacqueline Hill from J. Hill Associates. They developed the Leadership and Management Development Programme (LMDP) at Merlin in order to provide management and team development

and to build a stronger and more effective management culture. This framework of learning modules and support would be targeted at different levels of management. It also had to be flexible enough to take into account the ever-changing environment in which its culturally diverse and geographically spread staff work and the impact it has on their needs and availability to attend traditional learning events.

How do you think Michele and her team approach the challenges faced by Merlin, and what are the advantages and disadvantages of such an approach?

Once you have read this chapter, return to these questions and think about how you could answer them.

Introduction

Learning is a natural human behaviour. From our birth, we start learning – for example, to obtain new knowledge and to find out how to do things. We also learn how to be better at doing things and also learn how to learn faster, both of which are crucial aspects for improving individual, team and organisational efficiency. As Sadler-Smith (2006: 2) points out, 'learning is at the heart of the organisation', and the right provision of training may well be the difference between a company's merely surviving and its thriving.

Various learning theories have been formulated in a bid to provide a framework for influencing learning and learning outcomes. Understanding how they can be applied to the workplace is crucial to the design and delivery of the right training programme in the pursuit of the competitive edge.

LEARNING AND TRAINING

Although the terms 'learning' and 'training' are frequently used interchangeably, we would like to distinguish between the two (as adapted from Mayo and Lank, 1994, and Sloman, 2005):

- *Learning* is a self-directed, work-based process, leading to increased adaptive potential. It is employee-need-centred and the individual is the beneficiary from the start.

- *Training* is an instructor-led, content-based intervention, leading to a desired change in behaviour. It provides solutions to a learning need and is essentially skill-oriented.

In this context, it can be argued that learning is a knowledge-developed process through experience (Kolb, 1984). It is also a knowledge-skills-insight process. According to Honey and Mumford (1996):

> Learning has happened when people can demonstrate that they know something that they did not know before (insights and realisations, as well as facts) and/or when they can do something they could not do before (skills).

Common aspects of learning and training are:

- *knowledge* – what someone knows. Staff need to know what to do in their particular roles, and how to do it.

- *skills* – what someone can do. Knowledge in itself is rarely sufficient for satisfactory performance. Being competent at carrying out the task is as important.

- *attitudes* – the mental state of mind (positive or negative) affecting judgement, decision-making and motivation and most importantly, how work is carried out. It includes the employee's attitudes, emotions, values, feelings, motivation, beliefs and interests.

It is therefore in the interest of an organisation to increase employees' knowledge, skills and attitudes (KSA) and learning can thus be demonstrated as an end result or outcome of training (Mumford and Gold, 2004).

LEARNING THEORIES

This section introduces the basic principles and related concepts of the **behaviourist**, **cognitive**, **socio-cultural** and **humanist** learning theories, and summarises some of the more popular ones used in organisations for adult learning and training and development activities. Although there are many arguments online and in the corners of academia, it is important to realise that there is no right or wrong approach – just more effective and less effective styles for individuals, content and the context in which the learning takes place. There are many theories surrounding adult learning styles (see Coffield *et al*, 2004 for a comprehensive review). Using a learning style methodology can help provide a community with a common and consistent language within which individuals can state their needs and trainers can ensure that their sessions and learning interventions are reasonably balanced and likely to provide something for everyone.

What we need to consider by reviewing learning theories are:

- Effective learning requires some correspondence between experience and learning style.

- The individual learning style preference can be an obstacle to learning from certain types of learning experience.

Behavioural learning theory [1]

In general, learning theories have their groundings from behavioural experiments with animals. Most notable are the works of Pavlov (1927) and Skinner (1953), which propose that learning is a result of reinforcement through an individual's experience. Dogs normally salivate upon seeing food. What Pavlov did was to train dogs to salivate upon an additional stimulus – the sound of a bell ringing. The outcome of the training – or Pavlovian conditioning – is the observation of trained dogs salivating to the sound of a bell *without* the sight of food. Skinner (1953) furthered the study by training rats to operate a lever in order to release food in the cage. The formulation of the behavioural learning theory only included what could be measured – the stimulus and the resulting behaviour – and excluded any internal and cognitive activities in the learner's mind. (See also Chapter 3, *Personality*.)

These were important limitations, because stimulus-response conditioning experiments did not fully reflect the learning process. Further developments occurred through Gestalt psychology, which emphasises the study of experiences and behaviour as wholes rather than independently functioning, disparate parts. Kohler (1925) observed chimpanzees using a thought process to obtain food, either through making a long stick from smaller pieces, or stacking crates *and* using a long stick. This resulted in important findings – transferable to humans – on learning and problem-solving. It shows that the test subjects (in this case chimpanzees) displayed 'insight learning' when solving the problem of obtaining food by 'seeing it whole' rather than through trial-and-error attempts or reward-driven Pavlovian conditioning. Kohler's 'insight learning' introduces the concept of higher-level thinking – the 'Aha!' solutions to problems (Kohler, 1925).

Fellow Gestalt psychologist Lewin formulated his theory of *life space* and the general law of psychology from his observation of children's behaviour (Lewin, 1923). A classic example of such observation would be to watch children learning to sit on a stone. The thought process behind this simple task requires the child to turn its back on the stone in order to sit upon it. This loss of the visual cue makes the child rely on a cognitive process composed of internal rather than external incentives in order to complete the task. Lewin (1923: 226) argued that differentiation is 'a function of the conditions of the environment as well as of the individual peculiarities of the person', and formulated the general law of psychology $B = f(PE)$, according to which a person's behaviour B is a function (f) of a person's personality P and environmental situations E. In simple words, the behaviour of an individual can be expressed mathematically in a psychological topology according to the distributions of things in the environment with varying attracting or repelling forces.

Through learning, people can re-interpret their world and their relationship to it. A true learning culture continuously challenges its own methods and ways of doing things. This ensures continuous improvement and the capacity to change according to their personal characteristics, the different educational environments and their challenges to current and future personal and professional achievements. This continuous cycle of reflection is inherent to Lewin's *action research*, which involves a spiral of steps, 'each of which is composed of a circle of planning, action and fact-finding about the result of the action' (Lewin, 1948: 206). Essentially, action research is a process of testing, observing, thinking, changing and, in its simplest form, can be applied to practically anything one does. Figure 6.1 illustrates a simple action research cycle, which is reiterated as long as required. This cycle of steps was later adapted by Kolb and other researchers.

Cognitive theory [2]

In general, behaviourist approaches have been heavily criticised as being inadequate to examine the individual's internal mental activity. On the other hand, the works of Kohler and Lewin propose the presence of a cognitive higher order of thinking. More recent theories focus on the learner and his or her experiences by investigating the primary reason and way to obtain knowledge and further experience (training). These two elements inform the individual learning style. According to Riding and Rayner (2002: 51),

> learning style is an individual set of differences that include not only a stated personal preference for instruction or an association with a particular form of learning activity but also individual differences found in intellectual or personal psychology.

Figure 6.1 Action research

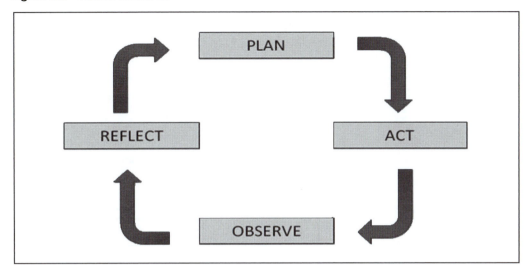

Source: adapted from Lewin (1948)

Putting learning into working context, it is important to consider that employees as individuals have their own ideas and beliefs about the environment they live in, and that they try to make the most sense out of it. This is called perception. Their perceptions shape what they believe about their reality – how to prioritise life and work events and make decisions accordingly. This 'individualist' reality determines their ability to learn, hence their learning style.

In a similar vein to Kohler's and Lewin's works, Jung (1923) formulated a model of cognitive styles or personality types to account for patterns of behaviour and thinking. This is divided into either introverted or extraverted, and further divided into four function types: thinking, feeling, sensation and intuition. Thinking and feeling are associated with a rational way of information-processing, while sensation and intuition were associated with an irrational manner. Adapting from Jung's theory, Myers (1962) developed a measure of cognitive styles since called the Myers-Briggs Type Indicator (MBTI). The instrument exists in three different versions (abbreviated, standard and long) and consists of a series of questions associated with the four bipolar discontinuous scales: extraversion/introversion, sensing/intuition, thinking/feeling, and judging/perceiving, as shown in Figure 6.2.

Witkin and Goodenough (1981) argued that cognitive style has more consideration for the manner than for the content of an activity. It is related to how information is processed rather than the content of the information. The individual differences in the way people perceive, think, solve problems and learn can be mapped to a cognitive style index (CSI) scale of intuition (right-brain orientation) and analysis (left-brain orientation) developed by Allinson and Hayes (1994). Although it represents a simplistic view of the individual's information-processing, CSI is one of the most reliable instruments (Coffield *et al*, 2004).

Kolb's experiential learning cycle

David Kolb (2000: 8) refers to learning style as a 'differential preference for learning, which changes slightly from situation to situation. At the same time, there is some long-term stability in learning style.' In light of this, he adapted Lewin's action research and developed his experiential learning model based on a 'learning cycle', as shown in Figure 6.3. Kolb's learning cycle aims to demonstrate that effective learning involves multiple interactions with experience and passing through all four stages, going through a continuous spiral (Kolb, 1984).

Figure 6.2   The Myers-Briggs Type Indicator

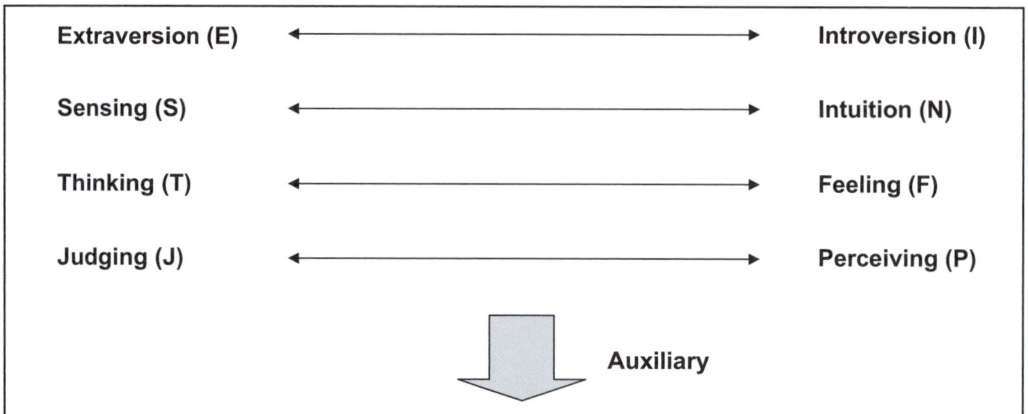

Extraversion (E)	⟷	Introversion (I)
Sensing (S)	⟷	Intuition (N)
Thinking (T)	⟷	Feeling (F)
Judging (J)	⟷	Perceiving (P)

⬇ **Auxiliary**

ISTJ	ISFJ	ISTP	INTP
INTJ	INFJ	ISFP	INFP
ESTJ	ESFJ	ESTP	ENTP
ENTJ	ENFJ	ESFP	ENFP

Figure 6.3   The four stages of the experiential learning cycle

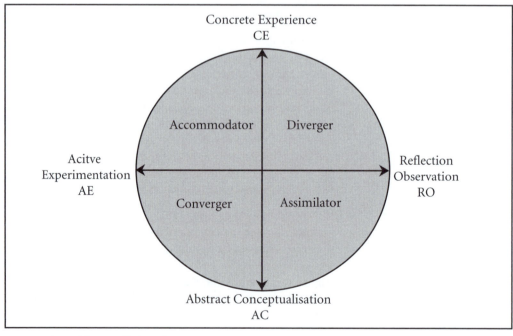

Source: adapted from Kolb (1984)

The four stages can be described as:

- *Concrete Experience* (CE): Carrying out a particular action and then seeing the effect of the action in this situation.

- *Reflective Observation* (RO): Understanding these effects in the particular instance so that if the same action were to be taken in the same circumstances, it would be possible to anticipate what would follow from the action.

- *Abstract Conceptualisation* (AC): Understanding the general principle under which the particular instance falls.

- *Active Experimentation* (AE): Applying through the action in a new circumstance within the range of generalisation.

To help individuals to assess their approach to learning, Kolb (1976) developed the Learning Style Inventory (LSI), which provides information on the individual's relative emphasis on the four abilities in the learning cycle. Through extensive empirical work, Kolb attempted to relate different subject disciplines to the quadrants of the learning cycle and hence to different forms of knowledge:

- Practitioners of creative disciplines, such as the arts, are found in the *Divergent* quadrant.

- Pure scientists and mathematicians are in the *Assimilative* quadrant.

- Applied scientists and lawyers are in the *Convergent* quadrant.

- Professionals who have to operate more intuitively, such as teachers, are in the *Accommodative* quadrant.

Applying theory to practice: Experiential experience

Visit the website for experiential learning: www.learningandteaching. info/learning/ experience.htm	Working in groups, critically assess how the experiential learning cycle can be applied to your own experience (academic or professional).

Honey and Mumford's learning cycle

During the years, educationists have developed different strategies in order to cope with various different student learning styles and techniques of learning, each style corresponding to each stage of the learning cycle. One important development came from Honey and Mumford (1982, 1996), who identified individual preference for each of the stages of the learning cycle (Figure 6.4). Different stages were related to different learning styles, and Honey and Mumford accordingly designed their Learning Style Questionnaire (LSQ) for managers and professionals. The questionnaire is different from the LSI in that it asks questions about general behavioural tendencies rather than just about learning. The questions rely on simple 'agree' or 'disagree' answers which probe the preferences for the four learning styles: 'activists', 'theorists', 'pragmatists' and 'reflectors'.

Activitists *(Do)*

- immerse themselves fully in new experiences
- enjoy the here and now
- are open-minded, enthusiastic, flexible
- act first, consider consequences later
- seek to centre activity around themselves.

Figure 6.4   Honey and Mumford's learning cycle

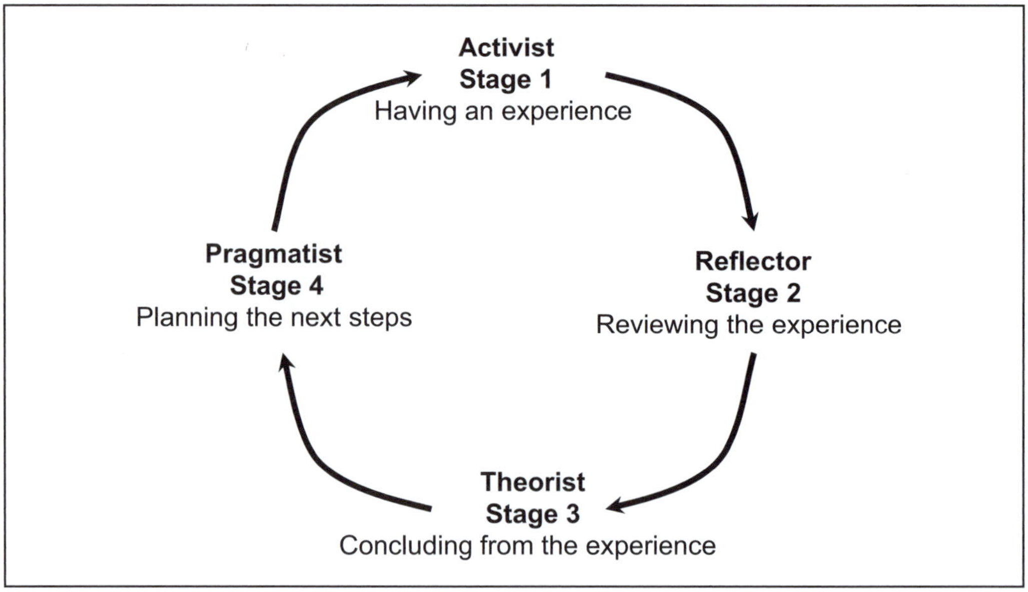

Source: Honey and Mumford (2000)

Reflectors *(Review)*

- stand back and observe

- are cautious, take a back seat

- collect and analyse data about experience and events, are slow to reach conclusions

- use information from past, present and immediate observations to maintain a big-picture perspective.

Theorists *(Conclude)*

- think through problems in a logical manner, value rationality and objectivity

- assimilate disparate facts into coherent theories

- are disciplined, aiming to fit things into rational order

- are keen on basic assumptions, principles, theories, models and systems thinking.

Pragmatists *(Plan)*

- are keen to put ideas, theories and techniques into practice

- search for new ideas and experiment

- act quickly and confidently on ideas, get straight to the point

- are impatient with endless discussion.

By knowing one's learning style, one can accelerate the learning process when undertaking activities that best fit one's preferred style. Knowing one's learning style can also help avoid repeating mistakes by undertaking activities that strengthen other styles. For example, if you tend to 'jump in at the deep end', consider spending time reflecting on experiences before taking action. However, we should also note that the categorisation of disciplines into learning styles would indicate a causality dilemma about whether a discipline promotes a particular learning style or vice versa.

Other models of learning style

Although the LSI and the LSQ are popular instruments, they are not perfect. Several studies (eg Allinson and Hayes, 1990; Duffy and Duffy, 2002) have failed to validate the four learning styles of the quadrants and newer models have been proposed such as the Curry's 'onion' model of learning style (Curry, 1983). This simple model is usually depicted as an inner core, representing the individual's information-processing style, that is surrounded by a layer of personality style and an outer 'skin' of instructional preferences. The inner core is more stable and significant in complex learning, while the outermost layer is easier to modify and influence, but less important in learning.

There are many more models and theories that are not mentioned here. While they may appear disjointed and confusing, researchers strongly believe that they all lie within a continuum of learning styles (Figure 6.5). At the left end of the continuum is the influence of genetics on fixed inherited traits and the interaction of personality and cognition. At the other end of the continuum, there is more emphasis on personal factors (eg motivation) and environmental factors and their influence on cognitive style.

Social and social-cultural learning theory [3]

Social learning theory focuses on the learning that occurs within a social context. It considers that people learn from one another, including such concepts as observational learning, imitation, and modelling. Much work on social learning theory comes from Bandura and Vygotsky, who specialised in the observation of children learning and playing. Because social learning theory involves both behaviour and cognitive ability, it can be considered a bridge or a transition between behavioural and cognitive theories. Crucially, people can learn by observing the behaviour of others and from the outcomes of others.

The classic example of social learning theory comes from the studies of children interacting with an inflatable 'bobo doll' (Bandura and Huston, 1961). Children first watched a film of someone beating a bobo doll. When placed in a room with a similar bobo doll, the children would also beat the doll, thereby imitating what they had watched. The important point here is that there was no stimulus or reward for the children for imitating, unlike the conditioning aspect of behavioural theory.

Another important concept in social learning theory is the existence of a 'zone of proximal development' (ZPD), formulated by Vygotsky (1978). This is the difference between what a learner can do without help and what he or she can do with help. At the start of learning, the individual relies on assistance from more competent peers (eg parents, teachers, coaches, experts). As learning occurs, the individual moves through the ZPD until learning is complete and he/she becomes independent. This can be easily demonstrated in the observation of children who, unable to solve a problem or tackle a task, will often turn to a more knowledgeable other for help. Language is used to communicate and receive instruction, and hence act as a facilitator of cognitive development. ZPD has been expanded to include the concept of 'scaffolding' outlined by Wood *et al* (1976). Scaffolding is the process through which a teacher

Figure 6.5 Coffield *et al*'s families of learning styles

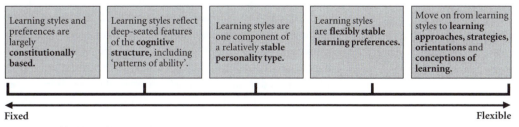

Source: Coffield *et al* (2004: 9)

or more competent peer gives aid to the student in her/his ZPD as necessary, and tapers off this aid as it becomes unnecessary.

Humanist theory

Another theory to consider here is the humanist adult learning theory (Maslow, 1954; Knowles, 1973; Rogers, 1969). This theory focuses on the emotional and personal development aspects of learning and posits that every person has a strong desire to realise his or her full potential. Maslow (1954) identified a hierarchy of needs (see Chapter 5) which is proposed to be important in motivation. At the bottom of the hierarchy are the basic needs of a human being – food and water and physical sensation. The next level is security and stability, which are important for the physical survival of the person. Once individuals have basic nutrition, shelter and safety, they attempt to accomplish more. The third level of need is for love and belonging, which are psychological needs: when individuals have no anxieties about physical needs, they are ready to share themselves with others. The fourth level is achieved when individuals feel comfortable with what they have accomplished. This is the esteem need level – the level of the need for recognition, success and status. The top of the pyramid – self-actualisation – occurs when individuals reach a state of harmony and understanding, and when they realise their needs to be and do that which they were 'born to do'.

The humanist theory of learning thus tends to be highly value-driven, and hence more like prescriptions (about what ought to happen) than descriptions (of what does happen). In this regard, the humanist adult learning theory emphasises the 'natural desire' of everyone to learn. Its underlying beliefs are:

- belief in people

- human choice towards behaviour.

Its view of learning is to fulfil one's potential, as directed by the learner.

By taking into consideration elements of the humanist theory, it is fair to say that employees are encouraged to take responsibility for their own learning. The trainer is now a facilitator in the learning process of the trainee. Accordingly, employees provide much of the input for their learning, which occurs through their insights and experiences. They are also encouraged to consider that the most valuable evaluation is self-evaluation, and that learning ought to focus on factors that contribute to solving significant problems or achieving significant results.

A common aspect of the different theories on learning places an emphasis on the realisation that something is required – knowledge, skills or attitudes – to perform at a higher level.

TRAINING NEEDS ANALYSIS

A training need is defined as the gap between the knowledge, skills and attitude possessed by the target individual or group and those needed to perform required roles in the organisation. The design of every training course should be based upon an understanding of those three factors and will depend heavily on the identification of these needs and the most effective response in meeting such 'training gaps'. This process is known as **training needs analysis** (TNA).

According to the *National Employers Skills Survey 2009*, the UK spent over £39 billion on training activities in 2009 (Shury *et al*, 2010). The average annual investment in training per trainee is £3,050, compared with £2,775 in 2007. While there is no shortage of training providers eager to get organisations to sign up to their training programmes, it is easy to see how businesses are concerned about the value for money of these often very costly activities. As argued by Lucy Kellaway in her Management column in the *Financial Times*, the real issue in training is not that employers do not spend enough on training, but that 'they do not pitch it right.' Indeed, many times it is down to a failure to identify the needs effectively and a failure to design appropriate training to meet the training gaps. McGehee and Thayer (1961) proposed that training should be pitched at three different levels: organisation, job, and individual.

Any training need must be justified in terms of improving how people (and by implication, the organisation) work. This requires an identification of what is not working so well, where it is not working, and how significant that deficiency is. A first step in assessing training needs is to analyse the needs of the organisation. Secondly, it is useful to carry out a job analysis: careful determination of job components, identifying what is missing to perform the job to the required standards, identifying what gaps can be filled through training, and what type of training, and ultimately prioritising training needs. Finally, wherever possible, it is valuable to assess individual training needs. This last analysis is difficult, sometimes, because the learners may not be accessible prior to the course. The following paragraphs describe each of the important stages.

Stakeholder analysis

It is important to identify all possible stakeholders with an interest in the training process, including the identification and assessment of the training needs. Stakeholder analysis in the context of needs assessment will reveal the importance and possible influence of the stakeholders in TNA, their type of participation, their interest and the possible impact on them. Although training is normally proposed from the management perspective, a lot of training has been designed without taking the needs of the participants into consideration, because managers make assumptions for others about what they should be required to learn (Hicks and Hennessy, 1997). Sometimes an effort is made to consider training needs, but information collected is not sufficient, or not obtained from the most appropriate sources. If the learners have not been involved, they may feel distant from the learning process, and de-motivated. They may not understand the concept of the training and be uncertain about what they will have achieved at the end. In short, the training is unlikely to be effective.

Research methods

This is a crucial stage in TNA. Correct identification of training needs requires research methods to assess what knowledge, skills and attitudes the organisation has and what it requires now and in the future. Various methods can be used, but the choice of specific methods will depend on the questions asked and the target level (organisation, job or individual). Examples of research methods are semi-structured interviews, questionnaire survey, diary records, focus group, and observation (Bryman and Bell, 2003).

Organisation-level needs

A clear understanding of the organisation's aims, responsibilities and strategy is a prerequisite to a consideration of needs. For example, for organisations that compete on the basis of quality, highly skilled workers are essential; for those that compete on cost, they are an unjustifiable extravagance.

Job-level needs

Identifying job-level training needs is often an important part of the 'planned maintenance' of an organisation and a necessary response to changing conditions and new problems. Each particular job will require an analysis of how important the job is, who will be doing it, how often the job needs to be done, and the knowledge, skills and attitude required to carry out the job, and what is lacking. The difficulty in learning the new job also has to be considered.

Individual-level needs

This stage is predominantly concerned with the individuals who require training and what their particular needs are. It is essentially matching the skills of the person to the skills of the job and determining what gaps exist. Even if structured and rational training is provided, it is important to estimate and determine whether training will have a positive or negative impact on the learner's performance. Indeed, this practice of performance management can create tensions and difficulties if it is perceived to be too controlling. Again, it is important to involve the learner as stakeholder in order to identify training gaps which the learner will accept.

Data analysis

Training needs analysis usually generates a large quantity of data. It is preferable to analyse data on the go because it facilitates the identification of important issues emerging during data collection which can be explored again later in more detail. Again, the data should reveal the knowledge, skills and attitudes at the present level and desired/future level and provide the evidence for proposing a training programme.

Stakeholder feedback

Identifying the wrong needs, or where the need is only partly related to training, can be wasteful and counter-productive. While stakeholders at different levels in the organisation might have different, if not conflicting, priorities, it is important that everyone involved in the TNA process has an opportunity to give feedback on the results through workshops, meetings or disseminated written reports in order to achieve a consensus on the training needs and the delivery of training.

TRAINING DELIVERY

In the previous section we highlighted the importance of training needs and how to identify these needs at different levels. This section aims to provide an overview of the broad range of learning and training methods. Some of these can be blended together depending on individual, team or organisational needs.

Many authors have categorised different types of learning and training methods available to individuals, teams or organisations based on various criteria. Some key frameworks are described in Table 6.1. Learning and training methods can be formal or informal and/or can be based on technology (computer, networking or e-learning). A systematic approach to learning is underpinned by learning theories (as discussed in the previous section) and by the concept of training and development within organisational settings.

Table 6.1:   Key frameworks for learning and training

Author(s)	Aim	Criteria
Marchington and Wilkinson (1996)	To provide a framework for the analysis of learning methods based on . . .	• the extent to which the methods are *individual-* or *group-based* • the extent to which the methods are *self-directed* or *participative* (andragogical) or *are controlled* by experts, ie trainers (pedagogical)
Hackett (2003)	To provide an analysis of the methods based on the extent to which the learning and training process is either trainer- or learner-centred and controlled	• *Training-centred methods*, such as a lecture, which is controlled by the trainer • *Learner-centred methods*, such as self-development questionnaires and learning logs, which are controlled by the learner • *Coaching*, which can be administered after mutual consensus of both trainer and learner
Mumford (1997)	To provide a review of learning and training methods based on their relationship to work	• *Off-the-job learning* options, such as lectures, case studies, role-plays, e-learning, etc • *Integrated learning methods*, such as on-the-job training, mentoring, action learning, work rotation and secondment

The frameworks presented in Table 6.1 show that learning and training methods can be *formal* or *informal* and/or can be based on technology (computer, networking or e-learning). A *systematic approach* to learning is underpinned by learning theories (as discussed in the earlier sections) and by the concept of training and development within organisational settings.

Although there are minor variations, most development learning and training systems adapt the following process.

1 *Analyse* the needs of the organisation and the individuals, and then identify the goals you wish to achieve in order to cope with any existing problems/issues.

2 *Design* a training and learning method or model to achieve your goals.

3 *Develop* the model into training programme (courseware).

4 *Implement* the programme.

5 *Evaluate* its effectiveness and review the first four phases if necessary.

The training includes:

● structured informal learning (work-based methods)

● formal training courses of various kinds and further education.

Informal learning

Informal learning is concerned with what people learn while at work. It is not focused on structured training provided by the company as part of the developmental process. Instead, it is more *experiential learning*, because the learners define how they will gain the knowledge they need (ie on-the-job training), depending on the challenges of work at different stages of their career. In this sense, employee development through informal learning can be achieved in incremental steps. It can be unplanned and unsystematic because it will not necessarily satisfy individual or organisational aims and needs (Armstrong, 2010).

Stern and Sommerlad (1999) have identified some characteristics of informal learning that can enhance the developmental process, shown in Figure 6.6.

The methods used below are highly relevant to individual needs, occur in the workplace, and vary depending on the learner needs, style and the relationship with the provider of the learning.

Figure 6.6 Informal workplace learning

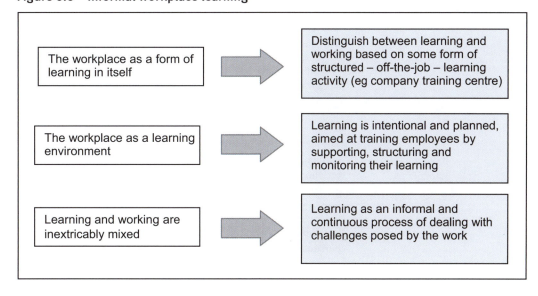

1 Competencies

Management competencies or capabilities are seen as a way of aligning the organisational objectives with performance management as identified in the selection process, appraisal and rewards, training and development (Holbeche, 1999).

One of the outcomes of the concerns of the 1980s was the establishment of the Management Charter Initiative (MCI), which went on to produce occupational standards for managers. Since then, various frameworks have been developed, which provide a specification of competencies, or abilities that managers in various roles and levels require, and that can also be used as a basis for determining development needs and for designing programmes leading to career development or the acquisition of a qualification.

Applying theory to practice: Training delivery and behaviourism

It is important to understand the different learning theories and their impacts on the training delivery. For example, behaviourism deals with cause and effect, and learning practices based on behaviourist theories predominantly use external stimuli to evoke a behavioural response. People therefore respond to reinforcement (such as rewards) within training – reinforcement is a motivator to participate in training. Because responses to stimuli are dependent on the individual, the instruction must be oriented to the individual and the effectiveness of rewards must be individually determined – that is: 'different strokes for different

folks'. Based on this behaviourist school of thinking, management development programmes should progress from the simple to the complex, and should include sensitisation, practice and feedback to managers and employees – potentially through the growing use of coaches and mentors at work. However, we should remain aware of the criticism of the behaviourist approach and its association with the ultimate/ruthless efficiency of industrial organisation and the rigid bureaucratic system.

2 Coaching, counselling and mentoring

Individual and management development can take place in many forms, some delivered by managers and some by internal or external coaches, or mentors. Training and development surveys by the Chartered Institute of Personnel and Development (CIPD) have highlighted a significant growth of the number of organisations using such personal assistance to develop at least some of their people's potentials. The three terms 'coaching', 'mentoring' and 'counselling' are often used almost interchangeably, but there are differences. Table 6.2 provides a comparative

Table 6.2:   The differences between mentoring, coaching and counselling

Mentoring	Coaching	Counselling
Helping to shape an individual's beliefs and values in a positive way; often a longer-term career relationship from someone who has 'done it before'	Helping another person to improve awareness, to set and achieve goals in order to improve a particular behavioural performance	Helping an individual to improve performance by resolving situations from the past
Ongoing relationship that can last for a long period of time	Relationship generally has a set duration	A short-term relationship, but can last for longer time periods due to the breadth of issues to be addressed
The agenda is set by the mentee, with the mentor providing support and guidance to prepare them for future roles	The agenda is typically set by the individual, but in agreement/consultation with the organisation	The agenda is generally agreed by the individual and the counsellor
Focus is on career and personal development	**Focus is generally on development/issues at work**	**Focus is on achieving specific, immediate goals**

Source: the CIPD

analysis of these informal methods of training and identifies their main differences (http://www.brefigroup.co.uk/coaching/coaching_and_mentoring.html).

The main focus of **coaching** is the improvement of the trainees' current skills and performance, but also it seeks to support career transitions (for a short video about a 'leader' as coach, visit YouTube: http://www.youtube.com/watch?v=7XGdT5DUyPI&feature=related). By adopting an objective perspective/attitude, coaches try to develop a structured dialogue with their coachees leading to sustainable solutions. Usually, line managers are asked to undertake the role of coach because it is the most efficient way of learning informally from more senior colleagues. The main focus of coaching is on the development of professional skills.

Coaching can be distinguished from **counselling**, which focuses mainly on providing support (through pastoral care and a series of workplace workshops) regarding employees' personal concerns such as motivation and self-confidence.

Senior managers or experienced employees can be assigned as **mentors** within the workplace. Their role is to set up regular meetings with their mentees in order to provide assistance regarding the improvement of their performance, the informal clarification of their role (especially for newcomers), job expectations, etc. It is a long-lasting relationship that aims to enhance the mentees' capabilities, understanding and advancement within their professional career.

3 Action learning

Most people learn best by doing. **Action learning** sets help to achieve this by making their members focus on solving live issues in their normal working environments and by trying out different approaches, with discussion and support from colleagues to help them reflect on their impact. It is a group process of learning as it aims to develop a group of people with different levels of responsibilities, skills and experience by focusing on dealing with an actual work problem within their professional environments and develop an action plan. According to the International Foundation for Action Learning (http://www.ifal.org.uk/brief.html, [accessed 11 March 2010]), it is based on the radical concept formulated as $L = P + Q$, according to which the learning process (L) is based on programmed knowledge (P) and a questioning insight (Q). This process is reflected in one single activity from the group which integrates:

- research into what is currently incomprehensible and requires resolution
- learning and understanding of any gaps the group has in its own knowledge in specific and relevant areas
- action to resolve the problem.

Action learning can be structured if it takes the form of regular meetings with group members for discussing possible solutions, actions and reflection on the impacts as well as providing feedback from peer observation/monitoring evaluation forms.

4 Project working

Increasingly, managers work in cross-functional teams, exposing them to different functions and enabling them to learn about different aspects of the organisation and ways of doing things. **Project working** is defined as a development process consisting of procedures and methods that guide teams in working effectively throughout an assigned project containing different functions. It aims to develop employees' learning about different aspects of the organisation and enhance their expertise in implementing effective action plans for dealing with difficult issues.

5 Secondments

Taking a role in another organisation through **secondments** for a year or two – or sometimes, in the case of senior people, non-executive directorships – is another way of broadening experience. Secondment is increasingly being recognised as valuable for learning and development. The term refers to a temporary move of one employee to another position and role within the same organisation (or in another organisation) for a year or two. Due to the increasing flexibility in working patterns, sophisticated organisations use this informal learning method as a constructive way of enhancing employees' performance as part of their talent management programmes, and as a strategy of developing employees' skill base in new areas. A secondment is therefore considered to be a career development opportunity which enables the employee/manager to test and apply specific skills in a different organisational environment. (For more benefits of using this method, see also the CIPD factsheet http://www.cipd.co.uk/subjects/lrnanddev/secondment/secondment.htm).

6 Performance and development reviews

Appraisals have been used by many organisations since the 1970s as a means by which managers (usually annually) record the performance and identify the potential and the development needs of their employees. Over the years, the process – which was formerly mainly concentrated on employee performance – has been transformed into a more rounded two-way discussion focusing on the development of the individual. The 'updated' development review enables both the reviewer and the employee to reflect on the performance and the current role, and together to develop action plans.

Most current organisations use a form of performance development review as part of their appraisal process. The **performance and development review** process seeks to relate individual contribution and career aspirations to the achievement of the business vision, aims and objectives. A key part of the performance management process is to enable employees to understand and critically reflect upon their own roles and current performance in relation to the overall strategy of the organisation.

7 360-degree feedback

Because appraisals or performance and development reviews can be conducted only by the line manager and they are based on their own viewpoint on their employees' past performance and potentials within the firm, such reviews are very likely to be perceived as subjective. The process of **360-degree feedback** or 'multi-rater' feedback is a tool that gives an opportunity for the employee to seek peer evaluation from various individuals with whom he or she has direct or indirect contact, such as peers, superiors and subordinates, and who can benefit from his or her services, such as customers and suppliers – based on a framework of competencies. The aim is for the process to provide a more objective evaluation of someone's performance and contribution to the organisation and the department.

8 Development centres

The purpose of **development centres** (sometimes known as assessment centres) is to focus on developing a holistic evaluation of employees' potential and development needs by exploring their personality, intellectual capability, behaviour and life values. Assessment centres and/or development centres can contribute effectively to training and development experience of the employees through work-related activities, role-plays, group work and psychometric assessment.

9 Succession planning

One of the most challenging tasks of the organisation is to identify employees with the right skills to undertake roles and projects that lead to key and top leadership jobs. **Succession planning** is a process by which one or more individuals (successors) are being identified for key jobs within the organisation. This process consists of a very structured career plan designed specifically for the successors, which seeks to provide – through education and other training methods – the necessary level of experience and degree of responsibility required for the targeted senior posts.

Education and training

1 Formal training courses

In large organisations especially, **formal training** is given in the form of various courses and workshops, particularly when it comes to first management jobs and as a precursor to promotion. The content of the courses will be heavily related to the role the individual is to fill, the type and size of the organisation, the resources that are available, the company's finance, and also its business strategy.

In the past, residential courses were used as part of the formal training delivery, but recently and increasingly, modules and/with work-based projects supported by coaching and mentoring are at the heart of formal training provision because they blend theoretical underpinning and practical experience. Such training may moreover be delivered both internally (training experts) or externally (business schools, training consultancies).

2 Management education

One of the most significant features of the past 20 years in the UK has been the growth in management education at university level. According to the CIPD, **management development** covers the entire structured process by which managers learn and improve their skills for the benefit of their employing organisations and themselves. As part of their development process, managers may be asked to attend a formal academic course (for example, MBA, or towards a professional qualification). A specialist business course can help managers to focus on key functions of the business, gain knowledge and critically evaluate the management techniques available, revise their current roles and their relationships with key stakeholders, but particularly to assess global challenges and labour market trends and how these issues affect their individual and organisational performance. These types of courses are undertaken as distance learning or part-time study and are mainly sponsored by the organisations.

3 E-learning and blended learning

Increasingly, organisations are seeking to supplement traditional courses by **e-learning**, which is the use of computers to deliver training, often delivered via corporate intranets.

There is no universally accepted definition of e-learning. For example, Pollard and Hillage (2001) defined e-learning as the delivery and administration of learning opportunities and support via computer, networked and web-based technology to help individual performance and development. The CIPD defined it as learning that is 'delivered, enabled or mediated using electronic technology for the explicit purpose of training in organisations'. The focus of these definitions is on the electronic forms used to deliver or transmit information as part of the knowledge transfer process.

Historically, the predecessor of e-learning was the 'correspondence course' (Stewart and Winter, 1994) or **distance learning** – paper-based learning material that was delivered through the post and that might lead to a professional or academic qualification. Like the correspondence course, e-learning provides large populations with the same material, and access is (even more) flexible so that people can learn in their own time.

Applying theory to practice: Early distance learning

Did you know that the UK's Open University was the world's first successful distance teaching university? Born in the 1960s – the 'white heat of technology' era – the Open University was founded on the belief that communications technology could bring high-quality degree-level learning to people who had not otherwise had the opportunity to attend campus universities.

Visit the OU website http://www.open.ac.uk/about/ou/p3.shtml for a brief overview of its historical development.

As 'distance learning' implies, there is no direct (face-to-face) contact with the provider of learning (trainer or tutor). The support that the student receives is nonetheless comparable with other forms of learning (formal or informal). However, what is important to the effectiveness of e-learning is the quality of electronic methods used (in the actual technology used and the student-friendly accessibility) and the ready availability of paper-based distance learning materials. The latter can be assessed for their effectiveness in terms of presentation (ie quality of paper, font size, colours, graphics, etc.), layout (structure), ease of using (plain English, clear sections, summaries and other supported aids) and interactivity (learner activities and exercises, self-assessment questions and tests and sample answers, recommendations for effective academic writing and language used, reflective summaries, etc) (Stewart, cited in Gold *et al*, 2010).

Against this, e-learning does not appeal to everyone, and it works better for 'hard' knowledge than for softer skills such as communication or leadership. But mixed with other forms of learning (such as 'blended learning', which is defined as the integrated combination of traditional learning with web-based online approaches – Harrison, 2009), it can be a valuable tool.

EVALUATION OF THE LEARNING AND TRAINING PROCESS

It is essential to evaluate the training process in order to assess its effectiveness in producing the desired outcomes as specified for the planned activity. The aim of the evaluation process is to make comparisons between the organisational and individual objectives in relation to the outcomes in order to establish appropriate methods of measuring the results of learning and development activities, and make recommendation on improving the effectiveness of training offered towards employee development. Accordingly, the evaluation process is focused on four main areas: planning, implementation, reactions and outcomes.

Evaluation is traditionally the final stage in a systematic approach aiming to improve performance through formative evaluation or making an assessment about value added and effectiveness (summative evaluation) (Gustafson and Branch, 1997).

Goal-based and **systems-based approaches** are predominantly used in the evaluation of training (Philips, 1991). Various frameworks for the evaluation of learning and development have been developed under the influence of these two approaches. The most influential framework in relation to the first approach has been developed by Kirkpatrick (Carnevale and Schulz, 1990; Dixon, 1996; Gordon, 1991; Philips, 1991, 1997). Kirkpatrick (1959) has attempted to measure the effectiveness of the training process by identifying four levels of evaluation: reaction, learning, behaviour and results (Figure 6.7).

Level 1: *Reaction* – Assess the level of satisfaction (reaction) of those participating in the training process.

Level 2: *Evaluate learning* – Assess the extent to which the objectives have been met by focusing on the application of knowledge, skills development or improvement and behavioural changes towards the organisational standards.

Level 3: *Evaluate behaviour* – Assess the extent to which specific learning objectives relating to the behaviour of the participants have been changed after receiving training.

Level 4: *Evaluate results* – Assess the added value of learning and training programmes against their cost. This is the ultimate level of evaluation based on the pre-training and post-training monitoring in order to measure the initial objectives in relation to the training outcomes.

A goal-based model such as Kirkpatrick's four levels may help managers and business consultants focus on the purpose of the evaluation, which could range from purely technical to more strategic. However, this model does not define the steps necessary to achieve goals and does not address the ways to utilise results to improve training (Eseryel, 2002). Nowadays, many organisations do not use this model exclusively – they usually utilise only Level 1 (reaction) and Level 2 (learning) because more complexities occur at the higher levels which this model is inadequate to deal with.

Figure 6.7 Evaluation of the training process

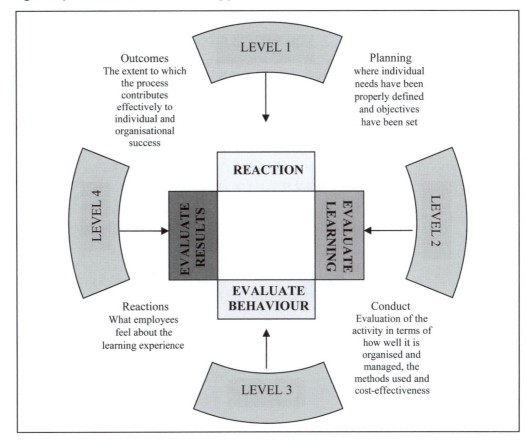

On the other hand, the systems approach seems to be more useful in terms of thinking about the context, the current situation and the identified planning, design and implementation of the programme as well as the measurement of the results. The most influential models include: the Context, Input, Process, Product (CIPP) model (Worthen and Sanders, 1987); the Training Validation System (TVS) approach (Fitz-Enz, 1994); and the Input, Process, Output, Outcome (IPO) model (Bushnell, 1990).

A key limitation of using the systematic approach is that it may not provide sufficient analysis of the dynamic interactions between the design and the evaluation of training. Few of the aforementioned models provide detailed descriptions or evaluation of the processes involved in each step. Furthermore, these models do not address the dynamic process of evaluation in relation to various interactions among people with different roles and responsibilities (Eseryel, 2002).

Future research should be focused on the existing barriers of training evaluation – how it is being integrated with the training design, how human relationships (collaborative processes) are managed during the evaluation process, and how they may be supported in terms of resources and time allocation. This will be helpful in assessing effectively the learning and development programmes in relation to current and future employee performance and organisational success.

Conclusion

Learning is complex. An aim of this chapter is to understand the various learning theories and their application to the design and delivery of training at the workplace. More often than not,

HR professionals have placed too much emphasis and reliance on training for training's sake, resulting in badly designed and delivered training, or based on the faulty diagnosis of training needs. One caveat to consider regarding learning theories is that they are not infallible. Few, if any, of the learning style questionnaires can measure an individual with complete accuracy. Furthermore, categorising and tracking learners by any category tends to stigmatise and stereotype learners, placing them in a box where they are prevented from developing to their full potential. Hence, if training is seen only in terms of models, theories, procedures, budgets, activities and roles, it will continue to disappoint and fail to deliver. In the corporate workplace, a 'one size fits all' approach might seem efficient in training delivery, but a tailored approach, while more costly, might be the key to winning the competitive edge.

E-learning, considered on its own, is ideal for the economics of tailored training if the learner's preferred style is known.

While there is too often a pressure to deliver measurable results of training, it is important to remind ourselves that even if training is at the heart of the organisation, people are the heart of training.

End notes

[1] See also Chapter 3.

[2] See also Chapter 3.

[3] See also Chapter 3.

REVIEW AND DISCUSSION QUESTIONS

REVIEW QUESTIONS

1 Why is learning important at work? What are the differences between learning and training?

2 What are the main characteristics of different learning approaches?

3 What are the stages of Kolb's learning styles? Please provide examples for each type.

4 What are the key differences between informal and formal learning?

5 What is the systematic approach to learning? Can you identify the main benefits for the organisation?

DISCUSSION QUESTIONS

1 How do you usually learn? Which learning style best describes your own preference? How can you *manage* your learning process once you know the different types of learning styles?

2 How would you develop training events based on different learning styles, in particular dealing with a diverse workforce from different backgrounds and nationalities?

3 How can training needs be analysed?

4 How will your learning at university be transferred to work?

5 What methods can you employ to motivate employees with different personalities and backgrounds to learn in the workplace?

FURTHER READING

Allinson, C. W. and Hayes, J. (2000) 'Cross-national differences in cognitive style: implications for management', *International Journal of Human Resource Management*, Vol.11, No.1: 161–70. This paper analyses the cross-cultural differences in learning styles based on the instrument of the Cognitive Style Index designed and proposed by the authors. The findings shed light on the implications for management.

Coffield, F., Moseley, D., Hall, E. and Ecclestone, K. (2004) *Learning Styles and Pedagogy in Post-16 Learning: A systematic and critical review*. London: Learning and Skills Research Centre. This report provides a systematic and historical review of the development of learning style theories and instruments.

Riding, R. and Rayner, S. (2002) *Cognitive Styles and Learning Strategies: Understanding style differences in learning and behaviour*, 5th edition. London: David Fulton. This text provides an analysis of managing diversity in education with a specific focus on individual differences in teaching, learning and special educational management.

CIPD Press Office [no date] http://www.cipd.co.uk/pressoffice/_articles/learning_ 100407pr.htm?IsSrchRes=1 This CIPD research reveals that many line managers are failing to support learning and development needs.

Buckley, R. and Caple, J. (1995) *The Theory and Practice of Training*. London: Kogan Page. This book provides a basic model of a systematic approach to training. It evaluates a structured approach with logical coherence which helps the learner ensure that his or her needs are effectively met.

Institute of Continuing Professional Development (2005) *Regulation Competencies: Is CPD working?* Research project. London: CPD Institute. Avaliable online at http://www.cpdinstitute.org/ storage/pdfs/CPD_research.pdf This interesting research was intended to examine and critique how CPD is being implemented within 23 professions across nine different sectors, and to assess how far these practices meet the changing expectations of both the professionals and the public alike.

 ## KEY SKILLS

DEVELOPING CRITICAL THINKING SKILLS AND REFLECTIVE LEARNING

By analysing the theories of learning and methods of learning and development this chapter tries to provide an insight to the kind of thinking that you should develop, which seeks to explore questions about existing knowledge on issues which are not clearly defined and for which there are no clear-cut answers. For example, as an HR manager you have to be able to provide support for your employees regarding their continuing personal and professional development. However, the degree to which you demonstrate this skill and service to your employees is dependent on the nature of the organisation and the resources (human and financial) that are involved in this process. But most importantly, you have to take into consideration the nature and context of self-development, which is different for different people and may in any case be restricted to specific roles and professional categories. It is essential for a good manager therefore to develop a critical appreciation of the principles of identifying and assessing the challenges involved in personal and professional development and reflective practice, and accordingly endeavour to be flexible (and, if possible, cost- and time-effective as well) when designing and implementing informal or formal ways of training and development for your targeted employees.

TEAMWORKING AND TEAM-BUILDING SKILLS

Teamworking and team-building skills are critical for your effectiveness as a manager, and even if you are not in a management or leadership role a better appreciation of group needs or understanding of teamwork can make you a more effective employee/colleague in that you could develop a strong synergy of individual contributions by taking into consideration individual needs and personalities, harmony in relationships among members, good communication channels and mutual collaborations/agreements regarding group goals and the allocation of roles.

PERSONAL DEVELOPMENT PLANNING

Personal development planning is a structural way of thinking about and planning for your future. This developmental process is twofold. Through informal and formal methods of learning, training and development it will help you to reflect first on your own personal aspirations (What do I want to achieve in life? What kind of person would I like to become?), and secondly on your future career (What are my personal goals and ambitions? What steps do I need to take in order to be successful in my role?). The advantage of adopting the personal development planning approach in your studies or work is that it increases your motivation by enabling you to a) gain a clear focus on your learning experience through developing a positive attitude and strategy for being successful in life; b) identify and discuss your development needs, skills acquisition, and training opportunities with your tutor or line manager; and c) boost your confidence about your qualities and capabilities and to explore your potential in both the short and the long term.

KEY SKILLS NEXT

PROFESSIONAL JUDGEMENT, DECISION-MAKING, PROBLEM-SOLVING AND SOCIAL RESPONSIBILITY

If you develop this key skill, you will be able to demonstrate an understanding of types of learning theories, professional knowledge and experience by using a systematic approach to your learning, training and development. More specifically, through this approach you will be able to describe key issues and criteria, identify key problems raised in your immediate environment, design frameworks to identify and analyse important information, seek support from senior colleagues and with their help develop an action plan to support learning and development. The synergy that emerges through collaboration constitutes an effective way by which a learning environment is built up through the effective interactions of individuals as an essential part of knowledge transfer. In this way it should be possible to engender a sense of social responsibility for all stakeholders (you, other students, tutors, colleagues, employers, customers, etc) who can benefit from the university's/organisation's services and actions through its people.

EMOTIONAL INTELLIGENCE, EMPATHY, SYMPATHY AND LISTENING

Within our social environments (university, businesses) we need to be more effective communicators to be successful in business and in our personal lives. The true basis of effective communication, relationships and understanding is empathy, sympathy and listening. These skills are vital for what we call emotional intelligence – the level of understanding that we can develop regarding other people, needs, wants and behaviours. HR and line managers are very likely to use these skills because they are in direct contact with their employees on a daily basis and as part of

their role are expected to provide emotional and technical support for the employees in order to facilitate their work. It is therefore essential to learn how to collaborate with others, to be able to appreciate their needs and aspirations, and to contribute effectively towards the successful implementation of their action plans.

LEADERSHIP: COACHING AND MENTORING

The key to leadership effectiveness today generally corresponds to the power of coaching and mentoring to lead individuals and teams to personal and organisational success. Through effective coaching techniques you can gain the loyalty and trust of others by making them feel valued by the team, and boost their self-confidence by letting them know that their actions and behaviour are appreciated and rewarding them accordingly. Effective mentoring is also important for leadership success because it helps you to identify your best potential and start investing in them for successful careers within the organisation. It is fair to say, then, that through acquiring this skill you will thus be able to identify the capabilities and merits of others, and by providing the appropriate support and encouragement you will help them – or help you (depending on your role) – develop an effective professional action plan.

NEGOTIATING, ARBITRATION AND CONFLICT RESOLUTION SKILLS

These skills may be required in any of a variety of forms, including efforts to address the difficulties of dealing with problematic collaborations and group conflicts at university or in the workplace; integrating conflict resolution ideas into your university experience; using role-play and good example practices to persuade other friends or colleagues to learn skills; identifying practical and effective responses to deal with personal animosities; and arranging for other individuals to act as mediators with their peers.

Ethical implications: Ethics and diversity

Working and managing relationships in a multicultural and international business environment is one of the most challenging issues that an effective manager may have to deal with on a daily basis, especially when asked to monitor employees' performance and/or to perform the role of mentor or coach for a group of employees. The different learning styles of people, cultures, and genders can affect the interpretation of behaviour in a negative way. Some might not respond positively to constructive feedback from a mentor or coach, and may even reject support offered in respect of continuous professional development. For example, a female

employee may feel uncomfortable when a senior manager asks her as part of a mentoring meeting to discuss her family commitments and how they might be affecting her professional development. Moreover, the extent to which individuals from different gender and/or cultural backgrounds appreciate the importance of key values within their professional relationships – such as honesty (transparency and integrity), respect, fairness, dignity, trust and confidentiality – depends primarily on the organisational culture and how effectively and ethically these values are demonstrated by its managing team in all their business dealings.

BEST PRACTICE

A systematic training and development approach should be focused on a variety of interactive learning methods and learning materials. Skills associated with facilitating the learning of groups and individuals are:

- creating appropriate and effective learning climates
- giving and receiving feedback
- providing one-to-one coaching and mentoring
- the use of a range of presentational and instructional skills
- supporting the learning of groups and individuals through blended learning and the use of technology.

The training intervention and all associated learning materials should be designed, developed and put into commission by using a systematic approach that is related to the identification of needs, and to the desired performance and actual performance of the individual.

An HR professional should act ethically and professionally with a strong commitment to retain equality and fairness in the design, formulation and delivery of learning and development within his or her organisation, and a commitment also to ensure the continuous personal and professional development of the workforce.

WORST PRACTICE

Indications of worst practice include:

- no consideration of individual differences in learning style
- a lack of consideration for the link between learning style and training design
- no enquiry addressed to all the different stakeholders in analysing training needs
- a lack of any formal approach in designing training delivery.

PART TWO

Groups and Teams

Chapter 7
Work Groups and Teams

Michael A. West and Joanne Richardson

Contents

Key Learning Outcomes

By the end of this chapter you should be able to:

- understand why team-based working is becoming increasingly prevalent in today's organisations
- define what a real work team is, and how it differs from other types of groups in organisations
- appreciate what the benefits of effective teamworking are, based on findings from the research literature
- understand the input factors influencing the effectiveness of teams
- understand the processes that affect the relationships between team inputs and team outputs
- recognise the distinct aspects of team effectiveness.

PRACTITIONER INSIGHT

Aston Business School

In 2007 a new **Executive Dean, Professor Michael West**, took over the leadership of **Aston Business School**. His aim was to bring renewed vigour and ambition to what the school could achieve. His vision was to make Aston Business School one of the most inspiring and innovative business schools in Europe, a world-class research centre, and one of the top three business schools in the UK. Underpinning this vision was a mission statement which focused on the provision of excellent learning and teaching, the generation of high-quality rigorous research, and a concentration on business partnerships. As part of the new mission, Michael wanted to ensure that Aston Business School was committed to developing and sustaining a community in which staff and students worked together in a motivating and supportive team-based environment. We spoke to Michael about how he worked to create and sustain effective teamwork in the Aston Business School management team.

Teamworking was at the heart of the future work design and structure of Aston Business School. Some staff within the school already worked in teams and had done so for many years. However, others were more accustomed to working on an individual basis, and the prospect of carrying out their work as part of a team was daunting for a number of them. In taking over as Executive Dean, Michael's first challenge was therefore to ensure that effective teamwork was successfully modelled and advocated by the school management team. In the first instance a new school management team had to be put together, working towards a new set of organisational objectives.

This involved selecting the right team members who had the appropriate knowledge, skills and abilities to bring to the school

management team. The task of the team was to ensure that all parts of the business school operated effectively and were working towards the achievement of the business school's mission. Given that the school was made up of five academic groups, a wide array of undergraduate and postgraduate teaching programmes, as well as a number of research centres, Michael recognised that a range of stakeholders were needed in the team. The team would therefore require input from a wide range of functions, including the teaching programmes, research centres, executive development, marketing, and staff management.

How would you recommend that Michael should go about designing the team itself and selecting the right members? Give some examples of what this team might look like and who these team members might be.

Once the school management team had been formed, Michael needed to ensure that the team would operate effectively, and therefore reflect the mission of the business school to create a collaborative team-based environment. This meant thinking about how certain team processes could be encouraged, and how others could be avoided.

Give some suggestions about which team processes you think are most important for the school management team to engage in, and how these might be facilitated. Further, which team processes are less likely to lead to effective outcomes, and how could Michael ensure that such processes are avoided or managed properly?

Once you have read this chapter, return to these questions and think about how you could answer them.

Introduction

Over the past 30 years, work groups and teams have become increasingly common in the workplace. Indeed, over the course of our working lives, most of us will at some point belong to one or more work teams in the workplace. According to Kozlowski and Bell (2003), team-based designs are becoming the 'norm' in many of today's organisations. In turn, traditional hierarchical structures have been seen to become inadequate, with many companies downsizing and de-layering to more team-based designs. But what exactly is **team-based working**?

Team-based working reflects the belief that by organising work in a way which formally optimises collaborative opportunity and capability, superior individual and organisational outputs can be achieved. West and Markiewicz (2004) describe team-based working as an approach to organisational design whereby decisions are made by teams of people rather than individuals, and at the closest possible point to the customer or client. The core building blocks of team-based organisations are teams; teams lead one another and form the basic units of accountability and work (Harris and Beyerlien, 2003). Management scholars have noted the widespread trend towards team-based structures (eg Muthusamy, Wheeler, and Simmons, 2005; Sundstrom *et al*, 2000), recent research reporting that 81% of manufacturing organisations and 79% of *Fortune* 1,000 companies are now using self-managed work teams (Thoms *et al*, 2002). So how can we explain the increasing popularity of teams in organisations?

To address this question it is first worth thinking about the type of tasks that organisations typically carry out in order to deliver products or services. Given the increasingly competitive climate in which today's organisations operate, the need to meet challenging demands under tight deadlines is paramount to their survival. Many of the tasks that organisations carry out are simply too large, complex and multifaceted to assign to a single individual working alone. For example, think about the work of an airline pilot, a surgeon, a professional cricketer or a front-line soldier fighting in combat. None of these individuals can successfully achieve his or her assigned tasks without the synchronised actions and collaborative efforts of the group of people surrounding them. The surgeon, for example, cannot begin a complicated heart operation without the help of an anaesthetist to administer the correct amount of anaesthetic and keep the patient stable throughout the surgery, a surgical assistant to hand over the correct apparatus at the appropriate time, or a recovery nurse to monitor the patient after the surgery and ensure that they remain comfortable. Such a demanding and complicated task requires a team of people with different skills to work co-operatively together, relying on one another to make effective and timely contributions towards the achievement of an overall shared goal. Quite simply, members of work groups and teams *need* each other.

This notion of interdependence is a critical concept when thinking about work groups and teams, and is discussed in more detail later in this chapter.

Beyond task complexity, there are also many other intuitively appealing reasons why organisations choose team-based designs. In a large-scale review of the research literature, Cohen and Bailey (1997) propose that there are a number of important reasons for implementing team-based working, including the following:

- Teams enable organisations to *develop and deliver products and services in a speedy and cost-effective manner*. Rather than working in an isolated and sequential fashion, team members can work interdependently and in parallel with one another, allowing for a more efficient and timely outcome.

- Teams are the best way to *endorse organisational strategy.* Rather than waiting for decisions to be made by senior management, teams with autonomy at a local level can respond more quickly and effectively to problems in the fast-changing environments encountered by most organisaitons.

- Teams enable organisations to *learn more effectively and retain this learning for longer periods of time.* Members of teams can learn from one another while working together, and pass on this knowledge to new team members. So when someone leaves an organisation, their knowledge is not lost.

- Teams promote *creativity and innovation* through the exchange of ideas and divergent perspectives between team members (West, Tjosvold, and Smith, 2003).

Research evidence supporting these arguments is discussed later in this chapter (see the section *Why work in teams?*). However, before this, it is important to define what we mean when we talk about work groups and teams, and why such clarity is important.

DEFINING WORK GROUPS AND TEAMS

Over the years, various attempts have been made to define work groups and teams (eg Alderfer, 1977; Guzzo and Dickson, 1996; Hackman, 1987; Hollenbeck *et al*, 1995). Some researchers have also gone to great lengths to distinguish between the terms 'work group' and 'team' (eg Katzenbach and Smith, 1998), while others use the terms interchangeably (eg Guzzo and Dickson, 1996) to refer to the same thing. In this chapter, we follow the later style.

A well-known and frequently cited definition of a team was provided by Kozlowski and Bell (2003: 334):

> Work teams and groups are composed of two or more individuals who exist to perform organisationally relevant tasks, share one or more common goals, interact socially, exhibit task interdependencies, maintain and manage boundaries, and are embedded in an organisational context that sets boundaries, constrains the team, and influences exchanges with other units in the broader entity.

Kozlowski and Bell's (2003) definition takes an organisational-level perspective, focusing on how a team interacts with, and is influenced by, external factors within the wider system. Considering the impact that the wider environment has on team functioning, and how teams interact with one another in multi-team systems (Marks *et al*, 2005) is becoming increasingly important in the team research literature.

Two other important characteristics for conceptualising teams can also be drawn from the definition above. Firstly, a team shares a number of *common objectives*. For example, think of a **multi-disciplinary team** of breast cancer care professionals. Despite performing different roles in the delivery of healthcare, they all share the common objective of working together to correctly diagnose and effectively treat a woman who is showing symptoms. The tasks that teams carry out should also be *interdependent*. For example, think of a Champions' League football team, working in a second leg match together to overcome a 1-0 defeat from the first leg. Although a striker may score the equalising goal, he relies on the midfielders to pass him the ball, who in turn depend on the defenders to challenge the opposition and protect their own goal. The overall performance of the team depends on the extent to which team members successfully interact, co-operate and anticipate each other's actions. Both of these important team characteristics are revisited in more detail later in this chapter.

The difference between 'real' and 'pseudo' teams

The trend towards team-based working has meant that the 'team' label has become intuitively appealing in organisations, given the general premise that teamworking will generate superior outcomes. Over the past 30 years, the discourse of 'teams' has become increasingly pervasive in organisational life (Learmonth, 2009). Managers generously assign the term to all sorts of collectives of individuals, with the assumption that just by doing so, superior outcomes will be generated. However, this can be problematic for organisations because despite the various definitions in the literature, in reality people have very different things in mind when they talk about teams (Hackman, 2002). Often people report that they are part of a team when they are merely working in close proximity to other people and have the same supervisor. What represents a team in one organisation can therefore be very different from that in another.

So what specific criteria distinguish a well-structured real team from a group of employees who report that they work as a team, but are in fact, only a team by name? Such groups have previously been identified as '**pseudo teams**' (Katzenbach and Smith, 1998; Dawson, Yan and West, 2008) or 'co-acting groups' (Hackman, 2002) and represent collectives of individuals that are characterised by incomplete or dysfunctional aspects of teamworking. **Real teams** are more than simply a collection of individuals co-acting with one another (Paris *et al*, 2000; Hackman, 2002). A 'real team' can be defined as:

> A group of people working together in an organisation who are recognised as a team; who are committed to achieving clear team-level objectives upon which they agree; who have to work closely and interdependently in order to achieve these objectives; whose members are clear about their roles within the team and have the necessary autonomy to decide how to carry out team tasks; and who communicate regularly as a team in order to reflect upon the team's effectiveness and how it could be improved.

Unpacking this definition, we can see that a 'real team' is one in which team members work closely and interdependently together towards clear, shared objectives which team members agree upon and are committed to. Real teams engage in regular self-regulation, usually during team meetings, in which they reflect upon their effectiveness and how this could be improved upon in future. They also have a degree of autonomy to manage their own work processes, and therefore implement changes to improve their performance. Further, real teams are recognised as 'teams' by the wider organisation, whereby it is clear who belongs to the team and who does not. Finally, team members are clear about what their role is in the team, as well as the roles of other team members. As with Kozlowski and Bell's team definition earlier, this definition also refers to the key characteristics of shared objectives and interdependence. Other 'real team' characteristics provided here include autonomy, reflexivity, boundedness and roles (Richardson, West and Dawson, 2008), all of which are discussed in later sections of this chapter. These characteristics all apply to different teams to differing extents, depending on the type of task they are doing as well as on external factors in the wider organisational environment.

What is most important is that team-based organisations comprise real teams. Research evidence from the UK National Health Service (NHS) suggests that individuals working in pseudo teams (whereby they report that they work in a team but the team does not have clear objectives and interdependence, and does not reflect upon team effectiveness) were likely to report lower levels of safety at work, and were more likely to suffer from poor psychological well-being than those not working in a team at all. It appears that not only are psuedo teams less effective at minimising workplace errors and improving safety in healthcare delivery, they are also more likely to experience low levels of satisfaction and well-being (Dawson, Yan and West, 2008). Conversely, individuals who did report working in real teams were more likely to benefit from greater psychological well-being. So if team-based working is to truly deliver the intuitively appealing promises it offers, it is critical that teams are 'real teams' and are characterised by the dimensions noted above.

Finally, when defining teams, the issue of team size must be considered. Kozlowski and Bell's (2003) definition suggests that teams must comprise at least two members. But how big should a team be? Researchers have offered various recommendations concerning the best size of team. For example, Scharf (1989) suggests that seven is the best size, whereas Katzenbach and Smith (1998) argue that teams should contain a dozen or so members. Indeed, some research has suggested that team effectiveness has a curvilinear relationship with team size, whereby too few or too many members can impede performance (Nieva, Fleishman and Reick, 1985), whereas other research has found that increasing size leads to improved performance indefinitely (Campion, Medsker and Higgs, 1993), or no relationship between team size and performance at all (Martz, Vogel and Nunamaker, 1992). Theories of group dynamics also point to the danger of the occurrence of 'process losses' in teams that have too many members, in which individual performance may decrease due to psychological phenomena such as social loafing, conformity or diffusion of responsibility. Overall, optimal team size is very much contingent on both the nature of the team task itself, and the boundaries imposed on the team by the external environment (Kozlowski and Bell, 2003).

Typologies of teams

Although a number of generic characteristics can apply (to greater or lesser extents) to all work groups and teams in organisations (eg common objectives, interdependency), teams can differ considerably in terms of what they do. Key dimensions upon which teams can differ include:

- *temporal duration* – Some teams may just work together for a few hours (eg surgical teams), whereas others have a clearly defined lifetime (eg an architect team working on restoring a building for six months) or may exist for many years, yet might only meet on a monthly basis (eg a board of directors).

- *physical proximity* – Some teams work together on a frequent face-to-face basis with high levels of physical interaction (eg a football team), whereas others may exist on a geographically dispersed virtual basis, relying on electronic means of communication and never actually coming together on a physical basis (eg an international team of academics working on a cross-cultural study).

- *task routineness* – Some teams perform highly routine and standardised tasks (eg assembly teams in a toy factory), whereas other teams must carry out highly strategic and ambiguous tasks (eg the Copenhagen Climate Council trying to set policies on carbon emissions for the next 20 years).

- *autonomy over work practices* – Whereas teams manufacturing cereal packaging might have little influence over how they carry out their tasks, top management teams typically have a high degree of control and discretion over decisions relating to their work.

- *reliance on technology* – Medical teams carrying out keyhole surgery, or design teams trying to develop a new keypad for a mobile phone, rely heavily on computer-aided technology, whereas sports or negotiation teams have low levels of dependence on such hardware.

As can be seen, there are multiple ways in which teams can differ in organisations. Over the years, a number of team researchers have proposed taxonomies or classification frameworks for organising different types of teams (eg Devine, 2002; Sundstrom, De Meuse and Futrell, 1990). Some of the most common team typologies used by researchers today, along with real-world examples, include:

- *production teams* – eg assembly teams in a car manufacturing plant; production process teams in a chocolate factory; teams in a printing firm producing thousands of copies of tomorrow's newspaper

- *service teams* – eg engineering teams that service boilers in hospitals; a hospitality team serving dinner at a wedding reception; advice centre teams for a financial services agency

- *project and development teams* – eg creative design teams in an advertising agency; a research team within a university; a software development team for a computer company

- *negotiation teams* – eg an international treaty team trying to agree about levels of nuclear arms ownership; a labour-management team in which trade union representatives negotiate pay rises with employers

- *action and performing teams* – eg cricket teams; a string quartet; an emergency response team; a famous hip-hop group performing live concerts across the world

- *strategy and policy teams* – eg a university committee setting standards on future research budgets; the United Nations Security Council drawing up new policies relating to international terrorist threats; a senior management strategy team making decisions about when to implement new products or services.

Tasks for teams

Teams need 'teamwork' (Hackman, 2002) – that is, work designed for a team. There is no point assigning a team with a task that could be just as easily completed by individuals working alone. The tasks that teams carry out should be those that are best performed by a team. The main factor that determines whether a team is required to perform a task is the degree of *task interdependence.*

Interdependence is the extent to which members of a team must work interactively and co-operatively in order to successfully complete a task (Stewart and Barrick, 2000). Under conditions of no interdependence, a task can be completed entirely by one individual. When the level of task interdependence is low, the need for team members to interact with one another in order to attain their goals is also low; consequently, teamwork behaviours such as communication and information sharing are required to a lesser extent. However, when task interdependence is high, the team's work must be arranged so that team members co-ordinate their efforts, interact frequently and closely and exchange resources in order to accomplish their task. Further, throughout the period of the task, activities and sub-tasks must constantly flow between team members in a back-and-forth manner. The extent of task interdependence typically increases when tasks themselves become more difficult. Teams can also be interdependent in terms of their goals and outcomes.

For example, think of a team of students who are working together on a business game simulation. The team will have to share and combine their individual knowledge, skills and abilities in order to successfully complete the multiple interdependent assignments that the task demands (eg financial calculations, marketing tasks, production output, human resource decisions). Given that the success of each sub-task is dependent on the completion of the others, the team is also likely to share a number of interdependent goals (for example, to gain competitive advantage or to be the most successful team). As a team, members are also likely to reap shared outcomes (for example, to receive collective feedback about the team's overall performance on the task, or be rewarded *as a team* with a high grade). Task, goal and outcome interdependence will therefore tend collectively to influence the extent to which team members must work together to perform effectively. When interdependence is high, a team will experience a shared sense of fate and will therefore 'sink or swim' together.

THE ORIGINS OF TEAMWORK

As already noted, teams represent the dominant work form in today's organisations. The theoretical rationale for team-based working is discussed later. A brief history of the study of groups and teams is first provided.

Teamworking is not a new concept. For thousands of years, humans have lived and worked together forming socially structured stable groups. Such tendencies have a clear evolutionary basis, given the survival benefits that groups could offer in prehistoric times, such as protection from predators, hunting food and the sharing of resources. As humans, we have an innate need for belonging and acceptance (Baumeister and Leary, 1995). Our social identity is largely formed through the groups to which we belong. This evolutionary perspective may explain why people who work in teams within their organisations often report higher levels of job satisfaction, learning and well-being than those who work alone.

Despite the historic origins of teamwork, scientific research into the area only began in the late 1930s when the Australian organisation theorist George Elton Mayo (1880–1949) carried out a series of research studies at a Chicago electrical company which were subsequently termed the 'Hawthorne studies'. The initial aim of Mayo's research team was to investigate the impact that physical working conditions have on employee productivity (Mayo, 1993). However, his observations revealed far more interesting results which have had a profound influence on the study of groups and teams ever since. The main findings from the Hawthorne studies revealed that:

- Work is typically viewed as a group activity rather than something to be done alone.

- Workplace interactions have an influential impact on much of our adult social life.

- Recognition, a sense of belonging, and security are more important than the physical conditions within which an employee works.

- By providing a team of employees with support and attention, and allowing them to participate in decisions, motivation and subsequent performance are likely to increase: this has become termed the 'Hawthorne effect'.

Findings from the Hawthorne studies gave rise to a new school of management known as the Human Relations movement, which has become the main subject in Organisational Behaviour.

THE EVIDENCE FOR TEAMWORK

There is a common belief that through combining the efforts of individuals within a team, the aggregates of individuals' contributions will be surpassed (West, Borrill and Unsworth, 1998). As was outlined at the beginning of this chapter, team researchers have proposed a number of reasons why organisations can benefit from being structured in teams (see Cohen and Bailey, 1997). Guzzo and Salas (1995) propose that the increase in team-based working relates to intended improvements in organisational productivity, customer service and an eventual beneficial impact on the bottom line. West and Markiewicz (2004) also argue that team-based working affords a number of primary benefits for organisations including:

- efficient processes

- flexible response to change

- improved effectiveness

- reduced costs

- increased innovation

- effective partnering

- customer involvement

- employee commitment and well-being

- skill utilisation.

But what research evidence is available to support such claims? In a recent review by Delarue and colleagues (2008), clear associations between teamworking and various important outcomes were drawn. These outcomes included worker outcomes, financial outcomes and operational outcomes, each of which is examined in more detail below.

Worker outcomes

As we noted earlier on in this chapter, working in groups is a fundamental human social behaviour and is basic to our species. So what evidence is there to demonstrate that people who work in teams are happier than those who work alone?

A number of studies have demonstrated that overall, the impact of teamworking on employee behaviour (such as absenteeism and turnover) and employee attitudes (such as engagement and motivation) is largely positive. For example, in a questionnaire of Canadian employees, Godard (2001) found that team-based working was positively related to job satisfaction, a sense of belonging, feelings of empowerment, and organisational citizenship behaviour. Other researchers have also found an association between teamworking and organisational commitment and job satisfaction (Batt, 2004; Batt and Appelbaum, 1995; Elmuti, 1997), as well as reduced absenteeism (Delarue *et al*, 2004) and lower employee turnover (Glassop, 2002). Overall, it appears that employees' experiences of the workplace are far more favourable when they belong to an effective work team.

Financial outcomes

Various studies have shown that teamworking is associated with greater financial performance, which is arguably the most convincing case for making the investment to implement team-based working in a profit-making organisation.

In a recent study, Barrick and colleagues (2007) reported that communication and cohesion among members of credit union top-management teams positively impacted the firm's financial ratios. Cooke (1994) also demonstrated that the introduction of teamwork had a significant effect on value added per employee. In a study of German organisations, economic value added significantly improved after the introduction of shopfloor participation involving teamwork (Zwick, 2004). And finally, in a valuable meta-analysis of 131 studies on organisational change, Macy and Izumi (1993) concluded that interventions with the best effects upon financial performance measures related to team development interventions and the creation of autonomous work groups.

Operational outcomes

Another important argument frequently cited for teamworking is increases in organisational efficiency, productivity and quality, given that team outcomes are believed to surpass the aggregates of individual efforts.

Research to support such claims was carried out by Levine and D'Andrea-Tyson (1990), who demonstrated that participation via teamworking leads to sustained increases in organisational productivity. Cohen, Ledford and Spreitzer (1996) also reported that teams which facilitate high levels of employee involvement have a significant impact on both efficiency and quality. Similarly, in a review of a large number of studies, Appelbaum and Batt (1994) concluded that team-based working can predict improvements in organisational performance, in terms of both efficiency and quality. In a subsequent study, the relationship between teamwork and improved quality is further confirmed (Batt and Appelbaum, 1995). The positive effects of teamwork on productivity have also been shown in a wide variety of organisational settings including the Australian economy (Glassop, 2002) and US steel mills (Boning, Ichniowski and Shaw, 2001).

Summary

Overall, evidence largely supports a positive case for team-based working. However, as was noted earlier in this chapter, the popularity of 'teams' and beliefs about what they can achieve has resulted in a very large influx of organisations restructuring into team-based structures. Yet depending on the tasks they carry out, not all organisations are suitable for team-based working. Furthermore, not all team-based organisations comprise work teams that are actually *real* and *effective.* If teamworking is not implemented and managed properly, there is a danger that our workplaces will be inhabited with 'pseudo' teams which have been shown to have potentially detrimental outcomes (Dawson, Yan and West, 2008). The aim of the next section is to understand how such circumstances can be avoided, in order to create environments in which the true benefits of teamworking can be achieved.

CREATING AND MAINTAINING EFFECTIVE TEAMS

Research into team effectiveness has commonly followed the input-process-output model (I-P-O; see Figure 7.1), a framework originally proposed by McGrath (1964) over 40 years ago. Many researchers have adopted this model for conceptualising teams, the general premise being that inputs affect outputs via the interaction that takes place during team processes. Thus interactions between team members (team processes) will influence input-output relationships (Hackman, 1986). More recently, researchers have extended and adapted traditional I-P-O models into more sophisticated representations, examples of which can be found in a comprehensive review of team research by Mathieu and colleagues (2008). However, here we present a traditional I-P-O consisting of the most important inputs, processes and outputs needed for developing and maintaining real and effective teams. Although it is arguable that such a simple two-dimensional model is insufficient for capturing the true complexities of real-world teams working in demanding and multifaceted environments, the model provides a useful framework for identifying the fundamental principles of effective teamwork.

Inputs [1]

Task design

The design of a team task is an important input for shaping how a team must work together, including what team member roles are needed, how workflow must be patterned, what sort of shared goals are established. Overall, the design of the task will determine, to a large extent, the general nature of team member interactions (Kozlowski and Ilgen, 2006). As we have already noted, the need for teamworking is very much dependent on the type of task a team is assigned. The task must best be achieved by a group of people working together, as opposed to individuals working alone. The task itself must therefore be sufficiently demanding and complex that it is best achieved by a team. This implies a high level of task interdependence (see the *Tasks for teams* section).

Further, in designing the team's task, a number of dimensions from Hackman and Oldham's (1976) Job Characteristics model are important to consider (see Chapter 14 for a full description),

Figure 7.1   An input-process-output model of team effectiveness

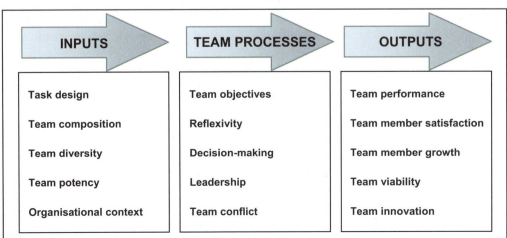

INPUTS	TEAM PROCESSES	OUTPUTS
Task design	Team objectives	Team performance
Team composition	Reflexivity	Team member satisfaction
Team diversity	Decision-making	Team member growth
Team potency	Leadership	Team viability
Organisational context	Team conflict	Team innovation

all of which can be applied to the team level. 'Task identity' implies that teams should be assigned complete tasks, which team members can see through from beginning to end. Providing a team with a complete task allows team members to identify more closely with the work they do, allowing them the opportunity to take ownership of the task and fully engage with it throughout the entire process.

Secondly, 'autonomy' suggests that teams should have a degree of control and discretion in deciding how to carry out their work. This dimension was also a key characteristic of 'real teams', as described earlier on in this chapter. Teams that have the opportunity to determine their own goals and decide how to execute their task will experience a higher level of internal motivation and determination (Spreitzer, 1995). Empowering teams to decide on their own course of action also means that decisions are made and implemented at the local level far more quickly, rather than waiting for senior management (who are typically removed from the day-to-day processes of the team) to make such decisions for the team.

Finally, the core job characteristic of *feedback* also has implications for how best to design a team task. It is important that a team receives regular, clear, timely and constructive feedback on their performance. Such feedback provides teams with information about the extent to which they have achieved their shared goals, and gives an indication of how they could improve their effectiveness in future. It is important that feedback is provided as soon as possible after performance, in order to ensure that it is still relevant to the team's current task and can have an optimal impact on the motivation and commitment of team members.

Team composition

Team composition is a second important input which influences team effectiveness. When selecting individuals to comprise a team it is critical to ensure that the team will possess the right knowledge, skills and abilities (KSAs) relevant for their specific task. For example, an airline crew will need a pilot to ensure that the aircraft safely reaches its destination, a co-pilot to provide technical support, communicate with air traffic control and monitor weather conditions, and a group of cabin crew members to provide a complete passenger service, ensuring safety, providing refreshments and managing difficult passengers. Each team member will bring different skills, knowledge and experience to the team, depending on their training and backgrounds. Without such a varied skill set, the team would not be able to complete its task. Teamworking not only provides the opportunity for team members to combine their range of KSAs in a collaborative manner, but also allows team members to learn from one another during the process.

Personality is also an important variable to consider in team composition. As is outlined in Chapter 3, mental ability and personality traits such as conscientiousness have been shown to predict job performance. It is therefore conceivable that a mix of different personalities within a team will also impact upon team effectiveness. Belbin's Team Roles model predicts just that. Belbin (1993) proposes that the most effective teams will comprise members who, between them, occupy nine key roles: implementer, co-ordinator, shaper, plant, teamworker, completer-finisher, specialist, monitor-evaluator and resource investigator. Belbin and his colleagues developed a questionnaire tool called the Belbin Self-Perception Inventory to help team members identify their preferred team roles. Although the reliability of the tool is questionable (Furnham and Gunter, 1993), and little direct empirical support has been found to support Belbin's model, wider research generally supports the premise that a mix of team member personalities and roles in teams will yield higher levels of effectiveness. For example, in relation to the 'Big Five' model of personality (see Chapter 3), researchers have found that in highly interdependent teams, hardworking and dependable team members are most desirable, because individual contributions are critical to team success (Mount *et al*, 1998). It might also be assumed that high levels of agreeableness within teams would be most desirable for team effectiveness. Although this makes intuitive sense, the research evidence does not support this. As will be seen in the following section on team processes, in some circumstances team conflict is actually beneficial to teams, because it can foster creativity. What research has shown us is that in the presence of one particularly disagreeable or aggressive team member or someone who is particularly low in conscientiousness, team effectiveness can be drastically undermined (DeDreu and Weingart, 2003).

Whatever the composition of the team, and the roles of individual team members, it is critical that team members have a clear idea of who belongs to the team and who does not. According to Hackman (2002), in order to work well together, team members must know who is in the team – a concept referred to as 'boundedness'. If individuals cannot reliably distinguish between who is in the team and who is not, and there is ambiguity about who shares accountability and responsibility for the completion of the team tasks, then a team will not be effective. Conversely, members of a bounded team are recognised by the wider environment as a team, identify themselves with that team and are clear about team membership. Because of this, bounded teams can begin to develop the collective momentum, social norms and specialised roles that characterise real teams (Hackman, 2002). Further, members are able to develop a sense of *entitativity*, which defines the degree to which they see themselves as belonging to one unit (Lickel, Hamilton, and Sherman, 2001).

Team diversity

Diversity is inevitable in work groups and teams. Characteristics on which team members might differ include KSAs, personality, gender, age, ethnicity, level of education, status in organisation, level of experience, and cognitive learning style, to name a few. So is it better to have homogenous teams in which all members are similar, or heterogeneous teams which contain multiple team-member differences? Over recent years, research has provided evidence for both cases. In a recent review by Van Knippenberg and Schippers (2007) two over-riding theoretical perspectives on diversity were identified:

- *the information/decision-making perspective*

  This perspective suggests that diversity is good for team performance, given that diverse teams have a greater pool of information to draw from for decision-making. For example, a team which comprises individuals from a variety of different educational backgrounds will have a far greater knowledge pool than a team whose members have all studied for the same university degree.

- *the social categorisation perspective*

  This perspective argues that diversity will be a source of inter-group bias, whereby team members will distinguish between those who are similar to themselves and those who are different. Such inter-group bias can create low levels of trust, co-operation and interaction between team members, which in turn will impact upon the quality of communication and overall performance of the team.

Overall, the reviewers conclude that when team processes are managed effectively, the impact of diversity on team outcomes is typically positive, and can lead to performance gains in the long term. As will be seen in the *Outputs* section, bringing together a group of people with diverse skills and backgrounds to carry out challenging and complex tasks has been shown to lead to greater levels of innovation.

The type and level of diversity required in a team is again very much dependent on the specific team task. Some teams will be far more homogenous than others. For example, in the Great Britain Olympic male swimming team, team members are all of the same sex and nationality, of a similar age range and of similar athletic ability. Conversely, an international team of academics working on a cross-cultural research project at various locations across the world is likely to be far more heterogeneous in terms of age, nationality, work experience and organisational status. Such a team might comprise one or more professors to oversee the project, a senior researcher to provide day-to-day supervision, a number of researchers to actually conduct the fieldwork, and a research assistant to provide administrative support. Depending on their various KSAs, each team member will therefore occupy a different role and carry out different tasks related to the overall completion of the project.

Team potency

Team potency is the shared belief within a team that it can be effective (Guzzo *et al*, 1993). This is sometimes also referred to as 'team efficacy'. Teams which believe that they can successfully meet their objectives demonstrate higher levels of motivation and persistence towards task accomplishment. Research evidence shows that team potency can positively predict team effectiveness (Campion, Medsker and Higgs, 1993). Positive moods can also spread rapidly throughout groups (George, 1990). If just one or two team members initially express their belief in the team's capabilities, therefore, this optimism can cross over to other team members and increase the team's overall potency. Bakker and his colleagues (2006) also found that positive interactions within a team foster energy and enthusiasm.

Think of a team in crisis – a team of bankers trying to perform well to avoid redundancy during an economic downturn, a lifeboat crew trying to rescue a family floundering on a boat in a treacherous storm, or a national security team having to deal with the aftermath of a terrorist attack. Working in such unstable environments is challenging and requires a high level of resistance and the ability to overcome adversity. So what keeps such teams together? The glue that binds effective teams is a high degree of commitment to a shared and meaningful vision, and a positive belief that the team can meet its goals and accomplish the task. If a team holds a positive belief about what it can achieve, team members are more likely to commit to the goals of the team and exert high levels of effort towards the achievement of those goals. Such potency is crucial if team members are able to inspire one another to work hard and to take personal risks on behalf of the team. As will be seen in the *Processes* section, team objectives have an important role to play in promoting such motivation and fostering a shared work approach. Other ways to improve team potency include training to develop team member KSAs. Improving a team's capabilities and demonstrating a commitment towards the learning and personal growth of team members will have a positive impact on the team's confidence, meaning that they will execute their work with greater levels of potency and optimism.

Organisational context [2]

Teams are typically embedded in larger organisational systems, and therefore their effectiveness will, to some extent, depend on wider contextual factors that impact on their team processes. Firstly, a team must be provided with adequate resources to carry out their task. Returning to the example of a surgical team, an operation could not be carried out without the correct apparatus for performing the specific procedure, enough clinical staff to provide care for the patient before and after the surgery, the availability of sufficient anaesthetic to keep the patient sedated and other drugs to provide pain relief, and a fully equipped operating theatre to provide sufficient space and light needed for the team to work in together. Very often such resources tend to be limited within organisations, leading to competition between teams and inhibiting them from performing their tasks properly. Teams must therefore operate as best they can within the boundaries of the wider organisation, including their policies and budgets.

Teams do not operate in an organisational vacuum (Hackman, 2002). What is needed for **team effectiveness** is not only real teams but a supportive organisational context that reinforces the team-based structure. Hackman (2002) argues that the likelihood of team effectiveness is increased when a team has an enabling structure that facilitates rather than ~~impedes~~ teamworking. He identifies three critical organisational systems that have particularly high leverage in supporting real teamwork. For a real team to be well supported, the organisation should provide an *educational system* that offers all the training and technical aids that a team may need, an *information system* that supplies data to help members to plan their team objectives, and a *reward system* that allows for positive consequences for good team performance (Hackman, 2002). Team-based rewards have particularly important implications for the development of effective teamworking and have been shown to improve performance (Tata and Prasad, 2004). Rewarding the team as a whole, as opposed to individuals, is critical if all team members are to be held jointly accountable for a specified output. Organisations seeking to implement teamworking should therefore make a concerted effort to reward team members equally, based on their collaborative efforts and collective performance. Such practices will help team members to recognise their interdependence and work together co-operatively, helping and supporting each other wherever possible.

Developing effective teamwork in organisations also requires that there is a climate for team-based working. According to Schneider (1990), organisational climate can be defined as the behaviours, processes and practices that an organisation supports and rewards. Where an organisational climate exerts low autonomy, high control and lack of concern for employee welfare, teamwork is unlikely to be effective (West and Markiewicz, 2004). Because of their inherent diversity, teams work best in environments that provide the flexibility and freedom to explore the divergent perspectives of team members. High levels of bureaucracy and control will stifle such creativity and inhibit innovative problem-solving. Organisations that actively encourage innovation and incorporate shared expectations of success in their values and culture thus may especially foster team effectiveness (Sundstrom *et al*, 1990). Furthermore, research by Galagan (1986) indicates that organisations which successfully implement work teams have similar cultures, often guided by the philosophies of senior management. Team-based working must therefore be supported throughout the entire organisational hierarchy.

Processes

Team objectives

Effective teams have a common purpose and shared vision about what they must achieve. Such a vision should be underpinned by a number of clear, shared objectives, which team members agree upon and are committed to. Clear team objectives ensure that everyone within the team is heading towards the same goal in a collaborative and efficient manner, as opposed to team members pulling in different directions, repeating one another's work, or even working in an antagonistic or competitive fashion. In teamwork, team members often interpret information and events differently, which can lead to confusion and disorganised responses (Kozlowski *et al*, 1999). If team members are uncertain about the values, goals and orientations of their colleagues, it is unlikely that the team as a whole will be able to articulate a clear vision which encapsulates a number of shared objectives (West, 2004). This is also difficult when ambiguity surrounds the task that the team must perform. The presence of unclear, ill-defined goals (or no goals at all) has been shown to be detrimental to team performance.

Team-level objectives provide a team with the incentive to combine their efforts and work closely together (Weldon and Weingart, 1993). When a team understands the demands of their task, the generation of a clear mission statement consisting of a number of specific and carefully stipulated objectives ensures that all team members share the same vision for their team and clearly understand the objectives by which it can be accomplished (Rousseau, Aubé and Savoie, 2006). A clear objective should incorporate specified goals which are connected to the purpose of the team and should specify the level of performance that team members are expected to achieve. Not only should team objectives be clearly articulated, team members should also be in agreement in terms of what the objectives should achieve. Further, the successful execution of tasks and completion of team objectives will require a degree of commitment from team members to ensure that each member contributes to the overall task in an appropriate way.

Overall, team-level objectives have been shown to be critical to team effectiveness and performance. Effective goal-setting behaviour in teams not only helps team members to realise their interdependence but has also been shown to improve and sustain higher performance, motivation and team-member satisfaction. Studies have also shown that group goals raise member effort. Teams should therefore always ensure that they develop clear, shared goals, which are agreed upon by all team members.

Applying theory to practice: Setting team objectives

In practice, the principle of 'SMART' goal-setting (see Chapter **5** for a description) is highly relevant for setting team-level objectives. To improve the clarity of team objectives, a team should hold regular team meetings during which all members take time to deliberately discuss and agree upon an overall vision for the team. The team should then discuss some short-term objectives through which this vision might be achieved. These objectives must be formulated by team members together in the team, making sure that they are specific, measurable, challenging and scheduled. This means stating them clearly, in numerical form (if possible), and within a designated time period. The team should also limit themselves to four or five objectives at a time so that team members can easily recall them off the top of their head. Teams should also try to set their objectives before they embark on a new task. Rather than launching straight into tasks, they should stop and take some time to plan how they will work together, as well as what they will do. Finally, it is important that every team member has a say in what the objectives are, and agrees with what is decided by the team. Collective agreement upon team objectives is important because it will encourage commitment to team goals.

Reflexivity

Struggling to co-ordinate efforts, overcoming task-related frustrations, becoming unclear about objectives and dealing with interpersonal conflicts are all common occurrences in teamwork. An effective way of overcoming such difficulties is team **reflexivity**. Team reflexivity is the extent to which members of a team overtly and collectively reflect upon their immediate and long-term objectives, processes and strategies and adapt them to current or anticipated circumstances (Carter and West, 1998). If teams are able to build self-awareness and monitor how team members interact and work with one another, it is more likely that they will recognise areas that need attention and development, and implement improvement plans accordingly (Tjosvold, Tang and West, 2004).

In order to initiate reflexivity, teams must meet together on a regular basis, during which they exchange task-related information. Teams may use a variety of different methods to transmit information, whether by scheduled meetings, emails, written reports, phone calls or talks in the hallway (Rousseau *et al*, 2006). However, for the purposes of reflexivity, face-to-face team meetings are likely to be the most effective medium. In a study looking at two different types of communication, Straus and McGrath (1994) found that when group consensus was required, computer-mediated groups who used technology as a form of communication did not perform as well as face-to-face groups. Regular face-to-face meetings will also help to build interpersonal bonds, mutual affective concern and a sense of shared identity which are important climate conditions for reflexivity. Indeed, research into newly formed nursing teams by Edmondson (1996) shows that learning from mistakes and devising innovations to avoid such mistakes in the future can only happen in teams that openly acknowledge and discuss their errors and how they could have been avoided. It should be noted that reflexivity requires a high degree of **participative safety**, since reflexive discussions are likely to reveal discrepancies between how the team is and how it should be performing. The effectiveness of the reflexivity processes will therefore improve as interpersonal team processes such as trust and potency develop, and as team members are more familiar with one another, and are more willing to share negative information relating to poor performance, errors or other task-related difficulties.

Under high levels of reflexivity, team members are motivated to engage in deep and systematic information-processing which helps them to combine and integrate relevant information to formulate creative solutions to problems and improved ways of completing their tasks (DeDreu, 2007). By reflecting upon strategies, task objectives and processes, reflexive groups can plan ahead, actively structure situations, have a better knowledge of their work and anticipate errors. Reflexivity is particularly useful for teams working in complex environments on difficult tasks because it helps them to recognise whether the way in which they are currently working corresponds with emerging challenges and external conditions. Deliberate reflection and discussion on anticipated changes can prompt teams to actively develop improved understandings and methods for the future. Research evidence has shown that teams which take time out to reflect on their objectives, strategies and processes are more effective than those that do not. For example, in a longitudinal research study, Carter and West (1998) monitored the performance of 19 BBCTV production teams over a year and found that reflexivity was a significant predictor of the creativity and team effectiveness (measured by audience viewing figures). Research interest in the area of reflexivity is rapidly increasing.

With regard to the Practitioner insight case study at the beginning of this chapter, think about how the concept of reflexivity could be introduced and implemented in the Aston Business School management team. What should the executive dean put in place to facilitate such reflexive behaviours in this team, and what might reflexivity achieve?

Applying theory to practice: What does team reflexivity look like in practice?

The team reflexivity process incorporates three key elements: reflection, planning and action/adaptation. Reflection refers to the awareness, attention, monitoring and evaluation of the object under consideration (West, 2000). In this stage, teams ask questions such as 'How could we have done things better?', 'How might we have approached this task differently, knowing what we know now?' or 'Do we communicate with one another using the most effective means possible?' Once this exploration stage is complete, teams can enter the planning stage, where intentions and courses of action are contemplated and decided upon. This second phase is characterised by detailed and ordered planning of what needs to be implemented or changed. Short- and long-term plans are established, and potential problems and pitfalls identified. Finally, the action/adaption phase involves the implementation of plans, and can be assessed on four dimensions: novelty (how innovative and new is the proposed change for the team, the organisation and wider stakeholders which it might affect?), magnitude (are the actions and changes on a small or large scale?), radicality (to what extent will the actions and changes impact on usual ways of working?), and effectiveness (will the action and changes achieve the intended objectives set by the team?).

Decision-making [3]

There is the general belief that teams will make better-quality decisions than individuals, given that they have a greater pool of knowledge and information to draw upon (see 'Team diversity' in the *Inputs* section). In light of the fact that many teams typically have a degree of autonomy over their work, and can therefore make decisions at a local level, it is important that decision-making processes are effective. However, research has identified various psychological phenomena called 'process losses' which can interfere with decision-making and lead to poorer decisions. These include:

- *social conformity* – As humans, we typically try to avoid conflict and confrontation. In group settings we therefore tend to go along with the majority opinion, even if it means withholding our own opinions which are contrary to the majority view: this is referred to as 'social conformity' (Brown, 2000).

- *status and power* – Each team member's opinions and contributions will hold different levels of importance and weight, depending on their status and power within the team. For example, a leader's opinion will typically be more influential and dominant, depending on the leadership style. Participative leaders, for example, will ensure that all team members have a say before they put their own opinions forward. French and Raven's 'bases of power' model (1959; see Chapter 13 for a full description) also suggests that individuals who are recognised by the team as having 'expert power' may be valued and attended to disproportionately when a team is faced with a particularly challenging decision that requires expert insight.

- *groupthink* – In an effort to avoid conflict and quickly reach a consensus between team members, it is common for groups to engage in a psychological phenomenon called **groupthink** (Janis, 1982). Groupthink typically occurs in close-knit groups who, perhaps without realising, sacrifice high-quality rigorous decision-making for the sake of maintaining social harmony. Leaders who tend to reject any opinions or views which conflict with their own are also likely to encourage groupthink, leading to potentially flawed decision-making.

- *group polarisation* – **Group polarisation** is the tendency for teams to make more radical, risky, controversial or extreme decisions than the average decision made by any one team member individually (Walker and Main, 1973). This is partly because all team members will be held jointly accountable for the outcome of the team's decision. As a result, each individual team member will not be solely answerable if things were to go wrong.

- *social loafing* – This is the tendency for individuals to exert less effort and commitment towards a task when it is not possible to decipher and evaluate each team member's unique contribution. **Social loafing** has important implications for team-based rewards, particularly if it is apparent that some team members are making substantially greater contributions than others, yet all team members are rewarded equally. Hardworking team members would find this particularly frustrating, which may result in the withdrawal of effort, motivation and commitment. Research has shown that when individual contributions are unidentifiable in overall team performance, individuals will put less effort into contributing to high-quality decisions during meetings (Karau and Williams, 1993). In order to reduce social loafing, clear team member roles should be assigned so that each individual has a meaningful and important contribution to make to the team task, which is recognised and valued by the rest of the team.

- *production blocking* – When teams come together to make decisions, it is common to carry out 'brainstorming' or 'mind mapping' exercises in which multiple ideas are generated in a boundaryless and inspired environment. The intuitive idea is that in such circumstances teams generate more ideas than individuals working alone. In fact, individuals working on the same activity alone can not only come up with more ideas than they would have done in a group setting, but the ideas themselves are typically of greater quality and creativity. This is due to the '**production blocking**' phenomenon that operates within groups. Diehl and Strobe (1987) argue that in team settings the competing and dominant verbalisations of others' suggestions can inhibit individuals from both thinking of new ideas and offering further ideas out loud to the group. Providing each team member with the opportunity to think about their own ideas on their own, before bringing the team together to share their thoughts, could therefore yield more effective decision-making.

Leadership [4]

Leadership processes play an instrumental role in effective teamwork. Indeed, there is considerable evidence to suggest that leaders affect team performance. Some researchers have even gone as far to argue that leadership (or lack of leadership) is a key variable in determining team functioning and whether team-based working systems are a success or failure (Katzenbach, 1997).

The type and style of leadership can differ significantly from team to team. Depending on the wider organisational culture, some teams might have a very clear and designated leader, whereas others might have a rotating leadership role or shared leadership between two or more team members. Leadership is not always needed in self-managed work teams because team members are able to take on management roles and direct their own work without the need for supervision. Whatever approach to leadership a team takes, it is important that it is clear and agreed upon by all team members. If a team is unclear about who their leader is, or there is conflict over the leadership role, this will act as a severe detriment to team effectiveness.

In more traditionally managed teams, which typically have formally appointed leadership roles, leaders play an important part in articulating an inspiring vision and clear objectives for the team, and expressing the positive beliefs and high expectations of the team. Such behaviours are crucial for fostering motivation, commitment and potency. Leaders should also express positive beliefs about team diversity, so that team members become accustomed to exploring each other's divergent perspectives and perceive the diversity within their team as an asset rather than a shortfall. As noted in the previous section, effective team leaders also actively encourage participation in decision-making. Information-sharing is critical for team effectiveness, so a leader must ensure that team members have the opportunity to discuss issues in an open and safe environment, without fear of embarrassment or of the rejection of their ideas.

Team conflict [5]

All teams experience conflict at some stage or another. Research has demonstrated that conflict is related to reduced satisfaction and productivity in teams (Gladstein, 1984). Similarly, the absence of conflict in decision-making groups and top management teams has also been linked to greater performance at both the team and organisational level (Bourgeois, 1980; Schwenk and Cosier, 1993). Despite these findings, other research indicates that some conflict within a team is actually desirable, because without conflict, teams can become stagnant, complacent and apathetic. Certain types of conflict have been shown genuinely to improve the quality of decision-making, and to have a positive impact on financial performance (eg Eisenhardt and Schoonhoven, 1990). However, this is only true for certain types of conflict in certain types of team tasks. The different types of conflict which may occur in teams should therefore firstly be considered.

Jehn (1995) distinguished between task conflict and relationship conflict. While relationship conflict, which is focused on interpersonal issues and incompatibilities, can be highly detrimental for team performance, task conflict, which is characterised by disagreements about the content of the team task, has actually been shown to be beneficial, because it reduces thoughtless argument while at the same time stimulating a rigorous and critical evaluation of the task (Jehn, 1995). Task conflict can actually minimise the process loss of groupthink that was described earlier in this section. Rather than accepting initial solutions, task conflict provides team members with the opportunity to question their assumptions and consider different approaches, thus allowing them to engage in effective questioning – a process which is termed '**constructive controversy**' (Tjosvold, 1998). Constructive controversy involves three key stages: the elaboration of views, the searching for understanding, and the integration of opposing positions. Task conflict can trigger such controversy and ensure that a team really understands the reasons for and implications of their decisions, having explored all the possible avenues.

It should also be considered that task conflict is not appropriate for all types of team task. For example, teams which complete straightforward, non-routine or highly standardised tasks will not benefit from routine task conflict, given that their tasks are typically prescribed and must be carried out in a specific way. However, teams which have been assigned non-routine and challenging tasks are more likely to require novel solutions and creative outcomes, and will therefore benefit from 'thinking outside the box'. Overall, task conflict can be beneficial for team creativity and innovation. However, interpersonal conflicts should be avoided and resolved as soon as they occur, so that teams do not become entrenched in ongoing disputes which divert attention, energy and focus from the task in hand.

Outputs

When team inputs and processes are successfully implemented and managed, a number of important team outputs should follow. Overall, the key output of the I-P-O model is team effectiveness. Team effectiveness has traditionally been conceptualised as having a number of key components: team performance, team member satisfaction, team member growth and team viability. **Team innovation** is also an anticipated output of the I-P-O model, given that effective teams often engage in creative team processes. Each of these outputs is examined more fully below.

Team performance [6]

As was detailed in the section *The evidence for teamwork*, effective teams generate high levels of performance and successfully achieve their intended objectives, whether these are based on improved financial performance, increased productivity, or high-quality outcomes. When team processes are effective, the productive output of the team meets or exceeds that quality, quantity and timeliness defined by the people who review, receive and/or use the output (Wageman *et al*, 2005).

Team member satisfaction

Teamworking satisfies the fundamental human need for belonging (Richardson and West, 2010). Individuals who are part of effective teams typically report higher levels of satisfaction, as well as improved role clarity and enhanced well-being (Mickan and Rodger, 2005).

Team member growth [7]

Team member growth is another key output of effective teamworking (West, 2004) and is important for the fulfilment of individual needs. Individuals who belong to effective teams have frequent opportunities to interact with their team mates, share information and knowledge, explore different perspectives and constantly learn from one another. Close interpersonal attachments can also form which enable a climate of trust and openness within a team. In turn, such satisfying and fulfilling relationships have a positive impact on the health and well-being of team members (Heaphy and Dutton, 2008).

Team viability

Team viability refers to a team's preference and capability to remain working together in the future. Effective teams will have long-term viability because of the trust and co-operation that their positive interactions and successful performances are likely to generate. When team members anticipate working together over a longer period of time, they are also likely to commit more effort and resources towards ensuring that the team remains intact. Hackman (1987) argues that members of teams without long-term viability will be more reluctant to work co-operatively, and may even burn out due to unresolved conflicts.

Team innovation

In today's complex and challenging organisational environment, a team must be innovative and creative if it is to survive and be effective. Innovation is the introduction of new ways of doing things or the implementation of new ideas, products or services in the workplace (West, 2002). Effective team processes, such as team reflexivity and constructive controversy, have been shown to positively impact on team effectiveness and innovation (Tjosvold, Tang and West, 2004).

Conclusion

Effective teamwork is a critical issue for today's organisations. Given the trend towards team-based structures, it is crucial that organisations ensure that they develop and support *real and effective teams*, providing them with the correct inputs, and facilitating effective team processes. Management should therefore pay close attention to their teams, ensuring that they possess the crucial characteristics of real teams: clear, shared objectives, interdependence, reflexivity, autonomy, boundedness, and clear roles for each team member. This ensures that organisations comprise real teams that can achieve the true benefits of teamwork, rather than pseudo-type teams which characterise a lot of the teams that exist in organisations today.

It should also be recognised that not all organisations need work groups and teams, depending on the types of tasks which they carry out. If tasks are simple, straightforward and require low levels of interdependence, work groups and teams are unlikely to be required. Implementing teams where they are not needed can be costly, unsettling and detrimental to worker-affective outcomes such as job satisfaction and well-being.

End notes

[1] See also Chapter 16.

[2] See also Chapter 11.

[3] See also Chapter 11.

[4] See also Chapter 10.

[5] See also Chapter 8.

[6] See also Chapters 5 and 17.

[7] See also Chapter 13.

REVIEW AND DISCUSSION QUESTIONS

REVIEW QUESTIONS

1 How can the increase of work groups and teams in organisations be explained?

2 What are the key characteristics of real teams?

3 List and describe six types of teams which are commonly found in organisations.

4 What are the key factors to consider when designing a new team?

5 Discuss six psychological phenomena which impact on team decision-making and how these could be avoided/ overcome.

DISCUSSION QUESTIONS

1 How might you help a team that has low levels of team potency?

2 What are the potential problems that could arise in a demographically diverse team? How could these problems be dealt with?

3 Should teams always endeavour to avoid conflict?

4 A team has never heard of reflexivity and is interested to learn more about it. How would you explain the concept of reflexivity to them, and what practical guidelines would you suggest for carrying it out successfully?

5 A newly formed team comes to you for some advice. One of their members feels that he is simply 'not a team player' and would prefer to work alone. How would you convince him of the advantages of teamwork, and what sort of skills would you suggest that he should seek to develop?

FURTHER READING

Carter, S. M., and West, M. A. (1998) 'Reflexivity, effectiveness and mental health in BBC-TV production teams', *Small Group Research*, Vol.5: 583–601. This article provides a closer insight into the concept of team reflexivity and the effects that it can have on team member well-being.

Hackman, J. R. (2002) *Leading teams. Setting the stage for great performances.* Boston, MA: Harvard Business School Press. Hackman's book provides lots of interesting examples of teams and has a practical focus. This book would be extremely interesting for anyone who has ever managed a team, and would like to know how to develop their team leadership skills.

Marks, M. A., DeChurch, L. A., Mathieu, J. E., Panzer, F. J. and Alonso, A. (2005) 'Teamwork in multiteam systems', *Journal of Applied Psychology*, Vol.90, No.5: 964–71. Multiteam systems are networks of two or more teams interacting with each other and working together interdependently in an organisation. Because team-based organisations comprise many teams, the ability of these teams to work together effectively is highly important if

the organisation is to meet its goals. This article introduces and discusses the concept of multiteam systems and provides empirical support for the theory.

Mohrman, S. A., Cohen, S. G. and Mohrman, A. M. (1995) *Designing Team-Based Organizations: New forms for knowledge work.* San Francisco, CA: Jossey-Bass. Mohrman and colleagues provide a thorough overview of the practicalities involved in designing and implementing team-based working in an organisation, covering important issues such as how to prepare organisations for change, and how to design an effective team-based reward system.

Salas, E., Goodwin, G. F., and Burke, C. S. (eds) (2009) *Team effectiveness in complex organisations. Cross-disciplinary perspectives and approaches.* London: Routledge. This book provides a comprehensive and detailed overview of some of the most recent and emerging trends in the area of teamwork. Particularly interesting themes covered include team psychological safety, team cognition and team learning.

KEY SKILLS

TEAMWORKING

When a newly formed group of individuals come together to work on a task, they have to work hard to become a team. Becoming a team requires that team members develop and exhibit a number of key skills that facilitate effective teamwork. For some, working alongside others is enjoyable, easy, and teamworking comes naturally. However, for others, learning to co-operate, trust and rely on others can be uncomfortable, difficult and often frustrating, particularly if they are used to working independently and prefer to be recognised for their individual achievements. Turning individuals into team players can take time, during which a number of teamwork skills must be developed. Key teamworking skills include:

Co-operation

Co-operation is fundamental in teamwork and forms the basis for team effectiveness. In order to achieve their shared goals, team members must realise that they will need to work collaboratively together, rather than working alone or even competing with one another.

Communication

If team members do not communicate, a job will not get done. Communication, in whichever form (face-to-face or virtual), is crucial in ensuring that information is shared and decisions are made. Communication should occur on a frequent basis, should be both formal (team meetings) and informal (small-talk in the lunch queue) and should adopt a supportive, friendly and warm style. Team members should pay close attention to one another, being aware of both verbal and non-verbal messages. In teams which have members who are speaking in their second or third language, team members should be tolerant and patient to ensure that everyone has the opportunity to express their opinion. Team-member views should also be elaborated and confirmed to ensure that the correct interpretation has been made. Finally, communication should be open and honest. Team members should feel safe to express their views in an open and honest environment, in which they will not feel punished, rejected or embarrassed by the team. In such a climate, team members are far more likely to be honest about difficulties they are having in meeting a goal, and admit any mistakes they may have made during a task.

Mutual respect

Given that teams are very often composed of a diverse group of individuals from different nationalities, backgrounds and professions, it is crucial that team members maintain a high level of mutual respect for one another. Very often, team members may perceive their own KSAs and contributions as having more importance, relevance or impact on the team outcome. Other team members might feel undervalued as a result, which will have a negative impact on team morale and motivation. Similarly, minority team members may not be listened to in team discussions, based on their status with the team or different professional backgrounds. Team leaders who explicitly recognise and openly acknowledge the unique contributions of every team member can help to build a team climate which fosters high levels of mutual respect and appreciation.

NEGOTIATION, ARBITRATION AND CONFLICT RESOLUTION SKILLS

Collaborative problem-solving is a key skill which is relevant to this chapter on teamwork. Teams are typically faced with complex and multifaceted tasks which require creative and mutually beneficial solutions. When a number of divergent perspectives are put forward, a team's interaction must ensure that everyone has their say, and that the discussion is not dominated by one or two individuals. In negotiating outcomes, a team leader should ensure that everyone has the opportunity to participate and that the outcome is a creative compromise which leaves everyone feeling that they made a meaningful contribution.

Conflict resolution is also an important key skill for a team to possess. If nobody has the skills to recognise and manage team disputes, conflicts can become entrenched and impact on the long-term productivity and potency of a team. Team conflicts must be recognised and dealt with as early as possible. If the conflict is related to the task, team members should take the opportunity to elaborate useful debates to come up with win-win solutions.

EMOTIONAL INTELLIGENCE, EMPATHY, SYMPATHY AND LISTENING

Emotional intelligence is very often discussed in the context of leadership. However, emotional intelligence within a team is also a highly desirable and valuable skill. The quality of team-member relationships is fundamental if a team is to develop high levels of trust and attachment. Team members must therefore be attentive to each other's unique needs and individual goals for learning and development. Team members with high levels of emotional intelligence are socially perceptive and can recognise and manage emotions in groups. They also have high levels of self-awareness and can therefore articulate their own emotions in a controlled and thoughtful manner. Such skills are vital in demographically diverse teams where different cultural signals and cues can create communication difficulties, which very often lead to misinterpretations, suspicion and even distrust. Emotionally intelligent team members can anticipate such problems early on and intervene to ensure that they do not develop into conflicts.

Secondly, effective teams, particularly those that have been established for some time, tend to demonstrate altruism and empathy towards members. This might involve the provision of instrumental support, such as helping a team member with a technical problem and teaching them a new technique. Other forms of social support which are more emotional and affective in nature could also be provided. This might involve lending a shoulder to cry on, and an understanding ear, or helping a team member through a difficult time in their home life.

Active listening is also an invaluable skill in teams. It is often typical for team members to resort to 'passive listening' during team meetings, whereby communicated information is not fully processed and explored but instead just acknowledged with a smile and a nod. Active listeners will instead pay close attention to what is being said, attempt to understand it and then evaluate it. This may involve reflecting the information back to the deliverer, ensuring that the correct interpretation has been made, and clarifying anything that is not fully understood.

Ethical implications: Fostering a climate of trust

In light of the highly collaborative nature of effective teamworking, a high level of trust is desirable in any team. Close interpersonal bonds and secure attachments between team members can help to foster a climate of psychological safety, openness and reciprocity, all of which are crucial if team members are willing to share information, compensate for one another and take personal risks on behalf of the team. Where trust and co-operation do not exist within a team, team members are more likely to act defensively and secretively, compete with one another over resources, and even sabotage each others' performances. A team leader must therefore ensure that they foster a climate of trust by articulating a shared vision, modelling fairness, consistency and support in their behaviour, and being open and honest with team members.

In effective teams, team members must also be willing to share the credit for outstanding achievements, whether this is in terms of management recognition or financial reward. As has been noted in this chapter, social loafing is common when team members are rewarded on the basis of their joint efforts. In such teams, hardworking conscientious team members may be taken advantage of while others contribute very little yet gladly share the credit and recognition. Over time, this inequity will impact on motivation and commitment, and may lead to the breakdown of trust within the team. It is therefore important that team leaders and team members monitor their own, as well as others', individual efforts and speak openly if they notice consistent unfairness or unethical behaviour such as bullying or harassment. Again, the ability to speak openly about such occurrences requires a climate of trust within the team. Team members should also be able to speak confidentially to their team leader or a manager outside the team without fear of being branded a trouble-maker or a whistleblower.

Taking your learning further

1 Campion, M. A., Medsker, G. J. and Higgs, C. A. (1993) 'Relations between work group characteristics and effectiveness: implications for designing effective work groups', *Personnel Psychology*, Vol.46, No.4: 823–50.

2 Cohen, S. G. and Bailey, D. E. (1997) 'What makes teams work: group effectiveness research from the shop floor to the executive suite', *Journal of Management*, Vol.23: 239–90.

3 Devine, D. J., Clayton, L. D., Phillips, J. L., Dunford, B. B., and Melner, S. B. (1999) 'Teams in organisations: prevalence, characteristics and effectiveness', *Small Group Research*, Vol.30, No.6: 678–711.

4 Guzzo, R. and Dickson, M. (1996) 'Teams in organisations: recent research on performance and effectiveness', *Annual Review of Psychology*, Vol.47: 307–38.

5 Kozlowski, S. W. J. and Ilgen, D. R. (2006) 'Enhancing the effectiveness of work groups and teams', *Psychological Science in the Public Interest*, Vol.7, No.3: 77–124.

6 Salas, E., Sims, D. E. and Burke, C. S. (2005) 'Is there a "big five" in teamwork?', *Small Group Research*, Vol.36: 555–99.

7 Sundstrom, E., McIntyre, M., Halfhill, T. and Richards, H. (2000) 'Work groups: from Hawthorne studies to work teams of the 1990s and beyond', *Group Dynamics: Theory, Research, and Practice*, Vol.4, No.1: 44–67.

8 West, M. A. (2004) *Effective Teamwork: Practical lessons from organisational research*. Oxford: Blackwell/British Psychological Society.

9 West, M. A. and Markiewicz, L. (2004) *Building Team-Based Working. A practical guide to organisational transformation*. Oxford: Blackwell/British Psychological Society.

BEST PRACTICE

An inspiring team leader

Catherine is a team leader at a large consultancy firm. Her team is made up of eight recruitment consultants all of whom are different in terms of their ethnic origin, age and educational background. Using her understanding of emotional intelligence, Catherine clearly sees this as an opportunity for innovation and has demonstrated an attempt to moderate diversity effects. She always encourages active participation in decision-making, listening carefully and considering each team member's contribution, thus allowing them to maintain a strong sense of belonging to the team. Due to the competitive nature of the job, interpersonal conflict often emerges between consultants within the team. However, Catherine understands that interpersonal conflict is detrimental to task effectiveness and always takes members to one side in order to identify each of their underlying needs, and resolves the problem through effective collaboration.

Catherine is in a position to demand respect from all of her team members. As a leader, she clearly communicates team objectives and designates tasks. However, she also acts as a servant to her team, providing them with support, help and guidance whenever it's needed. In terms of appraisal, Catherine provides her team with thorough and constructive feedback which members can then use to form a basis for their personal goals. Catherine also informally rewards her team for good performance, often bringing in treats on a Friday, and surprising members with afternoons off on special occasions. High levels of trust within Catherine's team provide members with the confidence and support they need to take new risks in trying to achieve their goals. For example, members often try different approaches to canvas-calling to see what is most effective in securing new clients. Catherine also rewards creative failure, consistently encouraging her team to be reflexive, to question why things didn't work out, and to revise them and try again.

WORST PRACTICE

A dominating team member

Within the Research and Development department of a large car manufacturer, six researchers have been asked to work on a project to come up with a new design for a steering wheel. The deadline for the project is just one week, and the team therefore needs to work quickly and co-operatively. All team members have an equal status within the organisation and come from the same professional background. Although one team member, Debbie, only joined the company two weeks ago, the others have worked together for a number of years and many of them enjoy socialising together outside work. However, they have recently been trying to avoid Richard, who they find uncommitted and lazy. They are also still annoyed about their previous project, for which Richard received the most credit and recognition from senior management, yet contributed very little in comparison to the rest of the team. However, instead of discussing their discontent openly with him, they have become increasingly defensive and uncooperative towards him.

During their first team meeting on the new project, the team decides that it would be best if they split up the task and work individually on different parts, bringing everything together at the end of the following week. They draw up a brief action plan and agree that they will send their own pieces of completed work to Debbie the day before the deadline, so that she can consolidate the work. Yet some of the key decisions about the product are left up in the air. Richard's role is also particularly

ambiguous, and the team purposely give him a difficult task which requires a lot of knowledge about how to use a particular piece of design software.

Over the week, most team members communicate on numerous occasions, but no one contacts Richard to inform him of their progress or to check if he needs help. In fact, as has happened in similar cases previously, Richard is having great difficulty in operating the software but does not feel that he can admit this to the rest the team out of distrust and fear of embarrassment. Instead, he keeps quiet, gives the impression that he knows what he is doing, and spends long days trying to figure out the program, to no avail.

The morning before the deadline, everyone completes and sends their work as promised, apart from Richard. Debbie is concerned that his work is missing, but in her efforts to fit in with the team and maintain harmony, she does not say anything, hoping that his lateness is commonplace. In the meantime, Richard hopes that the team will have covered his work and that he will get away without making a contribution – after all, no one seemed to mind last time. By 4 pm Debbie has still not received Richard's work and contacts the rest of the team. Angrily, the rest of the team work late into the evening to finish Richard's part of the work, knowing that his part is essential for the overall report, and fearing that they would all be punished if his part was not complete. Without consulting Richard, they report him to senior management.

Chapter 8
Conflict and Stress in Organisations

Alf Crossman

PART TWO

Contents

Key Learning Outcomes

By the end of this chapter you should be able to:

- define conflict and understand the four main frames of reference
- explain the different ways in which conflict can manifest itself
- understand the main methods of conflict resolution
- define the concept of stress and identify potential causes
- identify the symptoms of stress and know how to manage it
- explain the relationship between conflict and stress.

 **PRACTITIONER INSIGHT**

Fraser Birch Co. Ltd

Fraser Birch Co. Ltd is a family firm, established in 1923 and based in Bethnal Green in the East End of London. The company imports hardwood and plywood into the UK from South America, West Africa, Europe and the Far East. The company was run by two brothers, who were the shareholder directors, and a workforce of 12 employees. A few years ago there was a general acceptance that the company was stagnating. We speak to **Fraser Macfarlane** – who joined his father and uncle as the third director after graduating from university – about the conflict that arose when he joined the company.

Fraser Macfarlane was brought in to generate new ideas and to take the company forward. Previously, all decisions had been made by the two brothers. It soon became clear to Fraser that he was regarded as the 'new kid', and was not being fully involved in decision-making.

It was very obvious to Fraser that some key operational decisions had to be taken, such as hiring staff, adjusting prices to remain competitive, and obtaining additional transport for rush orders. Decision-making was slow because all the directors had to agree.

Fraser soon discovered that executive decisions he had taken were not being supported by the other directors.

The situation came to a head when a decision made jointly by Fraser and one director was overturned the next day – obviously the two senior directors had reversed the first decision without consulting Fraser. As a result of this incident, Fraser found his role increasingly difficult to fulfil. He began to experience cognitive problems, confusion and inability to think clearly, sleepless nights, as well as fatigue and loss of appetite. At home Fraser was irritable and withdrawn, putting pressure on his relationship with his wife and children. Previously very athletic and a keen runner, Fraser found himself without the energy to exercise to relieve the mental pressure. The situation was simply being compounded.

How would you classify the types of conflict that occurred in the above case study, and why did they arise? What do the physical and mental symptoms that Fraser experienced indicate? What action would you recommend to resolve the situation?

Once you have read this chapter, return to these questions and think about how you could answer them.

Introduction

This chapter is divided into three separate but inter-related sections of disproportionate length. The first section deals with conflict in organisations at the macro (organisational) level and at the micro (individual) level. One of the main problems we face with the subject is that conflict is often misconstrued – many perceive conflict to be inherently bad, whereas the reality may be somewhat different. This section identifies the nature of conflict and differentiates between **functional conflict** – that which is healthy – and **dysfunctional conflict**, which can be destructive. If we accept that conflict is a product of disagreement at either the macro or micro level on the basis of groups or individuals wanting to improve structures, systems or procedures, then it should be welcomed rather than discouraged. The chapter also addresses the way in which conflict manifests itself, and potential sources of resolution. The chapter is underpinned by other theoretical areas such as **equity theory** and **organisational justice perceptions**.

The second section in this chapter addresses **stress** in the workplace. Managers are often quoted as saying that 'a bit of stress is good for people'. This is a highly debatable position, and points of agreement or disagreement will depend on our understanding of stress and our ability to distinguish between 'stress' on the one hand and 'pressure' on the other. Theoretically, some stress can be productive, which used to be termed **'eustress'**, as opposed to that which is harmful, termed **'distress'**. In recent decades the use of these prefixes has been discontinued, leaving 'stress' as a generic, but arguably meaningless catch-all word. If we accept that individuals have different levels of mental and physical tolerance, there is then a distinct possibility that in the same situation one person might feel pressurised but another might feel stressed – and a manager might not be sufficiently skilled to differentiate between the two.

The final section in the chapter draws together the key aspects of conflict and stress theories and raises the potential for a causal link. **Personal conflict** over some moral or ethical issue, or **interpersonal conflict** between superior and subordinate or between peers, might lead to internal or interactional stress. The section explores ways in which these incidences of stress might manifest themselves, and how they might be managed. This section also draws attention to the potential connection between these constructs and the management of change, which appears in a later chapter.

CONFLICT IN ORGANISATIONS: POSITIVE OR NEGATIVE EFFECTS?

Conflict can be defined as a struggle between individuals or groups which arises out of the opposition they hold for each other's positions and ideas. One of the potential problems with conflict is the way in which it is perceived: there is a tendency to view conflict as a negative feature in organisations and in broader society. This may be partly due to the frequent and liberal use of the term by the media in relation to military situations – as in the 'Falklands conflict' or the 'conflict in Bosnia' – likewise, the use of the term in connection with industrial action, and the overt disagreements between management and workers otherwise referred to as capital and labour. In these contexts conflict is seen as an oppositional force resulting from the exercise of power by one party over another, from which it is difficult to discern any positive outcomes. To be able to fully understand conflict it is essential that we keep an open mind and accept that conflict is both caused by disagreement between parties and the subject of disagreement over its nature and causes and the harm or benefits it produces.

Conflict can be divided into two main variants, **cognitive conflict** and **affective conflict** (Jehn, 1995). *Cognitive conflict* is that which emerges when individuals or teams discuss and debate the task they are to complete. These individuals or team members debate their differing points of view and evaluate multiple approaches. The debate that is generated exposes any assumptions which are made or beliefs which are held, but in a constructive, even tolerant, manner in which the divergent views are honoured. Jehn (1995) suggests that this type of conflict improves the decision-making of the team and produces better outcomes on the basis of greater understanding and acceptance of the outcomes of detailed and reasoned decisions. *Affective conflict*, on the other hand, is more personal: it may emerge from personality clashes or where different individuals engage in power struggles, one-upmanship or brinkmanship. Affective conflict may also be the product of perceived inequitable treatment by employees, resulting in potentially disruptive actions by one or more to restore a sense of equity (Adams, 1965). Likewise, it may be as a result of low organisational justice perceptions (Greenberg, 1990). This type of conflict has a destructive, dysfunctional effect on the performance of individuals or groups because it distracts them from the more important aspects of the task. Affective conflict can also have a negative impact on job satisfaction – an example of this may be found in the Practitioner insight case study at the beginning of the chapter. More recently, it has also been argued that there may be an interaction between cognitive and affective conflict. Mooney *et al* (2007: 754) found evidence of cognitive conflict acting as a stimulant for affective conflict: the authors suggest that

> When teams stimulate debate and the open exchange of conflicting ideas, they may be inadvertently stimulating affective conflict as well.

As mentioned earlier, there is a tendency to see conflict as being necessarily bad and requiring to be either eliminated or suppressed. Indeed, this was the common perspective adopted by managers following classical management theorists such as Henri Fayol or Frederick Winslow Taylor. For example, in the early part of the twentieth century Henry Ford employed his own company 'police force', known as the Plant Protection Service, to keep order in his River Rouge factory. Potential sources of opposition and power – individuals who were considered to be dissidents or supportive of trade unions – were identified and fired. In recent decades there has been increasing support for view that conflict can have positive effects in organisations (Quinn, 1988; Baron, 1991; Amason, 1996). Likewise, Tjosvold (2008) expresses the view that conflict has positive attributes insofar as it can make a constructive contribution to teamworking and organisational effectiveness by combining the energy of different team members who use their experience and knowledge to introduce new ideas.

An absence of conflict in an organisation or a group within it can be as problematic as too much conflict. A lack of conflict may signal the presence of undesirable group dynamics such as groupthink (Janis, 1972). Groupthink is of particular relevance to conflict. Some groups develop such a high degree of cohesiveness that it can lead to consensus becoming so desirable that it inhibits critical thinking, which in turn can prevent open debate and the full evaluation of alternative courses of action. In such situations individuals tend to avoid conflict, often by simply falling in line with the leader or other dominant group members. As Cosier *et al* (1991: 7) argue, '"cognitive" conflict can be instrumental in preventing problems such as groupthink.'

Thus far the negative attributes of conflict have been discussed, but conflict may not necessarily be bad. Conflict may be described as having *dysfunctional* or *functional* properties, depending on whether it has a negative or positive effect. *Dysfunctional conflict* is likely to be in the form of protracted industrial action such as strikes, go-slows, and overtime bans which create long-lasting bad feeling between managers and workers. Reflecting on the signal-workers' strikes of 1994 (Crossman and McIlwee, 1995: 2), Vernon Hince – the then Deputy General Secretary of the Rail, Maritime and Transport Workers' Union – observed:

> While the dispute was eventually resolved, with considerable assistance from ACAS, relationships between the two parties directly involved will take years to heal.

Functional conflict, on the other hand, may occur between individuals or groups who disagree over the best way of achieving organisational goals or tasks, the end result being interactions which generate a variety of options and ideas which are then evaluated – a kind of brainstorming process – from which the organisation and workers can benefit. It is important to have an appropriate level of conflict: enough to stimulate creative thinking and self-criticism, but not enough to damage the group cohesiveness.

The importance of conflict study

There is no doubt that conflict is a powerful force within organisations. Indeed, we could argue that if conflict results in change for the betterment of the organisation and the people within it, then it is fundamental to their survival. We live in a world which is becoming increasingly diverse: society in general is more transient than ever before, and organisations mirror this trend. Contemporary workforces comprise individuals of different nationalities, religions, cultures, values and political preference. A retrospect on the first decade of the twenty-first century reveals a paradoxical situation. Workers – particularly 'professionals' – have more disposable income than ever before and a greater desire for leisure activity. At the same time, organisations have been demanding increased effort in the form of longer hours. Consequently, the likelihood of perpetually harmonious relationships is slight. Indeed, there is a growing literature on '**work–life balance**' which suggests it is time to review working arrangements and the demand placed upon employees. Although many organisations have adopted work–life policies and practices in order to attract better applicants and reduce organisational conflict in pursuit of enhanced organisational performance, evidence suggests this may not deliver the expected outcomes (Beauregarde and Henry, 2009).

The study of conflict is therefore important both for organisational success and individual well-being – a comprehensive understanding of the sources of conflict, how it manifests itself, and the strategies and tactics for conflict management is important. There are a number of prerequisites for conflict to emerge and exist. First, there must be a consciousness of differing interests, beliefs or values. Without this perception of difference conflict cannot arise.

According to Thomson and Murray (1976), conflict may be analysed using three dimensions: the *level* at which it occurs, the *dependent* variables, and the *independent* variables. The authors' conceptualisation of conflict is displayed in Figure 8.1.

The levels identify where the conflict occurs. The highest level is societal, the three lower levels can be organisation-related, but – as we will see later – the Marxist or radical view would be that conflict emanates from conflict in broader society. The dependent variables are the *attitudes and perceptions* of the parties, such as a sense of inequity or unfairness; *manifestation* in terms of their actions, collective or individual; and the *outcomes* generated as a result of the attitudes and actions. The independent variables explain how conflict can be grouped: 'process variables' refers to the actions relating to the particular issue and the thoughts and feelings which underpin them; 'contextual-structural variables' refers to the condition in which the conflict occurs; and 'procedural variables' relates to agreed rules designed to regulate the behaviour of the parties.

FRAMES OF REFERENCE

A frame of reference can be defined as the lens through which we view the world. The particular frame of reference we adopt influences our judgements of what is acceptable or unacceptable, what is right and what is wrong, both in the context of broader society and within the organisation. It is important to understand that there is no right or wrong frame of reference: they are simply different – the way in which we perceive things around us and form part of our sense-making machinery, or how we make sense of what is going on around us. Where different parties perceive the same phenomenon in a different way, conflict is likely to emerge, as Weick (2001: 9) observes:

> Organisations resemble puzzling terrain because they lend themselves to multiple, conflicting interpretations.

Figure 8.1   A classification of general approaches to the analysis of social conflicts

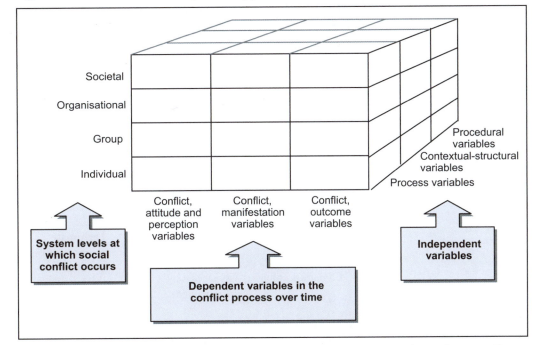

Source: Thomson, A. W. J. and Murray, V. V. (1976) *Grievance Procedures.* Farnborough: Saxon House. Reproduced with the authors' permission

The main frames of reference are the *unitarist*, the *pluralist* and the *radical*. The first two are mainly attributed to the work of Alan Fox (1966; 1973). These different frames of reference can be briefly described as follows:

- *Unitarist* – The unitarist frame of reference views the organisation as a harmonious whole in which there is a congruence of goals, values and **ideology**. This approach is regarded by some (Storey, 1992) as a central tenet of human resource management, which stresses the importance of commitment rather than compliance.

- *Pluralist* – The pluralist frame of reference is fundamentally different from the unitarist insofar as the organisation is seen as comprising a variety of stakeholders with divergent interests.

- *Radical* – The radical frame of reference is frequently (and somewhat inaccurately) referred to as the Marxist frame of reference. This view considers conflict to be the inevitable product of capitalism and the inequality it produces.

These frames of reference may be easily visualised. The construction company Taylor Woodrow, founded in 1921, now part of Taylor Wimpey plc, chose as its logo (until 2001) a silhouette of four construction workers pulling on the end of a rope, all in the same direction, to convey a strong sense of teamwork. This is a good representation of the key principles of the unitarist frame of reference in that it evokes a sense of psychological convergence where everyone wins. Imagine a situation where there are, once again, four workers pulling on the rope, but this time two are pulling at one end and two at the other – like a tug of war, each pair wanting to beat the other pair by pulling them into their own territory. This would suggest a more dysfunctional approach comprising winners and losers. Lastly, visualise a rope with two workers at each end – but now they are pushing towards and against each other. This represents an oppositional force through which the winning pair would overpower the losers by occupying their territory.

Some of the key features or concepts of the relationship between employees and the organisation are set out in Table 8.1. As you will see, there are fundamentally divergent perspectives within each frame of reference.

Table 8.1:   Frames of reference

Concepts	Frame of reference		
	Unitarism	*Pluralism*	*Radicalism*
Interests/goals	Common	Diverse	Oppositional
Conflict	Unnecessary	Inherent	Inevitable, due to class system
Power	Ignored as a concept	Crucial variable	Unequally distributed
Authority	To be maximised by management	To be shared	To be challenged by workers
Trade unions	Unnecessary trouble-makers	Legitimate representatives	Inadequate to fight capitalism
Communication	Controlled by management	Agreed systems and procedures	Underpinning the rights of capital

As far as interests and goals are concerned, within the *unitarist* frame of reference these are regarded as convergent or common. Conflict is regarded as bad and unnecessary, for such is the degree of psychological convergence that conflict should not exist at all: where it does, it is the result of poor **person-organisation fit** – the wrong people have been employed. Power is largely ignored as a concept on the ground that if all the parties subscribe to the same interests, the use of power is not an issue. What is more important is authority, which is used by management to inform and guide workers in the pursuance of joint goals. Representative organisations are viewed as unnecessary trouble-makers with their own agenda – after all, if capital and labour are in harmony, a third party to represent the interests of labour is not required. Communication is seen as an essential management tool for the purpose of giving information and direction to employees. One might argue this is on a need-to-know basis.

The *pluralist* frame of reference perspective is somewhat different. Interests and goals are seen as being diverse because the organisation comprises different groups following their own interests. Some of these interests may converge while others may conflict, and this convergence/divergence may change from time to time. As a result, conflict is perceived to be inherent in the relationship. Power is a crucial variable in the relationship, and the amount of power held by capital and labour varies – power represents a dynamic 'frontier of control' (Goodrich, 1975). Authority is something to be shared by the parties, and there is an expectation that this will be challenged from time to time. Communication is by way of agreed, often elaborate, systems and procedures. Representative organisations, such as trade unions, are seen as the legitimate representatives of labour, playing an important role in conflict management.

The *radical* frame of reference is founded on the Marxist view of the perceived inequalities in broader society and largely focuses on the class struggle between capital and labour. To this end the organisation is merely an arena in which a gladiatorial struggle is played out. Interests and goals are considered to be not only divergent but oppositional. Consequently, conflict is perceived to be the inevitable outcome of the unequal distribution of power, and managerial authority is considered something to be challenged by workers. Somewhat paradoxically, trade unions are not necessarily regarded as a means of achieving societal change. Indeed, Marx himself was concerned by the way in which the internal politics and structures of trade unions seemed to mirror the inequalities in society and the way in which they were only interested in the views of their members rather than of broader society. Radicals take a rather jaded view of communication, arguing that it is controlled by management and is used to underpin and strengthen the rights of capital.

A further frame of reference, the *interactionist* perspective, regards conflict as a positive force which is essential for organisational performance. What is important here is that conflict should be encouraged rather than eliminated, and it should be overt, constructive and carefully managed (Townsend, 1985). This follows the cognitive conflict approach discussed earlier in the chapter. So no single frame of reference is right or wrong – each is simply different.

CONFLICT SOURCES AND PROCESSES

The sources from which conflict emanates and the way in which it is handled are many and varied. A conceptualisation of the sources, processes and outcomes of conflict is set out in Figure 8.2. For the purpose of this model it is important to remember that conflict arises out of disagreement between parties. This manifests itself in a number of ways, some positive and others negative, so it is essential that we separate the conflict itself from the way in which it becomes manifest.

This model represents the dynamic and cyclical nature of conflict and the processes used to manage it. Paradoxically, some of the positive outcomes of conflict resolution may become sources of conflict in the future – a pay increase awarded today will have a limited life: in a year's time fresh conflict might emerge over the appropriateness of the current wage. The model represents a system that involves inputs, processes and outputs, with a feedback mechanism. As such, it is similar in nature to that proposed by Dunlop (1993).

In a similar manner, collective bargaining might not produce an acceptable outcome – there could still be conflict. In such circumstances the parties may then seek **third-party intervention** through **conciliation** in an attempt to settle their differences. This also may run in parallel with collective bargaining. If it is unsuccessful, the decision may be taken to refer the dispute to

Figure 8.2   A model of the conflict process

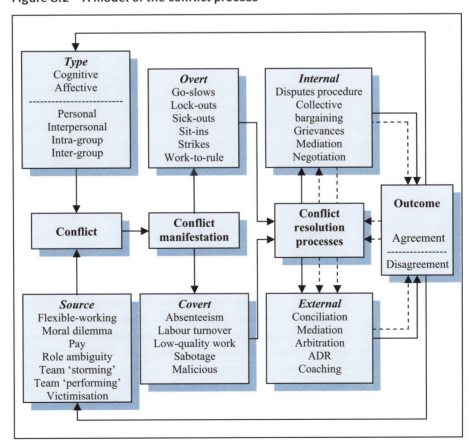

arbitration, so both internal and external methods may be used consecutively or concurrently to resolve the same conflict.

As noted earlier, conflict is essentially a process which occurs within and between different individuals as a result of the pursuance of different goals, values or objectives. In organisations different types of conflict can occur. As well as being cognitive or affective, as described above, it can be individual (personal or within-person conflict), between individuals (interpersonal conflict), within a group (**intra-group conflict**) or between groups (**intergroup conflict**).

Types and sources of conflict [1]

The personal conflict which an individual might experience can be born out of indecisiveness arising from competing internal values. For example, an employee aware of wrongdoing by his or her organisation may be faced with the **moral dilemma** of maintaining silence (Vandekerckhove and Commers, 2004) or of 'blowing the whistle' and reveal the wrongdoing. Considerations may be based on rational decision-making by the employee – the weighing up of the moral benefit of the revelation of wrongdoing versus the cost to the employee of any retaliation or sanctions the employer might invoke (Glazer, 1983; Poneman, 1994). The **whistle-blowing** decision will be based on the perceived seriousness of the wrongdoing, perceptions of intent, judgements of responsibility, and feelings of anger (Gundlach *et al*, 2008). These sentiments are in turn likely to be influenced by a sense of organisational citizenship, which may inhibit whistle-blowing (Lobel, 2009). Similarly, personal conflict may be created by divided loyalties, between the demands of work and those of the family. These may be time-related conflicts or affective-state related (Ilies *et al*, 2007). Personal conflict may also be the result of **role ambiguity**, where the individual's perception of their job is unclear or where there are competing claims on them. A manager may expect a subordinate team leader to behave as a manager, yet their team members may expect them to be 'one of the team', resulting in uncertainty and anxiety or stress.

Interpersonal conflict is that which occurs between individuals: superior and subordinate or peer to peer. It may be the result of role ambiguity when the individual's perception of their job is at variance with their co-workers' or manager's – see the Practitioner insight case study at the start of the chapter. The conflict generated interpersonally may be cognitive or affective in nature, but is more likely to be the latter. Interpersonal conflict may include personal attacks resulting in victimisation and harassment. Whereas this may be truly interpersonal, between individuals, there have been examples where an individual has been subjected to detrimental treatment by a group of workers – a worker who continues to work during strike action, labelled a 'scab', may be the subject of verbal and physical abuse. Likewise, individuals whose behaviour does not follow established group norms may be systematically ignored by colleagues, known as being 'sent to Coventry', in order to impose pressure for them to modify their behaviour and conform.

Intra-group conflict occurs within a group. It is similar to interpersonal conflict, but it invariably involves more than two individuals. Imagine a team of trade union negotiators preparing to meet with their management counterparts to bargain over issues such as pay awards or flexible working practices. Before meeting the opposition, the negotiating team must bargain among themselves to establish a common line, set priorities and establish their '**most favoured**' and '**fall-back positions**'. Imagine that the negotiating team was made up of representatives from different trade unions participating in 'single-table' bargaining over the introduction of flexible working arrangements which affected the participating unions disproportionately. Only when they have completed the intra-group bargaining are they in a position to meet the opposition in a united manner. As many trade union banners claim, 'Unity is Strength'. This type of conflict may also be associated with legitimate group dynamics, particularly the 'storming' phase of group development (Tuckman, 1965) and the intensity with which group members vie for power and influence or test each other's resolve. In this scenario the conflict is likely to be affective. In the 'performing' stage of group development the conflict is more likely to be cognitive as group members propose, debate and evaluate alternative courses of action.

Inter-group conflict is collective and occurs between different groups. In broader society this may be at the international level, between governments, or at the national level, between opposing political parties, government and opposition. Within an organisation inter-group conflict emerges from the differences of views between capital and labour. Sources of disagreement might be similar to those observed in intra-group conflict, but the groups involved, having established a common line internally, now interact with the other side. Examples of sources of conflict are annual pay awards where the union demands a specified percentage increase and management offers a lower amount. Essentially this is conflict generated out of what is referred to as the 'wage/effort bargain': disputes that arise over the perceived value of work and the distribution of organisational wealth. Pay is the most frequent source of conflict in organisations. As Hale (2009: 28) observes,

> In 2008, 99% of working days lost were due to disputes over pay. This accounted for 67% of all stoppages.

Hale goes on to note that 'Disputes over pay also include stoppages over feared or alleged reductions in earnings as well as disputes over pay increases.' In a world in which business is becoming increasingly global, conflict at the international level is a significant feature. Inter-group conflict may arise in mergers and acquisitions, particularly in multinational corporations where the integration of two or more deep-rooted cultures into a new culture, or an imposition of a dominant culture, becomes a source of negative, affective conflict which impedes organisational effectiveness.

Conflict manifestation [2]

When conflict occurs in organisations it does not necessarily manifest itself immediately – indeed, in some cases it may not be identified because the indicators may simply be regarded as something that is usual. High labour turnover, for example, may be normalised by managers and not seen as a problem, whereas other manifestations of conflict, such as strikes, may be more easily identified. In some situations individuals or groups raise their dissatisfaction openly; in others they just walk away. This behaviour is in line with the arguments put forward by Albert Hirschman (1970) in his seminal work *Exit, Voice, and Loyalty*. Although Hirschman's work is mainly associated with the actions of consumers and the choices they make in relation to the deterioration in the quality of goods or services, the underlying principles can be applied to the state of relationships in organisations.

Hirschman argues that individuals can make one of two responses to this deterioration: they can *exit* the relationship or they can *voice* their dissatisfaction. In behavioural terms, Hirschman's work is closely related to the 'flight or fight' found in other areas of the behavioural sciences. In an employment relationship which is believed by the employee to have deteriorated to the point at which there is no benefit to the individual, the choice is either to exit the organisation by resignation or to voice their concerns by making a complaint or raising a grievance. From the organisation's perspective, although it is less confrontational, *exit* does not give any indication of the reason for the deterioration in the relationship, whereas *voice* provides valuable information regarding the underlying causes. The choice of exit or voice is affected by a number of factors, including the state of the labour market. The more employment opportunity there is locally, the greater the likelihood of exit. In an organisation where there is no formal voice mechanism in place or there is a culture which discourages complaints, there is little choice but to exit. Where a voice facility exists through trade union or other collective representation, grievance or complaints procedures, cognitive conflict can be highly beneficial (Cosier *et al*, 1991) and, as a consequence, the use of exit is likely to be lower. As well as reducing labour turnover costs, this has the added benefit of informing the organisation of the reasons for the conflict and provides an opportunity for corrective action.

We can also categorise the manifestation of conflict as *overt* and *covert*. Overt manifestation is where the indicators are open and clearly observable, often following agreed procedures; overt action is frequently collective and organised, commonly referred to as 'industrial action'. The most familiar example of organised collective action is the strike, which results in a temporary cessation of work designed to put economic pressure on the management to concede to trade union demands. Other examples are the lock-out, in which the employer locks the premises denying access to all workers, even those who would like to go on working, and putting pressure on the union to concede to the management's terms. Less common forms of industrial action include the 'work-to-rule', where work rules and job descriptions are followed to the letter, resulting in the withdrawal of goodwill and flexibility. Workers may alternatively decide to occupy the employer's premises through a 'sit-in', which prevents the employer from maintaining production or the provision of goods or services using brought-in temporary labour. To avoid the loss of earnings associated with a strike, some employees may decide to go off sick *en masse* (a 'sick-out') – this can be as effective as a strike in terms of the disruption caused, and more difficult for the employer to monitor. The 'go-slow' involves workers working with minimum enthusiasm and work being carried out at a more sedate pace than normal. Conflict between British Airways and Unite – the trade union representing cabin crew – over pay and the introduction of new working practices resulted in an unusual form of conflict manifestation. The union balloted cabin crew members for strike action, of whom 81% voted in favour; the company successfully sought an injunction in the High Court arguing that the statutory balloting requirements had not been satisfied. The *Daily Telegraph* reported (Osborne, 2009) that 'disaffected cabin crew have resorted to pouring vintage wine down the sink on the plane and throwing away unused washbags' in what was described as passive resistance.

Covert conflict manifestation refers to action which, in most cases, is individual and spontaneous, rather than collective and organised, and escapes the notice of management. These indicators of conflict are frequently missed through normalisation – in other words, management see these things as normal occurrences and in doing so miss their true significance. As noted earlier, high labour turnover may not be seen as a problem and not investigated; this may be an accurate assessment. However, if turnover predominates in isolated areas, it may be indicative of conflict. Likewise, high levels of employee absenteeism or low quality of work may be attributed to low levels of employee motivation, commitment or loyalty. Again, this may be so, but the chances are that the underlying reasons are related to interpersonal conflict. A further manifestation of conflict is sabotage, usually – but not exclusively – involving the breakage of tools and machinery by employees who are disaffected or who harbour grievances about the way they are treated, their workload or other unresolved complaints (Koch, 1999). Whatever the manifestation of conflict, management must identify the causes and initiate an appropriate resolution strategy.

Disaffected employees may use any of a range of sabotage techniques. These include non-performance and fraud, and as extreme measures as putting rodents into food and needles into baby-food products (Analoui and Kakabadse, 2000). Imagine the full economic and reputational damage created by the latter example. Because incidences of sabotage are not as common as other forms of covert action, they can escape attention, but the potential disruption and damage should not be underestimated. In a similar vein, another form of conflict has emerged in some organisations – malicious compliance, through which employees interpret instructions from managers so literally and precisely that they create maximum inconvenience.

Applying theory to practice: Conflict in the workplace

Most people will have been involved in conflict in the workplace or observed it in other organisations. Essentially, conflict is the product of a disagreement between two or more parties which might manifest itself in different ways. As a manager or an employee, it is important to understand the type of conflict that has occurred, who is involved, and why it has occurred. Without knowing these things it is difficult to find an effective solution. The conflict which is most destructive is likely to be *affective* and between individuals or groups (interpersonal, intra-group or inter-group). The cause is likely to be dependent on the actual parties involved: interpersonal conflict may be related to personality differences or role ambiguity; intra-group conflict may concern flexible working arrangements; inter-group conflict may arise over pay demands. The way that conflict manifests itself provides clues to whether the conflict is overt or covert, which will in turn determine the potential conflict resolution processes to be employed (internal or external). There is little point in adopting a particular resolution strategy if it does not match the nature and source of the conflict. It would be inappropriate to instigate external conciliation or arbitration when an internal grievance hearing will settle the issue less formally and more rapidly.

Conflict resolution processes

Conflict resolution concerns the mechanisms, systems and procedures which can be used to overcome differences of opinion which are deemed sufficiently significant to reduce organisational performance. However, as Cosier *et al* (1991: 7) observe, 'In many cases, conflict resolution implies that conflict is undesirable.' As noted earlier, not all conflict is bad; some is constructive, functional – it should be encouraged. For the purpose of this section, the discussion of conflict resolution will focus on the dysfunctional form which can damage the organisational relationships.

The process of conflict resolution depends on the nature of the conflict and the parties involved. It is highly likely that individual conflict will be managed differently from collective conflict. Similarly, overt and covert conflict may necessitate different solutions. Some types of conflict are resolved by way of internal systems and procedures whereas other types may require the assistance of external agencies. The way in which conflict is handled may be prescribed by way of organisational policies and procedures, such as a grievance procedure, disciplinary procedure or **disputes procedure**.

According to Thomas (1992) there are five potential approaches to conflict resolution based upon a two-dimensional model – how assertive one party is in pursuing its own interests or how co-operative they are in satisfying the interests of the other party. The five approaches to conflict resolution are: *avoiding*, in which the parties are unassertive and uncooperative; *forcing/competing*, where the parties are assertive but uncooperative; *compromising*, in which the parties are in the mid-range on both dimensions; *accommodating* where they are co-operative but unassertive; and *collaborating* in which the parties are both assertive and co-operative. These behaviours are highly influential in both the way the parties develop and pursue their conflict resolution strategies and the outcomes that are generated.

Internal conflict resolution takes a number of forms. Within a unionised organisation the preferred method of conflict resolution is collective bargaining, through which employer and union representatives negotiate their way toward an agreement. Each party starts with an assessment of what they would like to achieve, the 'most favoured position', and the least they will accept, the 'fall-back position'. An accurate assessment requires considerable research and preparation. The outcome of collective bargaining will depend on the strategies adopted by the participants. In their seminal text *A Behavioral Theory of Labor Negotiations*, Walton and McKersie (1965) identify two contrasting approaches to **negotiation**: they term these *distributive bargaining* and *integrative bargaining*. Distributive bargaining is conflict-based – a zero-sum process through which conflict is generated over the way in which fixed-sum (financial) resources are distributed. The underlying assumption is a win-lose scenario – it is highly competitive and one party can only win at the expense of the other. In contrast, integrative bargaining is co-operation-based: the two sides are open with each other and co-operate towards mutual gain (Fells, 1998).

The resolution of conflict utilising internal processes may be through a prescribed grievance procedure. Most grievance procedures involve a number of stages through which an individual employee's complaint or grievance may be progressed. The underlying objective of grievance procedures is to resolve the conflict as soon as possible and as near the point of origin as possible to prevent it from escalating and to minimise the severity. The Advisory, Conciliation and Arbitration Service recommends that formal grievance procedures should only be used as a last resort; grievances are best dealt with informally at an early stage with the immediate line manager (ACAS, 2009a).

When the nature and extent of the conflict is such that the parties directly involved in the conflict cannot reach a mutual solution, it is common for them to seek independent assistance. Within the organisation this may involve an internal mediator – someone who is not involved in the conflict and who may be able to assist the parties in the reconciliation of their differences. In this scenario the mediator will assist the parties in reviewing the cause of the conflict and evaluating the potential solutions. The mediator is a facilitator: he or she may suggest courses of action for the parties to consider. Mediators do not impose solutions nor compel those concerned to follow them. Ultimately, it is up to those directly involved in the conflict to reach their own settlement.

Similarly, organisational conflict, whether interpersonal or inter-group, may best be resolved by the use of external independent advice. This is referred to as 'third-party intervention'. The two most common forms of third-party intervention are conciliation and **mediation**. Although they are similar in nature insofar as they are facilitative rather than decisional, there are important differences. The contemporary distinction between conciliation and mediation is that conciliation occurs when an application has been made to an employment tribunal or where an application is imminent, whereas mediation takes place without the tribunal backdrop (ACAS, 2009b).

Conciliation involves an independent person – the conciliator – working with the parties, either jointly or separately, the purpose being to assist them in seeing the issues clearly and to bring them to understand each other's positions in an objective way. In the case of individual conflict, conciliation is frequently used when an application has been made to an employment tribunal. In collective conflict it is more likely to be in relation to a dispute where, as noted earlier, collective bargaining has failed.

The term 'mediation' is frequently cited as a form of conflict resolution facilitated by independent third parties, and it is frequently used in a very liberal manner. Mediation may be utilised in cases of individual or collective conflict; it may also be used as an advisory intervention to prevent rather than resolve conflict. Technically, mediation may be slightly more prescriptive than conciliation; the mediator may make suggestions to resolve the conflict, whereas the conciliator may not. Mediation may sometimes be used by organisations as a preliminary measure, a halfway-house, prior to including an arbitration clause in a disputes procedure.

The most prescriptive form of third-party intervention is **arbitration**, in that for this type of conflict resolution the decision-making responsibility is delegated to the arbitrator. Arbitration comes in two main forms. The first is referred to as 'split-the-difference', 'traditional' or 'conventional' arbitration; the second is referred to as 'final-offer', 'last-offer', 'flip-flop' or 'pendulum' arbitration. In the first form of arbitration the arbitrator is able to occupy the middle ground between the two positions and may settle the dispute by simply splitting the difference, although arbitration decisions are rarely reached in this manner (Wood, 1985). In **final-offer arbitration** the arbitrator is denied the occupation of the middle ground and is expected to decide between the final positions of the parties. This raises a number of potential problems. First, it is not always possible to identify the final position of the parties – negotiations are frequently hard-fought battles, particularly within the distributive bargaining framework, which involve posturing. Expressions such as 'This is my final offer' or 'Not a penny more' are part of the negotiating ritual. If arbitration can be invoked by one party, they may, in doing so, pre-empt a potential settlement. Second, the negotiating behaviour of the parties might be influenced by the form of arbitration being used. If the agreed form of arbitration is 'split the difference' and the belief is that the arbitrator will decide on the mid-point, management may make an excessively low offer or the union an excessively high demand. Final-offer arbitration may encourage the parties to be more realistic in their expectations and adopt more responsible behaviour. In summary, in conventional arbitration the arbitrator has freedom to impose any settlement whereas in final-offer arbitration the arbitrator is constrained and must choose one position.

It might be argued that arbitration encourages the parties to abdicate their decision-making responsibilities. Certainly, if arbitration creates reliance or what has been termed a 'narcotic' effect, resulting in the parties not engaging in serious bargaining (Wirtz, 1963; Wood, 1985; Bolton and Katok, 1998), it might be to the detriment of the parties because conflict solutions reached on the basis of negation tend to be longer-lasting than those derived from arbitration.

Third-party intervention may also be referred to as 'alternative dispute resolution'. The main perceived benefits of the various methods, particularly conciliation and mediation, are economic and relational. It is generally accepted that third-party intervention or alternative dispute resolution is cheaper and less time-consuming than litigation (Fox and Stallworth, 2009; Lipsky and Seeber, 2000).

An additional form of conflict resolution is using external sources for 'coaching'. Although more usually associated with the use of external consultants for management and executive development, coaching is regarded by some (Fox and Stallworth, 2009) as a form of alternative dispute resolution. In its report on dispute resolution in the US energy industry, the Alternative Dispute Resolution Committee (2009: 197) noted that the Dispute Resolution Service was used 'in a coaching capacity' to assist in resolving two cases. The main difference between coaching and other forms of alternative dispute resolution is the participants. Whereas conciliation and mediation involve three parties, coaching is mainly restricted to two: the disputant and the coach. This particular intervention has been termed '**conflict coaching**' by Brinkert (2006: 522–3), who proposes what he terms a 'five Cs' model: 'client-disputant and coach communicating about conflict in context'. In essence the role of the conflict coach is highly relational; emphasis should be on understanding the conflict and the context in which it occurs. It is about sharing additional perspectives, not imposing them, in a conversational rather than didactic manner which fosters mutual trust.

Regardless of the form in which conflict manifests itself, it is essential that organisations formulate a strategy for minimising the incidence and producing a resolution when it does arise. This may comprise both internal elements, such as formal consultation, complaints, grievance, disciplinary and disputes procedures, and external elements, such as conciliation, mediation, arbitration and coaching.

WORST PRACTICE

Nothing but BlueSky all day long

Winston Jennings is the production manager at the BlueSky media publishing company. The star performer in the production team is Lucy Smarte. Lucy has consistently produced the quality and quantity of work that Winston needs, and she is quite prepared to work long hours. Other team members are not so reliable, so Winston gives the difficult projects – particularly those with tight deadlines – to Lucy. It is quite normal for her to be working on two or three high-profile projects simultaneously, but in the last six months this has escalated to four or five as the business has become more successful. Recently, Winston has noticed that Lucy has not been performing as well as he expected. She has become withdrawn and started avoiding other team members. She now often arrives late for work and looks tired, with bloodshot eyes. Winston calls a formal meeting to discuss her performance, during which Lucy becomes very irritable and defensive. He responds by telling her to 'Grow up and stop being such a pain.' If she has problems, she should leave them at home – and if she can't do that, maybe she should find another job. Lucy starts to cry and runs from his office.

Process outcomes

The outcomes of conflict resolution process may not always be positive – the chosen intervention may not bring about a solution. Collective conflict between a trade union and management over pay may not be resolved through collective bargaining, and the two sides may reach a stalemate: the best they can do is disagree, and the dispute continues. In these circumstances it would be normal to seek third-party intervention using conciliation, mediation or arbitration. A similar situation may arise between an individual and their organisation over unfair dismissal. Where the two parties are unable to reach a satisfactory outcome, the assistance of a conciliator may be sought, often as a preliminary to an employment tribunal hearing, in an attempt to reach a mutually agreeable solution and avoid having to present the case to the tribunal.

It is generally recognised that conflict resolution resulting from an active role in the problem-solving process by the parties themselves produces higher-quality and longer-lasting outcomes than those produced by third-party intervention, particularly in the case of imposed solutions through arbitration (Keashly and Newberry, 1995; Brett *et al*, 1996; Jameson, 2001). The outcomes of conflict resolution, whether internal or external, in the first instance may be simply categorised as agreement or disagreement. In the case of agreement, the current differences may be settled and life continues in line with the agreed terms. This may be a resumption of normal life, or the parties may decide that a lasting resolution is not possible and the only viable option is to dissolve the employment relationship. In the case of disagreement, the decision may be made to refer the conflict to an independent body through one of the interventions described above, or to advance the conflict to a higher level. As observed earlier, some outcomes may ultimately become causes of conflict – what is deemed acceptable now may not be so at some point in the future . . . and so the cycle of conflict continues. A conflict-based situation may be a stressful experience for the parties involved, whether this is personal conflict, over a moral dilemma, interpersonal or inter-group conflict, of an affective or cognitive nature, or inter-group conflict, such as a merger or an industrial dispute. Each individual involved will be affected by and cope with stress in different ways. These issues are examined in the following section.

Taking your learning further: Conflict and conflict resolution

Braverman, H. (1974) *Labor and Monopoly Capital: The degradation of work in the twentieth century*. New York: Monthly Review Press. This provides an account of the degradation of work in the twentieth century and the way in which conflict is created by the divergent objectives of labour and capital. Braverman argues that labour power has been largely eroded by the deskilling process, through simplification of tasks, and a more assertive management style.

Fox, A. (1973) 'Industrial relations: a social critique of pluralist ideology', in J. Child (ed.) *Man and Organization*. London: Allen &

Unwin. An excellent analysis of the pluralist and unitarist approaches to industrial relations and the way in which these explain the sources of conflict and its management in organisations.

Thomas, K. W. (1976) 'Conflict and conflict management', in M. D. Dunnett (ed.) *Handbook of Industrial and Organizational Psychology*, 2nd edition. Chicago, IL: Rand McNally. This chapter sets out the way in which conflict between parties may be managed and resolved, based on how co-operative or assertive each party may be, and develops a model of different approaches to conflict resolution.

STRESS IN THE WORKPLACE

The English word *stress* originates from a medieval French derivative of the Latin verb *stringere*, meaning 'to draw tight'. Although it can be argued that some stress is helpful, the negative effects of stress in the workplace cannot and should not be underestimated. In its *Stress at Work* factsheet, the CIPD (2009a) reports stress as one of the significant causes of workplace sickness and absence. The HSE (2009a) reports that in the 2008/09 reporting period, 415,000 individuals were affected by stress, anxiety or depression, which resulted in 11.4 million working days being lost – these three causes were the largest contributors to work-related ill health. Stress is also unbounded and cannot be easily compartmentalised. Stress in social life impacts on work, and work-related stress affects social life: advising a stressed employee not to bring their problems to work is unlikely to be understood nor acted upon.

Definitions of stress

As might be expected, stress has been defined in a number of different ways. Some definitions are neutral. Schuler (1984: 36), for example, suggests that stress is 'a perceived dynamic state involving uncertainty about something important', whereas others, such as the Health and Safety Executive (2009b), define stress in a negative manner as 'the adverse reaction people have to excessive pressure or other types of demand placed on them at work', or as 'an unpleasant emotional state' (Wagner and Hollenbeck, 2010: 107). Rarely do we find positively biased stress definitions – yet it is acknowledged that stress can create a positive state as well as a negative.

It is worth at this point dissecting stress into the positive and negative forms and exploring their attributes in order to enhance our understanding. Positive stress was termed 'eustress' in the 1930s by Hans Selye, the 'eu-' prefix being derived from the ancient Greek for 'good', as in 'euphoria', a good feeling. As Bal *et al* (2009: 10) observe, 'Eustress is the energy you feel when tackling a challenging assignment and feeling confident in your abilities.' This type of stress acts as a stimulus for success. Negative stress, on the other hand, is described as 'distress' – the harmful stress an individual might experience when engaged in challenging activities which are perceived to be beyond their capability or the result of poor working relationships. The positive and negative forms of stress are also sometimes referred to as 'hindrance-related' (distress) or 'challenge-related' (eustress) (Culbertson *et al*, 2010). Although the concept of positive stress may be encouraging, attempts to evoke it may result in more harm than good. The expression 'A little stress is good' springs to mind here: it has been argued that most people do well under moderate stress (Carmichael, 2009). The crucial point to understand is people's differential ability to cope with stress. The degree of resilience to stress may be related to personality, some individuals being more stress-prone than others. According to Friedman and Rosenman (1974), highly competitive individuals with a great need for achievement (Type A) tend to be more stress-prone than those with a more relaxed or balanced approach (Type B). In very simple terms, the difference between pressure and stress is an individual's confidence. Pressure for one person may be stress for another, and managers have to be able to differentiate between the two. Stress may also be categorised as 'acute' or 'chronic'. Acute stress may be physical or mental and tends to be short-lived: as soon as a stress event is over, the body returns to normal and relaxes. Chronic psychological stress occurs when the body is subjected to prolonged periods of high-intensity activity with which it simply cannot cope.

The causes and effects of stress

The causes of stress in the workplace are many and varied: *physical working conditions*, including temperature, noise, ergonomic design, virtual working, isolation, shift-patterns; *the nature of the work*, including intensity-overload/underload, repetitive routines, long hours, emotional labour (Wharton, 1996); *management style*, including inconsistency, demanding, setting unrealistic deadlines, autocratic behaviour, surveillance practices (Ariss, 2002), poor communication systems (Taylor *et al*, 2008), lack of feedback on performance; *uncertainty*, including during times of personal or organisational change (Lazarus, 1966: Fink *et al*, 1971), fear of job loss, role ambiguity (French and Caplan, 1970); *workplace relationships*, including between the employee and their manager, peers, subordinates and customers (Motowidlo *et al*, 1986; Sosik and Godschalk, 2000), victimisation and bullying (Vartia, 2001); and *conflict*, including moral dilemmas (Bird and Waters, 1989; Menzel, 1993), incompatibility between the demands of the job and the family (Kanter, 1977), **role conflict** (Deluga, 1989). Stress might also be created by a lack of confidence in our own ability to cope with a new situation or to achieve desired outcomes – you might experience this during your time as a student progressing from one level of academic study to another or having to make a presentation in front of an audience for the first time.

The effects of 'negative' or 'bad' stress are wide-ranging. They not only affect the psychological and physiological well-being of the individual experiencing stress, they also have a relational impact on the lives of colleagues, family and friends, and an economic impact on the effectiveness of the organisation.

Identifying and managing stress

Whether the causes are physical or psychological, stress manifests itself in two principle ways: physical and behavioural. In 1946 Dr Hans Selye – frequently described as 'the father of stress' – wrote what became one of the most influential articles in the field of stress and its understanding. Some 30 years later Selye (1977) commented that he was gratified to learn that his original article had been cited so frequently, but also to consider the progress in stress research since its publication. In his article, Selye (1946) proposed the 'general adaptation syndrome' (GAS) to describe the many and non-specific physical reactions of the body as a result of prolonged exposure to psychological (and physical) stress. The GAS comprises three stages: the *alarm reaction*, the stage of *resistance*, and the stage of *exhaustion*.

In the first stage, alarm reaction, an individual's defence mechanisms are stimulated, and the body releases adrenaline to combat the stress created by exposure to a new situation. This causes a range of physical symptoms – there is an increased heart rate and a higher volume of blood is pumped, faster breathing, perspiration and dilated pupils; there may even be muscle cramps, and nausea. You may have experienced some of these symptoms yourself in stressful situations such as exams. There are also psychological symptoms created by the release of chemical substances into the body which limit the cognitive abilities. When the source of stress is removed – as might be the case once physical or mental exertion stops – the body recovers and the symptoms disappear.

If the source of stress is not removed, the body goes to the second stage of the GAS – resistance – in which the initial signs of shock disappear. Through the secretion of additional hormones, the body responds by increasing blood sugar levels and raising the blood pressure, providing the body with rapid energy. Essentially, the body is now in 'overdrive' or being over-used. If there is no subsequent period of relaxation or respite, symptoms such as fatigue, irritability and anxiety will emerge. If the individual adapts to the situation or the source of stress is removed, the equilibrium will be restored. However, if the individual does not adapt or the source of stress remains, they will enter the third stage of the GAS.

In the third stage – exhaustion – the body's energy reserves become depleted by the prolonged exposure to stress and the production of coping hormones. Blood sugar levels decrease and the body's ability to tolerate stress is impaired, leading to mental and physical exhaustion, resulting ultimately in mental or physical collapse.

One of the primary difficulties for organisations and management is that of being able to identify the symptoms of stress and to take necessary action within an appropriate time period. It is still quite common for the telltale signs of stress to be overlooked, allowing the stress to build up until the inevitable breakdown occurs. It is then a case of cleaning up the mess which, by managerial vigilance, might have been avoided (Jacques, 1970). Although there may be a tendency to place the burden on employers and managers, effective stress management is also the responsibility of the individual, because they are likely to become aware of the early symptoms first – but they need to understand their full significance and not dismiss them.

Stress manifests itself in a variety of ways (CIPD, 2009a). The first signs of stress include fatigue, irritability, inability to concentrate, lapses of memory, anxiety, depression, withdrawal, headaches, increased smoking or alcohol consumption, high blood pressure, aggression, insomnia. Some of these symptoms are more obvious to co-workers than to the stressed employee. The steps an individual can take to reduce stress include reviewing their physical and psychological well-being through exercise, a healthy diet and avoiding excessive alcohol intake; personal organisation and planning to achieve a healthy work–life balance, prioritising tasks and scheduling work to avoid overload, planning regular breaks to relax and recharge; and developing emotional intelligence in order to become aware of the symptoms of stress and to manage their own emotions.

A manager, supervisor or co-worker who observes one or more of these behaviours should seek to identify the cause and provide assistance through workplace counselling and assistance programmes. It is also important for managers and supervisors to develop emotional intelligence to enable them to recognise atypical subordinate behaviours and identify potential causes. Not only will this help to reduce the incidence and impact of stress but employers have a legal obligation to protect employees' health, safety and welfare, which includes work-related stress. The Chartered Institute of Personnel and Development (CIPD, 2009a) advocates, among other things, a participative management style to reduce workplace stress. The Institute has also published a competency framework for managers for preventing and reducing stress at work

(CIPD, 2009b), which sets out key competencies, such as 'respectful and responsible: managing emotions and having integrity' along with sub-competencies of 'integrity', 'managing emotions', and 'considerate approach'. Arguably, the inclusion of these abilities among the broader management competencies can only have a positive effect in combating the growing trend in stress at work.

One of the most important aspects of stress management is the way it is viewed. Stress should not be viewed as an inherent personal weakness, the only viable solution to which is exit from the organisation. Organisations can introduce initiatives to reduce stress. These might include physical activities during breaks, planned breaks in computer use, attitude surveys which incorporate a stress dimension, and employer-sponsored health checks.

Applying theory to practice: Letting off steam in the radiator department

Steve Alleyne is HR Manager at Ellersby Engineering, which produces central-heating products. The results of a recent evaluation of absence and labour turnover statistics revealed higher absence and turnover among the 30 workers in the radiator department than elsewhere in the organisation. Steve consulted with the senior shop steward of the recognised trade union which led to a joint management-union organisation-wide staff attitude survey, part of which was a stress risk assessment following the Health and Safety Executive guidelines. This was followed by two focus groups. The finding of the survey and focus group highlighted a moderate level of stress in the radiator department, the main causes being: inconsistent demand as a result of poor scheduling, ranging from under-work to overload; a lack of consultation with workers over their workload; a lack of any formal means through which employees could voice their concerns; and authoritarian and dismissive behaviour by the department manager, who responded to complaints of overwork by saying, 'There are 2 million unemployed people out there just dying for your job – take it or leave it!' Working closely with the firm's Health and Safety Committee, Steve developed an action plan for the development and introduction of a Well-being at Work policy.

Taking your learning further: Stress

Cooper, C. L, Dewe, P. J. and O'Driscoll, M. P. (2001) *Organizational Stress: A review and critique of theory, research and applications*. Thousand Oaks, CA: Sage Publications. This text provides an analysis of the way in which changes to work and the employment relationship might increase worker and workplace stress.

Dijkstra, M. T. M., van Dierendonck, D. and Evers, A. (2005) 'Responding to conflict at work and individual well-being: the mediating role of flight behaviour and feelings of helplessness', *European Journal of Work and Organizational Psychology*, Vol.14, No.4: 119–35. This article explores the relationship between conflict, stress and personal well-being. The authors discuss the causes of stress, such as insecurity and interpersonal conflict, and argue that conflict is related to a deterioration in well-being.

Motowidlo, S. J., Packard, J. S. and Manning, M. R. (1986) 'Occupational stress: its causes and consequences for job performance', *Journal of Applied Psychology*, Vol.71, No.4: 618–29. This article explores the causes of occupational stress, such as role conflict and ambiguity. The authors discuss the way that stress can lead to depression, resulting in lower motivation and a negative impact on job performance.

CONFLICT AND STRESS: A POTENTIAL CAUSAL LINK

There is considerable research evidence which identifies conflict at work to be a significant source of stress (Parkes, 1989), with interpersonal conflicts being some of the most significant (Bolger *et al*, 1989; Dijkstra *et al*, 2005). If you refer to the Practitioner insight case study at the beginning of this chapter, you will observe that the interpersonal conflict that Fraser experienced ultimately resulted in symptoms of stress – sleeplessness, irritability with those closest to him, low self-esteem, withdrawal. Such was the level of stress he experienced that it had a negative impact on his performance.

It is also interesting to explore the relationship between organisational change and conflict and stress. There is ample evidence to support the view that organisational change is a source of conflict, particularly when employees believe that reorganisation and restructuring will result in job losses. In such circumstances it is not only the employees who lose their jobs that are likely to be in conflict with the organisation, but those who remain in employment, through resentment, anger, guilt and a sense of loss (McKenna, 2006). Some change – that which employees perceive to be beneficial – may be implemented with relative ease. Change which upsets the *status quo*, where familiar organisational structures, routines and relationships are replaced with uncertainty and perceptions of loss, may result in resistance and conflict in the various forms described earlier in the chapter. For some employees radical change can produce the same effects as bereavement in terms of the psychological impact, the degree of shock and cognitive disorientation. The potential impact of organisational change on individuals has been conceptualised as a multi-phase 'crisis' by Fink *et al* (1971), whose model is set out in Figure 8.3.

The authors propose four phases that individuals go through over time and the associated self-experience, reality perceptions, emotional experience, and cognitive structure in relation to significant change. Many of the effects set out in these components are similar to those associated with stress from other sources, such as interpersonal conflicts, work overload, and work–life balance. Although the model describes individuals' internal experiences, there will undoubtedly be external symptoms such as those described in the previous section. Consequently, the model provides a useful illustration of the potential relationship between the internal and interpersonal conflict that arises out of change and the individual stress that results.

Stress risk assessment

Assessing the risk of stress in the workplace is not only good management practice but a legal requirement. Under current health and safety legislation, employers are required to carry out risk assessments to minimise the incidence of stress at work. The most effective forms of assessment are those which involve employees in dialogue, either through a general staff attitude survey or one which is specifically related to stress. The Health and Safety Executive (2004) encourages organisations to be proactive in reducing stress at work and recommends six areas of assessment:

- the ability to cope with job demands
- adequate control over how the job is done
- the availability of adequate support from co-workers and superiors
- understanding of roles and responsibilities
- exposure to unacceptable behaviours
- involvement in organisational changes.

Figure 8.3 Phases of individual crisis

TIME

Phase	Self-experience	Reality perception	Emotional experience	Cognitive structure
Shock	Threat to existing structure	Perceived as overwhelming	Panic, helplessness	Disorganisation, inability to plan, reason or understand the situation
Defensive retreat	Attempt to maintain old structure	Avoidance of reality; wishful thinking	Indifference or euphoria (except when challenged, in which case, anger)	Defensive reorganisation. Resistance to change
Acknowledgement	Giving up existing structure; self-deprecation	Facing reality	Depression. Bitterness	Defensive breakdown: 1) Disorganisation 2) Reorganisation in terms of altered reality perceptions
Adaptation and change	Establishing new structure. Sense of worth	New reality-testing	Gradual increase in satisfying experiences	Reorganisation in terms of present resources and abilities

Source: Fink, S. L., Beak, J. and Taddeo, K. (1971) 'Organizational crisis and change', *Journal of Applied Behavioural Science*, Vol.7, No.1: 18. Reproduced with authors' and publisher's permission.

If the assessment reveals any problems or potential problems, the managers should consult employees to identify potential solutions. Risk assessment does not need to be a highly demanding or expensive procedure, and the benefits outweigh any costs involved. A cost–benefit analysis is likely to reveal that a workforce enjoying good mental and physical health results in reduced absenteeism, higher-quality work, more constructive relationships and greater employee engagement – all leading to improved organisational performance.

BEST PRACTICE

Engineering a less stressful relationship

Steve Jones, an engineering manager, was being criticised by Phil Symmons, his unit manager, because Steve's department had missed targets leading to the whole unit's failing. Phil also thought Steve's attitude was uncooperative and obstructive. Steve, however, believed he was doing a good job with what he had available, and thought that Phil was bullying him and obstructing his career development. This stress started to deeply affect his work and home life. On hearing about the situation, the Director brought in the HR department, who contacted Neil Scotton, an executive coach. Neil first met the Director and the HR manager to establish the concerns, expectations and boundaries. He then met Steve and Phil individually to listen to their perspectives. A joint meeting followed to define a clear objective outcome. The outcome agreed was that Steve should establish over the coming months whether he could demonstrate the competences of the grade he aspired to. The unsaid issue was that Steve and Phil each saw themselves as victims of the other's attitude and behaviour. The question 'How do you want them to feel at the end of each meeting?' was a breakthrough. They realised that their actions influenced events, and they had choice. The insight the coaching created meant that a healthy working relationship was restored.

Conclusion

The objective of this chapter was to provide an understanding of two principal concepts: conflict and stress in organisations. Conflict can occur at different levels and emanate from a variety of sources: frames of reference provide an important tool in the understanding of why conflict arises out of differing perspectives, goals, interests and values of the participants. Although conflict is frequently considered to be harmful, something to be avoided, there are times when it should be encouraged. Conflict in organisations can be positive *and* negative, functional *and* dysfunctional. Cognitive conflict within groups or teams may enhance the effectiveness of decision-making.

The way in which conflict manifests is multifaceted. Some forms are obvious indicators – strikes and work-to-rule, etc – whereas other forms, such as absence and labour turnover, may go unnoticed. Where it is perceived to be harmful, conflict may be resolved using a number of techniques, such as conciliation, mediation, arbitration and coaching, either individually or consecutively. The outcomes of conflict resolution may be a return to peaceful relations, an advancement to a higher level in the resolution process, or a recognition that no resolution is possible – in which case the relationship is dissolved and parties go their separate ways.

Stress is recognised to be a growing feature in organisations which results in significant psychological and economic damage. The causes of stress at work may be organisational change, interpersonal conflict between peers or between subordinates and superiors, work intensification or poor work–life balance. There are many physical and mental symptoms of stress. Some may be more noticeable to the individual whereas others may be more easily identified by work colleagues. Effective stress management is the responsibility of the individual and the organisations. The ability to identify the signs of stress, and knowing how to deal with them, is essential to preserve individual well-being and organisational performance.

End notes

[1] See also Chapter 7.

[2] See also Chapter 13.

Ethical implications: Ethics in conflict and stress

For many people, work is the most time-consuming activity in life, so it is essential that an organisation treats its employees ethically and responsibly. This does not mean that the needs of employees should override those of the organisation – the organisation has no obligation to provide employees with happiness or social welfare. What is important is to treat employees in a way that is morally right. Some conflict in organisations is helpful and makes a positive contribution to performance. However, when introducing a positive conflict stimulus or identifying that negative conflict has arisen, it is important that managers preserve the integrity of the organisation and ensure that the conflict does not have a detrimental effect on employee well-being. It is the moral responsibility of the organisation to minimise harmful, dysfunctional conflict through the application of appropriate policies and procedures. Similar ethical responsibilities surround the area of stress. Although employees have some responsibility for their own well-being, organisations, managers and supervisors should ensure that employees are not subjected to undue and prolonged stress as a result of conflict, work overload or unreasonable demands. A useful stance is provided by Epictetus (AD 55–135), who wrote, 'What thou avoidest suffering thyself, seek not to impose on others.'

REVIEW AND DISCUSSION QUESTIONS

REVIEW QUESTIONS

1 What are the four main frames of reference, and how do they explain conflict in organisations?

2 What are the four potential sources of conflict in organisations?

3 What are the three main forms of third-party intervention?

4 What are the technical terms used to describe positive and negative stress?

5 What are the three stages in Selye's General Adaptation Syndrome?

DISCUSSION QUESTIONS

1 Why should employers not dismiss high labour turnover as a normal aspect of organisational life?

2 Why should some conflict be encouraged in organisations?

3 Why might 'conflict coaching' provide a better outcome than the traditional forms of third-party intervention?

4 What are the effects of stress on the individual and the organisation?

5 In what ways might conflict and stress be related?

FURTHER READING

Baron, R. A. (1991) 'Positive effects of conflict: a cognitive perspective', *Employee Responsibilities and Rights Journal*, Vol.4, No.1: 25–36. In this article the author presents research findings in which managers reported beneficial effects of conflict.

Brinkert, R. (2006) 'Conflict coaching: advancing the conflict resolution field by developing an individual disputant process', *Conflict Resolution Quarterly*, Vol.23, No.4: 517–28. This article presents an argument for the use of executive coaching as a technique for conflict resolution.

Culbertson, S. S., Huffman, A. H. and Alden-Anderson, R. (2010) 'Leader-member exchange and work-family interactions: the mediating role of self-reported challenge- and hindrance-related stress', *The Journal of Psychology*, Vol.144, No.1: 15–36. This article explores the impact of positive and negative stress on leader-member relations.

Deluga, R. J. (1989) 'Employee-influence strategies as possible stress-coping mechanisms for role conflict and role ambiguity', *Basic and Applied Social Psychology*, Vol.10, No.4:329–35. In this concise article the author explores the relationship between stress and role conflict and potential coping strategies.

Dunlop, J. T. (1993) *Industrial Relations Systems*, Revised edition. Boston, MA: Harvard Business School Press. This book – one of the most influential in industrial relations – provides a framework for analysing the rule-making systems for conflict management.

Gerzon, M. (2006) *Leadership Through Conflict: How successful leaders transform differences into opportunities*. Boston, MA: Harvard Business School Press. A book which unites the fields of mediation and leadership.

Tjosvold, D. (2008) 'The conflict-positive organization', *Journal of Organizational Behavior*, Vol.29: 19–28. This article questions the commonly held view that all conflict is bad and sets out an alternative view highlighting the positive aspects.

Wood, J. (1985) 'Last offer arbitration', *British Journal of Industrial Relations*, Vol.23, No.3: 415–24. An article which critiques, in detail, the characteristics and uses of last-offer arbitration.

KEY SKILLS

There are a number of key skills that are necessary for effectively dealing with conflict and stress in the workplace. It is important to recognise that many of these skills have a broad application and are appropriate in a variety of situations. As we have seen in this chapter, conflict and stress can have both positive and negative effects and the deliberate introduction of both requires sensitivity and caution. And as you will have discovered in the chapters about individuals, each of us is different with different tolerance levels, coping abilities and strategies.

CRITICAL THINKING, REFLECTIVE LEARNING, EMOTIONAL INTELLIGENCE, NEGOTIATING AND PROBLEM-SOLVING SKILLS

As individuals, we need to develop our ability for *critical thinking* in order to apply reason and to make rational decisions. If, for example, we receive information about conflict between two individuals or a situation in which symptoms of stress are being exhibited, we need to analyse this information by deconstructing it down to component parts so that we fully evaluate its significance. It is highly likely that we will draw on additional information, theoretical or experiential, to synthesise this in our attempt to fully understand. If we have encountered similar situations previously, we may employ *reflective learning*. The information and knowledge we have absorbed is used to guide our thinking and formulate an appropriate course of action.

Conflict resolution and stress reduction requires *emotional intelligence*. As managers and co-workers we need to be aware of our own emotions and those of others, and be able to manage our emotions. This is particularly important during processes such as negotiations, conciliation, arbitration or **grievance-handling**. In such situations individuals need to be able to demonstrate *empathy* and understanding for others, and *sympathy* towards their requirements and any limitations that might constrain them.

In circumstances where two parties are in conflict, individuals require sound *negotiating skills* through which they can strive for a win-win outcome. This necessitates the ability to identify through verbal and non-verbal (emotional) indicators the various positions of the other party and to find common ground upon which to build an agreement to resolve the conflict. In acting as a third party in conciliation or arbitration, the individual should be able to demonstrate integrity through exercising *professional judgement* during the decision-making process. This of course relies heavily on critical and rational thinking described above and the employment of *problem-solving skills* based on a clear identification of the nature and extent of the problem, its causes and the potential solutions that will be acceptable to the parties concerned. Strong emotional intelligence skills will facilitate a constructive relationship between the parties and help to build mutual trust.

Likewise, in situations involving actual or potential stress, individuals need to exercise professional judgement in identifying the causes and extent of stress by reference to the symptoms exhibited. Taking appropriate action and making the right decisions requires a strong ethical approach which displays a strong *social*

responsibility towards the organisation and the individuals within it – in other words, doing what is ethically right, however difficult this might be. Once again this is achieved through critical thinking, a full evaluation of the issues, causes, potential remedies and the way these may be received by the parties. Doing the right thing may be advantageous for the individual and disadvantageous for the organisation, or indeed vice versa. If the decision-maker has formulated a solution based on sound critical thinking, rational analysis and reflective thinking, the outcome will be easier to justify to oneself and to others. What is important is that in the justification of the outcome to others, emotional intelligence is employed to ensure sensitivity towards alternative points of view, and that any differences of opinion are reconciled through integrative negotiation.

TEAMWORKING, LEADERSHIP, PERSUASIVE AND COACHING SKILLS

Little in organisations is conducted in isolation. If this were the case, conflict might not be such a contentious issue. Much of what happens in organisations is done collectively in groups and teams. *Teamworking* and the interaction between individuals in these organisational sub-structures is fertile ground for conflict and stress generation. As noted earlier in this chapter, cognitive conflict is generally considered beneficial to good decision-making, and the promotion of this may be within the role of the team leader. Strong *leadership skills* include the ability to stimulate desirable behaviours among team members and to facilitate the desired outcomes. This involves listening to the convergent or divergent views of the team and guiding them towards the desired outcome. It also involves promoting the sharing of ideas and the use of *persuasion* to overcome obstacles. Promoting positive, cognitive conflict for enhanced problem-solving and reducing negative, affective conflict is an important aspect of leadership. As you will have read in the chapter on groups and teams (Chapter 7), in the storming stage of team development conflict is inevitable as the team members vie for position and seek to establish the norms of behaviour. In such situations the leader's responsibility is to ensure that affective conflict is minimised. It is also the role of the leader to ensure that team members receive the support and development necessary to minimise conflict and stress and to enhance their performance. Using critical thinking, the leader should identify potential sources of conflict and/or stress within the team and designate appropriate action. This might involve interventions such as *coaching*. This may be developmental to improve the capability of an under-performing employee to avoid the onset of work-related stress; in contrast, it may be coaching for resolving conflict between two individuals which is negatively affecting their own performance and the performance of those around them. Both types of coaching require emotional intelligence on the part of the coach to fully engage with the coachee and to enable him or her, through questioning techniques, to develop the ability for self-awareness and self-evaluation to identify the causes and their own potential solution to the conflict or stress, rather than take a directive approach.

Chapter 9
Communication

Markus C. Hasel

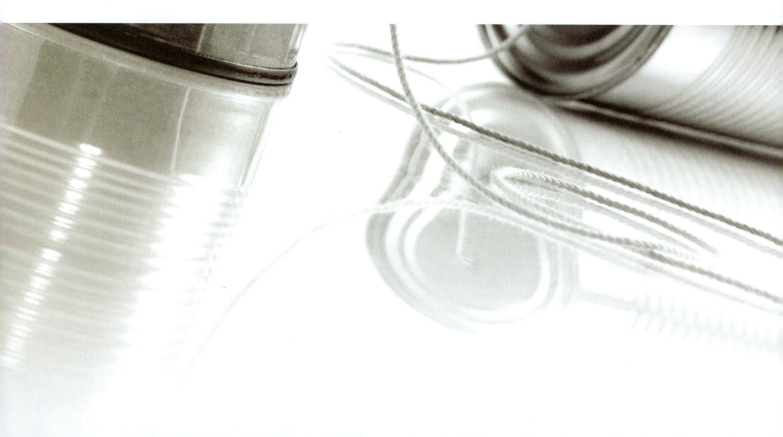

Contents

Key Learning Outcomes

By the end of this chapter you should be able to:

- appreciate the importance of communication
- describe the different ways to communicate
- appreciate that communication changes with time
- understand that communication depends on personal relationships
- appreciate the power of communication
- realise that some communication techniques are better than others.

PRACTITIONER INSIGHT

Xerox Europe

Xerox Europe is a Europe-wide operating enterprise that has expanded its business from photocopiers to business process outsourcing related to documents such as credit-card billing. An important part of the business is the learning and development team throughout Western Europe which provides staff within Xerox with training. We speak to **Darrell Minards, Head of Learning and Development**, about the main communication challenges that he faces at Xerox Europe.

One of the key challenges is tailoring training needs to cultural differences including considerations of language issues. Although the business language is English, people in non-English-speaking countries need to be trained in languages they are most comfortable with in order to make the learning experience a successful one. However, because communication is a crucial part of organisational life, the challenge lies in meeting organisational requirements and individual levels of language skills. The chosen language and communication style therefore has to be of value for both organisation and individual. For instance, leadership seminars are delivered in English, because participants need to communicate in the official business language – English – across the organisation. Despite any potential language barriers, it is crucial to communicate that training is available to people around the clock day and night.

What do you think the challenges are for cross-level communication by not training lower-level employees in English? What do you think can be done to resolve any related issues?

Another crucial change regarding communication within Xerox came about through technological developments. For instance, the financial crisis led to cost-saving measures that reduced travelling budgets. Xerox reacted by introducing forums for people to post their questions. Other members of the organisation are able to view answers and to reply, allowing boundaryless communication across countries. A recent example was a request by a trainer in the UK for a negotiation exercise that might be used in training events. After the request was posted on the forum, a trainer from Spain, who had never met the UK trainer, replied and suggested an exercise he had been using successfully in training.

What other kinds of technology do you think Xerox uses in order to reduce costs?

Once you have read this chapter, return to these questions and think about how you could answer them.

Introduction

Did you know that the first modern computer was built in 1939, was called 'Mark 1', and was followed by ENIAC, the first electronic computer without moving parts, four years later? Did you also know that we just communicated for the first time? Although you have not told me anything, I have told you something. Is that communication? It is unidirectional communication – as we will explore while going through this chapter.

The following chapter demonstrates the importance of communication, how to communicate verbally and in written form, and the different types and levels of communication. It also explains the differences, advantages and disadvantages, and even gives you an idea of when to use particular types of communication tools or techniques. By the end of the chapter, you should have a greater understanding of communication – one of the most important aspects in effective organisational work. If you are interested in understanding specific aspects of communication in more depth, you will find a list of articles and books for further reading at the end of the chapter.

ORGANISATIONAL COMMUNICATION

Communication is one of the core ingredients for societal life and any type of effective organisation, because we neither live nor work in isolation. Regardless of the level of communication, floor or executive level, the passing on and receiving of information is essential to organisational success. One of the main reasons organisations fail is a breakdown in communication. For instance, if floor staff no longer report customer complaints to their superiors, they are no longer able to communicate the message to higher hierarchical levels in the organisation, leaving the executive level unable to respond strategically to any issues such as changes in the market, lack of training of floor staff, or product-related complaints.

As a leader, it is crucial to communicate visions, strategies, plans, and possible changes to employees. It is similarly important to communicate in order to explore follower needs and expectations, or what the leader can do to improve teamwork or leadership in general. Adams and colleagues (1993) have estimated that for managers communication is one of their central tasks, spending 85% of their time engaged in some type of communication. Assuming that a manager is earning around £100,000 sterling, we could then estimate that £85,000 of the salary is paid solely for the manager's ability to communicate. Although it is not really as straightforward as this, because managers' communication is embedded in complex social and strategic environments, it still indicates the significance of communication and its value. The main issue, however, is that numerous managers, and others, are not entirely sure how to communicate most effectively. It is therefore crucial to determine when to use what type of communication, and what to communicate.

Employees, on the other hand, need to tell their managers and other colleagues what they expect from their jobs, what they consider important in their jobs, what they require in order to work more efficiently, and to be able to explore what the organisation can offer that may be beneficial to them, such as extra knowledge that makes work more successful. Imagine a consultant helping a company to develop a new product refusing to communicate with the team or the client. The project is doomed to fail.

Beyond these task- and job-related aspects, communication with supervisors, colleagues and clients is crucial in building and maintaining relationships. Think about communication this way: 'It is the glue, the underlying force that keeps the team, the organisation, the client relationships intact (if done correctly) and is a crucial element in maintaining relationships.'

The importance of communication in organisational functioning is shown by Reich (1991), who points out that rather than hierarchy, communication is the driving and decisive force in an organisation. Considering communication a tool of information acquisition, those communicating across all levels and with various people are those possessing a great amount of knowledge and information. Both are crucial for individual and organisational success. Information is power and communication a tool to acquire it. The interesting aspect of communication and information acquisition is that many people never personally meet those they communicate with. They are still able to build a communication network allowing them to acquire great levels of information useful to the individual, the department, and/or the organisation.

Communication beyond words [1]

Yet communication is not only verbal but also includes body language, clothes, and other behaviours. Body language suggests whether one is lying (usually the **sender** – ie the person who is communicating to/with you), interested (usually the recipient – ie the person you are communicating to/with) or genuine, or whether words match actions (eg imagine a salesperson trying to convince others to be a medical doctor). In a similar manner, the way one deals with other people is a form of communication. Presenting oneself as, for instance, rude, impatient, impolite, forceful or aggressive at the first encounter will leave the recipient perceiving one as someone who is rather negative and who should possibly be avoided consequently. Conversely, presenting oneself as open, polite, or willing to listen suggests that one is interested, trustworthy and genuine.

Clothes are also a type of communication. Imagine a first interview at a financial institution. Candidates will likely be wearing a suit and tie, and present themselves rather conservatively. Wearing jeans and T-shirt to the interview communicates a lack of respect of the firm's culture (ie appearing smart and conservative). The message will be 'I cannot be bothered to familiarise myself with your standards,' or 'I am not really interested in becoming part of your group.' Consider different professions – for example, bankers, lawyers and politicians dress in suits to look serious. On the other hand, media people are much more likely to dress in casual and trendy fashion. Their message is that they are creative, up to date, and that they know what the new trends will be to make, for instance, an advertising campaign a huge success. The police uniform makes a very clear statement of what others can expect from those wearing it.

Communication, regardless of its nature, only has one function: to achieve the desired goal. Whether this is to influence others, to develop new relationships or to maintain existing ones, communication is a powerful tool that, if used correctly, will yield great results.

Communication – more than just people

Although a lot of communication is an interpersonal process, it is also crucial for inter-firm and customer relationships. For instance, a managing director will likely avoid doing business with another company that refuses to disclose product details or the delivery time of the product, or that fails to communicate in any way, whether verbally or in writing.

Public relations departments, investor relations departments, and any other department that communicates with outside stakeholders (ie people who have some sort of interest in an organisation) are crucial to company success. Public relations departments which fail to communicate new product developments, social corporate policies or other company-related aspects, put the company's success in jeopardy. An investor relations department which does not communicate new developments that may act positively upon the company's financial results would lead to potential investors' unwillingness to invest in the company – all due to a lack of communication. The importance of these communication channels for organisational success is examined further in later sections.

CURRENT ISSUES IN COMMUNICATION

Despite – or maybe because of – the great importance communication plays for individuals, groups and organisations, it is difficult to master, and permanently changing. Instead of becoming simpler, the complexities surrounding communication are increasing. This is due to generation issues, problems occurring because of cultural differences, and technological aspects that are permanently changing. And while for some (usually younger generations) technological advancements are easing the way in which they communicate, older generations and those less technologically skilled may find them hindering or even impossible to grasp.

Technological developments [2]

Regarding the fast pace of society, and the changes accompanying it, it is likely that communication styles, techniques, and channels also go with the time – and indeed they do. Whereas past generations communicated through the use of letters, the telegraph, later followed by the telephone, modern society communicates via online networks and mobile phones. Although first thoughts may be that online communication via such media as Facebook or Skype are restricted to private use, the reality is that modern organisations use communication streams based on electronic means at least as much as private individuals.

Take the following as an example of how quickly things move in communication. In 1998 Townsend and colleagues pointed out that an increasing number of employees expect to be able to use teleworking to work from home. Although this is still a current phenomenon, with more people using some type of home office (just go to any coffee shop and count the number of people working on their laptops), the interesting aspect in their observation is the fact that they named four ways that enabled people to work outside their normal office space: the phone and fax, and computer modems and email. Consider today's alternatives – any type of communication over the Internet (such as Skype, mobile phones, email communication) no longer requires a computer modem: it has become part of so-called smart phones. In addition, we are now able to communicate with people visually over distance through tele- and video-conferencing. Consequently, managers have to be aware of technological developments and use them and train people if necessary to make work processes more efficient.

Globalisation [3]

Another significant change in recent years is the worldwide distribution of work collaborations and manufacturing processes. Before globalisation reached today's levels, communication across cultures and nations was not as profound. Keeping in mind that cultural differences may even differ strongly between two very close-knit and geographically proximal countries such as Germany and the UK, or the UK and the USA, it is crucial to become and remain aware of the differences that create and maintain a successful relationship.

House and Aditya (1997), for instance, point out that although the Japanese prefer written communication in difficult situations such as negative feedback on an individual's performance, Americans prefer direct face-to-face communication. Or take the so-called British understatement and compare it with US motivation-speak. These represent two different ends of the communication spectrum – but both are effective in their respective cultures. In a study comparing Germany and the UK, McCarthy (2005) showed that communication in German offices and businesses is a lot more formal than amongst their UK counterparts.

Considering the great number of business and collaborations between the two countries, it is crucial to be aware of the differences. This is not only to be successful in your business relationships but to avoid any potential issues leading to detrimental effects. For instance, being perceived as impolite by accosting a German business partner by their first name as common in the UK, or by using a strictly professional approach that leaves no space for personal exchange in Arab countries, where a successful business relationship is rooted in personal relationships different from Western professional approaches, are both examples of communication differences.

It is crucial for managers and employees alike to be aware of cultural differences. An inability to master cultural differences may have detrimental effects such as in various intercultural mergers. One recent example was the failure of Daimler and Chrysler due to a lack of genuine collaboration between German and US management. Part of these issues was finding a common basis through successful communication between managers from the respective countries. It led to unresolved problems between the two management parties, and consequently to the splitting up of the two companies.

Generation differences

This issue may not be as topical as technological developments or globalisation, simply because organisations have always comprised individuals from different generations, but the fact that younger people use a very different type of communication may often lead to significant issues between the age groups. Although the question is less content-specific in that the wording of what is spoken is similar, different generations expect different types of communication techniques. For instance, the use of first names in the workplace differs greatly among older and younger employees. Although this may not be true in all countries, the use of a first name among older employees in the Germanic countries Germany, Austria and Switzerland is almost never done. Yet among their younger counterparts the first name is often standard. This change is due to generational differences but similarly a change in communication culture due to the great influence of 'Anglo-Saxon' communication styles.

The generational question also arises in respect of leadership styles. Yu and Miller (2005) showed that leaders communicating with younger employees have to place greater emphasis on relationship-oriented aspects. Conversely, their older counterparts expect communication that focuses more on the task in hand.

Many changes in society and technological developments have led to changes, partly necessary, in the way in which individuals, groups and organisations communicate. Not only do these communication changes enable us to communicate quicker and more cost-efficiently, but they help us identify, understand and integrate better with unfamiliar cultures and societies. Awareness of these aspects is important for any future manager – and particularly for those looking to work in global corporations.

THE PROCESS OF COMMUNICATION

The core element of communication is the message. However, any message must be sent and received through the chosen communication channel. Regardless of the particular channel, a message is first *encoded*, then *transmitted* (through the chosen channel), and finally *decoded*.

Figure 9.1   The process of message transmission

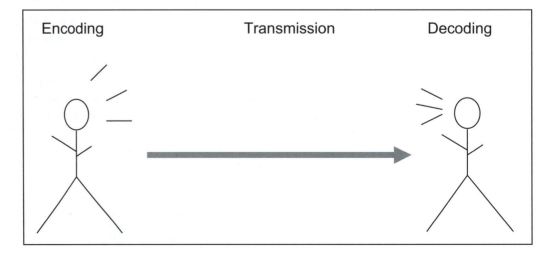

The success of the message in being received and understood as intended may, however, be limited. Firstly, issues may arise during **encoding** including the sender's unawareness of cultural differences, the use of jargon, wrong body language, or wrong tone, and this may happen not only in **verbal communication** but written communication as well – eg capital letters in emails, usually indicating that the sender is 'shouting', when no shouting is intended.

Issues may arise in the **transmission** process, such as noisy surroundings inhibiting the **receiver**'s ability to understand the message. Email communication may be interrupted or partly corrupted in the delivered email. Phone communication may be affected by a bad connection. There are numerous reasons leading to the transmission failure of a message.

Finally, the receiver may fail to decode the message. This may be due to a lack of familiarity with jargon, a different cultural understanding, misinterpretation of **non-verbal** cues, or previous experiences. For instance, although the sender (let's say, a supervisor) would like to assist an employee by sending a message, the employee may have previously worked under a manager who used task-related information in order to point out the employee's failures and shortfalls. The list of issues that may cause misunderstandings between the current sender and receiver is thus various and long. It is therefore of the utmost importance to remain vigilant when communicating.

Once the message is received, the same process occurs again – only this time in reverse order. The receiver now becomes the sender, giving the previous sender feedback on the message. The previous sender now becomes the receiver of this message entailing the feedback. Again, the same issues potentially arise. Difficulties may occur in the encoding, transmission or **decoding** phase inhibiting and potentially preventing the real message from being transmitted from sender to receiver. The best way in both cases is for the sender to check with the receiver what he or she thinks the content and intention of the message are. This type of feedback allows you to be clear that the message has been received as intended, and such feedback becomes infinitely more useful than when you are left in the dark about whether the message, its content, and the intention have been received as intended.

It is therefore crucial to be aware of possible shortfalls and hindrances in communication. However, one element is common to all types of communication that are successful, whether electronic, face-to-face, interpersonal, inter-firm, or any other type of communication: trust. Without trust, no communication will be effective. If one party is unable to trust the other party's words or other means of communicating, the sender will never successfully communicate his or her message to the recipient and the message will subsequently fall short of the desired effect. Fussell and Kraus (1992) pointed out that this interpersonal relationship – or as they put it, the two parties' shared understanding – forms the foundation on which communication is built and functions. This is important to keep in mind while you read about the different aspects of communication, and in your future development.

BEST PRACTICE

Unifying diversity

Consider a manager leading an international team made up of two Spaniards, two Brits, three Japanese and one Moroccan. In order to communicate effectively with the entire team, the team leader has to create a common team language. There are a number of cultural differences amongst the individual team members regarding their expectations. The Japanese expect to have an idea of where the team is heading without being greatly consulted. The Europeans are more likely to expect to be involved in decision-making. A culturally aware manager with a knowledge of effective communication will be sure to investigate what each culture expects in terms of communication, and adapt accordingly, but simultaneously attempt to create a common team communication style. Due to the difficulties associated with cultural differences, the manager will have to keep emphasising the importance of one style of team communication, while also allowing freedom in communication to the individual cultures. Hence, the most effective way to communicate with the entire team is a combination of cultural awareness and an emphasis on a common communication style when communication occurs amongst the entire team.

Information richness

When communicating, the sender must always keep in mind an aspect called **information richness**. Originally this theory was composed to be a prescriptive theory suggesting the importance of matching information requirements, such as a need for more clarity on a specific issue, and possible channels to transmit the message. It was soon realised to be a descriptive theory explaining, rather than suggesting, how managers communicate effectively, and highlighting the major role of electronic means of communication for organisational communication (Trevino, Lengel and Daft, 1987).

Trevino and colleagues also extended the theory by including situational constraints and symbolic considerations. By situational constraints they were referring to the amount of time available to convey the message and the place where the communication is to take place. Symbolic considerations explain the amount of authority to be communicated with the message. For instance, a leader communicating a message of high importance for strategic survival of the corporation will more likely convey a greater amount of authority with the message than when only referring to the departmental day out.

The functioning of the information richness theory is nicely displayed in the finding that due to greater levels of equivocality, senior management engage in more face-to-face communication than other managers (Daft, Lengel and Trevino, 1987). The list below shows the different types of communication in order of their information richness, with 1 the highest level and 5 the lowest:

1 direct verbal (face-to-face)

2 telephone (including voice-over IP, such as Skype)

3 letters, memos and emails addressed personally to the recipient

4 letters, memos and emails not addressed to one specified recipient (eg round-robin email)

5 numeric documents (eg a balance sheet).

The reasons for each medium's information richness are the sender's ability to receive immediate feedback, the number of cues including non-verbal behaviours (eg facial expression, body language, clothes, atmosphere between sender and receiver) that can supportively be included in the message, whether the message is personalised or general, and the level of language variety (eg intonation, tone of voice, speed of communication).

Referring

Although information richness enables sender and receiver to transmit a certain amount of information, successful communication only occurs when both have a mutual understanding of communication and the message. For instance, a banker might refer to dividends. Individuals with no financial acumen may ask, 'Dividend?' The banker would respond, 'The interest-type payment you will receive for holding your shares.' However, if the other party is also a banker, they might simply converse about dividends. This collaborative process of finding a common frame of reference is *referring* and aids in ensuring mutual understanding, increasing the likelihood that the other party will be able to decode the message.

Conversational references, however, are not set in stone. People adapt to each other's level of knowledge, with experts supplying necessary information and novices acquiring new information in order to raise the bar of reference. For instance, Isaacs and Clark (1987) showed in an experiment with 32 pairs of students at Stanford University that students learned about another's level of knowledge through repetitive referring and asking. The task involved 16 identical sets of postcards of common New York scenes given to pairs of students. One of the student pair described the order in which they had set up their cards, the other student trying to match their set in the same order through references given regarding the picture on each card. Students were unable to see each other and therefore only had verbal clues to the other's level of knowledge or reference. When the student describing the card order realised that the other student was unfamiliar with a particular sight, they added further information on, for instance, the shape of a building or another bit of information available from the picture on the postcard. The finding from the experiment showed that the more a pair worked together, the fewer words the pair needed to find a common reference and the more they adapted to the other's level of knowledge.

For any conversation and transmission of information, this process of referring is crucial. The superiority of verbal communication comes from the ability to quickly build up a common set of references. Written communication, due to its delay in feedback, requires previous knowledge of the other person's level of knowledge or the process of establishing a mutual understanding will take a lot longer. It is therefore important to keep in mind that when, for instance, starting a new job or having new members on the team, a manager's foremost responsibility is to establish a common frame of reference aiding in establishing effective communication and subsequently the best possible performance. Learning to establish a common reference is a valuable skill to be learned to perform successfully in any job. It makes conversing with others a more efficient process, allowing quicker decision-making and better leadership with both parties comprehending visions, strategies, or feedback.

Applying theory to practice: Levels of comprehension

Communication is a crucial part of organisational functioning. It is important in horizontal, vertical, internal and external communication. One aspect of effective communication underlying all types of communication is establishing mutual understanding, or a similar frame of reference. When communicating with another, organisational members should check that the frame of reference is similar to that of the other party, minimising potential misunderstandings. In communication, it ought not to be assumed that the conversational partner has the same level of knowledge and interprets a message as intended by the sender. Research has shown that individuals often overestimate the level of knowledge of the other person (Fussell and Krauss, 1992). It is therefore beneficial to check the level of mutual understanding on a regular basis before moving on to more complex issues or new topics, particularly when the topic of conversation is of high importance.

TYPES OF COMMUNICATION

The previous sections have given an overview of why communication is important, what has changed over the years, and the processes involved. In order to describe the impact and mechanisms of each type of communication and the meaning for individual, group, and organisational communication, the following section focuses on the different communication channels and illuminates their advantages and disadvantages. It explains the differences between official and unofficial as well as personal and organisational communication.

Synchronous v asynchronous communication

The way any individual can communicate is either via direct channels or indirect ones. Markus (1994) refers to direct communication – communication allowing for instant feedback – as 'synchronous'. Conversely, 'asynchronous' media describes communication not allowing for instant feedback. Synchronous channels include face-to-face communication and also more recently electronic communication such as email or messaging. A big advantage of synchronous communication is feedback. The sender usually gets instant (face-to-face) or slightly delayed feedback (electronic communication) regarding the message, but more important is the way it is perceived by the recipient. The importance of feedback is highlighted in a description by Schramm (1973: 51) as a 'reversal of the flow, an opportunity for communicators to react quickly to signs resulting from the signs they have put out'. Windahl and Signitzer (1992) went on to suggest that a lack of feedback is equal to a lack of dialogue. In other words, no matter what the nature of the feedback is, whether positive or negative, or even in an absence of feedback, the sender gets an idea of the other party's feelings and position. Whereas negative and positive feedback give a rather clear indication of how the receiver feels about the message, a lack of feedback tells the sender either to re-send the message or to clarify the message appropriately in order to receive any type of feedback. A lack of feedback may be due to the message's either not being perceived or not being understood. It is therefore the sender's job to adapt the message accordingly.

Conversely, asynchronous channels of communication minimise the potential to receive feedback or are accompanied by a delay of feedback from the receiver. Asynchronous channels of communication may be such tools as an intranet on which messages are posted but no immediate feedback is received. Another form may be via a messenger. The sender does not directly deliver the message and is therefore unable to immediately receive feedback from the receiver. The majority of indirect communication, however, is in the form of a written message not allowing for an instant form of feedback. It is important to keep in mind when deciding on the chosen form of communication how important speedy delivery, richness, and feedback are. With the increasing use of electronic communication, this aspect is gaining significance. The growing use of communication tools such as smartphones requires senders to be extra-aware of shortfalls as well as the advantages of electronic communication. The more important and complex the message, the less appropriate is the use of electronic communication.

Electronic mail [4]

Communication has evolved significantly over the last few decades. The development of electronic communication, particularly emails, has eased quick communication and enabled companies to save costs by minimising the need to travel or send out company newsletters. These cost-effective strategies have made electronic communication a significant aspect of organisational competitiveness. Yet the increasing use of electronic communication and electronic mail has also brought about a number of issues.

One of the major advantages, particularly considering the globalisation of projects and the increase in virtual teams, is the ability to call upon knowledge and expertise regardless of location or time. Finholt and Sproull (1990) emphasise the benefits of email for geographically dispersed teams, pointing towards the ability to create and sustain group identity despite the lack of physical proximity. Yet this type of group identity is weaker than group identity in teams within the same physical environment. It is crucial to keep both benefits and drawbacks in mind and weigh up what is of greater importance for the task in hand. In situations where the primary focus centres on merely receiving information from different corners of the world, communication based largely on electronic communication may suffice or be the better alternative. However, in projects requiring a great level of group cohesion, it is of the utmost importance to meet with all team members on a frequent basis.

Although email is a form of asynchronous communication, its fast transmission time allows for much shorter delays regarding feedback. Its information richness is therefore greatly increased, putting it onto a level of information richness between non-electronic written communication and the telephone. A few, however, have rated its potential use for senior management as less recommendable. Markus (1994), for instance, points out that due to the high levels of complex decision-making and strategic leadership at executive levels in organisations, the use of email is less feasible than for leaders and managers on a lower hierarchical level who will show greater involvement in non-equivocal and less complex tasks. Similar issues have been shown in relation to constraints on innovation. Electronic communication has rather detrimental effects on innovation, due to its lack of capacity for fast feedback and brainstorming (Gibson and Gibbs, 2006).

The social role of email has also been a point of interest. Markus (1992), for instance, found that the better the relationships are between group members and the better the group atmosphere, the more people want to engage in face-to-face interaction. In contrast, groups that appeared to be struggling with a tense group environment preferred to communicate via email. The explanation for this phenomenon is fairly simple. Considering the distance email creates between people, dealing with those one wants to minimise contact with becomes easier. In face-to-face and verbal interaction, not only are you giving out the message but you are also giving away behavioural cues: your voice and even your mood (including perhaps disappointment or anger) may be perceived by the other. It is much easier communicating with someone you do not like via email because there is no need for great levels of social interaction.

On the other hand, it is these email-related issues that lead to depersonalisation. Bordia (1997) showed that it creates anonymity amongst those communicating with each other. Although people do not engage in aggressive, rude or impolite behaviours, they certainly feel a lack of the social context you would experience when communicating with people face-to-face. Bordia also showed that despite the advantages of faster communication and the possibility of sending messages any time from any location, people became frustrated with email when attempting to solve complex issues. As with senior management, complex tasks require face-to-face or at least verbal interaction in order to react instantaneously to the message and clarify ambiguities. This not only takes a lot longer via email, but also due to the lack of information richness is inferior to face-to-face and verbal communication.

WORST PRACTICE

Misleading and misunderstanding

Due to the impersonal nature of email communication, people tend to discard any societal standards. Consider a manager advising one of the team members of an important meeting. The manager does not address the team member directly and does not take the time to spellcheck. The email is rushed and appears to be written in a hurry without much thought given to it. The email simply tells the team member to be in the meeting room at a specific time, yet does not explain what is expected nor who else is attending. The style of the message, even if unintendedly, transmits the message that neither is the team member an important individual, nor is the meeting of high importance. The manager has failed to address the member individually and to emphasise the importance of the meeting by using an impersonal, rushed style.

Other types of electronic communication

Email, even if it is the most prominent, is not the only electronic communication tool. Besides fax, which has been available for decades, the new forms of electronic written communication are much quicker and allow multiple receivers and senders to get involved. More recently, media such as Twitter have opened an entirely new world of communication – a world in which everyone is able to keep, if they want, the entire world informed about their whereabouts. Simultaneously, an infinite number are able to follow someone's tweets. The major limitation of tools such as Twitter is the limited amount that one can transmit, placing its information richness very low on the list. With technological developments this may, however, change, and organisations are increasingly using it to communicate with their followers or customers. The most prominent example is Barack Obama, who has used it to keep in touch with his followers.

Other recent developments include the likes of Facebook, MySpace, blogs, podcasting, and intranet platforms. The latter have in fact been around for many years. Intranets have been used to communicate organisational developments and allow organisational members to communicate their thoughts, stay in touch and work collaboratively over great distances. More recently, podcasting and blogging have become important tools for communication. IBM, for instance, has acknowledged the value of podcasting and put specific guidelines and policies in place to adapt to and adopt new technologies. Podcasting, as a management communication tool, satisfies two important functions. A company executive not only reaches employees worldwide but does so in a stimulating manner. The combination of various stimuli – namely, voice and appearance – linked to a message gives podcasting a high level of information richness.

In a similar manner, a blog enables an organisation to keep employees and customers informed of new developments, products or strategies. An increasing number of individuals and organisations use blogs to transmit their thoughts and to sell their services, reaching a great number of people. The advantage again is the possible combination of textual messages supported by graphic images reinforcing the information richness of the medium.

While podcasting and blogs are tools used in organisations, social platforms such as Facebook and MySpace are not usually thought of as organisational communication tools. However, organisations have realised the potential of these platforms and are using them increasingly for advertising purposes. Through the use of these channels, organisations are able to target, for instance, their marketing or recruitment at specific groups. It is important to note that these platforms are less likely to be used as direct communication channels for organisations, but instead more as platforms to communicate a message such as a new product to a wide audience. In a similar manner, business platforms such as LinkedIn are increasingly used to communicate open positions or to communicate with potential business partners. Information richness for all online platforms varies depending on the way a platform is used. Because of their flexibility in uploading videos, in podcasting, or merely in using them for written communication, online platforms have become increasingly important communication tools and can be used throughout a professional's life from finding a job to networking and marketing new products. These are cost-efficient and quick ways of achieving results that once took a considerable time.

Taking your learning further: Electronic communication

Gibson, C. B. and Gibbs, J. L. (2006) 'Unpacking the concept of virtuality: the effects of geographic dispersion, electronic dependence, dynamic structure, and national diversity on team innovation', *Administrative Science Quarterly*, Vol.51, No.3: 451–95.

Kiesler, S., Siegel, J. and McGuire, T. W. (1984) 'Social psychological aspects of computer-mediated communication', *American Psychologist*, Vol.39, No.19: 1123–34.

Markus, M. L. (1994) 'Electronic mail as the medium of managerial choice', *Organization Science*, Vol.5, No.4: 502–27.

van der Kleij, R., Lijkwan, J. T. E., Raskera, P. C. and De Dreuc, C. K. W. (2009) 'Effects of time pressure and communication environment on team processes and outcomes in dyadic planning', *International Journal of Human-Computer Studies*, Vol.67, No.5: 411–23.

Face-to-face communication [5]

A great part of daily communication in organisations is done through direct face-to-face interaction, which has consistently been shown to be the best means to communicate effectively. A number of reasons are responsible for its effectiveness (Huber and Daft, 1987):

- immediate feedback

- the ability to send multiple cues including spoken words and behavioural clues

- the adaptation of message to circumstances (environmental, situational or personal)

- language can be varied in terms of tone, intonation, speed, and flow.

While the sender is able to receive immediate feedback on his or her message, the sender is similarly able to receive cues on the likelihood of the feedback being understood and taken into account. This bi-directional channel of communication makes it forcefully effective – particularly the ability of either party to minimise misunderstandings and clarify ambiguities in a comparably short period of time. Face-to-face communication also allows the sender to communicate non-verbally through body language and/or facial expressions, or to support the verbal message with written communication media such as charts to back up the verbal message. This high level of information richness leads to its superiority over other forms of communication.

The importance is highlighted in various studies. As early as 1977, Allen showed that interpersonal communication is superior and preferred by engineers to collect and transmit ideas, thoughts and information from and to other group members. It might otherwise have been assumed that information in written form must be preferable because it can be consulted whenever needed. And this is indeed the case when it is important to keep information readily available. However, as a first point of contact, interpersonal communication is the preferred method.

Another study conducted a few years ago underlines the importance of face-to-face communication. Lurey and Raisinghani (2001) showed that virtual work (work teams that work in widely dispersed geographical locations and that rely on electronic means such as intranet platforms or email) was actually very difficult due to the absence of minimal face-to-face interaction, despite the fact that 80% of team members were communicating on a daily basis via email. Surprisingly, 86% pointed out that they either had no access to or simply did not make use of the only technique that might have mitigated these difficulties related to the lack of face-to-face communication: video-conferencing. The findings underline the significance of supplementing non-facial communication with facial communication tools to enrich and improve work relationships.

Verbal communication

Verbal communication may be in the form of face-to-face communication but may also occur via media such as the telephone or voice-over IP. Although its information richness is not as high as face-to-face communication, it is still a very effective way to communicate. Verbal communication via media such as the telephone or by electronic means may not allow the transmission of non-verbal cues, but the use of the voice to communicate a message enables the sender to use intonation and changes in speed and tone of voice. It also offers the chance to receive immediate feedback. A pause, vocal changes, a question, or an angry or happy response on the receiver's part are all types of feedback enabling the sender to adjust the message and the transmission accordingly.

Clark and Wilkes-Gibbs (1986) point out that due to the ability to receive immediate feedback, verbal communication allows the sender to monitor the encoding, transmission and decoding processes and, if necessary, add additional cues such as analogies, episodic bits or allusions in order to expand or clarify the message.

A word of caution: verbal communication does not always allow for immediate feedback. Consider a lecture with a speaker in front of a big audience. The possibility for instant feedback is limited. Usually the speaker sends his or her message and may receive delayed feedback after the speech has finished – but not during the speech, as would be possible in face-to-face communication, even involving more than two people.

Written communication

Written communication can be either personalised or impersonalised. The sender can choose to address a specific recipient or send a mass email, a company letter, an information booklet, or any other form of written communication. Although information richness may not be as high as with verbal communication, the advantage of written communication over verbal communication is the ability to consult the piece of information even after it has been received. Although at the time of transmission verbal and face-to-face communication is superior, a written message will remain beyond the initial interaction. Written forms of communication also allow for time to think, formulate, and edit the message, and minimise spontaneous reactions to a message such as shouting swear-words if one is dissatisfied.

Advantages and disadvantages

There is not necessarily a worst or best form of communication. The different types of communication vary in their effectiveness depending on the audience and the context (eg time and location) they are used in. Communication techniques have to adapt to the user as much as the user has to adapt to changes in communication. There is therefore no general recipe for successful and effective communication. It is much more a user-media-message-place-time interaction. While face-to-face interaction allows communicating with instant feedback and eases the process of solving complex issues, it requires geographical proximity. Company newsletters or online platforms enable instant and cost-effective ways to communicate with employees, other members of the organisation or customers, but are usually less rich in information.

For instance, the strategy of the computer-makers Dell to distribute their products via their online website allowed them not only to be more cost-effective than competitors but also to respond quickly to customer needs. Their strategy of communicating new products online and selling them online enabled them to minimise shipping costs (products had only to be delivered to the end customer, not to stores) and greatly reduce logistic issues because they can be dealt with in-house, and customers are able to give instant feedback on products on their company website. However, the need for face-to-face communication when dealing with complex issues is not satisfied if all communication is done online.

Gatekeepers

The importance of information and therefore communication is best understood when considering the great importance organisations place on gatekeepers – individuals able to collect information from external sources and translate it into assets valuable to the team and the organisation. Their important role in project success is shown by the significant impact gatekeepers have on product development. Verona (1999) reported a significant increase in product development productivity through gatekeepers. Tushman and Katz (1980) showed that local development projects were more successful if accompanied by a gatekeeper. However, they found contradictory results for research teams. Research teams who placed great importance on gatekeepers' communicating with external sources showed lower performance levels than their counterparts who primarily functioned without a gatekeeper. The difference appeared to be that teams who needed constant interaction with external sources performed worse than those teams who required external information less frequently.

Compare a gatekeeper to a bottleneck with a filter letting through only information that is of importance to the project team. This is very useful if a team desires specific information. Conversely, teams that require great levels of unfiltered input, such as research teams, need an open and constant communication flow. Remember from earlier that different types of media are more or less effective depending on the context. Gatekeepers, although generally important, also differ in their effectiveness depending on the context and the level of communication flow. It is therefore crucial to keep in mind that depending on the amount of raw information required by the team to perform, the use of gatekeepers should either be discouraged or encouraged.

Communication networks

Communication may flow through different networks. Depending on the task and the level of required communication between individual group members, communication networks – corresponding to linked paths by which information travels – may take any of four forms.

The most basic communication network is that of a chain. *Chains* are communication paths that do not require cross-level or complex communication. Chain networks are similar to assembly lines: communication is passed on in a sequential order from person A to person B to person C. Although this is ideal if tasks have to be performed in ordered stages, it does not allow for an exchange of ideas.

Circular networks are characterised by communication that flows as if it was travelling around an enclosed or isolated ring of people. People communicate with others who have similar characteristics, such as similar background, geographical proximity or areas of expertise. The drawback is that others, less similar, are unlikely to receive information. Conversely, it allows for communication to be concentrated within a particular frame of reference or context.

Communication in *hub-and-spoke networks*, also called *wheel networks*, always travels via a central member of the communication group, who in turn will pass on the information as and when required. There is therefore no need for individual members to communicate with each other and the information is controlled and gathered in one place. The hub or central focal point of information collection and potential filtering out of useless information is an advantage of wheel networks. However, the central collection of information may also lead to information only partly being passed on or not being passed on at all.

The most complex form of network is the *all-channel network*. This type of network is characterised by a high level of communication amongst all members of the group. People in all-channel networks communicate with those close to them, those superior to them, those working on a different task. This high-level communication network allows for brainstorming and the generation of a multiplicity of ideas. The great level of communication may, however, also lead to an overflow of information and information that bypasses particular members of the communication network.

Whereas the advantages of a hub-and-spoke (wheel) network result from a central person controlling all information and the information flow minimising communication overflow, the complexity of an all-channel network are the reverse in nature. The possibility that information may be repeated, that individual members may miss information or that communication never reaches them is much higher. Conversely, the exchange of ideas is much greater in a more complex network, because more people are involved in the communication process. It becomes clear that there is no worst or best communication network. Just as in respect of media and gatekeepers, the most effective network depends on the situation.

Taking your learning further: Verbal communication, gatekeepers and networks

Bolton, P. and Dewatripont, M. (1994) 'The firm as a communication network', *Quarterly Journal of Economics*, Vol.109, No.4: 809–39.

Cataldo, M. and Herbsleb, J. D. (2008) 'Communication networks in geographically distributed software development', *Proceedings of the ACM 2008 Conference*, San Diego, USA.

Cranefield, J. and Yoong, P. (2007) 'Inter-organisational knowledge transfer: the role of the gatekeeper', *International Journal of Knowledge and Learning*, Vol.3, No.1: 121–38.

Katz, R. (1982) 'The effects of group longevity on project communication and performance', *Administrative Science Quarterly*, Vol.27, No.1: 81–104.

Tushman, M. L., and Katz, R. (1980) 'External communication and project performance: an investigation into the role of gatekeepers', *Management Science*, Vol.26, No.11: 1071–85.

LEVELS OF COMMUNICATION

Horizontal communication

A lot of communication networks develop and subsist among same-level employees – ie among members of the same team, members of different departments, or members of different branches. The important facet of horizontal communication is that it occurs among people who are at the same level within the organisational hierarchy. Considering the level of teamwork and the nature of office design (with departments usually separated into independent units), an increased amount of horizontal and even more within-unit communication is understandable. Face-to-face interactions are higher within work units than amongt members working at different levels. One reason for the greater proportion of communication at the same level is the spatial proximity between members in the same department.

Another reason is the nature of work. Members working at the same organisational level tend to work within similar frames of duties and responsibilities. Consider a CEO and a personal assistant for a middle-level manager. The personal assistant will communicate much less with the CEO not only professionally but also privately, due to the different duties, work schedules and working hours. The personal assistant will, however, communicate with other personal assistants on a daily basis and maybe even privately. The personal assistant will have to communicate with other personal assistants to set up meetings, keep up to date on organisational developments affecting the manager they are working for, and will have to deal with the same issues regarding problems that arise with their superiors, departmental members or external sources. These common aspects determine the great amount of communication between assistants and the much lesser communication with the CEO.

Vertical communication

Communication may take place within a group but may also span different levels in the organisation. For instance, Manager B may have to inform the CEO of new developments in his or her department. Although the manager will communicate on a regular basis with other managers at the same level on common projects, common work commitments or similar interests, Manager B may only communicate with the CEO at strategic meetings.

However, vertical communication is a two-way process. Not only will Manager B inform the CEO of new developments, the CEO will in turn inform lower levels including Manager B of new strategies, new clients, developments in the market share or any other news. While the communication pathway from Manager B to the CEO is called *upward communication*, because the communication flow is directed upwards, communication initiated by the CEO and directed at Manager B is called *downward communication*, as the communication travels downwards.

An interesting aspect of vertical communication is that the more symmetrical the power relationship, the higher is the workflow (Mohr and Nevin, 1990). In this context, 'power relationship' refers to how much power one holds over the other, the level of information one holds, respectively, if one party possesses a much greater level of authority than the other party.

Consider the following scenarios:

1 A team member and a team leader have a very good personal and professional relationship and the team leader is happy to engage with the team member, involve her in decision-making processes, ask her advice, and value her feedback. (The team leader also has a good or neutral relationship with other team members.)

2 A team member has a bad personal and professional relationship with the team leader and the team leader wants neither to engage with the team member nor to involve him in decision-making processes or ask his advice, and does not value his feedback. (The team leader also has a bad or neutral relationship with other team members.)

3 A team leader has a good relationship with team members A and B but not with team member C. Whereas team members A and B are involved in decision-making, and the team leader is happy to engage with them and ask for their advice and feedback, team member C is involved in decision-making only when absolutely necessary; her feedback, opinion, and advice is not valued, and nor do the team leader and team member C enjoy engaging with each other.

4 A team leader has a very good relationship with team members A, B, and C and is happy to engage with them, involve them in decision-making and ask for their advice, and values their opinions and feedback, therefore creating a very good atmosphere amongst the team.

In which of these scenarios do you think communication is at its highest? Although power may not necessarily come to mind when reading the above examples, power develops through the process of viewing and treating a team member as equal by involving them in leadership processes such as asking for feedback, advice, and getting them to contribute to decision-making. The highest communication flow is therefore in scenario 4. Not only are all team members elevated to an equal level with the leader, but they also interact on a similar level with each other. None of the team members feels superior because he or she has a better relationship with the leader than others. Nor does any team member feel excluded and less important than any other. Communication therefore flow openly between team members and leader. (It will also flow freely between team members.)

Scenario 1 has the second highest communication flow. No member is excluded from the team, and the very good relationship between team leader and member allow the latter to feel equal to the leader, openly sharing her thoughts, opinions and information with the leader. The communication flow in Scenario 3 will be the third highest. Although one member has a bad relationship with the leader, the other two members have a good relationship with the leader, are involved in decision-making and possess a similar status to the leader. Scenario 2 shows the lowest level of communication. None of the team members has a good relationship with the leader, who is also unwilling to share his power with other members of the team. The willingness of the team members to share any type of information is therefore limited.

The above examples demonstrate how power influences communication. The more people feel they have equal power, the more likely they are to communicate. If individuals in the organisational hierarchy feel less powerful, the willingness to communicate may be inhibited because of their fear of rejection, of not being taken seriously, or that the other party is not open to any attempt at communication. On the other hand, leaders who perceive themselves as significantly more powerful than their team members are less open to communicating strategic goals or any other type of information (including personal communication) because their perception of the other party is as an inferior who is thus not 'worthy' of sharing important information with.

EXTERNAL COMMUNICATION

Communication does not only take place within an organisation. External communication is crucial for organisational success and survival. An organisation that fails to communicate properly or to communicate at all is doomed to fail altogether. Not only do management and people such as gatekeepers need to communicate with other organisations, organisational members need to ensure that the public and other organisations are informed of new products and changes in strategy, shareholders must be kept up to date, and the organisation has to be portrayed in ways likely to promote success for the organisation. There are various different ways an organisation can communicate with external stakeholders – those holding some type of interest in the organisation.

Investor relations

One of the main stakeholders that have to be communicated with are shareholders. Shareholders – those individuals, firms or governments that own a share in the company – must be kept up to date on a frequent basis. Investor relations departments are responsible for communicating with shareholders, but also with newspapers such as the *Financial Times*. The importance of external communication through investor relations departments can be observed daily when watching the London share index FTSE-100. The investor relations department's communication of news has a significant influence on whether a share price will rise or fall.

Consider the following. Recently, Porsche communicated to shareholders and the press that it was pursuing a takeover strategy. Its goal was Volkswagen, one of the biggest automotive companies worldwide. Consequently, the share price of Volkswagen increased to levels over 1,000 euros, briefly making it the most expensive share on the market. Porsche later announced that it was no longer able to take over Volkswagen due to financial constraints and some regulatory issues. As a consequence, Volkswagen's share price fell to levels around 150 euros, and Porsche's followed suit. The communication of investor-related information led to some of the most significant share price movements in only a few weeks affecting individuals, financial institutions and other companies.

This highlights the importance of communicating with investors for company value and success – further highlighted by the annual award for the best investor relations department. The criteria are communication with external stakeholders about company strategies, new product developments, and organisational changes.

Customer communication [6]

The number of stakeholders an organisation must communicate with is almost infinite, but one other very important group are the customers. Picture a car manufacturer failing to communicate new products to the wider public or existing and potential customers. The reason for car shows such as the Detroit Auto Show only serve one purpose – to communicate new products and organisational development.

One example of an organisation with effective customer relations is the Apple stores. Customers enter not only a world focused on communicating fun, innovation and easy usability, but a world of customer-friendly services, products and staff. Consider the Apple 'workshops' within the stores. Their mission: 'Apple will be there to help. We care about our customer and assist whenever we can.' Apple stores and workshops not only facilitate communication from Apple to its customers but also from the customers to Apple. Customers are able to directly communicate with the organisation through the floor staff and address concerns. As long as the concerns are passed through the ranks within the organisation, this two-way communication enables an organisation to quickly and effectively respond to customer concerns and suggestions.

Customer relations are essential for organisational success. Peppers and Rogers (1993) point out the significant cost savings of effective customer relationships. Acquiring a new customer is six to nine times more expensive than retaining customers through good customer relations. As in the Apple example, the direct contact with the organisation through helpful floor staff is the most effective way to directly communicate with and retain customers. The core element of good customer relations is, as the name suggests, personal relationships.

Good personal relationships also serve another purpose beyond receiving information from the customer. They allow the organisation to communicate with the customer, assist the customer, effectively resolve any potential issues, and inform the customer of new developments. As you may remember from the section on information richness, face-to-face and verbal communication are the most effective when dealing with numerous issues. The organisation is presented by a face (floor staff) or voice (customer hotline) and is able to actively show it is listening and taking the customer's concerns and suggestions seriously.

If it fails to do so, an organisation enters into what Fornell and Westbrook (1984) refer to as 'the vicious circle of complaints' – the breakdown of communications between customer and organisation. A willingness to listen permits the easing of customer concerns and enables the organisation to react. Conversely, an unwillingness to listen to customers leads to more customer complaints and the failure to solve potential issues. Through more effective customer relations, the number of complaints can be minimised and a greater number of existing customers retained. It is therefore in the interest of any organisation to communicate effectively with existing and potential customers.

Public relations

The perception of an organisation amongst the public is strongly influenced by the way it portrays itself: its corporate image. Alsop (2004) sums up the importance of public relations in the case of Altria Group and its subsidiary Philip Morris, the tobacco company. A few years ago, Philip Morris attempted to improve its corporate image by pointing out that its website offered various hints on how to stop smoking and the health effects related to smoking. The ad campaign referring to the website cost the company $250 million. The message, however, backfired when TV hosts such as Jay Leno criticised the apparent hypocrisy of a tobacco company offering health advice. Others perceived the communicated message as an attempt to steer people's image of the company away from its tobacco business towards a responsible company concerned about people's health.

The reason for Philip Morris to communicate its awareness and concern regarding health issues related to its products may at first seem counter-intuitive, but it was essential for the company's success. Alsop points out that Altria initially ignored any criticism in silence, not responding to any inquiries from the public or health organisations. In order to be perceived as an honest, sincere, and trustworthy company, it was crucial for the organisation to change its communication style and take a head-on approach to confronting issues raised by the public. The importance of sincerity and honesty was shown in a study on corporate reputation by Harris Interactive which demonstrated that communicating these traits is by far the best way to get external onlookers to perceive an organisation in a positive light.

The importance of communicating a positive corporate image has recently become crucial for many financial institutions. Remember the bank run on Northern Rock – it became essential to emphasise that savings were protected and people would not lose their money. Using public relations communications to avoid an even greater financial catastrophe was entirely necessary, calming things down and preventing further runs on the bank.

Organisations have learned a lot about the importance of communicating a positive corporate image for survival and success, yet it is a constant communication struggle to maintain a good public image, and it should therefore be high on a manager's agenda.

INFORMAL COMMUNICATION

Regardless of the type of communication, whether internal or external, there are two ways a message may be communicated: through formal and informal channels.

Some of the formal channels are described above, but a great deal of information is communicated through informal channels such as **gossip** and **rumours**. Whereas gossip is unverified information about people, rumours are unverified information about issues including job-related aspects such as potential downsizing, financial issues or politics. Both, however, grow from uncertainty and a lack of information.

Rumours

Ineffective or non-existent organisational communication, whether internal or external, offers ground for the development and spreading of rumours. Rumours are embedded in a vicious circle of lack of information, stress and more rumours. A lack of information and uncertainty lead to stress among organisational members. In order to counter the gap of information, individuals start communicating with each other, attempting to fill the gaps with their own 'information', assumptions and fears. Because it is the nature of rumours usually to consist of negative information, rumours themselves lead to increased levels of stress. However, as Bordia and colleagues point out (2006), rumours may also contain a positive message – usually corresponding to people's desires, such as a pay increase. Positive rumours may even lead to a brief increase in positive feelings such as satisfaction among team members. However, because rumours are by definition unverified facts, those rumours that do not come true inevitably lead to increased levels of stress and disappointment.

Rumours may, however, lead not only to stress but to a decrease in motivation and performance, and to a lower willingness to co-operate with other group members, particularly if the rumours surround organisational issues such as downsizing. Because of the mostly negative nature of rumours and the associated detrimental consequences, the management's task is to counter any rumours and openly communicate strategic missions and changes early. Rumours must be tackled as quickly as they arise, by clarifying or confirming them. Rumours are part of organisational life and are not in themselves a problem as long as management are aware of them and act early to minimise and prevent negative effects on employees and the overall organisation.

Gossip

Informal communication may also flow in the form of gossip – unverified information about people. In contrast to rumours, gossip is not about possible events but centres on personal, context-specific communication. It may be used to entertain, gain social control, and/or influence others' perceptions of a particular person or group. Rosnow (2001) viewed gossip as reliant on any one of three functions: influence, intimacy, and information.

The information function of gossip refers to the gathering of information about the situation of other colleagues. For instance, if you wanted to get some idea of why another person was promoted to a position you had yourself expected to be promoted to, you might talk to others over lunch. But rather than approaching the topic directly, you might work your way round to casually mentioning the promoted person's habit of spending long hours in the office and generally working overtime. Due to your lack of concrete knowledge on why the person has been promoted, your engaging in gossip in this way amounts to an attempt to fill in and explain the gaps in your own knowledge through your own suggestion and through finding out others' reactions and thoughts on the topic.

The second function of gossip, influencing, has as its primary goal the control of people. For instance, a manager may refer to some extraordinary abilities of another person recently promoted, indirectly implying what one needs to improve to become as successful as the person promoted.

The third function of gossip, intimacy, is used to create stronger interpersonal bonds between two parties. Through sharing information in the form of gossip, one party may attempt to build a more emotional relationship beyond the task-related work aspects, creating a closer interpersonal relationship.

Similar to rumours, however, gossip is often associated with negative information and outcomes. For instance, one may refer to a recently promoted colleague as someone evidently prepared to use unethical methods to get ahead, subsequently creating distrust amongst others and a reluctance to work with the promoted individual. This, in turn, may well undermine his or her ability to lead due to a lack of support from the employees, resulting in a lower individual and team performance.

Applying theory to practice: Dealing with gossip and rumours

When starting as a manager, ensure that you are kept up to date on information exchanges – including gossip and rumours – amongst your staff. By engaging with individual members and attending lunches and after-work gatherings, or simply by communicating with staff on a day-to-day basis, you will be able to keep abreast of anything that people deem worth gossiping and rumouring about. If you feel that there is some topic about which your team lacks any particular information and which may trigger off such gossiping and rumouring, quickly act upon it by clarifying what you can and heading off obvious misunderstandings. The most effective and simplest way is to hold regular meetings with all members of your department and allow time and space for questions and explanations.

Conclusion

Understanding the importance of communication is crucial for organisational success. Organisations and their members face a great number of challenges when trying to communicate effectively. A major challenge is not only that communication is a complex interpersonal process but that it occurs on all the different levels within and outside organisations. Although managers spend a lot of time engaged in one or other form of communication, it is a skill required at all levels of the organisation. Regardless of whether an organisational member wants to build relationships with other members, prepare for upcoming changes, market a new product or persuade others of the positives of the organisation, communication should always be shaped to suit the target audience.

Communication can be learned, but it is essential that organisations and their members are aware of changes such as globalisation and technological innovations to make the most of communication and to reach those it is meant for. Only then can organisations succeed both in successfully communicating and also in obtaining the great benefits that accompany the judicious use of this crucial organisational tool.

End notes

[1] See also Chapter 2.

[2] See also Chapter 16.

[3] See also Chapters 10 and 18.

[4] See also Chapter 16.

[5] See also Chapter 5.

[6] See also Chapter 13.

REVIEW AND DISCUSSION QUESTIONS

REVIEW QUESTIONS

1 Communication is a one-way process – true or false?

2 Is there one best way to communicate?

3 Is it important to communicate with external stakeholders?

4 Considering recent changes in technology, how has communication changed?

5 Is communication important for any other aspect of organisational functioning than teamwork?

DISCUSSION QUESTIONS

1 Develop a presentation about a coffee-maker for a marketing audience.

2 As a team think of the best ways to communicate strategic changes to external stakeholders.

3 You are a top management team. As a team think of a way to minimise gossip in the organisation.

4 Analyse the communication channels and media within your own team.

5 As a team, develop a new, innovative communication medium.

FURTHER READING

Alsop, R. J. (2004) 'Corporate reputation: anything but superficial – the deep but fragile nature of corporate reputation', *Journal of Business Strategy*, Vol.25, No.6: 21–9. A good evaluation of a number of corporate reputation failures.

Hooghiemstra, R. (2000) 'Corporate communication and impression management – new perspectives why companies engage in corporate social reporting', *Journal of Business Ethics*, Vol.27, No.1: 55–68. This article explains how and why an organisation needs to change its communication strategy.

Bordia, P., Jones, E., Gallois, C., Callan, V. J. and Difonzo, N. (2006) 'Management are aliens', *Group and Organization Management*, Vol.31, No.5: 601–21. This article is a good summary of different types of rumours.

Schweiger, D. M. and DeNisi, A. S. (1991) 'Communication with employees following a merger: a longitudinal field experiment', *Academy of Management Journal*, Vol.34, No.1: 110–35. This article investigates the challenges in communicating with employees following a merger.

Markus, M. L. (1994) 'Finding a happy medium: explaining the negative effects of electronic communication on social life at work', *ACM Transactions on Information Systems*, Vol.12, No.2: 119–49. An interesting study on the advantages and disadvantages of electronic communication and its perception amongst employees.

KEY SKILLS

Communication is a skill that can be acquired, but it has an important additional role in relation to other skills required in organisations – for instance, leading others, giving presentations, negotiating, teamwork, and decision-making. The ability to understand the audience, for instance, and how to communicate your message, is essential to the success of a presentation.

PRESENTATION SKILLS

Successful presentations are based on the ability to keep listeners engaged. There are numerous ways to make a presentation lively and keep the audience engaged using information-rich techniques, techniques that are lower in information richness, and a combination of the two. The major aspect of a successful presentation is the ability to combine methods in order to make the presentation an enjoyable experience.

Consider a presentation about a new car to an audience of engineers, and the same presentation to a marketing audience. Although both need to know about the new product, they will need different information, expect a different content and respond to a different style. Whereas the engineers will want to see figures and charts of the engine and other technical details, the marketing presentation will have to contain information on what new innovations are available to the customer, and the look of the car and its interior. The engineering presentation will therefore be more numbers-based, and the marketing presentation more photographically based. The secret of successful communication in a presentation is to transmit a message that is both significant and interesting to the audience.

LEADERSHIP SKILLS

Successful leadership originates from effective communication. For a leader to be most effective, he or she must engage in two-way communication. Not only does the leader need to communicate strategies, plans, visions or potential problems the organisation may face, but he or she must also listen to what organisational members have to say.

Consider the following example. One of the biggest car manufacturers in the world, General Motors, only recently filed for insolvency. Although the insolvency occurred during the greatest financial crisis since the Great Depression in the last century, the problems at General Motors (GM) had been homemade over many decades. Various GM consultants brought in by the company time after time raised the issue of inappropriate product development. For years GM management fired the consultants and ignored the necessity of producing smaller cars for the global market. If the executive board had listened to those advisers and even some of their own employees, they might well have been able to steer a course around the eventual insolvency.

In a similar manner, the same company spent the best part of its last year deciding on whether to sell its European subsidiaries or to keep them. The lack of downward communication regarding the future of the subsidiaries led the workers and their unions to strike and to refuse to continue working for the top management. Once top management had announced they would keep the subsidiaries – after months of uncertainty for workers over whether they were to be sold to another company or kept within GM – employees in the European subsidiaries immediately and wholeheartedly supported the strategy. None of these conflicts between workers and top management would have occurred had top management engaged with those at the forefront of the company. It is therefore crucial for leaders to communicate with their employees not once a year but on a constant and continual basis.

KEY SKILLS NEXT

MENTORING SKILLS

Mentoring may be part of leadership – however, it is only possible if the mentor is aware of what the mentee requires or is striving to achieve. The only way to explore the shortcomings or the needs of the mentee is to ask and listen. Open communication is a prerequisite for mentoring to occur. Consider a mentor unwilling to communicate with a newcomer in an organisation. They might meet once every few months and discuss for an hour what has happened in the time since their last meeting. The ability for change to take place is limited due to the lack of communication – particularly as communication in the context of mentoring acts as feedback to both mentor and mentee. The mentor gets information on what still requires to be done, the mentee on how to achieve the set goals and to progressively improve.

TEAMWORKING SKILLS

Teamwork, to be successful, also requires communication. Every organisation is made up of various teams that comprise individual members required to communicate in order to accomplish a common goal. Considering the close proximity of the majority of teams, communication is an absolute necessity – not only to create and maintain intact personal relationships but also to work effectively as a team.

Consider the following example. Team A work closely together and meet regularly to talk about progress and issues. However, members of Team A also communicate outside formal workplace meetings. Team B also work closely together and meet, but communication outside formal meetings is limited. Team C communicate neither in regular meetings nor outside the few meetings they do have. Considering the importance of communication to talk about task-related and personal issues, it follows that Team A is the most successful in terms of teamwork and in maintaining interpersonal relationships. Team B follows second, while Team C struggles even to maintain a good team spirit and to keep performance at acceptable levels. Because of the frequent communication in Team A, potential issues are quickly resolved, enabling its members to focus on the path ahead.

PROBLEM-SOLVING AND DECISION-MAKING SKILLS

Communication is again crucial to succeed in both these tasks. Similar to issues arising within teams, problems arising at a corporate level – as in the case of GM – have to be faced head-on and through communication at all levels. An open communication platform on the intranet, for instance, or a task force that communicates internally and externally may offer opportunities to exchange ideas and to gather information on how to resolve problems. The best decisions are often made through openness to ideas from different sides of the organisation. The example of GM, related above, suggests that the decision to change from bigger trucks to smaller vehicles might well have enabled GM to avoid insolvency. It was the potentially problem-solving decision that was avoided instead. All that decision required was effective communication, horizontally as well as vertically.

The above examples indicate the importance of communication for various organisational aspects. The list, however, is not exhaustive and might additionally have included other aspects, such as general management skills and negotiation skills.

Ethical implications: Using communication ethically

Communication is a powerful tool that must be used with care. Keep in mind, when you are communicating, that you have to be honest in what you are communicating. If, for instance, you need to communicate that part of your team will have to leave the organisation, be open about it. Also keep in mind that communicating opinions about others should, as much as possible, be based on facts. Gossip and rumours can have detrimental effects not only on an individual but on the organisation.

With the new technologies available, communication has become easier than ever. It is therefore important to use it carefully and selectively. By overusing the tools of technology you may overwhelm the addressee with your message. Try therefore to be selective in the type of media you use for transmitting your message, and use only a tool that is accessible and known to the recipient. For instance, if you want to communicate important strategic organisational changes, use media that are available to all those the message is intended to reach. In sum, use communication wisely, be selective, and focus on your audience's needs and interests.

PART THREE

Managing Organisations

Chapter 10
Leading and Influencing in Organisations

Yves R. F. Guillaume and Nils-Torge Telle

Contents

PART THREE

Key Learning Outcomes

By the end of this chapter you should be able to:

- define leadership and leadership effectiveness, and contrast leadership and management

- identify, explain, evaluate and contrast style, trait, contingency, leader-member exchange, and inspirational approaches to leadership

- assess whether and how cross-cultural differences affect leadership effectiveness

- evaluate whether leaders make a difference

- appreciate the importance of ethical leadership, and recognise individual and situational influences on ethical and unethical leadership

- show how organisations can develop leaders and leadership effectiveness.

 PRACTITIONER INSIGHT

Birmingham City Council

Birmingham City Council provides services for the most populous local authority in the United Kingdom and Europe, representing over 1 million people and employing more than 58,000 staff. It has revenue expenditures of over £3.5 billion a year, making it comparable to a FTSE-100-listed organisation.

Birmingham City Council has been working to strengthen its leadership capacity in order to provide the citizens of Birmingham with excellent front-line services while effectively managing internal and external demands. We speak with **Andy Albon, Director of Equalities and Human Resources** in Birmingham City Council, to explore the major challenges to building strong leadership in today's organisations.

Traditionally, career paths towards leadership roles emerged as non-managerial staff progressed into roles that involved the management of people, although little training was ever given in this area. Many people excel in non-managerial roles but on promotion need support, guidance and development in order to manage and lead other people effectively.

How then do we identify people who are good at managing other people? How do we train and prepare them for such roles? How do we motivate, reward and retain them? How do we make sure that they help us implement our overarching business strategy?

Responding to this challenge, Birmingham City Council has developed a leadership development programme called The Birmingham Way. This outlines how the organisation selects and develops its future leaders and builds strong leadership capacity, enabling future leaders to implement Birmingham City Council's overarching strategy to deliver excellent front-line services.

What does this leadership development programme look like?

What are the advantages and challenges of such a programme?

Once you have read this chapter, return to these questions and think about how you could answer them.

Introduction

In this chapter we look at what organisations should consider when selecting people for leadership positions, and at how they can develop effective and ethical leaders. We begin by defining leadership and highlight the difference between managers and leaders. We then examine different approaches to leadership, evaluate their validity and usefulness, and discuss how they can be applied in practice. Continuing on from this, we examine the implications of leadership in a global context. We then move on to consider whether leaders really make a difference in terms of a firm's bottom line and across different situations and persons. Next, we explore the ethical implications of leadership and consider what organisations can do to ensure ethical leadership. Finally, we discuss how organisations can identify and develop effective leaders. By the end of the chapter you should have a greater understanding of the role of leadership in organisations and organisational behaviour, and of what organisations can do to find and develop effective and ethical leaders.

THE NATURE OF LEADERSHIP

What is leadership?

In August 1994, 54 eminent leadership researchers from 38 countries met at the University of Calgary in Alberta, Canada, to initiate possibly the most significant – and perhaps also the biggest – research programme on Global Leadership and Organisational Behaviour Effectiveness (GLOBE) ever undertaken. After days of fierce and controversial debate, consensus with respect to a universal definition of organisational leadership was reached. We will adopt this universal definition of leadership for the remainder of this chapter, and accordingly define **leadership** as (House *et al*, 2004: 15):

> The ability of an individual to influence, motivate, and enable others to contribute toward the effectiveness and success of the organisations of which they are members.

This definition has five components. First, the definition highlights that we are looking mainly at leadership in organisations, and not at political leadership.

Second, it implies a distinction between the person who engages in leadership (ie the person who influences, motivates and enables others) and another person who is led (ie the person whom leadership is directed towards). Throughout this chapter we refer to people who engage in leadership as 'leaders' and those whom leadership is directed towards as 'followers'. Although leaders are often assumed to be persons with some degree of formally designated authority (eg a team leader, a supervisor, or a managing director), in this chapter we will see that in today's organisations leaders are often also persons with no formal authority (eg a subordinate who emerges as the informal leader of a group, a worker who motivates co-workers, or an employee who enables a superior to get the job done).

Third, the definition suggests that leaders influence the behaviour of other people. Because this does not necessarily require formal power, influence in organisations can be exercised top-down (eg by supervisor over subordinate), laterally (eg between supervisor and supervisor, or between subordinate and subordinate) or bottom-up (eg by subordinate over supervisor).

Fourth, defining leadership as an individual ability implies that it can be learned. However, as we will see below, this ability may be facilitated or impeded by personal characteristics (eg a leader's personality and intelligence) and situational characteristics (eg the task, one's formal and informal power, follower motivation and ability, and national and organisational culture).

Fifth, the definition distinguishes between effective and ineffective leaders. Effective leaders in organisations motivate and enable others to achieve organisationally relevant goals. These goals fall into three broad categories (Hackman and Wageman, 2005):

- whether the productive outputs of an organisational unit meet the standards of quantity, quality and timeliness of its clients

- the level of social integration within a unit (ie members' satisfaction with peers, job and leader; the level of co-operation; and members' commitment to the organisation, unit and leader), and

- the level of continuous learning and well-being of unit members.

Leaders and managers

The terms 'leadership' and 'management' are often distinguished. For instance, Kotter (1990) suggests that managers do the planning and budgeting whereas leaders establish direction; managers organise and staff whereas leaders align people; managers control and solve problems whereas leaders motivate and inspire; and managers produce consistency and order whereas leaders are concerned with productive or adaptive change. This distinction should not be taken too literally, however. It refers rather to the different functions that leadership and management serve in organisations. Both are essential for the effective functioning of organisations and the people in it. Accordingly, people in roles with formally designated authority (eg team leaders, supervisors and managing directors) often have to be both – effective leaders *and* managers. Conversely, the flattening of organisational hierarchies and the introduction of teamwork requires more and more non-managerial staff to take over leadership functions. Thus, effective managers often have to be effective leaders, but so more and more often do non-managerial staff. In keeping with this distinction, this chapter is about effective leadership in organisations and not about effective management.

APPROACHES TO LEADERSHIP

The trait approach [1]

Which innate qualities and characteristics set strong leaders – such as Napoleon, Gandhi, Churchill, Thatcher and Branson – apart from their followers? Is it their charisma, is it their courage, is it their strong will, is it their self-confidence, or is it something else? The search for characteristics that would differentiate leaders from non-leaders goes back to the earliest stages of leadership research and is called the **trait approach**. The nineteenth-century historian Thomas Carlyle, for instance, suggested that 'great men', such as Napoleon, have superior natural dispositions that set them apart from others and make them strong leaders. The beginning of the twentieth century saw a proliferation of studies that looked at which characteristics enabled people to rise to leadership positions and made them so influential. By the late 1940s Stogdill (1948) was already reporting on 124 studies that covered a wide range of characteristics, such as intelligence, alertness, initiative, self-confidence and dominance. In 1974 he reviewed (Stogdill, 1974) another 163 studies, conducted between 1949 and 1970, describing even more characteristics, extending the earlier list by such traits and skills as stress tolerance, social astuteness, dependability and co-operativeness. Despite the appeal it was not until very recently that researchers were able actually to show in a series of meta-analyses that the characteristics of a leader were indeed linked to leadership emergence and effectiveness. But let's look at the underlying idea first.

Applying theory to practice: Meta-analysis and correlation

Evidence-based management is an emerging movement aimed explicitly at using the current best evidence in management decision-making. Evidence-based management entails managerial decisions and organisational practices that are informed by the best available scientific evidence.

This chapter builds on its principles and critically evaluates leadership theories and approaches in the light of available scientific evidence. Today's most-used method of scrutinising the empirical validity of a theory or approach is *meta-analysis*, which combines the results of several studies that address a set of related research questions. This is normally done by identifying a common measure of 'effect size'. The effect size is a statistical expression of the strength of a relationship between two variables in terms of a numerical value, usually a correlation. This value can range from +1 to −1. A positive value expresses a positive relationship (ie the more of x, the more of y) between two variables, and a negative value a negative relationship (ie the more of x, the less of y). A value close to 0 suggests that there is no relationship. The higher the value the stronger the relationship.

For instance, from selection research you may have discovered that intelligence and job performance are correlated by about 0.3. This means that there is a positive and medium-sized effect of intelligence on job performance. In other words, the more intelligent a person is, the better is the person's job performance.

Effect sizes are usually given as a percentage of explained variance in another variable or in terms of correlations. Small effect sizes explain about 1% to 5% of the variance in the other variable (or are said to have a correlation of $r = 0.1$ to $r = 0.2$). Medium effect sizes explain 5% to 15% of the variance in the other variable (or are said to have a correlation of $r = 0.2$ to $r = 0.4$). And large effect sizes explain more than 16% of the variance (or are said to have a correlation of $r > 0.4$). In the social sciences – which is where leadership comes in – medium or large effect sizes usually indicate that there is strong evidence for a given theory or approach.

For more details visit the section on evidence-based management on our accompanying website for supplementary material.

How does it work?

Traits refer to relatively stable dispositions to behave in a particular way. Despite its name, the trait approach also suggests that leaders are more skilled than non-leaders. Skills refer to the ability to do something in an effective manner. Relying on the idea that traits can be organised around the Big Five personality framework (see Table 10.1), Judge and colleagues (2002) suggested that leaders are more open, conscientious, extraverted and less neurotic than non-leaders.

Open leaders, they suggested, may be more effective because they tend to be more creative, risk-taking and visionary. Conscientious leaders may be more effective because they have integrity, engender trust, show more initiative and persistence in the face of obstacles, and are better in goal-setting and monitoring. Extraverted leaders may be more effective because they are better communicators, have better social skills and are more assertive. Neuroticism may undermine leader effectiveness because neurotic persons are less likely to attempt leadership, are less inspirational and have lower expectations of themselves. Furthermore, Judge and colleagues suggested that persons who are more agreeable are more likely to rise to leadership positions because they are more personally appreciated. Once in a leadership position, however, agreeable leaders might be less effective because they are more passive and less assertive.

Table 10.1:   A description of the Big Five traits

Big Five factor	People who score high on this trait tend to be . . .
Openness to experience	Original, creative, daring, imaginative, independent
Conscientiousness	Careful, reliable, well-organised, conscientious, hardworking
Extraversion	Sociable, affectionate, fun-loving, talkative, friendly
Agreeableness	Soft-hearted, forgiving, sympathetic, acquiescent, lenient
Neuroticism	Worrying, nervous, high-strung, insecure, self-conscious

Source: adapted from McCrae and Costa (1987)

Relying on the idea that intelligence is the most reliable predictor of job performance, Judge and colleagues (2004a) suggested that more intelligent people are better leaders because they make better decisions, are better at explaining to people how they should do their job, and are better at recognising opportunities and potential problems.

Application

The message of the trait approach is straightforward. It suggests that leaders are born, and there is little organisations can do to develop effective leaders. Accordingly, what organisations should do is to select people with high cognitive abilities and a leader-like personality profile into leadership positions. As this chapter unfolds, we will see that this is only half the truth, of course. The style approach, which we examine next, will show that effective leadership can be learned (at least to some extent).

Evidence and evaluation

In sum, the trait approach helps us understand which people are more likely to rise to leadership positions and which people are the more effective leaders. Despite initial setbacks, two recent meta-analyses (see Table 10.2 for details) support the idea that personality and intelligence affect leader emergence and leadership effectiveness (Judge *et al*, 2002; Judge *et al*, 2004a). To date, only little research has been conducted that focuses on why this may be the case. Is it because people with certain characteristics and innate qualities are better in leading others? Is it because we perceive such leaders as being more effective, and that we are therefore more willing to accept them as our leaders? Or is it both? As we go along, we will see that both explanations may be valid.

Another shortcoming of the trait approach is that it fails to take situational variables into account. We will see later on that, for instance, the cultural context in which leadership takes place determines which characteristics are essential for effective leadership. Accordingly, it could be speculated that profiles of effective leaders vary across and within different organisations and industries.

The style approach

Responding to the failure of earlier trait studies, researchers started looking at actual behaviours that might distinguish effective leaders from non-leaders. Are effective leaders better in clarifying goals and explaining tasks? Are they better in motivating and understanding other people? Or are they better in doing all these things? The first and most important empirical studies in this research area were carried out at the Ohio State University and Michigan State University in the 1950s. To cope with the sheer number of possible leadership styles, researchers at both Ohio State and Michigan State came up with a two-fold taxonomy on the basis of which leadership behaviour could be described: a people-oriented leadership style and a task-oriented leadership style. Accordingly, this approach is often referred to as the **style approach**. This approach tries to clarify which of the two styles is more effective, or more precisely, which combination of the two styles is the most effective one.

How does it work?

The researchers at Ohio State (Fleishman, 1953) referred to the people-oriented style as *consideration* and the task-oriented style as *initiating structure*. Consideration behaviours are concerned with the social aspect of leadership and are focused on the leader–follower relationship. Supportive and camaraderie-building actions, as well as showing respect and trusting subordinates, are examples of consideration behaviours. Initiating structure is indicated by organising work, assigning tasks to subordinates and co-ordinating and scheduling work activities. Hence, initiating structure behaviours are task-focused. Since consideration and initiating structure were not conceptualised as the two ends of a bipolar scale but were described as independent behaviours, a leader can be high on consideration *and* high or low on initiating

Table 10.2:   The available scientific evidence for the most common leadership approaches*

Approach	Evidence
Trait approach *Personality*	Judge and colleagues (2002) demonstrated that the personality traits openness, conscientiousness and extraversion have a moderate positive effect on leader emergence and effectiveness, while agreeableness only predicted leader emergence. Neuroticism was negatively related to both leader emergence and effectiveness. The following table summarises their findings:

Effects of personality on leader emergence and leader effectiveness

	Leader emergence		Leader effectiveness	
Trait	*r*	*k*	*r*	*k*
Openness	.24	20	.24	17
Conscientiousness	.33	17	.16	18
Extraversion	.33	37	.24	23
Agreeableness	.05	23	.21	19
Neuroticism	−.24	30	−.22	18

Source: Judge et al (2002)

Intelligence	Judge and colleagues (2004a) showed in yet another meta-analysis that intelligence predicts leader emergence ($r = .25$, $k = 65$) and leader effectiveness ($r = .33$, $k = 14$).
Style approach	A meta-analytic study by Judge and colleagues (2004b) summarised the results of over 100 studies which looked at the relationship between consideration and initiating structure with various leadership outcomes. As can be seen in the table below, results support the idea that both consideration and initiating structure are important predictors of follower satisfaction and motivation and leadership effectiveness. In other words, leaders that are both people- and task-oriented are more effective, are better able to motivate their followers, and their followers are more satisfied.

Effects of leadership style on follower satisfaction and motivation and leader effectiveness

	Consideration		Initiating structure	
Criterion	*r*	*k*	*r*	*k*
Follower job satisfaction	.46	76	.22	72
Follower motivation	.50	11	.40	12
Leader effectiveness	.52	20	.39	20

Source: Judge, Piccolo and Ilies (2004b)

Contingency approaches *Fiedler*	Meta-analysing data from 10 studies and over 1,200 groups and their leaders, Schriesheim and colleagues showed some support for Fiedler's contingency model (Schriesheim *et al*, 1994). A meta-analysis conducted by Strube and Garcia (1981) showed that the LPC model is very robust and delivers statistical validity regarding the prediction of group performance. In this meta-analysis, 97 studies were investigated. However, a meta-analytical review conducted by Peters, Hartke and Pohlmann (1985) concluded that the model is supported by data obtained from laboratory studies but lacks validity regarding data obtained in real-world field studies. Taking all this together, research evidence yields mixed support for Fiedler's model, which has to be borne in mind when it is applied.
Situational leadership theory (SLT)	Although there is no published meta-analysis available from which one could assess the model's validity, a qualitative review has concluded that empirical research so far does not support SLT (Graeff, 1997). More research, and in particular a meta-analysis, is needed to reach a more conclusive verdict, but currently the model's validity is questionable, at best.

Table 10.2 NEXT

Approach	Evidence
Path-goal theory	Empirical research on path-goal theory has produced mixed results. For instance, a meta-analysis by Wofford and Liska (1993) showed that the relationships between leader behaviours and leadership effectiveness were indeed contingent on a number of situational variables. However, less than 50% of the relationships proposed by path-goal theory were supported. Podsakoff and colleagues reached a similar conclusion in yet another meta-analysis (Podsakoff *et al*, 1999).
Leader-member-exchange (LMX)	Empirical evidence from two meta-analyses supports the general tenets of LMX theory (Gerstner and Day, 1997; Ilies *et al*, 2007). A substantial effect has been found for LMX on externally rated subordinate in-role performance ($r = .3$, $k = 30$) and extra-role performance ($r = .37$, $k = 50$) and for LMX on overall subordinate satisfaction ($r = .50$, $k = 33$ studies) and organisational commitment ($r = .42$, $k = 17$). Narrative reviews support the idea that leaders are more likely to form high-quality relationships with their more competent and dependable subordinates and those that are similar in their attitudes and values (Liden *et al*, 1997). However, there is far less evidence to suggest that demographic similarities (ie gender, age, ethnic background) between the leader and follower affect the quality of LMX relationships.
Inspirational approaches *Charismatic leadership*	Empirical evidence generally supports the charismatic leadership approach. A meta-analysis of 36 studies (DeGroot *et al*, 2000) found a substantial effect of charismatic leadership on subordinate performance ($r = .3$) and a slightly stronger effect on followers' job satisfaction ($r = .4$). While the more specific tenets of attribution theory remain untested, most propositions put forward by self-concept theory are well supported by over 35 empirical investigations (Shamir *et al*, 1993).
Transformational and transactional leadership	Two meta-analyses support the main ideas of transformational leadership theory. Judge and Bono (2000) found that the Big Five traits had a moderate effect on transformational leadership (overall: $r = .4$, with the strongest predictors being agreeableness: $r = .28$ and extraversion: $r = .20$; $k = 15$). This supports the idea that transformational leadership theory is a behavioural theory, but that leaders with certain traits (eg extraverted and agreeable leaders) are more likely to display transformational leadership behaviours. Judge and Piccolo's (2004) meta-analysis summarises the findings of 87 studies and shows that non-transactional leadership (ie laissez-faire) undermines leadership effectiveness ($r = -.14$) and followers are less satisfied with their leaders ($r = -.13$). Transactional leaders' use of contingent reward results in greater leadership effectiveness ($r = .15$) and increases follower motivation ($r = .22$). Management-by-exception was more or less unrelated to follower satisfaction and motivation and leadership effectiveness. Controlling for these effects, transformational leadership had still a strong positive effect on follower motivation ($r = .32$), leadership effectiveness ($r = .37$) and follower satisfaction ($r = .52$). These findings support the augmentation hypothesis: transactional leadership leads to expected outcomes, whereas transformational leadership ensures that followers perform beyond expectations.

* r and k are statistical coefficients, commonly used in data analysis. r is the coefficient, describing the strength of a correlation between two variables – ie the greater r is (maximum value 1, minimum value 0), the more the two investigated variables are related to each other; k is a coefficient very often used in meta-analytic studies simply denoting the number of individual studies that were used and analysed in the meta-analysis.

structure, or vice versa. The Ohio researchers suggested that the most effective style is one that is high on consideration and high on initiating structure.

The Michigan studies were conducted at around the same time as the Ohio studies. They investigated the effect of managerial leadership behaviours on group processes and group performance (Katz, Maccoby and Morse, 1950). Similar to the Ohio State studies, the researchers at Michigan distinguished two leadership styles: *employee orientation* and *production orientation*. Employee orientation is very similar to the concept of consideration, in that it reflects a strong emphasis on interpersonal relationships, including helpful, supportive and appreciative behaviours. Production orientation on the other hand reflects behaviours that aim to increase work efficiency. Examples include planning and co-ordinating activities, setting performance goals and providing technical assistance. Production orientation corresponds to initiating structure from the Ohio studies. Unlike the Ohio studies, researchers at Michigan initially suggested that leaders are either employee-oriented or production-oriented but cannot be both. They later revised this idea, suggesting that the most effective leaders are indeed those who are both employee- and production-oriented.

Even today it is not entirely clear how a leadership style that is both task- and people-oriented results in higher leadership effectiveness. As we will see later on with the contingency approaches, one possible explanation might be that a more people-oriented style helps to inspire and motivate people and increases their self-efficacy, whereas a more task-oriented leadership style helps to remove barriers and enable people to accomplish their tasks.

Application

Different from the trait approach, the style approach suggests that effective leadership can be learned. Commercialising this idea, Blake and Mouton (1964) built their work on the Ohio and Michigan State studies and developed what they called the managerial grid. The managerial grid is an assessment tool on which a person's preferred leadership style can be assessed along the two dimensions of a leadership style that is more or less people- and task-oriented. Prescribing that the ideal leadership style is both task- and people-oriented, Blake and Mouton developed a series of well-evaluated trainings that help managers to develop the most effective leadership style. (For more details visit the Blake and Mouton website: the link is provided on this book's supplementary material website.)

Evaluation

The style approach marked a major shift in the focus of leadership. Unlike the trait approach, which suggests that leaders are born, the style approach implicates that leaders can be made. It also helps us understand that if we want to develop effective leaders, we need to train them how to be both people- and task-oriented. As can be seen in Table 10.2, meta-analytic research (Judge *et al*, 2004b) supports the idea that both consideration and initiating structure are important predictors of follower satisfaction and motivation and leadership effectiveness. As with the trait approach, however, there is little research available that might explain *why* such a style combination is most effective. Another shortcoming of the style approach is that it does not take all the contextual conditions into account. Do you really think that a task- and people-oriented leadership style is always effective, no matter whether the follower is motivated or not, and no matter whether job assignments are complex or simple?

The contingency approaches [2]

The three contingency approaches we discuss in this section – Fiedler's theory, situational leadership theory and path-goal theory – certainly suggest that follower, task and leader characteristics do matter. In a nutshell, these approaches argue that whether a people- or task-oriented leadership style is effective depends on the followers' personality, the job assignments followers are working on, and the amount of formal authority a leader possesses. These theories are therefore often referred to as **contingency approach** theories or models.

Fiedler's 'least preferred co-worker' theory

Motivated by the initially disappointing results of research conducted within the tradition of the trait and style approaches, Fiedler in the mid-1960s started developing his own leadership model (Fiedler, 1964; Fiedler, 1967). The underlying idea of his model is that there has to be a match between a leader's style and the degree to which the situation gives control to the leader. Accordingly, this approach is often referred to as **Fiedler's contingency model**.

How does it work?

In line with the style approach, Fiedler distinguished people as being either task-oriented or relationship-oriented. Different from the style approach, but in line with the trait approach,

Fiedler suggested that these orientations represent stable dispositions rather than actual behaviours. Accordingly, Fiedler proposed that people can be either people-oriented or task-oriented, but not both.

In order to measure a person's preferred leadership style, Fiedler developed the Least Preferred Co-worker (LPC) questionnaire. The questionnaire asks leaders to think of a co-worker with whom they can work least well. The leaders then have to describe this co-worker on a scale from 1 to 8 on a set of 16 bipolar adjectives (eg nice [8] – nasty [1], interesting [8] – boring [1], trustworthy [8] – untrustworthy [1]). Leaders with a people-oriented leadership style tend to describe their least preferred co-workers rather positively because for them good relationships are more important than high performance and productivity. In contrast, leaders with a task-oriented style tend to describe their least preferred co-workers rather negatively, because they are less interested in good relationships and more in high performance and productivity.

Fiedler further suggests that whether a task-oriented or relationship-oriented leadership style leads to high or low performance depends on the favourability of the situation. He defined the favourability of a situation as a function of leader–member relations (good versus poor), the leader's position-power (high versus low) and task structure (high versus low). *Leader–member relations* refers to the degree to which the leader has the support and loyalty of the subordinates and the relations are amicable and accommodating. *Position-power* reflects the authority of a leader to assess subordinates' performance and impose punishments on them or give out rewards. *Task structure* is the extent to which the requirements of job assignments are clear and spelled out (eg assembly-line work is a highly structured task, whereas research and development projects are highly unstructured).

As can be seen in Table 10.3, this leads to eight different situations that vary in favourability. For instance, the situation is most favourable when leader–member relations are good, when the task is highly structured and when the position-power of the leader is strong. In contrast, the situation is least favourable when leader–member relations are poor, task structure is low and the leader has low position-power. On the basis of a series of empirical studies, Fiedler showed that leaders with a task-oriented style were most effective in situations that were either favourable or very unfavourable to them (see Table 10.3). Leaders with a people-oriented style were found to be most effective in moderately or slightly unfavourable situations.

Table 10.3:   **Findings from the Fiedler model**

	Leader–member relations	Task structure	Leader's position-power	Most effective leader	Situational favourability
1	Good	High	Strong	Task-oriented	High
2	Good	High	Weak	Task-oriented	High
3	Good	Low	Strong	Task-oriented	High
4	Good	Low	Weak	People-oriented	Moderate
5	Poor	High	Strong	People-oriented	Moderate
6	Poor	High	Weak	People-oriented	Moderate
7	Poor	Low	Strong	People-oriented	Low
8	Poor	Low	Weak	Task-oriented	Low

Source: adapted from Fiedler (1967)

Application

The key message of Fiedler's model is that a leader's style has to match the situation. Because of this, organisations can create effective leaders by:

- selecting the right people to fit the right leadership situations

- modifying situations in a way that they fit the leader's style, or

- making leaders aware of their preferred leadership style and teaching them how they can modify the situations they are in.

In any case organisations would have to determine the preferred leadership style of their leaders and evaluating the fit between leader and the leadership position.

Evidence and evaluation

Fiedler's contingency model teaches us that there is more to leadership than just the leader. It is the first theory that takes into account task and follower characteristics, and shows that leaders with a people-oriented style might be more effective in different situations than people with a task-oriented style. However, as can be seen in Table 10.2, research evidence yields mixed support for Fiedler's model, specifically questioning its real-world validity (Peters *et al*, 1985). One of the major shortcomings of the model is that it is merely prescriptive and does not explain *why* task-oriented and people-oriented people are effective in different situations. Another problem with this approach is the validity of the LPC questionnaire. Among other things, most problematic seems to be the underlying idea that people can be either people-oriented or task-oriented, but never both. This is in sharp contrast with the Michigan and Ohio studies, which found, you may remember, that people may well use both leadership styles at the same time.

Situational leadership

In the late 1960s Hersey and Blanchard (1969) developed **situational leadership theory** (SLT), which has become the most popular leadership model among management and leadership development specialists. Every year over 1 million managers are exposed to it and more than 400 of the Fortune 500 have incorporated it in their leadership development programmes. Its popularity may well stem from the fact that the theory both provides some guidance on how leaders should behave in any given situation and is itself intuitively appealing.

How does it work?

Situational leadership is yet another contingency theory of leadership. It builds on the same premises as the style approach and suggests that there are two dimensions underlying any leadership behaviour: *directive behaviour*, which is similar to task-oriented leadership behaviours, and *supportive behaviour*, which reflects people-oriented leadership behaviours. According to SLT, crossing these two dimensions leads to four distinctive leadership styles: *supporting*, *coaching*, *delegating* and *directing*. As can be seen in Figure 10.1, a supportive leadership style is characterised by low directive leadership behaviours and high supportive behaviours. A coaching leadership style is characterised by leadership behaviours that are both highly supportive and highly directive. A delegating leadership style is characterised by leadership behaviours that are low supportive and low directive. A directing style is characterised by low supportive behaviours and highly directive behaviours.

Other than the style approach, SLT suggests that a combination of a highly directive and supportive leadership style is not always the most effective one. SLT instead states that the *developmental stage* of the follower has to be taken into account. A follower's developmental stage is a function of his or her willingness to accomplish a job assignment and his or her ability to fulfil the job assignment. Thus, the developmental stage of a follower is low when he or she is unwilling and unable to get an assigned task done, and it is high when the follower is both willing and able.

Figure 10.1 Hersey and Blanchard's situational leadership model

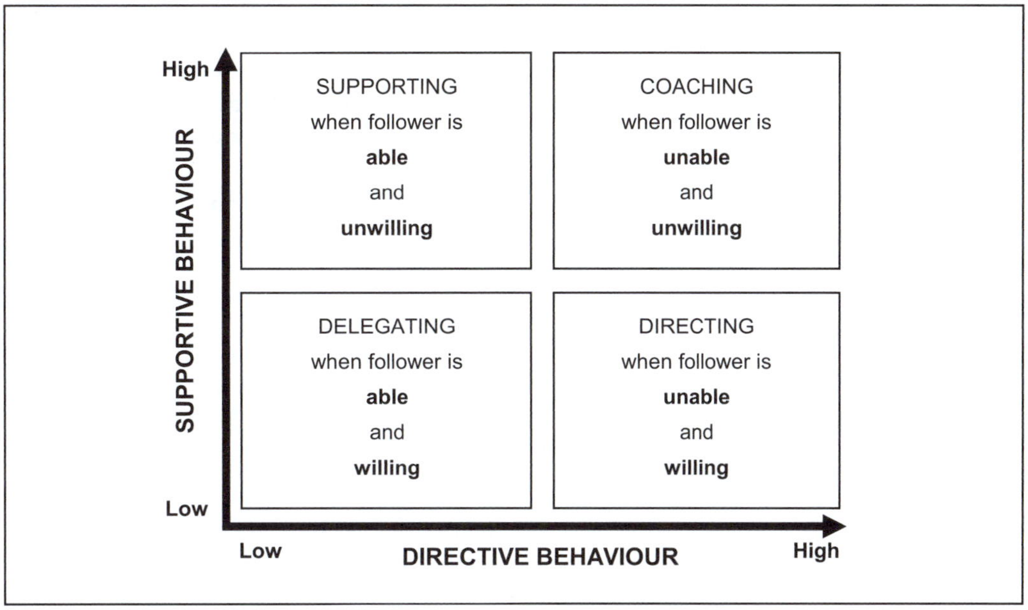

Figure content:

SUPPORTIVE BEHAVIOUR (vertical axis, Low to High)
DIRECTIVE BEHAVIOUR (horizontal axis, Low to High)

SUPPORTING — when follower is **able** and **unwilling**

COACHING — when follower is **unable** and **unwilling**

DELEGATING — when follower is **able** and **willing**

DIRECTING — when follower is **unable** and **willing**

Source: adapted from Hersey and Blanchard (1969)

SLT finally suggests that leadership styles have to match followers' developmental stages. Highly supportive behaviours are considered most effective when followers are unwilling, whereas behaviours low in support are most effective when followers are willing to fulfil their job assignments. Highly directive behaviours are considered most effective when followers are unable, whereas behaviours low in direction-setting are considered most effective when followers are able to accomplish assigned tasks. And from this it is evident (see also Figure 10.2) that a supporting leadership style is most effective when the followers are able but unwilling; a coaching style is most effective when the followers are unable and unwilling; a delegating style is most effective when followers are able and willing; and a directing style is most effective when followers are unable and willing.

Application

On the basis of SLT, Hersey developed a situational leadership training programme (for more details visit the website for situational training – the link is provided on this book's supplementary material website) which has proved immensely popular among training and development specialists. The training takes participants through a three-step process. For the first step participants learn to diagnose and analyse situations through the lenses of SLT. During this stage participants learn the underlying principles and how the model actually works. For the second step they are trained to select the right leadership style in a specific situation. For instance, participants are given little vignettes in which they learn that the follower was unable and/or unwilling to accomplish his or her job assignment. They are then asked whether a delegating, directing, supporting or coaching leadership style is the most effective one. For the last step they learn to apply these different leadership styles using a role-play methodology. Given the availability of such highly structured and well-designed training in combination with extensive marketing, it is not surprising that SLT became the most popular leadership training programme in the world.

Evidence and evaluation

Situational leadership theory focuses our attention on follower characteristics and suggests that leaders will only be able to motivate and influence their followers when they match their style to the followers' level of willingness and ability to accomplish their given job assignments. When you are unwilling to work, wouldn't you expect your boss to try to motivate you? On the other hand, when you do not understand what you have to do, wouldn't you expect your boss to explain it to you? Interestingly, neither of the three models we have discussed so far (the trait approach, the style approach and Fiedler's model) takes followers' characteristics into account. This seems to make intuitively good sense but, as you can see in Table 10.2, has hardly been empirically investigated, and the research that has been conducted is not in favour of SLT (Graeff, 1997). However, the main problem with SLT is that it is rather prescriptive and does not provide any rationale and empirical evidence for *why* a given style (eg telling) is best in a particular situation (eg when the employee is both unable and unwilling).

The theory we examine next endeavours to avoid such pitfalls by starting with a motivational theory of human behaviour on the basis of which it tries to deduce the leadership style effective leaders should use in a given situation.

Path-goal theory [3]

Path-goal theory was developed in the 1970s by House and colleagues (House, 1971; House and Mitchell, 1974). It is called path-goal theory because it suggests that the leader's job is to show the subordinates how they can achieve their work objective (show them the path they should follow to reach the goal). Leaders should remove any obstacles that may obstruct subordinate goal attainment and support followers with the information and resources necessary to achieve these goals. In return, this should lead to improved subordinate job performance and satisfaction.

How does it work?

Building on expectancy theory (see Chapter 5) path-goal theory suggests that followers will be motivated:

- when they believe that they are capable of accomplishing their job assignment (a situation known to theorists as *expectancy*)

- when they think that accomplishing their job assignment will be rewarded (*instrumentality*), and

- when they value the reward (*valence*).

The theory suggests further that these three components are contingent on whether the task is structured or unstructured, and on whether the followers perceive themselves as being able to accomplish the task. Moreover, in the tradition of the style approach, four different leadership styles are postulated: directive, supportive, participative and achievement-oriented. Using *directive leadership*, leaders schedule the followers' work, tell them what to do and when, and give appropriate guidance along the way. *Supportive leadership* is characterised by creating a friendly and comfortable work environment. *Participative leadership* involves consulting the opinions of the followers and taking them into account when decisions have to be made. *Achievement-oriented leadership* sets high standards and goals for the followers to achieve, challenging them to perform as best they can.

To explore the effect of the leader's behaviours on the components of expectancy theory, each situation is explained separately below (and see Figure 10.2).

When faced with an unstructured task, subordinates' expectations of accomplishing the organisational goals may decrease. The leader can increase subordinates' expectancy through the use of three behaviours: instrumental (directive) behaviour, participative behaviour, or achievement-oriented (or directive) behaviour. When faced with a structured task the leader can expect a decrease in valence. The task is routine, monotonous and provides little reward for a subordinate. Through the use of supportive leadership behaviour, the leader attempts to make the task more enjoyable by making the follower more comfortable or combining the routine

Figure 10.2 Path-goal theory (simplified)

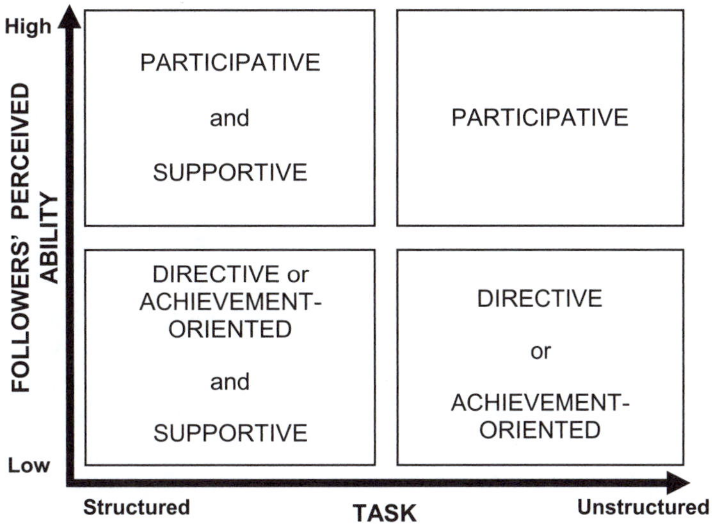

Source: adapted from House and Mitchell (1974)

task with an enjoyable task. And by making the task more enjoyable, the leader not only increases valence but also increases the subordinates' expectancy – their expectations of being able to endure the monotony long enough to accomplish the goal.

High-perceived-ability subordinates usually have high expectancy. Their decreased motivation may be caused by low valence. Task mastery may no longer provide a challenge or satisfaction for these subordinates. The leader can increase valence for these subordinates by involving them in the decision-making process. Allowing them to participate in decision-making processes increases their status in the organisation and extends their responsibilities. This may challenge them, boosting their sense of satisfaction. In this situation, motivation is increased through participative leader behaviours. Low-perceived-ability subordinates usually have low expectancy – limited expectations of accomplishing organisational goals. Instrumental or achievement-oriented leader behaviours are most effective in this situation. The leader's behaviours help the subordinate to identify the behaviours necessary for goal accomplishment. Instrumental behaviour indicates the exact behaviours required and is most effective for a subordinate with deficient skills (low competence). Achievement-oriented behaviours may be more appropriate in increasing expectancy for followers with low confidence.

Application

Path-goal theory was first and foremost an attempt by academic researchers to explain how and when different leadership styles lead to higher follower motivation and ultimately higher follower performance and satisfaction. Leaving aside for a moment whether the theory is valid or not, the theory could be taught to potential leaders, enhancing their understanding of how the task and personal characteristics of their followers interact and subsequently undermine or facilitate their motivation, and increasing leaders' knowledge of which leadership style ensures high follower motivation in any particular situation. However, because path-goal theory is seemingly complex and difficult to learn and apply, very few forms of management training have been developed on the basis of the theory.

Evidence and evaluation

Clearly, the strength of path-goal theory lies in its academic rigour. Building on a well-grounded theory of human psychological functioning (ie expectancy theory) it tries to explain what leaders should do to motivate their followers. Although overly complex and empirically little supported (see Table 10.2), it has served as a blueprint for a good number of theories and models that have subsequently been developed. Nevertheless, in its original formulation it has been criticised for not going far enough in incorporating the tenets of expectancy theory. For instance, you may have wondered earlier why directive leadership during tedious work increases subordinate motivation. In fact the original theory just does not explain it. Path-goal theory has also been criticised on a more fundamental level because it assumes, as does every other approach examined so far, that leadership is a top-down process initiated by the leader. The theories we investigate next challenge this idea and move the follower to centre stage.

Leader-member exchange (LMX)

So far we have suggested that for a leader to be effective, he or she has to have certain traits (eg extraversion and conscientiousness), has to display certain behaviours (eg consideration and structure) and has to adjust behaviours to the situation (eg task characteristics) and followers (eg ability and motivation). In other words, theories discussed so far focus on what the leader has to do to or with the follower in order to be effective. **Leader-member exchange theory** takes a different stance and focuses on the quality of the relationship between the leader and the follower instead.

How does it work?

Think of a leader you know. Does this leader have favourite followers with whom the leader gets along very well and others with whom the leader does not get along that well? Building on the idea that leaders tend to have such favourites, LMX suggests that leaders develop a different form of relationship with each of their followers (Graen and Scandura, 1987). In a high LMX relationship between a leader and a subordinate, there is a sense of mutual trust between the leader and follower, the follower receives a disproportionate amount of the leader's attention, and the follower is more likely to receive special privileges. A poor LMX relationship between a leader and a subordinate is characterised by the subordinate's being allocated less of the leader's time, getting fewer of the preferred rewards the leader controls, and by the relationship's being based on formal authority interactions.

Leaders develop relationships of different types with their followers, because they have a tendency to categorise their subordinates into 'in-group members' and 'out-group members' (Dienesch and Liden, 1986). Interactions with in-group members are characterised by high-quality LMX relationships and interactions with out-group members are characterised by low-quality LMX relationships and interactions. Leaders are motivated to categorise people into in-group and out-group members because of time pressure (ie they do not have the time to maintain high-quality LMX relationships with all their subordinates) and because they like some of their subordinates better than others (eg those that are competent, dependable, agreeable, but also those that share similar attitudes and values and those that have the same gender and ethnic background). In return, subordinates that have a high-quality LMX with their leader are more likely to make desirable contributions to their work role (ie lower absenteeism and turnover, higher task and extra-role performance) and hold more positive job attitudes (ie be more satisfied with their jobs, peers and leader and feel more attached to their organisation).

Application

In the light of these findings it seems important that leaders develop high-quality LMX relationships with all their employees. How can they achieve this? A field experiment (Scandura and Graen, 1984) showed that leaders can be trained to develop favourable exchange relationships with *all* of their subordinates. The training taught the leaders active listening skills, how to exchange mutual expectations and resources with their subordinates, and asked them to apply this knowledge in a half-hour one-to-one session with each of their subordinates. Leaders who took the training found subsequent gains in objective performance and satisfaction with their subordinates. So developing high-quality LMX relationships *can* be trained for and learned!

Evidence and evaluation

We can learn from LMX that high-quality relationships between leader and subordinates are essential for subordinates' well-being and their performance, but that leaders often fail to develop such high-quality relationships with all their subordinates. As can can be seen in Table 10.2, this is strongly supported by empirical evidence (Gerstner and Day, 1997; Ilies *et al*, 2007). While LMX helps us understand why leaders accord privileges to some of their subordinates, this is by no means any excuse for leaders to treat some of their followers less favourably. Instead, for the sake both of subordinate performance and well-being and also of simple fairness, leaders must reflect on these tendencies and make every effort to treat all their employees equally.

Inspirational approaches

Inspirational approaches look at the emotional and symbolic aspects of leadership. They help us understand how leaders inspire and motivate others to act beyond their immediate self-interests and to do more than they would normally do. The two main inspirational approaches are **charismatic leadership** and **transformational leadership** theory.

Charismatic leadership

Prominent examples of charismatic leaders include Winston Churchill, Mahatma Gandhi, Martin Luther King, Jr, Barack H. Obama, Richard Branson (CEO and founder of the Virgin Group), Steve Jobs (co-founder of Apple), Mary Kay Ash (founder of Mary Kay Cosmetics) and Oprah Winfrey (talkshow host and chairman of Harpo). These leaders are well known for the emotional impact they had on others by reaching out to the hearts and minds of people and for their willingness to take great risks to achieve their visions in spite of great odds against them. Such leaders often emerge in crisis situations, times of great uncertainty, or in new markets.

How does it work?

The German sociologist Max Weber (1947) referred to charisma as:

> a certain quality of an individual personality, by virtue of which he or she is set apart from ordinary people and treated and endowed with supernatural, superhuman, or at least specifically exceptional powers or qualities. These are not accessible to the ordinary person, but are regarded as of divine origin or as exemplary, and on the basis of them the individual concerned is treated as a leader.

Attribution theory (Conger and Kanungo, 1987) suggests that charisma is an attributional phenomenon. Followers attribute charisma to leaders if leaders advocate a vision that challenges the current status quo but is still within the latitude of acceptance by followers; if leaders act in unconventional ways, make self-sacrifices, take personal risks and incur high costs to achieve their vision; and if they are perceptive to others' abilities and responsive to their needs and feelings, and if they are able to influence them to accomplish great things that initially seemed impossible. Thus, according to the attributional approach, we might attribute charisma to Martin Luther King, Jr, because he criticised the then still existing policy of racial segregation in the United States and envisaged a future USA that had overcome it. (His famous 'I have a dream' speech is available via the link on the supplementary material website.) Despite threats to his life right up until his assassination he kept fighting for a USA in which every citizen had the same opportunities and equal rights, and in doing so encouraged many others to do the same.

Although attribution theory specifies the conditions under which followers attribute charisma to leaders, it does not explain how charismatic leaders inspire and motivate followers to become highly committed to the leader's mission and make them perform above and beyond the call of duty. This led to the development of *self-concept theory* (House, 1977; Shamir *et al*, 1993), which suggests that charismatic leaders are able to evoke and harness emotional reactions on the part of the followers. It explains why charismatic leaders are more liked, trusted and respected and able to exercise so much influence over their followers. Charismatic leaders achieve this by:

- articulating a common vision
- emphasising the value of attaining that vision
- providing hope for a better future and faith in its attainment
- expressing high expectations of the followers to attain the common vision, and confidence in the followers' ability to meet these expectations
- creating personal commitment to the vision.

The next time you watch *Braveheart*, listen carefully to Wallace's speech to the Scots army before the battle of Stirling Bridge (you can also find this speech on our website for the book's supplementary material) and focus on how Wallace envisages an independent Scotland, how he stresses the desirability of such a state, how he provides the hope that it will be realised one day, how he strongly believes in and counts on the Scots' ability to win the battle, and how he reinstates their self-confidence and gains their full commitment to sacrifice their lives for him and Scotland. These motivational processes are activated when a leader (in this case William Wallace) becomes a representative character and acts as a role model (as when Wallace leads the Scots into battle), and when he or she is able to align followers' interests, values and beliefs (in this case the Scots' desire to live in freedom) with the leader's activities, goals and ideology (as with Wallace's desire to win the battle and his vision of an independent Scotland).

Application

Are charismatic leaders born, or can we train people to have charismatic effects on followers? Max Weber's earlier definition would clearly suggest the former when he suggests that charisma is a divine gift (ie a personality trait). Both attribution and self-concept theory on the other hand would alternatively suggest that charismatic leadership can be trained for. In fact, there is empirical evidence (Howell and Frost, 1989) that undergraduate business students who have been trained to behave like charismatic leaders (by learning, for instance, how to articulate a vision, how to communicate high performance expectations, how to exhibit confidence in the ability of followers to meet these expectations, how to empathise with the needs of followers, how to project an optimistic and self-confident presence) may be attributed more charisma by their followers, and their followers may thereafter improve their task performance and be more satisfied. There is also evidence that a crisis and high levels of uncertainty facilitate the occurrence of charismatic leadership – in particular, if the leader is able to offer credible strategies for coping with it successfully (Pillai and Meindl, 1998). Nevertheless, personality traits such as a strong need for power, high self-confidence and a strong conviction in his or her own beliefs and ideals make it more likely that a leader will have charismatic effects on followers (House, 1977). Charisma is thus likely to be a function of trait, behaviour and situation.

Evidence and evaluation

The charismatic approach gives us a deeper understanding about the emotional reactions by followers to leaders, whereas earlier theories emphasise the rational-cognitive aspects of the leader-follower interaction. Understanding these emotional reactions helps to explain how charismatic leaders are able to transform the needs, values, preferences and aspirations of followers from self-interests to collective interests. As can be seen in Table 10.2, empirical evidence supports the idea that charismatic leadership has positive effects on followers' performance and satisfaction (Shamir *et al*, 1993; DeGroot *et al*, 2000). Despite its merits, it is questionable that the daily work of middle or lower-level managers requires charismatic leadership. Moreover, the charismatic leadership approach overemphasises the role of consideration for followers' emotional reactions. As we have noted earlier, in organisations it is often equally important that leaders guide and motivate their followers by clarifying role and task requirements. The transformational leadership approach, which is examined next, therefore integrates both consideration and initiating structure aspects.

Applying theory to practice: Activity

Watch the *Braveheart* clip again (it is on our website for the book's supplementary material). Using the leadership behaviour taxonomy presented in Table 10.4 characterise the leadership behaviour of William Wallace. Which transformational leadership behaviours does he display?

What effects does this leadership behaviour have on his followers

(eg in terms of their motivation to fight and their satisfaction with the leader)?

In order to succeed in the battle, why might it be important for William Wallace also to use transactional leadership behaviours (eg contingent reward and management by exception) to guide and motivate followers?

Transformational and transactional leadership

Transformational-transactional leadership theory (Bass, 1985) is a behavioural theory that integrates and extends earlier style and situational approaches and charismatic leadership theory. Bass (1990) suggests that the earlier approaches try to understand *transactional* leaders, whereas charismatic leadership theory is concerned with *transformational* leadership. Bass characterised non-leaders as *non-transactional*.

How does it work?

As it can be seen in Table 10.4, transactional leaders recognise what their followers want to get from their work and give them what they desire if they do their job well. They exchange rewards and promises of rewards for results and follower effort, and they respond to the self-interests of followers as long as the followers do their job by using a (1) contingent reward and (2) management-by-exception leadership style. Non-transactional leaders do not get actively involved in their followers' work. Accordingly, their leadership behaviour is described as (3) laissez-faire. In contrast, transformational leaders motivate subordinates to do more than the expected, raise awareness of the key issues for the group or organisation, and concern them with achievement, growth and development by using a leadership style that is characterised by (4) idealised influence, (5) inspirational motivation, (6) intellectual stimulation and (7) individual consideration.

Table 10.4: Behavioural dimensions of transformational and transactional leadership

Transactional leadership	(1)	Contingent reward: leader exchanges rewards or promises rewards for results and effort.
	(2a)	Management by exception (active): leader watches followers closely for mistakes and deviations from rules and takes corrective actions.
	(2b)	Management by exception (passive): leader intervenes only if standards are not met.
Non-transactional leadership	(3)	Laissez-faire: leader abdicates responsibility, delays or avoids making decisions, gives no feedback and makes few efforts to satisfy follower needs.
Transformational leadership	(4)	Idealised influence: leader provides vision and a sense of mission, acts as role model and gains respect and trust.
	(5)	Inspirational motivation: leader inspires, encourages others to raise expectations, reduces complexity in key issues and uses simple language to convey the mission.
	(6)	Intellectual stimulation: leader stimulates others to think, encourages their imagination and challenges the accepted ways of doing things.
	(7)	Individual consideration: leader develops others, provides challenges and learning opportunities, and delegates to raise their skills and confidence.

Source: adapted from Bass (1990)

Different from charismatic leadership theory, which may be characterised as a trait theory, transformational-transactional leadership theory is a behavioural theory (Bass, 1990). Rather than explaining why followers attribute charisma to leaders, transformational leadership theory identifies and describes behaviours that enable leaders to fully engage the subordinates and enthuse them to go above and beyond the call of duty. Moreover, charismatic leadership theory suggests that a leader's main concern is about being perceived as extraordinary by followers and making followers dependent on the leader for guidance and inspiration. In contrast, transactional-transformational leadership theory suggests that a transformational leader's main concern is about inspiring, developing and empowering followers to act in ways that support their group or the organisation rather than their self-interest. In line with these ideas, empirical findings (Kark *et al*, 2003) show that followers identify more with a charismatic leader, which in turn results in greater dependence on the leader. In contrast, followers identify more with their work group or organisation when they have a transformational leader, which in turn empowers the followers. Because of their empowerment, followers do not just do their jobs but strive for continuous improvement and innovation. They persist in the face of barriers or challenges and act more in the interest of their organisation than on the basis of self-interest or in the self-interest of the leader. Transformational leadership may thus benefit organisations far more than charismatic leadership.

Another important tenet of transactional-transformational leadership theory is that transformational leadership complements, but does not substitute for, transactional leadership (Bass, 1997). Known as the *augmentation hypothesis*, this implies that leaders need to be transactional to ensure that their followers accomplish their daily work, but that they need to be transformational for their followers to go beyond expectations. Effective leaders need therefore to be both transformational and transactional and show the full range of leadership behaviours (ie management by exception, contingent reward, idealised influence, inspirational motivation, intellectual stimulation and individual consideration).

Application

As with charismatic leadership, there is empirical evidence that suggests it can be learned (Barling *et al*, 1996; Dvir *et al*, 2002). For instance Barling and his colleagues conducted a field experiment in which a group of bank managers were given a one-day workshop and a series of four individual booster sessions teaching them transformational leadership, while a control group did not undergo this training. During their training sessions the bank managers were familiarised with the central concepts of transformational leadership, and discussed and role-played how it might be implemented in their work context. Some time afterwards, the bank managers who had attended these training sessions were found to have branches that performed significantly better and to have subordinates with a higher organisational commitment than the branches and subordinates of managers who had not attended the training sessions.

Evidence and evaluation

Transformational-transactional leadership theory helps us understand how leaders motivate subordinates to do more than the expected, raise their awareness of the key issues for the group or organisation and concern them with achievement, growth and development. The main propositions of transformational and transactional leadership theory are supported by meta-analytic research (Judge and Bono, 2000; Judge and Piccolo, 2004). However, although Bass (1997) considers transformational leadership to be effective in any situation or culture, the theory does not specify any condition under which transformational leadership may be less effective. For instance, because transformational leadership empowers people, it may be particularly effective when subordinates are concerned with complex tasks that call for continuous learning and creativity, although it may be less effective for simple tasks such as assembly-line work. Moreover, we will see later on that cultural differences may be another situational factor that undermines the effects of transformational leadership. We may also speculate that followers with a low need for growth may be more resistant towards transformational leadership than those with a high need for growth. Another caveat of transformational-transactional leadership theory is its descriptive-prescriptive nature. Accordingly, it does not question whether transformational leadership is ethical or not. For instance, one may well ask whether it is right that leaders should motivate people to do more than they are actually paid for by harnessing subordinates' needs for self-actualisation. Similarly, as we will see later, transformational-transactional leadership theory is not concerned with whether a vision, objectives or goals pursued by a leader will lead to success or disaster, and whether this might similarly imply unethical behaviours.

LEADERSHIP IN A GLOBAL CONTEXT [4]

Globalisation makes it more important for leaders to understand how to manage people with a different cultural background, as organisations become culturally ever more diverse or managers have ever more often to spend time abroad and lead people who are from a different cultural background. The approaches we have examined so far have assumed that leader traits and styles are effective regardless of the cultural context. We will see in this section, however, that leadership effectiveness is influenced by the cultural context in which leadership takes place. When you ask a British employee to list the characteristics of an ideal leader in order of importance, you are likely to get the following answer. The leader should be:

1 performance-oriented

2 inspirational

3 a team integrator

4 visionary

5 of high integrity

6 decisive, and

7 participative.

Were you to ask the same question of a follower in Germany, the answer you would get is that the leader should be:

1 of high integrity

2 inspirational

3 performance-oriented

4 decisive

5 participative

6 a skilled administrator, and

7 autonomous.

The differences in the attributes English and German followers value and the importance they attach to them are obvious.

We are all heavily influenced by the cultural context in which we grow up. Our parents, teachers and friends positively reinforce behaviours they find appropriate and question behaviours of which they do not approve. Accordingly, the culture in which we grow up shapes the way we think, feel and behave. Similarly, our culture shapes the way we think about leadership and how we tend to lead others. Introducing the idea of **culturally endorsed implicit leadership theories** (CLTs), researchers from the GLOBE research project (House *et al*, 2004; for more about this project see the GLOBE box below) suggest that members of a culturally defined group (eg the

English or the Germans) share common observations and values regarding what constitutes effective and ineffective leadership. If the *actual* characteristics of a leader match a follower's expectations about *ideal* leader's characteristics, the follower is more likely to recognise and accept the leader as a leader. Because both *actual* characteristics of a leader and expectations about *ideal* leader's characteristics are culturally endorsed, leaders are more likely to be accepted by followers that share the same cultural background, whereas they are less likely to be accepted by followers that do not share the same cultural background.

For an example let's go back to the one we were using. A British leader is likely to be performance-oriented because this is what he or she has learned is of primary importance in being an effective (British) leader. If this British leader then had to manage a German employee, the German employee possibly might have problems in accepting the British leader because he or she expects an effective leader first and foremost not to be performance-oriented but instead to display high integrity – which the British leader may not be particularly concerned to do.

Applying theory to practice: Project GLOBE

The Global Leadership and Organisational Behaviour Effectiveness (GLOBE) research programme is a multi-phase multi-method project in which investigators around the world are examining the inter-relationships between societal culture, organisational culture and organisational leadership. Approximately 170 social scientists and management scholars from 61 cultures/countries representing all major regions of the world are engaged in this long-term series of cross-cultural leadership studies.

In their paper 'Understanding cultures and implicit leadership theories across the globe: an introduction to Project GLOBE',

House *et al* (2002) outline the purposes of the GLOBE programme. The paper also features in this book's website.

The paper defines leadership effectiveness as a function of actual leader behaviours *and* followers' leadership ideals. Only when follower ideals and actual leader behaviour match, it is argued, do followers accept their leaders and leaders are effective. House and colleagues provide evidence for the idea that culture informs both follower ideals and actual leader behaviours, and that these therefore vary across countries. They conclude that what constitutes effective leaders can thus vary across the globe, making intercultural leadership much more difficult.

Is there then anything we can do about it? Extensive research (House *et al*, 2004: Project GLOBE) conducted among over 10,000 middle managers from over 60 different countries, identified around 100 attributes on the basis of which followers tend to categorise their leaders. These attributes fall into 21 different culturally endorsed leadership prototypes, such as integrity (eg trustworthiness), charisma (eg visionary, inspirational and motivating), team-integrating (eg communicative), self-protective (eg loner, asocial), malevolent (eg non-cooperative) and autocratic (eg dictatorial). As can be seen in Table 10.5, this research also showed that some of these ideal leader attributes are rated similarly as effective or ineffective in most cultures (the 'universal leadership prototypes'), whereas others varied quite substantially across cultures (the 'culturally contingent leadership prototypes').

Table 10.5:   Cultural beliefs about ideal leader attributes

Behaviours and traits universally considered facilitators of leadership effectiveness	Behaviours and traits universally considered impediments to leadership effectiveness	Culturally contingent endorsement of leadership attributes
Trustworthy	Loner	Individualist
Visionary	Asocial	Status-conscious
Inspirational and motivating	Non-cooperative	Risk-taking
Communicative	Dictatorial	

Source: adapted from House *et al* (2004)

What this means is that organisations that operate in a global context should select leaders who embody leadership attributes that are universally considered to facilitate leadership effectiveness and avoid selecting leaders who embody leadership attributes that are universally considered to impede effective leadership. Because some leadership attributes are culturally contingent, organisations should also ensure that they select global leaders who are open-minded and eager to learn and adapt their leadership style to different situations (Dalton and Ernst, 2004). When cultural differences between leader and follower are too great, however, it may be more effective to use indigenous managers rather than those from corporate headquarters whose culture does not fit the situation.

Before we proceed, let us shortly summarise what we have learned so far and see how it can be applied in organisations. Take a look, therefore, at the box below.

Applying theory to practice: Generating perfect leaders

The trait approach suggests that leaders are born. The style and the contingency approach suggest that leaders are made. Project GLOBE, the substitutes for leadership approach and Fiedler's contingency model suggest that leader effectiveness is a function of the match between leader characteristics, situation and followers. We have found that all these approaches are well supported by empirical findings. It thus appears that for leaders to be effective they have to have certain traits, they have to be able to adapt their leadership style to situational, task and followers' characteristics, and they have to be placed in positions that fit their profile best. So for organisations to ensure that their leaders are effective, they have to identify people with high leadership potential, train them how to adapt their leadership style to people, task and situational characteristics, and put them in positions that best match their leadership profile.

DO LEADERS REALLY MAKE A DIFFERENCE?

Ever thought about this question? Of course they do, you might say. Really? Well, the answer is yes and no.

The **romance of leadership** literature suggests that we have developed romantic notions about leaders and their effectiveness. Accordingly, we tend to overestimate the significance of their contributions. Because we believe that leaders should have the ability to control and influence the fate of their organisations, we tend to blame them for negative performance outcomes and give them credit for positive outcomes, no matter whether they are really responsible for them (Meindl *et al*, 1985). For instance, it might well be that an executive does everything right (or wrong), but that the economic conditions prevent this from being translated (or facilitate its translation) into increased (or decreased) bottom-line performance. This does not mean, however, that leadership makes no difference anyway. The empirical evidence presented throughout this chapter demonstrates a clear link between leadership traits and styles with objective measures of group and organisational performance (see Table 10.2 for a summary). Moreover, when reviewing the literature on executive leadership and organisational performance, Day and Lord (1988) were able to show that executive leadership explains as much as 45% of the variation in an organisation's performance – which is quite a lot!

The underlying idea of the **substitutes for leadership** approach is that characteristics of the subordinate (eg ability, professionalism, indifference towards rewards), of the task (eg that it is structured, provides its own feedback, is intrinsically satisfying) and of the organisation (eg it has clear, written goals and objectives, cohesive work groups, spatial distance between superior and subordinates) substitute for or neutralise the effects a leader's behaviours has on his or her followers' motivation, satisfaction and performance (Kerr and Jermier, 1978). Whereas substitutes make leader influence impossible and replace it, neutralisers simply make leader influence impossible. Table 10.6 summarises the most important substitutes and **neutralisers of leadership**. However, because a leader can affect most of these factors, another way in which leaders can motivate and influence follower behaviours is therefore by selecting the right people, designing tasks and jobs that are satisfying and intrinsically motivating for them, and implementing organisational structures, practices, policies and procedures that guide and direct employee behaviours.

Table 10.6:   Substitutes for leadership

Characteristics	Relationship-oriented leadership	Task-oriented leadership
– of the subordinate		
Ability/experience/training		Substitutes for
Professionalism	Substitutes for	Substitutes for
Indifference toward rewards	Neutralises	Neutralises
– of the task		
Is highly structured		Substitutes for
Provides its own feedback	Substitutes for	Substitutes for
Is intrinsically satisfying		
– of the organisation		
Clear, written goals and objectives		Substitutes for
Cohesive work groups	Substitutes for	Substitutes for
Spatial distance between superior and subordinates	Neutralises	Neutralises

Source: adapted from Kerr and Jermier (1978)

ETHICAL LEADERSHIP [5]

Remember the Enron scandal? Well, even if you do, it might be useful to see the video clip and the background information on Enron on this book's website for supplementary material. At the beginning of this chapter we suggested that the very essence of business leadership is to influence, motivate and enable others to contribute toward the effectiveness and success of an organisation. If these were the only criteria on the basis of which we were to evaluate leadership effectiveness, Enron ought to serve as an exemplar as to how organisations might develop excellent leadership capacities. As you may recall, Enron selected and developed leaders and had policies, procedures and practices in place that served one goal and one goal only – making profits at any price. Initially, this served the company quite well: starting as a small natural gas company, Enron became one of the world's leading energy companies in 2000, with over $100 billion in revenues and being named by *Fortune* 'America's most innovative company' and 'America's best company to work for' over six consecutive years. Filing a bankruptcy report at the end of 2001 when many of its management stratum were accused of fraud, money-laundering, insider-trading and conspiracy, the long-term effects of these practices were disastrous, however.

In this section we highlight the fact that there is more to effective leadership than just achieving organisational goals. What these goals are and the means by which they are achieved matter as well. This is the domain of **ethical leadership**, which is concerned with the kinds of values and morals organisations and their leaders find desirable or appropriate (Brown and Treviño, 2006). There are two main approaches on how to look at this issue: the **philosophical approach** and the **social scientific approach**. The *philosophical approach* helps us to understand what values and morals should be considered ethical and what should not. The *social scientific approach* helps us clarify who is most likely to become an ethical leader and how organisations and leaders can ensure that people behave ethically.

The philosophical approach

The underlying idea of the philosophical approach is to establish rules for how we should think about ethics and to uncover logical flaws in the way people think about ethics. To learn more about ethical decision-making you might want to read the chapter on business ethics (Chapter 18). Ethical decision-making can be quite difficult, and there are often no straight answers.

Because ethical decision-making is often also controversial, organisations and governments have started setting up what are known as ethics committees. The task of these committees is to provide leaders and employees with an overarching view of how business should be done, often in the form of a code of ethics (IBE [Institute of Business Ethics], 2007).

The social scientific approach

Do you think people at Enron did not know what constitutes ethical behaviour? Do you think teaching them about what is ethical and what is not would have made them behave more ethically? In fact, Enron had its own Code of Ethics that took up over 65 printed pages and every employee at Enron received this document on employment. Have a look at it on this book's supplementary website and you will see that all the unethical things leaders and employees did at Enron are actually described as unethical in this document. So it seems that knowing what is ethical and actually behaving ethically are two altogether different things. Below, we look at what organisations can do to make their leaders and employees behave ethically. It is part of the social scientific approach to ethics.

According to Grojean and colleagues (Grojean *et al*, 2004), a code of ethics becomes alive when organisations and their leaders establish a 'climate' that involves ethics. Such a climate refers to an organisation's policies, procedures and actual practices in regard to ethically correct behaviours and how ethical issues should be handled. The task of leaders in implementing such a climate for ethics is seven-fold. Leaders have to:

- establish clear expectations of ethical conduct

- establish leader and employee training and mentoring on what is considered ethical and what is not

- set the example by behaving at all times according to the code of ethics

- at all times highlight and communicate that the code of ethics has priority in everything employees are supposed to do

- provide feedback, coaching and support regarding ethical behaviour outlined in the code of ethics

- recognise and reward behaviours that are in line with the code of ethics

- remain aware that implementing ethical behaviours may be more difficult for some employees than for others.

While the implementation of a climate regarding ethics clearly speaks to the idea that ethical leaders are made, research has found a series of leader and situational characteristics associated with unethical behaviours. Relying on Kohlberg's research (1984) to the effect that people vary in their cognitive moral development along six stages (the highest stage of development being one at which a person's primary motivation is to fulfil internalised values and moral principles), it has been suggested that people at higher stages of moral development are more likely to behave and lead ethically. Despite its intuitive appeal, empirical research does not support this idea (McCauley *et al*, 2006), probably because there is a difference between knowing what is the right thing to do and actually doing it. Personality traits, on the other hand, have been linked to unethical leadership, such as low conscientiousness, high neuroticism, low emotional maturity and high narcissism (Brown and Treviño, 2006). Organisations should therefore not only ensure that an ethical climate is in place but also select leaders that have appropriate traits.

The box below summarises what organisations can do in order to facilitate ethical leadership.

Ethical implications: Inculcating ethics

Leaders have to be effective, certainly, but they also have to ensure that they behave ethically and that the consequences of their behaviours are ethical. One way to ensure that leaders behave ethically is to select people with a 'good' character (eg highly conscientious, emotionally mature and low on neuroticism) for leadership positions and to train them in ethical decision-making. The case of Enron shows, however, that even leaders with inherent good characters may get derailed when they are in a context that facilitates or even demands unethical behaviour, such as making profits at any price. But how can organisations be sure that leaders will behave ethically? Firstly, they need to establish a climate in respect of ethics. This means that policies, procedures and, more importantly, practices, have to be in place that highlight and communicate at all times that the code of ethics has priority in all the things leaders and their employees are supposed to do. Secondly, they need to ensure that leaders and employees adhere to the organisation's culture on ethics. Thirdly, organisations have to make sure that regular feedback, coaching and support regarding ethical behaviour as outlined in the code of ethics is provided, and that such behaviours are recognised and rewarded.

DEVELOPING LEADERS AND LEADERSHIP EFFECTIVENESS [6]

Companies such as General Electric spend over £1 billion annually in corporate management training and development, which they use to build strong leadership capacity throughout their organisation. Why do you think companies such as General Electric do this? And how do you think they do it? A recent study, which considered 1,279 companies with at least $8 billion in annual revenues from around the world, investigated what top-performing companies did differently for their high-potential future leaders, in comparison with middle- or poor-performing companies. (Details are on the supplementary website for this book.) In order to be effective, it turned out that leadership development has to be undertaken systematically, and it has to target both the development of individual leaders and the development of leadership capacity within the entire organisation.

Leader development

Leader development is defined as the expansion of a person's capacity to be effective in leadership roles and processes (Day, 2000). By investing in leader development activities, organisations hope to increase their human capital. The underlying idea of this is that effective leadership increases organisational and group performance. Training and developing individual leaders should thus increase organisational and group performance. For organisations, developing leaders includes enhancing their performance in current roles, improving their ability to carry out leadership tasks in ways congruent with changing organisational realities, and, for some, expanding their capacity to take on higher positions.

Throughout this chapter we have discussed various ways in which such training and development activities could be delivered. For instance, we have noted from the behavioural and situational approaches that leadership can be learned and that leaders might be given training in, for instance, what styles to use in a particular situation, how to appear more 'leader-like' to followers, or how to create situations that match the leader's style best. In the light of the high costs of such leadership development programmes and the pervasive link between personality and intelligence, with the ability to display and learn different leadership styles and adjust them accordingly, organisations often make their investment in leadership development and training activities contingent on a person's potential to emerge and act as an effective leader (Groves, 2007). For that reason organisations often assess the leadership potential of employees before they send them to expensive leadership training and development programmes. This often involves the use of assessment centres, interviews and extensive psychometric testing.

Leadership development

While the development of individual leader capacity is important, it is equally important to build leadership capacity throughout organisations. Not only are high-potential leaders and managers more likely to leave the organisation – because they enjoy much greater employment possibilities than other people – but the development of individual leader capacity does not build social capital, which refers to networked relationships among individuals that enhance co-operation and resource exchange in creating organisational value (Day, 2000). Day also summarises evidence which suggests not only that off-the-job leadership training programmes are overly expensive but also that leaders who attend these training events often fail to transfer the lessons learned to the workplace. Many organisations have therefore set up processes, practices, programmes and activities to create leader development systems, which are often referred to collectively as **leadership development** (in contrast to leader development).

Accordingly, Day suggests that for leadership development to be effective it has to be linked to an organisation's overarching business strategy, it has to identify individual training and development needs, and it has to take place in the context of work. This seems to be best accomplished by using a tripartite development strategy that links *assessment*, *challenge*, and *support* leadership development activities. Based on this idea and on empirical evidence from a meta-analysis (Collins and Holton, 2004), Day suggests that organisations should use a combination of the following six practices to facilitate leadership development in the context of ongoing work:

- 360-degree feedback
- coaching
- job assignments
- action learning
- networking, and
- mentoring.

In Table 10.7 we explain these developmental activites in more detail, give examples, discuss their overall purpose in the light of the tripartite development strategy, and highlight their strengths and weaknesses.

Table 10.7:   Leadership development activities

Leadership development practice	Description	Purpose	Strength/weakness
360-degree feedback	A method that systematically collects perceptions of a leader's performance from the entire circle of relevant viewpoints, such as leaders' self-ratings, peers, subordinates, supervisors and customers. Its main purpose is to facilitate leaders' self-understanding and highlight areas of development. Although 360-degree feedback provides a comprehensive picture of the leader's current performance and capabilities, it does not necessarily lead to individual development and learning. For 360-degree feedback to be effective, leaders have to accept it as relevant and useful, they have to be open to change, and they have to be committed to change.	Assessment	+ comprehensive picture, broad participation – overwhelming amount of data, no guidance on how to change, time and effort
Executive coaching	Practical, goal-focused form of one-on-one learning and behavioural change, usually with a professional coach or more senior manager. Its main purpose is to improve individual leader performance. Ideally, coaching is based on 360-degree feedback, identifies and sets specific developmental goals and facilitates goal implementation by focusing coaching on development experiences. While coaching helps leaders translate goals into actions and monitor goal achievement, it is very expensive and, depending on how it is sold, may stigmatise people as ineffective leaders.	Assessment	+ personalised, intensive – perceived stigma, expensive

Table 10.7:   NEXT

Leadership development practice	Description	Purpose	Strength/weakness
Job assignments	Provide stretch assignments in terms of role, function or geography. For instance, Gillette International sends its US managers overseas to work in other countries and operational areas before returning to a US assignment. Ideally, these assignments are linked to the developmental needs of the leaders, are facilitated by a mentor or coach, and prepare for assignments of greater authority. If job relevant, they tend to accelerate leader development and learning. However, they often lead to failure when the leader is not ready for them and may thus undermine career development.	Challenge	+ job relevant, accelerates learning – conflict between performance and development, no structure for learning
Action learning	Project-based learning directed at important business problems. For example, in General Electric's work-out programmes leaders are set a challenge (eg how to open new markets for a product). They then have to come up with an idea on how to tackle the challenge, champion the idea, and are held responsible for its implementation. Since action learning facilitates work-based learning and is tied to business imperatives, it is time-intensive and leadership lessons are not always clear. Support from mentors and coaches is therefore essential.	Challenge	+ tied to business imperatives, action-oriented – time-intensive, leadership lessons not always clear, over-emphasis on results
Mentoring	Advising/developmental relationships between a leader and a more senior manager. Although mentoring may develop informally, most organisations have a formal mentoring programme in place. Formal mentoring programmes pair a junior manager with a more senior executive outside of his or her direct reporting line. Other than a coach, a mentor can use his or her experience, network, influence and resources to support a mentee to successfully accomplish job assignments and action-based learning projects. Well-functioning mentor-mentee relationships may arouse peer jealousy and they may also lead to overdependence on the mentor.	Support	+ strong personal bond – peer jealousy, over-dependence
Networks	Help leaders to connect with others in different functions and areas. Networking supports organisations in breaking down barriers between functional areas. This facilitates the exchange of material and problem-solving resources across different functional areas and encourages leaders to form commitments with others outside of their immediate work group. Specific networking initiatives that have been implemented with the goal of leadership development are, for instance, a five-day seminar as part of Andersen Consulting's Worldwide Executive Program during which partners from all practice areas and parts of the world get the opportunity to meet and exchange ideas. Other ways to facilitate networking among leaders involve common training and job experiences. However, when not linked to specific training goals, the ad hoc and unstructured nature of such initiatives hardly contributes to the development of a leader.	Support	+ builds organisation – ad hoc, unstructured

Source: adapted from Day (2000)

In summary, for leadership development to be effective, it has to take place in the context of ongoing work, it has to be systematic, it has to combine proper assessment with developmental challenges and support, and it has to facilitate the development of both individual leader capabilities and organisational leadership capacity. Following these best practices, organisations can ensure not only that they develop the most effective leaders but also that these leaders are more likely to stay in the organisation and use their interpersonal competence to facilitate organisational and group effectiveness, as well as to build strong leadership capacity. The box below takes this a little further and examines how it can be applied in an organisational context.

Applying theory to practice: Leadership development programmes

Day's (2000) leadership development framework suggests that for organisations to build strong leadership capacity it is not sufficient to send individual leaders to training programmes that take place outside the context of work. Instead, they must have a leadership development programme in place that is oriented towards the development of leaders outside *and inside* the context of work. This should link all individual leadership development activities to an overall developmental purpose within the context of a strategic business challenge. Moreover, effective leadership development initiatives must identify leaders' developmental and training needs (eg through 360-degree feedback), must provide learning challenges (eg by assigning 'stretch' assignments) and must ensure support (eg via formal mentoring programmes).

Conclusion

We have come a long way. In this chapter we have looked at what organisations should consider when selecting people for leadership positions and how they can develop effective and ethical leaders. We began by defining leadership as the ability to motivate and influence others to attain organisationally relevant goals, and highlighted the difference between managers and leaders. We then examined the trait, style, contingency, LMX and inspirational approaches to leadership, evaluated their validity and usefulness, and discussed how they can be applied in practice. This was followed by a discussion of the implications of leadership in a global context, such as cross-cultural leadership and managing virtual and global teams. We then moved on to note that leaders make a difference in terms of a firm's bottom line, but that situations, task and follower characteristics may at times serve as leadership substitutes. Next we highlighted the importance of ethical leadership and that organisations should set up a climate regarding ethics in order to ensure that leaders and employees behave ethically. Finally, we found that for organisations to ensure leadership effectiveness, they must systematically develop their leaders and leadership capacity across the entire organisation.

End notes

[1] See also Chapter 3.

[2] See also Chapter 2.

[3] See also Chapter 5.

[4] See also Chapter 9.

[5] See also Chapter 18.

[6] See also Chapter 17.

REVIEW AND DISCUSSION QUESTIONS

REVIEW QUESTIONS

1 Identify and describe the main five leadership approaches.

2 Explain how organizations can identify and develop effective global leaders.

3 How do leaders affect organisational performance?

4 Which individual and situational factors affect ethical leadership?

5 How can organizations design a high performance leadership development system?

DISCUSSION QUESTIONS

1 Which leadership approach is most suited to explain leadership effectiveness?

2 Can there be an effective global leader?

3 Do leaders make a difference?

4 Is leadership unethical?

5 Are leaders born or made?

FURTHER READING

Northouse, P. G. (2009) *Leadership: Theory and practice*. Thousand Oaks, CA: Sage Publications. Easy to read, but comprehensive textbook on leadership.

Chemers, M. (2000) 'Leadership research and theory: a functional integration', *Group Dynamics: Theory, Research, and Practice*, Vol.4: 27–43. Short historical overview and integration of current knowledge in leadership effectiveness.

House, R. J., Hanges, P. J., Javidan, M., Dorfman, P. W. and Gupta, N. (eds) (2004) *Culture, Leadership, and Organizations: The GLOBE study of 62 societies*. Thousand Oaks, CA: Sage Publications. Very comprehensive summary of the GLOBE research project.

Day, D. V. and Lord, R. G. (1988) 'Executive leadership and organizational performance: suggestions for a new theory and methodology', *Journal of Management*, Vol.14: 453–64. Review showing how and when leadership affects organizational performance.

Brown, M. and Treviño, L. (2006) 'Ethical leadership: a review and future directions', *The Leadership Quarterly*, Vol.17: 595–616.

Summary and integration of current knowledge in leadership development with lots of practical examples and applications.

Day, D. V. (2000) 'Leadership development: a review in context', *The Leadership Quarterly*, Vol.11: 581–613. A short, but comprehensive review of current knowledge in ethical leadership.

Pierce, J. and Newstrom, J. (2008) *Leaders and the Leadership Process*, 5th edition. Boston, MA: McGraw-Hill. Collection of key readings, self-assessments, case studies and experiential exercises on leadership.

Yukl, G. (2010) *Leadership in Organizations*, 7th edition. Upper Saddle River, New Jersey: Prentice Hall. This textbook surveys the major theories and research on leadership.

Avolio, B. J., Walumbwa, F. O. and Weber, T. J. (2009) 'Leadership: current theories, research, and future directions', *Annual Review of Psychology*, Vol.60: 421–49. Review of more recent approaches to leadership.

KEY SKILLS

TIME MANAGEMENT

Research into the task-oriented leadership style has demonstrated that if a leader emphasises the importance of meeting deadlines, helps followers plan and schedule their work, makes it clear how they should do their job, highlights and communicates how they can anticipate problems, followers tend to be more motivated and satisfied, respect their leader more and do a better job. It is thus not only important that you adhere to deadlines and limit any unnecessary stress and inefficiencies, but it is also important when you are in a leader position that you help your followers and monitor their time management.

DEVELOPING CRITICAL THINKING SKILLS AND REFLECTIVE LEARNING

This chapter highlighted the importance of evidence-based management, which suggests that you should use the best available scientific evidence in management decision-making. This is a four-fold process. First you need to understand how a theory or approach works (eg how it explains leadership effectiveness). Then you have to assess whether there is any empirical evidence supporting the theory or approach (eg by considering the results of a meta-analysis evaluating the theory or approach). As a third step you have to evaluate the conceptual and logical underpinning of the theory or approach. Does it convincingly explain why, how and when a phenomenon occurs (eg in this chapter, leadership effectiveness)? Finally, you must assess whether the theory or approach can be applied in practice and in organisations (eg path-goal theory ticked all the previous boxes – yet it is so complex that it has never made its way into the portfolio of leadership training providers).

CREATIVE SKILLS

This chapter suggested that openness to experience, being inspirational and having a vision are essential ingredients of effective leaders. It is therefore important that you develop your creative skills if you want to become an effective leader. You must accordingly start training your skills to think 'out of the box'. For instance, every day before you go home, take five minutes to think about what you, others or the organisation could have done better to become more effective. Maybe you ought to keep notes about

that and revisit them from time to time. You will soon realise that it is not too difficult to see things differently.

PROFESSIONAL JUDGEMENT, DECISION-MAKING, PROBLEM-SOLVING AND SOCIAL RESPONSIBILITY

When you are in a leadership position, be aware that it is not all about goal attainment. First and foremost you should make sure that what you are doing, and the consequences of what you are doing, is the right thing to do and does not cause more harm than good. Also make sure that the people you lead do the same.

EMOTIONAL INTELLIGENCE, EMPATHY, SYMPATHY AND LISTENING

Research on the people-oriented leadership style demonstrated that if a leader emphasises the supportive and camaraderie-building actions as well as showing respect and trusting subordinates (examples of consideration behaviours), followers are much more motivated and satisfied and reciprocate respect and trust. Accordingly, when you are in a leadership position, make sure that you do not focus only on the task. You depend on your followers and their input, so make sure you consider them sufficiently.

LEADERSHIP, COACHING AND MENTORING

If you want to become an effective leader, you must first decide whether you really want to become a leader at all. Many people prefer to remain in non-leadership positions – which is fair enough. Also keep in mind that if you do not have a leader-like personality, it will be much more difficult and much less rewarding to lead other people. Nevertheless, this chapter showed that if you really want to, you can learn to become a more effective leader. Look at the various training models that were examined: perhaps you might want to try one of these or attend a leadership training programme. The most important thing is that you expose yourself to ever more difficult leadership challenges inside the work context. Also, make sure that these challenges are not actually beyond your capabilities. It might also be a good idea to seek the support and advice of a professional coach or a mentor.

BEST AND WORST PRACTICE

Best practice

- Use cognitive ability and personality tests to identify and select people for leadership positions.
- Train people so that they develop a repertoire of different leadership styles (eg people- and task-oriented styles, transactional and transformational leadership styles) and teach them how to adjust their leadership style to situation, task and follower characteristics.
- Have policies, procedures and practices in place that highlight and communicate at all times that the code of ethics has priority in all the things leaders are supposed to do.
- Have a leadership development programme in place that facilitates both leader and leadership development.

- Have policies, procedures and practices in place that highlight and communicate at all times that the organisational and group goal attainment has priority in all the things leaders are supposed to do.
- Invest in the development of individual leaders.

Worst practice

- Assume everybody has the potential to become a leader.
- Assume that a people-oriented leadership style is always effective.

Chapter 11
Decision-making

Michael Butler, Keith Bezant-Niblett and Karen Caine

Contents

Key Learning Outcomes

By the end of this chapter you should be able to:

- make better decisions and better understand others' decisions
- define decision-making by referring to a range of concepts
- understand the strengths and weaknesses of rational decision-making
- explain decision-making at the individual, group and organisational levels
- appreciate the role of creative processes in decision-making
- know how to apply each decision-making concept.

PRACTITIONER INSIGHT

Bisk Education

Business issue: how to sustain growth

This case study addresses the important business issue of how to sustain growth, and highlights the fundamental role of decision-making to drive growth. There are key decision points in the business life cycle where the optimal decision has to be found. The case highlights the problem of spotting such business opportunities in the first place – opportunities which most of us pass by unawares. The case goes on to highlight the need to regularly reinvent a business model (for example, through diversification and continuous improvement) as the market conditions change. At the heart of the case is the interaction of the founder with his management team to find the best possible answer to business issues as they arise.

Bisk Education: Key decisions that have built a major organisation

Nathan M. Bisk, Chairman of Bisk Education, is not only a lawyer and a Certified Public Accountant but an entrepreneur as well. He has combined his professional training with a penchant for identifying business opportunities and built an organisation that has become a world leader in online education.

At the time of the company's founding in 1971, the Uniform Certified Public Accounting examination had the lowest passing rate of any professional exam in the United States, an average of only 15% of the candidates passing on their first attempt.

Through his own personal experience and the general lack of success of his colleagues, he realised there was an opportunity to help others reach their professional goals with the creation of a new training organisation.

Originally, the Uniform CPA Examination was developed as a membership requirement for the American Institute of Certified Public Accounts (AICPA) and in 1952 became the standard credentialing tool for the profession throughout the United States. It was clear to Nathan that most CPA candidates needed a high-quality test preparation strategy (and a little bit of luck) to successfully complete the exam.

The solution, Nathan decided, was to develop a series of live training seminars to prepare candidates to pass the rigorous exam, which at that time took three days to complete. Because he was a good trainer, word of mouth and demand enabled him to book up training rooms to hold courses in other parts of Florida and neighbouring states. The business was a success, requiring the hiring of additional instructional staff.

Success and expansion brought with it a series of problems. Nathan could only be in one place at one time, and live instruction in multiple locations simultaneously was expensive. It contained too many uncontrollable variables, from maintaining the quality of the classroom setting to the skill of the instructor. There was also the fact that attendance at a live seminar was competing for time with the candidate's full-time job. This was also compounded by the inflexibility of having to be in a class at a fixed time.

PRACTITIONER INSIGHT NEXT

Faced with the desire to continue to grow the organisation and overcome the limitations that the seminar business presented, Nathan needed a new plan. Again identifying an opportunity in the marketplace, Nathan changed the business model by offering a self-study format, bringing the professor into the candidate's home. Utilising the technology of the day, audiotape cassettes, the new product consisted of textbooks and taped lectures on cassettes plus Nathan's unique 'solutions approach' that combined a detailed study plan and a time-management programme. This self-study model solved the problems of maintaining the quality and consistency of the material being delivered while providing an anytime, anywhere study format for the candidate.

During the transition from live seminars to a mail-order self-study business he would be competing with himself. For around three years he wondered if he had made the right decision – and history tells us he did. His employee mix changed from instructors to sales, administration and production staff.

Having aligned his company with the accounting profession, Nathan realised that after candidates passed the exam and became a Certified Public Accountant, the industry had an annual continuing professional education (CPE) training requirement. Here was another opportunity for Nathan to leverage the organisation he had built and the technical content he was publishing to generate a new source of income for his business. In the mid-1970s Nathan added CPE programmes to his product mix by repurposing the content he developed for his CPA Exam review products. Then in 1977 he released the first of its kind CPE audiotape self-study programmes.

By the early 1980s he had become an important training provider for many of the growing national firms of accountants. These key customers were telling him that accountants were too busy to attend traditional seminars to meet their continuing education requirements, and they were asking for programmes that could be administered in their offices. The answer was to add self-study courses in a video format taking advantage of the fast spreading VHS video-tape players that were becoming commonplace in homes and business. Staying on top of emerging technologies and information delivery methods, Nathan added computer-based courses in the late 1980s on floppy disk and by 1994 transitioned to CD-ROMs.

By the end of the 1980s and entering the 1990s Bisk Education had become dominant in the CPA market. Providing self-study solutions for both exam preparation and continuing education opened the door to establishing a national presence. The ever growing complexity meant for the first time that he had to appoint divisional managers, adding telemarketing sales staff, content editors, creation of an in-house video-recording studio and technology research and development staff. This stopped

the complexity becoming chaotic, and quickly he resumed a knowable business model as the company took the next step in its growth cycle. By 1993 the business was flourishing.

In 1995, something dramatic happened that made Nathan rethink his business model again. The Internet was starting to offer text-based educational programmes online. He realised something was happening in the market, but no one could agree at what speed of uptake people would wish to learn from courses provided on the Internet, as opposed to taking a traditional self-study course. He decided on trial and error. He kept the successful self-study course business running at full tilt, but invested in emerging technology and people who were unlike any he had employed before. Computer analysts and programmers in his organisation he could understand, but web designers and online graphics builders were very interesting folk to control. They didn't like to be told what to do: they preferred to be consulted and trusted. His organisation culture was changing fast, and he was moving from a command structure to a creative coalition of talented people. Along with the Internet came a new breed of marketers, telephone sales folk and student advisers. This **creativity** also meant that decisions were becoming empowered. A lot more framing of challenges was being considered, much more intelligence-gathering was taking place about this ever-changing marketplace, now being driven by the Internet. A lot more group decisions were happening through **consensus**, and conclusions were being driven by teams that comprised all parts of the 'new form' business. Feedback systems were being put in place, to understand how all parts of the organisation were reacting to the market. In 1995 Nathan introduced Internet-based online courses for exam preparation and continuing professional education for the accounting industry.

The given was that they were becoming a leader in the Internet provision of online learning programmes in accountancy. All of the expertise for these two businesses was contained in-house. The senior management team pondered over what other online learning businesses they could run. The constraint was growing another expertise in-house. They considered how they could harness external expertise in other places and use their undoubted core competence in Internet marketing and student sales to develop another 'knowledge development' business. In 1995, the University Alliance was born.

In partnership with a well-established and regionally accredited university, in 1997 he launched the first and only online MBA programme that included video lectures. This was quickly followed by a second well-established and regionally accredited university providing a number of undergraduate business degree programmes. These next programmes were unique in the online world because they were supported by streaming video lectures.

PRACTITIONER INSIGHT NEXT

Since that time, Bisk Education has been adding new university partners and programmes. Today, Bisk still runs a very successful CPA business, ranked number 2 in the industry, and has expanded the University Alliance portfolio to include eight of North America's top-ranked and regionally accredited universities offering more than 100 undergraduate, graduate and professional certificate programmes. Bisk is actively working to add more universities and programmes to its offerings.

Bisk Education has grown to become one of the USA's largest providers of professional education programmes to the accounting industry, the nation's largest provider of online executive education, and one of the country's largest providers of online degree and certificate programmes from leading colleges and universities. Bisk excels in programme content development, online learning technology and programme delivery, administrative management services, programme marketing, student recruitment and re-enrolment, student material fulfilment, technological support, student services and support, and publishing capabilities.

The business now is spending millions of dollars on Internet media and search engine advertising, and enrolling tens of thousands of students in the various programmes. Decisions are being made on a daily basis about infrastructure support systems, customer-facing technology, marketing promotions, target markets, student recruiting processes and countless other operational needs. The business is still based in Tampa, Florida, and currently employs over 720 people in two big facilities a small walk from the sea front. Nathan Bisk is still the President

and CEO, and now aged 70, has not the slightest intention of retiring.

> If you wish to research Bisk Education further, look at its websites:
> http://www.bisk.com/
> http://www.universityalliance.com/

How many decision-making styles can you identify in this case reading?

Do you think that decision-making has become more complicated as the organisation has grown?

What sort of decision-making style should Bisk Education be using in the future?

If you were running Bisk Education, what would be your next major decision? Would you:

- *grow the existing business by selling more programmes and courses to similar customers in North America?*
- *try to find a new customer base in the North American market to sell all their existing programmes and courses to?*
- *take their business model global and sell to Europe, and the emerging and developing world?*
- *transform its business again and reinvent how people learn, using new technology fast emerging on the market?*

Once you have read this chapter, return to these questions and think about how you could answer them.

Introduction

Decision-making is at the heart of all organisations. Organisations are judged by their ability to make decisions and execute them. Leaders in organisations are judged by others for their ability to make the right decisions at the right time. Organisational behaviour is about the ability to enable and enact decisions. Outside observers of the organisation will ascribe to it characteristics such as being cautious or risk-taking, and make direct links with the brand and the image in the market in which it serves.

Decision-making research is an exciting area – in flux, with lots of concepts and no overarching theory. This means that definitions of decision-making are changing. The *Longman New Universal Dictionary* of 1982 defines a decision as:

> a conclusion arrived at after consideration.

This leads to a decision-maker being characterised as decisive and having the power of deciding. It seems reasonable. However, here is a more up-to-date definition:

> You can look at an organisation as a locus for decision-making activity.
>
> (Hatch, 1997, p270)

> Decisions take place endlessly, so it is also possible at a given point in time to interpret an organisation as the product of its decisional history.
>
> (Hatch, 1997, p270)

The second definition emphasises the process of decision-making and how the process may be influenced – not just the outcomes. This chapter explores both definitions in more detail, arguing that both are needed, but in different organisational contexts. As a consequence, we define decision-making by referring to a range of concepts (and our list is not exclusive): in short, decision-making is the sum total of all available concepts.

In this chapter we aim to give the reader skills, knowledge and insights by highlighting the behaviour of people in decision-making in different circumstances. We do not advocate a 'one-right-way approach' but constantly emphasise the thought that all decisions are contextual, and therefore much care must be taken to assess all influences on the situation.

We start with a brief consideration of the cultural context of decision-making. We do this to emphasise that there is no one right way to make a decision because the person making a decision will prioritise certain methods as a result of their previous experience. This chapter, for example, selects certain decision-making concepts because of the authors' background, their personal and career trajectories. We discuss this more in the next section.

We then turn to the dominant concept of rational decision-making which outlines a clear decision-making process. We then point out why rational decision-making is not sufficient on its own – showing the boundaries it is subject to, and the **decision traps** people can fall into.

The next section looks at techniques to overcome decision traps and improve decision-making – firstly for individuals, then groups, then at an organisational level. Decision-making can be taken at different levels, and it is important to link a decision-making process to the appropriate level.

Finally, we examine creativity, and how it can improve decision-making at all levels. Having identified a variety of decision-making processes in the chapter and linked them to the appropriate level, we discuss creativity as an underlying process. Decision-making is about choices, and having the insight to make a good choice is crucial: sensing an issue or problem is emerging, framing the issue/problem in an appropriate way, thinking of options, completing a risk analysis linked to each option and effectively implementing a solution which may have several obstacles to be overcome.

Figure 11.1 captures the structure of the chapter, and the arrows indicate the flow of the content. In reality, when making a decision, you are the centre of the decision wheel, and you must use your judgement to decide which are the most appropriate concepts to use in your particular situation to maximise the chance of success.

CULTURAL CONTEXT

At the outset, it is important to recognise that the way we make decisions is shaped by how we have been socialised or brought up. The types of decisions that are made reflect our family values, the schooling we had, the community we were brought up in and the country that is our

Figure 11.1   The decision wheel – an outline of chapter content

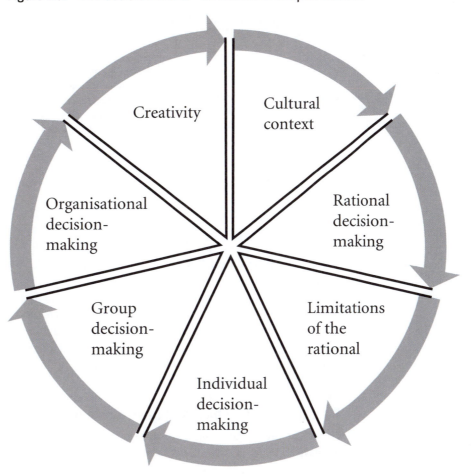

home. Decisions also reflect the value systems of the industry, organisation or occupation where we work. These influences are very important because they set the ground rules for what we consider to be right and wrong.

As Handy (1993) has stressed, the context, culture or environment in which a decision is made makes a huge difference. Decisions cannot be fully understood in isolation. For example, a group's decisions within an organisation could be influenced by the group's position within the organisation, its relationships with other groups, the characteristics and objectives of each of its members, the stage of development of the group itself and the criteria, importance and clarity of the task itself. These factors could affect the leadership style selected, the processes adopted and the team members' motivation. Again, in turn, these will affect the outcomes – the productivity and satisfaction of those concerned.

The authors are a product of a European and North American tradition. As a consequence, the concepts selected for this chapter reflect that tradition. This does not mean that they cannot be applied elsewhere – indeed, our students and participants in executive development workshops come from all over the globe.

The key point is that effective decision-making recognises the importance of diversity in all its facets, and especially multi-culturalism. Using the concepts in this chapter will help you make more effective decisions by appreciating and utilising multiple viewpoints. As an illustration of what can go wrong, however, we use the example of General Foods, which developed a misguided international strategy (see the box below).

WORST PRACTICE

General Foods

In the mid-1980s General Foods squandered millions trying to introduce Japanese consumers to packaged cake-mixes. They did not understand that only 3% of Japanese homes were equipped with ovens. When they then tried to promote the idea of baking cakes in rice cookers, they failed to realise that at the heart of the Japanese family was the availability of warm and ready rice. The rice cooker was always cooking rice, and no one in Japan could contemplate their being used for the baking of cakes.

RATIONAL DECISION-MAKING

Still today **rational decision-making** tends to be the 'default' mode for making decisions for many people. In our lectures and workshops, when people are asked to come up with an 'ideal decision-making process', they often come up with something resembling a rational process. When people explain (or justify) their decisions in retrospect, they often try to rationalise them as a way to prove that they were a good choice (at least in Western culture). It is important to understand that the aspiration toward the logic of rational decision-making (whether fully achievable in reality or not) has had a huge impact upon modern-day society. It is a response to past traditions and historical events.

Past traditions (which still have a role today)

Historical and literary sources reveal that when people had important decisions to make, they displayed a belief in divine intervention. For example:

- the **drawing of lots**: Tacitus records this ancient Germanic practice when important group decisions were being made

- by prayer: Shakespeare's Henry V spent the night before the Battle of Agincourt praying in what is called 'the dark night of the soul'

- in dreams: Artemidorus of Ephesus wrote *The Interpretation of Dreams* in ancient Greek in the second century AD, and the most recent English translation was published in 1990.

Although these methods may be categorised as historical decision-making, in reality some people still use some of these methods today. An Egyptian student in a recent MBA class emphasised that when he set up and ran his export business that he used a mixture of rational techniques and the three examples given above. Whether people consider them worthwhile decision-making techniques or simply a way of pushing away responsibility for a difficult choice depends on their individual beliefs.

Historical events

The **Industrial Revolution** had a profound impact on decision-making processes. It carried with it rational thought processes that started in the **Age of Reason**, when it was thought that if you worked hard enough, everything was discoverable and understandable, and that therefore with a series of logical decisions you would arrive at the right solution.

It is also important to realise that other cultures did not have the Industrial Revolution. Many other cultures around the world were born out of surviving on the land and from the environment. Effectiveness in the development of agriculture-based systems tends to lead to much more collectiveness of effort in the workforce, and a sense of a hierarchy of leadership based on thought and technical ability.

Until the late 1950s, at least in the West, it was thought that the ideal way of making decisions – the decision-making process to aspire to – was rational decision-making. This assumed that correct, or optimal, decisions could be reached by the consideration of data and with logical thinking.

The last hundred years have seen massive progress. Taylor in the 1920s worked with Ford to create the first modern production line. Work production methods were used in the World War II effort which enabled US shipyards to produce three cargo vessels every 14 days. Efficiency management was introduced into coal and steel industries that produced the cheapest raw materials the world has ever known. Business process engineering was applied to every work method, which was fine-tuned to the highest levels of efficiency and output. Efficiency became the mantra of so many businesses that exist today.

A rational model

There are a variety of versions of the rational decision-making model. They are good examples of a logical process because the decision-maker follows sequential steps, then returns to Step 1 to assess whether the objective has been achieved. Adair (2001), for example, proposes a five-step model, which we use to explore some of the limitations and benefits of this type of model.

Step 1: Define the objective

Because so many managers feel pressured by the belief that strong leaders arrive at decisions very quickly, and that efficiency means that you should never delay the workflow process, or stop the continuously moving production line, often little time is spent on defining the objective. All decisions must have a desired outcome. The result of all decisions should be measured in terms of gain, or improvement. It is vital that the precise objective of any decision is fully defined and understood before any progress is made. Lots of bad decisions are made because the objective is not really understood.

Step 2: Collect relevant information

Collecting relevant information is to a degree an extension of Step 1, but it is astonishing how many managers try to rely on experience, or past experiences, or the recommendations of a superior who is not close to the problem, to assume that they have sufficient information. Decisions are made to solve a problem, enact a change, or to advance the organisation. The pressure on leaders and managers to make these decisions is often immense, and often occurs because managers have to make many decisions in each day and each week. Step 2 advocates a period of reflection – a period when you consult with all relevant people involved on the situation that is leading to the decision that needs to be made, a period when historic information is collected, and a period when future alternatives could be considered. Implied in this recommendation is the notion that perhaps decisions are not made by one leader or manager, but that others pertinent to the decision are consulted or brought in to the decision-making process.

Step 3: Generate feasible options

Step 3 can only happen if Steps 1 and 2 are carried out fully and correctly. This challenges the well-held belief that there is an 'only-one-right-way solution'. Rational decision-making in its pursuit of the most efficient method does often favour the one best way, but the reality is there is always more than one feasible solution.

Step 4: Make the decision

This is the point at which a decision is made. For simple routine decisions you can arrive at this step in a matter of minutes, especially if you have full knowledge of the situation and all necessary business and technical knowledge. But even for these types of decisions the people involved in the decision must be closely consulted and considered.

Step 5: Implement and evaluate

It is no good if decisions are made but no one implements them. This implies that leadership must occur so that teams or individuals carry out the work. Unless you consider all aspects of the willingness and competence of individuals and teams to carry out the tasks as a result of the decision made, it is unlikely that the outcome will be the one described in Step 1, the original objective.

The case of a management consultancy

The main benefit of the rational model is that it is a clear decision-making process, with a procedure to follow. It is incorporated into many work processes, although it may appear in a more complex form. A good example is PA Consulting, which has a Business Solution Process Model it uses with its clients. 'Step 1: define the objective' is replaced in the Business Solution Process Model by the task goal of 'Gain entry and develop confidence with a client'. Steps 2 and 3 become 'Understand real issues', Step 4 becomes 'Choose solution', and Step 5 is subdivided into 'Plan implementation' and 'Deliver benefit'. There are further layers of complexity in that each PA task goal is linked to a set of core activities, supported by related skills and knowledge. For instance, in understanding the real issues of a client need, the management consultant, as a core activity, will have to collect relevant data, and one technique is to interview a range of staff who have knowledge of the organisational problem. The consultant will have to be skilled in asking appropriate questions and actively listening to the answers so that the interviewees feel listened to and so that the real client need is accurately identified.

In order to make sure you understand this building block of decision-making and learn to recognise the many ways that the rational model appears in organisations, you could visit the website of your favourite shop, download any statement on strategy (or other business process) and analyse it to see if it corresponds to the model or parts of it. This is not easy and will test your analytical skills because, as you see from the PA Consulting example, the stages of the rational model will be changed to suit the organisation's need. In PA Consulting they subdivided Step 5 into 'Plan implementation' and 'Deliver benefit' – it is then linked to core activities and skills/knowledge. To take the exercise further, you could then look for ways to improve the process used by your chosen organisation.

LIMITATIONS OF THE RATIONAL

Bounded rationality and awareness

In response to rational decision-making, from the 1950s onward, research – for example, by pioneers March and Simon (1958) – looked at how real life imposes limitations or '**bounded rationality**' on decision-making processes. We also explore some decision traps and emerging research from **evolutionary psychology**. Major boundaries to effectively implementing the five-step rational decision-making model include:

- Complexity and quality of information

  People can only keep so much information consciously in their heads, and can only bear a certain number of facts in mind when considering a decision. How many facts may vary – but for most people is probably generally less than 10. Once the information gets more complex than this, they will start to overlook things, or get confused over which options had which benefits and drawbacks.

  If a very large amount of information is related to a decision, or it is hard to obtain, there is a danger that more time will be spent collecting it and attempting to make sense of it than the decision is worth.

  Some desirable information may be impossible to obtain with any accuracy, and estimates may be needed or assumptions may have to be made.

Some of the information may be wrong.

Complexity and doubts over quality can lead to 'paralysis by analysis' – thinking on and on with no decision being reached at all.

- Disagreement

At any stage in the process people may disagree about what the objective should be, about how to collect data, about what data to believe, about which options are feasible, and so on. Even after agreeing feasible options and analysing them, the step to 'make a decision' may lead to disagreement as it suddenly becomes clear that not everyone is evaluating the decision in the same way. Even one person might have an internal disagreement where they find it very hard to decide between two apparently equally good (or bad) choices.

- Error

Sometimes people simply get things wrong. And in a complex situation that may lead to a snowball effect as one mistake leads to further incorrect assumptions elsewhere. Then people can get things very wrong indeed!

- Perception

People's decisions – and behaviour in general – are based on their perception of reality, rather than reality itself. And everyone's perceptions of a situation will be different because they, and their past experiences, are different. There are a wide variety of perception biases. Two obvious one are:

Stereotyping: This involves categorising people according to a group we believe they are part of, and assigning to them characteristics we associate with that group even if we have not experienced them in the individual. Taking some short cuts is common and necessary to cope with complexity – but overgeneralising incorrectly leads to poor decisions.

The halo effect: We can pick on one trait and give it a high importance, overlooking other evidence, and assume that the person will also have the other characteristics we believe are related even when we have not seen any objective evidence of their presence. These could be visual cues ('Someone dressed like that is bound to be loud, extraverted . . . and annoying') or behavioural – for example, associating warmth with humour, imagination, popularity and wisdom.

- Politics

Not all those participating may be approaching the decision with the same interests in mind. For example, they may have a personal agenda to look better than someone else in the eyes of their manager, or to secure the maximum possible available resources for their department, instead of necessarily looking for the optimal choice for stakeholders as a whole.

- Time

A rational decision could take a considerable amount of time – for example, while gathering complex information. In reality, most people are under time pressure and most day-to-day business and personal decisions must be taken quickly. Even major strategic decisions are likely to have a deadline of some sort.

Bazerman and Chugh (2006) supplemented the classic work on bounded rationality with the notion of bounded awareness, which is the unconscious process of ignoring important information, which can occur for a variety of reasons:

- Too focused

People who are very focused simply fail to see or remember things not relevant to their current task (such as only 21% spotting a woman with an open umbrella wandering amongst basketball players, because the audience of the video were concentrating on their experimental task of counting the number of ball passes).

- Change is gradual

  We notice sharp differences better than gradual ones.

- Failure to seek information

  We fail to seek it, especially if we are motivated to favour the decision the current information supports.

- Success

  If we are successful at the moment we tend to overlook information that could warn of pending problems ahead.

- Looking internally instead of at competitors

  You might, for example, plan to do what you can easily do well without realising that these may be the same things that your competitors also do well, and it could be worth investing the effort to do something harder that they can't.

- Failure to share information

  It is easier and often more socially rewarding to talk about shared information and experiences, rather than drawing out differences and unique information. So what only one person or the minority of a group know can be overlooked.

Decision traps

Because we cannot consciously and rationally consider every aspect of what we do, humans use short cuts, leading to the possibility of *decision traps*. These short cuts, called **heuristics,** often lead to faster, more efficient, decision-making. However, in certain circumstances assumptions can be misguided. Hammond, Keeney and Raiffa (2006) identify nine decision traps:

- Leaning toward the status quo

  People tend to default to not making changes. This becomes stronger if more options are presented – even if several options are better than the current situation.

- Anchoring around an initial suggestion

  There is a tendency to base options and decisions around an initially proposed position or value. This means that during negotiations, for example, the first party to suggest a price, a salary or the number of days holiday can influence the scale of the eventual decision.

- Not disregarding sunk (past) costs

  Once a situation has been committed to, and invested in with money or effort, people are reluctant to make a decision that goes against it. They find it difficult to look dispassionately at what is the best choice from this point forward. This can be at least partly due to a reluctance to appear to have made mistakes in the past – even when it is clear that a previous decision was the best choice at the time, and a better opportunity has arisen now. This bias can be very destructive in an organisation that has a low tolerance for errors.

- Overemphasising confirmatory evidence

  There is a tendency to seek out, or only pay attention to, evidence that supports a decision we want to reach. This can be partly because we tend to ask for the help and opinions of friends or other people who are likely to think in a similar way to us. However, we can also disregard information we are given if it disagrees with the view we have already formed.

- The framing trap

  The way a problem is put to us can affect the decision we make. If we look at a decision as a possible way of improving a situation, we will consider it, but are more likely to be risk-averse.

If the same decision is framed as a way of avoiding a problem or failure, we are more likely to take risks to avoid a bad outcome. In addition, if we frame a problem too narrowly, we may just make a decision about a symptom instead of resolving a root cause. Too widely, and we may give up because the decisions needed are beyond our powers.

- Overconfidence

We tend to be overconfident in our estimating and forecasting abilities, and it can also be difficult to check later whether we were right in order to help improve our forecast next time, so our confidence may continue undented even if our decision was logically wrong. For example, if we say there is an 80% probability that x will happen, and it does, then that still doesn't tell us if we had the probability correct. It could be that in fact x was very unlikely to happen and we were just very lucky. Only if the same situation is repeated will we start to build up statistics to support or refute our estimate. Also, if a decision is wrong, we may find other reasons why something different happened rather than question our own abilities. Overconfidence can lead to failure to collect key factual information because you are too sure of your assumptions and opinions.

- Too much prudence

Despite the overconfidence described above, we also tend to be cautious estimators and forecasters when committing ourselves in front of others – we may add in a bit of a safety margin. If this happens repeatedly through several levels in an organisation, the estimate to achieve something can be very inflated – possibly leading to a decision to reject a valid option because it appears too expensive. Alternatively, it might lead to senior management disregarding a real threat because several people in turn have tried to avoid overstating a forecast problem so that they wouldn't appear to be scaremongering.

- Relying on what we remember best

Basing decisions on the information we remember can cause bias, because the things we remember best tend to be the dramatic exceptions to the day-to-day norm, or the most recent happenings, so these will be given a higher weighting than they deserve when, for example, estimating the likelihood of something's happening in future.

- Traps acting in concert

All these traps either can affect us one at a time – or together in the same situation, which can make a decision-making error much worse.

The case of stock market boom-and-bust: the dot.com era

As a practical example of the psychological errors humans can make in organisational settings, we will focus on the problem of perception, which also highlights why we can take inappropriate risks. In particular, the focus is on how the brain deals with the fluctuations of Wall Street and other stock markets. We have just come through a global shock to the financial system, but one that has been studied is the US Nasdaq bubble of the late 1990s and its subsequent fall – this is the dot.com era, when boom became bust. When the market keeps going up, people are led to make larger and larger investments and don't think about the possibility of losses. But the market will turn and the reverse behaviour starts to happen – people can't wait to get out and assets are sold because of their declining value. This is known as fictive-error learning, which is linked to dopamine-rich areas of the brain such as the ventral caudate. When the market goes up, dopamine neurons are fixated on the profits the investor has missed and he or she feels regret at not having put in more money; and when the market collapses, the brain does not want to regret staying in. Over the long run, a randomly selected stock portfolio will beat the expensive experts and their financial models, but our emotions override this common sense (Lehrer, 2009).

Strangely, to improve your actual decision-making process you need to be both rational and aware of your emotions. As we have already seen, the main benefit of the rational model is that it is a clear decision-making process, with a procedure to follow. And as we have just explored, in other situations, being random in our choices can be just as beneficial. The difficulty is judging when to use each method – and this comes from experience and learning from the mistakes we all make.

Emerging research from evolutionary psychology

As a means of showing just how subtle our perception biases really are – so subtle that they are taken for granted and not sufficiently identified and challenged within organisational behaviour – we highlight emerging research from *evolutionary psychology* (EP). Such research is important because without it, organisations will function in potentially unethical ways.

Amongst a range of applications, EP is clarifying decision biases in recruitment and selection, an area where there has been surprisingly little research. Our evolution as social animals, which stresses the importance of interacting face to face, has led humans to read facial cues as a means of estimating future behaviour. Several biases have been identified (Senior, Lau and Butler, 2007):

- physically attractive people are perceived by others to possess positive traits

- attractive people are more successful at being hired than average-looking people

- attractive candidates are also recommended for higher starting salaries.

Linking perceptions of beauty to awarding higher status in organisations is unconsciously driven by wanting to support potential future mates. Male observers exhibit a specific processing bias toward attractive female faces. Female observers' reactions are more complicated. They selectively attend more closely to attractive women than average women because they may see them as intrasexual competitors. They favour attractive males, but their definition of attractiveness can vary through the menstrual cycle. Female attraction involves both physical and social aspects. During the follicular phase of the menstrual cycle (day 1 to 13), when conception is likely to occur, male faces that advertise social dominance are preferred. This can involve low pupil-to-brow distance, smaller eyes, a square jaw, thick eyebrows, and thin lips. Alternatively, during the luteal phase of the cycle (day 15 to 28), faces that advertise less social dominance may be favoured – for example, less mature-looking features such as higher-set eyebrows, rounder and larger irises, and narrower chins. The face seems to reveal genotypically 'superior' males.

Discussion of such decision-making biases in a work environment may be regarded as taboo within organisations. However, it is important to surface these evolutionary issues so that people are aware of the unconscious processes at work, how they might affect HR decision-making, and they can investigate how to avoid them and choose the best candidates for the organisation.

One possible answer to this dilemma is given later in the chapter. In the meantime, how would you solve the problem of unconscious and gendered decision processes within recruitment and selection?

Taking your learning further: Decision-making and the brain

Lehrer, J. (2009) *The Decisive Moment: How the brain makes up its mind*. Edinburgh: Canongate. This book is a very accessible, even exciting, with great examples. It has been a *New York Times* bestseller and a BBC Radio 4 book of the week. It raises a range of issues about how the brain makes decisions. We are constantly unconsciously learning most from our mistakes – which affect us much more than our successes. Once we have become an expert in an area through experience, we can generally trust emotions because they are communicating our unconscious wisdom built up from painful bad experience. However, we need to *think* when faced with novel circumstances, because our emotions may then well lead us astray. In fact, in well-known circumstances, our emotions are providing us with sensible solutions that would probably be quite rational if conscious.

INDIVIDUAL DECISION-MAKING

Now that we have covered many reasons why we cannot simply assume that with enough thought we can make purely rational decisions, it is time to review what help and advice there is to improve decision-making. We will start with decisions at the individual level, then move on to groups and organisations, before considering the role of creativity. At the individual level we will consider some ideas by Max Bazerman and Henry Mintzberg.

Reflexivity

Max Bazerman suggests that bounded awareness can be resolved by the awareness of boundaries and (evolutionary) decision traps and by reflective self-conscious enquiry about your own decision-making and that of others (**reflexivity**). People can find ways to avoid traps or cater for them. This is a continuous process because such awareness and behaviour changes influence subsequent situations.

Bazerman and Chugh (2006) suggest four activities: see, seek, use and share. Each activity is associated with further actions.

Seeing involves:

- asking different questions: 'What if ...?'

- getting an outside perspective.

Seeking incorporates:

- if there is no obvious disconfirming evidence, looking for it

- under-searching in most cases (for the sake of speed) but over-seeking when wrong decisions would have serious consequences.

Using promotes:

- consciously 'unpacking' the situation to consider a broad range of aspects

- assuming that the information will exist somewhere in the organisation – you are then more likely to find it.

Sharing requires:

- asking explicitly for people to contribute information

- creating structures that make information-sharing the default

- considering appointing someone to collect varied information.

Developing the 'What if . . .?' question, there has been a tendency for people to assume a need to 'overcome' emotional wants – and techniques to do this can be useful to help overcome bad habits that we really want to stop. However, Bazerman, Tenbrunsel and Wade-Benzoni (1998) point out that this may not always be the case, and on some occasions our unconscious mind may well be doing its best to make a valid point. This could be characterised as the difference between what you *want* to do versus what you believe you *should* do. When people are asked what they want, their responses will be emotional, affective, impulsive and hot-headed, whereas when they are asked what they should do, their responses will be more rational, cognitive, thoughtful, and cool-headed. That implies that the difference arises when your conscious rational cognition comes up with an answer that is different from your subconscious, emotional response.

They recommend being aware of any internal conflicts and trying to work out *why* you want what you want, or whether there is some flaw in the reasoning of your *should*. In other words, try to work out which one is wrong. You might, for example, decide that you ought to do what you 'want' because it is in fact the better option for you personally, even if perhaps other people who influence you might not like it and are trying to convince you of the 'should' option.

Synthesising decision-making

Henry Mintzberg argues that rational decision-making should be supplemented by other approaches. Mintzberg and Westley (2001) point out that the default for most people tends to be 'thinking first' or rational processing, because it assumes that the world is 'knowable'. But they believe successful people and organisations also need to include in their portfolio 'seeing first' and 'doing first', and to use each as appropriate to the situation and context.

Rational decision-making has already been discussed. Seeing first could be literally seeing (and understanding) something others may have missed, or it could be envisioning in your mind. Seeing first could involve seeing the result you want first, then working to get to it. When tackling a problem in a group, visualising the decision together (including producing pictures) draws out more about the opinions of those involved, is more memorable, and forces the resolution of differences better, than using words and thinking approaches.

Doing first involves trying things out that feel like they might be right, keeping things that work, discarding things that don't. It is particularly useful for situations with many unknowns – where thinking alone will not come up with the answer because there is not enough information. It is also a way of obtaining more information.

Thinking is primarily verbal, seeing is visual, and craft is visceral (uses 'gut feelings').

The case of Bisk Education

To show that Bazerman's and Mintzberg's ideas can be applied to real organisational situations, try to relate them to the case study at the start of the chapter. Nathan M. Bisk, Chairman of Bisk Education, is clearly, in Mintzberg's terms, a doer – he likes trying ideas out that will help to expand his business. More specifically, Nathan regularly asks Bazerman and Chugh's (2006) 'What if . . .?' question. For example, he saw the business opportunity of increasing the exceedingly low 15% pass rate for the Uniform Certified Public Accounting examination by introducing a quality test preparation strategy as the founding business model for Bisk Education. Nathan continued to ask the 'What if . . .?' question, evidenced by the continuous reinvention of Bisk Education. He regularly and consciously diagnosed the competitive position of his business in order to keep growing and keep winning market share.

A critique

The box below, however, shows that acting as an individual does not always work, and there is an important role for group decision-making. In other words, Nathan's individual business strengths are enhanced by having a team of people around him with complementary strengths. For instance, as Bisk Education grew, its employee mix changed from instructors to sales, administration and production staff.

Applying theory to practice: The rationale for group decision-making

Making important decisions successfully as an individual can be a difficult process. As part of the Creative Decisions for Effective Change module at Aston Business School, we ask MBA students 'What are the characteristics of an ideal decision-maker?' They regularly come up with a very long list of characteristics in just a few minutes. The 2010 class suggested:

Analytical skills	Logical and critical	Prioritises
Emotionally stable	Resilient	Practical
Observant	Creative	Self-knowledge
Openness	Communication skills	Consults others
Has goals	Long-term vision	Sees wider picture
Has a Plan B	Realises matters are rarely black and white	
	Knows and understands people, plays on the strengths of others	

Clearly, an individual who possessed all these characteristics would be able to apply the ideas of Max Bazerman and Henry Mintzberg. In reality, and reflecting on yourself, do you think one person can display all these characteristics, reliably, when making important decisions, especially if under pressure? Probably not. We hope this makes a good case for the role of groups in decision-making, where a variety of individuals contribute different strengths.

GROUP DECISION-MAKING

Because many of the benefits of group decision-making are explored in Chapter 7 *Work Groups and Teams*, we focus here on achieving consensus and **synergy** within a team. Before that, it is worth stressing the importance of groups to offset individual bias. We can do this by briefly returning to our recruitment and selection example drawn from recent research on evolutionary psychology. Having recognised that staff must be aware of the dangers of the beauty bias, but that other biases will also apply, it is then possible to offset the limitation by:

- convening interview panels rather than single interviewers, making sure that they include both sexes and are mixed regarding other attributes

- if possible, finding interviewers who will not be personally working with the applicant

- using other tests alongside interviews.

However, it cannot be taken for granted that groups work successfully together. There is a risk of **groupthink**, in which people conform too much instead of voicing opposing views (Janis, 1982). In Japan, for example, where consensus is valued highly, it is common for junior staff to speak first in a debate to avoid the risk that they will keep quiet rather than risking contradicting their seniors.

Another risk to be managed is that each individual in the team will see the world differently because of the way they perceive situations. Global working means that teams increasingly come from different cultures and often decisions are made about people in cultures other than from where they were born. The team is likely to comprise different genders, different age groups and different preferences about thinking, seeing and doing first.

It is in this diverse context that consensus and synergy becomes a managerial tool. Consensus and synergy is used by the authors in Aston Business School and Michigan State University. Consensus and synergy is linked to Hersey and Blanchard's (2007) stages in team formation: **forming, storming, norming and performing.**

Consensus

When working in teams, aiming for consensus can lead to the best decision in the circumstances and takes into account all viewpoints. Consensus is a unanimous agreement that everyone can accept and support. It leads to significantly higher-quality decisions, to more win-win solutions, and promotes feelings of ownership by all parties, all of which helps to improve the chances of successful implementation.

Consensus is established in a *forming* team and the conditions have to be created by the leader from the outset. It is often very hard to achieve, particularly in Western societies, because most individuals come to a forming team with a strong viewpoint often because of their background or specialism.

Consensus is particularly useful in complex decision-making involving many disciplines – for example, a complex project plan or when a decision has to be made concerning large numbers of people. Consensus is often the goal of politicians who have to make major decisions in relation to legislation or government policy.

How do you achieve consensus?

- Prepare your own position thoroughly in advance of a meeting when choices for action and activity have to be made. You must know the reason for your choice and the detail of the subject. You must also know the boundaries that you cannot cross, although thinking 'outside the box' by suggesting courses of action that have not been tried before, or that may have failed in the past because they were 'too early' or badly implemented, is often a good thing to do.

- You must recognise others' rights to explain fully their viewpoint and also understand that each person may have boundaries that are not the same as your own.

- You should recognise your rights to be able to assertively express your viewpoints. You should recognise other people's rights to assertively express their views. If others in the team, or those that could affect group behaviour, resort to aggression or submissive behaviour, you must do all in your power to ensure that the conversation returns to assertive behaviour as soon as possible. Mutual respect is a cornerstone of consensus.

- You must avoid conflict-reducing techniques as much as possible. In politics, voting on a motion or a package of changes will actually lead to conflict, and intransigent, intractable views. It is always better to try to talk to achieve the best decision in the circumstances, which may not coincide precisely with anyone's individual viewpoint, but can be accepted by all.

- You must realise that differences are helpful, and that often, by working to understand the differences, you will arrive at a better conclusion, and therefore a better decision.

Consensus is often seen by Western societies as being a slow process, in which people are waiting for a decision or outcome. By taking the extra time, however, the best decision is arrived at, after taking all circumstances into account. By rushing major decisions and taking a 'My opinion is the right course of action' viewpoint, individuals and teams can either all too often live to regret those decisions in future years, or have to change decisions and viewpoints quite quickly within months of the original decision being made.

Eastern societies, with their respect for levels of decision-makers and mutual respect for each others' views, often find the practice of consensus far better understood and far easier to implement.

Synergy

Synergy has been achieved when all team members have developed a mutual trust and respect for each other, and treat each other in an assertive way. The practice of synergy only works when the ground rules of consensus are rigorously applied, and teams have moved to the *norming* and *performing* stage.

How do you achieve synergy?

- The whole is greater than the sum of the parts. Two people can generally arrive at a far better decision than one person on their own (see Chapter 7). From our experience, if you can get five or six people to join in collective and consensus decision-making, a much better decision will be made.

- Active listening will be used by team members. By using good body language (eye contact) and supportive comments such as 'That's interesting' and 'Tell me more', the whole team is encouraging all members to be able to assertively express their knowledge and viewpoint.

- Each member of the decision-taking team can go on personal 'voyages of discovery'. Each person will leave the group session knowing something or understanding something better than they knew before.

- Individuals are taken into account and the group is not swayed by one or two dominant leaders, personalities or 'experts'.

The example of virtual teams

Increasingly, consensus and synergy is being carried out in digital media. Chat rooms are a place where problems are being solved by swapping information that leads to better-informed decisions. This has led to many organisations forming 'virtual teams' to make decisions, advance projects and solve problems. These virtual teams often include suppliers and customers, leading to 'end-to-end supply chain decision-making'. Virtual teamworking has become normal practice in most modern businesses of all sizes.

It was first pioneered by major organisations in the late 1980s and early 1990s, when computer-to-computer connectivity was established around the world. One early example is of the Research and Development arm of the Ford Motor Company, Visteon (subsequently spun off as a separate entity), which connected research engineers and scientists in the United States, Europe, Japan and India to jointly develop and design enhancements for their range of cars and trucks. The new car seats for the F150 truck, for instance, were designed by 10 teams in six countries, and these teams included first-tier suppliers who would be producing components and materials for the seats, who never met in person but used to talk and work daily on the development and design.

At the forefront of driving virtual teamworking today is Cisco, who have developed many applications on the computer platforms they provide to enable video-conferencing and virtual teamworking. As the Internet evolves, most smaller businesses are becoming adept at virtual teamworking, and lots of medium-sized company accounts in the USA are carried out and completed by accountants based in India. This requires almost daily interaction, but in most circumstances, the people involved never meet but have formed strong team relationships. As all elements of social media continue to evolve at dramatic speeds, individuals are fully used to forming social virtual teams.

Common interest groups – like people attracted to a venue where a celebrity is appearing – operate by mass texting. This technique is known as swarm-marketing. Various products are used to facilitate quick interactions between people with common interests. Skype has extended from private use into everyday business use. Facebook and MySpace have also crossed the boundaries from social media to business virtual networking and teams, and they are proven to have gained many people a job interview, or a contract, based on social as well as business dimensions. The LinkedIn business-based social website has also formed many interest groups, research groups and strong virtual teams.

A critique

Achieving consensus and synergy is not easy. As we have already noted, time is a pressing issue for organisations, and work groups may not allocate sufficient time to build towards consensus and synergy.

Another issue is the move for organisations in all types of industries to undertake projects as a growing part of their operations even when the primary 'productive' activity might be volume-based or operations-oriented (Keegan and Turner 2002). Co-ordination between the project group and the rest of the organisation and across organisations is often critical for ensuring that the knowledge gained in a particular project about, for example, consensus and synergy, is stored for use in other projects or that project routines are improved over time (Sydow, Lindkvist and DeFillippi, 2004). However, there has to be a process for knowledge-storing and improving routines (Sahlin-Andersson and Söderholm, 2002).

Team leaders need to think in current and future time. They must create the right environment for consensus and synergy in a current project (by devoting sufficient time within decision-making processes) and capture the learning of how they did it, if it went well, for future ventures (by establishing organisational processes of knowledge-storing).

ORGANISATIONAL DECISION-MAKING

As we have just seen, there are some decisions that must be made at the organisational level. We focused on the role of strategic leaders who create processes for knowledge-storing and improving routines across and between organisations.

Yet organisational decision-making brings new challenges of its own. Strategic decisions can be very difficult both to make and to execute successfully because they are also very costly to reverse – so it is extremely important to get them as right as possible. As Davis and Devinney (1997) point out:

- Strategic decisions whose success depends not only on successful implementation but also on the decisions made by others, involve major irrevocable commitments of unique resources (p15).

- Strategic decisions arise when the complexity and uncertainty is so large that no optimal or dominant decision can be found (p18).

- Strategic decisions arise when specific and complementary resources must be committed to specific purposes with high costs of reversing the commitment (p22).

- Contributions to the success and failure of strategic decisions are difficult to measure because the company's earnings include both a return to imperfectly contracted joint assets and a high degree of luck (p25).

- Effective strategy is based on the application of strategically valuable resources and assets in oligopolistic environments (p27).

Strategic decisions are likely to depend on the active co-operation of people who probably were not involved in making the decision themselves. The decision has to be 'sold' to them and their active participation obtained.

It is interesting to consider who makes strategic decisions. Top management often assume that they do, and should. However, in reality middle managers also make major strategic decisions on occasion, and *all* levels are involved in strategy, not least because of how they decide to allocate resources and effort (or not) to different initiatives. Strategy is also strongly affected by outsiders to the organisation: consultants, customers, regulators, shareholders and suppliers.

In such an environment, it is important to be able to analyse the change context and then categorise the type of decision to be made. By categorising the type of decision to be made, strategic decisions are broken down into more achievable tasks. Both the Cynefin model and the Change Kaleidoscope help here.

The Cynefin model

The Cynefin model helps the decision-maker to analyse the change context. Snowden (2002) developed the Cynefin model, suggesting that it is useful for organisations to understand where decisions should be made, depending upon the environment the organisation finds itself in, which has implications for leadership and power. The model identifies four environmental conditions each requiring different types of decision: the known state, the knowable state, the complex state, and the state of chaos.

The known state

This state links to our previous discussion about rational decision-making. All decisions can be based on predictable events. This means that events can be responded to easily using existing good practice systems. The leadership tends to be run by a strong management, making decisions from the centre, or the head office of the organisation, but relies on managers to implement the decisions.

The knowable state

This state is frequent when organisations are growing into new markets or into new geographies. It still assumes that the external environment is to a degree predictable and, as such, that most major decisions are based on sensing the situation by employing more analytical techniques to explore data sources, and response can be slower. The power at the centre is changed to a series of oligarchies, where leadership is exerted because of specific market expertise, product knowledge, new customer knowledge or new geographical knowledge. This creates complexity in communication and decision-making, and consensus and synergy play an increasing role.

The complex state

Nearly all organisations find themselves in a high degree of complexity, so research is undertaken to spot patterns, or the organisation is steered well away from the situation. The number of major decisions increases. Much more power is given to business units and functional areas, leaving senior management teams to co-ordinate activity. As complexity increases, so the chance for chaos rises.

The state of chaos

The recent global recession shows how chaos can be a problem that organisations have to be aware of and potentially manage. It was caused by bad loans to house-buyers in the United States, which led to the unpredicted near-collapse of the big banks around the world as debt could not be repaid, which in turn meant that many businesses could not raise finance as the money supply dried up. Because there is little time to act and react, and often because the situation in the organisation has not been experienced before, decisions are often based on experience and judgement with no research and no form of rational decision. These can be known as 'gut reactions' if they go right, and 'knee-jerk reactions' if they go wrong. Power returns to the centre as many being affected by the chaos look for a strong leader who often emerges from outside the old patriarchal leadership and can be seen as being charismatic, or tyrannical, or both.

The case of Bisk Education

The case study relates to the Cynefin model mostly in terms of the first three states. At times of business renewal, Bisk Education is in the complex state. In this state, the business is attempting to spot emerging patterns in the operating environment. For example, with the rise of the Internet, new types of workers were employed who, because of their expertise, had greater autonomy, but they still needed to be managed. Web designers and online graphics builders did not like to be told what to do – they preferred to be consulted and trusted, so Nathan moved from a command structure to a creative coalition of talented people.

As the new organisational structure settled down, Bisk Education moved through the knowable state to the known state. New good practice routines emerged and became standard operating procedures. In 1995 Nathan introduced Internet-based online courses for exam preparation and continuing professional education for the accounting industry. This involved a lot more group decisions which were happening through consensus driven by teams that came from all parts of the business and were supported by feedback systems to understand how all parts of the organisation were reacting to the market.

The Change Kaleidoscope

Having identified the state that the decision-maker is responding to, the Change Kaleidoscope facilitates the analysis of the change context in more detail (Balogun and Hope-Hailey, 2004). Eight design choices are used to prompt the decision-maker to improve the quality of their decision-making:

- Time – Will the decision be implemented in the long or short term?

- Scope – Does the change require a realignment or a transformation?

- Preservation – How much of current practices should be preserved?

- Diversity – Who should be involved in the decision-making process?

- Capability – What expertise is required?

- Capacity – Do staff have the appropriate skills and knowledge, for example?

- Readiness – Is there the need for change?

- Power – Does the decision-maker require support?

Having answered the questions, the decision-maker is encouraged to be even more specific, and future strategy should include:

- Change path: the type of change to be undertaken in terms of the nature of the change and desired end state

- Change start point: where the change is initiated and developed – eg top-down/bottom-up

- Change style: the management style of the implementation – eg highly collaborative/more directive

- Change target: people's attitudes/values, behaviours or outputs

- Change roles: who is to take responsibility for leading and implementing the changes

- Change levers: the range of levers and mechanism to be deployed.

The case of Bisk Education

If we return to the example of how Bisk Education responded to the rise of the Internet, we can see that strategic decisions are broken down into more achievable tasks. Making strategic decisions achievable is vital because, as Davis and Devinney (1997) point out, they involve major irrevocable commitments of unique resources and arise when the complexity and uncertainty is so large that no optimal or dominant decision can be found.

Ways in which Bisk Education broke down their strategic decision about the Internet into tasks that could be implemented include the following. Bisk Education decided that the scope of change was transformational, as Nathan moved from a command structure to a creative coalition of talented people. There was increased diversity of who should be involved in the decision-making process as web designers and online graphics builders became part of the new team structure. They were there because of their capacity, their specific skills as designers. All this created a change style that is highly collaborative.

A critique

It should not be taken for granted that the Cynefin model and the Change Kaleidoscope are the only change models that can help organisations. We have selected these because although they are relatively new, they have been around for almost 10 years and so have a provenance – that is, they have been applied and used in organisation development to improve organisation-level decision-making. The box below highlights an alternative approach which is gaining prominence as it demonstrates impact on organisational performance.

Taking your learning further: The Receptivity framework

Butler, M. J. R. and Allen, P. (2008) 'Understanding policy implementation processes as self-organizing systems', *Public Management Review*, Vol.10, No.3: 421–40. An alternative approach to organisational decision-making is the Receptivity framework. Like the Cynefin model, it seeks to link where decisions should be made and the environment the organisation finds itself in. Improving on the Change Kaleidoscope by providing a wider range of searching questions for the decision-maker, the framework has recently been transformed into a management tool: *Receptivity for Change Toolset – Identifying Transformation Potential in Dynamic Times*. The toolset also has the benefit of linking receptivity to change and organisational performance. To find out more about the toolset, visit www.thetransformationproject.co.uk.

CREATIVITY

Implied in the discussion about decision-making so far, but not overtly explored, is the role of *creativity* in decisions. Creativity is needed at all stages in the decision-making process:

- to have insight that an issue or problem is emerging – This is sense-making, which recognises that the organisational environment is changing and that a product or service needs to be modified or a new one developed.

- to frame the issue/problem in an appropriate way – Are you really tackling the right issue/problem?

- to think of options – Many issues/problems will have several potential solutions.

- to complete a risk analysis linked to each option – The temptation, given time pressures, is to do a cursory analysis, but insight may be required to understand more complex or chaotic influences.

- to effectively implement a solution which may have several obstacles to be overcome – Resistance to change is common, but given our bounded thinking, unforeseen events will emerge.

Creativity is a complex issue to understand. Here we focus on creativity as a process and a set of specific characteristics (creative thinking skills, expertise and motivation), which require practical application.

Creativity as process

Creativity is often viewed as a 'discovery moment'. However, it is much more of a process in which that moment has a place. The temptation as an individual, group or organisation is to expect insight straight away before preparing for the insight. Russell and Evans (1992) suggest that the following steps occur during the creative process:

- Preparation: analysing the task, gathering data, looking for patterns, trying out ideas and questioning assumptions

- Frustration: when we are unable to resolve the issue, feel bored, irritated or despondent and doubt our own ability

- Incubation: when we give up trying, put the issue on hold and hand it over to the unconscious mind

- Insight: the inspiration, the moment we normally associate with creativity

- Working out: testing our insights and giving them form.

The authors emphasise the need for process and the role of team approaches in facilitating the process, by taking students and executives to a modern art gallery as part of their module so that they experience and gain confidence about creativity in action. An exhibition at the gallery is used to stimulate individual ideas, which are then shared and, finally, teams create their own artwork using the same materials that the artist used in their exhibition. At the end of the session, we reflect on the creative process and relate it to the participants' working environments. It is energising for both participants and facilitators. Reading is suggested in the *Further reading* section at the end of this chapter.

Creativity as a set of specific characteristics

Amabile (1998) interlinks three sets of specific characteristics within creativity. The first two are related to the individual, but the third introduces the key influence of the manager in establishing an appropriate work environment. The first set of characteristics is creative thinking skills, which can be subdivided into:

- Personality traits:
    - Self-confidence
    - Independence
    - Intelligence
    - Risk-taking
    - Internal locus of control
    - Toleration of ambiguity
    - Perseverance

- Use of analogies

- Talent to see things differently (reframe).

The second set of characteristics is expertise in some area(s) related to the decision – but the relationship may not be obvious.

The last set is motivation, which involves:

- **Intrinsic motivation**, which works best

- Making the task:

  - interesting
  - involving
  - exciting
  - satisfying
  - challenging

- A supportive environment.

Creativity as practical application

Creativity can also take place at the organisational level. Mintzberg (1994) sees the organisation as a living, vibrant, people-centric organism, with the capacity to enable all to work together to solve problems and arrive at decisions. He sees innovation as central to the core of these living organisms, and all of the people as being central to the decision-making process of innovation. Because making the right decision right first time, every time, to match the precise situation is so important, Mintzberg started to research unexpected successes and unexpected failures in organisations. He came up with a list of the most important elements of innovation which will help in making the right decision to match the situation. It has generically become known as 'paradigm-busting'. We have converted the list into a set of questions which you can use to reflect on past decisions and improve your future decision-making (see the box below). This is a checklist for change and innovation. It has been successfully used in a variety of executive education workshops.

Applying theory to practice: Checklist of questions for change and innovation

For all unexpected successes, ask the questions:

- Why did we succeed?
- What can we learn from this success?
- What gems can we capture and 'institutionalise' before they fade?

For all unexpected failures, ask the questions:

- What can we learn from this?
- What may be changing out there, with competitors, and customers?
- What does it mean to us in terms of research, knowledge, learning or customer services?

For unexpected outside events, ask the questions:

- What is really going on out there?
- What does our world of customers really need?
- What has changed?
- How could it be relevant to what we do and what we might do?
- What could we do more of, less of, differently?
- How long have we got?

For incorrect assumptions about reality, ask the questions:

- What assumptions have we made in the past?
- What do people and customers really want from us now and in the future?
- What implications exist for us in terms of design, customer service or approach?

Processing the need, the following questions must be asked:

- What is relevant to this organisation?
- What does the world of people and customers need?
- What has changed recently in terms of our product or services?
- When did we last look at all the potential links?

To support the need for constant change, rational indicators need to be found:

- What signs of change are observable and researchable?
- What signs of new knowledge are there?
- What signs of new fashions, behaviours and trends are there?
- How can we move to exploit the external changes?
- Because technology is the fastest driver of change, where are new technologies most evident?

Conclusion

In this chapter we have shown you how to make better decisions and better understand others' decisions. This has been achieved by defining decision-making by referring to a range of concepts (see Table 11.1).

In particular, the strengths and weaknesses of rational decision-making have been discussed. The clarity and simplicity of a five-step rational decision-making model has been contrasted with the inherent bounded rationality that human beings possess, which leads us into numerous

Table 11.1: Summary of the chapter: the decision wheel linked to decision-making concepts and processes

The decision wheel	Decision-making concepts – the What	Decision-making process – the How
Introduction	Chapter argument	*No* 'one-right-way' approach
Cultural context	The role of context, culture and environment (Handy, 1993)	Our decisions are shaped by how we have been socialised or brought up – what is your cultural context?
Rational decision-making	Rational decision-making model	Clear and simple five-step process with a procedure to follow (Adair, 2001)
Limitations of the rational	Bounded rationality Decision traps Evolutionary psychology	Avoid heuristic biases Yet you need to be *both* rational *and* aware of your emotions (Lehrer, 2009)
Individual decision-making	Reflexivity	See, seek, use and share activities (Max Bazerman)
	Synthesising decision-making	Thinking, seeing and doing first (Henry Mintzberg)
Group decision-making	Consensus and synergy	Avoids groupthink (Janis, 1982) Good in virtual teams, using Skype, Facebook, MySpace and LinkedIn Requires time and knowledge-storing
Organisational decision-making	The Cynefin model (Snowden, 2002)	Analyses the change context
	The Change Kaleidoscope (Balogun and Hope-Hailey, 2004)	Categorises the type of decision – ie strategic decisions are broken down into achievable tasks
	The Receptivity framework (Butler)	Analyses the change context through the *Receptivity for Change Toolkit – Identifying Transformation Potential in Dynamic Times*
Creativity as . . .	Process	Five-step process (Russell and Evans, 1992)
	A set of specific characteristics	Skills, expertise and motivation (Amabile, 1998)
	Practical application	Asking key questions (see *Checklist of questions* above)
Conclusion	Service blueprinting	Nine practical guidelines (Bitner, Ostrom and Morgan, 2008)

decision traps. Fortunately, decision traps can be offset by various decision-making strategies at the individual, group and organisational levels.

At the individual level, reflexivity and synthesising decision-making have been highlighted. At the group level, we focus on consensus and synergy. At the organisational level, having noted the importance and challenges of strategic decisions, two models were explored to cope with the continuous change that organisations face (the Cynefin model and the Change Kaleidoscope). We also introduced an alternative approach, the Receptivity framework. Finally, the role and impact of creativity in decisions at all stages and levels of the decision-making process is made explicit.

All the decision-making concepts have been related to case studies. We have referred back to the case highlighted at the start of the chapter, Bisk Education, and introduced other high-profile examples, including practical applications of the theory introduced in the chapter. The decision-making concepts have also been critiqued so that you are aware of both their strengths and weaknesses.

As a means of capturing the ideas that have been addressed in this chapter, the example of **service blueprinting** is used. For service blueprinting to work, the employee is at the centre of the decision wheel that was introduced at the start of the chapter, and in any interaction with the customer, each segment making up the wheel must integrate.

BEST PRACTICE

Service blueprinting in Disney

It is important in most environments to get products and services aimed at specific segments of the population to market right first time, every time. Nowhere is it more critical to quickly get it right than within customer service. In many cases, service experiences are dependent on interpersonal and human delivery when a representative from a service provider meets a customer.

Service blueprinting is about individuals at the customer service interface (for example, car park staff in the Disney theme parks), who are empowered to make decisions to get the service absolutely right to match customer need. This may appear relatively simple, but how many of us have had poor experiences with front-line staff? This is both an individual and an organisational issue.

When individuals make service-based decisions, two events are happening. There is, first, a very strong underlying process, and second, most of the decisions are based upon the experience of the employee. The 'experiential' part is very important because it contains an understanding of the underlying needs of the customer, and the likely attitudes, beliefs and values that they will have. This part is supplemented by the employee's feeling empowered and supported by the organisation, represented by a manager at team level, who has relevant processes to be able to fulfil customer need. This is reflected by the recent statements of the Disney company, which said that everything employees do should create a set of memorable customer experiences.

BEST PRACTICE

Applying service blueprinting in practice

Mary Jo Bitner, Amy L. Ostrom (both Arizona State University) and Felicia N. Morgan (University of West Florida) (2008) recommend nine practical guidelines that will help you to blueprint a service of your choice. The nine steps are a clear decision-making process for applying blueprinting in practice, which links individual, group and organisational decision-making and which includes creativity as part of the process.

1 Decide on the company's service or service process to be blueprinted and the objective

Select the service or service process and the customer segment that will be the focus of the blueprint (external or internal) because different segments of customers may receive service differently. Make sure everyone is clear on the goals of the blueprinting process:

- for a new service it is likely to be to specify the desired service process, whereas
- for a currently offered service it is often to blueprint how the service is currently being offered.

The goals might include specifying specific role responsibilities.

2 Determine who should be involved in the blueprinting process

This stage requires some thought, and individual representatives of all groups involved in the design, delivery and support of the service – including in some cases the customer – should be included.

3 Modify the blueprinting technique as appropriate

Some blueprints might include:

- how customers interact with the company's technology
- how customers interact face-to-face with employees
- how customers interact with both technology and face-to-face
- special symbols that identify failure points, revenue-generating or cost-cutting opportunities or places where service quality perceptions could be enhanced can be incorporated

- any modification that enables better assessment of a particular service – eg time to perform each step
- considering how the blueprinting goals should be achieved.

4 Map the service as it happens most of the time

Focus on what typically occurs during the organisational service process and compare it to the ideal or competitor blueprints, depending on the goals.

5 Note disagreements to capture learning

Like consensus and synergy, participants will often come across points of disagreement about how the service works and how it is delivered to customers, but it is important to note these disagreements because they usually indicate problem areas within the service that are worth exploring.

6 Be sure that customers remain the focus

It is important that the customer stays top of the mind as the blueprint is being developed, not the team developing the blueprint.

7 Track insights that emerge for future action

Creating a blueprint leads to creative insights that can improve a service, which need to be noted as you complete the blueprint and then acted on later.

8 Develop recommendations and future actions based on blueprinting goals

Once the process of blueprinting the service is completed, recommendations for action can be compiled which are related to the goals of the blueprinting exercise.

9 If desired, create final blueprints for use within the organisation

Finished blueprints can be shared in the organisation and can be used for training and other purposes, and can be a resource for employees. The final blueprints should be shown to participants to make sure they are correct. The blueprints must also be updated over time.

REVIEW AND DISCUSSION QUESTIONS

REVIEW QUESTIONS

1 When is rational decision-making likely to work and when is it not? Give examples for both your answers.

2 Think of a recent decision you have made. Did you fall into any decision traps, and if you did, how can you avoid them in the future?

3 Think about the last time you were doing group work as a student, or in a team at work. Did the person leading the activity attempt to build consensus and synergy? If they did or did not, how did that make you feel? What would you do to empower your group and team members?

4 When you are listening to a news item about a high-profile organisation, is it represented as succeeding or not with its strategic decisions? If you were working at that organisation what would you do to improve decision-making?

5 When do you come up with your best ideas? When do you find it difficult to come up with ideas? How can you be more consistent in your decision-making?

DISCUSSION QUESTIONS

1 Once you have completed the Review questions, talk to a friend or colleague and compare your results. Are there differences, and what are the implications for decision-making?

2 Select an organisation of your choice and critically apply the various concepts of decision-making. Not all of them will be relevant, so select the most appropriate.

3 Returning to the case study, Bisk Education, critically evaluate its decision-making processes in terms of the ideas presented in this chapter. You may need to find out more information about the organisation.

4 Do you think there are cultural differences in decision-making processes? Give examples showing why you think so.

5 How will you integrate decision-making processes with other traditional areas of business and management? For example, if you are interested in accounts or marketing, give examples of how the concepts of decision-making could improve the performance of these areas.

FURTHER READING

Limitations of the rational

Kahneman, D. and Tversky, A. (eds) (2002) *Choices, Values, and Frames*. Cambridge: Cambridge University Press. Kahneman and Tversky shared an office at one time and asked each other hypothetical questions which helped to illuminate many of the brain's hard-wired defects. For example, when a person is confronted with an uncertain situation, the individual does not carefully evaluate the information. Instead, the decision depends on a brief list of emotions, instincts and mental short cuts. This is done to avoid the hard work of thinking, which does not necessarily speed up decision-making.

Senior, C. and Butler, M. J. R. (eds) (2007) *The Social Cognitive Neuroscience of Organizations*. Boston: Blackwell. For cutting-edge research on evolutionary psychology and how it affects different types of decision-making, read this. It is innovative because it uses neuroscientific methods to investigate organisations. It is

establishing a new field of research called organisational cognitive neuroscience.

Individual and group decision-making

Neale, M. A., Tenbrunsel, A. E., Galvin, T. and Bazerman, M. H. (2006) 'A decision perspective on organizations: social cognition, behavioural decision theory and the psychological links to micro- and macro-organizational behaviour', in S. R. Clegg, C. Hardy, T. B. Lawrence, and W. R. Nord (eds) *The Sage Handbook of Organization Studies*. London: Sage. This is a comprehensive review of the decision-making literature linking the individual level to the group level. It aims to ensure that organisational behaviour remains a field that is alive and here to stay – there is more to discover and apply in practical organisational settings. The aim is developed by taking a similar view to the one taken in this chapter – that managerial and collective cognitions are complex and highly influenced by context.

FURTHER READING NEXT

Organisational decision-making

Miller, S. J. and Wilson, D. C. (2006) 'Perspectives on organizational decision-making', in S. R. Clegg, C. Hardy, T. B. Lawrence, and W. R. Nord (eds) *The Sage Handbook of Organization Studies*. London: Sage. This is another comprehensive review of the decision-making literature but focusing on the organisational level. It develops themes under-explored in our chapter, such as power, implementation and interpretative approaches, because they are written about elsewhere in this book. Chapter 13, for example, evaluates *Power and Politics*.

Butler, M. J. R., Sweeney, M. and Crundwell, D. (2009) 'Facility closure management – the case of Vauxhall Motors, Luton', *International Journal of Operations and Production Management*, Vol.29, No.7: 670–91. This article is a case study from the private sector. It has rare access to decision-making processes and the purpose of the article is to detail the sequence and the results of the key strategic manufacturing management decisions made from the time of the announcement of the plant closure to the cessation of operations. The article also includes an analysis of the behaviour and motivation of all the staff involved in the closure management process.

Creativity

Butler, M. J. R., Wilkinson, J. and Allen, P. (2010) 'Exploring innovation in policy-making within central government: the case of the UK's Highways Agency', *Public Policy and Administration*, Vol.25, No.2: 137–55. This article is another case study which tracks the development and implementation of a new piece of legislation, the Traffic Management Act 2004. It also has rare access to the decision-making processes which drive innovation in policy-making within central government. It additionally develops another theme from this chapter: the appreciation of complexity in decision-making.

Adler, N. (2006) 'The arts and leadership: now that we can do anything, what will we do?', *Academy of Management Learning and Education*, Vol.5, No. 4: 486–99. As a counterpoint to the managerial case study given above, this article reveals the positive impact that the arts play in leadership development. When the editor of the journal received the manuscript of the article, it was immediately decided that this was an innovative approach to management learning and education and a special issue of the journal was commissioned.

Web links to seminal papers

The selection of web links is related to the selection of annotated Further reading:

Daniel Kahneman: http://nobelprize.org/nobel_prizes/economics/laureates/2002/kahneman-lecture.html. This link takes you to Kahneman's 2002 Nobel Prize speech. It is also available in text and video, and explains and reflects upon his work on the heuristics of judgement, risky choice and framing effects.

Max Bazerman: http://www.people.hbs.edu/mbazerman/working_papers.htm. Bazerman provides an opportunity to see his latest thinking by making copies of his working papers available.

Harvard Business School: http://hbswk.hbs.edu/topics/decisionmaking.html. Bazerman's work is set in the context of other research in decision-making at Harvard Business School. Again, working papers are available.

Michael Butler: http://academicsocialnetwork.ning.com/. One of the authors also uses a website to make his articles and other publications more widely available. The purpose of the website is to provide an opportunity to co-create ideas in 'Strategy Idea Space' by downloading evidence-based ideas (the publications), adapting them to your situation, then uploading your innovations to share with like minded-people.

The Transformation Project: www.thetransformationproject.co.uk. Michael Butler, in an ESRC-sponsored research project, is exploring how to transform decision-making processes in project management settings. Along with his team, he is co-producing two new management toolsets with project partners from all sectors and testing their impact on performance. The case studies show that quicker decision-making leads to senior manager agreement to project roll-out.

Other web links

http://www.youtube.com/watch?v=DyvXu3lSSG0: Henry Mintzberg has been mentioned several times during the chapter and this is a short clip on decision-making from one of his teaching sessions on the International Masters in Practicing Management (IDPM, www.impm.org). He explains the different approaches of thinking first, seeing first and doing first.

http://www.cognitive-edge.com/: Dave Snowden has been mentioned under *Organisational decision-making*. He founded Cognitive Edge in 2005 and develops new methods and tools to assist organisations with complex problems and opportunities.

http://www.slideshare.net/themoleskin/visual-and-creative-thinking: Kelsey Ruger, Pop Labs, presents ideas about visual and creative thinking – what we learned from Peter Pan and Willy Wonka. The link explains why visual and creative thinking are useful, what the myths surrounding them are, and ways to encourage them.

KEY SKILLS

This chapter focuses on the key skill of decision-making, and relates it to a set of underpinning skills.

DECISION-MAKING

Within organisational behaviour, decision-making is often neglected in favour of leadership or team skills because they are seen as being in demand by most employers and ambitious employees. Yet decision-making is a key skill. Without it, it is impossible to make a decision and an individual is left making a non-decision. Sometimes this is appropriate, because you have been asked to do something unreasonable or the original decision has been superseded by events and new decisions need to be made. At other times, a commitment to a course of action is required. Would Bisk Education have grown so effectively if the business opportunity had not been acted on, or a new business model created and reinvented as a response to the changing business environment? Nathan Bisk took appropriate decisions at the right time. It would be interesting to find out what mistakes were also made, because becoming a good decision-maker requires learning from experience. Lehrer (2009) finishes his book in the last paragraph (pp238–9) with:

> Of course, even the most attentive and self-aware minds will still make mistakes . . . but the best decision-makers don't despair. Instead, they become students of error, determined to learn from what went wrong. They think about what they could have done differently so that next time their neurons will know what to do. This is the most astonishing thing about the human brain: it can always improve itself. Tomorrow, we can make better decisions.

Decision-making can only be effective when underpinned by related skills.

REFLEXIVITY

Lehrer (2009) also gives a second piece of advice: to think about thinking, or be reflexive. He advocates this approach because it helps us to steer clear of errors – for example, the decision traps listed earlier. For him (p238), being reflexive involves:

> whenever you make a decision, be aware of the kind of decision you are making and the kind of thought process it requires . . . The best way to make sure that you are using your brain properly is to study your brain at work, to listen to the argument inside your head.

Earlier in this chapter, we noted how Bazerman and Chugh (2006) suggested four reflexive activities – see, seek, use and share – each activity being associated with further specific actions. The activities and actions interlink self-conscious enquiry and getting an outside perspective. There is an overlap here with team approaches, especially a team's capacity to develop through seizing learning opportunities.

CRITICAL THINKING

Because ideas about decision-making are in flux, illustrated by the range of concepts introduced in this chapter, it is important that a judgement is reached about which is the most appropriate concept to use at a given time. The decision wheel helps here, by summarising the different approaches that are available. However, the reader must, for themselves, appreciate the strengths and weaknesses of each concept in deciding the appropriate fit to the situation at hand. This chapter offers a guide, but the experience of the reader will add value to our interpretation. The capacity to weigh information up in the light of personal experience and to pursue independent learning is critical thinking in action.

ANALYSIS

Several concepts, but most obviously rational decision-making, benefit from being able to analyse, or the capacity to collect relevant information and interpret the information for patterns, before acting on it.

Spotting patterns is a problem-solving activity requiring insight. An integrative leadership style can be particularly favourable to creativity because it enables leaders to orchestrate expertise, people and relationships to bring new ideas into being (Mumford, Connelly, Gaddis and Strange 2002).

CONSENSUS AND SYNERGY

Making decisions with others leads to better decisions overall than working alone. In developing consensus and synergy, numerous skills are used: listening to others, understanding their points of view, learning from them and building upon them. This is emotional intelligence, demanding empathy and sympathy. It is also important to know your own point of view and needs and to make sure that you are also listened to. So negotiating, arbitration and conflict resolution skills are important to make sure that you and others have a balanced effect on the overall decision.

The same skills are also all needed at an organisational level. But at this more strategic level, attention not only needs to be paid to the decision itself but also to how a decision will be implemented – something increasingly dependent on other people. The capability to 'sell' or present the decision persuasively, both before it is made and afterwards, is therefore needed to convince staff of its merit.

Ethical implications: Moral behaviour and organisational behaviour

Although we acknowledge that some people might limit the role of business ethics – for example, on the grounds that acting morally is only justified if it promotes the manager's or organisation's best interests – we do not, however, subscribe to the view that taking other people's interests into account runs contrary to good organisational behaviour. Instead, we subscribe to the stakeholder view of justice, in that organisations have a wide constituency of interests to look after. The skills required for effective decision-making are compromised without the individual taking the decision displaying character virtue – that is to say, being credible and trustworthy. Consensus and synergy will not work without ethical behaviour, nor will the team aspects of analysis and reflexivity. The stakeholder view of justice includes the output of decisions, not just the process of decisions. Bisk Education would lose their customer base if they felt that the product and service did not meet their needs, did not do what it specified it would do.

Chapter 12
Equality and Diversity in Organisations

Maureen Royce

Contents

PART THREE

Key Learning Outcomes

By the end of this chapter you should be able to:

- appreciate the differences between equality and diversity
- identify the theories which attempt to explain discrimination at work
- understand the reasons why equality and diversity are important to organisations
- understand the business, legal and ethical pressures on organisations to manage equality and diversity successfully
- identify different mechanisms for delivering equality and diversity, recognising organisational needs and culture
- recognise the support available to organisations in developing equality and diversity initiatives
- evaluate the impact of equality and diversity initiatives.

 PRACTITIONER INSIGHT

The British Red Cross

The British Red Cross (BRC), incorporated by Royal Charter in 1908, was established with the broad remit of providing assistance for victims of armed conflicts. The BRC today enables vulnerable people at home and overseas to prepare for and respond to emergencies in their own communities through building resilience. **Practitioner Nalini Patel** reflects upon her own experience both as a 'diversity champion' within the BRC and with regard to the initiatives taken and challenges faced by the BRC to mainstream and evaluate its diversity initiatives.

The organisation is part of a global voluntary network responding to natural disasters, conflicts and individual emergencies. Its revenue-generating activities are fund-raising, donations and legacies, and income from its shops. Providing humanitarian support in emergency and conflict situations globally and looking to create sustainable resilience in health issues within marginalised communities in the UK, equality and diversity is an area of strategic importance to the BRC. Credibility with diverse and sometimes vulnerable groups will influence the success of its work within communities, so multicultural awareness and skills in managing diversity are a part of every division within the organisation. In its strategy document for 2010–2015 the BRC expresses its desire to make it easier for volunteers to join the organisation and to offer support and development to those taking up a volunteer role.

People from different backgrounds bring new skills, ideas and experience. And yet these differences can also result

in unfavourable treatment or discrimination. The Red Cross recognises that diversity initiatives must take both these factors into consideration to be successful. For example, an organisation that wishes to attract more disabled people as staff and volunteers must also demonstrate a commitment to being flexible and responsive to the needs of disabled people (www.redcross.org.uk). Evaluation of the internal culture and barriers to equality and diversity within the BRC in 2007 led to a drive to increase recruitment from diverse groups for paid and voluntary positions. Equality champions were appointed to encourage and evaluate initiatives such as the partnership with Scope to provide first aid training for people with disabilities. The Red Cross introduced the Living Diversity project, which created a variety of community programmes, many of which focused on reaching, and recruiting as staff and volunteers people from black and minority ethnic communities and disabled people. Some of the specific ways in which the BRC tries to engage communities include:

- holding meetings and events in alternative venues such as community centres
- having a presence at events such as disability conferences, youth networks and events aimed at black and minority ethnic communities
- creating publicity featuring people from all communities and which is available in accessible formats such as audio tapes and a range of languages
- publicising information to a wide audience through the specialist press, voluntary sector and professional black and minority ethnic business networks.

PRACTITIONER INSIGHT NEXT

In her interview, Nalini Patel discusses the importance of equality and diversity to the internal culture in the BRC, and introduces the idea of equality champions as a springboard for raising the profile of equality initiatives within a large organisation.

How would the initiatives undertaken by the BRC to include a more diverse range of people in the organisation be viewed by those in minority groups?

Why did the BRC feel they needed equality champions to support the growth of equality initiatives across the organisation?

Why would an organisation such as the BRC place particular emphasis on having an internal culture reflecting a philosophy of equality and diversity?

Once you have read this chapter, return to these questions and think about how you could answer them.

Introduction

This chapter is concerned with how people are treated in terms of equality within organisations. The chapter considers the premise that inequalities in relation to gender, ethnicity, disability and age are widespread within a wide variety of organisations containing diverse workforces, and that perceptions of inequalities and, indeed, fairness of treatment will impact upon employee motivation, the ability to work effectively in groups and teams, the quality of leadership, and the degree of stress experienced by employees. Although it is not the intention to examine all aspects of equality in detail, the focus of this chapter is upon gender and to a lesser extent racial equality.

The chapter begins with an explanation of the relevance of **equality** in relation to organisational behaviour, together with a definition of salient terms, and then considers a number of theoretical approaches universally adopted in order to explain the persistence of gender and ethnic inequalities both within the wider society and as reflected within many organisations. We thereafter go on to consider the nature of equality and **diversity** with regard to practices adopted in larger organisations and the extent to which organisational procedures such as 'equal opportunity' procedures are effective in reducing inequalities.

EQUALITY AND DIVERSITY IN THE CONTEXT OF ORGANISATIONAL BEHAVIOUR

Organisational behaviour concerns itself with identifying and understanding how people, groups and organisations behave. An essential part of this understanding relates to recognising the differences between people. We are all different. These differences may be visible or they may be harder to see and recognise. We might recognise that someone had a physical disability which prevented them from walking almost immediately, but it might take much longer to understand that the person we are trying to talk to is profoundly deaf and speaks fluently in sign language. Understanding differences in people and recognising that people are diverse is an important part of appreciating how organisations work. Although the term 'minority' is often used as a general term to bring together those who might be disadvantaged by being different, the numbers of people who may be included in such a list or category of 'difference' are increasing (EHRC, 2008).

It has been argued, for example, that the definition of **gender identities** in the workplace is reflected in the predominantly male culture of organisations where the feminine gender identity is suppressed or marginalised. In this context, Thompson and McHugh (2002: 337) contend that:

> Women managers especially are often required to adapt to masculine models of management, or risk being viewed as exceptions to women in general... Women's labour in organisations has often been an extension of domestic labour, as in the example of secretaries who act as office wives, protecting their charges from unnecessary interference and strain, making tea, buying presents, even cleaning their bosses' false teeth.

Much of the early work on equality in the UK focused on those groups recognised to be disadvantaged (Kirton and Greene, 2000). Primarily, these were women and people from minority ethnic groups. Later, recognition was given to other groups of individuals recognised as being disadvantaged and included disability, equality relating to **sexual orientation** and age. Increasingly, broader definitions of exclusion including socio-economic indicators and, more recently, human rights have become part of the wider equality debate. Beyond the UK, identification of the groups which might be considered to be disadvantaged varies greatly from one country to another, where the reasons for potential exclusion might be based on religion, language and/or education and may also be subject to change over time. In the UK, the government set up commissions to advise on matters of equality. The Equal Opportunities Commission, the Commission for Racial Equality and the Disability Rights Commission represented the rights of individuals and groups and advised on policy and legislation until 2007, when the Equality and Human Rights Commission (EHRC) took over the role of these commissions but with a broader remit to additionally represent equality in sexual orientation, age and religion. Such commissions exist because government, organisations and individuals recognise the need for specialist research and expertise in the area of equality and diversity. In Malaysia (Patrickson and O'Brien, 2001) there is no formal framework for managing equality and diversity behaviour in organisations, whereas in Australia (De Cieri and Olekalns, 2001) the commission structure strongly resembles the UK model. Just how effective commissions and legal frameworks have been in advancing equality of opportunity is discussed later in the chapter. In trying to create an environment that will support equality and diversity, organisations have to recognise that they may not control attitude but can control behaviour: policies to manage behaviour and provide education to influence behaviour are seen as part of the management role in organisations.

Although the UK population and work-base may be demographically more diverse than previously, it is problematic for organisations to manage this diversity if as organisations they themselves are relatively un-diverse. Where management structures lack diversity it is difficult to create a diverse and multicultural organisational environment. This is where we link to Chapter 17 and the role of human resource management (HRM). In order to build a diverse workforce we first have to create a climate for diversity (Hicks-Clarke and Iles, 2000). Once organisations are prepared for diversity and see the strategic advantages of it, they can look to their HRM policies in recruitment, selection and training as well as specific equality and diversity policies to introduce greater diversity into the organisation and create a climate in which diversity can thrive.

Equality, then, is what we hope to achieve through equality and diversity policy and practice. Diversity or difference is what we have. Diversity may be visible or invisible, but from an organisational viewpoint there is a need to understand how to work with a diverse population to ensure that there is equal representation at all levels in the workforce and that there is not just tolerance but respect for the differences of others (Carr-Ruffino, 2007). The 2009 CIPD factsheet concerning discrimination, equality and diversity uses statistical evidence to suggest that we need to continue to work hard as organisations in understanding equality and diversity because, despite our efforts, the outcomes to date are far from impressive. The CIPD factsheet suggests that in the UK unemployment is twice as high among people from ethnic minorities, although there are relatively more Chinese, Indian and black African graduates than white graduates.

It could be argued that the earlier focus on objectives aimed at avoiding discriminatory practice and fair play have been overtaken by the reality of demographic changes and global markets. This means that increasingly organisations must be multicultural and understand diversity in order to understand their customer and client base and workforce. In introducing the chapter we have recognised the importance of appreciating the differences between people and the relevance of equality and diversity to modern organisations. Evidence presented in this chapter suggests that companies are increasingly striving for racial, ethnic and workforce balance for legal, ethical and economic reasons. In the next part of the chapter we look in more detail at definitions of equality and diversity to develop further understanding.

DEFINITIONS AND THEORIES CONCERNING EQUALITY AND DIVERSITY

To understand how organisations have responded to the challenges of creating a culture of equality, there has to be some understanding about the theory linking to the more traditional ideas around equality and the newer, more business-focused concepts around diversity. The relationship between diversity and equality of opportunity has been explored by many authors in the field. Kandola and Fullerton (1998), Kirton and Greene (2000) and Torrington *et al* (2007) have all considered showing the comparative differences between equality of opportunity and managing diversity. Table 12.1 provides definitions and an overview of the differences concerning equality and diversity.

Essentially, equality is seen as being focused on the nature of the disadvantage in terms of gender, ethnicity, disability and age. However, this view of equality may create **stereotypes** by considering, for example, all people with a disability under the same umbrella policy. This implies a one-size-fits-all approach and denies the reality of differences between people who may belong to the same category in equality terms. Criticism of this labelling process led to thoughts about how to address the individuality and differing needs of individuals. To understand the nature of the difference between equality and diversity, imagine that the categories of race, sexual orientation, age, gender, disability are all placed together in a box which defines their reasons for being there. Equality processes keep these groups together in their 'box' and makes assumptions about the needs and requirements of the individuals based on the label for the box. But it is easy to be concerned about this and to think that although people with a disability, or women, or older workers may have some issues in common, there will also be many issues that are quite specific to the career aspirations, skill set and personality of the individual concerned. Diversity removes the individuals from the box and considers that all people are different in their own way, and that in looking to respond to individual differences rather than trying to address group issues, organisations will be more successful in creating an environment in which people can be comfortable with their difference and contribute to the best of their ability. In the next section we look more closely at perspectives concerning equality and diversity and what they mean in an organisational context.

Perspectives regarding equality

This section deals with gender and **ethnicity**. With regards to gender, there are a number of interesting and important theories which attempt to explain and justify differences between men and women. These theories can be placed into two categories. The first category is based on biology and the sexual division of labour, and the second category is based on the premise that **gender roles** are culturally rather than biologically produced and that we may label as the social construction of gender roles.

There are also theories which examine the basis of inequalities between men and women. Inspired by the development of the women's liberation movement, attention is focused upon the subordinate position of women in society and the feminist approaches which attempt to

Table 12.1: Comparative and behavioural aspects of equality and diversity

Equality	Diversity	Implications for organisational behaviour
Group focus – concentrates on the nature of the potential disadvantage	Individual focus – ability of all to achieve full potential	Organisations need to decide whether to focus resources on known aspects of disadvantage – eg race – or whether to put resources into developing the potential of all
Perceived as a minority interest – issue raised by those with a reason to be interested in equality. Exclusive policies – removing barriers	All included, broader involvement – no one is excluded. Inclusive policies – nurturing potential	Equality is not always seen as being of strategic importance and may be sidelined to relatively low positions in the organisational hierarchy. Senior management in organisations often lack diversity and so the more universal appeal of individual rather than interest-based focus is more attractive
Focused primarily on issues that may not link to organisational strategy. Policies may be piecemeal, not related to each other or to organisational strategy	Business a priority – seen as part of the business strategy	Economic self-interest – that diversity improves business success is a strong strategic argument. Equality policies may not easily integrate with other areas of strategy
Seen as specific to HR or equality expert	All have responsibility	With an 'expert' role it can be easy for employees to see equality as a job for someone else – diversity confers responsibility. However, it may be easy to give responsibility, but when everyone is responsible there may be little accountability for progress
Legal compliance	Best practice	Legal compliance is usually minimal compliance and looks to protect the organisation from being outside the law rather than a more positive outlook on benchmarking against the best organisational behaviour in equality terms
Integration is the aim	Inclusion is the aim	Organisations may recruit 'difference' but their internal policies and their training may have a culture of 'sameness' so that the differences are integrated and become lost. A diversity approach seeks to value the difference and maintain it for what it can bring to the organisation

explain this type of inequality. There are three main feminist approaches that can be identified:

- radical feminism
- Marxist and socialist feminism
- liberal feminism.

Biology and the sexual division of labour [1]

Basically, the argument here is that biological differences between men and women lead them to occupy different social roles and exhibit different types of behaviours (the so-called **sociobiological** explanation). In terms of sexual behaviour, for example, men are more likely to be promiscuous, whereas women will be more circumspect in their pursuit of a 'suitable' male. Men will, in competing for the attention of women, be more assertive, physically stronger, more competitive and ultimately more dominant than women. Because of her biological function – that of childbearing – a woman is tied to the home base, and because of her physique, the woman is limited to less strenuous tasks. This **sexual division of labour**, it is claimed, is universal and accounts for the role of women in industrial society, which is basically that of bearing and nursing children and providing them with warmth, security and emotional support in the home. In contrast to this, the male breadwinner spends his working day competing in an achievement-oriented society. The stress that this incurs in the male is relieved by the female through the provision of love, consideration and understanding. Sociobiological explanations of behaviour have been heavily criticised by feminists as a spurious attempt to provide 'scientific' justifications for male power. More specifically, Oakley (1981) argues that:

- Gender roles are culturally rather than biologically determined.

- Evidence from a number of different societies shows that there are no tasks (apart from childbearing) which are performed exclusively by females.

- Biological characteristics do not bar women from particular occupations.

- The mother role is a cultural and not a biological construction. Evidence from several societies indicates that children do not require a close, intimate and continuous relationship with a female mother figure.

The social construction of gender roles [2]

This explanation of male/female differences rests on the assumption that gender roles are culturally rather than biologically produced. In other words, humans learn the behaviour that is expected of males and females within their society. Gender is socially constructed in the sense that differences in the behaviour of males and females are learned rather than being the inevitable result of biology and is part of the **gender socialisation** process. Initially, the parent–child relationship is important, and Oakley (1981) identifies four ways in which socialisation into gender roles takes place:

1 The child's concept of himself or herself is affected by manipulation. For example, mothers tend to pay more attention to girls' hair and dress them in 'feminine' clothes.

2 Differences are achieved through the involvement and direction of boys and girls towards different objects, which is particularly obvious in the provision of toys: girls are given dolls, soft toys and miniature domestic objects and appliances to play with, whereas boys are given toys that encourage more practical, logical and aggressive behaviour such as bricks and guns.

3 Parents and others such as primary school teachers use such verbal epithets as 'You're a naughty boy,' or 'That's a good girl.' This leads young children to identify with their gender and imitate adults of the same gender.

4 Male and female children are exposed to different activities. For example, girls are particularly encouraged to become involved with domestic tasks. In addition, much research has documented how stereotypes of masculinity and femininity are further reinforced throughout childhood and adult life. Portrayals by media advertising of men and women in traditional social roles have been criticised by feminists.

The feminist preoccupation with the position of women in society – which they argue is a subordinate one – has generated a vast, but by no means unanimous, literature that can be broadly categorised into the three approaches described below.

Radical feminism

Radical feminism supports the contention that men are responsible for the exploitation of women. Women are seen to be exploited because they undertake 'free' labour for men by carrying out childcare and housework, and because they are denied access to positions of power. Another argument that is commonly put forward is that society is regarded as **patriarchal** – dominated and ruled by men. This means that because men still dominate occupationally, politically and within society generally, it follows that society's values are male values and women's values are subordinate to them.

Marxist and socialist feminism

Women's exploitation is not attributed entirely to men but to capitalism, which is the main beneficiary. Housework and the 'job' of mother is 'oppressive' unpaid work from which capitalism benefits through the production of wealth. The exploitation of women in paid employment, and their generally subordinate position in the occupational hierarchy is held to be a consequence of the emergence of private property and the resultant lack of ownership of the means of production, which deprives women of any power.

Liberal feminism

This approach suggests that gradual change in the social and economic systems of society will lead to an improvement in the position of women. According to this perspective, no one benefits from existing gender inequalities – both men and women are harmed as the potential of females and males alike is suppressed. For example, many women with the potential to be successful and skilled members of the workforce do not get the opportunity to develop their talents, while men are denied some of the pleasures of having a close relationship with their children. The explanation for this state of affairs lies not so much in the 'structures' and institutions of society as in its culture and in the attitudes of individuals. Socialisation into gender roles produces particular expectations of men and women, while discrimination prevents women from having equal opportunities. The liberal feminist agenda includes:

- the creation of equal opportunities in all spheres and particularly in education and work contexts

- the aim of creating equal opportunities pursued through the introduction of legislation and the changing of attitudes: measures such as the Sex Discrimination and Equal Pay Acts help to tackle discrimination

- the elimination of sexism and stereotypical views of women and men from children's books and the mass media.

Although the least radical of feminist perspectives, the liberal agenda could still lead to considerable social change – and at the very least, the changes it advocates could create the conditions whereby women have the same access as men to high-status jobs.

Explanations for gender inequality within the organisational workplace

Gender inequality within the workplace comprises important disadvantages experienced by women as compared with men in paid employment. These include:

- lower levels of remuneration

- greater likelihood of being in part-time work

- higher concentration of employment at lower occupational levels

- employment in low-status jobs.

A number of explanations for these inequalities – which we now briefly consider – focus upon the organisation and often reflect conditions within the labour market.

Human capital theory

Human capital theory argues that the apparent lack of commitment shown by women to paid employment is the cause of the disadvantages they suffer in the labour market. Because women are likely to abandon or interrupt their careers at an early age, they have less incentive to invest their time in lengthy programmes of training or education and are therefore of less value to employers than their more highly trained and more skilled male counterparts. For this reason, women will have less experience of their jobs than men, which makes it difficult for women to be promoted to higher-status and better-paid jobs. Women's lack of training, qualifications and experience resulting from the demands of childcare all contribute to their disadvantaged position in the labour market. The two main factors that have a positive influence upon women's career progression are a fully uninterrupted working life, without any break whatsoever, and being regarded as 'promotable' by 'having the ability and commitment to appear a long-term prospect, particularly through being able to work long hours' (Kirton and Greene, 2000: 46). Women are thus seen as being at a considerable disadvantage when the model of employment is based on the full-time male employee.

Dual labour market theory

Dual labour market theory distinguishes between the primary labour market, which is characterised by high pay, job security, good working conditions and favourable promotion prospects, and the secondary labour market, comprising lower-paid jobs, poor job security, inferior working conditions and few opportunities for promotion. Both may exist within one organisation, but transfer from one to the other is difficult, if not impossible. Secondary-sector workers are more dispensable and easily replaced – and a high proportion of these workers are women. The relatively low status of women in society and their tendency not to belong to trade unions weakens their position further and makes it particularly difficult for them to get a foothold in primary-sector employment. Once recruited to the secondary sector, women are likely to remain captives in it for the rest of their working lives. There are, however, some limitations and important exceptions which are not considered by the dual market approach:

- Some women in skilled manual jobs (for example, in the textile industry) are low-paid even though their work may be very similar to primary-sector men's jobs.

- Many women do have jobs in the primary sector, but not in manufacturing industry, as in the case of nurses, teachers and social workers.

- Dual labour market theory cannot adequately explain why women gain promotion less often than men, despite doing the same jobs.

Reserve army of labour

A Marxist explanation of the traditional role of women both within and outside the labour market argues that capitalism requires a spare pool of potential recruits to the labour force. Because of their inbuilt contradictions, capitalist economies experience cycles of boom and recession accompanied by increases in labour demand during the former and shedding of labour during the latter phase of the cycle. Improvements in the efficiency of production technology together with market demands to produce new products also requires a 'reserve army' to provide the necessary labour flexibility to deal with these changes.

One of the main functions of the reserve army is to reduce the wages of all members of the labour force as unemployed workers compete for jobs, thereby allowing employers to reduce wages and increase the rate and extent of exploitation. Beechey (1983) identifies a number of ways in which women have traditionally been particularly suited to the needs of this reserve army:

- Traditionally, women are less likely to be unionised and so are less able to resist redundancy than men.

- Women's jobs are least likely to be covered by redundancy legislation, making it more likely that women rather than men would be redundant at lower cost to the employer.

- Traditionally, unemployed women may not be eligible for state benefits if their husbands are working, and hence would not appear in the unemployment statistics: 'Women who are made redundant are able to disappear virtually without trace back into the family' (Beechey, 1983: 203).

- Traditionally, women were prepared to work for less pay than men, even in equivalent jobs, because they could rely upon their husbands' wages as the main source of income for the family.

While the reserve army explanation appears to take into account at least some of the fluctuations in the employment of women during the course of the twentieth century – for example, in appearing to account for the increased employment of women during the two World Wars – the theory may not adequately explain why a significant proportion of women are able to retain their jobs during periods of recession. Gardiner (1992), for example, argues that according to substitution theory, there are advantages to the employer in allowing women to retain their jobs during times of recession and rising unemployment since they are a comparatively cheap substitute for male workers.

Explanations for ethnic and racial inequality within the organisational workplace

Although most Western nations are becoming more ethnically diverse, divisions and inequalities between ethnic and racial groups continue to persist and are mirrored in the workplace. The term 'race' is often used in an ambiguous and imprecise way, and there have been various attempts to establish racial categories based on biological differences – some researchers have distinguished four or five categories, whereas others have identified dozens. Obviously, there are clear physical differences between human beings and some of these differences are inherited. But the question of why some differences and not others become matters for social discrimination and prejudice has nothing to do with biology. Racial differences should therefore be understood as 'physical variations singled out by the members of a community or society as socially significant' (Giddens, 1998: 146). Differences in skin colour, for example, are treated as significant, whereas differences in colour of hair are not. Racism is prejudice based on socially significant physical distinctions. A racist believes that some individuals and groups are superior or inferior to others as a result of these racial differences.

'Ethnicity' refers to the cultural practices and outlooks of a given community of people that set them apart from others – that is, makes them culturally distinct from other groups in society: they are seen by others to be distinct. Different characteristics may serve to distinguish ethnic groups from one another, but the most usual are language, history/ancestry, religion, and styles of dress or adornment. Ethnic differences are therefore entirely learned. There are many ethnic minority groups, and it is generally accepted that members of a minority group are disadvantaged as compared with the majority population and have some sense of group solidarity, of belonging together. The experience of being subject to prejudice and discrimination usually heightens feelings of common loyalty and interests. Members of minority groups frequently tend to see themselves as separate from the majority and are often physically and socially isolated from the larger community. Many minorities are both ethnically and physically distinct from the rest of the population, as, for example, are West Indians and Asians in Britain.

Psychological interpretations of prejudice and ethnic inequality [3]

There are two main explanations for ethnic differences and inequality of treatment. The first is based on stereotypes and scapegoats, and the second is based on the authoritarian personality.

CHAPTER 12 Equality and Diversity in Organisations

- Stereotypes and scapegoats

Prejudice operates mainly through the use of stereotypical thinking – that is, thinking in terms of fixed and inflexible categories. Stereotyping is often closely linked to the psychological mechanism of displacement, in which feelings of hostility or anger are directed against objects that are not the real origin of those feelings; people vent their anger against 'scapegoats' (people blamed for things/events which are not their fault). **Scapegoating** is common when two deprived ethnic groups come into competition with one another for economic rewards. Those who direct racial abuse and attacks against blacks, for example, are often in a similar economic position; they blame blacks for grievances of which the real causes lie elsewhere. Scapegoating is normally directed against groups that are distinctive and relatively powerless, because they make an easy target. (Protestants, Catholics, Jews, Italians, black Africans and others have played the unwilling role of scapegoat at various times throughout Western history.) Finally, scapegoating frequently involves projection defined as the unconscious attribution to others of one's own desires and characteristics.

- The authoritarian personality

Adorno *et al* (1950) argued that some individuals may possess certain personality traits which predispose them to stereotypical thinking and projection, and as a result of their research diagnosed a personality type which they termed the 'authoritarian' personality. The researchers developed a number of scales which, they argued, could determine levels of prejudice. On one scale, for instance, interviewees were asked to agree or disagree with a series of statements expressing strongly anti-Semitic views. Those who were diagnosed as prejudiced against Jews also tended to express negative attitudes towards other minorities. People with an authoritarian personality tend to be rigidly conformist, submissive to their superiors and dismissive towards inferiors, and tend to be highly intolerant in their religious and sexual attitudes and beliefs.

The research has been criticised but, at the very least, the ideas of Adorno *et al* are valuable in assisting understanding of authoritarian patterns of thought in general and the psychological bases of prejudiced attitudes in particular.

Sociological interpretations of prejudice and ethnic inequality

The psychological mechanisms of stereotypical thinking, displacement and projection are found amongst members of all societies, and help to explain why ethnic antagonism is such a common element in different cultures. However, they tell us little about the social processes involved in discrimination. Sociological concepts relevant to ethnic conflicts and disadvantage in society include *ethnocentrism*, *ethnic group closure*, and *resource allocation*.

- Ethnocentrism

Ethnocentrism is defined as a suspicion of outsiders combined with a tendency to evaluate the culture of others in terms of one's own culture. Combined with stereotypical thought, ethnocentrism can give rise to particularly virulent forms of racial prejudice or racism. Outsiders are conceptualised as aliens or barbarians or as being morally and mentally inferior.

- Group closure

There is often a strong association between ethnocentrism and **group closure**. 'Closure' refers to the process whereby groups maintain boundaries separating themselves from others. These boundaries are formed by means of exclusion devices which accentuate the divisions between one ethnic group and another and include:

- limiting or prohibiting intermarriage between groups

- restrictions on social contact or economic relationships such as trading

- the physical separation of groups into 'voluntary' ghettos.

- Resource allocation

Groups of equal power may mutually enforce lines of closure – their members keep separate from one another, but neither group dominates the other. More usually, however, one ethnic group occupies a position of power over the other, and in these circumstances group closure combines with resource allocation, such that the dominant group controls the distribution of wealth and material goods. Some of the fiercest conflicts between ethnic groups centre on lines of closure between them, precisely because these lines signal inequalities in wealth, power and social standing. The concept of closure and unequal resource allocation assists our understanding of a whole range of differences, 'not just why the members of some groups get shot, lynched, or harassed, but also why they don't get good jobs, a good education or a desirable place to live' (Giddens, 1998: 215).

Race, labour markets and the organisational workplace

As with gender, the existence of a dual labour market, where the secondary market comprises a relatively high proportion of ethnic minorities, is an important distinguishing factor. Workers of ethnic-minority origin have also consistently suffered a disproportionately high level of unemployment. It would, however, be unhelpful to consider ethnic minorities as one homogeneous group, and the following factors suggest that there is a high degree of differentiation:

- With regard to unemployment, Pakistanis, West Indians and Guayanese do particularly badly, irrespective of their qualifications, while male Indians appear to be the most successful group in terms of using their qualifications to escape unemployment.

- Those with Indian origins are consistently better qualified than any other minority group, and as well qualified as, if not better qualified than, the white population.

- Those with Pakistani or Bangladeshi origins, and particularly the women from these two groups, are the least qualified of all.

- The West Indian and Guayanese population traditionally have the highest employment rate for any group.

In a survey concerning the distribution of the different ethnic groups between different types of employment undertaken in 1997 (Modood *et al*, 1997), profound and enduring inequalities in employment were found to exist along a number of variables such as type of work and industry, hours, shifts and supervision.

Taking your learning further: Ethnicity, race and gender

Rex, J. and Mason, D. (eds) (1988) *Theories of Race and Ethnic Relations*. Cambridge: Cambridge University Press. This edited book of readings examines theories of race in more detail. The book is a well-established text and brings together internationally known scholars from a wide range of disciplines and theoretical traditions, all of whom have made significant contributions to the field of race and ethnic relations. As well as identifying important and persistent points of controversy, the collection reveals a complementary and multifaceted approach to our understanding of race and ethnicity.

Greer, G. (2006) *The Female Eunuch*. London: Harper Perennial. A new-cover re-issue of probably the most famous, most widely read book on feminism ever. First published in 1970, *The Female Eunuch* is a landmark in the history of the women's movement and is a searing examination of women's oppression. The book is a worldwide bestseller, translated into over 12 languages.

Some evidence concerning gender and ethnic equality

Evidence of inequalities is derived from research by the former EOC (2006) and the EHRC (2008). Taken together, the evidence reveals persistent and deep-rooted inequalities within gender and ethnic groups.

Gender evidence: labour markets and organisations

With regard to gender, women workers are still concentrated in poorly paid routine occupations such as clerical and secretarial work. Far more women than men are in part-time occupations. To be sure, women have recently made some inroads into occupations defined as 'men's jobs', but only to a limited extent. Women are under-represented in all the higher managerial and professional grades. Those women who are successful economically have to fit into a world of 'maleness' and masculine value systems where they feel they do not fully belong. One of the major factors affecting women's careers is the male perception that for female employees, work comes second to having children. The EHRC report (2008) entitled *Sex and Power* notes that there has been very little change in women's representation at senior levels in most large organisations compared with the situation in 2003. The box below provides an example of discrimination with regard to women managers.

Applying theory to practice: Gender stereotyping and women leaders in HC

The theories concerning gender stereotyping, patriarchalism, biology, and the gender division of labour are relevant to some degree or other in the example provided below.

HC is a large multinational computer software manufacturer based in the United States. Consultancy undertaken within this organisation revealed that gender stereotyping concerning women leaders and managers was rife and took a number of forms, including:

- *Conflicting perceptions* – Women business leaders are perceived as being either fallible and prone to making mistakes or too hard-hitting and therefore disliked. In other words, those who act in a manner consistent with gender stereotypes are considered too soft; those who go against them are considered too strong.

- *Higher challenges and standards, fewer rewards* – Women leaders face higher standards than their male counterparts and receive less reward. Often they must work doubly hard to achieve the same level of recognition for the same level of work and 'demonstrate' that they can lead.

- *Competent but disliked* – Women exhibiting traditional leadership skills such as assertiveness tend to be seen as competent but not personable or well-liked. Those who adopt a more stereotypically feminine style are liked but not seen as having valued leadership skills.

The consultancy report suggested that organisations need to develop strategies to remove the pervasive and damaging impact of gender stereotyping from the work environment to take advantage of the expanding pool of female leadership talent.

Evidence concerning ethnicity

Ethnic minority groups in common with a significant proportion of the female labour force are disadvantaged with regard to qualifications and employment opportunities, levels of pay, differential recruitment policies and practices, and trade union membership. Not only do ethnic minorities find access to organisations difficult, but once inside they generally find themselves discriminated against for reasons that are social rather than economic in origin, and for criteria that include not just skin colour but religious and political affiliation also (Doeringer and Piore, 1971; Commission for Racial Equality (CRE), 2007). The box below provides an example of worst practice with regard to race discrimination and harassment in the organisational workplace.

WORST PRACTICE

Racial discrimination at work

Racism at work can be direct or subtle, conscious or unwitting. It can come from your boss, from the people you work with or be built into the way your organisation works. Racist behaviour can be against the law. It takes a positive commitment from the whole organisation – managers and staff. When employers and unions work together it can make a real difference. Motor Factoring is a small to medium-sized (SME) single-workplace motor components company based near Birmingham, UK. Racism was endemic at Motor Factoring. The new HR manager identified the following problems with the Asian workers who were:

- being called names
- overlooked for promotion
- denied training
- denied overtime and other benefits
- only offered unpopular shifts
- shouted at
- bullied
- selected for redundancy

- denied holiday entitlement.

This resulted in the Asian workforce experiencing some or all of the following:

- loss of confidence
- stress
- humiliation
- insomnia
- low morale and motivation
- anxiety
- physical sickness
- bad work performance
- time off work and even long-term sickness leave.

The consequences of this for Motor Factoring were:

- disharmony in the workplace
- unhappy workers
- reduced output
- reduced profits
- high sickness levels.

Diversity

The CIPD (2008) defines diversity as 'valuing everyone as an individual'. The relationship between diversity and equality of opportunity has been explored by many authors in the field. Kandola and Fullerton (1998), Kirton and Greene (2000) and Torrington *et al* (2007) have provided evidence showing the comparative differences between equality of opportunity and managing diversity. Managing diversity theorists recognise that through recruitment and training practice we send out strong cultural messages that may discourage those who are different. A diversity approach incorporates a belief that differences should be seen as strengths that can add competitive advantage to the organisation. Traditional approaches to equality tended to view difference as, if not a weakness, then as something that had to be supported through policies or that could be diluted during training to produce behaviour conforming to cultural norms. Carr-Ruffino (2007) argues that managing diversity means celebrating difference by valuing what it can bring to an organisation. A further difference is that managing diversity is based on an economic and business case for recognising difference rather than equal opportunities practice, which tends to look either at the moral case for treating people equally or at minimum legal compliance. The CIPD (2008) suggests that diversity contributes to creating an environment in which people from all backgrounds can work together harmoniously by combating prejudice, stereotyping, harassment and undignified and disrespectful behaviour.

Notwithstanding the claimed benefits of an effective diversity policy, the proliferation of cases within the public arena involving a large number of employees suggests that many organisations are, in practice, either not taking the espoused rhetoric of equality and diversity seriously enough at best, or ignoring good practice at worst (see the box below).

Applying theory to practice: High-profile cases

You may be able to identify some of the underlying theoretical perspectives and workplace inequalities which these high-profile cases reveal.

Discrimination in the workplace is a serious issue and there have been many cases brought before employment tribunals over the years. Some are won and some are lost, but there are a few that will always be remembered.

Sex discrimination in the city (sexual stereotyping/biological explanation and gender division of labour):

Investment banker Julie Bower took her company Schroder Securities to court in 2002 claiming that her male counterparts were given much bigger bonuses. She won her case and received £1.5 million – which caused a sensation at the time.

Ann Southcott (theory concerning age inequality):

In 2007 66-year-old Ann Southcott became the first person to win an age discrimination case at an employment tribunal. She was dismissed form her clerical job at Treliske hospital in Truro the day before the Employment Equality Regulations (Age) came into force. This meant that instead of getting one month's pay for every year she had been there, she received just 11 days' pay. She won her case and was reinstated with back pay.

Abbey race discrimination (theory concerning scapegoating):

At the end of 2008 Balbinder Chagger won a record £2.8 million in a race discrimination case against high-street bank Abbey. He claimed that as a former employee he had been held back because of his race and was made redundant in 2006. The record payment took into account his future loss of earnings from his £100,000-a-year job.

Mohammed Sajwal Khan (theory concerning religious discrimination):

In 2003 a bus cleaner was the first person to win a religious discrimination case under the new equality legislation. Mohammed Sajwal Khan asked his employer NIC Hygiene for extended leave to go on a religious pilgrimage. His manager told him it had been granted, but when he returned from his six-week trip he was suspended. The subsequent tribunal found in his favour.

Table 12.2 identifies the main advantages and disadvantages to both employee and organisation of equality and diversity approaches.

Not all organisations are in a position where they are able to fully embrace diversity thinking. They may still be trying to develop good practice equality processes and struggling to meet legal requirements. Their workforce may be relatively un-diverse, and time and culture change will be needed to create a climate where workers who are different from the organisational norm can feel comfortable and appreciated. The first steps in developing diversity lie in a strong commitment to the equality process, so the two approaches are, in many ways, interdependent. Strong commitment to diversity will often spring from a clear, well-monitored and developed set of equality processes and policies.

Table 12.2:   Advantages and disadvantages of equality and diversity approaches

	Advantages to the employee	Advantages to the organisation
Equality approach	Clarity of process, support of peer group sharing issues relating to aspect of difference	Process-based initiatives are easier to evaluate although outcomes are now reported with respect to racial diversity and disability
Diversity approach	Perceived as an individual with individual needs. Not stereotyped with assumptions made based on aspect of difference	Where *all* are treated as diverse there is less need to foster specialist provision – may reduce specialist provision to legal minimum
	Disadvantages to the employee	**Disadvantages to the organisation**
Equality approach	The ' offering' of the organisation may not be appropriate or relevant to the individual	Resourcing specialist support to identified minority groups. Perceptions of unfairness from those not benefiting from specialist provision
Diversity approach	May lose positive support or resources allocated previously to identified minority groups	Unreal expectations related to diversity provision. Lack of understanding, training and resources to develop diversity culture

FACTORS INFLUENCING THE DEVELOPMENT OF EQUALITY AND DIVERSITY IN ORGANISATIONS

Equality and diversity are essential to the growth and survival of organisations whether they are global corporations or small family business units. The range difference in the population mosaic and rapidly changing demographics mean that organisations cannot afford to remain culturally unaware of the extent of diversity in their customer base and in their workforce. Allard (2002) asserts that 'diversity is not an option', but that engaging with issues of equality becomes a necessity in the face of increasing globalisation and technology. As our work structures become virtual and decentralised, our need to work within a cultural framework of acceptance of difference becomes imperative to achieving organisational goals.

We now turn to the business, legal and ethical reasons for organisations to become involved in equality and diversity.

Business drivers for developing equality and diversity

Organisations are aware of their responsibilities and activities which place them in the public view. For private-sector organisations there is fear that having a poor reputation for equality will diminish the reputation of the company and impact on its ability to sell goods and services within an increasingly diverse population. Trevor Phillips, chairman of the EHRC, believes employers need to recognise equality and diversity as a method of improving business performance by utilising the skills and talents of the entire workforce (Chubb and Phillips, 2007).

McCloud and Lobel (1992) recognise that minority views stimulate consideration of non-obvious alternatives in work settings. This view is supported by Jackson (1992), who considered that problem-solving styles produced better decisions through the operation of a wider range of perspectives and a more critical analysis of issues. As firms reach out to a broader customer base, they need employees who understand particular customer preferences and requirements (Morrison, 1992). The insights and cultural sensitivity that women and ethnic minority employees bring to a marketing effort improve an organisation's ability to reach different market segments (Cox and Blake, 1991; Richard, 2000). The concept of human capital is that people have skills, experience and knowledge that provide firms with economic value. As other sources of competitive advantage – such as technology – become easier to emulate, the crucial differentiating factor between firms can be how human resources work in an organisation (Pfeffer, 1994). Cultural diversity in human capital serves as a source of sustained competitive advantage because it creates value that is both difficult to imitate and rare. If an organisation overcomes resistance to change in the area of accepting diversity, it may be well positioned to handle other types of change (Iles and Hayers, 1997). An organisation with a diversity of perspectives should have more creativity and an ability to respond quickly to an uncertain external environment. However, organisations may not fit easily within a static definition (Kirton and Greene, 2000).

Creating a diverse workforce increases the diversity of skills in organisations and creates a positive reputation for the organisation which may consequently lead to an increase in the number of potential employees (Kandola and Fullerton, 1998). An example of this is Jaguar Land Rover, which has employed more women in order to reflect the growing number of women in its customer base (Broughton and Strebler, 2008). Organisational vision is seen as a key concept in diversity practice by Ross and Schneider (1992) and Rossett and Bickham (1994). They conclude that if diversity is to become a business issue, the organisation must have a clear vision of what it intends to achieve and the message must be clearly communicated that diversity is a business – as opposed to a moral or ethical – objective. For managing diversity to be seen as an organisation-wide strategy, the diversity policy or strategy must be clearly seen as having an impact on business goals. A diverse workforce can help to inform the development of new markets or products. Where the role of the organisation is to provide a service to a community, perhaps in health or education, diversity can help organisations to understand and relate their service to the culture of different groups and individuals within that community, so improving the quality of the service overall.

In human resource management (HRM) terms, managing diversity is seen as being a more integrated approach linked to achieving business goals. Equal opportunities policies may fail to link effectively with other strategies such as appraisal practice or reward. In terms of linking to business strategy, equality and diversity policies work with business excellence models and initiatives such as Investors in People, which particularly look to develop areas of individual competence (CIPD, 2008). Managing diversity is seen as a tool for encouraging the integration of HRM strategy areas to deliver the objective of a diverse workforce where difference is valued and recognised throughout all the organisational processes.

Legal drivers for developing equality and diversity

Although the role of diversity and equality in achieving commercial success has been considered by academics and HR practitioners since the 1980s, responses by organisations have not always been driven by the business imperative. For some organisations, the implementation of legislative requirements based on fear of litigation has been a driving force for the development of equality and diversity policy. Typically, organisations in the 1990s did not address diversity beyond what was required by law and, in the UK, by the Equal Opportunities Commission (Cox, 1991).

The CIPD (2008) survey shows that for over one-third of organisations surveyed legal pressures were the main driver for managing diversity, which suggests that minimum legal requirements correspond to the primary position taken. Movement away from minimal compliance requires a major culture shift, and this will be discussed further when we look at delivery mechanisms for equality and diversity policy. In the UK the managing diversity agenda followed a widely publicised report about the public scandal of racism within the police force over its failure to properly investigate a racist murder (MacPherson, 1999). The subsequent legislation in the UK – the Race Relations (Amendment) Act, 2001 – required institutions to develop proactive policies on racism and ethnicity and has had an influence on perceptions of the need to be able to show how policies are actively being integrated into the organisation at all levels.

Richard (2000) argues that human resource practitioners can add value by generating a cultural mix in the human resource base. Policies linked to adherence to legal requirements develop from an HR base in many organisations, so to develop away from mere avoidance of legal penalty the role of the HR department in equality becomes another aspect of organisational behaviour to be examined. Table 12.3 outlines the main UK legislation governing equality and diversity.

Ethical and moral drivers for developing equality and diversity

Ethically and morally, equality is seen as the correct thing to do (Knouse and Stewart, 2003). The social justice argument is based on the belief that everyone should have a right to equal access to employment and when employed should have equal pay and equal access to training and development. Organisations with a moral imperative driving their equality practice are also likely to ask for strong positive equality behaviours from individual members of staff and place a high value on promoting a culture not just of avoiding discrimination but of valuing and appreciating difference (Carr-Ruffino, 2007) and creating a working environment that is free of harassment or bullying behaviour. Where ethical and moral drivers are the main force in determining organisational behaviour, the organisation must simultaneously produce coherent policy in the area and also recognise that individual members of staff have unavoidable responsibility. Pursuing equal opportunities initiatives does not always bring immediate tangible results either for the organisation or for the individual. A degree of ethical commitment is therefore necessary to combat institutional forms of discrimination. 'Equal opportunity' issues such as discrimination, harassment and equal access are fundamentally about respect for individuals and groups with socially diverse backgrounds. They demand an ethical response

Table 12.3: A summary of relevant discrimination legislation

Name of legislation	Description
Equal Pay Act 1970	Gives an individual a right to the same contractual pay and benefits as a person of the opposite sex in the same employment where the man and the woman are doing like work, work rated as equivalent under an analytical job evaluation study, or work that is proved to be of equal value.
Sex Discrimination Act 1975	Makes it unlawful to discriminate on the grounds of sex. Sex discrimination is unlawful in employment, education, advertising or when providing housing, goods, services or facilities. It is unlawful to discriminate because someone is married or in employment, or within advertisements for jobs.
Race Relations Act 1976 (Amendment) Regulations 2003	Introduce new definitions of indirect discrimination and harassment, new burden of proof requirements, continuing protection after employment ceases, new exemption for a determinate job requirement and the removal of certain other exemptions.
Disability Discrimination Act 1995	Outlaws the discrimination of disabled people in employment, the provision of goods, facilities and services or the administration or management of premises.
The Sex Discrimination (Gender Reassignment) Regulations 1999	Seeks to prevent sex discrimination relating to gender reassignment. It clarifies the law for transsexual people in relation to equal pay and treatment in employment and training.
Race Relations Amendment Act 2000	Places a statutory duty on all public bodies to promote equal opportunity, eliminate racial discrimination and promote good relations between different racial groups.
Employment Equality (Religion or Belief) Regulations 2003	Protects against discrimination on the grounds of religion and belief in employment, vocational training, promotion and working conditions.
Employment Equality (Sexual Orientation) Regulations 2003	Protects against discrimination on the grounds of sexual orientation in employment, vocational training, promotion, and working conditions.
Gender Recognition Act 2004	Seeks to provide transsexual people with legal recognition in their acquired gender. Legal recognition follows from the issue of a full gender recognition certificate by a gender recognition panel.
Disability Discrimination Amendment Act 2005	Introduces a positive duty on public bodies to promote equality for disabled people.
Employment Equality (Sex Discrimination) Regulations 2005	Introduce new definitions of indirect discrimination and harassment, explicitly prohibit discrimination on the grounds of pregnancy or maternity leave, and set out the extent to which it is discriminatory to pay a woman less than she would otherwise have been paid due to pregnancy or maternity issues.
Employment Equality (Age) Regulations 2006	Protect against discrimination on grounds of age in employment and vocational training. Prohibit direct and indirect discrimination, victimisation, harassment and instructions to discriminate.
Racial and Religious Hatred Act 2006	Seeks to stop people from intentionally using threatening words or behaviour to stir up hatred against people because of what they believe.
Equality Act 2006	Establishes a single Commission for Equality and Human Rights by 2007 that replaces the three existing commissions. Introduces a positive duty on public sector bodies to promote equality of opportunity between women and men and eliminate sex discrimination. Protects from discrimination on the grounds of religion or belief in terms of access to good facilities and services.
Equality Act 2010	Is the most significant piece of legislation to be introduced for many years. It is there to strengthen protection, advance equality and simplify the law. The main provisions of interest to local government are: • the introduction of a new strategic socio-economic duty to reduce socio-economic inequalities • a new public equality duty that will extend the public duties to age, sexual orientation, religion or belief, or transgender status • the extending of anti-age discrimination rules to include goods, facilities and services, stopping people being unfairly refused insurance or medical treatments based on their age, for example • age discrimination provisions do not come into force until 2012 for the private sector and later for health and social care.

from individuals within the organisation in the sense that they require a personal commitment to ethical action as well as a simultaneous, co-ordinated institutional response (Clifford and Royce, 2007).

The box below illustrates ethical issues with regard to the '**glass ceiling**' and the '**sticky floor**'.

Ethical implications: The glass ceiling and the sticky floor

Perhaps the main ethical issue in equality matters is inequality itself. The chapter has identified a number of equality issues concerning gender and ethnicity/race. The '**glass ceiling**' is an important issue, and is concerned with promotion to top management and the thwarted career aspirations of female managers when they fail for no apparent good reason to attain it. Frustrated aspirations at this level lead to a decline in morale and performance levels (Ngo *et al*, 2003). In the international context, particularly but not exclusively as far as developing nations are concerned, we have the converse of the glass ceiling – the so-called '**sticky floor**'. Many workers, particularly women workers, find themselves stuck to it. Examples include migrant workers of many different ethnic origins in the UK, low-paid female workers in unskilled service-sector jobs, garment workers in Sri Lanka and Chinese garment workers in Canada and the USA (Brooks, 2002). Many of these workers are employed in small factories and workplaces, often of a transient nature, whose employers either ignore or flout any equality legislation that may exist. For these workers the only motivation to work is to satisfy subsistence needs for themselves and their families.

DELIVERY MECHANISMS FOR EQUALITY AND DIVERSITY

The positioning of equality and diversity within organisations varies tremendously and is a matter of some uncertainty. Some organisations have bespoke equality experts or departments, in others the role is embedded within the HR function. Some organisations seek to mainstream equality and diversity, making it the responsibility of every manager, team leader or staff member, while others look to voluntary support for equality issues from those with interest, knowledge or experience in the form of 'champions'.

In the following section we review some alternative forms of equality and diversity delivery and use some evidence from the UK higher education system to give examples of how the theory works in a practical environment. You should also be able to relate much of the material we have covered concerning diversity towards answering the questions in the Practitioner insight case study concerning the British Red Cross at the beginning of the chapter.

Organisational policy and human resource management [4]

We noted earlier that human resource management has a role in generating a cultural mix, a diverse workforce. However, although we certainly need to have equality-focused recruitment and selection processes to build cultural diversity, there is the additional matter of how to maintain diversity once those we recruit are subjected to the cultural norms and to training within the organisation. HR practitioners need to review the communication and performance systems within their organisations to ensure that organisational objectives are understood by a diverse audience, and that the efforts to translate these objectives into practice are performance-managed in a way that will allow for diverse approaches. Yet the management focus on equality and diversity has often been limited in range. Funding mechanisms and priorities, particularly in times of recession, have given a minimal incentive for senior managers to view equality and diversity funding as a commercial priority.

HR departments have a role in showing by example how equality practices and policies within the institution impact on their own culture and behaviour. The big question for HR departments has not been the writing of a mission statement showing diversity values or of creating policy but one of delivery at the local level. Coherent HR in all areas is dependent on local support, but perhaps equality and diversity requires particular focus on ensuring that the team leaders and individuals understand the importance and benefits of making positive changes in this area.

In examining the development of local support for equality issues, there is recognition of the role played by the human resource management (HRM) function in developing integrative HRM policies to support change and diversity. We can take an example from the UK higher education system. All post-1992 universities in the UK were perceived in the 1990s (the Fender and Dearing Reports) as being in need of strategic and integrated HRM planning. Accordingly, additional funding was provided by HEFCE (Higher Education Funding Council for England and Wales) to encourage such development. The funding provided through the HR strategy pot from HEFCE provided resource for post-1992 universities to improve and develop areas of their service. Among the projects approved was one targeted at creating specialist equality co-ordinators at local level for both academic, services, technical and ancillary staff. Throughout the life of the project, issues about decision-making at strategic level slowed progress and became sources of tension and frustration.

Warner and Crosthwaite (1993) reviewed the differences in HR structures in HE. Although most HR and personnel directors or senior managers reported themselves (Warner and Crosthwaite, 1993) as participating at the highest level, a review of structure suggested that, in reality, many were one step or one committee away from the most powerful and key decision-making committee. Dibben, James and Cunningham (2001) point to senior management commitment as being the key element in turning equal opportunities policies into practice. The importance to all organisations of having a strategic link to the highest decision-making body of the organisation is shown through this example – where there was a break in this link, delays and communication issues resulted. The co-ordinator project looked at a vision to break free of the 'marginalised' nature of equal opportunities complained of by Dibben *et al* and bring life to a set of paper policies that were already exemplars of good practice within the sector. Earlier research into diversity and equality initiatives in UK universities reveals a fairly haphazard approach to strategy and considerable variation between strategies (Jewson and Mason, 1992; Neal, 1998). Dibben, James and Cunningham (2001) point to the marginalisation of equality practice in the sector while De Lowerntal (2003) and Cornelius (2002) highlight the environmental constraints and requirements in mainstreaming diversity initiatives. In looking at the university sector it was possible to understand the barriers to achieving an integrated structure to support diversity.

In looking at developing organisational policy on equality and diversity, barriers inherent in moving from strategy and policy to delivery and practice can be identified. De Lowerntal (2003: 11) points out the risk of isolating practice, professional expertise and knowledge from the individual members of the workforce, who may perceive equal opportunities to be in the hands of 'professionals who already have a good awareness of legislation and practice'.

Diversity writers such as Kandola and Fullerton (1998) have recognised for some years that to recruit diversity is only one part of the process. Creating a climate for diversity (Hicks-Clarke and Iles, 2000) requires the institution to have a supportive culture and awareness to sustain that diversity. In common with many organisations, however, the resources to deliver diversity in practice are dissipated between institutional functions. Given a scarcity of resources, the development of a personalised ethical framework at the level of the individual becomes increasingly important. Strategy and policy statements may be robust in principle but the test of delivery is in the responses individual employees see on the ground. It is this perception about the delivery of equality and diversity behaviours at local level that will ultimately measure the success of the policy. A self-conscious fear of doing something wrong has created the danger of not doing anything at all or of leaving it to those with some expertise in the area. In developing good practice, academics and administrative staff need to challenge their existing practices and behaviour, and Parker, Naylor and Warmington (2004) recognise the importance of self-review among workers and stress the importance of informal learning in meetings and discussions in the field of equality awareness.

A further issue in relation to the development of good practice is that of the risk of over-specialisation and concentration of expertise. Cornelius (2002: 127) for example, argues that:

> Organisations that rely primarily on building equality and diversity expertise within specialist nodes may end up reducing the spread of equality and diversity information organisation-wide.

There is a dilemma, then, about policy development and delivery. Where this is driven by HR and/or a specialist equality unit, there may be knowledge-based or independence-related advantages but there is also a very real risk that this important work is left only to those who already know something about it. This makes it difficult to create culture change and to have widespread understanding about positive diversity behaviours.

An example of a 'best practice' policy is that of Marks & Spencer, as given in the box below. Procedures such as diversity and equal opportunities procedures stem from policy and emphasise the formal means whereby equality and diversity problems affecting individuals and groups within the organisational workplace may be resolved. However the case of Hannah, also in the box below, indicates that many of these problems could be resolved more informally.

BEST PRACTICE

The M&S equal opportunities statement

Marks & Spencer is committed to an active Equal Opportunities Policy from recruitment and selection, through training and development, appraisal and promotion to retirement.

It is our policy to promote an environment free from discrimination, harassment and victimisation where everyone will receive equal treatment regardless of age, colour, disability, ethnic or national origin, gender, marital status, religion or sexual orientation. All decisions relating to employment practices will be objective, free from bias and based solely upon work criteria and individual merit.

The company is responsive to the needs of its employees, customers and the community at large and we are an organisation which uses everyone's talents and abilities where diversity is valued.

Source: Marks & Spencer plc: Equal Opportunities Statement (2005)

The case of Hannah

Hannah experienced a considerable amount of **sexual harassment** from male colleagues. She decided enough was enough and did something about it. Hannah always wanted a career as a 'high flyer' in a financial institution and had the skills and qualifications to succeed. Jobs in the financial sector in the City (of London) are male-dominated, but this did not deter her. She made sure she dressed professionally and resolved to give male colleagues 'a run for their money'.

Hannah made a bad start, facing male hostility and resentment. Initially, no sexist comments were made. Male colleagues were just 'cold and resentful'. The situation deteriorated rapidly for Hannah. Nothing she did was right in the eyes of her male colleagues. Subtle sexist comments gave way to overtly sexual jokes and insinuations which were insulting.

'It was past the point of making a joke of it, so I tried to talk to the ringleader and asked why he was being like that. He played innocent and apologised for any "misinterpretation" – but nothing changed. In fact, I think he just wound up his friends more and the harassment became more frequent.

'Their behaviour was getting to me so much that I dreaded going into work and slipped into a state of depression. I knew I couldn't let them win, so I finally plucked up the courage to do something about it. I started keeping notes of everything they said and did so that I had a good record. Then I made an appointment and approached my boss about it. I expected him to be unsympathetic, but actually he took my complaint very seriously. The grievance was dealt with in-house and the men received disciplinary action and were moved to different departments. It felt great that somebody was on my side and that I had stood up for myself. Since then I have been treated as an equal by my new colleagues and am happy and thriving in my role. I would advise anyone who is being discriminated against to find the courage to speak up. It's not your fault, it shouldn't be tolerated, and you can get back your life and your confidence back.'

Mainstreaming

The aim of **mainstreaming** diversity is to ensure its integration within all aspects of the organisation, rather than for it to remain as a flagship policy or mission statement. Efforts to mainstream immediately raise the question of individual behaviour at a local level and the extent to which institutional strategy is able to support the individual employees in developing diversity practices. This is particularly the case when there is a minimal central role for co-ordination and promotion of initiatives. The primary interest of the management in the business case for diversity and equality does not necessarily translate into consistent action, while the delivery of an integrated policy of mainstreaming equality and diversity requires the enthusiastic support of networks of activists for whom the career structure holds limited rewards for such participation. Mainstreaming advocates placing the responsibility on all groups as power-holders to challenge discriminatory practice and develop positive equality-based behaviours. It does not rely on those suffering the consequences of discrimination to resist and challenge the power of the organisation. In this sense it could be regarded as a development of radical equal opportunities theory, and can be used to close down support for specialist equal opportunity units, on the basis that 'integration' of equal opportunities into established organisational procedures is a superior form of delivery. From the beginning there was always a fear in European circles that mainstreaming might be welcomed by management as an excuse for throwing responsibility for equality and diversity onto the workforce itself (Rees, 1999). Allied to this is a concern that without appropriate support and resources there may be too much uncertainty to proceed beyond a basic minimalist level.

One of the concerns relating to mainstreaming as a delivery mechanism is examined by Jackson (2006), who established that equal opportunities did not fall neatly into the established structure of many organisations. Jackson noted tensions developing between devolved HR responsibility to line management and the central control perceived as a necessary security blanket against tribunal and court cases. It was difficult, given the potential risk of failing to meet legal compliance, to empower local teams to develop equality and diversity practice specific to their own particular needs. Jackson believed equality and diversity was an area of 'unpredictable boundary' (Jackson, 2006). Clifford and Royce (2007) also reveal tensions within and between the activist groups whose interests, knowledge and skills may be impressive, but who also have a very varied personal agenda which may be distant from the primary objectives of the organisation. The commitment of individuals may be conditional, constrained by the minimal financial support and also by minimal support from the organisation. Achieving strategic cultural changes within an organisation places responsibility on both senior management and all employees, and mainstreaming as a strategy attempts to co-ordinate effort on equality and diversity without localised specialist input.

The attempt to realise an approach to mainstreaming and managing diversity that was originally – and remains – constrained by the very conditional commitment of both management and staff, and the strict control of resources, remains a key theme and determinant of success. In order to successfully mainstream there must be local knowledge and understanding about the nature of equality and diversity issues, and a one-day training session or online check of knowledge will not be sufficient to sustain action at the local level. By absorbing equality and diversity into managerial structures there is a danger of reducing the impact due to limited visibility. This is a negative view of mainstreaming and Cornelius takes a more positive stance, stating that mainstreaming equality and diversity within line management was not so much about addressing the rights of diverse groups of employees but more a matter of embedding diversity to achieve greater business success (Cornelius *et al*, 2000).

Voluntary involvement and diversity champions

Organisations that utilise diversity champions are tapping into unused resources and adding skills and value to the organisation that otherwise would not be recognised (Dass and Parker, 1999). Positioning outside the mainstream hierarchical structure can inject people, ideas and diversity but may also lead to isolation and alienation. Clifford and Royce (2007) indicate that there may be a difficult choice to be made in challenging the organisation for inappropriate behaviour when seeking as an individual to further career ambitions within the same organisation being criticised. A diversity champion has to be willing to challenge the norm in order to be effective (Kirton *et al*, 2007) and may be seen as an outsider within the organisation (Lorbiecki, 2001). Using diversity champions as a method of building capacity in equality and diversity helps create a deeper understanding of problems that minorities face in that diversity champions may be from a minority themselves and provide opinions from that perspective. Lawrence (2000) argues that diversity champions will have a moral bias when arguing the business case due to their own opinions and experiences. Due to the personal interest in equality and diversity, the diversity champion will get personal satisfaction from the role. However, there is not a monetary reward, which can cause conflict because it can take time away from their day-to-day job.

SUPPORT FOR EQUALITY AND EVALUATION OF THE IMPACT OF EQUALITY INITIATIVES

Support for the development of equality and diversity strategies comes internally from the senior management team of organisations and externally from bodies such as the Equality and Human Rights Commission (EHRC). The EHRC's annual budget is £70 million, which is twice the funding of the three previous commissions together. The shift to a single commission was not unique to the UK – human rights commissions in the USA, Canada and Australia already had responsibility for all anti-discrimination issues. The EHRC was informed by a global policy trend in which multiple discrimination grounds are addressed by single equality bodies. The EHRC became functional in 2007. However, it was established 18 months earlier to enable transition from the previous commissions – the Commission for Racial Equality, the Equal Opportunities Commission and the Disability Rights Commission (Gurr, 2009). While the Commission may be better placed to manage multiple facets of discrimination or disadvantage, the counter-argument is that it may have breadth but lack depth and expertise and deliver a lower quality of service due to a lack of specialisation (Niven, 2008).

This brings us back to the debate about equality and diversity at the very beginning of this chapter. Diversity has breadth but may lose out on specialist consideration of types of difference – the same accusation is levelled at the EHRC. The EHRC is currently looking at restructure options including creating lead commissioners to support expertise and reduce criticisms of 'one size fits all'. Townsend and Wilner (2009) argued that the idea of creating a single body was met with caution by the then existing commissions, which were unconvinced about the relevance of human rights to their agenda and feared marginalisation within a body with a broader remit – diluting the intent and message (Spencer, 2008). By 2009, the EHRC was examining options for appointing commissioners to lead each of its activity areas (Townsend and Wilner, 2009). If this was to be implemented with tailored objectives for each area, it would diminish the problem of 'one size fits all'.

External support from the Commission has been somewhat fractured. Meanwhile, organisations are having to continue to progress and evaluate more carefully the outcomes from their equality and diversity initiatives. In discussing continuation funding, the 'evidence' for impact may become a point of tension within an organisation. In order to continue to receive support there must be evidence of outputs, and in an organisation where business imperatives are the driver, those outputs are also intended to link to bottom-line profitability. Discussed in terms of their 'performance', champions, volunteers and specialist equality units may be threatened by 'managerialism', which Walsh (2002) claimed has handcuffed equal opportunities within many organisations.

It could be argued that the failure to evaluate effectively becomes a natural consequence of a lack of resources applied to equality initiatives, but it remains a key concern that the effort in bringing equality and diversity projects to life may not be mirrored in monitoring both visibility and effect. The effort in equality and diversity appears still to be directed towards the launch of new policies and initiatives but the longer-term outcomes are not always evaluated. Saunderson (2002: 84) suggests that equal opportunities policies tend to be 'venerated, eulogised, then simply shelved and sidelined'.

Taking your learning further: Managing diversity

Ellis, C. (2006) 'Diverse approaches to managing diversity', *Human Resource Management*, Vol.33, No.1: 79–109. This article reviews the emerging pitfalls of new organisational diversity programmes. Three pioneering corporate programmes are examined closely, and a discussion of the purpose, the process, and the impact of these programmes is offered. Original survey data reported here suggest that exposure to diversity issues affects workplace attitudes such as motivation, job satisfaction and morale.

Golembiewski, R. T. (1995) *Managing Diversity in Organizations*. Tuscaloosa, Alabama: University of Alabama Press. An established text of immense relevance to the student and practitioner alike. The book focuses on a key issue that organisations are facing: diversity. The author identifies the many forces and factors that cause diversity – such as ethical, political, philosophical and demographic – and details historical and contemporary approaches.

Conclusion

In this chapter we have examined a wide range of issues concerning equality and diversity which affect every organisation, however large or small, within national and to some extent global contexts. Given the breadth and variety of equality and diversity perspectives and practices, the chapter has focused mainly upon gender and race/ethnicity. However, the importance of other equality areas such as disability and age must be acknowledged. Equally as important – but outside the scope of this chapter – are social class differences within the wider society which are reflected within organisations and workplaces and are expressed by means of a variety of individual and group conflict scenarios. We have specifically looked at different theories and perspectives which are brought to bear upon equality and diversity together with the extent to which equality and diversity issues are managed within organisations.

We conclude that the management of diversity in organisations is not to be left to the top-down direction of managers, but neither can it be guaranteed by the bottom-up challenge of the 'oppressed'. The 'mainstreaming' (however understood) of diversity and equality issues towards personal responsibility will be more easily achieved in a culture of support and empathy with the aims of equality and diversity. There may be difficulties in maintaining this level of responsibility if employees feel themselves to be isolated. This will depend on the particular mix of powers, supports and tensions across the hierarchies within a specific organisation, and the financial and social resources made available.

End notes

[1] See also Chapter 11.

[2] See also Chapter 2.

[3] See also Chapter 4.

[4] See also Chapters 15 and 17.

REVIEW AND DISCUSSION QUESTIONS

REVIEW QUESTIONS

1 Summarise the main perspectives concerning gender, as described early in the chapter.

2 What do you think are the main inequalities concerning gender and race/ethnicity in the organisational workplace?

3 Explain what is meant by the term 'diversity'.

4 What do you think should be the main features of an organisation's diversity policy?

5 Identify the likely organisational behaviour effects of both gender and racial harassment upon the individual concerned.

DISCUSSION QUESTIONS

1 Discuss the importance of equality and diversity within the context of organisational behaviour.

2 Which of the theoretical perspectives concerning either gender or race/ethnicity are most relevant to our understanding of gender or race/ethnic inequalities in the organisational workplace?

3 Explain what is meant by the terms 'glass ceiling' and 'sticky floor', and justify these terms within a global context.

4 How important are ethical issues with regard to equality and diversity? Justify your answer.

5 Discuss the importance of equality initiatives within the workplace.

FURTHER READING

Daniels, K. and Macdonald, L. (2005) *Equality, Diversity and Discrimination: A student text.* London: CIPD. This text is used to offer a mixture of a strong practical focus and a clear academic approach to create a balance of theory and practice, and is one of the few accessible, up-to-date and student-focused texts in the market that specifically features this subject area.

Kirton, G. and Greene, A.-M. (2004) *The Dynamics of Managing Diversity.* Oxford: Elsevier Butterworth-Heinemann. This is one of the first texts to respond to growing academic coverage of the topic of diversity management at degree level. The text considers new working practices, statistical information and equality and diversity law, as well as including case studies and information on international policies outside the UK and Europe.

Jones, J. and Clements, P. (2008) *The Diversity Training Handbook: A practical guide to understanding and changing attitudes.* London: Kogan Page. This book sensitively addresses thorny issues by providing clear guidelines for dealing with stereotyping, racism,

homophobia, sexism and disability, and is replete with practical applications.

Scott, J., Crompton, R. and Lyonette, C. (2010) *Gender Inequalities in the 21st Century: New barriers and continuing constraints.* London: Edward Elgar. This book shows there are new barriers and constraints that are slowing progress in attaining a more egalitarian society. Taking the new global economy into account, the contributors in this book examine the conflicts between different types of feminisms, revise old debates about 'equality' and 'difference' in the gendered nature of work, and propose new and innovative policy solutions.

Dipboye, R. L. and Colella, A. (2004) *Discrimination at Work: The psychological and organizational bases.* New Jersey: Psychology Press. This book brings together, in one volume, a review of the research on discrimination based on race, age, sexual orientation, gender, physical appearance, disability, and personality.

KEY SKILLS

TIME MANAGEMENT

Generally, time management refers to the development of processes and tools that increase efficiency and productivity of both managers and employees in a timely manner. Time management is therefore often thought of or presented as a set of time management skills. The theory is that once we master the time management skills, we'll be more organised, efficient, and happier. In relation to the management of equality and diversity, as with any other topic and issue within the organisational behaviour area, the following subset of skills in relation to time management are important.

- Goal-setting – What are the organisation's goals in relation to equal opportunity and diversity, and what time-scale should be adopted for implementation and periodic review?
- Planning – How timely is the organisation's planning in terms of selection, recruitment, career progression and redundancy in order to ensure fairness and non-discriminatory practice?
- Prioritising – What are the priorities for ensuring that the practice of equal opportunities and managing diversity match the policy?

DEVELOPING CRITICAL THINKING SKILLS AND REFLECTIVE LEARNING

These skills are extremely important in relation to equality and diversity. With regard to theory, the literature concerning both equality and discrimination contains many different perspectives which may be criticised and reflected upon. For example, you may wish to reflect upon the theoretical perspective which emphasises biology as the basis for gender difference. In physical terms, to be sure, there are clear differences, but is it valid to argue that because of these differences men are socially and culturally 'superior' to women? You may also wish to reflect upon the extent to which society itself reinforces difference through socialisation and gender stereotyping. With regard to race and ethnic difference, social psychological theories such as Adorno's 'authoritarian personality' and theories concerning group closure and scapegoating are of relevance.

Many of these perspectives can be used to help understand 'bad practice' in many organisations. These practices include sexual and racial harassment, overt discrimination not only in relation to gender and race but also with regard to age, religion, sexual orientation and disability. In addition, equal pay issues, promotion prospects concerning the 'glass ceiling' and 'sticky floor' can be understood in relation to established theoretical perspectives.

Finally, it is important to be critical of any organisation that espouses 'equal opportunity' in terms of policy, but where the practice is out of kilter with that policy (reality versus rhetoric).

TEAMWORKING

Teamworking is important in almost every organisational behaviour-related context.

With regard to diversity and difference, the practice of group- and teamworking necessitates the ability of team members to understand and appreciate difference in others. This should help promote respectful and mutually productive behaviour within the team. In many organisations, it is also the team leader's responsibility to ensure that any conflicts or disagreements within the group for whatever reason are quickly and efficiently resolved. Related skills include relationship-building, emotional intelligence, negotiation, co-operation, influencing, compromise and decision-making skills.

PERSONAL DEVELOPMENT PLANNING

Personal development planning or PDP means creating opportunities to think through, in a structured way, such questions as:

What do I really want to achieve from life?

What kind of person do I want to be?

Am I clear about my personal goals and ambitions?

Am I making the right decisions to get me where I really want to be?

In relation to equality and diversity, the PDP should include a commitment to non-discriminatory and non-prejudicial behaviour.

NEGOTIATING, ARBITRATION AND CONFLICT RESOLUTION SKILLS

Of importance here are negotiating and conflict resolution skills. In relation to equality and diversity, these skills should be part and parcel of every manager's portfolio. Arguably, line managers are often the key to successful conflict resolution. In the light of the widespread incidence of sexual and racial harassment in the workplace, the line manager's skills concerning negotiation and conflict resolution increase the prospects of such incidents being resolved informally at the most important and fundamental stage. Should the problem or incident remain unresolved at this stage, the affected employee may well attempt to get the problem resolved formally through procedural means, or even be tempted to turn to outside bodies like ACAS or employment tribunals (in the UK) to achieve an equitable outcome.

LEADERSHIP, COACHING AND MENTORING SKILLS

These types of skills are essential requirements for the effective management of equality and diversity and therefore involve the active participation and contribution of all managers. Leadership, coaching and mentoring skills help to sensitise both managers and employees to the often delicate issues surrounding discrimination and harassment and draw on a wide range of other related skills. For example, a manager would typically need to be emotionally intelligent, lead other team members and identify and plan their own development needs as well as of those who they review, coach or mentor, and so reflective learning and listening skills are likely to be required. They may also play a leading role in negotiations, arbitration and conflict resolution. These types of skills are usually acquired from a combination of sources, including personal experience, management development programmes and learning from the behaviours of their colleagues and their own coaches or mentors.

Chapter 13
Power in Organisations

Ed Rose

Contents

Key Learning Outcomes

By the end of this chapter you should be able to:

- define power and recognise the main characteristics of power
- identify the various bases of power and apply them to an organisational context
- evaluate the main theoretical approaches pertaining to both power and control
- explain the nature of, and the practical issues concerning, power and control within call centre workplaces
- appreciate the significance of the empowerment process
- understand the nature of organisational politics.

PRACTITIONER INSIGHT

Challenges for a public sector organisation

Liverpool City Council provides public services and political leadership for the city of Liverpool. The leader of the Council is the most senior elected member in the Council. The leader provides vision, direction and drive for the city and directs the strategic policy and budget aims of the Council. The leader is a key figure in the Council's relationship with central government and works with both public and private partners to ensure the delivery of high-quality services to the community.

After he or she has been appointed at the annual general meeting, the leader recommends for approval the names of the councillors who are to serve on the executive board and allocates their roles and responsibilities. The leader also represents the Council to the region, business and voluntary sectors and local, national and international organisations by negotiating, advising and working in partnership with them as appropriate.

The leader is appointed each year by the Council at its annual general meeting and is usually the leader of the party with the most councillors. The present leader is Councillor Warren Bradley. The leader chairs meetings of the executive board, which is responsible for the key decisions that affect the whole city, and oversees work in relation to co-ordination of the promotion and marketing of the city as a whole.

The leader has responsibility for the overall performance and conduct of the Council and for external relations. He or she works with the chief executive to ensure that elected members and officers are working effectively together to meet the Council's targets. The leader is also responsible for producing the Council's forward plan, which gives details of the likely key decisions to be taken by the executive board during the course of the next four months.

THE CHALLENGES

The challenges faced by the city of Liverpool have been shaped by the Council's vision for the city. These challenges involve power relationships at all levels of the organisation. We manage these relationships through consultation and empowerment.

OUR VISION

- Liverpool City Council is committed to working in partnership from a basis of sound financial and strategic planning to achieve a thriving international city that can compete on a world stage as a place to live, work and visit.
- To do this we will address three long-term challenges and aims, to be underpinned by ten priority themes reflecting the ambition, challenge and complexity of Liverpool. These challenges are ongoing but subject to revision as they are incrementally resolved.

CHALLENGE 1: GROW THE CITY'S ECONOMY

- Make Liverpool a first choice for investment and growth by working with the private, not-for-profit and public sectors quickly and effectively, with an emphasis on quality of infrastructure.
- Promote enterprise, trade and jobs.
- Exploit the city's wider cultural advantage to attract and retain visitors, workers and residents.

PRACTITIONER INSIGHT NEXT

CHALLENGE 2: DEVELOP OUR COMMUNITIES

- Provide sustainable communities through access to decent homes and best practice in environment management, including recycling, street cleansing and environmental enforcement against dereliction and environmental detractors.
- Challenge crime and antisocial behaviour, safeguarding young people from becoming perpetrators or victims.
- Increase people's sense of influence in decisions affecting their lives and communities through open, fair and accountable neighbourhood-driven processes.

CHALLENGE 3: EMPOWER OUR RESIDENTS

- Ensure safeguarding and inclusion of the most needy and excluded groups in the city, providing equality and real opportunity for improvement and enhanced quality of life.
- Confront barriers to employment and training through lack of access, deprivation, discrimination and poor health to increase the proportion of the city's labour force in employment.
- Develop first-rate education and training from early years to increase the skill base of our workforce and further position Liverpool as a prime destination for graduate retention.

OUR WORKERS

- Liverpool City Council values its workforce and seeks to empower them as far as is practically possible. We have a very good relationship with the main trade unions and we offer trade union representatives and employees generally the opportunity to participate in decisions affecting their work.

OUR NEW VALUES AND PRINCIPLES

- We take pride in our city and our achievements and are committed to working together for the benefit of citizens, customers and the residents of Liverpool.
- We are committed to providing the best services we can.
- We recognise diverse viewpoints and will communicate clearly and openly about our decisions and actions, including the reasons for those decisions and the outcome of any consultation.
- We will work in a manner that reflects integrity and a sense of corporate and environmental responsibility.
- We will act with respect and courtesy at all times and this will be demonstrated in our actions and our communications. We will strive to resolve issues at the earliest opportunity.
- We will promote these principles through leadership and example.

What do you consider to be the bases of power of the leader of Liverpool City Council?

Do you think that the leader of the City Council has political influence?

To what extent do you think that the concept of empowerment is applicable to this case example?

Once you have read this chapter, return to these questions and think about how you could answer them.

Introduction

Power is a crucial process within organisations and enables managers to get things done through others. However, power can be abused in many ways owing to the unequal but inevitable distribution of power relationships at all levels of the organisation. Power, if fairly distributed, may also empower employees with the responsibility and autonomy to make decisions they otherwise would not make. Power is closely related to control and is also regarded as a dynamic political process.

The chapter begins by offering some definitions of power that have stood the test of time. The chapter then goes on to identify and evaluate the different types and bases of power and how these may be applied within an organisational and workplace context. We then proceed to examine the associated notion of control from the standpoint of both management and non-management perspectives. The context of the call centre workplace is considered in relation to theoretical and experiential issues concerning power and control. The nature of **empowerment** is then examined in terms of theoretical and practical issues, and the chapter ends with a consideration of organisational politics.

DEFINITIONS AND CHARACTERISTICS OF POWER

Power, as a concept, has a long and rich academic tradition in European and American social science, evident from the early twentieth century onwards. A number of similar 'classic' definitions have been offered which are both relevant and enduring. We may consider the following:

- Power is simply *the probability that a person will act as another person wishes*. In this context, Gerth and Mills (1976) state: 'This action may rest upon fear, rational calculation of advantage, lack of energy to do otherwise, loyal devotion, indifference or a dozen other individual motives' (in Coser and Rosenberg, 1976: 149).

- For Max Weber (1947: 152), power is: 'The probability that one actor within a social relationship will be in a position to carry out his own will despite resistance'.

- Tawney (1931: 229) defines power as 'The capacity of an individual, or group of individuals, to modify the conduct of other individuals or groups in the manner in which he desires, and to prevent his conduct being modified in the manner in which he does not'.

The definitions of power given above indicate a number of significant features or characteristics which these definitions share, the more important of which are:

- Power always refers to a social relationship between at least two people, parties or 'actors' and is never an attribute of just one of them.

- The exercise of power relies ultimately upon the ability to apply negative sanctions if the other party does not comply.

- Power always involves asymmetrical relations and, in this respect, always involves inequality. This unequal relationship is based upon the inequality of resources that the parties bring to the power relationship.

- The resources that can be turned into power are many and varied. For example, they may involve control by financial means, privileged access to knowledge, through ownership of property or through control of production and distribution of services.

- The concept of power has often been confused with influence. Power implies the exercise of influence on the actions of others, but not all influence involves power, even though all power involves influence.

- One of the most common analytical mistakes is to make the assumption that power is present only if and when it is used, that it exists if it is observable in the exercise of control or the imposition of sanctions. This is called **manifest power**. However, power does not have to be observed in action. Power can be hidden, or latent. This means, for example, that company chief executives have **latent power** to close call centre operations in the UK and 'offshore' them to countries where labour is cheaper than in either the UK or the USA.

- Another mistake in the analysis of power is to equate it wholly and entirely with **authority**. When the actions of power-holders are considered legitimate by those subject to their command, power is said to have become authority. Whereas power compels, authority rests on consent. This issue is considered briefly in the following section.

POWER IN AN ORGANISATIONAL CONTEXT: AN OVERVIEW

Power is widespread, observable and elusive at the same time. Power penetrates the very fabric of human society and permeates its institutions, its politics and its social structure. Clearly, organisations of all types – whether they are business organisations, public sector and local authority organisations, military or charitable organisations – are imbued with power structures and relationships. By their very nature, most organisations are structured in such a way that power is seen to be acceptable and legitimate by the people who work in those organisations.

An organisational structure, as manifested by the organisational chart or 'organogram', may be represented by a diagram of a reporting hierarchy that is commonly used to show relationships among employees, titles and groups. An organisation's power structure is normally typified by dominance and subordination which that structure tends to legitimise. This legitimate or 'acceptable' face of power is termed 'authority', although in everyday language the terms 'power' and 'authority' are often used interchangeably. Another way of considering authority is not only as legitimate power but also as formal power. According to this interpretation, therefore, power is both formal and acceptable to all organisational participants. However, as we shall see, not all power is legitimised within 'real-world' organisations. Organisations and the people who work in them do not necessarily function according to external rules or internal norms of behaviour. For example, an employee may be bullied at work and this occurs when someone, often a manager, intimidates a subordinate.

Power is invariably associated with **control** since power can be understood in relation to control over the actions and behaviour of people such as employees with or without their consent. Within all organisations which are driven by the managerial requirements for efficiency and effectiveness in getting results, together with the need to co-ordinate activities and processes geared towards output maximisation, hierarchical control is seen as imperative. The focus here, then, is not only upon structures of control but also upon control as a process that is integral to the way most organisations operate. Control issues are considered in further detail later in this chapter.

TYPES AND BASES OF POWER IN ORGANISATIONS

There are a number of types or forms of power that manifest themselves in all organisations. Some forms of power are, however, found mainly in particular types of organisation such as prisons or the armed forces. One of the earliest and arguably the most influential contributions to the power literature is that of French and Raven (1986), who developed a framework which identifies the sources of interpersonal power that managers and others use to influence subordinates, other employees and organisational stakeholders.

French and Raven's framework

French and Raven identified five forms of power that managers may use. These are called reward, coercive, legitimate, referent and expert power. The first three (reward, coercive and legitimate) relate to an individual's position or status within the organisation and are collectively known as **position power**, whereas referent and expert power are concerned with power residing in the individual but which is independent of the position of that individual: this is known as **personal power**. French and Raven describe power relations between individuals in an organisational context and use the terms 'agent' and 'target'. The *agent* is the power-holder (usually a manager) whereas the *target* is the person (usually a subordinate) who does something that is required by the agent.

Position power consists of the following three types:

- *Reward power* – Reward power is the extent to which an agent or manager can use pay and non-pay rewards of an extrinsic or intrinsic nature (see Chapter 5). The manager believes that the target – a colleague or subordinate – has the ability to provide her or him with desired outcomes. Reward power is, however, limited to the manager's actual ability to supply the desired outcomes. For example, managers control the rewards of promotions, salary increases and bonuses in such ways that reward power is intended to result in improved performance provided that the employee sees a clear and strong link between performance and rewards. Other examples include the use of compliments, praise and enriched jobs. The effective use of reward power depends upon what is specifically being offered as a reward and how clear the link is between behaviour and reward.

- *Coercive power* – Coercive power is power that is based on a person's ability to punish another person through the application of negative sanctions, causing an unpleasant experience for the target person. The exercise of such power is often characterised by the use of force. Coercive power exists more commonly in the minority of organisations where other forms of power are considered less effective in yielding a desired outcome. Examples of these types of organisations are to be found within the armed forces and within certain corrective institutions such as prisons. Nevertheless, coercive power exists to a much lesser extent in most other organisations including business organisations where legitimate power or authority is largely exercised. Examples of coercive power can range from a manager making 'unreasonable' requests of a subordinate who may have no other choice than to comply with that request, to verbal abuse, harassment and bullying.

- *Legitimate power and formal authority* – The authority structure of an organisation is partly characterised by the formal positions or status of the power-holders and the enactment of their roles based upon the contract of employment. It is the contract of employment which spells out the rights, duties and obligations of both employer and managerial and non-managerial employees. Legitimate power is concerned with a mutually accepted perception that the power-holders (managers and supervisors) have the right to influence subordinates who in turn accept the legitimacy of their obligations to carry out routine instructions and requests. The formal authority structure confers legitimate power upon all positions of responsibility throughout an organisation from the chief executive downwards. This type of authority structure is illustrated by the example of the leader of Liverpool City Council in the Practitioner insight case study at the beginning of the chapter.

The formal authority structure of an organisation may also be synonymous with **bureaucracy**, both as reality and as a concept. The concept of bureaucracy was first proposed by Weber (1947), and although it has been criticised from various standpoints, it remains a valid analytical framework for larger organisations. The four main characteristics of bureaucracy according to Weber are:

- a well-defined division of administrative labour among persons and offices
- a personnel system with consistent patterns of recruitment and stable linear careers
- a hierarchy among offices such that the authority and status are differentially distributed among managerial and non-managerial employees, and
- formal and informal networks that connect managers and other organisational employees to one another through flows of information and patterns of co-operation.

There are two subcategories of *legitimate power*, described as process and information power. **Process power** is characterised by control over methods of production. For example, an organisation may appoint a financial auditor to examine and report back upon the efficiency of a production process. **Information power** is concerned with the extent to which managers need access to information and become dependent upon those who hold such information. In the exercise of their legitimate power, managers need to access information in order to perform their day-to-day activities. The need for information thus provides a source of power for those who hold it.

There are also two main categories of *personal power*, termed expert and referent power. Expert power exists when the agent has specialised knowledge or skills that the target needs. For this type of power to work, three conditions should be met. First, the target must trust that the expertise given is accurate. Second, the knowledge involved must be relevant and useful to the target. Third, the target's perception of the agent as an expert is crucial. Managers with specialist knowledge and non-managerial specialists may exert power and influence over others who require their specialist knowledge. Nevertheless, expert power is limited by the degree to which this expertise is irreplaceable.

Referent power is, in general, unquantifiable and elusive and is based largely upon interpersonal attraction. The agent has referent power over the target because the target identifies with or wants to be like the agent. In some cases the referent power of the agent is illusory, as typified by the 'halo effect' (or charismatic spell) that may be cast on the target by the agent, but which is effectively a perceptual error or dysfunction. An individual such as a manager who is considered to be either charismatic or a 'good role model' would be a typical way of considering the nature of referent power.

Morgan's sources of power

As a refinement of French and Raven's classification of power types and sources, Morgan (1996) identifies 14 sub-types, the most important of which are presented below.

- *Formal authority* – The most observable type of formal authority in most organisations is bureaucratic and is typically associated with the position held within the organisation and is equated with French and Raven's legitimate power. This type of authority is only effective if it is legitimised from below.

- *Control of scarce resources* – If a resource is in scarce supply and an individual is dependent on its availability, it can almost certainly be translated into power. For example, if the supply of labour required to perform skilled work is scarce and the employer urgently requires that labour, the bargaining power of those workers will be correspondingly greater than otherwise, and the price of that labour to the employer will increase.

- *Use of organisational structure, rules and regulations* – There are, of course, many rules and regulations in most organisations. A typical example of rules is those appertaining to discipline and the power that stems from the disciplinary process. Should an employee commit a disciplinary offence, such as being persistently late to work, the employee will be disciplined or 'punished' according to the disciplinary procedure of that organisation.

- *Control of decision processes* – Of importance here are the principles or premises guiding decision-making which tend to be low-profile and embedded in cultural assumptions, beliefs and practices about 'who we are' and 'the way we do things around here' (Morgan, 1996: 178) or 'custom and practice'. The decision-making process is more visible and comprises the ground rules guiding that process. However, Morgan notes that 'organisation members can manipulate and use [the process] to stack the deck in favour of or against a given action.'

- *Control of knowledge and information* – The extent to which knowledge and information is controlled within an organisation is, at least partly, dependent upon the positions held by individuals and groups. In this context Brooks (2009: 238) maintains that 'by choosing to control the timing, destination and quality of information, it is possible to define or influence the organisational agenda and create dependencies.' This is exemplified by the 'gatekeeper' role whose power extends to information control. For example, senior finance staff control the organisation's financial resources as well as defining and controlling (and possibly manipulating) information about the use of these resources. The banking crises of 2007 and 2008 have drawn attention to the extent to which the financial resources of certain banks by their senior financial managers and executives are manipulated.

- *Control of boundaries* – Boundaries represent the interface between different elements of the organisation where collaboration between these elements, functions and units within the organisation result in 'boundary transactions' and 'networking', thereby enabling individuals and groups to accumulate varying amounts of power. Astute managers may form networks of informal allies in order to pacify potential adversaries or persuade would-be collaborators. Such networks are used for information and the acquisition of power through being well informed and for accessing other sub-networks, thereby encouraging the dependency of others (Brooks, 2009).

- *Control of technology* – The extent to which and the method by which managers exert control over subordinates is a crucial factor in determining the way in which those subordinates react to such control. Managerial control over the **technology** used to produce goods and services, and, more recently, how customer services and sales employees working in call centres respond to customers within the call centre context while being subject to extensive technological surveillance, is examined in greater detail below.

- *Gender and the management of gender relations* – Gender inequalities remain commonplace within many organisations and within the wider society (see Chapter 12). The main type of gender inequality is pay-related, where the pay gap between men and women employed in many organisations is still wide. In addition, there are fewer women managers and senior employees than there are men in these positions. A great deal of research in this area suggests that there is a level beyond which women perceive they cannot advance career wise – the so-called **glass ceiling** phenomenon. Senior male managers may well thus wield more power over their female counterparts (Longhi and Platt, 2008).

Taking your learning further: Power relationships

Hardy, C. (2005) 'Understanding power: bringing about strategic change', *British Journal of Management*, Vol.17, No.1: 3–16. This article shows how a better understanding of the use of power can provide the energy to ensure strategic action by driving the organisation and its members through the strategy-making process.

Kelly, C. (2007) 'Managing the relationship between knowledge and power in organisations', *Aslib Proceedings*, Vol.59, No.2: 125–38. This paper looks at the factors that constitute a legitimate use of power in the Western organisational context of the twenty-first century, which in turn engenders the development of trust within employment relationships.

POWER AND CONTROL [1]

The association between power and control has been referred to earlier in this chapter. Control has long been regarded as an important part of the management process within organisations and was recognised as such by Henri Fayol (1949) as long ago as the early twentieth century. Control remains one of the major management functions together with forecasting, planning, organising, commanding and co-ordinating.

Child (1984) and Child and Faulkner (1998) made an influential contribution to the study of control and identify two elements of control. These are control as a process, and control as a system.

- *Control as a process* – Control within an organisation is a general process whereby 'management and other groups are able to initiate and regulate the conduct of activities so that their results accord with the goals and expectations held by those groups' (Child, 1984: 136). This is generally regarded as the main focus of managerial control in that goals, such as performance goals, are set and are expected to be achieved and maintained.

- *Control as a system* – A control system is a mechanism intended to ensure that targets are achieved and will continue to be achieved. The control system 'is aimed at ensuring that a predictable level and type of performance is attained and maintained' (Child, 1984: 136). In this context it is important to note that control is exercised not only by managers but also by other employees such as front-line workers, technical and administrative staff and professional groups. Control may also be countered by varying degrees of individual, or more commonly collective, employee 'resistance' such as resistance to change or merely resistance to the very notion of what may be perceived by employees as the excessive exercise of control on the part of managers (Thompson and McHugh, 2002).

BEST PRACTICE

Power distribution

For a business to be successful, power should be judiciously and equitably distributed in order that employees are involved in the development of the business, that communications with employees are effective, that flexible working and policies encouraging equality and diversity are in place, that realistic targets are set which reward achievement and that employee development and training policies and practices are effective. Employees are often in a position to see where improvements to working methods can be made or when market demands are changing. For example, production staff will be aware of inefficient production processes, while customer service staff will know common sources of complaints. With regard to employee development and training, More Than Insurance – a subsidiary of Royal Sun Alliance – offers its call centre staff an ongoing training programme entitled the Motor Sales Module, which comprises a range of knowledge, action and emotional labour categories, examples of which are:

- Product knowledge: 'Full knowledge of relevant products/ service range. Understanding of relevant functional procedures – eg referral process'
- Sales skills: 'Selling and call-handling skills. Full knowledge of relevant products/service range. Awareness of competitor product offerings and how they are differentiated'
- Call-handling: 'Telephone techniques, ACD knowledge, problem-solving, communication, sales awareness, objection-handling. Professional, courteous, positive, calm; resilience, empathy, enthusiasm'
- 'Customer champion': 'Selling and call-handling skills. Full knowledge of relevant products/service range. Effective written and oral communication skills. Follows through for the customer; shapes customer expectations; takes proactive action for customers; is confident in familiar situations; co-operates willingly'.

Levels of control [2]

According to Child there are two levels of control exercised within organisations. The first level concerns all those operations with which an organisation is conceivably involved with, in both national and global contexts. Within any one organisation these operations include its capital, the nature of its assets, its strategic involvement in its product and labour markets, its local, national and global communities, labour markets and relations with suppliers and government. The ability that management in particular has to exercise power within organisations derives primarily from control at this strategic level. This level of control permits management either to redeploy and extend capital investment through further ventures in times of economic upswings, or to retrench and selectively close the organisation's operations during periods of recession. Examples of the latter include the outsourcing of UK call centres in recent years and, during the recession of 2008–2011, wholesale closures of many workplaces within private manufacturing and services.

The second level of control is that of the production process within an organisation, within both private manufacturing and services and the public sector, and is concerned with how employees perform their work. Control mechanisms exist in order to facilitate the reduction of costs, increase productivity and enable rapid adaptations and responses to national and international market changes. However, there may well be a fundamental conflict of interest between managers on the one hand, who are employed to fulfil the strategic goals of the organisation, and by doing so legitimise the organisational control system, and non-managerial employees on the other, who may in certain ways resist, either actively or passively, individually or collectively, the real or perceived constraints placed upon them by, for example, regular and periodic performance appraisals. One of the most pervasive of control mechanisms is that of *technological control*, which will be considered within the call centre context.

Management control strategies

Management control is, by definition, a downward process and applies to all power- and authority-based relationships within formal and informal organisational contexts and hierarchies. The process of management control is outlined in Figure 13.1.

Figure 13.1   The process of management control

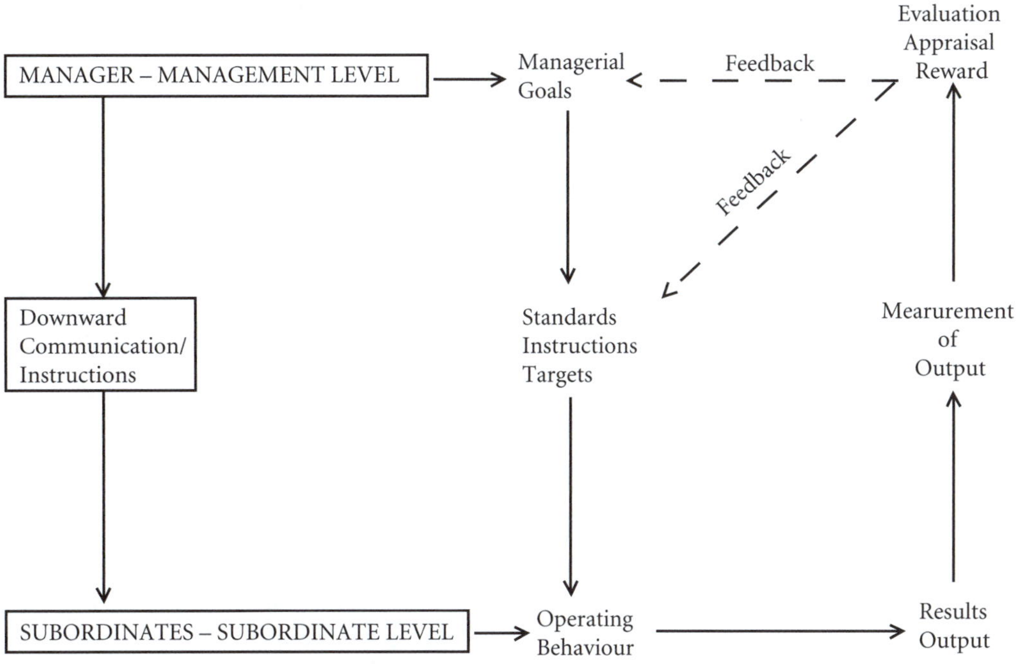

Source: adapted from Child (1984: 159)

As shown in Figure 13.1, the manager has goals for her or his subordinates which normally establish certain standards such as output targets or instructions and guidelines concerning how the work should be undertaken. The work is then done by subordinates resulting in measurable outputs, which are then evaluated and appraised at regular performance appraisal meetings at which feedback is provided. Feedback may be either positive (reward inducing) or negative (punishment inducing). Rewards may be both financial, as with the award of bonuses, and non-financial, as with mere praise, and are intended to be motivational. Punishments may comprise feedback, suggestions and guidelines for the improvement of performance. However, if performance is routinely not up to standard, the subordinate could also be disciplined. Child (1984) identifies four main strategies of control comprising personal centralised control, bureaucratic control, output control and cultural control.

● *Personal centralised control* as a strategy involves centralised decision-taking, direct supervision, personal leadership founded upon the possession of charisma or technical expertise, and reward and punishment, which reinforces conformity to personal authority. This strategy is more prevalent in smaller organisations where the owner also manages. The centralisation of decision-making and initiative around a leadership figure is a fundamental characteristic of this approach where control is exercised largely by personal supervision of work. A major criterion in allocating rewards and punishment is likely to be obedience to the leader's authority. As organisations develop and grow in terms of size and complexity, top managers will find increasing demands upon their time and this combination of factors will move management away from personal centralised control to bureaucratic control or output control.

● *Bureaucratic control* involves the breaking down of tasks into easily definable elements, formally specified methods, procedures and rules applied to the conduct of tasks, budgetary and standard cost-variance accounting controls, technology designed to limit variation in conduct of tasks, with respect to pace, sequence and possibly physical methods, routine decision-making delegated within prescribed limits, and reward and punishment systems which reinforce conformity to procedures and rules. A particular feature of this type of control includes the design of reward and punishment systems which reinforce the control strategy. Compliance can be rewarded by upgrading, improved status, favourable employment benefits and job security.

- *Output control* is concerned with jobs and units designed to be responsible for complete outputs, specification of output standards and targets, the use of 'responsibility accounting' systems, the delegation of decisions on operational matters, and rewards and punishments linked to the attainment of output targets. This strategy focuses upon the identification of tasks that have a measurable output or criterion of overall achievement. Rewards and punishments can be linked to the attainment of performance expressed in output terms, and in this way a direct incentive is created for workers to meet and exceed targets. Output control strategy is also concerned with assisting the delegation of operational decision-making, thereby obviating the need for bureaucratic controls or reliance on close supervision. Another term for output control strategy is 'managerial and technological control' (Rose and Wright, 2005), as used in the call centre context considered later in this chapter.

- *Cultural control* entails the development of strong identification with management goals, semi-autonomous working with few formal controls over work, a strong emphasis on selection, the training and development of personnel, and rewards oriented towards security of tenure and career progression. This type of control is exercised mainly by professional service organisations which are staffed by professional employees and trained specialists. The rationale of this strategy is one of maintaining control by ensuring that members of the organisation accept as legitimate, and willingly comply with, managerial requirements. Such organisations are also characterised by a strong focus upon selection and training of recruits, and the willingness of recruits to accept the mission, values and culture of the organisation.

Applying theory to practice: Management control strategies

Examples of how the theory of control may be used in practice:

Personal centralised control in a growing company

The growth of the organisation requires supervisors rather than the sole owner/manager to oversee day-to-day operations, and centralised decision-making becomes divorced from close supervision. The authority of the leader generally rests upon the rights of ownership or upon particular personal qualities such as charisma or technical expertise.

Bureaucratic control in a large organisation

Bureaucratic control predominates in both public sector and large private sector organisations. The rationale for this type of control is the attempt to ensure predictability by specifying how workers should behave and carry out their work. Formalisation in the sense of written definitions of jobs and procedures is the most characteristic feature of bureaucratic control.

Output control

Examples of measurable output include the number of calls taken or received in call centres, assembly- or sub-assembly-line production and an end product. Once outputs or criteria for overall achievement have been identified, it is possible for management to specify output standards or targets.

Cultural control

An example of an organisation in which cultural control is applied is one that is staffed mainly by professionals, such as a legal services firm, whose members will demonstrate high levels of commitment to their professional association, in this case the Law Society. Members, by dint of their legal skills, may be granted considerable degrees of flexibility in determining their responsibilities.

The characteristics of an effective control system

Traditional organisational behaviour texts such as Luthans (2006) and Hicks and Gullett (1977) identify a number of enduring characteristics which define an effective control system. It is important to note that control systems have both positive and negative outcomes, and that an effective control system will tend to minimise the negative aspects of such a system. Mullins (2006), following Luthans and Hicks and Gullett, identifies six important characteristics of an effective control system.

- *Understanding* – A meaningful control system 'is one that can be understood by those that are involved in its operation' (Mullins, 2006: 430). This involves a positive relationship between the control system and the activities and technical expertise of employees. Measurable outcomes such as performance outcomes should be unambiguous and clearly recognised.

- *Conformity* – Controls should 'conform to the structure of the organisation and be related to decision centres responsible for performance' (Mullins, 2006: 430). In order to achieve this, managers need to have all relevant information in relation to their functional activities in order that they can control more effectively the range and depth of their responsibility.

- *Minimisation of deviations* – This concerns deviations from required standards of performance. Minor deviations may be permissible as long as they are seen to be atypical. However, corrective measures should be in place in order to minimise them.

- *Critical activities important to the success of the organisation* – The control system should flag up important activities crucial to success. On the other hand, the control system should not necessarily be all-inclusive and include unimportant or trivial activities that may be unnecessarily time-consuming and uneconomic in their execution. For example, a manager of a retail store has to have information with regard to stock levels, stock placement and the amount and different types of goods sold.

- *Flexibility* – An effective control system should be flexible and 'must yield information which is not influenced by changes in other factors unconnected to the purpose of the control system' (Mullins, 2006: 431). For example, if new technology is introduced which enables improved computer surveillance of employee activities, the control system should be flexible enough to respond by reducing the number of supervisors.

- *Consistency* – An effective control system should be 'consistent with the objective of the activity to which it relates' (Mullins, 2006: 431). This means that the organisation's control system should not only be able to detect deviations from the planned standards of performance, but also provide indicators for improvement. For example, within the local authority context, it is important that all departments – such as housing – monitor spending to ensure that spending budgets are maintained and to ensure that financial and other resources are directed towards housing in priority areas such as maintenance of the housing stock. It is the responsibility of management to identify and determine the form of corrective action needed in order to tackle and solve any problems arising from spending allocations to priority areas.

Control as divisive [3]

Hill's (1981) account of control and subordination within the employment relationship concerning managerial and non-managerial staff remains one of the most comprehensive analyses of the control concept in relation to the work situation. Citing Wright (1976), Hill identifies three dimensions on which the exclusion of labour from control is meaningful. The *first dimension* relates to the fact of economic ownership within modern globalised capitalism and is concerned with the direction of investments and resource allocation. Within the call centre industry, for example, companies tend to direct investment in their call centres to areas of relatively high unemployment, where labour is cheap, interchangeable and controllable. Other factors such as 'regional accent' play a secondary role. More recently, global resource allocation in the call centre industry has led to the phenomenon of offshoring, which involves the transfer of human and capital resources to the Far East, and most notably India, where labour is even cheaper and control over labour is, if anything, even tighter than within the UK context.

A *second dimension* of control over labour power, according to Hill, is achieved by managerial control exercised through the hierarchy of supervision over those who are directly and indirectly involved in the production of goods and services. This dimension of control concerns the 'appropriation of command' of the physical apparatus of production, 'whereby employees are deprived of their autonomy in the immediate activity of production and of control over the instruments of production' (Hill, 1981: 11). In practice, this is achieved by increased division of labour, by new technology which may deskill and/or replace labour, and by the supplanting of traditional supervision methods – for example, by electronic surveillance within the call centre context.

A *third dimension* and characteristic of control, as a corollary of appropriation by management, is a certain 'dehumanisation' of work and feelings of alienation that stem from it (Blauner, 1964). The antithesis of managerial control in all its guises is 'worker control', where employees collectively own the means of production. However, since outright worker control is a fanciful notion within a capitalist society, and recognising the power imbalance between employees and employers/managers, the control terrain, it may be argued, is permanently in the hands of the employer and, by proxy, management. This is not to deny that there are forms of worker influence over management decision-making in existence, such as the 'partnership' system within the John Lewis retail group. There are, in addition, mitigating factors which may ameliorate the nature and extent of the exercise of managerial control over employees which include human resource management interventions (see Chapter 17), skill levels, organisational design characteristics, local and national labour market factors and the extent to which there is scope for individual and collective negotiation concerning the 'frontier' of control.

However, none of these three dimensions identified above points to the development of a 'neutral' organisational control system whereby objectives are shared and there are no conflicts of interests and where 'control becomes in principle only a matter of co-ordinating different people's contributions and adjusting these in the light of progress achieved and/or changing circumstances' (Child, 1984: 139). Under these conditions, control can be regarded as a technical matter in which an exercise of power is not necessarily involved in certain types of organisation such as a workers' co-operative. The so-called 'optimistic vision' (Frenkel *et al*, 1999) whereby management control relations have been supplanted by strong ties among work colleagues, which while questionably characteristic of **post-bureaucratic** organisation is emphatically untypical of customer service operations, including call centres, within an essentially bureaucratically structured organisation.

Following on from this, a significant assumption in analysing control in most organisations is that control is much more than just a technical matter. The control process embodying management control strategies and practices engenders varying degrees of conflict, consensus and resistance, as Child (1984: 138) suggests:

> There is a conflict of interests inherent in the employment contract which, if it remains at the forefront of employees' minds, will tend to sustain an active and probably collectively organised resistance to managerial control. Such resistance will appear to those engaged in it to offer the best hope of protecting their interests in terms of, for example, the balance between effort required and payment offered. . . Competitive pressures [may] oblige managers to exercise more stringent control in an attempt to reduce costs, increase productivity and respond more swiftly to market changes, and may heighten employee resistance even to the point where the continued viability of the whole productive unit is at risk.

POWER AND CONTROL: THE EXAMPLE OF THE GLOBAL CALL CENTRE

The call centre is a relatively recent phenomenon which has changed the complexion of the British, American, and indeed the global workplace. The growth and application of telecommunications and computerised systems in the field of customer services, sales and information has been nothing short of spectacular during the past 15 years, and in 2009 employed 374,000 people nationwide, made up of front-line centre agents and operators comprising 87,000 staff and customer care occupations comprising 287,000 staff (Datamonitor, 2009). With regard to future growth, Datamonitor forecasts growth to well over 500,000 agent positions by the end of 2010 and an increase in employment of 3.5% between 2008 and 2013 (Datamonitor, 2009). Areas in which call centres are expected to grow are local government and the outsourcing sector. Call centres (or contact centres, as they are also known) integrate computer and telephone technology, designed to provide clients with fast and accurate services, and also to monitor, tape-record and measure staff performance. Centres are turning increasingly to 24-hour, seven-day operations as they compete with each other for customers and customer loyalty. Call centres are the consequence of companies across a whole range of services (banking, insurance and other financial services are probably the most visible) focusing more sharply on the needs of individual customers. In order to gain a competitive edge, and in order to offer this level of 'individual' service, the call centre was created to centralise all customer activities.

Most call centres with operations in the UK are located outside London and the south-east. The supply of greenfield sites, coupled with regional grants and lower wages, make migration of large 'tele' operations like British Airways ticket sales and London Electricity enquiries inevitable. Regional accents are also important – studies show that the UK public perceives the Scottish accent to convey reliability, whereas other accents such as the 'Brummie' (Birmingham) twang may hint at criminal tendencies (Fernie and Metcalfe, 1998).

Call centres are far from uniform and have many differentiating features, which are summarised in Table 13.1. The majority of call centres deal with incoming calls. The employee or agent answers a call that is automatically directed or routed to him or her (calls are 'force-fed' so that the agent has no control over whether or not to answer a call, and as soon as one call is dealt with, another is put through) and any relevant information required is computer-processed. All time is monitored – whether the agent is actually dealing with calls, in between calls, or unavailable for whatever reason. The technology that makes this possible is called 'automatic call distribution' (ACD). The new technology behind the centres enables management to wring every last ounce of productivity out of the workforce. Not a moment is wasted. For outward calls the computer does all the dialling and can detect and automatically drop calls if there is no reply. Sophisticated 'predictive software' allows computer-generated judgements concerning the length of the average call and calculates how many calls it needs to make in order to provide potential customers for the available workforce. Calls, whether outbound or inbound, are completely scripted; the computer prompts the operator through a series of questions to ask a customer. Supervisors can listen in at any time to check whether an employee – who will be expected to deal with several hundred clients a day – is adopting the correct (cheerful) tone and displaying enthusiasm for the job, sometimes referred to as 'emotional labour' (Hochschild, 1983).

Table 13.1:   Differentiating features of call centres

Type of call centre	Description
In-house	Part of a larger organisation and handles calls for that organisation only.
Outsourced	Usually a company in its own right, which handles work from a variety of clients. An increasing number of UK companies outsource their work to companies in India and other countries.
Type of work	Inbound (receive) or outbound (solicit) call-handling or a combination of the two.
Degree of service	Embraces single function (outbound sales soliciting) or multiple functions such as sales, service, enquiries and technical matters.
Unionisation	Smaller call centres which are often outsourced are more likely to be union-free.
Size	Call centres vary in size from very small with ten or so handlers to very large with hundreds of handlers, depending upon nature of the business and volume of work.
Type of employment	Non-standard employment is common in call centres, which may employ predominantly agency workers (common in outsourced call centres) who may also be part-time. Many call centres employ a mix of permanent and temporary full-time and part-time handlers.

The monitoring of behaviour and measurement of output, according to some research, at least equals if not exceeds the worst supervisory excesses of the traditional assembly line. Fernie and Metcalfe (1998: 7) describe the control process in the following terms:

> The tyranny of the assembly line is but a Sunday school picnic compared with the control that management can exercise in computer telephony. Indeed, the advertising brochure for a popular call centre is titled *Total Control Made Easy*. Critics refer to them as new sweatshops and battery farms. Agents' activities are monitored in real time by the supervisor. Real-time screens display status information such as the number of existing calls in queue, how long the oldest call has been waiting, how many agents are on calls and how many are logged out or unavailable.

Fernie and Metcalfe use the analogy of Bentham's **Panopticon**, which Foucault (1979: 53) adopts as a metaphor for the emergent workplace and which describes the sort of supervisory power and control process within workplaces that is evident in call centres:

> All that is needed, then, is to place a supervisor in a central tower and to shut up in each cell . . . a worker. They are like so many cages, so many small theatres, in which each actor is alone, perfectly individualised and constantly visible . . . Visibility is a trap. . . Each individual is securely confined to a cell from which he is seen from the front by the supervisor, but the side walls prevent him from coming into contact with his companions. He is seen but does not see; he is the object of information, never a subject in communication . . . This invisibility is the guarantee of order . . . There are no disorders, no theft, no coalitions, none of those distractions that slow down the rate of work, make it less perfect . . . Power should be visible and unverifiable.

The research by Fernie and Metcalf (1998) and others such as Baldry *et al* (1998) provides support for the '**sweatshop**' **view** of call centres as being a contemporary version of the nineteenth-century sweatshop or those dark satanic mills or some sort of Orwellian construct. Most of these contributions adopt the Foucault perspective, emphasising the disciplinary implications of call centre work and the subservience of employees to the 'electronic panopticon'. Taylor and Bain (2007) provide another description of this type of work:

> For many employed in the sector, the daily experience is patently of repetitive, intensive and frequently stressful work, based on Taylorist principles, which can result in employee 'burnout'. These pressures are exacerbated through the performance of 'emotional labour'. Individual employee performance is measured and monitored to an unprecedented degree by means of electronic surveillance, augmented by more traditional supervisory methods.

The negative effects of call centre work may be greater for some types of worker than others and be more evident in some types of work situation than others (Deery *et al*, 2004). It is important to note, however, that not all researchers share the pessimistic views of those cited above espousing what we may label the sweatshop view. An alternative perspective suggests that the relationship between call centre staff and the customer means that the employer is highly dependent on the social skills and emotional labour of staff to ensure that customers are treated well. This implies that the employment relationship has to be managed with care (Frenkel *et al*, 1998, 1999; Rose and Wright, 2005), and that management need to balance the requirements of productivity and performance with a concern for customer satisfaction, focusing upon the quality of interaction between staff and customer. To that end, employers may well utilise the rhetoric, if not the application, of human resource management (HRM) policies in order to emphasise employee commitment and initiative through, for example, 'empowerment' techniques (Rose and Wright, 2005). This alternative perspective therefore emphasises a more positive image of call centre work, which embraces the idea of a semi-professional, empowered worker who uses information technology as an opportunity to tailor services to the client while simultaneously using and developing their own skills, and which arises as a consequence of management wanting to customise the product or service to the requirements of the customer.

Frenkel *et al* (1998, 1999) suggest that this approach thus contains elements associated with professional identity and knowledge of what the customer needs, and this has to be reconciled with standardised and bureaucratically imposed performance and productivity criteria. The type of organisational model Frenkel *et al* (1999) advocate under these circumstances is called 'mass customised bureaucracy'.

Control in call centres: the application of Child's criteria [4]

Within a call centre context, control is both multidimensional and heterogeneous. The matters to be controlled range from tangible items, such as the number of calls made and call waiting times, to the less tangible and more subjective, such as the quality of CSR-customer interaction. Child (1984) identifies two major structural criteria of control which may be transposed to the call centre workplace, both of which are related and complementary. The first criterion concerns the centralisation-delegation field. Call centres are relatively horizontally structured and there are, in fact, comparatively few levels of management and modest scope for delegation of responsibility either within the management structure or between management and team leader. In effect, the team leader has little effective responsibility for team members. Indeed, centralised authority and control are vested in the technologically based call centre architecture.

The second criterion of control revolves around the formalisation-informality continuum. In many respects, extreme formality prevails in the form of Taylorism (measurement), targets and written-down quantifiable components and targets associated with the employment relationship. These include a variety of formalised controls such as call centre employee recruitment, selection, training and regular appraisal meetings, the latter of which may be used punitively, as a method of discipline (Callaghan and Thompson, 2001). Control as formalisation, also known as bureaucratic control, is, according to Edwards (1979), rooted in the social and hierarchical structure of the organisation rather than in the personal authority of the manager, and offers management a means of 're-dividing the workforce and tying it to impersonal rules and regulations' (Thompson and McHugh, 2002: 106).

On the other hand, there is a veneer of informality that resides in the team and team leader. The team leader represents the human face of call centre authoritarian power or '**hegemonic despotism**' (Burawoy, 1979), who may 'cheer as well as chivvy but ultimately judges performance' (Rose, 2002: 45). A further control criterion explored by Child is that of the degree of supervisory emphasis. In order to supervise closely, the traditional factory or office required relatively narrow **spans of control**, the purpose of which was similar to formalisation in that it imposed checks or limits on the discretion that subordinates can use. The extent to which this dimension of control is relevant within the call centre environment is, however, questionable, given the mediation of the customer within the standard manager/supervisor-employee relationship, the insinuation of the notion of employee commitment as a form of internalised control that does not rely upon observing rules or upon external rewards and sanctions, and the prevalence of electronic surveillance and other technical controls obviating the need for close supervision in the traditional sense (Russell, 2008). Table 13.2 describes the main characteristics and elements of control and power in the globalised call centre workplace.

The main elements of the model described in Table 13.2 include both horizontal (team) and vertical (management) dimensions. The horizontal dimension of the model is highly prescriptive and describes a desired situation which does not and arguably cannot exist in its pure form within call centre workplaces barring a major culture change, and as such, requires equally elusively high levels of employee commitment to peers and organisation. The vertical dimension describes panoptic control systems more typical of many service and sales call centres. Each of the characteristics common to both dimensions (locus of work task analysis, direction of work tasks, evaluation of work done, mode of sanction and reward, and form of surveillance and its disciplinary role) is equated with one of Edward's/Child's three control categories. The workflows relevant to call centres and customer service/sales work are the **service and sales**

Table 13.2:   A call centre control model

Vertical (top downwards): info-normative and output-procedural	
Control characteristics	*Type of control*
Nature of work task analysis Individual, tending to team. Managers establish initial team norms on the basis of average human and productive capacities; must ensure minimum level of conformance with respect to attaining these managerially defined norms.	*Personal* In most instances. Often but not always centralised, involving direct supervision based on technical expertise with reward and punishment reinforcing conformity to personal authority.
Direction of work tasks Mainly standardised and formalised. The times needed to perform standardised and formalised work tasks are aggregated and expressed in both team and individual forms. To some limited and variable extent, individuals may experiment to establish their own ways of working within their team.	*Bureaucratic* In the majority of instances and involves breaking down of tasks into easily definable elements; formally specified methods, procedures and rules applied to the conduct of tasks; reward and punishment systems to reinforce conformity to procedures and rules.
Evaluation of work done Rational and individual. Evaluation of performance undertaken on an individual and rational basis through work monitoring embedded in the technological infrastructure and architecture of the call centre. Performance information widely publicised within and between teams often via public display.	*Technological* Whereby the use of technology is designed to limit variation in the conduct of tasks, with respect to pace, sequence and physical methods such as telephonic skills. Widespread use of monitoring equipment facilitates control from afar.
Mode of sanction and reward Superior to subordinate. The output of work monitoring identifies both 'good' and 'poor' performers. Managers can then act accordingly to sanction poor performers or undertake remedial interventions such as re-training and dismissal.	*Personal* Via performance and appraisal interviews and assessments on a regular basis involving line manager but not normally the team leader.
Form of surveillance and its disciplinary role Panoptic (obedience). Surveillance incorporated into the technology of production; provides a high degree of transparency; instils a high degree of self-discipline in relation to the achievement of minimum targets. Customer/CSR (service and sales) output surveillance.	*Technological and bureaucratic* Controls to enforce discipline and standardised performance output. Emotional labour used as a control mechanism also incorporated into training activities used to develop social skills.
Horizontal/lateral relations within teams: socio-normative	
Control characteristics	*Type of control*
Nature of work task analysis Team – individual. Team should go beyond minimum expectations and optimise its performance around the best performer.	*Personal* In that the team leader, who 'motivates' the team as a whole and encourages better team performance by understanding reasons why better performers outperform their peers.
Direction of work tasks Within the team, details of individual performance that exceeds the minimum levels are identified and rationalised so that they become the new norm for the whole team.	*Personal* As this requires the consensus of the team whereby the team normalises its performance around better workers. Desirable but unrealistic.
Mode of sanction and reward The team develops formal and informal means of sanctioning and rewarding its members' behaviour.	*Personal* In practice can only be limited to 'prizes', awards and bonuses which supplement basic pay.
Form of surveillance and its disciplinary role Team members conduct intense surveillance of each other's activities; instils a high degree of self-discipline making team members strive to improve their own performance at norms set near the level of the most able; other forms of peer group pressure brought to bear on those seen to be letting the team down.	*Personal* Unrealistic within a call centre context where peer surveillance would require a major restructuring of work activities and a major culture change.

Source: based on Rose (2009: 56)

workflow identified as two of three ideal typical workflows within an information society by Frenkel *et al* (1999). In this respect Frenkel *et al* identify three forms of control, each of which is associated with a particular workflow. The first form of control is the **info-normative**, which is characteristic of service workflows and in which IT-generated information forms the basis for control. The normative element is provided by facilitative and supportive supervision on the part of team leaders. **Output-procedural control** is typical of sales workflows, where 'output measurement based on customer decisions (to apply and qualify for loans, for example) is complemented mainly by enforcement of company procedures' (Frenkel *et al*, 1999: 81). Finally, **socio-normative** control exists in the relatively highly skilled contexts of knowledge workflows, exceptional in call centre work environments, where management and peers (or co-workers) influence the work process simultaneously and where peer or co-worker influence is expected to be the main characteristic of socio-normative control.

EMPOWERMENT

In recent years there has been a steady increase in interest in empowerment as an academic concept and a practical management strategy and device. Empowerment is both a process and a management tool and is seen as encouraging and facilitating employee motivation. In essence, empowerment may be defined as the granting of greater autonomy, freedom and self-control over individuals' work, and providing individuals with increased responsibility for decision-making in order to perform their jobs and job-related tasks more efficiently. Empowerment is also concerned with the political process of sharing power within an organisation in such a way that individuals learn to believe in their ability to do the job. The central idea of empowerment is that individuals closest to the work and to customers should make the decisions, and this makes the best use of employees' skills and talents and enhances their self-efficacy or self-worth and effectiveness. Empowerment can be considered to be effective not only with regard to managers and other employees but also with regard to customers and clients. The example of Liverpool City Council (at the beginning of the chapter) also includes an 'empowerment challenge' which targets residents and, in particular, needy and excluded groups.

Two contrasting views concerning empowerment

The literature dealing with employee empowerment points to a diversity of academic and practitioner perspectives which fall into two broad camps comprising the critical (or cynical) camp and the prescriptive or managerial camp. On the one hand, according to a critical perspective, empowerment is regarded as nothing less than a tool which assists in the control and manipulation of employees. This is a valid, if rather cynical, perspective and suggests that there is very little actual power or control vested in non-managerial employees who management may regard as being empowered. From this standpoint it could be argued that there is no real 'power' afforded to employees, outside the narrow scope of task-related decisions aimed at satisfying external customer needs quickly without having to refer to management. Wilkinson (1998: 49), for example, asserts that 'management have defined the redistribution of power in very narrow terms … strictly within an agenda set by management…' A further critical viewpoint is that empowerment schemes which are occasionally the result of an organisational restructuring involving a reduction of hierarchical levels within it, add a further burden of responsibility on employees without increasing their remuneration or enhancing their status and that empowerment therefore 'becomes a euphemism for work intensification' (Hyman and Mason, 1995: 387).

The view that empowerment is chimerical or illusory is further reinforced by Hollinshead *et al* (2003) and Rose (2008). Hollinshead *et al* (2002: 324), for example, point out that 'developments in the late 1980s and 1990s suggest that the process [of empowerment] only appears to give employees greater control and in reality remains dominated and restricted by management.' That empowerment is allegedly illusory is also reinforced by Argyris (2006) and Hales and Kildas (1998: 93). The latter state that:

the overwhelming impression to be gained from the literature is that empowerment entails some additional employee 'choice' at the margins of their jobs, rather than any substantial increase in employee voice.

The prescriptive or managerial argument stresses that empowerment is an essential factor which assists in the achievement and maximisation of individual and organisational potential. For example Goldsmith *et al* (2002: 145) suggest that

> it is predominantly about encouraging front-line staff to solve customer problems on the spot, without constant recourse to management approval.

Whereas Bowen and Lawler (1992), cited in Lashley (2001: 334), take the view that it is about 'management strategies for sharing decision-making power'. Empowerment occurs at both individual and group levels (Conger and Pearce, 2009). At individual level empowerment is experienced when followers engage in effective self-leadership, where self-leadership is defined as 'a process through which people influence themselves to achieve the self-direction and self-motivation needed to perform' (Houghton *et al*, 2003: 126). According to Conger and Pearce (2009), empirical studies of empowerment in practice suggest that it has a powerful and positive influence upon individuals. At group level, empowerment is experienced when the group effectively practices shared leadership, which is defined (Pearce and Conger, 2003) as:

> a dynamic, interactive influence process among individuals in groups for which the objective is to lead one another to the achievement of group or organisational goals or both.

Empowerment in practice: success criteria and obstacles

Following the framework of Spreitzer (1995), the empowerment process comprises the four dimensions and requisites of meaning, competence, self-determination and impact.

- *Meaning* – This relates to an employee's values and beliefs and the extent to which they are congruent with the employee's work role and those of the organisation. This engenders a positive outlook in the employee which is necessary if the empowerment process is to be successful.

- *Competence* – This encapsulates the belief in the ability to do the job competently. The absence of this belief means that the employee is likely to feel inadequate and hence lack a sense of empowerment.

- *Self-determination* – This is concerned with the employee having control over the way the work is done. The absence of self-determination implies an absence of empowerment.

- *Impact* – This is the belief held by an employee that her or his job is making a positive difference within the organisation. Without the sense of contributing towards an organisational goal, employees are unlikely to feel empowered.

WORST PRACTICE

Disempowerment

Here we are not concerned with the abuse of power but rather with managerial incompetence in the use of power and resources thus adversely affecting all employees. To achieve bad practice, all you need to do is to minimise the effect and contribution of the workforce. This was the case within one French car components company, Distelle, which went bust in 2006. Among the things it was doing wrong were:

- limiting the information the company gave out. This is particularly potent. If employees do not know what is going on, how can they become involved?

- asking for suggestions, and then ignoring them

- promising things but not delivering them. The company promised a reward for suggestions, but then ensured that the rewards were not delivered. The company also undertook to provide feedback – which was not forthcoming.

Employees need to experience positively all four of the empowerment dimensions in order to feel truly empowered, thereby enabling organisations to reap the benefits from empowerment efforts in terms of increased employee effectiveness, higher job satisfaction and less stress at work.

There are a number of obstacles to overcome in order to put empowerment principles into practice. Conger and Pearce (2009) suggest the following guidelines for managers and leaders:

- *Confidence and positive expectations* – Managers should express confidence in employees and set high performance expectations because there is a clear link between positive expectations and effective performance.

- *Opportunities to participate in decision-making* – Participation in decision-making is concerned with the extent to which employees can influence managerial decisions affecting employees' work and other matters of concern to employees. This means that any effort to consult with employees should ensure that employees have a say and a vote in order to influence the final decision. Participation allows employees to have ownership of the decisions which affect them. This in turn will increase levels of responsibility amongst employees.

- *Autonomy* – Allowing employees greater autonomy to manage themselves often brings beneficial results. In many instances, employees tend to be held back or stifled by bureaucratic rules and processes which prevent greater autonomy or self-management both at individual and team levels. For example, a debt collection agency had a rule whereby a manager's signature was required to approve deferred payments arrangements for defaulting customers. This had the effect of making front-line workers feel powerless. When the rule was dropped, front-line workers felt empowered and collections increased.

- *Inspirational and meaningful goals* – When managers set inspirational or meaningful goals for individuals and groups, the greater is the likelihood that individuals and groups 'own' the goals and take personal responsibility for them.

Taking your learning further: Dimensions of empowerment

Wilkinson, A. (1998) 'Empowerment: theory and practice', *Personnel Review*, Vol.27, No.1: 40–56. This article examines significant problems with much of the prescriptive literature on empowerment, in that there is little detailed discussion of the problems employers may experience implementing empowerment or the conditions which are necessary for such an approach to be successful. It is assumed that employees will simply welcome the new way of working.

Rose, E. and Wright, G. (2005) 'Satisfaction and dimensions of control among call centre customer service representatives', *International Journal of Human Resource Management*, Vol.16, No.1: 136–60. This article looks at the dimensions of control in call centres in relation to satisfaction.

ORGANISATIONAL POLITICS [5]

As we have seen, power and authority is not evenly distributed among individuals and teams in organisations. This means that there is a power imbalance which is legitimised by the authority structure of the organisation. Organisational politics are absolutely central to a great deal of what normally goes on in organisations. The term 'politics' often conjures up images of shady deals, behind-the-scenes 'plotting' as portrayed by Machiavelli as long ago as the sixteenth century in his classic work *The Prince*. The Machiavellian view of politics is most certainly a valid one, but one that is often regarded in negative terms. For a more positive interpretation of organisational politics, it is necessary to identify two relevant definitions.

Definition 1

Organisational politics is the art of using influence, authority and power to achieve goals and, according to Pfeffer (1994: 7):

comprises activities taken within organisations to acquire, develop and use power and other resources to obtain one's preferred outcomes in a situation in which there is uncertainty or disagreement about choices.

Mayes and Allen (1977) adopt a similar definition whereby political behaviour refers to actions not officially sanctioned by the organisation that are taken to influence others in order to meet one's personal goals which may or may not correspond to team or organisational goals.

Definition 2

Organisational politics are fundamentally concerned with the management of meaning (Pettigrew, 2002). As Clegg *et al* (2008: 264) point out:

> Actors in these political relations seek to legitimate the ideas, values and demands that they seek to espouse while simultaneously denying or decrying those that they seek to oppose. Thus power is ultimately deployed in games of organisational symbolism. It is wrapped up in the myths, beliefs, language and legend – the stuff of organisational culture.

Power and influence tactics

As the first definition suggests, political power is inextricably associated with influence, which is the process of manipulating the thoughts, behaviour and feelings of another person. That other person could be the line manager (upward influence) or subordinate (downward influence) or colleague/fellow co-worker. As a refinement to Definition 1, influence involves three actors: the manager or boss (upward influence), the employee or subordinate (downward influence) and the team or co-worker (lateral influence). Research has indicated that the most frequently used tactics are consultation, rational persuasion, inspirational appeals and ingratiation. Upward appeals and coalition tactics are used less frequently and exchange tactics are rarely used (Yukl and Falbe, 1992). Influence tactics are adopted by individuals in order to control others' impression of them – this tactic is commonly associated with 'impression management'. Examples of this tactic include gaining influence by image-building and attempts to gain support for important initiatives and projects. Ingratiation is a crucial tactic and can take many forms including flattery, conforming to prevailing opinions and adopting subservient behaviour. Exchange as an influence tactic is mainly concerned with providing favours in order to create a favourable impression. For example, attempts to influence subordinates often involve assigning tasks or changing behaviour, and with co-workers the objective usually comprises requests for assistance. With superiors, influence attempts are often made to seek approval, resources, political support or personal advantage. Rational persuasion and coalition tactics are used most often to get support from peers or co-workers and superiors in order to change departmental or company policy. Consultation and inspirational appeals are particularly effective in order to gain support and resources for a new project. Overall, the most effective tactic with regard to achieving objectives is rational persuasion. Pressure is the least effective tactic (French *et al*, 2009).

The effectiveness of influence tactics therefore depends upon the person who is to be influenced and the extent to which the influence attempt is successful. The various tactics used for different people in varying situations and circumstances as previously identified are summarised in Table 13.3, and how some of these tactics can be put into practice is outlined in the box below.

Table 13.3:   Power and influence tactics in organisations

Influence tactic	Description	Outcome
Rational persuasion	Use of logical argument and evidence to emphasise potential benefits to the organisation. Expert, information and referent power enhance the effectiveness of rational persuasion.	Works when there are shared rather than incompatible objectives. Technological, administrative and management change are possible outcomes.
Apprising	Use of information and logic to emphasise the benefits of a request or proposal made by superior to subordinate.	Will further career prospects, improve skills and facilitate the performance of the job-holder.
Inspirational appeals	Attempt to encourage enthusiasm and commitment on the part of employees by linking a request to the employees' needs, hopes, values and ideals.	For example, employees asked to work longer hours on a special project producing large quantities of influenza vaccine in order to save many lives.
Consultation	Increasing an employee's commitment in carrying out a request by involving and consulting the employee as to how the task should be undertaken.	This is a form of negotiation, the aim of which is to produce a 'win-win' situation which benefits both parties.
Exchange tactics	This could take the form of an offer to the employee to reward the employee if she/he does what is requested. Associated with reward power.	Pay increase, promotion, help and information, providing political support, 'putting in a good word'.
Collaboration	Resources or help offered if a request or proposal is carried out. A joint effort to achieve the same objective.	Provision of equipment or technical advice to achieve a goal.
Personal appeals	Carrying out a favour based on friendship or loyalty. Example of referent power.	Varied.
Ingratiation tactics	Making employee feel accepted and appreciated by giving out compliments, being friendly and helpful and showing respect before making a request.	Can strengthen friendship and make the target person more willing to consider a request.
Pressure tactics	The use of threats, warnings, demands, repeated requests and frequent checking to ensure that the employee has complied with a request. Sometimes associated with coercive power.	May undermine working relationships and can therefore be counterproductive.
Coalition tactics	An indirect influence tactic whereby the assistance of others (coalition partners) is sought in order to influence a person. Normally used in combination with other influence tactics.	Depending upon the other direct influence tactics used in combination with coalition tactics, the outcome(s) will vary.

Applying theory to practice: Influence tactics

Indispensability – Valued contributions provided by a person with specific skills increase indispensability and influence. For example, a computer programmer who is the only person who knows computer passwords and has the technical expertise to deal with crashed computers is highly indispensable.

Non-substitutability – This is closely related to indispensability, and means that if an employee is the only one perceived to be capable of bringing a quality or skill to the organisation, that employee is non-substitutable. For example, the process of 'headhunting' potential chief executives assumes that the person being headhunted is non-substitutable and that she or he will be politically influential.

Centrality – Centrality refers to how much of an employee's work and contributions is part of the core values of the organisation.

Thus, the greater the degree of centrality, the greater is a person's political influence.

Association with powerful managers – Association with top managers who have greater power and influence may increase the power of associated employees and other personnel.

Building and managing coalitions – A coalition is a group of people who join together to try to influence a decision. Coalitions are formed when no one person is powerful enough to achieve her or his goals single-handedly.

Influencing decision-making and controlling the agenda – By influencing decisions, the direction of the organisation may be changed. Agendas shape decisions and by controlling the agenda, a manager exerts control even before decisions are formulated.

Conclusion

Power is an essential organisational characteristic and there are many theoretical perspectives and practical ramifications concerning the exercise of power. Control is closely associated with power and managers use control systems in order to facilitate and optimise employee efficiency and output. Empowerment is an example of the distribution of power and authority through delegation. The political process is a reflection of power imbalances within organisations and is concerned with, among other things, the degree of influence that can be wielded by managers and others.

In this chapter we have examined power in its varied forms, and the practical applications of power have been demonstrated. In examining control, we considered control systems within the global call centre and the impact of managerial and technological control upon the call centre workforce. Finally we considered empowerment as a managerial attempt to increase the authority, responsibility and autonomy of employees, and organisational politics as a means of influencing employee behaviour.

End notes

[1] See also Chapter 4.

[2] See also Chapters 2 and 14.

[3] See also Chapter 8.

[4] See also Chapters 9 and 16.

[5] See also Chapter 16.

REVIEW AND DISCUSSION QUESTIONS

REVIEW QUESTIONS

1 How would you explain the importance to management and to organisational behaviour of power as a concept?

2 What, in your opinion, is the purpose of a management control system?

3 Identify the characteristics of a good control system.

4 What would you describe as the main features of power and control in the global call centre workplace?

5 Identify five examples of resistance to power and control.

DISCUSSION QUESTIONS

1 Discuss how the various bases of power can be applied to an organisation of your choice.

2 What do you think are the likely consequences of electronic supervision and surveillance within the global call centre workplace?

3 To what extent do you think that power is a political process?

4 Discuss the advantages and disadvantages of empowerment and the factors that have to be taken into consideration for its successful implementation.

5 How important are the various control strategies adopted by the management of an organisation?

FURTHER READING

Buchanan, D. and Badham R. (2008) *Power, Politics and Organizational Change: Winning the turf game.* London: Sage. This text provides a fascinating insight into power and political processes. The authors emphasise the context in which managers initiate change, how it is achieved, and how actions are accounted for. The text is written in an engaging and lively way.

Gerth, H.H. and Wright-Mills, C. (2009) *From Max Weber: Essays in Sociology.* London: Routledge.

Pfeffer, J. (1994) *Managing with Power: Politics and influence in organisations.* Boston, MA: Harvard Business School Press. This seminal text provides an in-depth look at the role of power and influence in organisations. Pfeffer shows convincingly that the effective use of power is an essential component of strong leadership.

Clegg, S. R., Courpasson, D. and Philips, N. (2006) *Power and Organisations.* London: Sage. This book pays due regard to the need to provide an overview of various theories, traditions and bodies of empirical research on organisational power, and does so in an engaging narrative style. The book is excellent for students of organisational behaviour who wish to expand their knowledge in this field.

Child, J. (1984) *Organisation: A guide to problems and practice.* London: Harper & Row. This text, now rather dated, contains one of the best chapters ever written dealing with control in organisations. The text is also very good for other areas of organisational behaviour.

French, J. P. and Raven, B. (1986) 'The bases of social power', in D. Cartwright and A. F. Zander (eds) *Group Dynamics: Research and theory.* New York: Harper & Row. This is useful for more detailed reading dealing with the bases of power.

Owen, J. (2007) *Power at Work: The art of making things happen.* Harlow: Pearson. This book is a 'hands-on' practical handbook which deals with the skills that can be learned and used to advantage by managers and others.

KEY SKILLS

NEGOTIATING, ARBITRATION AND CONFLICT RESOLUTION SKILLS

Of particular interest are negotiating skills which are central to the acquisition, maintenance and extension of an individual's and group's power base. You will, as a manager, be expected to exercise many, if not all, of these skills. For a manager, negotiation is crucial to a number of areas and contexts where the exercise of power and influence are required. These contexts include the employment relations arena where management and employee negotiating teams (usually comprising trade union representatives) engage in 'power play' and negotiate across a range of issues such as pay and new working practices. The aim of this type of negotiation is to produce a 'win-win' situation in which neither side loses face. Other negotiating contexts include negotiation concerning an individual grievance on the part of an aggrieved employee and where the grievance interview represents the interplay of political skills in order to achieve a desired outcome for the aggrieved employee. The skills that are specific to negotiation are also those skills that are used in a variety of other contexts and situations within the organisation. In other words, these skills are transferable and generic. A summary of a selection of these skills are:

Persuasion – Persuasion is based on approaches that respect the other person or persons within both negotiating teams, making it easier to understand, but not necessarily agree with, the other's point of view and argument. Persuasion should not be confused with manipulation, which is based on stealth whereby, intentionally or otherwise, the other person is tricked into accepting your way of thinking. For example, persuasive skills can be used by a union negotiating team to put forward the reasoning, facts and arguments to justify and support their demands. Similarly, the management negotiating team will persuade by reasoned argument concerning its offer

Note-taking skills – Taking accurate notes will assist negotiators by providing a record of what has been said and to and by whom, for identifying important arguments and amendments, and for checking the accuracy of salient contributions concerning what has been agreed, or what has yet to be agreed, before and after adjournments.

Listening and observing – An obvious attribute which can be the key to a successful negotiation outcome, listening is important in attempting to identify verbal signals and clues, weaknesses and strengths in arguments and general errors in the other party's case. Listening carefully to what the other party is saying will reveal clues and ideas about how to move the negotiations forward and requires practice and skill. A good listener may also be able to ascertain the real messages from apparently negative statements. For example, the statement: 'There is no possibility of my agreeing at this stage' might reveal the real message: 'Give me a little more time and I might be able to agree.'

Questioning and probing skills – During face-to-face negotiations, the parties will have certain objectives designed to probe the other side's position, test their commitment and willingness to move, uncover hidden blockages to progress and assess what reciprocal

responses may be necessary. This tactical method of obtaining movement and influencing the outcome is common to all types of negotiation situation.

DEVELOPING CRITICAL THINKING SKILLS AND REFLECTIVE LEARNING

The concept and practice of power, control and political processes in organisations requires you to think critically and reflect upon what you have learnt. As a student you need to consider power to be a concept that can be approached from both a management and an employee perspective in addition to considering the extent to which this and related concepts can be applied in practice. As a manager you will need to develop critical thinking skills as part of your role, and this is as true of power relationships as it is with any other aspect of organisational behaviour and human resource management. A manager who wields power and exercises control wisely will utilise the skills associated with reflection and critical thinking. In essence these skills include informational and knowledge skills in order to be well informed, judgemental and analytical skills, skills associated with developing and defending a reasonable position, and skills of enquiry through asking appropriate questions.

PROFESSIONAL JUDGEMENT, DECISION-MAKING, PROBLEM-SOLVING AND SOCIAL RESPONSIBILITY

Power, control and political processes within organisations require skills of judgement, decision-making and problem-solving. As organisations become more complex, there is an increasing need for staff, including managers, to develop specialist knowledge and skills which are needed to exercise power and control effectively and enhance the quality of the decision-making process. Delegation of power – in order to empower employees, for example – entails decisions and professional judgement about the tasks that could be performed better by other staff; the opportunities for staff to learn and develop by undertaking delegated tasks and responsibilities; and guidance, support and training, patterns of communication and effective monitoring and review procedures.

TEAMWORKING

Team- or group-working is often normal practice in most organisations and as a student you will have been part of a learning group in a tutorial or workshop. In terms of power and control within any organisation, the team leader has formal or legitimate power vested in her or him by the organisation and will also have a degree of personal power. In practice, the exercise of such power requires certain skills which encourage both the formal and informal leadership role. Effective team leaders are good at controlling people and events and co-ordinating resources, and have the energy, determination and initiative to overcome obstacles and bring competitive drive to the team. Team leaders give shape to the team effort and recognise the skills of the individuals and how they can be used.

Ethical implications: Ethics and power

Ethics in general involves an analysis of the basic concepts and fundamental principles of human conduct. It includes study of universal values such as the essential equality of all men and women, human or natural rights, obedience to the law of land, and concern for health and safety and, increasingly, also for the natural environment. With regard to organisational power, ethics may also be equated with corporate social responsibility (CSR). Ideally, CSR as policy and practice would function as an integrated, self-regulating mechanism whereby an organisation and its management would monitor and ensure the organisation's observation of legal and ethical standards, and of international expectations of appropriate behaviour. Questions to be asked concerning the ethics of power-related behaviour are:

Does the behaviour produce a good outcome for people both inside and outside the organisation?

Does the behaviour respect the individual rights of all parties?

Does the behaviour treat all parties equitably and fairly?

To be considered ethical, power-related behaviour must meet all these three criteria. The ethical use of power is one of the most sensitive topics within the business world owing to headline cases such as Enron and Tyco International, whose executives' behaviour was criminally unethical. In the case of Tyco, two chief executives abused their power by pilfering around $600 million from the company, including a $2 million toga birthday party for the wife of one executive on a Mediterranean island and an $18 million Manhattan apartment with a $6,000 shower-curtain. After a four-month trial, the executives were convicted in June 2005 on 22 counts of grand larceny, falsifying business records, securities fraud and conspiracy.

PART FOUR

Organisational Structure

Chapter 14
Organisational Design, Structure and Work Organisation

Scott A. Hurrell and Vincenza Priola

Contents

Key Learning Outcomes

By the end of this chapter you should be able to:

- understand key classical paradigms in organisational structure: Taylorism, Fordism, bureaucracy, functional and divisional forms, and their impact on work organisation

- consider newer paradigms in organisational design and work organisation: post-Fordism/post-industrialism, adhocracies and McDonaldisation as well as co-operatives

- critically evaluate the evidence for the uptake of 'new' organisational forms and the extent of continuity in more traditional organisational forms

- understand how different forms of organisation relate to different economic models and types of production – eg mass production, flexible specialisation and the knowledge economy

- understand the impact that organisational structure, design and work organisation have on employees.

PRACTITIONER INSIGHT

Robertson Bell Talent Management Consultancy

Robertson Bell Talent Management Consultancy is an organisation that specialises in recruitment, training, facilitation and coaching across sectors but typically in highly skilled and professional occupations. **Jacqui Cowing, an executive director**, is herself a specialist in helping organisations to develop design and structure solutions to ensure success in changing economic and social climates, focusing on professional and managerial work. We speak to Jacqui about her views on traditional organisational structures and how she feels organisations should be structured in order to facilitate the creativity and innovation of employees.

Jacqui believes that traditional organisational structures and their underlying principles are unsuitable for the demands of twenty-first-century business. In the current fast-paced climate driven by globalisation and large-scale technological innovation, organisations increasingly need to show creativity, innovation and even intuition in order to remain competitive. Jacqui's work has, however, revealed that many organisations are poorly placed to embrace these challenges in part because of the way in which 'rationality' and the rule of logic has come to dominate organisational thinking and, subsequently, their structures. Traditionally, organisations have been designed along 'mechanistic' grounds leading to organisational forms that are highly bureaucratic, rigid, difficult to transform and unresponsive to the innovative potential of their workforce.

Such organisations encourage 'violent obedience' amongst workers rather than creativity, and experience atrophy rather than growth. In Jacqui's eyes, what is needed is for organisations to move towards more 'organic' forms where collaboration and personal development are encouraged rather than stifled.

In meeting this requirement for organic forms of organisation, Jacqui believes that a workforce is needed that has a sense of meaning and purpose, achieved through employee well-being. In short, employees will feel scared to express their views and contribute to organisational innovation if they do not feel happy, safe and valued at work. Jacqui thus believes that organisations should move away from purely profit-driven motives, towards a more ethical mindset. This ethical mindset not only considers the treatment and well-being of employees but also, in turn, the organisation's wider social and environmental impact.

Jacqui thus sees challenges for today's organisations in facilitating the creativity and innovation of employees through more flexible and organic structures that have the ethical treatment of employees at their core.

How do you think organisations may meet the challenges that Jacqui identifies?

What do you think the implications are for the management of people?

Once you have read this chapter, return to these questions and think about how you could answer them.

Introduction

The manner in which organisations are designed and in which work is subsequently organised has substantial impacts on organisational behaviour for both employees and managers. Organisational design affects matters as diverse as the motivation of individuals, reward strategies, recruitment and selection and power relations, all of which are discussed elsewhere within this book. The aim of this chapter, however, is to outline some of the main paradigms in organisational design, structure and work organisation and to discuss the implications that these have for individuals and organisations. In doing so the chapter will show how contemporary organisations are designed and structured before questioning the extent to which 'newer' organisational forms have replaced more traditional ones. This discussion is framed within a historical perspective, essential for understanding today's methods of designing organisations and work.

DOMINANT CLASSICAL IDEOLOGIES IN ORGANISATIONAL STRUCTURE AND DESIGN 1: TAYLORISM AND FORDISM [1]

The Industrial Revolution from the late eighteenth century was a defining event in organisational design. The Revolution was driven by new technology shifting the focus of work from agriculture to manufacturing and into specialised factories – a departure from the agrarian, itinerant and more individualised patterns of work that individuals had previously engaged in (Edgell, 2006). The **division of labour** was now highly specialised, with individuals having tightly defined jobs within a management-defined system. Work was also now separate from family and personal life in terms of space, relationships and culture, whereas previously work tended to be organised around the household. Marx and Engels (2004) were critical of the organisation of 'masses of labourers, crowded into the factory, organised like soldiers', 'enslaving' workers (*ibid*: 12–13) in work that was ultimately dehumanising (Baldry *et al*, 2007). 'Rationality' was the order of the day and was taken to its logical conclusion in three modes of structuring organisations and designing work that dominated thinking for over a century: **Taylorism**, **Fordism**, and bureaucracy.

The rise of Taylorism

Frederick Winslow Taylor was to have a profound effect on organisational design. Born in 1856, Taylor was a steel engineer by trade, securing a job at the Midvale Steel plant in Philadelphia as a gang boss (effectively a foreman) by 1879 (Kanigel, 1997). During Taylor's time, workers were generally paid piece-rates based upon output, the management reducing rates if workers produced at a volume such that wages became too high. To avoid rate cuts, workers would limit output and informally agree production levels amongst themselves, termed '**soldiering**' (*ibid*). Any man (and manual workers were almost exclusively men at this time) producing more than this informally agreed level, effectively made his co-workers look lazy.

Taylor was determined to resolve the problem of soldiering by (as was his somewhat tactless way) *telling* the men to work harder and engaging in a swathe of sackings (Taylor, 1947). Workers were, however, reluctant to work any harder – but eventually some fell into line and production increased (*ibid*). That is not to say that Taylor did not face risks: he was threatened with physical violence (especially as he took the none too wise option of walking home next to a deserted railway track and the even less wise option of making this well known) and sabotage was also common (Kanigel, 1997). He caused further resentment by introducing fines for breakages and other misdemeanours while telling the workers that he would at all costs get a 'fair day's work' from them (Taylor, 1947). Taylor was clearly not an especially emotionally intelligent man and some of his actions would probably have made famously aggressive TV chef Gordon Ramsay blush. Even in these less enlightened times, however, a different tack was needed to prevent all-out war.

Table 14.1:   The characteristics of scientific management

Braverman (1974)	Grey (2009)
• The gathering of knowledge about work processes by management • Removing the 'brain work' of planning and organising from production workers and transferring it to management • The use of knowledge *by management* to control each stage of the organisation and execution of work	• A science of each element of work • Division of labour between workers and managers separating the planning and execution of work tasks • Scientific selection and training of workers to follow managerial instructions • 'Co-operation' between workers and managers with managerial authority not questioned

'**Scientific management**' was thus born at Midvale. Taylor conducted a number of scientific experiments on machines to determine optimal production conditions, turning these into managerially dictated instructions to workers (Kanigel, 1997). Knowledge was removed from workers and handed to management – subsequently reducing the need for management to *trust* workers (Braverman, 1974; Grey, 2009). Taylor subsequently turned his attention to how fast *men* could work in his famous time and motion studies. These studies examined the time taken to perform each *part* of a job rather than the whole job itself, breaking jobs down into discrete elements. This **micro-division of labour** was not in itself new and is generally attributed to Adam Smith's (1776) (theoretical) discussion of increasing productivity within pin manufacture. Taylor diligently *implemented* this micro-division, creating 'instruction cards' for each job – detailing the exact nature and sequence of tasks for any activity and the time that these should take (Taylor, 1947). 'One best way' was thus created for each activity; 'The workman didn't have to think out the job anew; management did it for him' (Kanigel, 1997: 208). Table 14.1 shows how Braverman (1974) and Grey (2009) describe the characteristics of scientific management.

Work under Taylor was undoubtedly physically arduous, but he paid premiums for those that did it his way because 'You had to pay to an ordinary capable man, a first-class man in order to get him to work like the devil' (Kanigel, 1997: 209). It is also the case that Taylor's highly systematised approach removed the negative effects of the caprice and favouritism of gang leaders and also led to a safer working environment (Grey, 2009). Despite the many criticisms levelled at Taylor's system, there was a notion of fairness and consistency – although Taylor of course dictated the level of both 'fair' work and a 'fair' reward. Workers could also expect to be treated by well-established rules. The use of Taylor's approaches became increasingly widespread and Henry Ford most famously adapted his principles.

Ethical implications: Taylorised workplaces

Taylor's principles have clear ethical implications in terms of the (maximum physically possible) level of output he was trying to extract from workers and the dehumanising nature of removing all thought from the work. Scientific management was understandably unpopular, causing widespread industrial unrest (Braverman, 1974; Grey, 2009). Indeed, Taylor was sacked from the Bethlehem Steel Plant in 1901, partly because of worker resistance to his methods (Kanigel, 1997). Ethical concerns over Taylor's practices even led to a US congressional investigation. This investigation concluded that work practices should not be imposed upon unwilling workers without an attempt to gain consent; that stopwatches could *not* determine a fair day's work; and that Taylorism was basically dehumanising – reducing workers to machines (*ibid*). Taylor remained unrepentant. The obvious riposte is that workers were paid more for this extra effort – but were they paid enough, and even if they were, did it justify the effort levels required? Braverman (1974) cites the example of one experiment where Taylor increased productivity by almost four times but only increased compensation by 81%. These same ethical implications remain today in Taylorised workplaces (see *The limits of post-Fordism* below).

Extending Taylorism: Fordism

Henry Ford is famous for pioneering the moving production line in 1914 (Braverman, 1974). Although Ford himself denied being influenced by Taylor and Taylor himself referred to Ford's cars as 'cheaply and roughly made' (Kanigel, 1997: 496), the parallel between the two systems is undeniable. Upon the introduction of the production line, discrete, highly fragmented and simplified operations were conducted sequentially via the use of specialised machines, with a car manufactured at the end of the process (Edgell, 2006). Taylor's work was less revolutionary and although he had attempted to turn skilled jobs into fragmented tasks, he had largely kept the machinery the same (Braverman, 1974; Kanigel, 1997). However, clear similarities exist – the standardisation of tasks, the micro-division of labour, managerial control over the pace of work, and the separation of planning from execution. Furthermore, the analogy of the organisation with the rational machine was perhaps even more evident under Ford than Taylor, with the speed of work dictated not just by managerial decree but also by the machinery (ie the assembly line) that workers used. Also, wages in Ford were higher than competitors', doubling to $5 a day in 1914 (Edgell, 2006). Although Beynon (1975) states that this rise was in part to stave off unionism, placate dissatisfied workers and reduce turnover and absenteeism, the fact remains that Ford appeared to follow Taylor's prescription of a 'fair day's work for a fair day's pay' – however much the true degree of 'fairness' may be questioned.

With Ford's methods, so began the age of mass consumption. Fordism allowed economies of scale generated by mass production of low-cost standardised products (Coriat, 1992). Indeed, one remark attributed (perhaps incorrectly) to Ford is that customers could have the model T car in any colour they wanted – as long as it was black. Braverman (1974: 147) notes that after the introduction of the production line Ford's 'Model T' production rose by 10 times in three months, and that by 1925 as many Model Ts were produced in a day as had been in an entire year of early production. Cars were now affordable to a greater number of people than ever before, as were other products once these concepts were extended to other industries. The net effect of these changes was that more individualised and autonomous craft production was undercut and gradually marginalised (Bradley *et al*, 2000). The principles of Ford allowed capitalism to thrive, bringing prosperity to nations, companies and individuals. Large standardised workplaces were now the norm (Braverman, 1974) alongside rigid formal job descriptions (Flecker and Hofbauer, 1998) and hierarchical managerial control (Boreham, 1992).

Critiques of Taylorism and Fordism

Despite the prosperity generated from Fordism, the movement has attracted strong critics. It is clear from Marx's critique of industrial organisation that Taylor and Ford's methods lead to mass, specialised workplaces and, conceivably, to work that was unfulfilling and dehumanising. It can be argued that Taylorism and Fordism leads to workers who are 'alienated (ie isolated and estranged from their work), deskilled and bored' (Bradley *et al*, 2000: 34; see also Blauner, 1964). Taylor and Ford believed that workers were motivated by economic needs alone, and thus measures to prevent **alienation** were considered unnecessary (a little shortsighted, given the resistance to these methods). The question remains over whether the relative wage premium attached to Taylor and Ford's organisational principles would ever make up for its alienating nature.

Perhaps the most ardent critique of Taylorism and Fordism was the sociologist Harry Braverman in his seminal 1974 polemic entitled *Labor and Monopoly Capital*, and subtitled *The Degradation of Work in the Twentieth Century*. Braverman bemoaned many of the changes in work resulting from increased rationalisation of organisational structures and processes. This discussion was placed against the backdrop of the ever-expanding conglomerate corporation engaging in vertical integration and consuming parts of their supply chain. A manufacturing company, for example, might purchase primary materials producers or transportation companies. As organisations grew, so did the increasing number of subdivisions within them, finance and marketing becoming the most powerful alongside personnel management, legal and purchasing.

In Braverman's eyes the spread of Taylorist and Fordist principles was inexorable, driven by the need (or desire) for tighter management control. Most famously, Braverman demonstrates how traditionally skilled 'white-collar' clerical work had suffered at the hands of Taylorism. Braverman revealed that the growing complexity of organisations had instigated exponential growth in clerical workers in the USA from around 100,000 in 1900 to 10 million in 1970. As clerical work became a mass occupation, however, workers were given increasingly narrow remits under conditions of reduced autonomy. Braverman compared clerical work directly to the Fordist factory with 'streams of paper' replacing manufacturing components organised in a 'continuous flow like that of a cannery, the meat packing line, or the car assembly line' (p301). Clerical workers were also subjected to increased demands for speed, with work intensifying to allow greater volumes to be completed. The net effect of these developments was 'the progressive elimination of thought from the work of the office worker ... reducing mental labour to a repetitive performance of the same small set of functions' (p319).

Braverman subjected service and retail work to a similar critique, stating that occupations such as chambermaids, porters, janitors and dishwashers were no longer distinct from manufacturing labour. Perhaps one of the most striking examples was a US restaurant chain that stated that it was not skilled chefs that were required but rather 'thawer-outers' of pre-prepared frozen food (p370). Supermarkets provided Braverman with a further battleground as jobs became ever more specialised and automated, epitomised by semi-automated checkouts that still exist today 'accept(ing) ... the assembly line or factory pace in its most complete form' (p372).

Braverman believed that work had become dehumanised as management effectively separated the hand (ie the worker) from the brain (management) while asking for greater levels of effort. He bemoaned the manner in which skill was becoming degraded by the organisation of work and the 'destruction of craftsmanship during the period of the rise of Scientific Management' (p135). Management were now in command, removing any control that workers had over their labour and alienating them in the process. That is not to say that workers did not sometimes resist such changes, typically through industrial action, but Taylorism was, in Braverman's eyes, fundamentally ruining work and society. This pessimistic view of work is generally referred to as the '**deskilling thesis**'.

Although Braverman's thesis is lucid, well argued and stands up to contemporary empirical investigation, there are still criticisms that must be highlighted. Firstly, his account was written over 35 years ago and centres around descriptions of work in the USA – although his ideas still have global resonance today. His conceptualisations of work are also broad-brush and although backed up by many examples may be over-generalised and ignore any countervailing '**upskilling**' trends (Bell, 1976). Furthermore, the extent to which **craftwork** as a means of organising production can be generalised in the way Braverman does is highly questionable, many commentators doubting it was *ever* the norm (see Edgell, 2006: 53–8 for a review). Although Braverman does note worker resistance, scholars have also criticised him for overstating the power of managers and the powerlessness of workers (Edgell, 2006). Finally, Braverman has been accused of 'gender blindness' (*ibid*: 55). He largely ignored how skill has traditionally been conceptualised by patriarchal society to over-value the skills of 'male' (eg technical and manual) work at the expense of 'female work'.

Taylorism and Fordism rationalised work through the micro-division of labour, tight control by management, the separation of thinking and planning from execution, and, eventually, control through technology. Critics of the methods consider it to be a dehumanising system that exploits workers and intensifies work, whereas their supporters point to efficiency gains, savings for consumers and increased productivity and prosperity. These forms of organising work are generally associated with large, complex multi-division organisations – as is a second classical ideology in organisational design: **bureaucracy**.

DOMINANT CLASSICAL IDEOLOGIES IN ORGANISATIONAL STRUCTURE AND DESIGN 2: BUREAUCRACY

Weber and rational-legal authority [2]

The development of bureaucracy has its origins in the work of Max Weber, writing in the late nineteenth and early twentieth centuries, but remains equally relevant today. Weber had a keen interest in how economy and society were organised and especially the operation and structure of authority within institutions (Parsons, 1947; Grey, 2009).

Weber (1947) identified three forms of 'legitimate' authority: charismatic, traditional and rational-legal. *Charismatic authority* (like charismatic leadership) is the most personal, with authority residing in the 'sanctity, heroism or exemplary character' of the leader and/or followers' trust and belief in them (p328). Charismatic authority may not always be associated with positive beliefs, an extreme example being the rise of Adolf Hitler. Examples of charismatic authority still exist in organisations today through high-profile entrepreneurs and founders such as Virgin's Richard Branson and Apple's Steve Jobs. *Traditional authority* is less personal and rests on the 'sanctity of traditions … and status' (Weber, 1947: 328). An example of such authority would be hereditary royal families, or the church (Grey, 2009). In traditional authority, it is the office or position that is respected rather than the individual holding that office, although it is still that person in whom authority resides. What Weber was most interested in was *rational-legal authority* tied up with the rule of law. Within such a system, authority resides not with individuals' charisma or respect accrued through the traditions of an office but instead in a 'legally established impersonal order' (Weber, 1947: 328).

These kinds of authority can coincide, and Weber was aware that no society had ever shown a 'pure' form of any single type of authority (*ibid*: 329). Take, for example, Barack Obama. He arguably has a large amount of charisma – indeed, his critics may argue that he obtained his office (and subsequent Nobel Peace Prize) through this at the expense of substance. The office of President of the United States also has a strong tradition and a commensurately high status. There is a fantastic moment in an episode in the first season of the US political drama *The West Wing* where fictional US President Jed Bartlett (played by Martin Sheen) invites his closest employees and advisers to attend a party at which he is cooking chilli. President Bartlett gets a far from enthusiastic response to this invitation to taste his cooking, to which he (jokingly) urges his staff to look down at the huge presidential seal depicted on the Oval Office carpet, then look back up at him. He then invites his staff to the party again, receiving a much more (mock) excited response. Through his invoking the tradition of the office, the staff fall into line. The office of the US President also has legal authority, the Constitution of the United States providing clear rules as to the scope and limits of the authority of the president. Returning to *The West Wing* example, however: President Bartlett clearly had no *legal* authority to compel his staff to attend his party. Furthermore, both Richard Branson and Steve Jobs clearly cannot rely on their charismatic authority alone to manage large and disparate organisations, meaning that other kinds of authority have to be embedded in Virgin and Apple too.

Weber's (1947) work on rational-legal authority led to an analysis of the organisation of bureaucratic administrative functions that were, in the spirit of Fordism, the norm at the time. Although it must be noted that much of Weber's work appears to describe public administration, he believed that bureaucracy was apparent in private enterprises and even charitable and religious organisations. In this sense, when Weber talked about 'laws', this did not apply only to government statute but also to rules formulated within organisations. Subsequently, the authority granted to those in bureaucratic offices is impersonal and comes from the laws or rules themselves. The characteristics of bureaucracy for organisational design and staffing practices are shown in Table 14.2.

Table 14.2:   Weber's characteristics of bureaucracy

Organisational design principles	Work and staffing practices
• Bureaucracies are a continuous organisation of official functions bound by rules. • Each office has a specified sphere of competence involving a clear division of labour between that office and other offices. • The authority to carry out functions within each office is clearly defined. • The organisation of offices is hierarchical with clear lines through which activities are passed. • The rules that regulate offices are *technical*. To rationally apply rules, officers require specialised training. • Officers do not own the organisation but act rationally on its behalf to avoid any conflicts of interest. • Administrative rules and actions are recorded in writing.	• Officers are subject only to the authority of 'impersonal official obligations' imposed by others in the organisation. • Officers should remain objective and independent in applying administrative rules and laws. • Officers are remunerated through fixed salaries and a pension. Salaries are graded hierarchically and reflect the responsibility of the office. • Each office has a related career structure. Promotion is based on seniority and/or performance judged by superiors. • Offices are filled by 'free selection' and on the basis of technical qualifications and suitability.

Weber was full of praise for bureaucracies (p337):

> The purely bureaucratic type of administrative organisation ... is, from a purely technical point of view, capable of attaining the highest degree of efficiency and is ... formally the most rational known means of carrying out imperative control over human beings.

Indeed, Weber unanimously claimed that 'for the needs of the mass administration of today it [bureaucracy] is completely indispensable' (*ibid*). Weber believed, however, that bureaucracy also had wider social benefits. He thought the rational and unbiased technical recruitment referred to in Table 14.2 led to a meritocracy and a reduction in class privileges. He further posited that if systems were based on technical knowledge and 'concrete facts', administration would be fair and impartial, leading to a just and equitable society which considered the welfare of those within it.

Critiques of bureaucracy

The very terms 'bureaucrat' and 'bureaucracy' today often conjure up images of inefficiency, irrationality and even unfairness – the antithesis of what Weber proposed. Perhaps the most famous critique of bureaucracy is by Robert Merton (1957). Prominent within this critique was Merton's use of **'trained incapacity'**, meaning that bureaucrats' strengths and training might actually become their weaknesses. If organisations wish to change or find themselves operating under changed conditions, for example, the very nature of bureaucratic training is likely to mean that staff cannot easily adapt. Indeed, if you turn to the Practitioner insight case study at the beginning of this chapter, the inability of bureaucratic organisations to keep up with change is seen by Jacqui Cowing as a major barrier to success. Trained incapacity also means that bureaucrats are unlikely to be able to deal with any circumstance that falls outside of the conditions within which they have been trained, leading potentially to irate customers and clients. In this sense, Merton highlighted the manner in which bureaucrats begin to see the application of rules as the primary *purpose* of the job rather than as a means through which to achieve organisational objectives. Merton believed that trained incapacity and attitudes towards rule enforcement were inevitable given that bureaucracies effectively offer a career for life. In order to progress within such a structure the bureaucrat has to conform, leading to conservatism and the reinforcement of values which may themselves be dysfunctional.

Applying theory to practice: Trained incapacity and bureaucracy: 'Computer says No'

We're sure all readers will be able to recall times dealing with (for example) local councils, call centres or even (dare we say it?) university departments where inflexible officers' strict adherence to seemingly irrelevant rules causes immense frustration. 'Trained incapacity' and bureaucratic principles thus still have a huge (and immensely irritating) impact on our everyday lives. The principle is illustrated perfectly in David Walliams' 'Computer says No' character, Carol Beer, from the comedy series *Little Britain*. This human automaton seemingly lacking any personality or initiative (originally working in a bank but also eventually as a travel agent and a hospital receptionist) types all customer queries and requests into a computer before mindlessly announcing the computer's invariably negative response with the aforementioned catch-phrase. This character is not simply a comedy creation but an accurate social commentary on bureaucratic-type roles and also the type of disempowered low-autonomy work that is seen in many service settings, such as Taylorised call centres (see *The limits of post-Fordism* below).

Merton's final critique centred on the impersonal '**bureaucratic personality**' needed for 'rationality'. In Merton's eyes, however, impersonality led to the alienation of those whom bureaucrats deal with, who come to see them as detached or aloof. The bureaucratic personality is itself reinforced by the fact that bureaucrats are necessarily given a definite sphere of authority that they may apply over-zealously. The caricature of the enthusiastic petty public official with a seemingly unimportant job is a familiar one. (Traffic wardens are, for example, often accused of this, sometimes leading to 'polite' requests that they should 'Get a real job'!)

Additional to Merton's critique are a number of general points, although the potential list is almost endless. The first point relates to how one defines 'rationality'. The notion of bureaucracy is predicated upon rationality, but who decides what is 'rational' within a bureaucracy? Indeed, the Practitioner insight case study at the beginning of the chapter highlights how Jacqui Cowing believes 'rationality' may impede organisations. Rules and laws are decided upon by those who operate at the highest levels, and what is rational for them may of course not be rational for other people (see Grey 2009: 24–7 for an excellent overview). Furthermore, the rational machinations of bureaucracy are often used for irrational ends – Ritzer (2004) cites the horrific and extreme example of the Holocaust, which was performed to the highest levels of efficiency.

Weber may also have been naïve in terms of his vision of a meritocracy where officers were selected and promoted 'impersonally', based purely on their technical ability. Nearly everyone has worked in an organisation where people have been selected and promoted on the basis of nepotism, or because they are more skilled in 'impression management' (Huczynski, 2004) than actually doing the job, or for some reason other than their ability or suitability for the position. Indeed, within one of our own pieces of research (Hurrell, 2009) in a bureaucratic, quasi-public-sector scientific research organisation, one disgruntled respondent noted that 'People who are full of shit get promoted around here!'

A further critique is whether impersonality is *ever* possible. You only have to browse through the newspapers for evidence of bureaucratic processes that do not fit the impersonal model, usually taken from politics. High-profile examples in the UK include Home Secretary David Blunkett resigning in 2004 after revelations about his fast-tracking a visa application for an ex-lover's nanny, and Cabinet Minister Peter Mandelson resigning in 2001 after allegedly trying to interfere in the passport application of Indian billionaire Srichand Hinduja. Although these are high-profile examples, the principle holds in less well-publicised examples and outside of public life.

The question also remains whether the impersonal nature of bureaucracy is even desirable. Although most people would agree that any system that eliminates capricious and arbitrary action is beneficial, the total elimination of any emotion on the part of bureaucratic workers also has its problems. Consistent with Marx, Blauner and Braverman, many other authors have decried the 'dehumanising' removal of human emotion from work. In its aim to achieve objectivity, the more the bureaucracy is 'dehumanised', the more completely it succeeds in eliminating from official business any feelings and emotions such as love, hatred, irrationality and anything that is personal and escapes calculation (Weber, 1947: 215). Although rationality, dehumanisation and impersonality are part and parcel of bureaucracy and are appraised for their special values, one may question whether work in practice can ever be totally rational and controlled, as indicated in the opening Practitioner insight case study. During the last 20 years, in fact, various authors (eg Albrow, 1994, 1997; Bolton, 2005; Fineman, 2000, 2003; Hochschild, 1983) have highlighted how much of what people do at work is concerned with how they and others feel about it. Fineman (2003) asserts that all organisations are emotional arenas in which 'feelings shape events shape each other'. Emotional energy is important in creating a sense of belonging and feelings to workers' organisational world and roles (Fineman, 2003). Organisations and work practices can generate fun, pride and exhilaration, but they can also make us bored, stressed, depressed and anxious.

Finally, Weber's model of bureaucracy posits that people passively accept and then apply rules but ignores the manner in which managers and employees may actually bend the rules to mutual benefit. Gouldner's (1954) study of mine and factory workers, for example, revealed how local managers engaged in what is known as an 'indulgency pattern', effectively ignoring some organisational rules and showing leniency towards workers. Workers, in turn, reciprocated with hard work and co-operation. Problems occurred, however, when a new manager tried to break this indulgency pattern and introduce Taylorised work practices and a 'punishment-centred bureaucracy' for those who would not obey (Gouldner, 1954a). The actions of the new manager eventually led to a wildcat strike and the plant temporarily closed (Gouldner, 1954). The indulgency pattern was rational for *both* managers *and* employees, whereas the new punishment-centred bureaucracy was rational for senior managers *only*, and failed. A similar example can be found in Burawoy's (1985) discussion of 'making out' where managers turned a blind eye to employees' fixing the piece-rate through soldiering as it ultimately benefited the work environment. Rules are not passively accepted givens, and human dynamics and interpretation can lead to organisationally efficient outcomes which do not follow the 'rational' rules of bureaucracy.

It must be noted that however much we can criticise Weber's model, he was fully aware that it was only an ideal type and would probably never exist in its purest form. For example, he believed that equality of treatment and impersonal application of rules was 'the spirit in which the *ideal* official [emphasis added] conducts his office' (Weber, 1947: 340). It is an apparently convenient 'cop-out' for a seemingly prescriptive formula of organisational success, but it is a necessary one. Weber was aware that imperfections may occur, but nevertheless it is doubtful whether he would have expected the notion of bureaucracy ever to have the negative connotations that it has today.

Functional versus divisional structures in classic design

The classic **mechanistic** designs discussed so far are what may be termed *functional* structures in that they are designed, as Weber and Braverman suggested, around functional specialisms (for example, planning, production, finance and marketing). Such designs are highly centralised, decision-making cascading down from a few senior officials (Chandler, 1962), with a narrow 'span of control' (Ouchi and Dowling, 1974) in that managers supervise only a few people. This leads to highly complex hierarchical and 'tall' organisational structures with many layers of management. A generic example of a functional organisational structure is given in Figure 14.1, which also indicates how functions may be subdivided further, using finance as an example.

As well as the general disadvantages of bureaucracy noted above Chandler (1962) states that managers are promoted from within the functions where they spend their entire careers and thus do not tend to have a grasp of the wider business or other functions. This led to inflexibility and an inability to deal with changing competitive conditions even in the early part of the twentieth century (*ibid*), reflecting Merton's concept of 'trained incapacity'. Indeed, the opening Practitioner insight case study highlights how such structures constrain organisations still today. Such functional '**siloing**' can potentially mean that organisational goals are ignored at

Figure 14.1   An example of a functional (bureaucratic) organisational structure

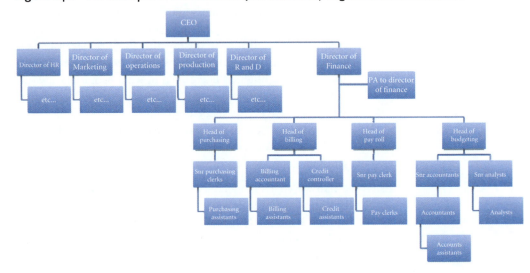

the expense of narrow functional concerns, leading to organisational inefficiencies (Lambert *et al*, 1998).

A variation on the functional organisation is a *divisional* structure where organisations may be organised around market divisions (for example, products or services) rather than functions (Mintzberg, 1980). Divisions in this type of structure are theoretically given a high degree of autonomy (vertical decentralisation) and answer to small corporate centre (*ibid*). Fontaine (2007) provides an example of Boeing as a divisional organisation where the three product divisions (Commercial Airline, Military Aircraft and Private Aviation) each have their own research and development, sales, accounting and production functions (represented diagrammatically in Figure 14.2). The stated advantage is that divisions are more responsive than overly centralised functions because each division has shared accountability, with divisional workers frequently exposed to multiple functions (*ibid*). Organisational identity may thus be much higher (at divisional level, at least) than in a functional structure. It is for this reason that many of the graduate programmes to which some of you will be applying expose trainees to a number of areas of the business within a short time.

Mintzberg (1980) believed, however, that *within* divisions the functional structure still tends to be adopted, because divisions remain a single set of systems designed to meet specific goals set by the corporate centre. He thus believed that divisional organisations remained bureaucratic,

Figure 14.2   An example of a divisional organisational structure (eg Boeing)

Source: Fontaine (2007)

with many of the problems noted above. Organisations may also choose to mix **divisional** and **functional structures** so that some parts of the organisation fit the divisional model more than others. For example, Fontaine (2007) did not specify whether HR and marketing were also organised divisionally in Boeing.

Divisional structures may also be used in **multinational corporations (MNCs)** that are ever more common in a globalised world (Rollinson, 2001). In this respect, MNCs are those that *operate* in a number of different countries rather than those that simply *trade* in a number of countries (*ibid*). The divisional form can allow a degree of autonomy to subsidiaries operating outwith the home nation, enabling targeted products and services (*ibid*) and even a degree of local cultural integration (Wood *et al*, 2009). Ghoshal and Noria (1993) describe this localised MNC structure as **differentiated**, and a generic example is presented in Figure 14.3. An example of such a differentiated organisation is General Motors (*ibid*), which is headquartered in the USA but owns distinct brands with their own operations and products throughout the world, such as Vauxhall and Opel in Europe and Daewoo in South Korea (General Motors, 2010).

Problems still exist with multinational divisional organisations, in no small part because their size sometimes means that the corporate centre may on occasion reduce the autonomy of international subsidiaries and impose homogeneous policies throughout the organisation. Organisations following such an approach may more correctly be termed 'international' than 'multinational' (Rollinson, 2002) and find it difficult to operate in cultural contexts outside the home country (Hofstede, 1993). It is also the case that, as with the general divisional structure described above by Mintzberg, an MNC may still revert to more functional forms within national divisions with associated problems. Figure 14.3 considers the possibility that national divisions may themselves be organised on a functional or divisional basis. In light of the complexities involved in managing MNCs, the pressures towards increased central control may even become *more* intense the larger an organisation gets, as Braverman suggested for domestic US organisations.

Whether an organisation is functional, divisional, domestic or multinational, the structural and design issues discussed above remain mechanistic and rather monolithic. The question is, therefore, whether such methods of structuring organisations still remain viable.

Figure 14.3 An example of a divisional MNC organised at country level

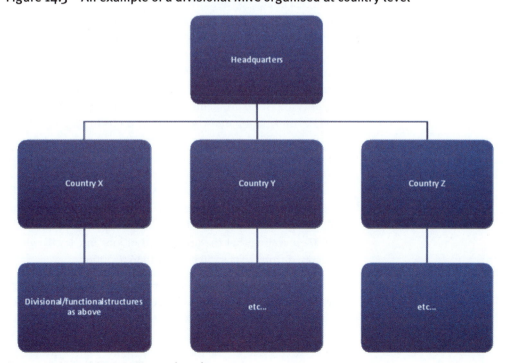

Source: Adapted from Rollinson (2001)

Taking your learning further: Organisational structure

Braverman's (1974) book *Labour and Monopoly Capital*, discussed at length in the main text, is of particular note. This excellent critique of classic forms of managing work provides numerous vivid examples and is written in an engaging and thought-provoking manner.

Gouldner's (1954) study of *Industrial Bureaucracy* in a gypsum mine and factory is a further classic text. This in-depth case study analyses the developments of administration within the plant, identifying three types of bureaucracy: 'mock bureaucracy' (the indulgency pattern and non-enforcement of the rules), 'representative bureaucracy' (where rules are mutually enforced and obeyed), and 'punishment-centred bureaucracy' (where managers regularly attempt to enforce the rules but workers resist). These classics identify homogenising principles (Braverman) and subtleties in both organisational practices and workers' reactions (Gouldner).

Mintzberg's (1980) article in *Management Science* entitled 'Structure in 5s: a synthesis of the research on organisational design' provides a succinct and highly readable overview of the principles of classic organisational structure, such as bureaucracy and divisional forms as well as the 'newer' adhocracy structure discussed below.

Ghoshal and Noria's (1993) *Sloan Management Review* paper 'Horses for courses: organisational forms for multinational corporations' provides a thorough overview of the factors that have to be considered when structuring MNCs, and provides a typology to characterise such organisations.

NEW FORMS OF MANAGING WORK AND ORGANISATIONS

Changing economic models

There has been much written about 'new' forms of organisational design that are considerably removed from the mechanistic organisational forms discussed above, motivated by supposed changes in the economic and market structure. One such change is the shift from the Fordist economy of mass production and consumption to the so-called '**Starbucks economy**' (Penn and Zalesne, 2007). In such an economy, consumer choice and less standardised products have become increasingly important – as epitomised by the huge variety of choices and customisation options available in Starbucks, which reportedly has over 87,000 'beverage combinations' (Cocco, 2008). A related trend is the increase in service industries throughout the world and the decrease in manufacturing – leading Korczynski (2002: 1) to claim that 'all advanced economies are dominated by service industries'. Perhaps, therefore, the breeding grounds of traditional organisational forms are dying out.

A further change is the shift towards what is called the '**knowledge economy**'. For over 30 years, starting with Daniel Bell (1976), commentators have been heralding an 'upskilling' across developed economies. Upskilling means that competitive advantage is based on education, technical skill, creativity and innovation, rather than on cost and economies of scale (*ibid*; Reich, 1992; Crouch *et al*, 1999). This knowledge may still be found in tangible products (for example, computer software and hardware) but also in the work of 'symbolic analysts' who identify and solve problems and broker strategic services (such as business consultants) (Reich, 1992). Information and communication technologies are essential for work in the knowledge economy, with knowledge workers engaging in 'systematic activity that traffics in data, manipulates information and develops knowledge' (Despres and Hiltrop, 1995: 3). Developments in technology have been seen as one of the most important drivers of economic and organisational change (Burnes, 2004; Green, 2006). Indeed, within the UK between 1979 and 1999 the highest growth occupations were engineer, technologist and computing professionals (Goos and Manning, 2003). There is further broad support for Bell's upskilling thesis, with Felstead *et al* (2007) revealing that the proportion of jobs in the UK which required a degree or higher had increased from 20% to 30% from 1986 to 2006.

Within both Starbucks and knowledge economy models it is proposed that the 'old' mechanistic organisational designs are no longer viable – as suggested also by Jacqui Cowing in the chapter's opening Practitioner insight case study. This is especially the case in a shrinking globalised world where communication is instant and the need for change is reportedly constant (Burnes, 2004; Ritzer, 2004). In the eyes of many writers we are therefore moving into the age of **post-industrialist** or **post-Fordist** organisational forms.

Post-Fordist organisational designs

One of the earliest studies that identified 'new' organisational forms was that conducted by Burns and Stalker (1961). We have already highlighted how they classified organisations following Fordist or bureaucratic models as 'mechanistic'. At the other end of the continuum, however, they identified 'organic' organisations that are considerably more flexible. Such organisations allow greater discretion for individuals and groups over how work should be carried out. **Organic organisations** are, in theory at least, more democratic, with greater room for negotiation and more involvement of workers along the lines described in the Practitioner insight case study at the beginning of the chapter. Critically, however, Burns and Stalker did not believe that organisations strictly adhered to one type or another or that their design would necessarily remain constant. The two ideal types lay on a continuum, with organisations showing a mixture of characteristics, and organisations could also move along this continuum as circumstances dictated.

One change that initiated the shift towards more organic organisational forms was the move to **flexible specialisation** from the 1970s (Piore and Sabel, 1984). This move effectively challenged the Fordist model of production and consumption representing an epochal change and the 'second industrial divide' (the first being the move to mass production) (*ibid*). The flexible specialisation thesis proposed that organisations' competitive advantage lay not in economies of scale but rather in 'economies of scope' – ie on the variety of products that could be produced rather than the volume (Boxall and Purcell, 2003: 93). Organisations were seeking 'to develop more versatile equipment which can be switched easily from the production of one model to another … day to day *in response to market demands*' (Piore, 1986: 158, emphasis added). Flexibly specialised organisations were resultantly seen as able to serve smaller niche markets in the way that Fordist organisations could not (Boxall and Purcell, 2003).

The move towards flexible specialisation necessitated a shift in organisational design, along the lines of Burns and Stalker's organic type. Organisations following the flexibly specialised route, according to Piore (1986), followed a matrix structure such that work was organised around particular projects rather than following strict functional or divisional lines. Organisational 'components' were also given greater autonomy over their functioning and direction (p158) in an extension to the divisional organisational form. The system also required greater overall co-ordination to eliminate waste, the components delivered to the production line 'just in time', as in many Japanese organisations of the period (p159). Work practices also needed to change, with the 'elimination of narrow job assignments' alongside increased training, job security, profit sharing and worker involvement in decision-making (p160). Piore believed that these developments in sum would lead to upskilling and a reduction of monotonous and repetitive work. Because of the greater connectivity between organisational components, design tasks (for example) were now to involve 'rank and file workers' as well as designers and engineers (p159). The very flexibility demanded by the system and greater levels of involvement meant that workers themselves had to be 'functionally flexible' to carry out a variety of tasks (Atkinson, 1984).

A similar and related concept was the move towards **Japanisation** or '**lean production**'. This move sought to improve organisational efficiency through eliminating waste in production processes, epitomised by Japanese car manufacturers (Womack and Jones, 1996). Such a system utilised the **just-in-time (JIT) systems** described above. To increase efficiency and eliminate faulty goods, the Japanese notion of *kaizen* (continual improvement) was built into work practices (Bradley *et al*, 2000). Workers were organised in teams to share knowledge about the details of production to facilitate co-operation and work more effectively. The *kaizen* system also used worker involvement schemes such as 'quality circles', where workers collaboratively suggest solutions to problems (*ibid*). Lean production requires multi-skilled workers who are committed to the long-term goals of the organisation, reaching its pinnacle with *nenko*, the notion of employment for life (*ibid*). The overall effect is, reportedly, mutually beneficial.

Workers receive job security and a better quality of working life while management increase productivity (*ibid*). The increased commitment shown by workers also leads to decreased turnover and associated costs.

The emerging 'knowledge economy' model also has organisational design implications. In response to this economic change, organisations have supposedly become flatter and more collegiate to facilitate knowledge transfer and creation, as suggested in the Practitioner insight case study (Despres and Hiltrop, 1995). Layers of the hierarchy that defined functional organisations are stripped out to increase creativity and responsiveness to market conditions, alongside the use of interdependent semi-autonomous teams that replace rigidly prescribed individual roles (*ibid*). These changes relate in part to the difficulty of managing creative and/or professional knowledge workers (described by Scarbrough, 1996: 35, as 'herding cats'), allowing them the space to autonomously develop ideas. Mintzberg (1980) described project-based organisations as 'adhocracies' which display little centralised control. In an **adhocracy**, professionals may reside in a functional structure for 'housekeeping (ie logistical) purposes' but their work is deployed on a market (ie project) basis through decentralised teams. In this form the adhocracy shows 'the least reverence for classic theories of management' (p337) discussed above.

One way in which Mintzberg believed that an adhocracy could be run is through a matrix structure. In such a structure, functional and divisional groupings are combined concurrently on particular projects. One example of a matrix structure is the scientific research firm Silex (Hurrell, 2009). In Silex, specialist divisions (such as geology, seismology and cartography) were formerly in existence alongside functional groupings such as ICT, administration and technical support. These divisions and functions were then combined on particular project teams. An example is given in Figure 14.4 where staff in the seismology and cartography divisions and IT function are working together in project team A, and staff in the geology division and administration and technical support functions are working together in project team B. Such a simple schematic does not, however, begin to do justice to the complexity of a true matrix structure or adhocracy. (Staff from one division may be working on multiple project teams, for example.)

The logical conclusion of these innovative organisational forms is what Charles Handy (2002) called the 'age of unreason' (contrast this with the rationality of Fordism and bureaucracy). Handy believed that various forms of new organisation would emerge in the future such as the **shamrock organisation**. This organisational form consists of a small contractual core of career-minded professionals, technicians and managers supported partly by the *contractual fringe*, providing specialist freelance knowledge services on short-term projects (Handy, 2002). Handy

Figure 14.4   An example of a matrix organisational structure

Functions			
Divisions	IT	ADMINISTRATION	TECHNICAL SUPPORT
SEISMOLOGY	PROJECT TEAM A		
CARTOGRAPHY			
GEOLOGY		PROJECT TEAM B	

believed that, as a result of freelancing, fewer and fewer people would go to definite places of work and 'club centres' would arise where workers occasionally dropped in to share ideas or perform specific tasks which could not be done elsewhere. These changes led to Handy's vision of '**portfolio people**', with multiple skill sets selling their expertise to numerous organisations at the same time on specific projects.

Handy's portfolio people may even have found themselves working in '**virtual organisations**'. Such organisations may follow the concept of the adhocracy but are also characterised by employees who are 'physically dispersed ... working together regardless of location or who "owns" them' (De Sanctis and Monge, 1999: 693). Diverse workers can thus be linked electronically by ICT on a contract-by-contract basis in an ever-changing, 'boundaryless' organisation with no clear structure (*ibid*). These virtual, dynamic relationships may also be evident between *organisations* as well as workers. De Sanctis and Monge give the example of Barclays' 'virtual global bank' that electronically linked together existing networks of smaller local banks. Advances in ICT thus mean that the traditional industrial model of a definite and separate workplace is no longer standard nor essential. Workers or contractors can 'telecommute' from anywhere given the appropriate communication technology (Handy, 2002). For Handy, at least, the traditional organisation was being replaced by much more ethereal designs, and the virtual organisation is the epitome of this process.

THE LIMITS OF POST-INDUSTRIALISM/POST-FORDISM

The post-Fordist shift described above has severely limited applicability to much of what is going on in organisational design. Firstly, it must be noted that Burns and Stalker did *not* describe a step-change towards organic organisational forms, identifying few 'pure' organic organisations. They also noted that organisations chose to implement mechanistic or organic structures depending upon what worked best for them in their given environment. Burns and Stalker's theory was thus a **contingency theory** eschewing narrow best practice prescriptions in favour of highlighting how structure is dependent upon particular organisations' needs.

In terms of bureaucracies, one only has to look around to see that they have certainly not died out. Many public bodies, including universities, have bureaucratic structures and often a seemingly 'jobsworth' mentality amongst their officers. (You must all have stories of such experiences!) Furthermore, even within private companies, bureaucracy is rife. Again just think of your experiences when, for example, phoning your mobile phone company. Each different part of a query has to be dealt with by different departments who seemingly do not have the expertise or autonomy to help on any other matters (see also the 'Computer says No' example in the *Applying theory to practice* box above). This being 'passed on' between departments reflects the trained incapacity and silo mentality discussed above. Bureaucracy is so prevalent today that a book has even been published in its defence (Du Gay, 2000)!

The extent of lean production has also been overstated, Bradley *et al* (2000) noting that its uptake outwith Japan was limited to a few large multinational corporations (typically car manufacturers) on greenfield sites. Even where such methods were introduced, many of the supposed benefits can also be questioned. The use of lean production, for example, did not halt the Japanese economic crises of the 1990s. Furthermore, the claim that lean production leads to working 'smarter not harder' is also questionable. Critics claim that work is simply intensified, so that managers exert greater control over employees, especially as the trade union counterbalance is frequently removed from the workplace (Stewart *et al*, 2009). The upskilling allowed through lean production may also be a myth, commentators noting that workers simply experience horizontal job enlargement through an addition of low- or semi-skilled tasks to their core work (*ibid*). The moves towards work intensification and multi-tasking also means that *fewer* employees are required, leading to insecurity and job losses rather than *nenko* (*ibid*; Bradley *et al*, 2000). Bradley *et al* conclude that many aspects of Taylorism remain in lean production (for example, work intensification and 'one best way' dictated by management), and that ultimately it has failed to live up to its promises.

As stated above, the knowledge economy is also seen as a key driver of new organisational forms. Indeed, the Practitioner insight case study example is examined in the context of highly skilled work. The knowledge economy model can, however, be questioned. Goos and Manning (2003, 2007) reveal that although there has been growth in highly skilled jobs such as health professionals, engineers and technologists, there has also been strong growth in lower-skilled sales assistants, checkout operators, cooks, waiting and bar staff and health assistants. A polarised labour market with both 'lovely' and 'lousy' jobs is thus apparent (Goos and Manning, 2007). The extent of upskilling can also be questioned. Despite an increased demand for graduates, Felstead *et al* (2007) reveal that in 2006 the number of people in the UK with degrees outstripped demand by employers by 1.1 million. Furthermore, 25% of graduates believe that their degree is not necessary to do their job, suggesting that their skills may not be being put to best use (*ibid*). Perhaps more worryingly, employers' demand for people with no qualifications outstrips supply by over 5 million (*ibid*)! Clearly, the upskilled knowledge economy is only partial, with many low-skilled jobs remaining. Even within Handy's shamrock the flexible labour force exists. Such workers are typically low-skilled and low-paid, working under poor employment conditions and subject to the whim of changing market conditions (Kalleberg, 2000).

Many authors have highlighted continuity in classically designed organisations. Perhaps the most famous is George Ritzer's (2004) **McDonaldisation thesis**. Within this work Ritzer outlines how McDonalds' organisational principles are being taken up by many other businesses and are also, inexorably, 'coming to dominate more and more sectors of American society as well as the rest of the world' (p1). The principles that Ritzer describes as epitomised by McDonald's are:

- *efficiency* – McDonald's focuses on speed and efficiency in the delivery of their product. Workers follow discrete steps within tightly defined work processes for serving customers and making food (Leidner, 1993).

- *calculability* – McDonald's focuses on the size of their products since customers quantify the value that they receive and the efficiency of eating at McDonald's. Because workers' jobs vary so little, the focus is on how quickly tasks can be carried out, with workers 'expected to do a lot of work, very quickly for low pay' (Ritzer, 2004: 14).

- *predictability* – McDonald's offers standardised products and customers know that wherever they go the products will be largely the same. Workers also behave in predictable ways – for example, following scripts when serving customers ('Would you like to "go large"?', 'Have a nice day!').

- *control through non-human technology* – Customers are controlled to be in and out as quickly as possible. Workers are explicitly and directly controlled through technology for maximum efficiency and standardisation (for example, timers and automated equipment used when preparing food).

Does any of this look familiar? Ritzer is describing a Fordist environment designed to service mass markets of standardised products in a highly centralised MNC. Ritzer even identifies the ideas of Taylor, Weber and Ford as essential precursors of McDonaldisation, with workers reduced to dehumanised 'robots' on production lines. As a result, Ritzer sees McDonaldisation as inevitable if organisations want to expand, and gives myriad examples where these principles have been put into place, from Starbucks, to childcare centres, to doctors' and dentists' offices, to tax assessment centres and even within higher education. In Ritzer's analysis, Fordist production methods are not only continuing but may even be *expanding*.

Applying theory to practice: Examples of McDonaldisation

Ritzer (2004) identifies the pervasiveness of McDonaldisation into spheres in which it may seem undesirable. For example, in Kindercare – a childcare organisation – employees have little or no childcare skills or qualifications and 'teach' a curriculum dictated by an instruction book. Even lessons may thus be scripted and deskilled. Ritzer also identifies the dehumanising quantified nature of modern university mass education. He believes that the huge numbers of students living in 'mass dorms' and attending 'mass lectures' makes it difficult to meet other students (this seems a little unrealistic), let alone develop personal relationships with lecturers. To this he adds the use of machine-graded multiple-choice exams and posting students' results impersonally by national security number. Lecturers are also subject to impersonal, quantifiable ratings from student course evaluations scored on closed quantitative scales (such as you will probably be asked to fill in at the end of the course you are reading this book for) and even through assessments of the 'impact' of their publications. Even within healthcare the move has been towards quantity rather than quality of patient care, with doctors' salaries even linked to productivity. Many of these are US-specific examples and may have limited generalisability – but some may be familiar to you and remain thought-provoking nonetheless.

An obvious criticism might be that Ritzer is overstating his point and that the move to McDonaldisation is not as ubiquitous or inexorable as he claims. However, he is aware of non-McDonaldised organisations and that not all organisations follow the McDonald's model in its totality even where they implement some of the principles. Whether or not one agrees with the extent of his analysis, the fact remains that Ritzer convincingly identifies a large degree of continuity with large mechanistic organisational forms and subsequent mass production across all aspects of economic and social life.

Other writers have also identified the continuity of traditional organisational forms. Much research has been directed at call centres, themselves a seemingly ubiquitous component of modern life. (Who has not seemingly spent hours on hold or been bounced endlessly between departments when phoning for assistance?) Some have classified call centres as 'knowledge work' given its reliance on technology and the management of information. However, such work does not *create* knowledge but simply transfers it (Warhurst and Thompson, 1998). Indeed, within such centres anything other than routine tasks are generally referred to superiors or specialised departments (*ibid*). Weber's principles of demarcation and hierarchy thus remain alongside a functional organisational form. As in McDonaldisation, many customer interactions are scripted – employees have little autonomy and are tightly monitored through electronic management control systems (see Taylor and Bain, 1999, 2000; Baldry *et al*, 2007). Work is also highly intensified, the calls automatically routed one after the other. Employees are also expected to adhere to strict time guidelines for each call, leading to what Taylor and Bain (2000) call 'a production line in the head'.

WORST PRACTICE

It is very difficult to identify 'best' and 'worst' practice because management often choose *contingent* organisational designs to fit their purpose and environment (Burns and Stalker, 1961). It is, however, possible to identify good and bad practices in terms of the effects on workers. This chapter is littered with examples of 'bad' practice where organisations are structured so that work is dehumanising, deskilled and dissatisfying. An illustrative example, according to Scarbrough (1996) was call centre work in Direct Line. Here systems guided their employees through sales or customer queries on computer screens, in a predetermined step-by-step manner, with occurrences outside of those displayed seen as too complicated for the operator and passed on to a superior. Operators were deskilled by this technology because all thinking was done for them by the system. Baldry *et al*'s (2007) study of call centres also revealed work processes where managers tightly surveyed and monitored calls in the face of exacting and ever-increasing targets. Worker outcomes included poor satisfaction and morale, stress, high turnover, sickness and absence. If managers structure organisations along Taylorised lines, not only may staff suffer but ultimately the organisation can incur costs as well.

A notable paper by Boreham (1992) also reveals the myth of post-Fordist organisational forms. Presenting data from seven differing countries (Australia, Britain, Canada, Germany, Japan, Sweden and the USA), Boreham identifies two key proxies for 'post-Fordist' management: employee autonomy and employee participation in organisational decision-making. His results reveal that non-managerial employees generally reported low levels of autonomy and decision-making power, even when they were experienced and skilled workers. Boreham concludes that Fordism has not been replaced and that, 'the contemporary workplace appears to be one in which it is hierarchy that matters' (p21). Although this paper is a little out of date, his findings are borne out by more recent data. Green (2006) states that between 1986 and 2001 the proportion of UK workers reporting they had a 'great deal of choice' over how they worked declined from 52% to 39%. Similarly, Felstead *et al* (2007) show that between 1992 and 2006 the proportion of workers reporting that they had a 'great deal of influence' over their work likewise declined significantly. These data suggest that the autonomous/high-trust post-Fordist organisation is not only more thinly spread than some believe – it is actually in decline.

So what of teamworking and multi-skilling, other essential components of the post-Fordist work organisation? The nationally representative Workplace Employment Relations Survey (WERS) conducted in 2004 revealed that 72% of all British workplaces formally engaged in teamworking (Kersley *et al*, 2006). However, this figure tells us little. Only 51% of establishments extended teamworking to all employees and it was most common amongst highly skilled professionals. Furthermore, only in approximately one-third of workplaces did teams display all of the following characteristics of 'true' teamwork: responsibility for specific tasks, dependence on the work of each other, the ability to rotate tasks and the making of joint decisions on how work was to be done. When adding whether teams could autonomously appoint their own leaders, the proportion of workplaces in which that occurred fell to only 4% (*ibid*: 89–91)! The data also revealed that only 21% of establishments had groups of non-managerial employees meeting to solve organisational problems, which was again most common amongst higher-skilled and professional employees (the kind of employees considered in the Practitioner insight case study). These data reveal that a minority of British workplaces displayed some post-Fordist work elements, typically in relation to higher-skilled knowledge workers, but that these practices were certainly not widespread.

The extent of virtual organisations and **teleworking** are also questionable. De Sanctis and Monge (1999) reveal that very few organisations are purely virtual. Virtual organising was instead partly evident in *some* external relationships, multi-functional teams and/or physically distant telecommuters in *some* organisations. The extent of teleworking is also quite low, as shown by data collected across the EU15. Only 4% of EU employees could be classified as mobile teleworkers (working 10 hours or more away from the home or office a week and using an Internet connection while doing so); only 3% were self-employed and teleworked from a home office (for example, as portfolio workers); and only approximately 2% teleworked from home on one or more day a week (SIBIS, 2003). These figures were even lower in the accession states that had not joined the EU at the time. Even where technology is used in the workplace, Bradley *et al* (2000) reveal that it does not necessarily improve organisational effectiveness or productivity or make workers' lives easier. Indeed, they report that increased use of technology is often associated with an increase in stress and pressure.

If IT is not widely used to facilitate virtual organisations or teleworking, how is it then being used? Baldry *et al*'s (1998) study of three modern offices heavily reliant on IT found 'team Taylorism' (p168) in supposedly multi-function teams. Although one public sector organisation and a finance company did allow teams to complete entire work processes (for example, receiving, processing and finalising a claim), the work itself remained repetitive and monotonous. In another public sector office teams did not complete the whole work process, each tightly defined stage of dealing with a query being carried out by a separate team. Within each organisation technology, used to impose and meet expanding targets, led to an increase in the amount, speed and intensity of work and ever-greater supervision, control and discipline from managers. Baldry *et al* are left to conclude that the 'obsession with targets and measurements of output would have delighted F. W. Taylor' (p172), and that far from the post-Fordist ideal, these organisations more readily resembled a 'Dickensian sweatshop' (p182). IT can thus reinforce traditional bureaucratic and Taylorised work environments as well as newer post-Fordist organisations.

A further way technology may be used in a fashion that is detrimental to employees is the increased outsourcing and **offshoring** of certain organisational functions, often for reasons of cost (Noon and Blyton, 2007; Legge, 2007). Thus far outsourcing has been discussed in terms of specialist knowledge services, but this is only part of the story. Now many organisations in the developing world are outsourcing low-skill work to low-wage economies, effectively treating employees as if they are external to the organisation and as expendable as any other resource such as machinery. Contemporarily, it is particularly call centre and back-office (routine data processing) operations that are being offshored, although other services reliant on IT such as HR and payroll are also being offshored as well as higher-skilled jobs such as software development and research (Noon and Blyton, 2007; Gilmore and Williams, 2009). Gilmore and Williams estimate that between 2004 and 2008 almost three-quarters of a million financial services jobs were offshored from Western Europe to lower-cost countries such as India, China, Israel, the Philippines, Eastern Europe and South Africa. Clearly, such moves create insecurity and job losses for employees in the home nation, providing further evidence of how IT can be used to control employees and fragment organisations.

Taking your learning further: Post-Fordism and 'new' organisational forms

Burns and Stalker's (1961) book *The Management of Innovation*, which contains the mechanistic–organic continuum, is of course a classic study in the field of organisational design and structure. What is particularly notable about the study is the identification of the uptake of different forms depending upon the environment in which the organisation operates rather than trying to prescribe a 'one best way' approach à la Taylor.

Bell's (1976) *The Coming of Post Industrial* Society, in which the upskilling thesis was presented, is perhaps one of the texts that most stimulated discussion about the advent of the knowledge economy and associated organisational developments.

Despres and Hiltrop's (1995) article 'Human resource management in the knowledge age' in *Employee Relations* is a notable article on

'new' organisational forms in such upskilled knowledge work. The article describes many of the characteristics of post-Fordist organisations discussed here, and although it is open to the critique of overstating the concepts, it remains a good starting point.

Taylor and Bain's (1999) article 'An assembly-line in the head' in the *Industrial Relations Journal* is something of a stark contrast to Despres and Hiltrop's. This article provides an excellent critical discussion of work in a call centre and shows how even 'new' work concerned with managing information is subject to Taylorist and Fordist principles.

These readings thus show the development of post-Fordist ideas and also, in Taylor and Bain's case, a critique.

ALTERNATIVE ORGANISATIONAL FORMS [3]

While most organisational behaviour textbooks focus on work and management in traditional commercial organisations, they often fail to acknowledge alternative forms of organisations that are characterised by a higher level of employee involvement. This section explores organisations such as co-operatives, share ownership companies and partnership organisations.

A **co-operative** is an autonomous organisation owned and controlled equally by the people who use its services or who work at it. Its ethos is the achievement of economic democracy. Members are voluntarily united for their mutual benefit to meet their common economic, social, and cultural needs and aspirations through a jointly owned enterprise. Although the reformer Robert Owen is considered the pioneer of co-operative ideas – in 1810 Owen and his associates bought a mill in Wales, introduced better conditions of work and offered high discounts and profit sharing to the employees – the first recorded successful co-operative enterprise was the Rochdale Society of Equitable Pioneers, founded in England in 1844 by a group of 28 weavers and other artisans in order to open their own food store. By the 1860s co-operatives were fully established in the United Kingdom and modelled on the 'Rochdale Principles', which are still found in today's co-operatives. The organisational model of the co-operative is widely popular in the USA as well as in Europe. In the EU in Italy, France, Spain and Germany co-operatives often represent a significant percentage of total trade (in fact, Wilson, 2010: 364, reports that in Italy co-operatives account for 30% of the total trade). The International Co-operative Alliance's (2004) *Present Application of the Rochdale Principles of Co-operation* can be seen in Table 14.3.

Table 14.3:   The characteristics of co-operative organisations

Feature	Characteristics
Open membership	Membership should be wide open to admit all people to the enjoyment of the benefits of co-operation. Legislation can, however, allow co-operatives to limit the number of their members.
Democratic control	The principle of 'one person, one vote' applies without any reference to the amount of shares or other capital interest held by individuals. Committees of management or representatives are democratically elected.
Dividend on purchase	Net surpluses are generally distributed to members and/or allocated to reserve funds and/or allocated to the provision of welfare services to members.
Limited interest on capital	Where share capital exists within the organisation, either a limited rate of interest is paid or else no interest is paid out to shareholders.
Political and religious neutrality	With a few exceptions, generally co-operatives are neutral in politics and religion. The exceptional societies might either act in collaboration with political parties or religious associations.
Cash trading	Trading by the organisation is usually made with cash rather than credit, although short-term credit (eg 30 days) may be available to co-operatives.

Although co-operatives are certainly associated with a sense of ownership, often the financial constraints and the level of technology available influence working practices, limiting workers' control over their jobs. Cornforth *et al* (1988) found that when co-operatives were successful, workers were satisfied, highly involved, positive about their products, services and colleagues, and they found their work much more stimulating than traditional employment. However, co-operative working was also intense, requiring a high emotional involvement, and was often characterised by severe financial concerns. Positive aspects such as more flexibility and employee control were often counterbalanced by low pay and long working hours. Although co-operative work has some problematic aspects, overall, co-operatives offer more egalitarian working practices and a high level of identification with organisational values.

Other forms of employee financial participation are share ownership and partnership, in which the company is owned partly or wholly by its employees. Unlike co-operatives, share ownership companies are generally managed by a trust, and the profits are shared with employees. Although there are successful examples of wholly employee-owned organisations (eg the John Lewis Partnership in the UK, and W. L. Gore & Associates, Inc., in the USA – the developer of Gore-Tex waterproof and breathable fabrics), more often participation consists of a mixed ownership where the company's shares are also available on public stock markets. Several large corporations have arrangements for employee participation in the form of **employees' stock ownership plans** (ESOPs), offering share schemes to employees who have been with the company for a certain length of time. Such plans are funded through contributions deductable from employee participants' pay, which are then invested in company shares. ESOPs are widely available employee benefit plans and, in many countries, are associated with significant tax benefits for the company and the employees.

While share ownership is often represented as a means to increase commitment (Kelly and Kelly, 1991) and productivity (Robinson and Perotic, 1997) the research evidence is mixed. Wilson's (2010) review suggests that benefits resulting from share ownership were not seen by employees as an essential element of pay but 'just another type of bonus' and therefore did not generate higher commitment. Often the employee stake is too small to bring about a sense of ownership, and although employee shares offer some financial participation, such schemes are not generally associated with participation in decision-making or with increased control over one's work processes and practices (*ibid*).

Employee involvement was introduced in the mid-nineteenth century to prevent or inhibit trade union membership and participation. An example of successful employee ownership in the UK is the John Lewis Partnership, which comprises the John Lewis department store chain, Waitrose, the supermarket chain, and the direct consumer services company Greenbee. The business was founded in 1864 by John Lewis and developed into a partnership by his son John Spedan Lewis in 1920, when the profit-sharing scheme was introduced along with a representative staff council. Today there are 70,000 partners, mostly full-time, who share the company's profits (http://www.johnlewispartnership.co.uk). The company's website (*ibid*) provides a wealth of information on the company's history, philosophy and strategy as well as documents and recordings of the founder's views and employees' testimonials.

Such alternative organisational structures, despite the concerns raised above, certainly provide, in theory, a greater sense of democracy, ownership and involvement. These alternative organisational forms show different ways in which organisations can be structured and management can be practised to achieve a less hierarchical and bureaucratic structure and a more egalitarian workplace.

BEST PRACTICE

Autonomy at a call centre

Jenkins *et al* (2010) present a type of call centre very different from those discussed throughout this chapter. 'VoiceTel' provides outsourced reception services for a number of clients. Managers organise receptionists in small teams, each with a leader, who negotiate their own identity and precise way of working. Each receptionist has up to 40 diverse clients to answer calls for and on whom they have to have considerable knowledge, while also having some knowledge of teammates' clients. Receptionists are free to negotiate the exact nature of service directly with the client and to gather knowledge on their clients in a similar manner. Similarly, there are no scripted prescriptions for how

calls should be answered: receptionists are free to use their skill, judgement and knowledge of their clients' needs. There are no performance measures, targets or time-limits attached to call-handling. The jobs are high in discretion and autonomy, multi-skilled, and not monotonous, the workers in turn showing high degrees of job satisfaction and organisational commitment. Jenkins *et al* conclude that management in VoiceTel had been successful in implementing a successful 'high-commitment' organisational design, inconsistent with Taylorism. Although VoiceTel is a unique case study that may not easily be generalised, it provides an excellent example of 'good' practice, nonetheless.

Conclusion

This chapter has shown that as organisations grew, management sought to 'rationalise' them through mechanistic organisational designs that many, such as Braverman, have highlighted as dehumanising and detrimental to workers' well-being. Clearly, managing large organisations is highly complex and managers need to somehow co-ordinate activities in some way, but are Taylorism, Fordism, bureaucracy and functional organisational structures necessarily the answer? These 'rational' designs may also have 'irrational' outcomes: there are many examples of dysfunctional bureaucracies and also of resistance to the imposition of Taylorism. Mechanistic organisational forms are, however, efficient at servicing mass markets through offering low-cost products. With the advent of flexible specialisation and the knowledge economy, it has been argued that organisations themselves are becoming 'post-Fordist', 'organic' and flexible, and some (such as Handy and 'virtual' organisational writers) are now questioning whether organisations will even retain any form of concrete structure. It is also argued that the greater autonomy and creativity allowed in such organisations is beneficial to the motivation and well-being of workers (see Chapter 5), a view that is shared by Jacqui Cowing in the Practitioner insight case study at the beginning of the chapter. Evidence, however, shows that the take-up of post-Fordist organisational designs is patchy and that the changing economic modes of organising behind these apparent changes can be questioned. Some writers, such as Ritzer and Baldry and his colleagues, have revealed that traditional mechanistic organisational forms not only continue but are even *expanding*, colonising new spheres of employment such as services, where their applicability may at first sight seem unlikely.

The effect of the continuation of mechanistic forms leads Warhurst and Thompson (1998) to conclude that the post-Fordist 'paradigm shift' has not occurred (p20):

> Most workers are struggling to survive in and make sense of routine jobs and there are few employees commuting from electronic cottages or happily hawking their portfolios around companies.

Virtual organising is rare, and Handy was wrong – which is not overly surprising because he is a speculative 'futurologist' and most of his analysis appears to be plucked out of thin air. (Read *The Age of Unreason* and see what you think!) What should be clear, however, from the evidence presented in this chapter is that the old and new co-exist. One way of dealing with this complexity is the use of the term 'neo-Fordism'. Edgell (2006) believes that McDonaldisation is a form of neo-Fordism differentiated from traditional Fordism by the involvement of the customer in work processes, by the juxtaposition of mass production, choice, quality and low prices, and by attempts to organise work on a team basis. Call centres and other new organisations where post-Fordism is not apparent may also be described as neo-Fordist because differences with the traditional Fordist model are apparent. Some of the pitfalls of Fordism and Taylorism for organisations and employees may be avoided by new organisational forms, but analysis has shown that many of the negative effects remain. However one presents it, continuity in traditional organisational structures and designs remains, and Fordism, neo-Fordism and post-Fordism co-exist.

End notes

[1] See also Chapter 2.

[2] See also Chapters 2 and 13.

[3] See also Chapter 16.

REVIEW AND DISCUSSION QUESTIONS

REVIEW QUESTIONS

1 What are the defining characteristics of Taylorism and Fordism?

2 How is bureaucracy similar to Taylorism and Fordism? How does it differ?

3 What are the characteristics of functional and divisional structures? How do these differ from adhocracy?

4 How does Braverman's deskilling hypothesis relate to Taylorism, Fordism and bureaucracy?

5 Which economic models have supposedly motivated movement towards 'new' forms of organisation? What 'new' forms of organisation are these changes related to?

6 What are the key points of Ritzer's McDonaldisation thesis?

DISCUSSION QUESTIONS

1 Were Taylor's methods morally objectionable?

2 Is bureaucracy doomed to be inefficient?

3 Is McDonaldisation inevitable?

4 What does the call centre tell us about contemporary organisations and the organisation of work?

5 Why do managers remain attracted to classic mechanistic organisational forms when there are organic alternatives available?

FURTHER READING

Grey, C. (2009) *A Very Short, Fairly Interesting and Reasonably Cheap Book About Studying Organizations.* London: Sage. This amusingly written book is an excellent introduction to learning about organisations, their effects on people and their place in society.

Handy, C. (2002) *The Age of Unreason.* London: Random House. Worth reading as an indication of how management gurus conceive the future of organisations. A good example of rhetoric and reality not marrying!

Ritzer, G. (2004) *The McDonaldization of Society.* Thousand Oaks, CA: Pine Forge Press. A modern-day classic. Accessible and full of enlightening examples, this book debunks many of the ideas associated with post-Fordism.

Thompson, P. and Warhurst, C. (eds) (1998) *Workplaces of the Future.* Basingstoke: Macmillan. A comprehensive, critical collection analysing the 'new' workplace, the extent of change and the effects of organisations on employees.

Thompson, P. and McHugh, D. (2002) *Work Organisations*, 3rd edition. Basingstoke: Palgrave Macmillan. A comprehensive, illuminating and critical text covering all major aspects of organisations, how they work and the effects they have on those within them, in depth.

KEY SKILLS

THINKING CRITICALLY AND LEARNING REFLECTIVELY

This chapter has highlighted the manner in which much management rhetoric is often taken at face value without proper consideration. Critical evaluation of the evidence, however, reveals a rather different picture. Such skills are also important in the workplace – for example, when evaluating a proposal it is essential to interrogate the evidence rather than taking presenters' claims at face value. Similarly, if a consultant is trying to sell your organisation a design 'solution', then it pays to have people who can think critically. In such situations it is essential to ask yourself questions such as: Will the proposed system really have the benefits that it claims? Is the proposed solution really applicable for this organisation?

SOCIAL RESPONSIBILITY AND ETHICS

From its inception Taylorism has raised ethical questions regarding its effects on workers. Newer developments also raise ethical questions. Perhaps nowhere is the requirement for ethical decision-making more important today than when making offshoring decisions, for example. As suggested in the Practitioner insight case study, these considerations should always be forefront in the eyes of managers not only for ethical and humanitarian reasons but also because negative impacts on workers will eventually affect the company. For example, dissatisfied employees may leave, and the company incur recruitment costs. Exhausted and stressed employees may need time off sick, further costing the organisation. Treating workers badly will affect not only workers' morale, health and company performance but could also impact negatively upon the company's reputation. Think, for example, of the effect that the US Congressional investigation must have had on Taylor. This loss of reputational capital could lead to decreases in sales or future problems in recruiting staff. A critical, analytical, ethical and socially responsible mind can potentially alleviate many of the problems that are caused by workers' negative reactions to work design before they even occur.

ANALYTICAL SKILLS AND DECISION-MAKING

The above key skills highlight the importance of analytical skills in building up an evidence base, critically evaluating the evidence and eventually making decisions. Analytical skills are essential in organisational structure issues – for example, critically interrogating the claims of consultants, as noted above, or gathering evidence on the manner in which certain organisational structures may be linked to organisational performance or how these may impact upon employees. Through analytical skills decision-making can be improved so that informed decisions ultimately make an evidence-based contribution to organisational success.

NEGOTIATION AND CONFLICT RESOLUTION SKILLS

Taylor and Ford imposed their work practices upon employees without adequately consulting them or justifying their actions, and many organisations today still do this, raising yet more ethical concerns. The Congressional investigation into Taylor's methods was particularly damning in this regard. Through consultation and joint determination (as in co-operatives), improvements may be made, reducing any conflict and ultimately benefiting both managers and employees.

EMOTIONAL INTELLIGENCE, SYMPATHY, EMPATHY AND LISTENING

The above negotiations will not be successful if employees can tell that managers are not interested in listening to them or in understanding their position. By picking up on such frustrations through emotional intelligence, managers can tell whether or not their negotiating tactics are working. If not, perhaps empathy is lacking and more effort is needed to put themselves in the employees' positions. Remember, it was noted above that Taylor seemed devoid of emotional intelligence (empathy or sympathy) and he certainly did not listen to his workers. These would have been factors in the large-scale opposition and industrial unrest he encountered. Decisions that are unsympathetically and unilaterally enforced are not likely to ultimately benefit the organisation.

Chapter 15
Organisational Culture and Change Management

Vincenza Priola and Scott A. Hurrell

PART FOUR

Contents

Key Learning Outcomes

By the end of this chapter you should be able to:

- understand the meaning of organisational culture, and its complexity
- evaluate the various implications that different perspectives on organisational culture have on the understanding of work organisations
- analyse how differences in national culture affect work and organisations operating across national boundaries
- critically reflect on how organisational culture plays an important role in the management of employee diversity
- reflect on the implications of change interventions on the culture of the organisation
- understand the processes involved in managing organisational change
- evaluate various ways in which change can be implemented and the impact that these might have on employees' experiences of work.

PRACTITIONER INSIGHT

Truflo Marine

Truflo Marine is a specialist designer, manufacturer and supplier of high-integrity valves, actuators and pressure-reducing stations for critical seawater, nuclear and naval marine applications. It was established in Birmingham in 1962 and offers exceptional experience and expertise to engineers and buyers involved in critical flow control solutions. In May 2006, the international engineering business IMI plc bought the Truflo International Group. Over the intervening years Truflo Marine has gradually been integrated into one of the main IMI business platforms: Severe Service.

We speak to **Clayton Manley,** who has been at Truflo Marine for over 10 years and became the Managing Director in 2009, about Truflo Marine's culture and the integration process within an international group (IMI plc) with its Head Office in the USA. 'Quality, integrity and reliability' is at the heart of Truflo Marine's mission, defining the nature of the products and embedded within its company culture. Because Truflo Marine manufactures products that are critical to the safety and performance of nuclear submarines, the marketplace and the nature of those products underpin its culture. The products, and the processes that underpin them, must be right and fit-for-purpose; they have

to be trusted by all stakeholders. A problem within a product could ultimately cost someone's life.

As Truflo Marine is changing in order to better integrate with a much larger business and expand its sales to new markets, it is also working towards the introduction of a more innovative and continuous improvement (CI) culture, where individuals and teams are empowered to implement best practice and change in their areas. This is supported with a robust continuous improvement framework (the Business Excellence model) through targeted training, ensuring that individuals have the tools, techniques and confidence to implement their own ideas for improvement.

What do you think are Truflo Marine's challenges in integrating within IMI plc?

What could be the advantages and disadvantages of the buy-out for Truflo Marine management and its workforce?

How do you think the company manages in practice the process of empowering individuals to support the emphasis on continuous improvement?

Once you have read this chapter, return to these questions and think about how you could answer them.

Introduction

Although the concept of organisational culture is currently widely accepted and recognised, it represents one of the newest topics in the field of organisational behaviour. In fact, most of the literature defining culture and investigating how it develops has originated since the 1980s. As suggested by Thompson and McHugh (2002), the credit for reviving the issue of corporate culture mainly goes to US management gurus Peters and Waterman (1982) and Deal and Kennedy (1982), connected to the management consultancy firm McKinsey, and to the academic William Ouchi (1981). Ouchi is known for developing the '**theory Z**', which refers to a distinctive type of organisational culture that represents a US adaptation of the Japanese management style also known as 'hierarchical clan' culture, which has been adopted to various extents by organisations such as IBM, Procter & Gamble, Hewlett-Packard, Kodak and Rockwell International, among others.

Although the literature on organisational culture has proliferated since the early 1980s, the idea of cultural elements in organisational life is not new. The notion of culture in relation to organisations was present in Taylor's 'scientific management', which aimed at breaking the subcultures of the shop floor and creating a culture of management (see the previous chapter). Similarly, the human relations school had important cultural objectives in terms of developing an environment in which workers were appreciated. However, it was only in 1952 that Elliott Jaques (in Linstead *et al*, 2009) first used the term 'culture' in relation to work organisations. The growing emphasis on culture in the 1980s and 1990s coincided with a more general shift away from a concern on structure and economy towards 'softer' managerial issues. While earlier discussions acknowledged the benefits of developing a 'strong' organisational culture, academic debates proliferated around definitions and the tangibility of the concept itself. In an attempt to define culture, earlier writers made a distinction between culture and climate, suggesting that the former is more stable and enduring as well as more difficult to define and evaluate than climate. Climate is generally measured quantitatively through employee surveys, whereas culture can only be studied using the anthropological methods of **ethnography** used to study human cultures and societies.

This chapter aims at discussing how organisational culture has been defined and understood by researchers in relation to the point of view they adopt. In doing so, the chapter problematises issues associated with processes of culture 'creation' and development as well as processes associated with interventions aimed at managing change in general and culture change in particular. In addition, the chapter discusses the importance of national cultures in organisations and explores how the ways in which organisations manage diversity are highly influenced by the core values and beliefs that make up the organisational culture.

UNDERSTANDING ORGANISATIONAL CULTURE

Organisational culture is a contested concept and one of the most difficult to define. Just as it is difficult to define culture in a sociological and anthropological sense, it is also extremely difficult to construct a comprehensive definition of organisational culture. If culture in general is what makes us humans, organisational culture is the 'feeling' part of an organisation or, as Hatch (2006) suggests, it is the way of life in an organisation. Culture defines the basic organisational values, and communicates to new members the behaviours and actions that are encouraged, the ways in which things ought to be done, and the behaviours that are discouraged.

It enhances the stability of an organisation and helps members to interpret organisational life while it also provides them with a sense of identity.

A review of the literature on culture brings to the fore the myriad definitions that have been offered by organisational theorists. As examples we present here three widely reported definitions:

> Culture is a pattern of beliefs and expectations shared by the organisation's members. These beliefs and expectations produce norms that powerfully shape the behaviour of individuals and groups in the organisation.
>
> Schwarts and Davies (1981: 33)

> A set of understandings or meanings shared by a group of people. The meanings are largely tacit among members, clearly relevant to the particular and distinctive to the group. Meanings are passed on to new group members.
>
> Louis (1980)

> Organisational culture can be thought of as a glue that holds an organisation together through a sharing of patterns of meaning. The culture focuses on the values, beliefs and expectations that members come to share.
>
> Siehl and Martin (1984: 227)

Since these and most other definitions associate the concept of culture with beliefs, values, expectations and meanings that are shared by organisational members, we can argue that culture cannot be dictated by top management, although it can certainly be influenced by the company founders. Organisational culture is tied to more fundamental beliefs, values and shared meanings that are both created by and reflected in the key symbols such as ceremonies, stories, language (in the form of jokes, metaphors, legends, etc) which are recognised by organisational members (see, for example, Schein, 1985). It is also reflected in the norms and rules, in the organisational philosophy and climate. Think about two widely different companies such as Apple Inc. and IBM. Apple (founded in the 1970s) offered an alternative corporate culture to the traditional bureaucratic, hierarchical organisation more typical at the time, adopting a flat rather than tall hierarchy, an image associated with anti-establishment and innovation, a casual dress code (legend says that Steve Jobs, one of the founders, often walked around the office barefoot even after Apple was a Fortune 500 company), and a philosophy focusing on aesthetic design and distinctive advertising campaigns. Such culture highly differentiated the company and placed it in opposition to IBM, one of its stronger competitors. IBM has a sales-oriented business culture supported by 'uniformed professionals' who observed the strict dress code of 'dark (or gray) suit, white shirt and a sincere tie' (Smith, 1999: 24) until the 1990s when CEO Louis V. Gerstner Jr relaxed these codes, implementing a 'business casual' dress code. Such changes in the dress code do not affect the organisational culture, but the more or less formality of a dress code still reflects the formalised, 'professional', sales-oriented business emphasis of IBM's values.

Culture distinguishes organisations and is often referred to as 'how things are done around here' (eg Drennan, 1992), but although it is reflected in key organisational symbols it is important to point out that these symbols are not the culture itself – they are the means of transmitting and maintaining the culture. A variety of other measures, most often HR practices, also contribute to the transmission and the endorsement of the company culture. Such measures include recruitment and selection processes, appraisal systems, training and development, company-wide initiatives and community programmes. New members are often selected on the basis of a match between their values and those of the organisation or, when this is not the case, they go through a process of socialisation leading to the learning and internalisation of such values (see, for example, Pascale, 1985; Anderson and Ostroff, 1997).

Figure 15.1   Schein's three levels of culture

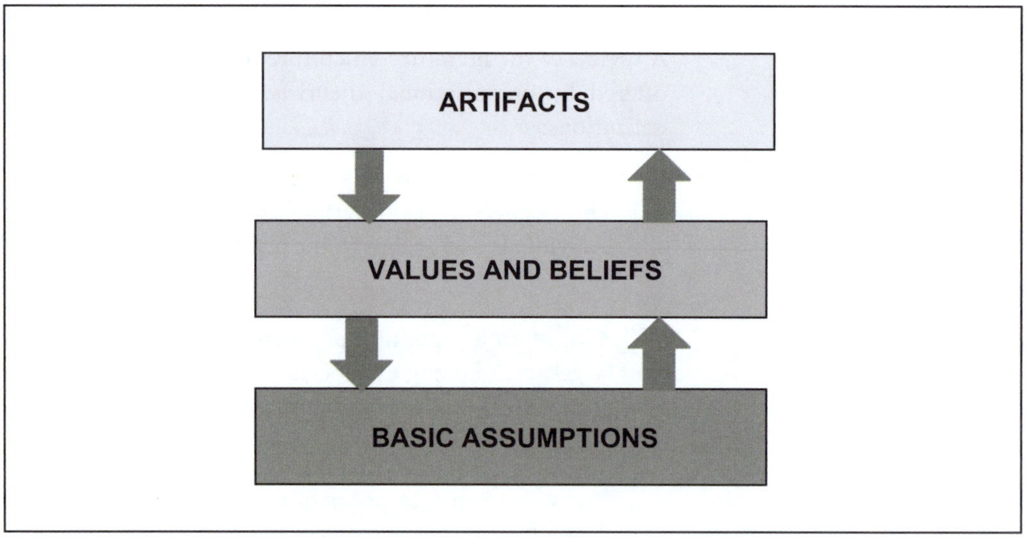

Source: adapted from Schein (1985) *Organizational Culture and Leadership*. New York: Wiley & Sons, p14

Edgar Schein's model of organisational culture

One of the most influential theories of organisational culture is that formulated in the 1980s by Edgar Schein, a US social psychologist. Schein suggests that culture in organisations exists on three levels, starting from the deepest level of **basic** beliefs and **assumptions**, followed by **values and behavioural norms**, which are followed by the superficial level, consisting of the most visible of all cultural elements: the **artifacts**. Figure 15.1 offers a representation of Schein's three levels of culture.

The superficial level of *artifacts* consists of visible manifestations of an organisation's culture such as physical (eg office layout, dress code, location and appearance of the building) and material objects (eg corporate logos, mission statements, company brochures, advertising material, annual reports) and the level of technology. The physical environment mutually contributes with the socially constructed environment (eg behaviours such as rituals and celebrations, language, symbols, stories and myths, metaphors) to create an organisation's artifacts. There are obviously many forms and types of artifacts observable in organisations and the above suggestions are only a few examples. Such artifacts are considered the manifestations and indicators of the deeper level of culture, and thus are used as a guide to understand an organisation's values and therefore its culture. However, because they are distant from the core assumptions and predispositions, those who are attempting to understand an organisation's culture can also misinterpret artifacts.

As mentioned above, mission statements are considered cultural artifacts. Consider, for example the mission statement of Barclays Bank Plc:

> Barclays' strategy is to achieve good growth through time by diversifying its business base and increasing its presence in markets and segments that are growing rapidly. This is driven by the Group's ambition to become one of a handful of universal banks leading the global financial services industry, helping customers and clients throughout the world achieve their goals. The strategy is based on the principles of earn, invest and grow. ... Barclays' five guiding principles are key to the way the business operates: Winning together ..., Best people ..., Customer and client focus ..., Pioneering ..., Trusted ....
>
> (Barclays Plc, http://group.barclays.com/About-us/Who-we-are-and-what-we-do/Our-vision-and-strategy)

Do you feel that this information provides a good source of access to understand the Bank's culture? What does this statement tell you about its organisational culture? Can you discern some of the Bank's values by reading its mission statement only?

Although information such as mission statements and company literature, combined with other artifacts, can undoubtedly give an insight into an organisation's culture (eg in the case of Barclays above, an emphasis on growth, expansion to different markets and the aspiration to be a world leader in financial services, which reflects some of the company's values), culture can only be fully understood as the product of a historical process investigating the company's development through time and studying a variety of aspects. In addition, it is worth adopting a more critical eye in examining company literature (eg mission statement, brochures, etc) in that there is often a gap between the good intentions expressed and the realities of the organisation's practices (Brown, 1998).

Values are placed at a deeper level than artifacts and are located between these and the basic assumptions. They refer to the principles and standards held by an organisation, are linked to the moral and ethical codes, and refer to what the members of an organisation care about (Hatch, 2006). The cultural values determine the *behavioural norms* expected, thus allowing organisational members to know what is expected of them in a variety of situations. Schein (1985) suggests that a leader's beliefs can become collective beliefs with time through the medium of values, and that the members of a culture hold values and conform to norms because they are supported by their underlying beliefs and assumptions.

Cultural values and norms are more difficult to detect than the artifacts and often, without an accurate historical analysis of the company, their understanding and analysis may be highly challenging and/or might lack truthfulness. Take the examples of companies such as Nike, Gap and Mattel. In 2010 these companies appeared in lists of the world's most ethical companies (eg ethisphere.com), however, in the late 1990s they were subjected to very strong criticism and high-profile negative campaigns for producing their goods in Asian sweatshops. Such sweatshops – or sweat factories – employ workers who often work long hours for a low wage in a substandard working environment which may have hazardous materials and situations and might employ child labour. Without detailing the specific cases of the companies mentioned above, one has to consider how in less than a decade such companies are now considered highly ethical. The reasons are to be found on the companies' responses to the negative PR such accusations have generated since the late 1990s. In their responses, in fact, these companies put forth statements of corporate social responsibility, described new ethics and compliance programmes and inaugurated various other measures, including factory inspections, to defend their practices. Nike specifically (De Tienne and Lewis, 2005: 362):

> presented its assertions of fair employee treatment, good factory conditions, and equitable company-wide standards through many mediums including a labor report, its statement of corporate responsibility, personal letters, website segments, college visits and newspaper releases.

Without the wider historical and contextual information – including various court rulings culminating in a highly contested US Supreme Court case that in 2003 accepted the Nike argument – an examination of Nike's ethical values from the inside (eg company documents, company interviews) would provide a different cultural analysis.

The *basic assumptions* are at the core of the organisational culture and are implicit, deeply rooted and often unconscious. They guide members' perceptions, feelings and thoughts and are highly difficult to detect and change. Basic assumptions are generally concerned with broad beliefs about nature and humanity. Different assumptions held by organisational members lead to different perceptions of what is central to the organisation's life. Schein (1985: 86) lists the following seven basic cultural assumptions – examples for each of them are reported in brackets:

- the organisation's relationship to its environment (the way in which the organisation perceives itself to be dominant, submissive or harmonising in relation to its environment)

- the nature of human activity (the orientation towards either high achievement or a more fatalistic approach to life: this point differentiates between those for whom work is primary to their life and those who value their private life more)

- the nature of reality and truth (differences in how people view truth either as decided by pure dogma or by the wisdom of trusted leaders)

- the nature of time (the orientation of individuals and organisations in terms of past, present and future)

- the nature of human nature (assumptions held at company level on whether people are fundamentally lazy or highly self-motivated – see McGregor's theory X and theory Y)

- the nature of human social arrangements (referring to assumptions about the correct ways to distribute power and to organise society – eg competitive versus co-operative values)

- the difference between homogeneity and diversity (whether the organisation emphasises diversity and innovation or conformity).

One interesting point worth noting is that in Schein's model the arrows not only point upward from the basic assumptions to the values and the artifacts; there is also the suggestion that the artifacts can transform the basic assumptions that produce them (the arrows pointing down). Furthermore, Schein suggests that the culture of an organisation reveals itself when presented with problems and challenges, rather than in its routines. This has obvious implications for the methodologies used to study organisational culture. As briefly suggested in the introduction, in order to observe the cultural dynamics in periods of change and problems you cannot rely on self-report questionnaires. One has to be part of the organisational life (at least for a period of time) and to experience the cultural processes. This is only possible when an ethnographic approach is used.

PERSPECTIVES ON CULTURE

The above discussion has given an insight into the complexity of organisational culture as a concept. This section explores and distinguishes between various approaches to the study of culture in organisations. There is a fundamental distinction between those who study culture. Some authors and researchers (eg Kotter and Heskett, 1992; Deal and Kennedy, 1982) believe that culture is an objective reality that can be measured and manipulated to increase organisational performance and effectiveness (the *modernist-objectivist perspective*). On the other hand there are those authors and researchers (eg Morgan, 1986) who think of culture as a metaphor developed for understanding organisations (the *symbolic-interpretivist perspective*). Such distinctions refer not only to the existing dissent about the nature of culture but also to the lack of consensus about its amenability to managerial manipulation (Wilmott, 2000). In fact, authors such as Ackroyd and Crowdy (1990) and Legge (1994) raise concerns regarding the possibilities of managing and changing culture in organisations despite the efforts of practitioners who continue to offer culture change programmes and initiatives.

Culture is understood by researchers, theorists, practitioners, managers and employees according to the viewpoint they adopt. Joanne Martin (1992), in an attempt to consolidate a diverse array of theoretical and empirical research on culture, provides a meta-theoretical framework to clarify and challenge the assumptions that have guided diverse and conflicting perspectives to the study of culture in organisations. She distinguishes between three perspectives that are dominant in organisational culture research, and explains how the different theoretical points of view affect the ways in which not only culture is perceived and studied but also how people's behaviours are influenced by their own viewpoint and those of the people around them. Martin also suggests that these three social science perspectives come to different conclusions about how culture changes and therefore make implications for managing cultural transitions difficult to understand. The three perspectives examined in Martin's (1992) book are labelled *integration*, *differentiation*, and *fragmentation*.

From an **integrationist perspective**, culture is manifested in a company's values and is seen as a mechanism which integrates and holds together different individuals and groups – it is 'what people share – the social glue that binds organisational members together' (p8). The focus of this approach is the commonalities that are shared by members (eg language). The basic characteristics of organisational culture from the integrationist perspective are consistency, clarity and organisation-wide consensus leading to a single shared culture. 'Organisations can differ in the extent to which they have a culture' (p9) and employee commitment and control generated by the culture ensure organisational effectiveness. This is effectively a 'unitarist' view of the employment relationship, believing that management and employee goals are the same and that managerial authority should not be questioned (Fox, 1974).

The social scientific view based on **differentiation perspective** emphasises differences and diversity. It acknowledges the existence of a highly differentiated vision of culture where subcultures exist within a dominant culture, sometimes in harmony, sometimes in conflict. Power dynamics and conflict of interests among groups (eg management and the shop floor) are the key concepts explored by this perspective. The focus within this perspective is on the *lack* of consensus, the inconsistencies and the aspects of culture which are initiated by the lower hierarchical organisational levels (non-management). In relation to the act of doing research, attention is paid to the cultural manifestations that are not consistent with each other. Such inconsistencies can be of *action* (eg promotion on merit is actually on the basis of who you know), *symbolic* (eg when the language contains metaphors that are in conflict with the company's values) and *ideological* (eg when the company's values are in conflict with each other). Such a perspective is also consistent with a 'pluralist' view of the employment relationship, recognising that managers and workers may well have very different goals and values from one another – meaning that conflict is natural (Fox, 1974).

'From a **fragmentation perspective** the confusions, paradoxes and unknowns' encountered every day in organisational lives 'are salient and inescapable' (p9). Ambiguity is seen as the essence of any cultural description and is a permanent and a continuing state. Culture is considered a metaphor for organisational life rather than a variable to manipulate. People fluctuate between subcultures because they are faced by unclear and inescapable contradictions. Organisational researchers adopting this perspective aim at capturing these complexities.

Each of these three perspectives emphasises some aspects of organisational behaviour rather than others, and the understanding of each perspective's assumptions helps to explain why disagreements are so deep and vehement. At the same time it helps to understand the complex relationship between an organisation's culture and the behaviours of its members. Culture is not separated from the people but it is the product of the interactions that exist within the workplace. In addition, one must consider the co-existence of several cultures or subcultures within an organisation (eg departments, hierarchical levels, geographical locations) and how they might influence the 'corporate culture' (whether one believes that there can be *one* culture). Appropriately, Linstead and Grafton Small (1992, in Linstead *et al*, 2009: 157–8) distinguish between 'corporate culture' and 'organisational culture', suggesting that the former is:

> devised by management and transmitted, marketed, sold or imposed on the rest of the organisation, with both internal and external images including actions and belief – the rites, rituals, stories and values which are offered to organisational members as part of the seductive process of achieving membership and gaining commitment.

Organisational culture, they argue:

> grows or emerges within the organisation and emphasises the creativity of organisational members as culture-makers, perhaps resisting the dominant culture.

Organisational culture can, therefore, be fragmented and is the outcome of sense-making processes which take place when organisational members attempt to achieve an understanding of their workplace (Linstead *et al*, 2009).

CULTURE AND CONTROL

Organisational culture has been subjected to critique, particularly from a sociological perspective, highlighting contradictions within the rhetoric of those management writers who emphasise the high level of autonomy employees experience in companies characterised by strong cultures (eg Peters and Waterman, 1982). Critical perspectives argue that cultural control is instead just another way to manipulate the workforce and achieve higher productivity. Culture certainly exerts influence on organisational members in that the beliefs and values which shape the employees' behaviour, and are internalised, are not recognised as overt management (see Ray, 1986). In this sense, culture can and does exercise one of the most powerful forms of control because it combines compulsion with perceived freedom – it replaces the direct technical control and close personal supervision of Taylorism with *indirect* control (Thompson and McHugh, 2002). The bureaucratic control described by Weber in the previous chapter (1947) becomes cultural or **normative control**, providing the basis for the employees' desired behaviour (Ray, 1986).

Organisational interventions aimed at creating cultural strength, participative management, employee involvement and participation, commitment and total quality have all been acknowledged as key factors for successful organisations (see the example of 'flexible specialisation' and Japanisation in the previous chapter). However, in order to allow autonomy, employees have to be 'programmed centrally first', with accurate selection identifying those who fit in (Weick, 1987). Selection is then followed by extensive induction and training which communicates company goals, develops a sense of community and instils identification with company values and standards. Along these lines, normative control is associated with symbolic management to the extent that commitment has been internalised by employees (to various degrees), thus negating the need for direct or technical control, at least in part. Consequently, there is a contradiction between the level of autonomy that employees are allowed in 'strong culture' organisational rhetoric and that which they are *actually* allowed, contrary to the prescription of many popular management gurus (such as Peters and Waterman, 1982).

The conception of corporate culture as a self-disciplining power (using Foucauldian terminology) has its limits, which have been explored by many empirical studies. In reviewing such studies Thompson and McHugh (2002) argue that cultural control complements rather than eliminates the need for bureaucratic and/or technical control, and that an array of cultural and more traditional rules and sanctions are used by management to extend the levels of identification between the employees and the organisation. The discussion on McDonaldisation in the previous chapter provides the example. McDonald's tries to elicit strong identification with the organisation through a customer-focused culture, has instantly recognisable artifacts which constitute the brand (such as Ronald McDonald and the 'golden arches'), and even allows a degree of employee involvement through quality circles, yet still relies upon classical bureaucratic and technical control systems.

Examples such as the above demonstrate not only the complex and multifaceted nature of organisational culture as a concept but also how it is linked to other aspects of organisational life such as 'brand' and 'branding', and how it is strongly embedded in more current developments of **employee branding** strategies. Employee branding refers to the processes by which workers are encouraged to buy into symbolic representations of organisational values by, for example, consuming the company's products or 'living the brand' away from the workplace (Miles and Mangold, 2004). In this way employees, through both display and performance, are increasingly being induced to represent the brand image both within the workplace and without. It is clear from this that cultural values and branding values have overlapping aspects while remaining separate concepts (see Brannan, Parsons and Priola's 2011 book *Branded Lives: Identity and work in the era of the brand* for an exploration of employee branding in practice).

In addition, the aspect of employee internalisation of culture is not that simple and straightforward because there may be limits to the extent to which commitment is internalised. Sinclair (1991) argues that for public sector organisations the establishment of a strong cultural control system is difficult. Public sector employees, such as professionals in the health service or in education, traditionally have stronger identification with trade unions, professional bodies, peers, and clients, and weaker identification with the employing organisation. Wedded to these identity factors, professionals also exert considerable expert power, identifying strongly with a body of knowledge or expertise and are more likely to be oriented to ethical rather than commercial values (see, for example, Muzio *et al*, 2007). These professionals strive for higher levels of autonomy or freedom, attribute a high intrinsic value to their vocational career, and do not generally need a strong identification with the organisation they work for. Although Muzio *et al* (*ibid*) identify increasing market and government pressures that are somewhat changing certain professions' sense of identity, many of the characteristics noted above remain salient. The limits of the effects of corporate culture as a control system have been highlighted in other contexts as well where employees have been shown to comply with organisational goals without internalising the values (see Hopfl's 1992 study of British Airways, and Ogbonna and Wilkinson's 1990 study of UK supermarkets).

BEST PRACTICE

Cultural leadership

Literature on culture and change has highlighted the importance of leadership in the success of mergers and acquisitions. Bligh (2006) has conducted a study of a large north-eastern US healthcare system that went through a full-scale merger involving 12,000 employees in four large hospitals and seven smaller facilities. Bligh (*ibid*) examined the role of leadership in facilitating post-merger cultural change and how employees interpret successful leadership. Her study shows that in order to achieve cultural integration employees need to be psychologically committed to the goals and the rationale for the consolidation. To create this buy-in leaders can exercise an important role in helping employees to see how upcoming changes can create a successful service and lead to better-quality care. Employees need to believe in the underlying ideology of the

merger and identify with its core components. Cultural leadership can help increase employees' acceptance of post-merger cultural changes. The case study suggests that in relation to cultural leadership the following actions are important:

- active team-building across previous site affiliation
- utilising employees' input in post-merger changes
- providing outlets for loss and renewal
- creating realistic (rather than high) expectations of challenges and opportunities.

Another crucial finding that emerged from Bligh's study is the important role of organisational leaders (at all hierarchical levels) in influencing how employees interpret the post-merger cultural changes and how leaders can be instrumental in creating cultural integration as well as counter-cultural resistance.

NATIONAL CULTURES AND ORGANISATIONS [1]

When we examined Schein's three levels of culture, we listed seven basic cultural assumptions which are deeply rooted at the core of an organisation's culture. Such assumptions are certainly influenced (much more than artifacts) by the larger cultural systems and the societies in which the organisations operate. One widely cited author who studied cultural differences between nations and how they influenced the culture of a large US multinational corporation (IBM) is Geert Hofstede. Hofstede (1990) proposes a theory of cultural relativism, suggesting (p392) that:

> it slowly became clear that national and regional cultures do matter for management. ... In fact these differences may become one of the most crucial problems for management – in particular for the management of multicultural, multinational organisations, whether public or private.

Hofstede's work focused on national cultures and how their differences were expressed in the attitudes of IBM's employees operating in the firm's international subsidiaries (at the time of the study, 1967–1973, IBM operated in 49 countries). Findings from the survey, which involved approximately 100,000 employees, showed a pattern of beliefs and values that were explained by using a four-dimensional model for national cultures. He labelled these four dimensions 'power distance', 'individualism-collectivism', 'uncertainty avoidance' and 'masculinity-femininity' (Hofstede, 1980).

- *Power distance* refers to the extent to which inequalities of various kinds, such as power, wealth, status and prestige, are accepted by the members of a nation. In relation to leadership in organisations, for example, it relates to the scale of accepted centralisation of authority and autocratic leadership. Examples of countries with low power distance are north European countries, such as Finland, Denmark, the Netherlands, Austria, Norway, Germany, Sweden, Switzerland, Ireland and Great Britain. The USA, Canada, Australia, New Zealand and Israel also report a low power distance.

- *Individualism-collectivism* refers to the degree to which individuals in a nation are expected to act independently or to subordinate their self-interest to the good of the group. In countries such as the USA (and all those with low power distance seen above), individualism is seen as a source of well-being, whereas in countries such as Mexico, India, the Philippines and Venezuela it is seen as undesirable.

- *Uncertainty avoidance* refers to the level to which nations and societies encourage individuals to cope with high levels of uncertainty and risk or whether they create institutions to avoid risk. Technology, legislation and religion play a role in the definition and character of uncertainty tolerance. Examples of countries with a strong uncertainty avoidance are Belgium, Greece, Portugal, Japan, Italy, Spain, France and many South American countries such as Chile, Argentina, Venezuela, Brazil, Colombia and Peru.

- *Masculinity-femininity* corresponds to the clear distinction between gender roles in society. In masculine nations men are expected to be more assertive and women more nurturing; such societies promote performance and achievement. Feminine nations encourage interpersonal relationships, quality of life and concern for the environment. Examples of feminine countries are Finland, Denmark, the Netherlands, Norway, Sweden, Chile, Portugal and the former Yugoslavia.

Hofstede's dimensions are graphically represented as intersected (the individualism and power distance indexes are the axes of one graph and the uncertainty avoidance and masculinity indexes are the axes of a second graph). Particularly evident is the fact that collectivist countries have always large power distance. See Figures 15.2 and 15.3 below, which show the allocation of the 40 countries to each quadrant emerging from the intersection of the four dimensions.

Figure 15.2 lists the positions of the 40 countries investigated by Hofstede in relation to the two scales of power distance – PDI (range of scores: 11–94) and individualism – IDV (range of scores: 12–91).

Figure 15.3 lists the positions of the 40 countries investigated by Hofstede in relation to the two scales of masculinity – MAS (range of scores: 5–95) and uncertainty avoidance – UAI (range of scores: 8–112).

Hofstede's study has been criticised for its methodological flaws. Some of the problems reported in Hofstede's study, for example, refer to its validity and reliability: a self-report questionnaire was the only method used to gather data (Kieser, 1993; Søndergaard, 1994) and only limited generalisation is possible from a small sample taken in a particular time in the specific context of a single organisation. Schein (1990) also questions whether something as abstract and complex as culture can be measured with survey instruments at all. Hofstede's findings have on the other hand been replicated and confirmed by other studies – but he himself remains aware of the limitations of his own methodological approach (Hofstede, 2002).

Figure 15.2   Positions of countries on the power distance and individualism dimensions

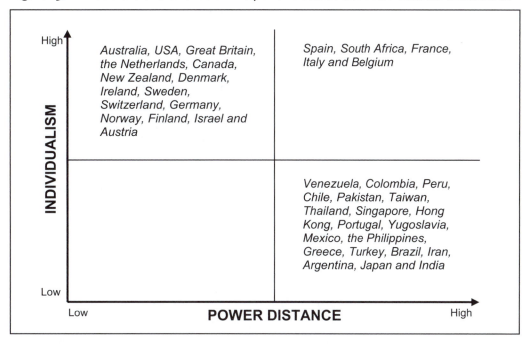

Source: adapted from Hofstede (1980: 223)

Figure 15.3 Positions of countries on the masculinity and uncertainty avoidance dimensions

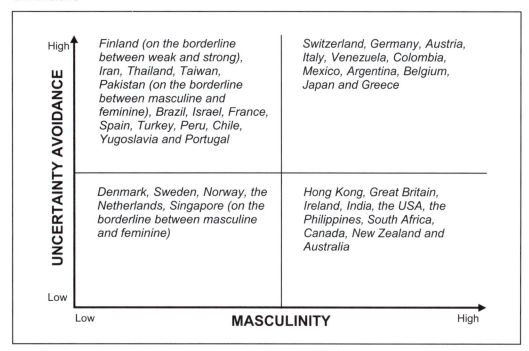

Source: adapted from Hofstede (1980: 324)

Hofstede's study has certainly contributed a great deal to highlighting how the concept of national identity, with its tacit and unconscious sets of beliefs, supplies important information that is rooted in organisations' cultural practices. Hofstede's (1993) analysis also shows the problems in trying to export management practices developed within one national culture to other cultures, using US management as an example. As Wood *et al* (2009) suggested in the discussion of MNCs (see previous chapter), a highly 'ethnocentric' approach to managing global companies without attempting integration in each operating country may lead to substantial problems in each locale.

Moreover, as noted above, other studies conducted with different methodologies have reported findings similar to those from Hofstede's work. Hampden-Turner and Trompenaars (1993), through their multinational consultancy firm, presented scenarios with ethical and practical dilemmas to more than 15,000 managers. On the basis of the responses to such scenarios they identified seven cultures of capitalism that were assessed in relation to national cultures. They too used a dimensional framework to explain their findings, and two of these dimensions are equivalent to two of Hofstede's dimensions: individualism versus communitarianism and equality versus hierarchy. Additionally, their central argument is also similar to Hofstede's in suggesting that one society's beliefs will regulate the economic activities of the nation.

ORGANISATIONAL CULTURE AND DIVERSITY [2]

Hatch (2006) makes an important point with reference to the centrality of the notion of *sharing* in the development of the concept of culture. She suggests that a closer look at the term 'sharing' reveals two contrary meanings. The first has to do with common experience, and therefore involves similarity among people. However, sharing also means to divide something into pieces (shares) and distribute them among people. This second meaning emphasises separateness, 'doing something separately together'. As Hatch (2006: 206) asserts:

> just as sharing a meal does not mean that we all eat exactly the same food, sharing cultural patterns does not imply that all members have the same cultural experiences and understanding. Sharing culture means that each member participates in and contributes to the broad pattern of culture.

So the contribution and experience of each are different. If, according to Hatch, culture depends upon community and diversity, while allowing for similarity, it both supports and depends upon differences.

According to Parker (2000), organisations are not unitary entities but are made of subcultures in which organisational identities are continually contested (similar to Martin's differentiated and fragmented approaches above). Power and inequalities – of gender, race and class, for example – play an important part in organisational culture. Organisations differ according to the gender, race and class (hierarchical) regimes and express values and behaviours appropriate for each gender, race and class of employees. Thus, organisational culture influences the treatment of diversity and inequalities with women, minority groups and working classes all having differential access to power and resources. Organisational practices and behaviours might make diversity more or less acceptable (for an overview see Gatrell and Swan, 2008).

The level of female labour market participation in the UK currently stands at around 45% of total employment (Duffield, 2002, in Brannan and Priola, 2009); while approximately 10% of the UK working age population is made up of ethnic minority groups (NAO, 2008). Despite these demographic labour market trends, however, organisations are still dominated by white men and masculine Western values (Brannan and Priola, 2009; Priola, 2009). Racial and gender inequalities have been confirmed in relation to practices of recruitment (Bygren and Kumlin, 2005), training, progression and promotion (Maume, 1999), appraisal and reward (Wilson and Nutley, 2003) and work structure and content (Wilson, 2010). Wilson-Kovacs *et al* (2006: 684) have highlighted the need to:

> document in greater detail the range of obstacles corporate cultures raise in the advancement of minority groups to senior positions as well as the difficulties individuals from these groups encounter once they are selected for such appointments.

Wilson (2010: 245) reports an Equal Opportunities Commission document which shows that the culture of the workplace is the main reason why Bangladeshi, Pakistani and black Caribbean women in the UK who want to work find it difficult to achieve their ambitions. Examples of such cultural obstacles are the repetitive questioning about fasting, clothing, eating habits and religious beliefs; the uniformity of dress codes which impose Western fashion: and the fact that the women felt obliged to participate in out-of-work activities that made them uncomfortable (eg going to the pub). Organisational culture is generally more significant in the management of diversity than the existence of written HR policies, particularly whenever there is a discrepancy between an organisation's policy and/or rhetoric and its practices.

As acknowledged by Priola (2009), the analysis of organisational diversity can focus on the processes and practices which contribute to the construction of gender, racial and/or class identities (as well as sexual orientation and disability) within specific occupational positions, organisations and sectors. In such cases the analysis of the organisational cultures becomes intertwined with the analysis of the diversity processes and practices. Wilson (2010) suggests that organisations perceive and manage meanings in relation to difference both consciously and unconsciously. In her case study research of three organisations she found that in one organisation there was a deliberate construction of meaning in company publications aimed at representing gender and race mixed images. In another company there was a positive but unofficial construction of homosexuality as creative, which had a positive effect. However, she asserts that generally there was an unconscious conformity to the image of the white, heterosexual, able man. Janssens and Zanoni's (2005) study of four service organisations also showed that organisation-specific understandings of diversity are based on the way in which employees' socio-demographic differences affect the organisation of work in positive or negative ways and how the differences can or cannot be used to attain organisational goals. These understandings of diversity, in turn, influence the organisational approaches to diversity management. The importance of the role of culture in shaping individual and organisational understandings of diversity is clear.

From a practitioner point of view, Guidroz *et al* (2009) conducted a survey of 7,500 employees of a large consumer goods company with its headquarters in Europe and based in 60 countries. They suggest that an organisational culture that encourages involvement and creates a sense of ownership is important in the management of diversity. They also assert that a consideration and incorporation of the organisational culture in designing a diversity management programme is important for improving the employees' perception of diversity management and for achieving a positive outcome.

Managing a diverse workforce is challenging. However, it can be supported by a culture of openness and supportiveness where any issue related to diversity can be brought into the open and discussed constructively. Within such a culture employees are encouraged to be exposed to a variety of viewpoints and are supported in balancing personal and professional needs and feel appreciated for bringing into the workplace a unique combination of background influences.

This part of the chapter has focused on organisational culture, exploring the range of features associated with an organisation's system of values and behaviours. Organisations are, however, dynamic systems and their culture is influenced by a combination of factors including the founder's vision,[3] the nature of the business, the markets in which it operates, the national culture and the level of technology. When changes occur in any one of these factors, some of the characteristics of culture will have to change. The next few sections discuss the management of change in organisations and how change can affect organisational culture.

MANAGING CHANGE [4]

Thus far in this chapter we have focused on a somewhat static picture. Although in the chapter on organisational structure and work design we traced the historical development of how organisations and work have been designed, we did not focus in detail on how organisations may move from one structural form to another or, up until this point, how organisations may go about initiating culture change – although the difficulty of such change has been alluded to above. To this end, a brief discussion of change management is needed because it is an important consideration in contemporary organisations. Change management may itself cover any number of initiatives – for example, mergers and acquisitions, restructuring (including downsizing), entering new markets, developing new products and services, introducing new technology, changing organisational processes, and changing how work is organised, although the list is potentially endless. It will be impossible to go into depth on all of these or to consider all the possible effects on the culture of organisations, but one can intuitively appreciate that any change will have an impact on the organisational culture. The sections below explore some general principles that can be identified in the management of change as well as the efforts that organisations can make to minimise the impact on employees during the frequently stressful and highly uncertain process of organisational change.

The need for change

The drivers of organisational change are many and varied and are increasing all the time due to, for example, globalisation, changes in competitive pressures and the economy, and constant developments in technology. Rollinson (2005) provides a comprehensive list of the drivers of change and divides them into factors external (the wider environment and the task environment) and internal (process and people factors) to the organisation:

- *The wider environment* is furthest removed from the organisation and includes the role of demographics and changing social values that can impact on consumers and markets. For example, ageing populations create certain consumer needs and affect product markets accordingly. Changes in the wider environment tend to be slow and often occur over many years.

- *The task environment* covers external factors that are closer to the firm and includes the economy, customers and markets, suppliers, competitors, regulatory groups, and technology. Clearly, one of the biggest environmental factors affecting organisations in recent years, for example, has been the global recession due to the 'credit crunch'. This in turn affected the behaviour of customers and markets, suppliers and competitors as they too struggled to cope with challenging economic conditions. Furthermore, organisations have to deal with regulations and pressures for change from a growing number of sources including local, national and international governments (such as the EU), consumer groups, employers and industry associations, charities and pressure groups, and trade unions. Finally, technology is constantly changing and not to keep abreast of it can often be hugely costly for organisations.

- *The internal environment* of the organisation is broken down into process and people factors. The former of these factors may include internal innovations that allow new markets to be entered or improvements in products and service delivery. A change in ownership or expansion of the organisation may also necessitate a change in internal structures and processes. People factors include those that affect the composition and behaviour of the workforce. The increasing participation of women and employees from various ethnic groups in the UK, for example, has led to increased use of diversity management techniques, as discussed above.

Rollinson's factors highlight that change may be internally or externally driven and that changes driven by one set of factors may also lead to changes in another set of factors. The drivers of change should thus not be seen in isolation. For example, as organisations respond to the need to reduce costs in a time of recession, suppliers may have to be changed or internal innovations may be necessary. In a worst-case scenario, redundancies may even have to be made, leading to changes in the work of those who remain and also to the attitudes and behaviour of the 'survivors' of redundancy (Burke and Cooper, 2000). Unfortunately large-scale redundancies were all too common worldwide during the latest economic downturn, especially during 2008 and 2009.

The sets of internal and external factors outlined above also suggest how organisations may be either reactive or proactive regarding change. Organisations may reactively respond to the environment, proactively predict the environment and change before the environment does, or even proactively attempt to change the environment in which they operate. Child (1997) refers to proactivity in dealing with the environment as 'strategic choice'. Child identified some organisations displaying 'environmental-determinism' that *reacted* to their environmental conditions with little agency and saw the environment as constraining. Other organisations, however, *interact* with their environment, displaying greater choice and agency in their actions with the outside world. To use a different typology, Miles and Snow (1978) identified some organisations that were simply 'reactors' as opposed to others who carefully developed long-term strategies that worked best for them given their expertise, circumstances and environment.

The outcome of Child's strategic-choice perspective for change management is that 'key actors are seen to play a particularly important role in *initiating, shaping and directing* strategic reorientations towards the environment' (p65, emphasis added). This allows the organisation to be in a much stronger position in dealing with change as, in theory, they have greater control over the process than those who are simply swept along by environmental changes. Indeed, Hamel and Prahalad (1994) believe that by actively taking control of their organisation's futures, senior managers may be able to avoid some of the more disastrous consequences of large-scale rapid transformation, such as downsizing and redundancies. Rather than simply blaming difficult economic conditions for large-scale layoffs in the US recession of the early 1990s, for example, Hamel and Prahalad blamed 'senior managers who fell asleep at the wheel and missed the turning for the future' (p124). These authors believe that if managers had more proactively considered the future, some of the downsizing crises that certain organisations (such as IBM and General Motors) encountered during the troubled economic times could have been avoided. They finish on a haunting note (p128):

> Given that change is inevitable, the real issue for managers is whether change will happen belatedly, in a crisis atmosphere, or with foresight in a calm and considered manner; whether the transformation agenda will be set by a company's more prescient competitors or its own point of view; whether transformation will be spasmodic and brutal or continuous and peaceful.

There are of course criticisms of the strategic-choice paradigm, most notably to the effect that organisations will generally not have complete freedom of choice and will generally have to face some kind of environmental constraints. Indeed, Child (1997) points out that strategic-choice theory has often *wrongly* been interpreted as implying a total absence of environmental determination. Contrary to Hamel and Prahalad's (1994) views, there are also some environmental events that are impossible to accurately predict – for example, the extent of the recent economic downturn. Some natural events are yet harder to predict still – the eruption of the Icelandic volcano in 2010 that grounded flights across Europe and that cost the airline industry millions of pounds being a prime example. Hamel and Prahalad's engaging piece may also be setting up an ideal that is nigh on impossible to implement. Despite these criticisms, however, the issue of whether organisations proactively or reactively change in line with their environments is an important issue in the analysis of change management.

Lewin and change management

Whatever an organisation changes, for whatever reason, and whether its behaviour is proactive or reactive, models of managing change can be applied. Perhaps the most famous of these models is by Lewin (1947). Lewin was a humanist psychologist who sought (amongst other things) to examine the ways in which social conflict could be resolved, believing that change was one situation in which conflict may occur (Burnes, 2004). In Lewin's eyes, managing change required consideration of the individual (for example, an employee), the group in which the individual belonged (for example, a team or department) and the organisation as a whole, if it was to be effective (*ibid*). To this end Lewin proposed two key models through which change management should be viewed: force field analysis and the three-step model.

Force field analysis

Lewin (1947) proposed that an organisation existed in a state of dynamic equilibrium, with forces operating to maintain the status quo in it at any one time. Two sets of basic forces operated to maintain the status quo: *driving forces* (such as those explained above) and *constraining forces* operating against these driving forces. The constraining forces might include, for example, resistance by employees or pressure from interest groups that are opposed to any changes planned by an organisation (eg environmental groups protesting about airport expansions). Lewin proposed that it was only through understanding what the constraining forces were, why they existed, and how they should be overcome that change could happen (Burnes, 2004). In identifying, understanding and removing the constraining forces, Lewin proposed that collaboration between those driving and resisting change was essential. In Lewin's eyes individual and group learning was essential in enabling people to understand and interpret the world around them (*ibid*). People should be involved in change initiatives and learn why they are necessary if constraining forces are to be removed, rather than management's simply *telling* people what change is required and how it is to be implemented.

The three-step model

Once constraining forces have been identified and understood Lewin proposed that the management of change should follow three stages as shown in Figure 15.4. The stages are:

- *Unfreeze* – In this stage the current equilibrium must be destabilised to allow old behaviours to be discarded and the new behaviours required for the change to be learned. This stage can be very difficult for those experiencing change to deal with, and may lead to a high degree of uncertainty and emotional reactions in individuals.

- *Move* – This is the implementation stage during which individual learning is key to develop the new behaviours that are required by the change process. The exact form of this stage may be highly uncertain and it is very difficult to plan exactly how it will occur.

- *Refreeze* – Lewin believed that change processes may be very short-lived if they are not properly reinforced, and this is essentially what the refreezing stage is concerned with. This stage involves establishing a new (possibly temporary) equilibrium through reinforcement in the wider organisational environment. In order for new behaviours to remain in place, reinforcement is required through organisational culture, norms and practices, the likes of which are discussed above.

It must be noted that Lewin's model is rather simplistic and he is somewhat vague on exactly *how* organisations should implement change. His work has been developed into contemporary theories of **organisational development (OD)** that focus in more detail on the nature of systems

Figure 15.4   Lewin's three-step model of change

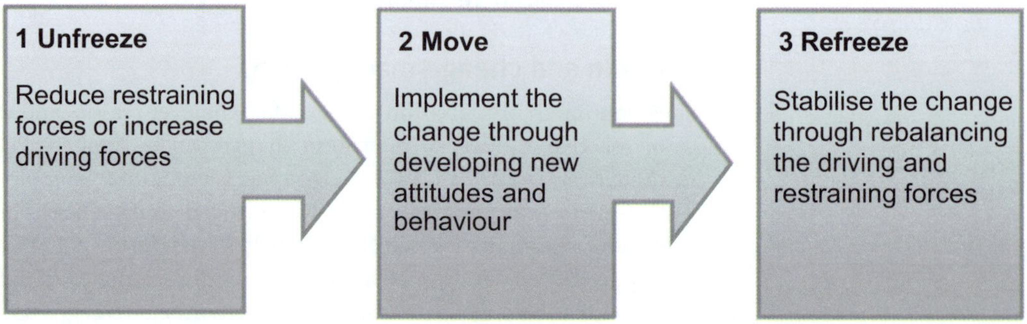

and processes that are required to manage change (see, for example, Cummings and Worley, 2005; Rollinson, 2005). However, one could argue that narrow prescriptions of the 'one best way' to manage change are rather naïve, and that Lewin's models allow underlying principles to be developed while leaving the precise implementation of change to individual organisations in a manner which best suits them. Yet it is also the case that even in the more detailed recent theories of OD the underlying principles of Lewin still hold good – for example, communicating with employees openly about the change process, empowering employees to act, promoting learning within employees and focusing on system-wide cultural changes to ensure the ongoing stability of change initiatives (Hurley *et al*, 1992). Lewin's humanitarian approach, at least in theory, therefore lives on.

There are, however, criticisms that can be levelled at Lewin's approach and the manner in which it is implemented in OD today. Most notably, even though Lewin's approaches emphasise learning there is an assumption that the approach that management has chosen is the correct one and that employees should 'learn' this. There is thus, despite an attempt to consider the perspective of employees, still a normative unitarist assumption that management and employees are striving for the same goals, with management authority not questioned (Fox, 1974) and within an integrated culture (Martin, 1992). The extent, therefore, to which true learning is achieved through Lewin's approach is highly questionable. Lewin's approach also claims to be humanistic and his methods for managing change appear to be so. Yet it can be argued that the uncertainty caused by the 'unfreezing' stage is harmful to individuals. Schein (1996), for example, believed that to unfreeze a status quo, anxiety has to be created in individuals before they can change. Although it is questionable whether individual uncertainty can ever be removed from the change process, the fact remains that because of the underlying unitarist assumptions, the true humanism of Lewin's model can be questioned. A final criticism is that Lewin's model, OD and much of the discussion so far have all focused on *planned* change, assuming that, whether reactive or proactive, management consciously identify a discrete change initiative and attempt to implement it, which may not always be the case (see below). Despite these criticisms, however, Lewin's model remains an integral contribution to the change management literature (see *Further reading* at the end of the chapter).

Planned change and emergent change

The literature and various approaches to **planned change** highlight the fact that in the realisation of intended change outcomes management go through a list of steps, phases or stages allowing the monitoring and guidance of the change process. Although such an approach can be reassuring, more recently it has been challenged. The **emergent change** school (see Burnes, 2004), in fact, believes that change is dynamic, contested, unpredictable and can never be truly planned. Kanter *et al* (1992) believe that organisations are never truly 'frozen' and are fluid, constantly changing entities. Similarly, Burnes (2004) sees change as a bottom-up process rather than top-down – one in which workers continuously adapt in response to changing conditions. In the emergent model, change is an organic, ongoing, collaborative process within the organisation. Within this approach Senge (1990) sets out the theory of the constantly evolving 'learning organisation'. Although authors often distinguish between these two approaches, in practice both planned and emergent change coexist often simultaneously (eg management may start a planned change which then moves into an emergent mode, or vice versa).

CULTURE AND THE MANAGEMENT OF CHANGE [5]

Given the emphasis of culture within this chapter and the above discussion of Lewin and OD, it should be relatively easy to see how important culture is in the change management process. As we have seen, culture concerns, at the deepest level, the underlying assumptions as to what an organisation is and how it should operate (Schein, 1985). These underlying assumptions are then in turn reinforced through shared beliefs, values and further assumptions and displayed at the most superficial level through organisational artifacts such as jargon, ceremonies and symbols (*ibid*) (for example, Google's distinctive logo and reference to its staff as 'Googlers'). The basic premise regarding change is, therefore, that unless the underlying assumptions of culture are changed, 'the way we do things around here' will not change (Carnall, 2003). Changes in these underlying assumptions may then be displayed through changed attitudes and beliefs and organisational artifacts, but OD theorists argue that the key to change initiatives is that they take place at the *deepest* cultural level in order to permeate the organisation and become the new norm (Smircich, 1983). It is for these reasons that many change management theorists, such as those noted above, believe that culture rather than systems or structures is the key to successful change management.

Critics, however, state that because of the deeply ingrained manner of organisational culture which is often developed over a number of years, changing it is easier said than done and often takes a very long time (Carnall, 2003). Also, it has been noted already that change can cause considerable upheaval to individuals, and because culture includes underlying assumptions about the way that 'things are done around here', this may cause particular uncertainty. In view of the difficulties and dangers inherent in changing culture, Deal and Kennedy (1982) propose that culture change should only be engaged in under particularly extreme conditions, including where the environment is undergoing fundamental or turbulent change (for example, in banking, where the recent global economic downturn resulted in new regulations and a strength of feeling towards the industry that necessitated a re-evaluation of the way in which its business was conducted); where an organisation is growing rapidly; or where the performance of an organisation has been in long-term decline. In other circumstances Deal and Kennedy warn against culture change. Carnall (2003), however, states that culture should always remain a consideration in change initiatives even if the culture itself is not being changed. This is because if the change initiative is out of step with the culture of the organisation, it is likely to fail. Furthermore, if the culture of the organisation is too conservative (such as in bureaucracies, for example), individuals may be especially resistant to change, making it highly difficult to implement. Culture thus remains a strong consideration in change management, however difficult it may be to change the culture itself.

MINIMISING THE IMPACTS OF CHANGE ON INDIVIDUALS [6]

As with Lewin's model it is commonly understood that individuals go through a number of transitional stages during any kind of change. Williams *et al* (1989) describe these stages as *exiting* an old state of affairs, *transit* (the change process itself), and *entering* a new reality, whereas more psychological approaches have focused on the individual's dynamic and emotional experiences when going through change. Tannenbaum and Hanna (1985) describe somewhat emotively the three stages as *homeostasis and holding on*, *dying and letting go*, and *rebirth and moving on*. Kübler-Ross' (1973) model, developed in the area of terminally ill patients, has been adapted to interpret the individual's experience of change in organisations. The stages are: *denial, anger, bargaining, depression*, and finally *acceptance*. Similarly, the seven-stage individual process described by Spencer and Adams (1990) also involves many emotional hiccups along the way, including 'sinking into the pit' and feelings of despair before people finally accept change, move on and find meaning in the new reality. What is common in all of these above models is that:

- Individuals take time to accept change.

- They go through a psychological and emotional process in doing so.

- During the process, feelings of emotional distress, helplessness and meaninglessness are common.

- Eventually, individuals come to accept change and may even find meaning in their new situation.

Some writers, however, point out that not everyone 'moves on' after a change process. Rather than finding new opportunities in change, therefore, some individuals experience negative feelings of 'survival' instead (Stuart, 1995). These negative feelings may involve a desire to seek revenge and retribution for the upset caused during the change process, denying the new reality, or even feelings of self-loathing (*ibid*). The experience of 'survival' during change has been most readily applied to redundancy situations, where it is argued that even those who survive downsizing may themselves experience negative feelings towards the organisation. Weiss (2001) argues that as well as generally experiencing increased workload because of redundancies, 'survivors' may also grow to distrust the organisation, feel anger and experience uncertainty, a lack of security and a loss of identity. All of these negative attitudes can then negatively impact on the individual, their performance and eventually the organisation.

Whether the effects of change management on the individual are short term or longer term, the fact remains that organisations should try to reduce these negative effects. Indeed, Woodward and Hendry (2004) found that one-third of senior managers involved in change programmes did not consider the effects on individual employees at all! Perhaps the most straightforward manner in which to manage individuals during change is to simply allow them time to go through the psychological processes described above in the hope that they will end up experiencing meaning and engage with their new situation, rather than feelings of survival and resentment. There is of course the problem with this approach that a positive outcome cannot be guaranteed. A further way is to implement some of Lewin's recommendations regarding allowing people the opportunity to engage in social learning about the change process and their new surroundings rather than prescribing how they should feel and act. Certainly, Rogers (1967) believed that the only way to influence individuals' behaviour is to allow them to learn by themselves rather than more organisationally directed methods such as training. The criticism above, however, must be noted – that the true extent of learning allowed in a managerially determined unitarist change process can be questioned. A further potential technique is to provide employee assistance programmes (as with stress management – see Chapter 8) to try to nullify the negative consequences of change. A key problem with this approach is, however, that it does not address the problem at source.

Consideration of the **psychological contract** and perceptions of **organisational justice** may also be pertinent in managing the consequences of change. The psychological contract is referred to as 'the perceptions of mutual obligations to each other held by the two parties in the employment relationship, the employer and the employee' (Herriot and Pemberton, 1997: 151). Periods of change are likely to alter the perceptions people have of organisational justice in relation to work outcomes and the procedure by which these outcomes are allocated and the terms of the obligations that individuals feel the organisation has towards them. Changing perceptions and standards could lead to a breach in the psychological contract and subsequent negative outcomes for the organisation (such as increased absenteeism, turnover, and reduced effort by employees) (see, for example, Herriot and Pemberton, 1997). The psychological contract defines the acceptable standards on which justice is predicated. When individuals perceive that the mutual obligations are met, they are likely to perceive that justice exists, even when the outcomes might not be to their advantage. However, when there is a perception that these obligations are breached, people are likely to perceive that an injustice exists (Cropanzano and Prehar, 2001). For these reasons organisations should very clearly communicate with employees during the change process to explain the rationale and outcomes of change and to ensure that no 'mixed messages' are apparent (Guest and Conway, 2002; Stiles *et al*, 1997) (see the *Worst practice* box below). It should be noted, however, that such communication may be inconsistent with the above point about allowing individuals the space to learn about their new surroundings, and thus any communication should also allow such learning.

WORST PRACTICE

Changing performance management

Stiles *et al* (1997) provide evidence of three UK companies (in distribution, telecommunications and banking) who were changing their performance management systems in response to wider changes in their environments. In each organisation traditional notions of job security were being replaced by a culture of security contingent on the achievement of targets linked to organisational strategy. The rhetoric in each organisation was that managers and employees would jointly decide performance objectives – but employees felt that objectives were imposed. Against a backdrop of downsizing and restructuring it was also felt that even good performance would not mean an employee's job was safe. New appraisal systems were also seen as inconsistent, lacking in transparency, and not providing the promised development or rewards. Because the organisations gave employees 'mixed messages' and implemented organisational changes in a top-down manner without employee consultation, trust in management was low and employees were uncommitted and dissatisfied. These processes were thus largely reactive to external pressures, poorly communicated and implemented, and imposed upon employees with little concern for their views and well-being. Given the recommendations for managing change presented in this chapter, Stiles *et al* (1997) thus present a picture of poorly managed change.

Perhaps the best way to avoid the negative consequences of change is to *involve* employees in organisational decision-making in order to increase buy-in with change initiatives from the beginning (Morgan and Zeffane, 2003). Indeed, Morgan and Zeffane argue that direct involvement with senior-level management during change initiatives is the most likely method through which trust between management and the workforce can be maintained. Given the relative paucity of employee representation at workplace level and above in the UK (Kersley *et al*, 2006) – and in other Anglophone countries such as Australia (Morgan and Zeffane, 2003) – the extent to which this currently happens, however, is doubtful. An alternative to direct involvement is to involve trade unions who collectively represent workers in the change management process, to try to reach mutually agreeable outcomes, such as in Jaguar Land Rover during the recent recession (see the *Applying theory to practice* box below).

Applying theory to practice: Jaguar Land Rover

A recent example of how the involvement of employees can be achieved in practice is the actions of Jaguar Land Rover and the Unite and GMB trade unions in the UK, to try to deal with the effects of the recent global recession. Although in January 2009 compulsory redundancies were made by the manufacturer (especially amongst managers and agency staff), managers and employee union representatives worked together to mitigate further job losses through other measures, such as a four-day week and a one-year pay freeze (AFP, 2009). This proposal was then democratically put to the union members who voted 70 to 30 per cent in favour of the measures (*ibid*). Although the threat of job losses was clearly a key factor in the employees' decision, employees were given a voice during this time of turbulent change with a resultantly more favourable outcome. Indeed, the approach was recognised internationally (EFILWC, 2009). It must be noted, however, that further job losses in Jaguar's Liverpool factory were required later in the year, disappointing the unions. These redundancies were, however, voluntary, in keeping with the initial agreement. The Unite union also appeared to be more critical of the level of government support given to the factory than of the employer (Unite, 2009).

The extent to which employees experience the negative effects of change management or see it as an opportunity rather than a threat may of course depend on their individual characteristics (see Chapter 3). Indeed, managerial interventions are always subject to individual reactions. The fact remains, however, that change management is a stressful and potentially damaging process for employees, and management should do their utmost to try to minimise the pernicious effects of change through the techniques described above. Managers should emphatically explore and understand the reasons for employees' resistance to change. Because resistance to change is part of the way in which people respond and interpret their identity and their sense of organisational purpose, such processes could inform managerial decisions affecting the dynamics of change in a positive rather than negative way.

Conclusion

The main concern of organisational culture research in the 1980s and 1990s was creating or changing the organisational culture to achieve excellence in performance. This corresponded to a political period (Reaganism in the USA, Thatcherism in the UK) of liberal consensus and glorification of the enterprise, which favoured the rise of the corporate culture. However, following the cases of corporate scandals in the late 1990s and early 2000 (eg the Enron collapse, followed by the dissolution of Arthur Andersen LLP, the collapse of Tyco International, WorldCom and Adelphia), questions have emerged over whether excellence in performance can also correspond to excellence in ethics. One of the benefits of the 'excellence' and corporate culture literature has been to bring attention to the fact that organisational culture is such an important area of study (Thompson and McHugh, 2002). Further and more recent studies have in fact captured the complexity of culture, which is about subcultures, interaction, language, symbols, rituals, meaning, socialisation, sharedness and diversity. It is fully embedded in the organisational activities and is affected by power relations, gender, ethnicity, class and national cultures as well as the structure and the strategy of the organisation.

End notes

[1] See also Chapter 10.

[2] See also Chapter 12.

[3] Anita Roddick, the founder of the Body Shop, is an example of how the founder's vision can influence an organisation's culture. Her human rights and environmental activism have shaped the values and production systems of the Body Shop by prohibiting animal testing on all their products and ingredients, and by being one of the first to promote fair trade with Third-World countries.

[4] See also Chapter 17.

[5] See also Chapter 16.

[6] See also Chapters 4 and 8.

REVIEW AND DISCUSSION QUESTIONS

REVIEW QUESTIONS

1 Which are Schein's levels of organisational culture?

2 How is the concept of organisational culture linked to organisational diversity management practices?

3 What are the different drivers of change that Rollinson identifies? Give some examples of each.

4 What are the three stages of managing change identified by Lewin? What happens at each stage?

DISCUSSION QUESTIONS

1 Think of an organisation you know well and describe its artifacts. Can you discern the organisational values and basic assumption from such artifacts?

2 If you were asked to conduct a cultural analysis of a specific organisation to which you are given full access, how would you go about studying and documenting its culture?

3 Do you think it is possible to understand an organisation's culture without knowing its history?

4 Can an organisation successfully change its culture?

5 How may an organisation go about minimising the harmful effects of change on employees?

FURTHER READING

Martin, J. (1992) *Cultures in Organizations: Three perspectives.* New York: Oxford University Press. This is an interesting text exploring multiple viewpoints in the study of culture.

Smircich, L. and Calas, M. (1987) 'Organisational culture: a critical assessment', in F. Jablin, L. Putnam, K. Roberts and L. Porter (eds) *The Handbook of Organizational Communication.* Beverly Hills: Sage Publications. This chapter provides an excellent assessment of the influential research on organisational culture.

Burnes, B. (2004) *Managing Change.* London: FT/Prentice Hall. This is perhaps the most comprehensive book available on change management and takes the reader from underlying theoretical

concepts of organisation through to specific paradigms and techniques for managing change.

Hughes, M. (2006) *Change Management: A critical perspective.* London: CIPD. This includes material relevant to the management of change from the employee and organisational perspective. The chapters on individuals and change and resistance to change are particularly useful.

Rollinson, D. (2005) 'Organisational change and development', in *Organisational Behaviour and Analysis: An integrated approach.* London: FT/Prentice Hall. This chapter gives an excellent introductory overview to the theory and process of OD.

KEY SKILLS

CRITICAL THINKING SKILLS, AND REFLECTIVE LEARNING

Developing critical thinking skills and reflective learning has been encouraged throughout the chapter by demonstrating that, generally, organisational processes and practices must be understood from different perspectives in order to achieve a comprehensive view. The managerial perspective is not the only one to take into consideration when exploring a concept nor when making decisions. Thinking skills and reflective skills are fundamental for students as well as managers whose decisions will affect not only their subordinates but also many internal and external stakeholders. Thinking critically includes seeking various sources of information and exploring all evidence. It also helps in making informed knowledge claims and decisions.

PROFESSIONAL JUDGEMENT, DECISION-MAKING, PROBLEM-SOLVING AND SOCIAL RESPONSIBILITY

The importance of professional judgement, decision-making, problem-solving and social responsibility has been emphasised in this chapter. Issues associated with the effects of culture as a control system, the implications of change interventions for the workforce, the importance of culture in managing diversity have all been explored with the intent to stimulate greater personal judgement and social responsibility. All employees – and managers in particular – can and do influence the culture of their workplace by developing their understanding of the workplace but also by challenging existing practices. Professional and personal judgement, informed decision-making, offering solutions through a problem-solving approach are all fundamental in influencing the culture of one's workplace. A concern for performance is not all that matters for the success of organisations – as discussed in the chapter and as demonstrated by the Enron and other corporate scandals. Morality, ethics and social responsibility also contribute to the success of an organisation and the acceptance of its values by the employees.

NEGOTIATING, ARBITRATION AND CONFLICT RESOLUTION SKILLS

Negotiating, arbitration and conflict resolution skills are fundamental skills for managers. Cultural values and behaviours can be challenged by employees: negotiation is needed to produce a situation to which all involved can contribute their perspective. High levels of negotiating, arbitration and conflict resolution skills are needed for managers to influence not only their subordinates but also the higher levels of decision-making when changes are implemented. Such changes might take place in the industrial relations sphere where management and employee representation (generally trade unions) engage in arbitration and bargaining, but also might alternatively concern the management of minor changes where employee representation is not included. As seen earlier in the chapter, unilaterally enforced changes will not have a successful outcome.

Ethical implications: Ethics and organisational culture

There are various viewpoints that one can take up in considering the ethical implications of studying and 'participating' in organisational culture. On the one hand there are ethical implications associated with using people to achieve a certain goal (see the section on culture and control). On the other hand, because organisational culture refers to the values and behaviours encouraged in organisations, ethical values can be considered an important or less important part of the organisation's culture. Traditional management thought has avoided the rightness or wrongness of corporate actions, acknowledging the neutrality of managerial work. However, no managerial act is morally neutral and such a perspective has been challenged more recently with the growing popularity of corporate social responsibility (CSR). The ways in which managers act can be judged honest or dishonest, and the effects of managerial decisions are likely to be judged in moral terms by others. Managerial acts can have serious consequences for others' lives and for the environment, and organisations should create a culture which emphasises ethical standards, social consciousness and care. An ethical organisation is one which shows sensitivity to human values, to differences and to conflicts of interest which characterise managerial decisions. The example of Arthur Andersen, one of the 'Big Five' accounting firms until the 1990s, demonstrates how companies can struggle in achieving a balance between independence and the desire to grow. Arthur Andersen LLP provided auditing, tax and consulting services for large corporations. However, in the 1980s it rapidly expanded its consultancy practice and audit partners were continually encouraged to seek consulting opportunities from auditing clients. Such conduct created significant conflicts of interests which undermined Andersen's faithfulness to accounting standards, culminating in fraudulent accounting and auditing and the voluntary surrender of its licence to practice in 2002.

Chapter 16
Technology in Work Organisations

Michel Ehrenhard, Huub Ruel and Tanya Bondarouk

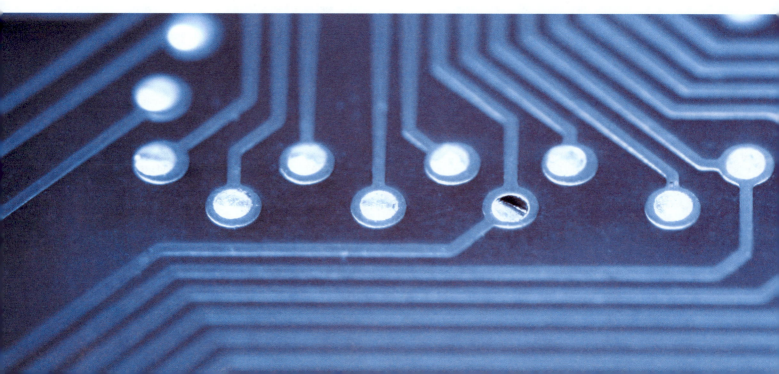

Contents

PART FOUR

Key Learning Outcomes

By the end of this chapter you should be able to:

- describe different types of technologies used in work organisations
- identify and explain some of the ways technology shapes work organisation
- understand the impact of technology on collaboration within and across organisations
- understand what motivates employees to accept and use technology in the workplace
- understand which of various change roles can be combined when implementing technology
- describe technological developments that may have a large impact on the future organisation of work.

PRACTITIONER INSIGHT

Belgian Government Ministry

At the turn of the millennium the **Belgian Federal Government** initiated what was called the Copernicus Reform Programme. The main reason for this programme at that time was the poor level of service provided by governmental authorities, yet the results of the programme, in terms of improvements in both effectiveness and efficiency, themselves remained disappointing until 2008. In that year, the financial crisis hit hard and accordingly had an enormous effect on the Belgian Federal Government's budget. For the first time in decades, budgets for government spending – in particular, the payroll – were announced to be due to be cut the following year. This led to a high sense of urgency for reform and created a strong impetus to organise differently. In particular, large benefits were expected from the implementation of e-HRM: web-based applications for human resource management within the Ministry. We spoke to **Jan Samin, the head of HR at the Belgian Ministry of Public Health**, about the new e-HRM project that he initiated in 2005.

When Jan started in 2004 at the Ministry of Public Health, the personnel administration was a mess. For the HRM department to be considered an equal partner at top management level Jan was fully aware that HRM administration services would have to become and be seen to be excellent. Lessons had been learned the hard way, for previously the belief had prevailed that when e-HRM tools were made available, the employees would simply start to use them. But this turned out to not be the case in respect of the e-HRM tools that had been purchased and installed in the early 2000s.

So in 2005 Jan initiated a new e-HRM project in which this time there was a much stronger emphasis on change management in order to achieve a much higher user adoption of the new e-HRM tools. With the prior bad experiences in mind, he had to prevent

the provider of the IT services from inhibiting the commitment of users to the project. During the 'go live' stage – the stage in which the system became fully operational – the service provider was pushing too hard and wanted to go too fast for users in an effort to meet budget and time pressures. At this point the HR director sensed that the e-HRM team and the wider organisation were just not ready for going live. He therefore boldly stepped in and caused some fairly severe disruption by putting the 'go live' on hold. A project like this, which was intended to evolve HRM from a paper-based function into a web-based function, needed clear and intensive communication. The HR director set up a new campaign aimed at increasing awareness among employees of the upcoming e-HRM implementation. It was of the utmost importance that the goals were clear and that commitment was built up for achieving them. By means of a marketing campaign with posters, mailings, screen pop-ups, and entertainment, the e-HRM initiative was 'sold' to managers and employees. The HR director also wanted top-down (management to employees) communication to be replaced by more bottom-up (employees to management) communication. Employees were supported in starting discussion groups on HRM issues and on how HRM might be improved by web-based HRM applications.

These initiatives of course took extra time, cost more, and led to delayed implementation of the system. However, this was largely compensated for by the eventual positive introduction and well-received implementation of e-HRM by managers and employees.

What would you have done if you were in Jan Samin's position?

Why do you think it is important to have employees involved in an e-HRM project?

Once you have read this chapter, return to these questions and think about how you could answer them.

Introduction

Most, if not all, work in contemporary organisations is entwined with all sorts of technologies. These technologies range from office technologies, such as email, to computer-aided design in engineering and robotics in production. In particular, over the recent decades, information and communication technologies (ICT) have had far-reaching consequences for how we do our work. Primarily, ICT enabled both the shift from a production- to a knowledge-based economy and the opportunity for anytime-anywhere collaborations that made the world substantially smaller. This chapter focuses mainly on ICT because they are the predominant form of technology with which both contemporary employees and students work. First, we describe three different types of technologies to provide the reader with an overview of different types of ICT, after which we discuss from a number of perspectives how managers and employees deal with technology in their daily work.

We start our brief description of various types of technology in work organisations by distinguishing between a) **transactional** and operational information systems, b) management information systems, and c) **collaborative** and group work technology. Then we discuss how employees accept and use technology – in particular from the perspective of the dominant paradigm in this domain: the unified theory of acceptance and use of technology (UTAUT). Next, we describe three possible approaches to implementing work-related technology. We explore the more traditional planned approach by which technology induces change by redesign; the advocate approach in which change is a process of negotiating interests and building coalitions; and the facilitator approach by which end-users find technology appropriate to them by attributing shared meaning. Finally, we provide an insight into two important developments that will have – if they have not already had – a profound impact on work organisations. These developments are **offshoring** and outsourcing in relation to globally distributed work, and **social media** in relation to collaborative work and interaction with customers.

VARIOUS TYPES OF TECHNOLOGY IN WORK ORGANISATIONS

A basic knowledge of the various types of technologies available to work organisations is necessary in order to understand the effects of technology on employees. We therefore first provide an overview by classifying ICT into three different categories based on the purpose for which they are used. For example, **functional** and transactional **information systems** are used to assist employees in the execution of a specific demarcated task, whether in production, service or support. **Management information systems** on the other hand provide higher-level and integrated information – often called a managerial dashboard as it compares to a car dashboard with speed, oil temperature, and fuel meters – which can be used for managerial decision-making, often with the goal of improving performance. Additionally, we have distinguished a third category in the form of information systems that are used to improve collaboration and communication among professionals, often across organisational boundaries.

Functional and transactional information systems [1]

Traditionally, information technologies were designed within different functional areas – finance, marketing, logistics, HRM – to support and improve processes within these areas. However, in modern organisations many business processes have cross-functional areas and in many cases cross-organisational boundary implications – for example, purchasing through electronic exchanges with suppliers. Organisational structures have become flatter through the intensified use of information systems. All this can result in the integration of information systems to serve multiple purposes (communication, co-ordination, and control), and in the use of integrated information systems in all functional areas.

Basically we can distinguish four main characteristics of a functional information system:

- *it is composed of smaller systems* – A functional system consists of several smaller information systems that support activities performed in the functional area (eg performance management in HRM).

- *it is either integrated or independent* – The specific information system applications in any functional area can be integrated to form a coherent departmental functional system, or they can be completely independent. Alternatively, some of the applications within each area can be integrated across departmental lines to match a business process.

- *it is interfacing* – Functional information systems may interface with each other to form an organisation-wide information system, sometimes forming an '**enterprise system**' (these are discussed more thoroughly in the next section). Some functional information systems may interface with the external environment. For example, recruitment information systems may collect data from external recruitment sites.

- *it is supportive of different levels* – Information systems may support the three levels within organisations: operational, managerial, and strategic (see Figure 16.1).

In all functional areas there are transactions that are handled by the **transaction processing system** (TPS). Some TPSs occur within one area, whereas others cross several areas (such as payroll). The primary goal of a TPS is to provide all the information needed in accordance with legislation and organisational policies to keep the business processes running. Specifically, TPSs are held responsible for avoiding errors, monitoring, collecting, storing, and processing information for all routine core business transactions. These data shape inputs to functional information systems in the form of 'data warehouses', customer relationship management, and other systems.

Figure 16.1   The functional information system areas and their integration

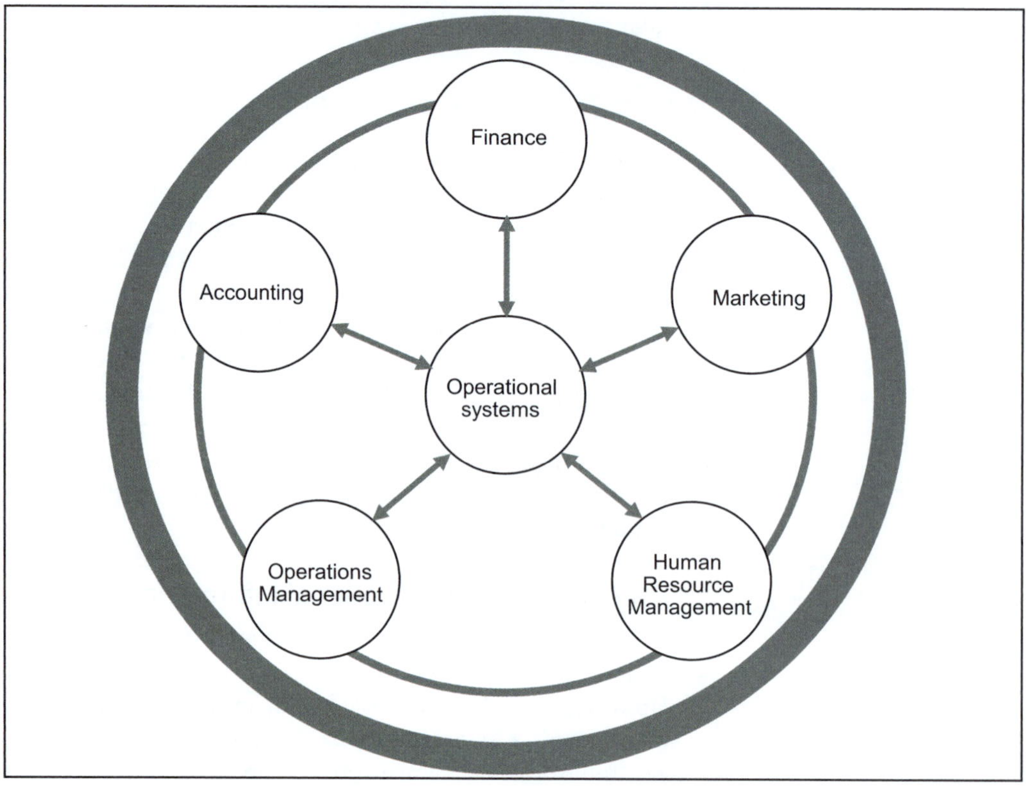

To meet the expectations and requirements of the business, TPSs have certain characteristics, which are listed below:

- the ability to process large amounts of data

- internality – the sources of data are internal; the output is aimed also at an internal audience, with a high level of detail

- the ability to process the data/information on a regular basis (daily, weekly, yearly)

- the ability to operate at a high speed with a high volume of information

- structured and standardised data

- the need for high security, accuracy, data protection, and attention to such sensitive issues as information privacy

- the core abilities of enquiry processing, seek options and report-generating functions.

Functional information systems can be built in-house, or they can be purchased from a few large vendors (SAP, Oracle, Microsoft, IBM, etc) or dozens of small vendors. In any case there is a need for their integration with other functional systems, and TPSs. As mentioned earlier, for many years most information systems applications were developed independently, within different functional areas. This created potential problems with sharing information and interfacing different applications, especially when the business processes were carried out in several departments. On top of that, many companies developed their own functional systems to fulfil processes. However, to build information systems for business processes but with cross-functional applications requires a special approach. Combining several packages from several vendors may not be practical or effective. One possible approach to integrating information systems is to use existing *enterprise resource planning* (ERP). However, ERP requires a company to accommodate its business processes to what the software can do. As an alternative to ERP, companies can choose the best available systems on the market and integrate them, or use some of the home-grown systems and integrate them. Whatever approach is chosen, integrating functional information systems helps to reduce uncertainty, minimise errors, share information, and improve efficiency.

Frequent cross-departmental integration is one of the ways to integrate information systems, and involves the creation of front-office and back-office systems. 'Front-office' refers to customers who face the system (such as marketing, recruitment, and advertising). 'Back-office' refers to activities related to order fulfilment, accounting, payroll, shipments and production. When a company is about to integrate its functional information systems, it should consider several issues:

- The integration of stand-alone functional information systems is a major problem for many companies, along with the issue of willingness to share information that may challenge existing rules and norms.

- Transaction processing deals with the core processes in an organisation. It must receive top priority from management in resource allocation, balanced against innovative applications, because the TPSs collect and order information for other applications.

- Many ethical issues are associated with the topic of information system integration. Professional organisations relating to different functional areas (finance, marketing, HRM, production) have their own codes of ethics. These codes should be taken into account in developing integrated functional systems.

Management information systems

Management information systems are intended to support managers in their decision-making (see Chapter 11 for more on decision-making). For this purpose, management information systems usually synthesise information from operational and functional information systems. This integrated information can then be used to develop management reports or real-time managerial dashboards, in which managers can drill down into real-time information on organisational performance. Also, information from outside the organisation can be pulled together to provide managers with up-to-date information on markets and the wider environment. In this section we first focus on performance management and managerial information overload, and then discuss enterprise systems, which constitute the most prominent and comprehensive form of contemporary management information systems.

In Chapter 5 we learned about motivation and how managers try to motivate their staff to improve performance. An important aspect within motivation is the role of feedback given to both managers and employees. Management information systems fulfil an important role in providing feedback because it has the power to enable greater transparency and, additionally, the potential for greater control (Kohli and Kettinger, 2004). Also, the literature on performance management recommends that organisations do more than simply collect data concerning their performance. It suggests in addition that when they are confronted with their results, organisations may feel an impetus towards understanding and using data strategically to improve their performance. In this sense, a management information system is an important tool in following the Deming (1986) plan–do–check–act cycle. Managers are thus able to intervene in a production or service process, based on information synthesised in management information systems, and to track the consequences of their interventions. In 1964, management guru Peter Drucker had already used the concept of 'managing by results' to refer to such interventions as what lies at the core of what a manager should do. Specifically, managing by results can be defined (Ehrenhard, 2009: 48) as:

> managers' use of performance information – derived from measures related to managerial goal-setting – to support their decision-making for reaching desired outcomes and to give account to stakeholders.

However, a substantial part of the modern-day workforce consists of professionals who need a wide degree of autonomy to do their work. Successful performance management therefore holds that managers need to strike a fine balance between control and autonomy. Otherwise, too much interference with professional work will lead to resistance and power plays (see Chapter 13 for more on power issues). On the other hand, too little attention could also have a detrimental effect in that employees could feel that their efforts were going unacknowledged (see also Chapter 10 on leadership). Additionally, knowledge workers usually have an advantage over their supervisors because their performance is difficult to gauge in concrete measures of output. For this purpose, Ehrenhard (2009) has defined one coercive and one enabling variant of managing by results. The former, coercive variant focuses on setting a specific, measurable and time-bound target for employees' output – eg the number of chairs assembled in an hour or the amount of mail delivered in a day. The latter, enabling variant focuses on an employee's ability to undertake certain behavioural and associated learning, and leaves room for open constructive discussion about obtaining outcomes. Note that the choice of either of the two variants depends on the context, but also on the developmental orientation of the manager. For instance, in the case of football, whereas one might be happy to win matches and perhaps even a championship by playing poorly, sooner or later teams that genuinely focus on learning and improving will overtake and beat one's own team (see Chapter 6 for more on learning).

However, it is not only employees who might have issues with performance measurement. Often, system engineers believe that the more information is provided, the better for the organisation. Yet Nobel Prize-winner Herbert Simon (1997: 242) has pointed out that:

> in designing systems there was a tendency to give top management access to all this information [...] The question was not asked whether top or middle management either wanted or needed such information, nor whether the information could in fact be derived.

So information collection can simply be yet another burden in organisational life. We must therefore consider that 'the key to the successful design of information systems lies in matching the technology to the limits of the attentional resources' (Simon 1997: 248). Information technology thus provides a number of ways to support managerial decision-making, although we should be careful not to overload managers with information. For most managers today, however, having performance information readily accessible is the exception rather than the rule. This development was especially driven by enterprise resource planning systems and was further encouraged by the arrival of *enterprise systems.*

Enterprise systems appear to be a dream come true because they promise seamless integration of all the information flowing through an organisation – financial and accounting information, human resource information, supply chain information, and customer information (Davenport, 1998). The market for enterprise systems grew enormously during the 1990s. Most of the Fortune 500 companies have already installed enterprise systems (Kumar and Van Hillegersberg, 2000). Enterprise systems can be distinguished from other types of (large) information systems by four main traits:

- they integrate the information flows within the organisation

- they are commercial packages (ie vendors put them on sale)

- they consist of best practices, and

- because every organisation is in essence unique, some customisation is always required.

However, due to the sheer size and reach of enterprise system packages, complications during implementation tend quickly to arise. Most notorious is the impact on the organisation as a whole. Davenport (1998) points out that enterprise systems have profound business implications, and that offloading responsibility to technologists is particularly dangerous because technical challenges are not the main reason that enterprise systems fail. Companies often neglect to reconcile the technological imperatives of the enterprise system with the business needs of the enterprise itself. Also, the business often has to be modified to suit the system (Davenport, 1998). This means that the organisation's business processes have to be re-engineered to fit the best practices that comprise the system, which considerably adds to the expense and risk of introducing an enterprise system (Kumar and Van Hillegersberg, 2000; Markus and Tanis, 2000). Moreover, vendors try to structure their systems to reflect best practices, but it is the vendor, not the costumer, who defines how 'best' is interpreted (Davenport, 1998). This means that the adopting organisation is dependent on the vendor for updates of the package (Markus and Tanis, 2000). Furthermore, achieving full integration depends a lot on the configuration of the system and the choice for installing just one system instead of modules from multiple vendors (Markus and Tanis, 2000).

Besides these organisational impacts of enterprise systems, organisations also have good reasons to avoid adopting or even to abandon enterprise system implementation. Two reasons often mentioned are that the packages on the market lack fit with the specific needs of an organisation, and that enterprise systems have the tendency to inhibit flexibility, growth and decentralised decision-making. Also important are the available alternatives – for instance, sophisticated data warehousing or using middleware to change a system's architecture (Markus and Tanis, 2000). Furthermore, enterprise systems also have a direct and paradoxical impact on an organisation's formal structure and culture. On the one hand organisations by using them are capable of streamlining their management structures, creating flatter, more flexible, and more democratic organisations. On the other hand, they also involve the centralisation of control over information and the standardisation of processes, which are qualities more consistent with hierarchical command-and-control organisations with uniform cultures (Davenport, 1998). To sum up, the main reasons for not adopting an information system also hold for enterprise systems: high cost, no competitive advantage, stifling of innovation and of bottom-up initiatives, and resistance to change.

Collaborative and group work technology [2]

Collaboration occurs throughout modern organisations. It can be defined as the interaction, communication, and collective accomplishing of tasks by people within or across organisations. In today's world where the Internet is all around, collaboration has come into its own as time and place have pretty well evaporated as barriers to it.

In many collaborative situations, technology is a facilitator, providing the platform, applications and functionalities to effectively collaborate. In its most basic form – for example, in decision-making processes – the people involved may all be invited to express their opinions on the issue at stake by email. Thereafter, decision-making may be assisted by a summary of ideas and opinions sent to all involved, resulting in a final decision supported by all team members. A more advanced example of technology-facilitated collaboration is the combined development of new product ideas via video-conferencing – having video and audio for the widely (perhaps even globally) dispersed team members at their disposal. Both examples, simple and advanced, are common in modern organisations of which most are international businesses as well.

Technology-facilitated collaboration can be seen in various work situations ranging from email correspondence between employees linked by a given task, online document-sharing, to online cross-functional, cross-departmental and cross-organisational projects. Organisations use technology-facilitated collaboration to save costs, to improve organisational communication, to remove hierarchical layers, and to enhance product development (Bajwa *et al*, 2008). Furthermore, networked structures to impose more decentralised decision-making and teamwork have been introduced that were facilitated by technology. Besides internal collaboration, the Internet and web-enabled applications have spurred collaboration between organisations – for example, in inter-organisational product development and service delivery. Outsourcing and offshoring have made a huge leap due to the availability of web-enabled technologies. On top of this collaboration with customers in products and services design has become more common through the availability of technology-facilitated collaboration. Adoption of this technology came hand in hand with the rise of the knowledge economy.

Technologies to facilitate collaboration are called collaborative technologies or groupware technologies. We define them as information-technology-based applications or built-in functionalities that facilitate and/or induce collaboration between end-users.

There are many variations in collaborative technologies available in the marketplace. The traditional type of collaborative technologies was designed to enhance group performance through the support of communications, interactions, and the flow of information and expertise. But nowadays collaborative technologies are aimed at enabling teamwork or project work in different time/place scenarios. Moreover, many new technologies have built-in sharing and collaborative functionalities, and with more and more technologies being web-based and being sourced through, for example, Google, collaborative and sharing behaviour is in serious demand. It remains, however, a matter for organisation-wide implementation requiring change management and an effort to create a shift in the mind-set of managers and employees to share and collaborate easily.

Because collaboration is considered critical in modern organisations in order to be and to stay competitive, collaborative technologies have become attractive tools in recent years. For example, the World Bank uses these tools extensively. Already by the early 2000s it was using 50 advanced video-conference systems every day to communicate with up to 150 sites across the globe; it was using more than 30 distance-learning centres, more than 800 distance-learning conferences, and more than 100 communities of practice to facilitate global virtual teamwork. Along with this, the organisation was by then already successfully using intranets (an online network within the organisation) for real-time in-house collaboration, and extranets (an online network between selected organisations) to support communication with clients and other stakeholders. With the deployment of collaborative technologies the World Bank aimed to obtain a competitive advantage, to cut costs, to flatten the organisational structure, to become more flexible, and to be thoroughly networked.

Three main benefits of collaborative technologies have been described by Bondarouk (2004). Firstly, collaborative technologies are assumed to give better support to data exchange, project management, and document retrieval, and to promote better co-ordination between personnel. Better and quicker decision-making is considered a crucial benefit in adopting collaborative technologies. Quicker response times and quicker problem-solving information on ideas, questions, and comments presented by all involved should certainly improve a company's productivity (Ellis and Wainer, 1994) and in turn result in cost savings.

The second most acclaimed benefit of collaborative technologies is that they improve the communication among the users (ie employees, team members) of the technologies. Communication is assumed to become richer, easier, and more frequent. However, it is also acknowledged that although communication, in whatever form, can be helpful, it can also be a distraction or even be unhelpful (Mark and Wulf, 1999). This is actually well known to many email users. Good work may often demand freedom from interruption, and teamwork is sometimes enhanced by less communication rather than more. Collaborative technologies may therefore produce unwanted negative results (Dale, 1994).

Finally, by extensive sharing of resources and data, collaborative technologies are assumed to decrease individual and unnecessary hardware and software needs (Yen *et al*, 1999).

These assumed advantages, or possible benefits, ascribed to the use of collaborative technologies often become the main forces behind the implementation of them in organisations.

ACCEPTANCE AND USE OF TECHNOLOGY

Technology cannot work without the intervention of human beings – this holds true for all technologies, not just for information technology. Stressing only the technical aspects is very likely to result in failure. Research has shown that overlooking the user side is a highly significant reason why technology may not bring the expected outcomes or may even bring about the opposite of what is expected – eg higher costs rather than cost savings.

Social scientists have developed models that identify the factors explaining why users are willing to adopt or reject a particular technology – known as user-acceptance models. Research on the issue continues. As Kukafka *et al* (2003, p218) put it:

> Designing an effective approach for increasing end-user acceptance and subsequent use of information technology (IT) continues to be a fundamental challenge that has not always provided straightforward solutions.

Existing user-acceptance models suggest that various factors have a significant influence on users' acceptance and use of information technologies. Users' perceptions and expectations of the system are assumed to be the key factors (Li and Kishore, 2006). Venkatesh *et al* (2003) have integrated eight prominent user-acceptance models into a unified theoretical model (UTAUT) that captures the core elements of those models. They concluded that the UTAUT model outperformed the existing models in explaining user acceptance and adoption of technology. Let us therefore look at the UTAUT model in more detail (see Figure 16.2).

The UTAUT model assumes three determinants of behavioural intentions (to use some technical terms) – performance expectancy, effort expectancy, and social influence – and two direct determinants of use behaviour – intention and facilitating conditions. UTAUT also includes four moderators – age, gender, experience and voluntariness of use – which are assumed to influence the direct relationships between determinants and behavioural intention and use behaviour. The UTAUT model is presented by its developers (p467) as 'a definitive model that synthesises what is known and provides a foundation to guide future research in this area'.

According to Venkatesh *et al* (2003: 447):

> Performance expectancy is defined as the degree to which an individual believes that using the system will help him or her to attain gains in job performance.

Figure 16.2   The unified theory of acceptance and use of technology (UTAUT)

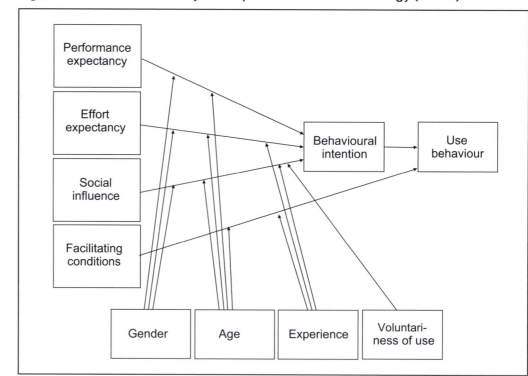

Source: adapted from Venkatesh, Morris, Davis and Davis (2003) 'User acceptance of information technology: toward a unified view', *MIS Quarterly*, Vol. 27, No. 3: 447

It is the strongest predictor of intention in both voluntary and mandatory settings. Venkatesh *et al* (2003) assume that the influence of performance expectancy will be moderated by both gender and age.

And on effort expectancy (p450):

> Effort expectancy is defined as the degree of ease associated with the use of the system.

Venkatesh *et al* (2003) assume gender, age and experience to work in concert. They therefore hypothesise that effort expectancy will be more salient for women – particularly those who are older and who have relatively little experience with the system.

And on social influence (p451):

> Social influence is defined as the degree to which an individual perceives that other important people believe he or she should use the new system.

In mandatory settings, social influence has shown to be important only in early stages of individual experience with the technology, its role eroding over time and eventually becoming irrelevant the longer the stage is sustained. The role of social influence in technology acceptance decisions is complex and subject to a wide range of other contingent influences. Venkatesh *et al* (2003) assumed a complex interaction that involved the moderating variables (gender, age, voluntariness of use, and experience) simultaneously affecting the social influence–behavourial intention relationship.

And on the facilitating conditions (p453):

> Facilitating conditions are defined as the degree to which an individual believes that an organisational and technical infrastructure exists to support use of the system.

However (p454),

> When both performance expectancy constructs and effort expectancy constructs are present, facilitating conditions become insignifcant in predicting intention.

Venkatesh *et al*'s (2003) study indicated that beyond what is explained by behavioural intentions alone, facilitating conditions do have a direct influence on use. So when moderated by experience and age, facilitating conditions will have a significant influence on use behaviour.

Consistent with all of the intention models that were reviewed by Venkatesh *et al* (2003), they hypothesised that in the end it is behavioural intention that determines technology use.

As stated above, the UTAUT model represents a fusion of the most prominent user-acceptance and user-adoption theories, and would seem the best model to explain user acceptance of technology. However, we must remain conscious of the fact that the model was developed and tested in a Western cultural context. In today's global economy, in which Asian countries are emerging as economic powerhouses, it is important to be cautious about the model's predictive power in non-Western cultures. Further research into factors that explain why users will or will not accept and use a new technology is still needed.

IMPLEMENTATION OF TECHNOLOGY

Chapter 15 examined the management of change in general, and the relationship between culture and change in particular. In this section we more specifically focus on the management of technological change, in particular the implementation of new technologies in an organisation. The previous chapter explained how difficult change can be. Implementing technological change is not that different. The introduction of new technologies in work organisations can be a distinctly arduous task.

Usually, new technology is introduced with the stated objective of performance improvement in terms of achieving greater efficiency or effectiveness. Nonetheless, new technologies in practice often conflict with vested interests, deviate from understood ideas and intentions, or are simply badly designed. Even when a technology is up and running, problems may arise due to changes in the environment or merely to a lack of maintenance. For these reasons, Markus and Benjamin (1996) in their seminal paper describe three **change agent roles** in technology-enabled change processes: the traditional role, the advocate role and the facilitator role. These roles focus respectively on designing and planning the change, building a coalition for change, and creating shared meaning. In addition, Markus and Benjamin (1996) emphasise that playing a single, fixed role as implementer or change agent has negative consequences for organisations as well as for the credibility of change agents themselves (see the *Applying theory to practice box* below). Indeed, in practice a change agent should combine a number of these roles to implement the change. The design role is most suitable for moderate to fast improvements in (economic) performance, whereas the other two roles are more suitable for learning and building organisational capabilities (Beer and Nohria, 2000).

Applying theory to practice: The roles of the technological change agent

Markus and Benjamin's (1996) framework may be used to identify the separate roles that can be played by those who want to implement technology-related – in particular, information-systems-related – change in organisations. Markus and Benjamin propose that implementation is most effective when a change manager is able to combine a number of roles instead of sticking to one approach. However, in practice those particularly involved in technology implementation tend to stay in an 'engineering' role and pay too little attention to the social processes of power and meaning that surround technology implementation. Also, depending on the specific context and technology, more emphasis could be given to one role over the other. In the case of office technology, perhaps an off-the-shelf training programme would suffice, whereas the implementation of an enterprise system would have much more far-reaching implications for (almost) everyone in the organisation and would therefore require a combination of all three roles.

Applying theory to practice: Change agent roles in technology-enabled change processes

For managers of technology-enabled change processes or change agents, the three change agent roles can be very useful. Being aware of the meaning and implications of the three different roles – traditional, advocate, and facilitator – allows a change agent to switch between them during a change process. In different stages of a change process, applying the most effective role will make a change process proceed more smoothly. For example, the traditional role, designing and planning the change, may work best when subordinates involved may express feelings of uncertainty and goal ambiguity. The advocate role may work well when the change agent needs support for the change. She or he will try to get relevant influential players 'on board'. The facilitator role may work well in the stage where the change process needs to create enthusiasm and involvement on the part of as many people targeted by the change as possible.

Applying the change agent roles is not easy because a person can have a natural preference for one of the roles and can therefore find it hard to apply other roles. This may take training. Another risk of the change agent roles approach is that it demands a good assessment by the change agent of what the situation at hand requires, and to know exactly when and how to switch between roles.

Designing and planning the change [3]

As noted earlier, when we examined the benefits and downsides of collaborative technologies, the users of technology in organisations do not just voluntarily use new forms of technology because these technologies may impose new and very different ways of carrying out the targeted uses. Information technologies available in the marketplace tend to 'promise' to bring benefits but then 'forget' that the benefits only emerge once the technology is actually in use.

According to the 'traditional' plan-based view of implementation, new information technologies in the workplace only yield the assumed benefits if the organisation is analysed for a specified 'technical problem' and solutions to it are presented in the form of proposed changes to organisational structures, work processes and technologies. This usually implies that the existing ways of working and collaborating are to be regarded as insufficient: redundancies and inefficiencies in work processes may be cut away, processes may be standardised, and the organisational workforce may be downsized. The focus is thus mostly on quantifiable improvements in efficiency and effectiveness. Most of the work in this domain is done by process engineers and technological experts. Employees, team members and managers will have to adopt a new methodology in carrying out their work and achieving their team or department goals. The redesigned method is from that point based on the support of an information system and only then can the desired benefits of the new system be obtained.

This process of implementing new information technology may be described as deterministic, in the sense that an information-system-based redesign of the work processes is determining the expected output of a team of users. Following this view, users are not considered stakeholders or people who may give meaning to an information system and who, on that basis, may decide for themselves how to use the information system.

Building a coalition [4]

In addition to the (re)designing and planning of the technology and the accompanying changes in organisational structures and processes, it is also necessary to make genuine changes in the behaviour of the people of the organisation. We referred earlier to Kohli and Kettinger's (2004) description of how information technology has the potential for greater control. Besides being able to steer the organisation in a certain direction, control also implies that the management of existing technology – and even more the implementation of new technology – is an inherently political process. The level of politicking will particularly depend on the vested interests in an organisation (Pfeffer and Salancik, 1974). An obvious example of a potential conflict of interests occurs when new technology will enable service workers to deal with customers directly instead of having to refer them to account managers. Both Fligstein (1991) and Greenwood and Hinings (1996) have emphasised that significant organisational changes can only be fully realised either when those in power are in favour of them or a new group of people gain control.

In this context, power is often defined negatively as constraining. When power is exercised top-down, (top) management constrains the choices employees have. When power is exercised bottom-up, employees resist change. Let us go beyond either of these one-sided views and follow the British sociologist Anthony Giddens (1986), who defines power as 'the capacity to make a difference'. In other words, power can both be enabling and constraining. Specifically, Giddens perceives power as the capacity to allocate human and material resources. Command over people is then labelled authoritive power, whereas command over the distribution of objects or goods is labelled allocative power. This view does not, however, imply that people will always follow commands: people always have a choice, even if some options come at high cost, such as the loss of the job.

In particular, for those aiming to implement technology, the question arises as to how power can be an enabler for the desired changes. Most importantly, following Greenwood and Hinings (1996), a coalition must be set up in support of the changes. Building such a coalition is easier said than done because the aforementioned interests are not always aligned. Contradictions in interests may in turn lead to conflict which will be detrimental to successful implementation. But what is often overlooked in the power literature, with its focus on protagonists and antagonists of change, is the role of the silent majority. In other words, when interests are at stake, people might actively resist – but there is usually a silent majority who passively resist. Passive resistance implies that people are not against the change *per se* but have a tendency either to fall back into previously routine behaviour or to simply give other projects a higher priority and so withhold effort (Ehrenhard, 2009). Successful change managers therefore direct a substantial amount of their efforts towards winning over the silent majority and then investing in sustaining their commitment to the desired change. That way a tipping point can be reached for the desired changes to diffuse through the organisation.

Change managers in the role of advocates (see Markus and Benjamin, 1996) usually try to change the attitudes or behaviour of a person by means of argument, reasoning, or, in certain cases, active listening. 'Selling' the issue also plays a particularly important role (Dutton, Ashford, O'Neill and Lawrence, 2001). Important factors to consider when selling an issue are the packaging or framing of the issue, who to involve and who not to, and the timing. Likewise, but with reference to both inside and outside the organisation, Rao (2009) describes how people he calls activists construct 'hot causes' that arouse emotions and exploit 'cool mobilisation' which together through improvisation strengthen a shared identity as the basis for collective action. In other words, members of a defined group 'join hands' in a coalition to achieve sustainable change in relation to technology implementation. For example, use of the Internet only peaked long after the technology had first become available precisely because users could experiment – for instance, by building web pages which in turn created a need for better search engines to find one's way through the chaos. Similarly, text messaging peaked with programs such as ICQ, and later MSN, which are now being replaced for example by Facebook and Twitter. (The implications of social media are discussed in greater detail later in this chapter.)

Creating shared meaning [5]

In recent years there has been a growing recognition in managerial literature that, ultimately, it is the actors' perceptions of organisational processes, filtered through existing mental frames, which form the basis of the formulation and interpretation of organisational issues (Hodgkinson, 1997: 626). Further, social cognitive research shows that people act on the basis of their interpretations of the world, and in doing so they enact particular social realities through giving them meaning (Bartunek and Moch, 1994). Mental frames (representations) of reality are seen to preclude and challenge the processing of information through sense-making and sense-giving processes, when people face new actions, and interpret and communicate their thoughts about them. (For an overview, see Hodgkinson and Sparrow, 2006.)

An understanding of the users' interpretations of information and communication technologies (ICT) is critical to an understanding of their interactions with the systems. To interact with the

ICT, people have to make sense of them, and in this sense-making process they develop particular *assumptions, expectations, and knowledge* of ICT, which then shape subsequent interpretations. Even if these assumptions, interpretations and frames of reference are taken for granted and rarely studied or reflected upon, they nevertheless play an important role in influencing and structuring how people think and act towards ICT. Cognitive frames have been related to managers' performance (Goodhew *et al*, 2004; Jenkins and Johnson, 1997; Laukkanen, 1994), decision-making (Axelrod, 1976), performance appraisal (Gioia *et al*, 1989), strategic behaviour (Dutton and Jackson, 1987), strategy formulation (Hodgkinson and Johnson, 1994), the exercise of power (Bartunek and Ringuest, 1989), leadership (Lord and Maher, 1991) and organisational performance (Thomas *et al*, 1993).

Orlikowski and Gash (1994) outline the core tenets of an analytical approach centred on the concept of technological frames to study interpretive processes related to the use and roles of information systems in organisations. Their central idea was to explore how people – users of the technology – make sense of information systems and how their interpretations impact on their actions involving information systems. From sociological studies of technology innovation, they drew out the concept of relevant social groups that include individuals who have similar experiences with technology. The main conclusion of their study was that differences in frames of understanding among relevant social groups ('technologists' and 'users') related quantifiably to problems such as misunderstandings, scepticism, resistance and poor use of technology. The implications of this for future practice therefore included 'early articulation, reflection, discussion, negotiation, and possibly change' of inconsistencies in those frames of understanding in order to reduce the incidence of unwitting misinterpretations and errors caused by incomprehension around the work with IT (Orlikowski and Gash, 1994: 202).

Frames related to the organisational applications of information systems concern the knowledge and expectations of contextual organisational data like business values (Davidson, 2002), motivation and criteria for success (Iivari and Abrahamsson, 2002), technological change and strategy (Barrett, 1999; Orlikowski and Gash, 1994). Frames related to incorporating information systems into organisational practice focus on how change occurs due to technological innovation (Davidson, 2002). Communities of actors engaged in similar tasks might work to similar (congruent) information systems frames if, through training sessions or storytelling, shared socialisation, comparable job experience and mutual co-ordination, people come to understand rules in similar ways.

Many authors suggest that it is well worthwhile examining the cultural contexts of the IT-related assumptions of key relevant groups: managers, employees, and information systems specialists. 'Culture' here is understood as an emergent process of reality-creation through shared knowledge and cognition (Geertz, 1973; Walsham, 1993). Such a perspective on culture shifts our understanding towards how individuals interpret and understand their experiences. Culture is conceived as derived from the commonalities and interactions among the *subcultures* (Barret, 1999). Subcultures may be distinguished on the basis of their sets of understandings, assumptions and interpretations of information systems. In some studies language is identified as one of the key characteristics: subcultures define themselves and set boundaries by developing a specialised (professional) language. Use of it expresses membership and status, and may provide a basis for identification (Iivari and Abrahamsson, 2002). It is important that subcultures include socially transmitted patterns of behaviour characteristic of particular groups, and therefore denote collective social identity, mutual engagement, shared experiences, and common frames of reference for interpreting and negotiating meanings.

It is to be assumed that information systems frames are unlikely to be shared across all different subcultures. Following Orlikowski and Gash (1994), we articulate the notion of *congruence* in information systems frames as referring to the alignment of frames across subcultures. By 'congruence' we do not refer to identical but to related content, values, and categories. A variety of terms has been used to express the idea of the congruence of cognitive frames, addressing in parallel ideas of collective cognitive maps (Axelrod, 1976), collective cause maps (Bougon *et al*, 1977) and strategic and organisational consensus (Fiol, 1993; Floyd and Wooldridge, 1992).

Incongruence, on the other hand, would mean crucially different, or even opposite, assumptions about the key aspects of information systems management. To the extent that frames differ across subcultures, problems such as misaligned expectations, contradictory actions, resistance, and scepticism may occur (Orlikowski and Gash, 1994). Researchers stress the importance of the social context and power exercise in shaping congruent or incongruent frames. Barrett (1999) thus observed that appropriate leadership in the adoption of an IT system was needed to ensure congruent frames among the project groups. Further, empirical studies suggest that in cases where the power asymmetry favours those proposing an organisational change, they affect the frames of key relevant groups by drawing on expert power (Barrett, 1999; Davidson, 2002).

TECHNOLOGY AND THE FUTURE OF WORK

Knowledge work constitutes a large part of Western economies, but is still on the rise especially in the emerging economies. In this section we focus our attention on two important developments for the future of work. First of all, we discuss how work is becoming more and more globally distributed. Products can be produced in locations thousands of miles away from where they are assembled and sold. Customers in Great Britian may be attended to by people in call centres in Pakistan. Second, we discuss a development that is very much of increasing significance: social media. Companies are still experimenting in how social media may be used to enhance collaborative work or improve service to customers.

Offshoring and outsourcing [6]

Over the past decade, low-wage countries have developed vibrant, export-oriented software and IT service industries. Attracted by available talent, good-quality work and, most of all, low cost, companies in high-wage countries are increasingly offshoring software and service work to these low-wage countries. Trade (together with automation) has caused many jobs in the manufacturing sector to be lost from the West, and many developing nations in East Asia to increase their wealth and industrial prowess since 1970. Changes in technology, work organisation, educational systems, and many other factors have caused service work – previously regarded as immune to these forces – also to become tradable. This rapid shift to a global software-systems-services industry in which offshoring is a reality has been driven by advances and changes in four major areas:

- *technology* – including the wide availability of low-cost high-bandwidth telecommunications and the standardisation of software platforms and business software applications

- *work processes* – including the digitalisation of work and the reorganisation of work processes so that routine or commodity components can be outsourced

- *business models* – including early-adopter champions of offshoring, venture capital companies that insist the companies they finance use offshoring strategies to reduce capital burn rate, and the rise of intermediary companies that help firms to offshore their work

- *other drivers* – including worldwide improvements in technical education, the increased movement of students and workers across national borders, the lowering of national trade barriers, and the end of the Cold War and the concomitant increase in the number of countries participating in the world market.

'Offshoring' is the term used here. It is a term that applies best to high-wage countries that outsource work overseas – that outsource for instance to India, China, Malaysia, the Philippines and many other places. Cross-cultural issues discussed in Chapter 15 also have a most profound effect on offshoring due to the cultural distance between Western and Eastern countries. Germany, for example, also sends work across its borders, including to Eastern Europe, but there is no water – no shore – to cross. Some of the work that is offshored is sent to entrepreneurial firms established in these low-wage countries. In other cases, multinational corporations (MNCs) headquartered in high-wage countries open subsidiaries in the low-wage countries to work on products and services for their world market.

There are at least six kinds of work sent offshore that are related to software and information technology:

- programming, software testing and software maintenance

- IT research and development

- high-end jobs such as software architecture, product design, project management, IT consulting, and business strategy

- physical product manufacturing: semiconductors, computer components, computers

- business process outsourcing/IT-enabled services: insurance claim processing, medical billing, accounting, bookkeeping, medical transcription, digitisation of engineering drawings, desktop publishing and high-end IT-enabled services such as financial analysis and reading of X-rays, and

- call centres and telemarketing.

The United States followed by the United Kingdom are to date the largest offshorers, but other countries in Western Europe, Japan, Korea, Australia, and even India send work offshore. The countries that receive the work fall into four categories:

- those that have available a large workforce of highly educated workers with a comparatively low wage-scale (eg India and China)

- those that have special language skills (eg the Philippines can serve the English and Spanish customer service needs of the United States by being bilingual in these languages)

- those that have geographical proximity ('nearsourcing'), familiarity with the work language and customs, and relatively low wages compared to the country sending the work (eg Canada accepting work from the United States, the Czech Republic accepting work from Germany), and

- those that have special high-end skills (eg Israel's strength in security and anti-virus software).

There are many drivers and enablers of offshoring. These include:

- The dot-com boom years witnessed a rapid expansion of the worldwide telecommunications system, making ample low-cost broadband available in many countries at attractive rates. This made it possible to readily transfer the data and work products of software offshoring.

- Software platforms were stabilised, with most large companies using a few standard choices: IBM or Oracle for database management, SAP for supply chain management, and so on. This enabled offshoring suppliers to focus on acquiring only these few technologies and the people who were knowledgeable in them.

- Companies are able to use inexpensive commodity software packages instead of customised software, leading to some of the same standardisation advantages as with software platforms.

- The pace of technological change was sufficiently rapid and software investments became obsolescent so quickly that many companies chose to outsource IT rather than invest in technology and people that would soon have to be replaced or retrained.

- Companies felt a competitive need to offshore as their rivals began to do so.

- Influential members from industry, such as Jack Welch from General Electric, became champions of offshoring.

- Venture capitalists proclaimed the benefits of entrepreneurial start-ups in using offshoring as a means to reduce the 'burn rate' of capital.

- New firms emerged to serve as intermediaries, to make it easier for small and medium-sized firms to send their work offshore.

- Work processes were digitalised, made routine, and broken into separable tasks by skill set – some of which were easy to outsource.

- Education became more globally available with model curricula provided by the professional computing societies, low capital barriers to establishing computer laboratories in the era of personal computers and package software, national plans to build up undergraduate education as a competitive advantage, and access to Western graduate education as immigration restrictions were eased.

- Citizens of India and China, who had gone to the United States or Western Europe for their graduate education and remained there to work, began to return home in larger numbers, creating a reverse diaspora that provided both countries with highly educated and experienced workers and managers.

- India has a large population familiar with the English language, the language of global business and law.

- India has accounting and legal systems that are similar to those in the United Kingdom and the United States.

- Global trade is becoming more prevalent, with individual countries such as India and China liberalising their economies, the fall of Communism lowering trade barriers, and many more countries participating in international trade organisations.

There are also a number of reasons why a company might not wish to offshore work:

- The process of the job cannot be made routine.

- The job cannot be done at a distance.

- The infrastructure is too weak in the vendor country.

- The offshoring impacts too negatively on the client firm, such that the client firm may lose control over an important work element, may lose all its in-house expertise in an area, or may suffer too great a loss of worker morale.

- The risks to privacy, data security or intellectual property are too high.

- There are not enough workers in the supplier firm with the requisite knowledge to do the job. This is what happens, for example, when the job requires application domain knowledge as well as IT knowledge.

- The costs of opening or maintaining the offshore operation are too high.

- There are cultural issues that stand between the client and vendor.

- The company can achieve its goal in another way, such as outsourcing within its home country or consolidating business operations.

Globalisation of, and offshoring within, the software industry will continue and without doubt increase. This increase will be fuelled by information technology itself as well as government action and economic factors, and will result in more global competition in both lower-end software skills and higher-end endeavours. The business imperatives – profits, shareholder value, and inter-company competitiveness – will continue to play a dominant role. Current data and economic theory suggest that despite offshoring, career opportunities in IT will remain strong in the countries where they have been strong in the past, even as they grow in the countries that are targets of offshoring. The future is, however, one in which the individual will be situated in wider global competition. The brightness of the future for individuals, companies, or countries is centred on their ability to invest in building the foundations that foster innovation and invention.

Social media [7]

Social media are another important development, additional to the global distribution of work in the form of offshoring and outsourcing. Substantial improvements in the technological infrastructure for communication have caused a shift towards online service delivery – a development of which we are just at the beginning. Already, considerable attention has been drawn to a specific group of technological developments known as Web 2.0. Web 2.0 has enabled user-driven online services, such as Wikipedia, Twitter and LinkedIn. Essential for these technologies is that they rely on user interaction and collaboration – which is why the term *social media* is commonly used for these types of social-behaviour-enabling technological channels or platform.

In particular, a number of different Web 2.0 technologies can be identified. For instance McKinsey (2007) has identified blogs, podcasts, collective intelligence, Wikis, mash-ups, Really Simple Syndication (RSS), social networking, peer-to-peer networking (P2P), and web services. Blogs are web logs in which one or more people write an online journal or keep a diary, and which might attract millions of followers. Twitter is an example of micro-blogging, which means that only short messages ('tweets') can be posted. Podcasts are similar to blogs, except that they are audio- or video-recorded instead of text-based. Collective intelligence relies on the expertise of a group to support decision-making – for instance, by rating ideas, tagging interesting articles, or in the form of collaborative publishing. Wikis are a specific form of collaborative publishing, where a large number of users can contribute and review each other's work. Interestingly, the highly regarded scientific journal *Nature* found that of the Internet encyclopaedias the English-language Wikipedia came very close to the *Encyclopedia Britannica*, perceived as the worldwide standard, in terms of the accuracy of its science entries (Giles, 2005). Mash-ups collect content from a number of different online sources to generate a new service – for instance, a website that offers tickets from a number of airlines. As opposed to mash-ups, RSS enables users themselves to aggregate information by subscribing to distributions of news, blogs, podcasts, etc. Well known to the public is social networking, which refers to systems in which users can share information about their background, skills, preferences, and the like. Additionally, users can decide which information is public and which information they share only with their network. Celebrated examples of social networks are LinkedIn and Plaxo for business relations, Facebook and MySpace for family and friends, and Flickr and again MySpace for specific interest groups: photographers and musicians respectively. Furthermore, P2P is one of the oldest forms of social media and simply entails the sharing of data openly over the Internet or within a closed user group. Core to P2P is that data is shared over a large number of machines instead of one. Finally, web services enable different systems to share information or conduct transactions with one another.

Obviously, these technologies can serve a large variety of purposes. What, though, are the benefits specifically for companies? In a McKinsey (2009) survey among 1,700 executives from around the world, 69% indicated that their companies gained measurable benefits, such as more innovative products and services, more effective marketing, better access to knowledge, lower cost of doing business, and higher revenues. Basically, social media can bring more employees into daily contact at lower cost. Furthermore, they can increase knowledge integration by encouraging participation in projects and idea-sharing. Also, they can be used to strengthen relations with customers, suppliers and other parties outside the organisations. No wonder that according to Forrester Research (Young 2009) investments in social media are expected to grow more than 15% annually over the next five years despite the economic turmoil. The McKinsey (2009) survey also found that the three most important practices for successfully using Web 2.0 for internal purposes are: integrating the use of Web 2.0 technologies into employees' day-to-day activities, senior leaders' role-modelling/championing the use of technology, and providing informal incentives.

Naturally, social media do not provide only benefits. For example, Constantinides (2010) points out some of the drawbacks that are mentioned in the literature. First of all, since essentially many people can equally contribute, there is a risk that large amounts of low-quality information will lead to research becoming like looking for a needle in a haystack. Also, intellectual property rights could easily be threatened. Moreover, the boundary between advertorials (advertisements and publicity statements presented as if articles printed in independent journals) and less-biased contributions might be difficult to discern. One way to prevent this kind of threat would be to add some means of rating content and/or contributors. Secondly, there is the risk of sharing too much information. Both companies and individuals could have their privacy or data-protected information severely compromised. For example, if an organisation fired an employee, this person could put documents online that are damaging to the reputation of the company or that provide market competitors with commercially useful information. The major problem is that when information is put online, it is almost impossible to remove. Information quickly spreads over the network and might be stored in an enormous amount of different systems. Thirdly, based on what was mentioned in the previous paragraph, employees need to be encouraged to use social media for the benefit of the company. In practice, however, companies are more ambiguous on the use of social media during working hours. A clear demarcation between private and company interest is often difficult to make – for instance, in the case of business-oriented social networking sites or contributions to wikis. Social media, like all technologies, can be used for many different purposes in many different ways.

Conclusion

Technology plays an important role in work organisation. This chapter has provided insight into a number of technologies for work in and between organisations and individuals. Since information and communication technologies are by far the dominant forms of technology in work organisations, we focused on them specifically. We distinguished between traditional functional and transactional information technologies, management information systems, and collaborative and group work technology. Next, we discussed the acceptance and use of technology, mostly by explaining the central concepts of the unified theory of acceptance and use of technology model. The authors of the UTAUT model synthesised various texts on technology acceptance and use and, based on a meta-analysis, derived the central concepts of their model. Precisely because of this rigorous synthesis, the UTAUT model is the primary contemporary model for technology acceptance and use.

Thereafter, we discussed three perspectives on the implementation and management of information systems. Based on these three perspectives, three roles can be fulfilled by those implementing and managing information systems. First of all, information systems and accompanying changes to organisational structures and processes must be designed and planned. But when the plan or design is complete, the changes do not occur automatically. Change managers have to consider both conflicting interests and contradicting frames of meaning. A strong coalition for change must be built to overcome vested interests, for which a number of approaches have been discussed. Likewise, a number of ways to create shared meaning have been elaborated upon. Readers who would like to go into the different paradigms on technology and change in more depth might consider reading the paper described in the box below.

Taking your learning further: Paradigms on technology and change

Liker, J. K., Haddad, C. J. and Karlin, J. (1999) 'Perspectives on technology and work organization', *Annual Review of Sociology*, Vol.25: 575–96. This paper takes you one step further by summarising and synthesising a variety of theoretical paradigms that look at the relationship between technology and the nature of work.

Finally, we discussed two important developments for the future of work. Offshoring and outsourcing are already having a powerful effect on the distribution of work. Companies always look for an optimal mix between skilled and cheap labour and supportive economic regimes. On another dimension, social media provide numerous opportunities for individuals and organisations to connect with others both within and outside their organisations.

End notes

[1] See also Chapter 5.

[2] See also Chapter 7.

[3] See also Chapter 15.

[4] See also Chapters 13.

[5] See also Chapter 2.

[6] See also Chapters 13 and 14.

[7] See also Chapter 14.

REVIEW AND DISCUSSION QUESTIONS

REVIEW QUESTIONS

1 How can management information systems be used to motivate employees?

2 What is the main reason that enterprise systems have such an enormous impact on organisations?

3 Why is it logical to organise ICT applications by functional areas?

4 Why are transaction processing systems a major target for restructuring?

5 What are the drawbacks of collaborative technologies?

DISCUSSION QUESTIONS

1 How would you go about building a coalition for change when implementing a management information system, in particular an enterprise system, which primarily serves the interest of management?

2 Which of the three approaches described in the section on the management and implementation of technology would you emphasise as a change manager responsible for implementing social media such as wikis into an organisation?

3 Explain how Web applications can make the customer king/queen.

4 Discuss the need for application integration and the difficulties of doing it.

5 If you analyse the financial crisis of 2008, what role in it would you give to information and communication technologies (ICT) and offshoring processes? Also, how did ICT accelerate or rectify some of the problems?

FURTHER READING

Bondarouk, T. V., Ruël, H., Guiderdoni-Jourdain, K. and Oiry, E. (2009) *Handbook of Research on E-Transformation and Human Resources Management Technologies: Organizational outcomes and challenges*. Hershey, PA: Idea Group. This book provides practical, situational, and unique knowledge on innovative electronic HRM technologies that add competitive advantage to organisations.

Burgelman, R. A., Christensen, C. M. and Wheelwright, S. C. (2009) *Strategic Management of Technology and Innovation*, 5th edition. New York: McGraw-Hill/Irwin. This edition continues to take the perspective of the general manager. The book examines the interaction between different levels of general management in application to the management of information technologies in the workplace.

Koot, W., Leisink, P. and Verweel, P. (2003) *Organizational Relationships in the Networking Age. The dynamics of identity formation and bonding*. Cheltenham: Edward Elgar. The volume puts an emphasis on the emergence of a feeling of social discontinuities and transformations, and the role in these processes of information technologies.

Torres-Coronas, T. and Arias-Oliva, M. (2005) *E-Human Resources Management: Managing knowledge people*. Hershey, PA: Idea Group. The volume provides a unique view on managing workforce in the new global and digital environment.

Turban, E. and Volonino, L. (2010) *Information Technology for Management. Transforming organizations in the digital economy*, 7th edition. New York: John Wiley & Sons, Inc. This edition addresses the tactical and strategic principles of management information systems in light of the new developments such as Web 2.0, mobile devices, on-demand computing, and real-time data alerts.

KEY SKILLS

TIME MANAGEMENT

Time management is essential in technology implementation because a longer-than-planned project duration will almost automatically lead to higher costs and potentially substantial budget overruns. Especially in the case of enterprise systems, project teams may be as large as 200 people: because of the number of interdependencies, a minor delay in small sub-parts of the project can have major effects on the implementation project as a whole. Additionally, the longer it takes to get the system up and running, the shorter the time a new system might provide a competitive advantage. On the other hand, when deadlines are set too tight, short cuts might be taken in the implementation under time pressure – for instance, by spending less time on testing and fine-tuning. This could lead to real problems, if not a total halt of the system, in the up-and-running phase.

DEVELOPING CRITICAL THINKING SKILLS AND REFLECTIVE LEARNING

These skills are especially important when implementing change. The Liker, Haddad and Karlin paper described in the *Taking learning further* box goes into more depth on a theoretical level and should thus contribute to the reader's critical thinking skills. However, which approach works best will depend not only on a sound knowledge of a number of paradigms and approaches, nor on an in-depth mapping of the vested interests and dominant frames of understanding in the project situation, but also on the personal preferences of the change manager. Most learning therefore takes place when reflecting on experiences in technology management and implementation practice. For this purpose one must continuously sharpen one's critical thinking skills. This implies among other things that one has constantly to consider if the chosen means are genuinely contributing to realising the programme objectives and the broader organisational strategy.

TEAMWORKING

Most technology is both implemented and maintained by teams. In respect of time management, we have already emphasised how interdependencies will influence the progress of technology implementation. The same holds true for technology maintenance. Nonetheless, teams are known to be better at both ideas generation and responding flexibly to developing solutions. Problems that arise may thus be identified and tackled early on – that is, when the team has enough diversity. A team consisting solely of technologists will have difficulties understanding users that are less familiar with the system. In relation to users of technology, we have already described how collaborative technologies support teams in their work. Furthermore, we have outlined how important continuing technological development will affect teamwork, if it is not doing so already – for instance, in the case of offshoring, where global teams may collaborate over large distances. Obviously, social media provide a whole new dimension to working in teams and to collaboration in cross-organisational networks.

CREATIVE SKILLS

This chapter has outlined three broad approaches to technology management and implementation. However, technology implementation is at least as much an art as it is a science. Because of the constantly changing circumstances that are inherent to the social processes surrounding technology implementation, one has to be able to improvise one's way around contingencies that arise due to the abundance of unforeseen conditions in technology implementation practice. As we have outlined before, cognitive frames have an important role in technology implementation, so the ability to think out-of-the-box will strongly improve the chances of successfully implementing technology. Also, although often neglected, creative skills are important in technology maintenance. For example, a printer-producing company attempted to document their repair workers' knowledge so they could draw from this database in the case of problems. What they found in practice was that the repair workers' practices were actually impossible to document due to their great reliance on improvisation in problem-solving.

EMOTIONAL INTELLIGENCE, EMPATHY, SYMPATHY AND LISTENING

Of course professional judgement, decision-making, problem-solving and responsibility are all key skills that are essential to managing and implementing technology. Yet these skills in relation to technology implementation are not particularly different from other organisational issues. However, we have already stressed how, during technology implementation, a change manager attempts to change attitudes, cognitive frames and behaviours – for example, by means of argument, reasoning, structured listening, and 'selling'. We therefore focus here on emotional intelligence, empathy, sympathy and listening. Above all, being able to understand others through emotional intelligence and empathy are key to building coalitions and creating shared meaning. Also, early concern for others in the form of sympathy and listening to their issues *and* genuinely giving attention to these issues will prevent problematic choices early on and mitigate most resistance to technology implementation.

NEGOTIATION, ARBITRATION AND CONFLICT RESOLUTION SKILLS

Negotiation, arbitration, and conflict resolution skills are essential skills for those attempting to implement new technologies in work organisations. First of all, employees and managers have to find an optimal solution for their organisation which also serves both their interests. Yet most importantly, implementers, change agents, project managers, or whatever, need to able to negotiate, arbitrate and resolve conflicts with top management for resources, with users to improve their transition process, and with suppliers not only for a good price but especially for good after-sales services. Usually, top management's attention and resources decrease rapidly when a new technology gets to the up and running phase, even though it is only then that the full impact of the new technology is felt by the entire organisation.

Ethical implications: ICT management and ethics

Imagine that we are looking for a policy that protects a piece of intellectual property that is the result of customisation within an ERP package. A number of questions that do not have obvious answers then emerge. Is it really intellectual property which can be owned, or is it more like a derived formula, an algorithm, which is not owned by anybody? If a computer program is intellectual property, is it the expression of an idea that is owned (traditionally protectable by copyright), or is it a process that is owned (traditionally protectable by patent)? Clearly, we need a proper conceptualisation of the nature of a computer program in order to answer such questions.

And if it is a policy we are after, a typical problem in ICT ethics arises simply because there is quite often a policy vacuum in respect of how computer technology should be used. Often, either no policies for conduct in these situations exist or the policies that do exist seem inadequate. ICT ethics includes consideration of both personal and social policies for the ethical use of technology. Sometimes it is necessary to go right back to basics. For instance, assuming software *is* intellectual property, why should intellectual property be protected? In general, the consideration of alternative policies forces us to discover and make explicit what our own value preferences are.

BEST AND WORST PRACTICE

Best practice	Worst practice
• A multi-perspective system of ICT management	• A lack of ICT planning
• The adoption of selection practices with a high level of reliability, validity and sensitivity	• A lack of top management commitment
• Involving different stakeholders in the implementation of ICT	• No user involvement
• Following up feedback with coaching, training and development	• Not providing individuals with feedback
• Adhering to fair and balanced procedures	
• Organising focus group discussions	
• Enjoying top management commitment	

Chapter 17
Human Resource Management and Organisational Behaviour

Rory Donnelly

Contents

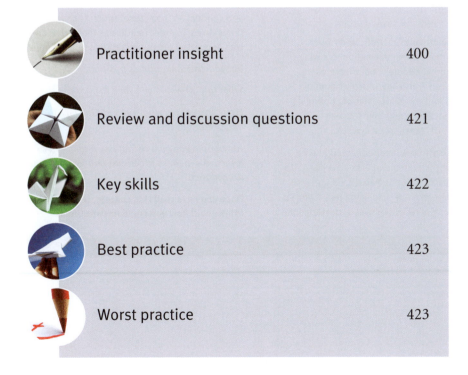

Key Learning Outcomes

By the end of this chapter you should be able to:

- define human resource management and be familiar with developments both in theory and in practice

- evaluate different approaches to HRM and discern variations in HRM practices/strategies within and between organisations

- recognise the variety of roles that HR managers and line managers are required to play in the delivery of HRM

- identify and explain some of the ways in which HRM shapes organisational behaviour

- appreciate the importance of a continuous and integrated approach to performance management

- understand the rationale behind the use of different recruitment, selection and appraisal methods, and identify some appropriate techniques.

 PRACTITIONER INSIGHT

ITIS Holdings Plc

ITIS Holdings Plc is a leading provider of traffic and travel information, delivering valuable traffic information to a wide variety of businesses, government bodies and private users. In December 2007 ITIS acquired Trafficlink, the UK's leading distributor of traffic incident and travel information, providing over 42 million people with access to real-time journey information across all modes of transport each week.

Following the acquisition of Trafficlink, the headcount at ITIS increased from approximately 50 staff members to over 250. Up until this point, the company had never had an HR manager, so only limited HR processes were in place: line managers followed a commonsense approach to dealing with issues of performance

and conduct as they arose, rather than referring to any set procedures. In order to address these challenges, **Caroline Eden** was appointed the organisation's first **HR manager**.

Put yourself in Caroline's position.

What role(s) would you seek to adopt as the HR manager?

What procedures would you put in place for managing conduct and performance?

How would you ensure that line managers were engaged effectively in these processes and followed the correct procedures?

Once you have read this chapter, return to these questions and think about how you could answer them.

Introduction

Chapter 2 highlighted some of the interactions and distinctions between the fields of human resource management (HRM) and organisational behaviour (OB). Building on this analysis, this chapter focuses squarely on HRM and on its role in shaping behaviour within organisations.

The chapter begins by defining HRM and tracing its development as a field of study and practice, before examining and critiquing different approaches to the management of human resources. We then move on to consider the strategic role of HRM and HR managers in directly shaping OB and organisational performance. This is achieved through an analysis of the core elements of a continuous and integrated performance management system. By the end of the chapter, readers should have a greater understanding of the role of HRM in managing performance and organisational behaviour, which is of fundamental importance irrespective of the organisation an individual works for or the role that he or she performs.

DEFINING CONTEMPORARY HUMAN RESOURCE MANAGEMENT

Human resource management is a key function in all organisations, from large to small, with or without a specialist or formal department in place. However, that said, the practice of managing employment is characterised by substantial heterogeneity, with variation occurring within and between organisations as well as the national contexts in which they are embedded. Over recent years, the practice and study of HRM has matured as the term has become more widely recognised and adopted by workers, organisations and academics in the UK and abroad, yet it is still relatively difficult to define what the term 'human resource management' actually means. This is largely because the definition of the term has traditionally been subject to debates over the extent to which HRM merely represents a rebranding of personnel management, or rather, a new and distinctive model of employment management (Legge, 1995).

The phrase was initially coined in the USA in the mid-1960s, when it began to appear synonymously alongside the term 'personnel management' in American texts (Kaufman, 2008). After several decades, the concept was formally differentiated from the related fields of personnel and industrial relations by the Harvard framework of human resource management (see Beer *et al*, 1984). In contrast to these conventional approaches, HRM increasingly began to be promoted as a fresh, more integrated and proactive model for the management of employment. Workers were viewed as assets instead of a cost to be minimised. HRM started to be seen as an entire system, combining and aligning a range of HR practices. From this basis it became vaunted as a distinct and superior management ideal in influential, but now heavily criticised, texts such as *In Search of Excellence* (Peters and Waterman, 1982) and *Competitive Advantage Through People* (Pfeffer, 1994).

The term started to appear in UK literature in the mid-to-late 1980s (Hendry and Pettigrew, 1986; Guest, 1987; Storey, 1989). At this juncture, the introduction of this US management concept generated scepticism and lively debate. Many were highly critical, branding HRM as little more than 'rhetoric' (Strauss, 2001). This was partly in response to the perception that HRM threatened long-standing industrial relations groups and could be used as a mechanism to weaken and subvert the role of trade unions in British workplaces (Guest, 1987; Purcell, 1995).

Such criticisms were assisted by the somewhat ambiguous and contradictory definition and model of HRM imported from the USA. Some perceived the import to be little more than old wine in new bottles (Legge, 1995), whereas others saw HRM as a substantively different model founded on **unitarism**, **individualism**, high commitment and strategic alignment (eg Guest,

1987; Storey, 1995). Despite broadly performing the same functions, a number of qualitative differences between personnel management and HRM have been identified, which are highlighted in Table 17.1 below. Of these differences, it is important to note the devolution of the HR function to line managers under the HRM model, which leads to a strong focus on the *management* of managers (Legge, 1995; Storey, 2007). In addition, whereas personnel management has conventionally been associated with managing the employees of an organisation, HRM can involve managing employees as well as those who would not formally be classified as the company's direct or permanent 'employees' (for example, temporary contractors and agency staff), because of the increasing complexity of employment arrangements in today's organisations.

Although these distinctions have been identified, it is important not to view these differences as representing a fundamental break between personnel management and HRM. Rather, Bach (2005) contends that what we are actually seeing is a transition from personnel management through to human resource management. In an organisational context, this transition may be slow and may not be seamless, uniform or unidirectional, because not all of the above aspects of HRM may be adopted by an organisation, which may oscillate between a personnel and an HR management approach. Moreover, just because an organisation decides to adopt the term 'HRM' does not mean that it actually does what it says on the tin, as it were.

In light of the lack of a clear separation between these management approaches, the definitional boundaries between HRM and personnel management continue to remain unresolved. Correspondingly, the focus on these boundaries has become less contentious since the 1990s and support has grown for adopting a broad, generic and value-free definition of HRM (Kaufman, 2008), encompassing 'all those activities associated with the management of the employment relationship' (Boxall and Purcell, 2003: 1). Over recent years, the term has arguably overtaken 'personnel management' in organisations and universities, and debates have since moved on to focus on more substantive issues – namely, the impact of HRM on organisational performance, organisational behaviour and individuals' experiences of work (Legge, 2005).

Table 17.1:   The differences between personnel management and HRM

Management focus	Personnel management Workforce-centred (employee needs)	HRM Resource-centred (management interests)
Time and planning perspective	Short-term, reactive, *ad hoc*, marginal	Long-term, proactive, strategic, integrated
Psychological contract	Compliance	Commitment
Control systems	External controls	Internal self-control
Employee relations perspective	Pluralist, collective, low trust	Unitarist, individual, high trust
Preferred structures/ systems	Bureaucratic/mechanistic, centralised, formal defined roles	Organic, devolved, flexible roles
Roles	Specialist/professional	Specialist/professional but also *integrated into line management*
Evaluation criteria	Cost minimisation	Maximum utilisation (human asset accounting)

Source: Bach, S. (ed.) (2005) *Managing Human Resources: Personnel management in transition*, 4th edition, p6. Oxford: Blackwell

THE DEVELOPMENT OF HRM MODELS AND STRATEGIC HRM

Along with identifying differences between HRM and personnel management, academic debate has also focused on patterns of HRM practice, with distinctions drawn between 'soft' and 'hard' models (Storey, 1989; Legge, 1995). The soft model builds on the notion that employee skills and abilities constitute valuable assets which provide organisations with a critical source of competitive advantage. Emphasis is therefore placed on developing these assets and generating the degree of motivation, commitment and satisfaction needed for high performance. In order to achieve these aims, the soft model to some extent advocates a framework for the treatment and effective management of employees. This concept of an ideal template is reflected in the notion of 'best practice' HRM, under which a bundle of soft HR practices are prescribed to maximise the link between HR activity and business performance (see Pfeffer, 1994).

The hard model, on the other hand, allows for a range of different practices and styles and adopts more of a calculative approach to the link between HR and business performance. Employees are simply seen as commodities or resources, like land or capital, from which managers seek to extract maximum profit through exercising flexibility and managing their employees as they see fit. From this perspective, where employees are fairly easy to replace, they are typically treated as disposable assets and so relatively little investment is made in their development or in fostering their commitment. Only when staff or particular groups of employees are in short supply or are central to the achievement of an organisation's goals are they treated well, in which case the boundaries between hard and soft styles can become distorted within an organisational setting.

As a consequence, it is difficult to neatly categorise an organisation as adopting either a soft or a hard model. Within a consultancy firm, for example, some practices may be consistent with a soft model whereas others may have more in common with a hard version of HRM, because there may be inconsistencies and even contradictions in a firm's approach to managing human resources. There may be a degree of separation in the way in which consultants are managed relative to administrative staff, the former managed according to a soft HRM style and the latter managed in a somewhat harder fashion. Furthermore, there are also likely to be differences in the way in which particular groups of consultants are treated, with variation according to grade, status or the type of consultancy services delivered. In addition, there is likely to be variation along these lines between different consulting firms and the approaches adopted are unlikely to remain static, as practices are often influenced by external factors, such as economic and competitive conditions.

The practices that are adopted by an organisation are therefore typically contingent on its particular circumstances, such as the types of workers that it manages and their importance to its activities, the labour markets in which it competes, its strategy and its size. Consequently, a 'best fit' approach is often more suitable than the application of a universal framework of 'best practice', because it enables an organisation to tailor its practices to suit its needs and those of its staff.

However, it is important to recognise that the adoption of practices associated with either approach is differentiated and can be characterised by a spectrum of adoption, some organisations utilising a frequently changing hodgepodge of practices, vacillating between aspects of hard and soft HRM. To quote Kaufman (2008: 41–2): 'While some companies "walk the talk", view employees as organisational assets, and make HRM a strategic driver of competitive advantage, many others have significantly scaled back their investment in employees and HRM or continue to practise people management in a largely tactical, administrative and cost-focused manner.'

The adoption of such practices can be linked to an organisation's business strategy. The application of a clear and consistent position on the management of human resources is, however, not evident in all organisations, many assuming an *ad hoc* and reactive approach that can lead to a disconnect between an organisation's strategy and its HRM policies and practices. This is despite growing evidence supporting the importance of the role of an integrated business and HR strategy in enhancing organisational performance (Becker and Gerhart, 1996; Gelade and Ivery, 2003; Pauwee, 2004).

In identifying and examining this link, the academic literature on strategic human resource management has increasingly begun to adopt a firm-level focus, concentrating on the overall approach adopted by an organisation in the management of its human resources and the bundle of HRM practices that are adopted in combination. This is in part because the nature of an organisation's resources and the manner in which they are managed shape worker behaviour and performance as well as broader organisational success. More recent research, however, points to the need to go a step further by differentiating between different groups of employees and customising the practices adopted accordingly.

From a strategic HRM perspective, the focus has traditionally been on 'best practice' and 'best fit/contingency' strategies of HRM (see above). The best practice approach advocates the adoption of a high-commitment style of labour management, irrespective of an organisation's characteristics or its particular business or competitive strategy (Pfeffer, 1994). The Harvard model noted above has advanced a less prescriptive variant of this viewpoint (see Beer *et al*, 1984). The model provides an analytical framework for assessing the role of 'situational factors' and 'stakeholder interests' in shaping human resources strategies, some of which may constrain the choices available to management.

The best fit or contingent approach to strategic HRM centres on two types of fit. *External fit* focuses on the link between an organisation's business and HR strategy, whereas *internal fit* concentrates on the integration and application of all HR policies and practices in a coherent and consistent manner. Fombrun *et al* (1984) promote a basic framework to illustrate these two forms of fit. In terms of internal fit, they argue that selection, appraisal, development and reward practices can be used in combination to generate desired employee behaviours, in order to achieve an organisation's performance goals and acquire a means of competitive advantage. Each of these functions of human resource management, and how the practices associated with these functions can be used to target or shape organisational behaviour, is discussed later in the chapter.

While Fombrun *et al*'s (1984) framework follows a logical thread, it is important to recognise that it may not always be possible for HRM to deliver desired behaviours or performance because of the extent of change required, the characteristics of an organisation's existing workforce and their reactions to any changes. Indeed, the framework has been criticised for not taking account of employees' responses and how this affects their behaviour. Moreover, an organisation's strategy may develop organically over time rather than being the product of rational design, and the adoption of a strategy may not be driven solely by an organisation's business or competitive strategy but also by its HR strategy and its human resources.

Links between the implementation of different types of business strategies and the role of associated HRM practices in matching desired behaviours have been highlighted. For example, in their well-known paper, Schuler and Jackson (1987) operationalised three business strategies identified by Porter (1980) to outline required behaviours and the HRM practices needed to reinforce such behaviour. Others such as Miles and Snow (1984) have focused on the behaviour of specific workforce segments – in their case senior managers and chief executives, because of the direct and high-level role that they play in shaping organisational performance. However, there is relatively little empirical evidence to support these links or gauge their impact on organisational performance. Nonetheless, the recognition that an organisation may differentiate its strategies and practices according to different segments of its workforce is important and will be explored further in the following section, which provides an insight into the contribution of the resource-based view of the firm to the field of strategic human resource management.

THE RESOURCE-BASED VIEW AND ITS APPLICATION

The notion that individuals represent resources alongside capital and land, as previously mentioned, is reflected in the resource-based view (RBV) of the firm. The RBV of the firm focuses on the interrelationship between organisational resources, strategy and performance and the achievement of sustained competitive advantage rather than the pursuit of immediate strategic goals. The basic tenet of this perspective is that resources must fulfil four interconnected criteria, if they are to meet this objective (Barney, 1991). These are detailed and explained in Figure 17.1.

Organisational resources meeting these criteria typically consist of a bundle of physical and human assets. Although both types of assets can be deployed by an organisation to gain strategic advantages, not all resources are equally important to performance, and it is argued that the most valuable ones are typically human resources (Galbreath and Galvin, 2004). This view supports the argument that human resources constitute an organisation's greatest asset and source of competitive advantage, and that as a result they should play a key role in shaping and not just implementing an organisation's business strategy. Indeed, unlike the best fit view, which emphasises the role of HR practices in generating competitive advantage, the RBV of the firm concentrates on the importance of the role of *human capital* (defined as the stock of skills and knowledge embodied in individuals) and the need for it to drive the adoption of appropriate HR practices, because this capital, which is often *intangible* (non-physical and difficult to measure), can be harder to copy than practices alone and so provides greater long-term advantage. Such resources therefore add value and so represent an investment rather than a

Figure 17.1   The link between resource characteristics and sustainable advantage

Valuable
To be of value, the resource must make a difference and add value to an organisation's activities, either by enabling it to outperform its competitors or by offsetting its own weaknesses. If these criteria are not fulfilled, the resource is unlikely to create value or sustain an organisation's competitive advantage.

Rare
The resource must also be by definition rare or insufficient, because if all organisations were able to access or obtain the resource, then the value and advantage offered would ultimately become negligible.

Imperfectly imitable
If a valuable resource is controlled by a single organisation it can provide a source of a competitive advantage. In order for this advantage to be sustained, it must be very difficult if not impossible for competitors to perfectly replicate. Resources that are easy to copy confer no advantages.

Non-substitutable
Even if a resource is rare, potentially value-creating and imperfectly imitable, it must also be difficult to substitute. Otherwise it may be replaced or become obsolete or unnecessary and consequently lose its long-term value.

cost. That said, not all human resources and the roles that they perform are of the same strategic importance to an organisation. Moreover, as Barney and Hesterly (2007) have since pointed out, an organisation must be organised, ready and able to make use of resources that are valuable, rare and inimitable, if it is to achieve competitive advantage.

Drawing on this view and its relevance to the management of human resources, Lepak and Snell (2008) argue that the strategic value of human capital and its rarity varies between different groups of workers and that as a consequence this should influence the modes of employment used by an organisation, as well as the configuration of the human resource practices it adopts. As stated previously, today's organisation can choose to use internal employees as well as those who are formally employed by external parties (ie temporary contractors or agency staff). The type of relationship and the HRM practices adopted are therefore likely to vary along these lines as well as the uniqueness and value of these resources to an organisation. On this basis, Lepak and Snell (2008) distinguish between four modes of employment and the HR practices recommended for the strategic management of workers employed under these modes.

1: Knowledge-based employment

The knowledge and human capital held by these individuals is likely to be viewed as being central to an organisation's activities and to provide the most significant contribution to its strategic objectives. Examples would include professionals, functional managers, scientists and analysts. The employment offered to these individuals is likely to focus on generating long-term *commitment* through extending employment security to this core group of employees. In order to foster this commitment, an organisation is likely to adopt a soft style of HRM, invest heavily in the training and development of these individuals and allow them to participate in decision-making and exercise discretion over their work. Recruitment is likely to focus on aptitude rather than achievement, and appraisals of performance are likely to emphasise ongoing development to generate desired organisational behaviours. These individuals are likely to be well rewarded, with the long-term nature of the relationship supported by stock options.

2: Job-based employment

This mode of employment is likely to be used for employees whose knowledge and human capital is of strategic value but is not necessarily rare and so does not offer a strong basis for competitive advantage. There is an incentive for an organisation to employ these workers to perform predetermined tasks and routines because there is a need to staff the roles that they fulfil. Examples include administrators, drivers and customer service representatives. The HRM style can range from soft to hard. Less investment is likely to be made in training and development, and the degree of participation and discretion available to these employees is often limited. Recruitment of these individuals is typically based on their ability to perform these tasks/routines rather than their specific knowledge, skills or competences. Appraisals often focus on short-term results and *productivity* targets, while pay is likely to reflect market rates for the job. Where performance incentives are used, they are likely to be linked to the achievement of targets outlined in individuals' appraisals.

3: Contract work

The knowledge and human capital held by these workers is typically neither rare nor of great strategic value to an organisation. Examples would include clerical workers, support staff and temporary workers. The tasks undertaken by these individuals are likely to be of limited scope, purpose or duration, and so an organisation may opt to use temporary staff instead of hiring permanent employees to perform these jobs. These workers are likely to be managed using a hard style of HRM, due to economic aspects of the employment contract. Where training is provided, it is typically limited as is the extent of participation and discretion available to individuals performing these tasks. Instead, greater emphasis is likely to be placed on ensuring worker *compliance* through enforcing preset standards, rules and regulations. These workers are normally paid on an hourly basis and/or the completion of specific tasks.

4: Alliances/partnerships

These employment arrangements may be used where organisations rely on alliances/partnerships for human capital that is rare but of insufficient value to warrant offering these individuals permanent employment, because this would represent a high and unnecessary cost relative to instrumental *collaboration*. Examples would include an organisation's use of external management consultants or software engineers. The services provided for an organisation by these individuals are likely to be knowledge-intensive in nature and may involve the *joint production* of services, products or solutions. Emphasis would therefore be placed on team-building and the maintenance of collaborative high-quality relationships rather than investing in the development of the alliance partner's human capital. The value of these relationships means that these individuals are likely to be managed using soft or a combination of soft and hard measures, depending on the nature and basis of the relationship. These individuals or the external companies that they work for are likely to be paid on the basis of the time spent on the project, the successful completion of a project and/or the degree of the gains achieved.

Lepak and Snell (2008) therefore discern a relationship between human capital and the strategic adoption of HRM and employment practices. The interaction between the value and uniqueness of human capital, modes of employment and the configuration of HRM practices under this matrix are illustrated in Figure 17.2.

The decision to pursue one or more of these employment modes is likely to be shaped by a range of factors, including an organisation's competitive strategy, labour market and external pressures as well as the national legal, social and institutional environment in which the organisation operates. However, as with the other models discussed above, the boundaries between these modes are not always clear-cut within organisations. There may be a temptation to categorise an organisation or certain types of workers as knowledge-based – for instance, a management consultancy firm and its consultants (note that in this context consultants would constitute

Figure 17.2 Lepak and Snell's HR architecture

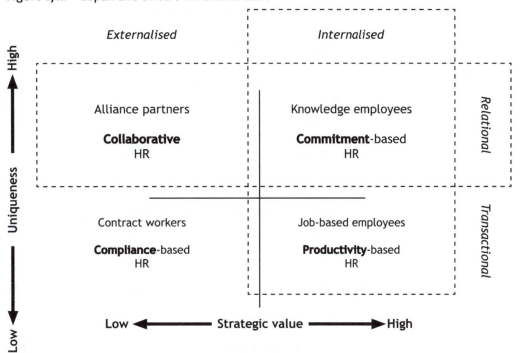

Source: Lepak and Snell (2008) 'The HR architectural perspective' in Boxall, P., Purcell, J. and Wright, P. (eds) *The Oxford Handbook of Human Resource Management*, p.214, Fig 11.1. By permission of Oxford University Press.

employees rather than alliance partners) – but within such a firm some consultants may hold unique knowledge and create innovative and valuable services, whereas others may perform work that is more job- and routine-based. Furthermore, knowledge-based employees are not always extended substantial discretion and autonomy, because there may be a greater focus on regulating their productivity. In addition, the framework prescribed for this mode of employment focuses primarily on the internal and dyadic relationship between an organisation and its employees. Yet these employees can have strong relationships with external clients, which can generate challenges for organisational commitment, because an individual may choose to go and work for a client or operate independently of the firm by setting up his or her own business or by operating as a freelancer/contractor (Donnelly, 2010).

THE TASKS AND ROLES PERFORMED BY HR MANAGERS [1]

In organisations in which they are present, HR managers clearly play a role in the management of human resources. The nature, degree and prominence of this role is, however, likely to vary from firm to firm. At one end of the spectrum, HR managers may play a limited and marginal role primarily focusing on administration, whereas at the other end of the spectrum, they may play a leading role in shaping an organisation's business strategy at board level.

Differences in the roles played by HR managers and the development of these roles have been identified in the literature. Building on previous analyses, Ulrich *et al* (2009) identify five HR roles or tasks to be achieved that focus on the creation of value: employee advocate, human capital developer, functional expert, strategic partner, and leader. These roles are explained below.

Employee advocate

Employees are seen as being crucial to an organisation's success. This role effectively positions HR managers as employee representatives or even champions. Often this involves understanding and responding to employee needs and concerns, as well as monitoring and ensuring fair treatment and employee well-being.

Human capital developer

As with the employee advocate role, employees are seen as being critical to an organisation's success, but human capital developers primarily focus on preparing and equipping employees for the future. Part of their role requires them to coach employees so that they develop desired attitudes and behaviours.

Functional expert

HR practices are seen as creating value. Functional experts not only administer these practices, they also deliver efficiencies through, for example, the use of IT and the development of policies and interventions which expand the roles of these 'functional experts'.

Strategic partner

The role of strategic partner is multifaceted. HR managers must therefore fulfil a variety of roles, acting as business experts, change agents, knowledge managers and consultants.

Leader

Where HR managers are able to take up a leadership role, they must fulfil each of the first four roles. In addition, they must lead the HR function, demonstrate its value, collaborate with other functional actors and departments, ensure corporate governance, and monitor the activities of their HRM staff and ultimately the organisation's line managers.

Each of these roles is important to the HRM function. However, HR managers and HRM departments may encounter difficulties in balancing and reconciling these roles – for instance, catering to employee needs at the same time as pursuing organisational interests. Indeed, because of this, there may be a preference to move away from the employee advocate/champion role (Francis and Keegan, 2006). They may also encounter constraints over the degree to which they are able to perform these roles. For example, the scope to play a leadership role may be constrained by the importance attached to HRM within an organisation and other leaders' and departments' views on the value of the HRM function and its role, as well as competing priorities.

In addition, line managers also play a direct and important role in the delivery of HRM, and so the roles of employee advocate and human capital developer may not be the sole preserve of HR managers. Indeed, it is arguably through the delegation of operational and non-specialist HR tasks to line managers that HR managers are able to perform the more strategic roles identified by Ulrich *et al* (2009) above. This can, however, lead to a lack of integration and consistency in HRM practice. Line managers may lack the skills or interest to perform these activities, and there may be tensions over ownership, because HR managers may wish to retain control over elements of the delivery of HRM, while line managers may be reluctant to take on these tasks or be resistant to the intensification of their workload, perceiving them instead to be the responsibility of HR managers. Lack of role clarity, skills, understanding and partnership can therefore undermine the HRM function and make it more difficult for an organisation to successfully implement a desired HRM strategy.

THE MANAGEMENT OF PERFORMANCE AND BEHAVIOUR [2]

The alignment of the roles played by line and HR managers together with strategic objectives in relation to performance and organisational behaviour can be facilitated through the operation of an effective and internally consistent performance management (PM) system. Building on the framework devised by Marchington and Wilkinson (2008), a PM system ought to be viewed as a holistic and continuous process, integrating a number of core HRM functions, including: HR resourcing and induction, performance review and appraisal, the enhancement and reinforcement of standards through the use of reward, training and development and relevant procedures, and the provision of support and counselling for those not meeting the criteria or standards set. See Figure 17.3 below.

We now concentrate on each of these components of a PM system and analyse the role of HRM in targeting and generating desired organisational behaviours. These components are examined in a step-by-step sequential manner in this chapter, but it is important to note that the influence of these measures depends on an individual's standing within an organisation. For example, recruitment and selection may not apply to an employee who has been with an organisation for some time, unless of course he or she is put forward or being recruited and selected for a different role or promotion.

1: HR resourcing and induction

The recruitment of human resources is a crucial but often challenging and expensive process. Around four-fifths of the organisations sampled in the CIPD's *Resourcing and Talent Planning* survey (2010) experienced recruitment difficulties, whether in the public, private or voluntary sectors. The majority of them did not have a formal resourcing strategy in place to manage future labour demand and supply or desired organisational behaviours, a fact that is unlikely to assuage these difficulties. This may be due to the short-term orientation of many organisations in the UK and the ongoing volatility of the economy. However, the lack of a formalised approach is short-sighted, because the development of a carefully designed plan can facilitate greater integration between an organisation's business and HR strategy and the improved management of associated expenditure.

Figure 17.3   Performance management

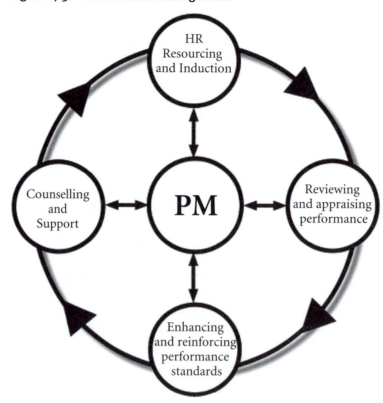

Source: Adapted from Marchington and Wilkinson (2008)

Findings from the CIPD's survey (2010) would suggest that the average recruitment cost is around £2,930 per employee, the amount spent varying according to seniority, role, sector and organisation. For the recruitment of senior managers/directors, the average expenditure is £8,333, with the range spreading from £250 to £100,000!

These costs can also easily escalate and be difficult to manage and ascertain. For example, if the chosen candidate does not take up the job or leaves after a short period of time, the process may have to be repeated. If a poor recruitment decision is made, indirect costs may be incurred if an individual delivers unsatisfactory customer service or if there is a need to retrain or take disciplinary action against a poor performer, which may ultimately lead to the individual's being replaced by a new recruit should their performance fail to improve. It is therefore essential for organisations to make the right resourcing decisions.

Before recruiting new staff, it is important to first examine whether alternative options are available, for the cost of recruiting staff can be high and just because an individual leaves does not necessarily mean that he or she should automatically be replaced. For example, it may be possible for the previous incumbent's role to be automated through the use of technology or divided among colleagues through the reorganisation of working patterns or the use of overtime. This may mean that it is not necessary to hire anybody or that if a new recruit is still needed, his or her role could be performed on a part- rather than full-time basis or maybe even subcontracted to an external agency if the role is no longer of core significance to the firm (see Lepak and Snell's framework above). If the outcome of this analysis is to recruit, an organisation may then choose to recruit from its internal workforce and/or the external labour market. Internal recruitment sends a positive message to an organisation's staff and can enhance motivation and commitment; so many organisations advertise available positions in-house (79% of organisations in the CIPD's 2009 *Recruitment and Retention* survey advertised all their vacancies internally).

However, it is good practice to consider external candidates alongside internal ones in order to widen the pool of recruits, reinforce an organisation's commitments to diversity and equal opportunities, and ensure that the best candidate is recruited.

Recruitment methods

There are a wide variety of recruitment methods available to organisations and most use a combination of methods. The selection of appropriate methods is likely to be shaped by an organisation's recruitment strategy, the sector in which it operates, the number, type and behaviour of workers it wishes to recruit, and the costs associated with each recruitment method. Some of the methods used by employers are noted in Table 17.2, together with an indication of the extent to which they are adopted.

A small number of these methods are highlighted at this point because of their role in targeting desired behaviours. As Table 17.2 reveals, corporate websites have become an increasingly popular recruitment tool over recent years. This is partly because they provide organisations with direct control over job advertisements that can be displayed and updated in real time and can be viewed internationally to maximise the field of applicants, which can be advantageous when an organisation faces difficulties in recruiting enough staff from its domestic labour market. An organisation's website may also serve to draw applicants who identify with its strategy and so may be more committed and motivated to achieving its goals.

A related development includes the use of social networking sites for recruitment, because these sites can be used to recruit individuals who demonstrate certain characteristics or behaviours. For instance, IT companies may use innovative and contemporary methods of recruitment such as Web 2.0 (ie SecondLife) to reach out to innovative and creative individuals, while consultancy firms may use LinkedIn or Facebook to attract individuals adept at social networking (eg linkedin.com/companies/deloitte and facebook.com/ IBMUKcareers).

Table 17.2 also demonstrates that many organisations are increasingly using recruitment agencies because elements or even the entire recruitment process can be outsourced to an agency, potentially enabling cost and time efficiencies to be achieved. In addition, an agency may have an existing database of suitable candidates demonstrating the types and levels of behaviour desired by an organisation. A firm may recruit the individual(s) put forward by the agency on a permanent or temporary basis, depending on how important their knowledge is

Table 17.2: Methods used to attract applicants (%)

	2009	2008
Own corporate website	78	75
Recruitment agencies	76	78
Specialist journals/trade press	55	62
Employee referral scheme	46	47
Links with schools/colleges/universities	34	36
National newspaper advertisements	31	42
Search consultants	31	33
Physical posters/billboards/vehicles	8	10
Radio or TV advertisements	7	6
Social networking sites (such as LinkedIn)	7	N/A

Source: CIPD (2009)

likely to be the organisation (see Lepak and Snell's framework above), and this may change during the course of the relationship, from a temporary to a permanent basis. When an organisation wishes to hire particular individuals to take up a senior position, perhaps from a competitor firm, or when it does not wish to publicise its recruitment plans, it may opt to use a search consultant or 'headhunter' to gain access to their network of contacts and to assist in the hiring and negotiation process.

Additionally, although not featured in the table, an organisation may choose to recruit on a responsive or word-of-mouth basis. Word-of-mouth recruitment typically centres on candidate referrals or recommendations made by employees, providing an indication of the individual's likely behaviour and their fit with the organisation, role or job. A responsive technique is often adopted in retail and catering businesses, whereby applicants may submit their CV on a speculative basis. Such an approach may be useful for identifying candidates with an interest in working for the organisation and who demonstrate proactive and flexible behaviour.

In practice an organisation uses a variety of recruitment methods in attempting to attract the right candidates. Once the applicants or candidates are known, it is necessary to select the best individual(s). As with recruitment, a number of methods are available to employers. A selection is highlighted in Table 17.3, along with some data denoting the degree to which they are used.

Each of the above methods offers its own advantages. However, no method of selection is even close to being 100% perfect because they all have their drawbacks, and so organisations typically use a range of methods to offset these weaknesses and assist in the decision-making process. Along with practical considerations relating to the criteria for selection as well as cost, timeliness and convenience, the adoption of appropriate methods is also likely to be influenced by the following variable factors:

- the extent to which the method enables differences between candidates' ability to perform a job to be accurately determined (ie the degree of *sensitivity* offered by the method) – For example, a certain level of competency or set of behavioural characteristics may be needed, so if a job requires strong mathematical skills, numeracy test scores would allow individuals' performance to be ranked and compared, while personality tests could be used to identify and measure the strength of desired traits

- reliability, which refers to the consistency of a method, particularly with regard to the application, administration and outcome of the method, irrespective of the person performing the method or the point in time at which it is carried out

- validity, which is defined as the correctness of the inferences that can be drawn from a selection method

Table 17.3:   Methods used to select applicants (%)

	2010
Interviews following contents of a CV/application form	64
Literacy and/or numeracy tests	43
Personality tests	44
Assessment centres	42
Group exercises (for example, role-playing)	30
Pre-interview referencing	16
Video CVs	1

Source: CIPD (2010)

- the degree to which objectivity and subjectivity play a role in shaping decisions

- the extension of equal opportunities, so that particular groups or individuals are not advantaged by the use of a certain method relative to other groups.

We now examine a number of the methods identified in Table 17.3, with reference to the advantages and disadvantages of these methods and the factors highlighted above. As shown in the table, interviews in combination with CVs/application forms constitute the most commonly adopted methods of selection. The receipt of CVs/application forms can generate the information an organisation needs to initially shortlist candidates, and can speed up the process, particularly when an application is submitted online. Interview(s) with short-listed candidates can then be performed to gain a greater insight into a variety of factors including an applicant's career experience, attitudes, objectives and behaviour. Some of the advantages of interviews are that they can be arranged at relatively short notice and can be performed face to face, over the telephone or via the Internet through the use of video-conferencing software. They can be structured and/or offer flexibility to elicit evidence of desired characteristics or experiences and can include a variety of different questions and forms. Interviews or questions may be *behavioural* and *situational* in orientation, so candidates may be asked to provide specific examples of behaviour to demonstrate a required competency or behaviour relevant to the specific job vacancy they are being interviewed for. This is based on the premise that past action provides an indicator of behaviour on the job. Examples would include:

- 'Tell me about a recent situation in which you had to deal with a very upset customer or co-worker.'

- 'How would you deal with a colleague with whom you seem to be unable to build a successful working relationship?'

- 'When would it be appropriate to bring in your supervisor when dealing with an angry customer?'

In an interview it is advisable to approach such questions in the following manner. First, begin by providing a brief description of the problem, challenge or situation. Then explain what action you took and why you decided to take that action, before providing a description of the outcome, its success and what you learned from the experience.

Although such questions and interviews are widely adopted and can be useful, they are not without their drawbacks, which are substantive. A candidate may provide fictional examples or manufacture their answers according to what they perceive the interviewer or organisation to be looking for. An individual's responses may also be unique, making comparisons between candidates problematic, and their responses may be subjectively interpreted and influenced by personal liking, stereotypes and first impressions. Some of these problems may be assuaged through the use of structured questions to allow direct comparison and multiple interviewers to reduce subjective bias, but this may remove some of the benefits of flexible one-to-one interviews.

Google makes extensive use of interviews in its selection process (visit http://www.youtube.com/watch?v=w887NIa_V9w). If candidates make it through each stage of the process, numerous employees at the firm as well as representatives from the HRM department interview them. However, the employee interviewers in this process may not all be professional, highly trained or experienced interviewers. The interviews may be valid in gaining an insight into whether an individual is likely to be able to fit into the organisation and perform the roles required of them, but consistency or reliability is likely to be low, because of the unique and heterogeneous nature of these interactions. Subjectivity, personal liking and bias may influence evaluations and there may be a tendency to recruit 'corporate clones' demonstrating uniform behaviours. This may be the intention behind the interview process, but diverse behaviours and perspectives can enhance innovation. So whichever form of interview arrangement is adopted, it is unlikely to avoid the problems that are typically associated with the interviewing process.

Other methods that are useful for predicting likely behaviour and performance on the job include tests and group exercises. Ability tests can be used to measure a candidate's aptitude. This can include assessments of mental or cognitive reasoning to identify whether a candidate has the potential to successfully perform the role and to what standard and how likely they are to approach the resolution of problems. Literacy and numeracy tests can be used to assess an individual's attainment levels in these areas and consequently provide an indication of whether they are likely to be able to perform the role and to what level. These types of tests provide accurate and objective test data, but an individual may arrive at the right answers through luck or repeated practice, and there is the potential for some groups to be disadvantaged by the types of questions asked or the way in which they are formulated (Searle, 2003; Newell, 2005).

Personality tests are useful in gaining an insight into how individuals are likely to behave, but candidates may tailor their responses to fit the anticipated attributes of the role, and their actual behaviour may be modified by contextual factors, raising questions over the reliability of personality tests. For example, if an individual is applying for a sales or customer service job, he or she may choose responses that demonstrate a degree of extroversion, because this is likely to be required for this type of role. In some situations or settings an individual may behave in an extroverted manner, whereas in others, he or she may demonstrate a high level of introversion. Moreover, as with ability tests, the characteristics or level of aptitude identified by an organisation in a given area may not actually be necessary to perform the role successfully, raising questions over whether they provide a valid indicator.

Group-based exercises can be used to evaluate individuals' skills and behaviour. This is because they provide an insight into how candidates get on with other team members, how they apply themselves to new problems, how they express themselves, what role they play in a team, and whether they are able to influence others and how they do this. These types of exercises can also be used to identify training and development needs (see relevant section below). However, individuals may alter their behaviour during such exercises and it may be difficult to assess an individual's contribution in isolation from the contributions or parts played by other team members.

Often these types of tests and exercises are used in graduate recruitment to enable organisations to differentiate between candidates. For example, there may be minimum application requirements, such as a 2:1, but this standard may vary across disciplines and between universities and so there is a need to be able to rate and compare applicants. Some of these tests can be performed online, but they are typically performed at an assessment centre, because qualified professionals are required to administer, grade and provide feedback on many tests. One of the key advantages of assessment centres is that they enable multiple selection methods such as interviews, tests and exercises to be performed simultaneously in a defined period of time. However, assessment centres are costly to run and so are likely to be used for large-scale recruitment rather than for the purposes of hiring a single individual.

Taking your learning further: Tests in the selection process

Wolf, A. and Jenkins, A. (2006) 'Explaining greater test use for selection: the role of HR professionals in a world of expanding regulation', *Human Resource Management Journal*, Vol.16, No.2: 193–213. This paper provides an insight into some of the reasons that influence the choice of tests in the selection process.

Induction

Once candidates have been selected, they then generally go through an induction process. During this process, a new recruit is typically welcomed to the organisation and introduced to its goals, its structure, the ways it works, and its policies and procedures (ie terms and conditions of employment, and health and safety), together with the roles to be performed by the recruit and required performance standards and targets. A recruit may also go through induction training and identify training and development needs with his or her line manager.

The quality, length and depth of this process can vary substantially between organisations and the roles for which individuals are recruited. For example, an induction may range from being basic, short and unstructured through to being comprehensive and systematic. Indeed, the process can be viewed either as an initial event or as an ongoing process in which new recruits are socialised into an organisation's culture and adopt its values (Marchington and Wilkinson, 2008).

From an OB perspective, this can enable required types and levels of behaviour to be reinforced and internalised. The process can be critically important in strengthening an individual's identification with colleagues and the organisation, and so can assist with retention. Induction is therefore attracting increasing attention, many organisations seeking to enhance their induction process in order to improve retention (CIPD, 2010).

2: Reviewing and appraising performance

The performance standards and targets established at an induction are likely to be monitored and reviewed on an ongoing informal basis and/or at periodic formal reviews. These targets and behavioural standards may change or be renegotiated as an individual's career progresses with an organisation, and so assessments of performance are conducted throughout an individual's employment with an organisation.

Informal feedback delivered by an individual's manager or colleagues can be very valuable in terms of development, but this can often be provided on an *ad hoc* basis and may not be substantive. Formal reviews are typically performed every 12 months, but they may be held on a more frequent basis depending on how long an individual has been with an organisation, their performance standards and an organisation's particular approach to performance management.

Formal reviews are commonly performed on a one-to-one basis, although other evaluators of an individual's performance may be involved in the process. An organisation's HRM department may design the structure and format of these reviews, but the review typically involves or is performed by an individual's supervisor or immediate line manager. The factors subject to appraisal can vary, but are likely to cover dimensions such as personality, competencies, behaviour, goal achievement and job performance. In terms of OB, behaviourally anchored rating scales (BARS) and behavioural observation scales (BOS) may be used to assist in the evaluation and measurement of performance.

The BARS system involves breaking down a job into its key tasks and identifying behaviours that are important for completing each task, rather than looking at more general employee characteristics (eg personality). A range of possible behaviours is then identified for each task, before placing these on a scale with performance labels (ie 'ineffective' to 'excellent' performance). The performance of an individual against these scales is then rated for each task. The BOS system adopts a similar approach. Desired job-related behaviours are identified and the frequency with which employees engage in each of these behaviours is rated. Both systems let employees know the types and levels of behaviour that are expected of them, and both give managers the opportunity to rate the performance of individuals and provide them with specific behavioural feedback. However, ratings may not always be accurate because managers may encounter difficulties in rating individuals' behaviour and their evaluations may be influenced by bias and subjectivity, so these systems typically offer low reliability (Spence and Keeping, 2010). Indeed, as a result of this, those being appraised may contest the ratings awarded.

These ratings and appraisals can be used to inform training and development needs as well as reward levels. However, they are often perceived by line managers and employees to be little more than an administrative exercise, because appraisal forms are often archived until the next review rather than being referred to throughout the course of employment as a continuous process of improvement. This means that issues of performance can often be neglected until the next appraisal, and fluctuations in an individual's performance may be overlooked. In addition, such appraisals are widely used for both reward and development purposes, which can conflict, because an individual may shy away from highlighting areas of development needed to enhance performance because it may affect the level of rewards he or she receives.

As well as one-to-one reviews with a superior, an individual's performance may be appraised by a number of other actors who are likely to evaluate an individual's performance from different perspectives. For example, an individual's peers, subordinates, internal or external clients or even external assessors may review his or her performance. Individuals may even evaluate their own performance. These different viewpoints are likely to influence how an individual's performance is evaluated and on what bases. As an indication, an individual's peers may hold very distinct views relative to their line manager or clients. Each of these perspectives offers its own advantages and purposes, but taken in isolation can be influenced by subjectivity and bias.

In order to obtain a more rounded and holistic view, many organisations therefore use a multi-source or 360-degree approach to feedback, which integrates these perspectives. This appraisal structure is illustrated in Figure 17.4.

The relevance of each of these sources of feedback is likely to vary depending on the nature of the role performed by the individual being assessed and how he or she fits in with the organisation. For instance, the acquisition of an external customer's perspective may be extremely valuable if an individual provides customer services, whereas for other roles it may be less relevant or even irrelevant. The adoption of such a system can also be expensive, particularly as an external specialist organisation may be commissioned to administer the process, and so 360-degree feedback is typically used to develop managerial-level staff and enhance their self-awareness.

The acquisition of different perspectives serves to reduce bias in comparison to assessment being performed by just one individual and may provide more valid feedback. These perspectives are also usually collected in a confidential and anonymous manner, and so may be more direct and to the point. However, this may guide the nature of the reviews provided, because reviewers may use it as an opportunity to voice their personal grievances with their manager, as subjectivity and personal liking are likely to play a role in influencing the evaluations provided. Alternatively, a reviewer may not feel that they can be totally honest just in case their manager is able to identify the source of any negative comments, and so may be concerned about their potential reaction and shape their responses accordingly. Consequently, the reviews provided may not be accurate, relevant or valid. That being said, the review provided is likely to have a greater chance

Figure 17.4   360-degree feedback

of being accepted by the individual under review because it originates from a variety of standpoints. This is particularly likely to be the case where such feedback is mutually reinforcing. The outcome of this feedback can then be used to identify behavioural strengths and areas where development is needed.

Taking your learning further: 360-degree feedback leading to action

Luthans, F. and Peterson, S. J. (2003) '360-degree feedback with systematic coaching: empirical analysis suggests a winning combination', *Human Resource Management*, Vol.42, No.3: 243–56.	This paper emphasises the importance of building on the feedback provided by appraisals rather than just filing it away.

The system has become increasingly popular, and in fact many organisations now perform what is known as 720-degree feedback, whereby a second 360-degree appraisal is performed to assess whether an individual's behaviour has changed and to what extent, as a result of the feedback and training provided following the first 360-degree appraisal. However, the process may be perceived as a bureaucratic exercise in that it can generate a great deal of information which can make it difficult to discern a clear picture, especially where there may be conflicting and/or unclear feedback. The likelihood of this is increased by the tendency for reviewers who are untrained or have received limited training, and who may not fully engage with the process or see much value in it. Although there is a greater chance that the feedback will be accepted, this does not mean that it will not have a demotivating effect or that the individual being appraised will be any more interested in or committed to changing his or her behaviour. Nevertheless, the outcome of the review may influence reward levels, training and development and whether an individual needs counselling or support to help them achieve the desired behaviour or performance levels.

3: Enhancing and reinforcing performance standards

In this section we examine how pay and training and development can be used to enhance employee performance, and we follow up with some of the strategies used by organisations to reinforce performance standards.

Pay as reward

As well as being a key factor in attracting and retaining staff, pay and reward can influence levels of employee performance. With the increasingly individualised nature of pay determination, many organisations now operate pay systems that focus on individual effort and that reward desired organisational behaviours, particularly in the private sector – although it should be noted that for many employees pay is not determined in this manner, and it may be that even within an organisation that adopts such a pay system, it is only certain groups that are rewarded in this way (eg only senior management staff).

Often the aim is to encourage employees to actively contribute to the achievement of an organisation's goals through creating shared interests, linking business objectives with staff rewards. This can be done by offering bonuses or incentives above an individual's base pay for meeting or exceeding standards, which are normally set at induction or following a review meeting by an individual's line manager. The nature and level of these incentives are likely to vary according to the role performed by individuals and their status.

Returning to the example of a consultancy firm, one of the core objectives of this type of organisation is typically the provision of outstanding client service, because this is likely to increase the fee income generated by the firm. A range of incentive measures may be adopted to achieve this objective, the type and level of reward differentiated between groups within the organisation. Fee-earning consultants may be rewarded on the basis of the firm's overall performance, the performance of their team and their own individual performance, with the form and level of rewards related to an individual's role and the degree of their contribution to the organisation's objectives. As knowledge-based workers, fee-earning consultants may be offered equity to enhance their motivation and strengthen their long-term commitment and the link between individual and organisational performance (see Lepak and Snell's framework above). The type and level of these incentives would vary according to seniority, because an individual's status is likely to reflect his or her importance to the firm and the degree to which he or she generates creative and innovative services (Donnelly, forthcoming). For junior consultants, the emphasis may be on an immediate cash incentive rather than a long-term reward, whereas the administrative staff may receive a premium on the basis of their efficiency and productivity, because they perform more routine job-based work.

However, the link between reward and an organisation's business objectives may not always enhance motivation or performance. If a reward is on the basis of team performance, not all members are likely to contribute equally to its success. Although peer pressure is likely to play a role, some individuals may not pull their weight, whereas others may put in considerably more effort relative to their colleagues and so feel that their contribution has not been fairly recognised or rewarded. This may have a *sorting effect* because those who do not perform well may leave, but equally if the contribution of high-performers is not rewarded on a relative basis, they may become demotivated and seek employment elsewhere.

Individuals may also become demotivated if they perform well but their contribution is not adequately rewarded because of the firm's poor overall performance or because of factors beyond their control. In the banking sector, bonuses can account for a significant proportion of an individual's reward package. In light of the banking crisis, many workers in this sector have faced rising uncertainty and have had to work harder to generate efficiencies and improve performance in order to meet their employer's changing business objectives. Nevertheless, despite increasing effort and performance in this challenging environment, many of these workers saw their bonuses cut back and their bank shares become less valuable and in some cases even diluted during the crisis. For example, Deutsche Bank reduced its bonus payments by 60% in 2009, while Lloyds Banking Group cut its annual bonuses at the same time as stretching its performance targets.

Such a situation is far from ideal, because it is likely to impact on the commitment and motivation of bank workers as well as the degree of change in behaviour that may be accomplished, because pay is often used as a change management tool. Indeed, expectancy theory centres on the notion that individuals will alter their behaviour if they perceive that doing so will be adequately rewarded. Moreover, this may generate significant implications for banks, where this impacts on the motivation and commitment of knowledge-based employees who are top performers and are central to a bank's activities. Consequently, it is important for an organisation to offer additional rewards on top of pay and bonuses, including career development opportunities, flexible working arrangements and benefits such as pension payments, holidays and healthcare as part of a 'total reward' package. This is because individuals can be motivated to contribute to an organisation's goals and exercise discretionary effort through a combination of extrinsic (ie pay or recognition provided by an employer) and intrinsic factors (ie self-motivation through job pride or a sense of professionalism).

Training and development

The training and development needed to improve performance standards is also likely to be highlighted by an individual's line manager during the induction and/or review process. The type of training provided together with the degree of investment is likely to vary according to the importance of an individual's role and his or her contribution to the achievement of its objectives. In terms of organisational behaviour, this might involve enhancing behaviours or competencies in a number of focused areas. Examples of some of the types of behaviour identified for development might include:

- communication and interpersonal skills

- assertiveness

- teamworking and team-building

- leadership and management

- attitudes and motivation

- sales, customer relations and customer service

- time management and work–life balance.

Strategies to reinforce performance standards

A number of techniques can be used to develop these behaviours, such as business games, simulation exercises and role-play. Each of these can be used for behavioural modelling and behavioural development. Behavioural modelling uses observation as the basis for engineering changes in attitudes, behaviour and interpersonal skills. The need for such changes may have been identified in an individual's review. As part of this technique, a process or desired behaviour would be demonstrated, with specific learning points or critical behaviour highlighted. Those undergoing this form of training would then typically replicate the behaviour through role-plays or other kinds of simulation exercises, with the aim of reinforcing such behaviour on the job. Often this technique would be used for the development of sales and interpersonal skills.

Like modelling, behavioural development can be achieved through the kind of simulation exercises listed above, as well as training and lectures. However, it can also be achieved on the job through coaching, shadowing, mentoring and/or job rotation, which can clarify behaviours and attitudes that are expected from the employee and enable continuous development. In addition, an employee may still be productive while being trained, and on-the-job training can cost less relative to off-the-job training, particularly where it is carried out by an external training organisation. The degree of engagement and impact of this training can then be evaluated at an individual's next formal review.

Where employees do not meet minimum performance standards, it may be necessary for the standards to be reinforced through the use of procedures designed to deal with poor or ineffective performance. An individual may fail to meet these standards due to personal reasons – in which case, an organisation may offer support services to assist the individual in reaching the required standards (see the section below). If an individual's poor performance is a result of unwillingness or inability to perform the work as required, appropriate procedures are necessary. For example, an individual's attendance levels may be unsatisfactory, requiring his or her punctuality and attendance to be managed more closely, depending on the reason(s) for the absence. An individual's poor performance that stems from a lack of capability and that fails to improve following warnings and opportunities to improve may ultimately lead to dismissal if alternative work is not available. See Marchington and Wilkinson's (2008) text for a more in-depth analysis of performance management and the procedures used to tackle sub-standard performance (see also Chapter 7).

4: Support and counselling

As mentioned above, poor performance related to personal problems can be avoided or alleviated by the provision of support from line managers and colleagues as well as support and counselling services, which are often outsourced to external organisations with professionally accredited staff. The services may constitute an element of an organisation's employee assistance programme (EAP) alongside a range of other services, including legal and financial advice (for an example of the types of services provided as part of an EAP visit http://www.youtube.com/watch?v=_7qgE3kJQNU). The purpose behind offering these services is typically to help employees resolve concerns that may affect their performance, health and well-being.

Marks & Spencer, for example, offers its staff a range of confidential services to help them deal with personal situations either at home or at work. An independent 24-hour helpline offers staff general counselling support and advice on legal and financial problems, as well as abuse, relationship difficulties and state benefits. Such schemes offer advantages to both organisations and employees. However, the take-up of these services by employees is often low, which together with cost, may in part explain why only a minority of organisations offer such services.

Conclusion

HRM plays an important role in shaping organisational behaviour. This chapter has provided an insight into the development and growth of HRM as a management framework and field of study, relative to the traditional field and practice of personnel management. We examined some of the hard and soft dimensions to HRM, together with best practice and best fit approaches to the application of HRM practices in organisations.

We then reviewed the emergence of the concept of strategic human resource management and the resource-based view of the firm. This perspective emphasises the importance of viewing employees as an organisation's key resource and source of sustainable competitive advantage. The development of this view by Lepak and Snell (2008) highlights the need to examine the architecture of the firm and how an organisation may tailor its practices and modes of employment according to the relative importance of different worker groups to an organisation's strategic objectives.

Focusing on the interaction between HRM and organisational behaviour, we then examined the strategic role of HR managers and the functions that they perform in targeting and stimulating desired behaviours. This prompted an analysis of the mechanisms comprising a performance management system and the need to adopt a continuous and multidimensional approach to the generation of desired behaviours and performance standards. The analysis revealed the need for HRM to adopt different practices for different groups, and ultimately pointed to the need for HRM to be responsive to workers' individual needs if they are to identify with an organisation's objectives and adopt the types of behaviour conducive to high performance and organisational success.

End notes

[1] See also Chapters 10 and 12.

[2] See also Chapters 3, 6, 7, 10 and 15.

REVIEW AND DISCUSSION QUESTIONS

REVIEW QUESTIONS

1 What differences can be discerned between HRM and personnel management?

2 What models and modes of employment are associated with soft HRM?

3 How are contract-based workers likely to be managed?

4 What are the advantages and drawbacks of one-to-one interviews? How might some of these disadvantages be overcome?

5 What are the benefits of Internet-based recruitment and selection?

DISCUSSION QUESTIONS

1 What methods would you use to recruit and select call centre workers, and why?

2 When would you use group-based exercises? Provide three different examples.

3 What methods and measures would you use to appraise the performance of a team manager?

4 What types of reward mechanisms would you use to help sustain the commitment of a lawyer?

5 How would you enhance the role and effectiveness of line managers in the delivery of HR management?

FURTHER READING

Armstrong, M. and Baron, A. (2007) *Managing Performance: Performance management in action*. London: CIPD. This text covers the management of performance and provides survey findings that reveal how organisations manage their employees' performance, together with clear practical advice.

Hutchinson, S. and Purcell, J. (2007) *Line Managers in Reward, Learning and Development*. London: CIPD. This text, based on research undertaken in six large public and private sector organisations, explores issues surrounding the role of line managers in two critical areas of human resource management: reward and development.

Legge, K. (2005) *Human Resource Management: Rhetorics and realities*. London: Palgrave Macmillan. This text analyses the role and place of HRM in contemporary organisations and examines the changes and developments that have taken place since the first edition was published in 1995.

Mabey, C. (2006) 'Closing the circle: participant views of a 360-degree feedback programme', *Human Resource Management Journal*, Vol.11, No.1: 41–53. This paper provides an insight into participants' experiences of 360-degree feedback and the implications for practice.

Marchington, M. and Wilkinson, A. (2008) *Human Resource Management at Work: People management and development*, 4th edition. London: CIPD. This excellent user-friendly leading text provides a comprehensive analysis of HRM at work and is particularly useful for those pursuing CIPD accreditation.

KEY SKILLS

TIME MANAGEMENT

It is critically important to effectively manage your time so that you successfully meet your deadlines and limit any unneeded stress and inefficiencies. Often you will have to deal with a number of competing priorities that have to be completed at different stages or even all at the same time. The key to successful time management is organising and planning your work schedule at a personal level, although this may have to be in line with the requirements of your boss, colleagues or clients/customers. In order to do this, it is a good idea to keep an up-to-date written or electronic diary, and it may be useful to think about how you currently spend your working time by logging your activities over a few days. This may, for example, highlight a need to take calls and respond to emails at certain times of the day in order to avoid continuous interruptions to your working patterns, if the nature of your work permits it. Your work schedule may also mean that it will be necessary to manage the expectations of your colleagues and may require you to protect your planned time by declining additional work. If you do take on extra work, it is important to know as much as possible of the requirements of the task by finding out what is involved and what the needs and expectations are of the person asking you to do the work. For instance, people may ask you to do something 'now' when 'later today' would be perfectly acceptable. The management of your time at work is important because it will help you to be more effective and successful, and will assist you in achieving a better work–life balance.

CRITICAL THINKING SKILLS AND REFLECTIVE LEARNING

This chapter has demonstrated the need for you to think critically and reflect on what you have learned. Because an HRM policy or practice works in one organisation does not necessarily mean that it will have the same effect in the organisation that you work for. A new management development or system may be appealing, but it may represent little more than a rebranding of what has been done in the past and may generate increased costs and similar or even new types of problems. It is therefore important to apply critical thinking and draw on what you have learned from your studies and your experiences.

TEAMWORKING

Even if you do a lot of work on your own within an organisation, it is likely that teamworking will be an important element of your job. Teamworking offers extensive benefits and so it is important that you fully engage and communicate with other team members in order for the team to be successful and meet its objectives. This can require the use of a wide but interrelated range of 'soft skills', including group working, relationship-building, emotional intelligence, negotiation, co-operation, influencing, compromise

and decision-making skills, each of which can be developed through group assignments and teamwork in class.

PERSONAL DEVELOPMENT PLANNING

While it is important to have a career plan and objectives, the feedback provided by line managers or other appraisers is likely to be of value in helping you to achieve these goals. It is therefore important that you use this feedback effectively by devising a strategic plan to enhance your personal development. This should be continuously reviewed and updated because it is likely that your developmental needs will change as your career progresses.

EMOTIONAL INTELLIGENCE, EMPATHY, SYMPATHY AND LISTENING

These types of skills are commonly associated with the nature of the work performed by HR managers, but they are typically required of everyone in their daily interactions. The degree to which these skills are likely to be required may vary according to the type of work being performed and an individual's role. For example, nurses, counsellors and call centre operatives are likely to require strong skills in these areas. As noted in the chapter, line managers often require these skills in providing an initial base of counselling support and such skills can be important in managing, motivating and relating to staff. These types of skills can be enhanced through development. For instance, listening skills can be improved by 'active listening' techniques, games and exercises.

NEGOTIATING, ARBITRATION AND CONFLICT RESOLUTION SKILLS

These skills are particularly relevant to the roles performed by HR managers and are typically refined through practice. Guidance on how to approach these aspects of the job can be found on the CIPD's website (www.cipd.co.uk) as well as the Advisory, Conciliation and Arbitration Service's website (www.acas.org.uk).

LEADERSHIP, COACHING AND MENTORING SKILLS

These types of skills are required of all managers, including HR managers. They draw on a wide range of skills, including many of those listed above. For example, a manager would typically need to be emotionally intelligent, lead other team members and identify and plan their own development needs as well as those of who they review, coach or mentor, and so reflective learning and listening skills are likely to be required. Managers may also play a leading role in negotiations, arbitration and conflict resolution. These types of skills are usually acquired from a combination of sources, including personal experience, management development programmes and learning from the behaviours of colleagues and from coaches or mentors.

Ethical implications: Equal opportunities for all

When selecting between candidates, it is important to provide equal opportunities for all those applying for a position. Not doing so may lead to claims of unfair treatment and discrimination. A failure to handle the process in an ethical manner may also attract bad press and have a negative impact on an organisation's public image. For example, the clothing firm Abercombie& Fitch has faced numerous court cases relating to the discriminatory nature of its recruitment, selection and employment practices. In 2004 it settled a class action suit for $40 million. As part of the settlement, the company agreed to create an office of diversity and to recruit more employees from ethnic minority backgrounds. In 2009, an employee named Riam Dean in the UK won a harassment case against the company. She had been asked to work behind the scenes rather than on the shop floor because she had a prosthetic arm, which was not perceived to fit the look portrayed by the retailer. Such cases and the findings upheld against the firm are unlikely to have benefited the company's business, image or ethical credentials.

BEST PRACTICE

The John Lewis Partnership was established in the nineteenth century (johnlewispartnership.co.uk). The organisation is based around a partnership business model. Currently, it employs in the region of 70,000 partners in its upmarket retail operations Waitrose, John Lewis and Greenbee. In 2009, it recorded an annual turnover of nearly £7.4 billion, an increase of 6.5% on the previous year.

The partnership aims to be an employer of distinction. In line with this commitment, the organisation operates a soft model of HRM, extending a range of benefits to its members. These include:

- fair treatment – a commitment to diversity and equal opportunities
- work–life balance support – flexible working, career breaks, extended leave and a flexible retirement policy
- competitive pay, including a partnership bonus
- extensive benefits (a non-contributory final salary pension scheme, life assurance, discounts, generous holiday entitlements, ticket subsidies, education subsidies, bursaries for the pursuit of excellence, voluntary charity secondments and a range of subsidised clubs and facilities to suit the needs of its members)
- training, promotion and career development opportunities.

Through investing in its members, the partnership has grown from strength to strength. Having established a formula for success, its expansion is forecast to continue over the coming years.

WORST PRACTICE

ClaimsCo was once the UK's biggest 'no win, no fee' personal injury claims firm. It expanded very rapidly in the early 2000s, the number of employees tripling within just 18 months. To many it appeared to be a veritable success story. It had managed to win its clients six-figure settlements, it had donated £6 million to a well-known children's charity, and its staff appeared to be well rewarded because they were treated to lavish events.

The company originally started up on the basis of targeted selling through newspapers, TV ads and call centres. However, in order to fuel the organisation's growth, this strategy changed and its sales staff were instructed to engage in doorstep selling, visiting shopping malls and hospital casualty departments to drum up business by telling members of the public that if they had been in an accident, they could be entitled to thousands of pounds' worth of compensation by registering a claim. This pressure to increase sales figures, combined with commission-based rewards and poor HRM procedures led to the organisation's overnight collapse. The company's demise was attributed to a number of factors, including the HRM policies and practices adopted:

- Promotion to managerial positions was not on the basis of merit, competencies or experience but rather family membership.
- The company's recruitment and selection procedures failed to identify fraudulent behaviour among staff.
- ClaimsCo set unrealistic targets for its sales force. Some members of staff fabricated claims in order to reach these targets.

When the company suddenly went into administration, many members of the organisation received text messages warning them that they would not receive their salary for that month. These messages were then followed shortly afterwards by texts informing them of their immediate redundancy.

PART FIVE

Emerging Issues

Chapter 18
Ethics: Issues and Developments

Ed Rose

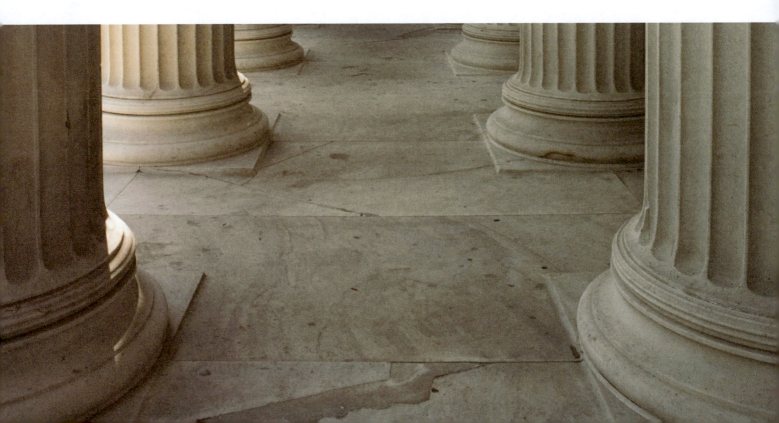

Contents

Key Learning Outcomes

By the end of this chapter you should be able to:

- identify the main issues concerning definitions of ethics
- outline the context of business ethics within organisations
- explain the ethical issues underpinning organisational behaviour
- consider ethics in relation to organisational behaviour practices.

Introduction

This chapter considers some of the ethical issues and dilemmas which affect organisational behaviour. The chapter is unlike the other chapters in this book and comprises more of a thought-provoking piece which provides a perspective on ethical concerns generally and, more importantly, in relation to organisational behaviour. It is, therefore, essential to note at the outset that although there are particular problems concerning ethical behaviour in terms of both policy and practice within the domain of organisational behaviour, these problems can only be fully appreciated within the broader context of business ethics. Most of the chapters in this book have identified ethical problems and issues, and this chapter will attempt to bring these together in an integrated way.

There is no doubt that what constitutes ethical behaviour, and how such behaviour is managed within organisations, are two of the major current and emerging issues confronting organisational behaviour and business generally. The significance of business ethics will unquestionably intensify over the coming years as a result of globalisation, the impact of global recession and the consequences of stealthy climate change. The chapter begins with an overview of the problems and definitions of business ethics, and this is followed by a more detailed consideration of business ethics in relation to organisations. We then go on to explain in more detail the ethical issues which underpin organisational behaviour as a multi-disciplinary area of study. Lastly, the chapter examines ethics by means of thought-provoking questions in relation to the practices associated with the various organisational behaviour topics identified within the chapters of this text.

ISSUES CONCERNING DEFINITIONS OF ETHICS

There are, to be sure, problems and difficulties concerning the definition of ethics. This is because ethics embraces much of what we do and think at societal, organisational, workplace and private levels. There is no single 'code of ethics' which is applicable to all situations and contexts we may find ourselves in. Perhaps the most widely encompassing statement of what ethics is derives from Baron (2006: 693):

> Ethics is the study of moral judgements about the rightness of actions and rules of behaviour. At the societal level, ethics is intended to contribute to mutually beneficial modes of conduct as an alternative to government regulation and enforcement. At the organisational level, ethics is a guide to managerial decision-making and policy formulation. At the individual level, ethics provides a basis for justifying one's actions, evaluating the actions of others, and reasoning about moral issues.

Baron also suggests that ethics comprises three 'systems' which may be termed *utilitarian*, *rights* and *justice*. These systems relate to perceptions of what is 'good' and 'right' and are important guides to firms (and organisations in general) and managers in the evaluation of alternative courses of action.

Utilitarianism

Utilitarianism has its origins in the work of Jeremy Bentham (1789) and John Stuart Mill (1861) and emphasises the need for ethical principles to be part of the free enterprise system. In this instance, it is regarded as ethical to attempt to maximise everyone's well-being, whether this is to be achieved by government, by private enterprise and markets, or by a combination of both. Utilitarianism focuses upon the consequences of an action or decision and is the direct opposite of self-interest. In relation to organisational behaviour, the ethics of decision-making is considered in Chapter 11. In summary, utilitarianism holds that:

- the *consequences* of actions are judged as to whether the *actions* are morally good

- these consequences are therefore assessed in terms of human well-being

- human well-being is in turn evaluated in terms of individual preferences

- whether an action is 'right' is judged by how much well-being or good it produces, and

- the action is considered morally justified if it maximises collective well-being.

Rights

Rights and liberties do not, in the main, stem from the consequences of utilitarian action but are enshrined within the framework of democratic society. Rights include certain basic liberties such as the right to freedom of speech and the right to equality of opportunity, together with basic general rights of freedom, autonomy and equality. Rights also entail *obligations* on the part of those deemed responsible for enforcing them. For example, human resources managers have an obligation and responsibility to apply equal opportunities policies where appropriate (see Chapter 12).

Justice

Theories of justice arising from the work of Rawls (1971) are concerned with how different individuals stand relative to each other in relation to rights, liberties and utilitarian consequences. Perceptions of fairness from an individual perspective are important in this instance. Baron (2006) notes that there are three main components of justice theories: *distributive justice*, *compensatory justice*, and *retributive justice*.

Distributive justice

Distributive justice is concerned with providing incentives that contribute to the well-being of society and with providing a fair and just distribution of rewards of those contributions. In essence, as Velasquez (1998: 105) contends, the basic principle of distributive justice is that 'equals should be treated equally and unequals unequally'. This implies that, for example, individuals should receive the same pay if their productivity is the same and different pay if their productivity is different, irrespective of race or gender. Equity theory of motivation illustrates the point quite well (see Chapter 5).

Compensatory justice

Compensatory justice is concerned with whether and how a person should be compensated for an injustice, and involves the notions of fairness or equity and restitution for the individual. The issues relevant for organisational behaviour are many and varied and include instances of perceived and actual injustice, such as bullying, prejudice and harassment at work.

Retributive justice

Retributive justice is not specifically related to most organisations within a business context because it is concerned with punishment for actions that are contrary to a moral rule or societal well-being. For this reason, retributive justice is not considered further in this chapter.

BUSINESS ETHICS AND CORPORATE SOCIAL RESPONSIBILITY

Business ethics and corporate social responsibility (CSR) are dealt with in greater detail in the next main section of this chapter. We consider here some of the approaches to defining these areas. So far, we have looked at ethics in general and we now focus upon the business arena. However, as with ethics in general, definitions of business ethics and to a lesser extent CSR are rather problematic. Business ethics and CSR are very much related to each other in that the implications of both can have consequences for national and multinational organisations operating within a global market where cultural differences exist across borders. There may, for example, be differences between a national culture and a specific organisational or corporate culture (see Chapter 15 for an explanation of organisational culture).

With regard to business ethics, Clegg *et al* (2008) identify two strands.

- *Strand 1* – Business ethics is 'the reflection on the ethical behaviour of business organisations' (Clegg *et al*, 2008: 408). The focus is upon the ethical consequences of individual and organisational behaviour. This definitional strand supports the view that the pursuit of economic interests within the framework of national law will inevitably lead to ethical behaviour following the adage that 'good ethics is good business'. Hence, ethical behaviour is merely the following of and observing the rules for doing good business.

- *Strand 2* – The definition of business ethics is compromised by those who argue that the pursuit of economic self-interest in terms of profit is incompatible with ethical and moral principles.

Johnson *et al* (2008) introduce the notion of *ethical stance*, which is the extent to which an organisation exceeds its legal minimum obligations to its stakeholders (employees, customers, suppliers, government, society and the local community). The authors advance a three-level model which places business ethics and CSR within a process which incorporates an organisation's ethical stance at level 1, CSR at level 2, and individual manager ethics at level 3. This model is considered in greater detail in the next section of this chapter.

Corporate social responsibility is defined as the view that organisations should behave ethically in relation to the environment both locally and globally, the local communities in which their workplaces are based, the quality of working life and the wider society. The growing prominence of CSR within the managerial and academic domains is a reflection, at least in part, of the social, political and environmental impact of modern organisations. The focus of research and practice has been mainly upon larger, global organisations because they tend to have a higher profile than smaller, nationally based organisations. Larger organisations operate in diverse international and global markets and are increasingly under intense political scrutiny in the light of well-documented incidents indicating abuse of corporate responsibility and ethical standards by specific companies and business leaders. Such incidents include the misappropriation of pension funds, the repression of workers in developing countries, environmental incidents, and bribery and corruption associated with deals to obtain large government contracts.

THE CONTEXT OF BUSINESS ETHICS AND CORPORATE SOCIAL RESPONSIBILITY WITHIN ORGANISATIONS

This part of the chapter considers business ethics and corporate social responsibility (CSR) within large business organisations and non-governmental organisations as they impinge upon organisational behaviour. There are two approaches which are relevant to our understanding of how organisations espouse their ethical rhetoric and whether or by what means the rhetoric is translated into reality. These approaches are known as *normative ethics* and *the descriptive approach.*

Normative ethics

Normative ethics is concerned with the 'oughts' of ethical behaviour and governs how the organisation and its management should behave according to certain rules and codes. Hence, managing ethics is achieved through formalised codes of conduct. However, it should be borne in mind that the rhetoric associated with an organisation's ethical code may be difficult to live up to in practice. An example of the rhetoric of an ethical code of conduct is provided in the box below, using the example of BP. However, for various reasons, the reality may not equate with the rhetoric.

The rhetoric of the ethical code of conduct of BP

At BP our aspirations are: no accidents, no harm to people and no damage to the environment. We are committed to the protection of the natural environment, to the safety of the communities in which we operate, and to the health, safety and security of our people.

The underlying philosophy of the code is that there should be no gap between what we say and what we do. A crucially important element of this is the commitment to an open culture where people feel secure in seeking advice and in raising concerns. If you are unsure of what to do in particular circumstances or concerned that the code is being broken, you have a responsibility to speak up. The code explains the mechanisms to do this, including the *Open v Talk* process, and the protections to ensure that retaliation against those who do speak up will not be tolerated. Our reputation, and therefore our future as a business, depends on each of us, everywhere, every day, taking personal responsibility for the conduct of BP's business. Together we can show the world that BP is a company united by strong clear values and the highest standards of behaviour. It is on that basis that we will be judged – not only as a company that delivers excellent financial returns but also as a great company we are proud to work for.

In addition to fully complying with all legal requirements, we will constantly strive to drive down the environmental and health impact of our operations through the responsible use of natural resources and the reduction of waste and emissions. These challenges apply to all parts of our business and to all facilities, plants, refineries and offices – wherever we operate in the world.

Source: http://www.bp.com/liveassets/bp_internet/globalbp/STAGING/global_assets/downloads/C/coc_en_full_document.pdf

---

The descriptive approach and cultural relativity

The descriptive approach does not rely upon normative guidelines as to what ought to be applied in practice but the intention at this point is rather to monitor and describe what actually happens. Important here is the fact that because many organisations operate in a global market and therefore have outlets, subsidiaries and workplaces in many countries, awareness of *cultural relativities* is crucial to the continued success of these organisations. In essence, cultural relativity as far as business ethics is concerned means that what may be considered ethical in one country may be regarded as unethical in another.

However, we should also recognise that culture changes, often swiftly, over time, and that this may explain some of the swings towards and away from issues of corporate ethics and responsibility. For example, changes in the treatment of and attitudes towards women and their abilities in the workplace is something we have seen develop gradually over the past century in the UK and most developed economies. These changes are closely associated with *values* and *attitudes.* Values are often regarded as the standards by which things are judged and serve to shape individuals' and organisations' beliefs and attitudes. Examples of organisations not taking an initial ethical stance with regard to labour conditions in countries which provide the source of its products that it markets in developing countries include Primark, Asda and Tesco (see the box below).

Primark, Asda and Tesco have ethical dilemmas

Primark: cheap and cheerful at an ethical cost?

After fresh revelations of holes in its supply chain ethics, Primark is working overtime to stitch its reputation back together. Primark is battling to save its reputation after more revelations of illegal labour practices and poor working conditions in its supply chain emerged in January 2010. One of Primark's UK suppliers was found to be employing illegal workers and paying staff less than the minimum wage. The authorities are investigating the incident, which happened at Manchester-based knitwear factory TNS. Primark is having to explain itself also to the Ethical Trading Initiative (ETI), the UK body set up to improve supply chain working conditions, which it joined in 2006. The incident came just months after it emerged that Primark clothes were being made in India by factories using child labour. Primark sacked three suppliers in Tirupur that had subcontracted the work to the factories using children after the news came out in June 2009.

Asda and Tesco: cheap gear

Britain's second largest supermarket chain launched an investigation in 2010 into allegations that workers who make its clothes in Bangladesh are being forced to work up to 80 hours a week for as little as 4p an hour. Asda, one of three major discount clothing retailers accused of breaching international labour standards, said it would audit its suppliers in relation to the pay and conditions of Bangladeshi garment workers who supply British companies. Employees of factories making clothes for George at Asda, Tesco and Primark said their wages were so low that despite working up to 84-hour weeks, they struggled to provide for their families. There were also reports of physical and verbal abuse by supervisors and of workers being sacked for taking sick leave. All but one of the eight workers interviewed, from seven different factories, claimed they were forced to work 12-hour days and sometimes all night to finish an order. Workers from factories supplying all three retailers said they were refused access to trade unions and claimed that in the previous month, four colleagues had been dismissed for trying to organise a union.

The three retailers are among the most powerful clothing brands in Britain. In 2009, a report estimated the country's burgeoning value-clothes market to be worth £7.8 billion. Asda was reportedly the biggest player with 17% of the market, Primark second with 15%, and Tesco fifth after Matalan and New Look with 11%. All three retailers have signed up to the Ethical Trading Initiative, a voluntary code of conduct which sets out basic rights for employees, including a working week of no more than 48 hours, voluntary overtime not exceeding 12 hours a week, and payment of a 'living wage'. They say they are doing their best to improve workers' rights. However, one factory owner in Bangladesh, who supplies only to the US and German markets, said that buyers gave him little choice but to keep wages low. Mohammed Lutfor Rahman, chairman of the Luman Group, said: 'Buyers who come to Bangladesh tell us, "We are businessmen – we want to make money. If we see cheaper prices in China, we will go there."'

Source: adapted from: http://www.guardian.co.uk/business/2007/jul/16/supermarkets.retail2 and http://www.ethicalcorp.com/content.asp?ContentID=6364

Johnson *et al* (2008) present a three-level framework which encompasses business ethics and CSR. These levels comprise:

- the ethical stance
- corporate social responsibility (CSR)
- individual manager ethics.

The ethical stance

An organisation's ethical stance is the extent to which it exceeds its legal minimum obligations to its stakeholders and to society at large. An ethical stance goes beyond the normative and represents not only the policy but the practice of good ethical conduct. Johnson *et al* consider an organisation's ethical stance to be one which develops and intensifies over time. The ethical stance progression itself involves four stages. Each stage of the process incorporates a widening range of stakeholder interests and 'includes a wider range of criteria involving a longer period over which outcomes are judged' (Johnson, *et al*, 2008: 234).

The first stage identifies the minimum obligations towards the short-term interests of shareholders and encompasses the minimum legal obligations of the organisation. This first stage does not, of itself, constitute an ethical position but is a necessary, if not essential, condition for ethical progression.

The second stage broadens the focus to incorporate stakeholders. As was indicated earlier, there are many stakeholders associated with every organisation and they include any or all of the following:

- guarantors
- investors
- funding bodies
- distribution partners
- marketing partners
- licensors
- licensees
- approving bodies
- regulatory authorities
- advisers and consultants
- employees: staff, managers, directors, non-executive directors
- customers
- suppliers
- the local population (community)
- the regional general public
- the national general public
- international communities.

The shareholders will recognise that their interests would be enhanced by the positive management of relationships with other stakeholders. For example, an organisation's engagement in charitable donations while not necessarily producing shareholder gains in the short term, would, to be sure, enhance the organisation's reputation and visibility which in turn would, at the very least, other things being equal, not endanger the long-term profits and share price of the organisation.

The third stage considers the interests and expectations of the multiple stakeholders we have identified. The actions of these organisations would be likely to include a refusal to offshore jobs and services to countries where wages are lower, contracting with 'fair trade' suppliers, not selling antisocial products, and maintaining employment by operating less efficient workplaces which might otherwise have closed down. The box below provides an example of the ethical policy and stance of a high-profile UK bank. The Co-operative Bank relaunched its ethical policy incorporating its ethical stance in 2009, 17 years after the policy's inception in 1992.

The ethical stance of the Co-operative Bank

Our new Bank Ethical Policy for 2009 – because the world doesn't stand still

It is vital that we regularly update our Ethical Policy so it continues to reflect our customers' views on issues that are important to them. Last year, as part of the fifth review of our bank Ethical Policy, we invited customers to tell us what they did or did not want to see their money financing.

A record number of customers took the time to participate, demonstrating that customers continue to value our ethical approach to banking. In fact, they issued us with an overwhelming mandate to take a tough line on some of today's most pressing issues. Our revised Policy, launched in 2009, includes nine new statements reflecting these views:

'We will not finance any organisation that advocates discrimination and incitement to hatred.'

'We will not finance the manufacture or transfer of indiscriminate weapons – eg cluster bombs and depleted uranium munitions.'

'We will not finance organisations that fail to implement basic labour rights as set out in the Fundamental ILO Conventions – eg that use child labour or that actively oppose the rights of workers to freedom of association, eg in a trade union.'

'We will not finance organisations that take an irresponsible approach to the payment of tax in the least developed countries.'

'We will not finance organisations that impede access to basic human necessities – eg safe drinking water or vital medicines.'

'Furthermore, we will support fair trade and the provision of finance to the working poor in developing countries, via microfinance.'

'We will not finance any business whose core activity contributes to global climate change, via the extraction or production of fossil fuels (oil, coal and gas), with an extension to the distribution of those fuels that have a higher global warming impact (eg tar sands and certain biofuels).'

'We will not finance any business whose core activity contributes to the development of nanotechnology in circumstances that risk damaging the environment or compromising human health.'

'We will not finance any organisation involved in the exploitation of great apes – eg in experimentation or general commercial use.'

Source: adapted from: http://www.goodwithmoney.co.uk/ethical-banking/

The final stage of the ethical stance progression is concerned with the extent to which ethically driven policies and practices shape and re-shape society. This may not be achievable by any but the largest organisations and raises issues concerning power and accountability (see Chapter 13). A few successful global organisations such as Microsoft and Google may fall within this category but are, nevertheless, constrained by financial and shareholder interests. The extent to which shareholder and financial interests can be circumvented is provided by the example of the Bill and Melinda Gates Foundation (see the box below). The argument here is that the existence of the Foundation would not have been possible had it not been for the business and financial success of Microsoft. Nevertheless, the success of Microsoft has been compromised by what the US Department of Justice and the European Commission argue are unethical practices. The latter institutions argued that Microsoft used monopolistic business practices and anti-competitive strategies including refusal to deal and 'tying', which resulted in Microsoft placing unreasonable restrictions with regard to the use of its software. Microsoft also allegedly misrepresented its marketing tactics in order to bolster its monopoly position. Both the US Department of Justice and the European Commission found the company in violation of antitrust laws. The European Commission submission can be found at: http://ec.europa.eu/competition/antitrust/cases/decisions/37792/en.pdf

The Bill and Melinda Gates Foundation

The Bill and Melinda Gates Foundation is the largest transparently operated private foundation in the world, founded by Bill and Melinda Gates. The Foundation is driven by the interests and passions of the Gates family. The primary aims of the Foundation are, globally, to enhance healthcare and reduce extreme poverty, and in the USA, to expand educational opportunities and access to information technology. The Foundation – based in Seattle, Washington – is controlled by its three trustees: Bill Gates, Melinda Gates and Warren Buffett. Other principal officers include Co-Chair William H. Gates, Sr and Chief Executive Officer Jeff Raikes. It has an endowment of US $33.5 billion as of 31 December 2009. The scale of the Foundation and the way it seeks to apply business techniques to giving makes it one of the leaders in global philanthropy. In 2007 its founders were ranked the second most generous philanthropists in the USA.

For 14 of the last 16 years Bill Gates has been the richest person on Earth. More than a decade ago he decided to start handing over the 'large majority' of his wealth – currently £36 billion – for the Foundation to distribute, so that 'the people with the most urgent needs and the fewest champions' in the world, as he and his wife Melinda put it on the Foundation website, 'grow up healthier, get a better education, and gain the power to lift themselves out of poverty'. In 2006, Warren Buffett, currently the third richest person in the world, announced that he too would give a large proportion of his assets to the Foundation. Its latest accounts show an endowment of £24 billion, making it the world's largest private foundation. It is committed to spending the entire endowment within 50 years of Bill and Melinda Gates' deaths. Last year it awarded grants totalling £2 billion. As well as its money, it is the organisation's optimism and the fame of its main funder – in 2008 Bill Gates stopped working full-time for his computer giant Microsoft to concentrate on the Foundation – that has given it momentum. In May 2010 an editorial in the revered medical journal *The Lancet* praised it for giving 'a massive boost to global health funding . . . The Foundation has challenged the world to think big and to be more ambitious about what can be done to save lives in low-income settings. The Foundation has added renewed dynamism, credibility, and attractiveness to global health [as a cause].'

Source: http://www.gatesfoundation.org/about/Pages/foundation-fact-sheet.aspx

Corporate social responsibility

Corporate social responsibility (CSR) has been adopted as a formal policy goal by many businesses. Those organisations that commit themselves to CSR often adopt sustainable development goals that take into account economic, social and environmental consequences of their various activities. Along with management ethics, the importance of CSR has been given a high profile as a result of scandals involving Enron, WorldCom and other large organisations in which executives were accused of serious financial misdemeanours and fraudulent transactions that benefited them personally. CSR policies and practices embrace a wide range of context, stakeholders and employees. The box below provides details of the various CSR policies and practices operated by many organisations within the private, public and voluntary sectors.

Policies and practices concerning CSR

Global and local environments

- Funding local community projects
- Helping to improve the local environment
- Control of pollution
- Energy-efficient recycling of waste materials
- Energy conservation
- Product improvement using recycled materials

Direct community involvement

- Community involvement projects
- Support for arts and education
- Promoting and supporting local health initiatives
- Charitable donations to local causes

Employee engagement

- Providing adequate employee training
- Improving health and safety
- If subcontracting, providing adequate codes of behaviour and equal treatment for employees on non-standard contracts
- Providing personal counselling for assistance with alcohol and drug addiction
- Ensuring adequate medical care and insurance

Equal opportunities

- Ensuring minority employment
- Ensuring adequate promotion opportunities for a diverse workforce
- Eradicating 'glass ceilings' and 'sticky floors' (see Chapter 12)
- Ensuring that any policy concerning equal opportunities is reflected in practice

> **Products, service and suppliers**
> - Ensuring and guaranteeing the safety and quality of product and/or service
> - Not outsourcing to call centres to improve customer service
> - Ensuring product sustainability
> - Ensuring fair terms of trade
> - Boycotting unethical and irresponsible suppliers
> - Guaranteeing an ethical subcontractor code

The limitations of CSR

It has been argued that it is in the interests of shareholders and shareholder value that businesses appear to be concerned about CSR. However, it has also been argued by critics that CSR is often seen as 'a tool of corporate greenwash, a rhetorical device employed by corporations to legitimise the corporate form and accommodate the social consciences of its consumers' (Clegg *et al*, 2008: 420). Other criticisms include:

- CSR is vague and can mean different things to different corporations and organisations within different settings and contexts. For example, business organisations that contribute funds and donations to the local community for charitable purposes can be seen to be operating in an ethical and socially responsible way. However, this diverts funds away from shareholder interests because those funds could have been ploughed back into the organisation, re-invested, or used to improve the pay and conditions of the workforce.

- Another criticism is that because organisations in the UK, Europe, the USA and elsewhere operate under a framework of corporate law and are therefore legally, if not socially, responsible for their actions, this by itself strongly implies a sufficient moral and ethical stance for any specific organisation. One dilemma this raises is the difficulty in distinguishing between what may be deemed 'responsible' action which benefits the community, environment and other stakeholders thereby demonstrating a concern for society, and actions that are designed to enhance the reputation of an organisation.

- Finally, it is essential to note that 'cultural relativism' should be considered where laws, customs, morals and ethics differ between countries on a global scale. CSR policies in one country may therefore not be wholly applicable in another country.

ETHICAL PROBLEMS AND PRACTICES UNDERPINNING THE FIELD OF ORGANISATIONAL BEHAVIOUR

As we have indicated earlier in this chapter, ethical behaviour and corporate social responsibility (CSR) are concerned with the 'outward face' that organisations show to customers, clients, their other varied stakeholders and society as a whole. There are increasing pressures upon organisations to adopt ethical stances, not only externally but also internally, and there appears to be a clear trend that demands that government officials, workers in general and the organisations they represent all act in accordance with high ethical and moral standards. This section of the chapter is concerned with ethical managerial behaviour which impinges specifically upon the areas of organisational behaviour covered in this book, together with the ethical dilemmas raised. An ethical dilemma or problem occurs when an individual is compelled to make a decision that requires a choice among competing sets of principles or alternatives. Such a situation may arise when a member of an organisation has to make a decision whether to do something that could be considered unethical but which benefits the individual, the organisation or both.

Perhaps too often, business ethics is portrayed as a matter of resolving conflicts in which one option appears to be the clear choice. For example, case studies are often presented in which an employee is faced with whether or not to lie, steal, cheat, abuse another, break the terms of a contract, and so on. However, ethical dilemmas faced by managers are often more true-to-life and highly complex, with no clear guidelines to resolve them. The resolution of ethical dilemmas often involves a choice between alternatives (which is why each is a dilemma). These alternatives include:

- determining the extent of conflicts of interest upon those affected by a decision

- determining real alternative actions that are equally justifiable, and

- determining the consequences of a decision or an action upon the various stakeholders.

Examples of ethical problems and dilemmas include:

- conducting personal business during work time

- discouraging a good employee from taking another job by withholding information

- allowing the unsafe disposal of hazardous waste

- giving bribes in order to secure a contract.

In addition, managers encounter ethical dilemmas in various work and organisational contexts, particularly in working relationships with superiors and employees, customers, competitors and suppliers.

The box below provides some examples of real-life ethical dilemmas.

Examples of complex real-life ethical dilemmas

'A customer (or client) asked for a product (or service) from us today. After I told him our price, he said he couldn't afford it. I know he could get it cheaper from a competitor. Should I tell him about the competitor – or let him go without getting what he needs? What should I do?'

'Our company prides itself on its merit-based pay system. One of my employees has done a tremendous job all year, so he deserves strong recognition. However, he is already paid at the top of the salary range for his job grade and our company has too many people in the grade above him, so we can't promote him. What should I do?'

'Our company prides itself on hiring minorities. One Asian candidate fully fits the job requirements for our open position. However, we're concerned that our customers won't understand his limited command of the English language. What should I do?'

'My top software designer suddenly refused to use our email system. He explained to me that as a Christian, he could not use a product built by a company that provided benefits to the partners of homosexual employees. He'd basically cut himself off from our team, creating a major obstacle to our product development. What should I do?'

'My boss told me that one of my employees is among several others to be laid off soon, and that I'm not to tell my employee yet or he might tell the whole organisation, which would soon be in an uproar. Meanwhile, I heard from my employee that he plans to buy presents for his daughter and a new carpet for his house. What should I do?'

'My computer operator told me he'd noticed several personal letters printed from a computer that I was responsible for managing. While we had no specific policies then against personal use of company facilities, I was concerned. I approached the letter writer to discuss the situation. She told me she'd written the letters on her own time to practise using our word processor. What should I do?'

'A fellow employee told me that he plans to leave the company in two months and start a new job which has been guaranteed to him. Meanwhile, my boss told me that he wasn't going to give me a new opportunity in our company because he was going to give it to my fellow employee instead. What should I do?'

Ethics and organisational behaviour

Most of the areas and topics of organisational behaviour addressed by this book also present ethical dilemmas. The focus here is mainly upon the internal dynamics of organisations and the dilemmas are considered in relation to the chapter topics as they appear in the book. The dilemmas are posed as questions which may also serve as discussion points. Chapters 3 to 13 are covered in this section.

Individuals: personality, perception, attitudes and emotions, motivation and learning

These topics are considered together because they relate to the individual and individual attitudes, attributes and behaviour. The topics cover Chapters 3–6. Salient questions which may be construed as ethical dilemmas include:

- Should employees be punished for making mistakes? If so, for what types of mistakes should they be punished? Are there mistakes for which they should *not* be punished, and if so, what are they?

- Should all employees be given the opportunity to learn new skills, and if so, why? Should some employees have greater learning opportunities than others, and if so, when should this occur?

- Do individuals with highly authoritarian and compliant personalities behave unethically? One example which may assist your response is provided in the box below.

- Are accurate perceptions always necessary? In what situations (if any) is it less important to ensure that perceptions are accurate?

- Would a customer service representative's behaviour in a call centre be considered unethical if she or he were to provide her or his judgement concerning advice to a customer rather than reading from the prescribed script? This dilemma is part of what is regarded as 'emotional labour' and 'emotional dissonance' (see Chapters 4 and 13).

Authoritarian personality and unethical behaviour

The authoritarian personality suggests a certain inflexibility of belief, conforming to conventional values and a recognised source of authority. This type of personality is more likely to prevail in organisations whose values expect unquestioned obedience to inflexible rules and conducts of behaviour. Legitimate authority is regarded as absolute (see Chapter 13). It may be argued that individuals with highly authoritarian personalities display levels of obedience which may result in unethical behaviour. Within the armed forces and specific military organisations, for example, authoritarianism is a required personality trait and has been associated with 'crimes of obedience' and unethical behaviour (Hamilton and Kelman, 1990). Milgram (2005: 12) noted that: 'The essence of obedience consists in the fact that a person comes to view himself as the instrument for carrying out another person's wishes, and he therefore no longer sees himself as responsible for his actions.'

Crimes of obedience have also been linked to leader characteristics. Hinrich (2007) states:

More recently, researchers who have explored the phenomena of crimes of obedience have examined leader characteristics that would make a leader prone to issuing unethical directives and that would predict success at influencing followers to obey those directives. This approach suggests that crimes of obedience could be reduced through selection techniques designed to keep certain people out of leadership positions or by altering the ethical behaviour of those in leader positions through training. Very seldom is the focus placed on non-leaders, and in most leader-focused studies, followers are generally depicted as a homogenous group.

An example of this type of unethical behaviour in a non-military context is given by French *et al* (2008: 102), who state: 'Under instruction, Arthur Andersen employees shredded documents to cover up the impending corporate scandal that allegedly led to the demise of one of the US's largest accountancy organisations and sparked the Enron scandal.'

Groups and teams, conflict and stress, and communication

These topics cover Chapters 7, 8 and 9.

- Is it appropriate to exclude some members from teams when status and long-term rewards (such as promotions) are based largely on team performance?

- What types of sanctions should be imposed on those team members who are engaged in social loafing? Who should apply those sanctions (if any)?

- Do organisations have a responsibility to offer assistance to employees in order to cope with stress, such as providing more leave and flexible work arrangements?

- Do managers and others who are central to communications networks within the organisation have a responsibility to convey important information they receive?

Managing organisations including leadership, decision-making, equality and diversity, and power and politics

Topics covered here comprise Chapters 10 to 13. Arguably, these topics pose some of the greatest ethical dilemmas for individuals in organisations.

- Are ethical leaders more effective than leaders who demonstrate unethical behaviour?

- What is more important: employee productivity or leaders' exhibiting ethical behaviours? Is ethical behaviour more important even if the result is poor performance?

- Under what circumstances is it ethically appropriate to use coercive power?

- Does the wielding of both political and non-political power have ethical consequences for the organisation and its members? See the box below for an explanation.

- Is the decision-making process within organisations entirely unethical, or is it the consequences of decision-making which could have ethical implications for the organisation?

- Are there any circumstances in which it is appropriate to discriminate against a particular category of individuals either at the recruitment stage or within employment itself?

Ethical or unethical power?

The misuse of power at every level of the organisation could have unethical consequences, so every organisational member has a responsibility to work in an ethical and socially responsible manner. The distinction between non-political and political power is important in this context. Non-political power is exercised through the formal authority structure of the organisation which incorporates formal rules and procedures and is directed towards formally sanctioned goals, whereas political power often operates outside the formal organisational structure and processes and may be directed towards non-organisationally sanctioned goals. The political process and the criteria which determine whether the political act is ethical or not is represented in Figure 18.1 below, adapted from Velasquez *et al* (1983).

Figure 18.1 A process for analysing political behaviour in organisations

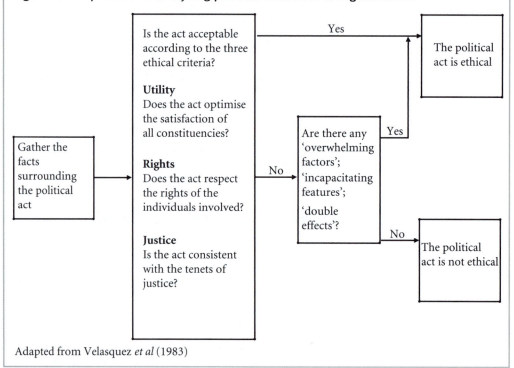

Adapted from Velasquez *et al* (1983)

The utilitarian, rights and justice aspects of ethics are described earlier in this chapter. They include criteria to determine whether the political act is ethical or otherwise. Figure 18.1 also indicates that, exceptionally, some behaviour, while not satisfying the utility, rights and justice criteria may still be ethical if that behaviour fulfils the 'overwhelming factors' requirement and criteria. This 'special case' may therefore be regarded as ethical or otherwise, depending upon:

- the extent and nature of the conflicts that may exist amongst the relevant criteria as, for example, where the behaviour results in a mix of 'good' and 'bad' outcomes
- the extent to which conflicts exist within criteria as, for example, where a behaviour uses questionable means to achieve a positive end
- the extent to which the individual manager or employee is unable to use any of the criteria owing to, for example, inaccurate or incomplete information.

Conclusion

Ethical issues and dilemmas are increasingly prevalent within most organisations and concern all organisational members in a variety of ways. Yet such issues have attracted little attention in most organisational behaviour texts. Much of the focus in the non-organisational-behaviour literature has been upon larger, often global organisations and corporations where a number of high-profile cases and scandals highlighted by the media have been analysed.

This chapter has sought to clarify the nature of ethical behaviour and corporate social responsibility (CSR). There appears to be considerable unanimity in the literature concerning definitional aspects of ethical behaviour and corporate social responsibility, and the chapter reflects this orientation. In relation to organisational behaviour we have identified the constituent areas which present actual and potential problems and dilemmas for management practice. There can be no doubt that ecological and other pressures upon organisational members to act in a socially responsible way will increase in future years.

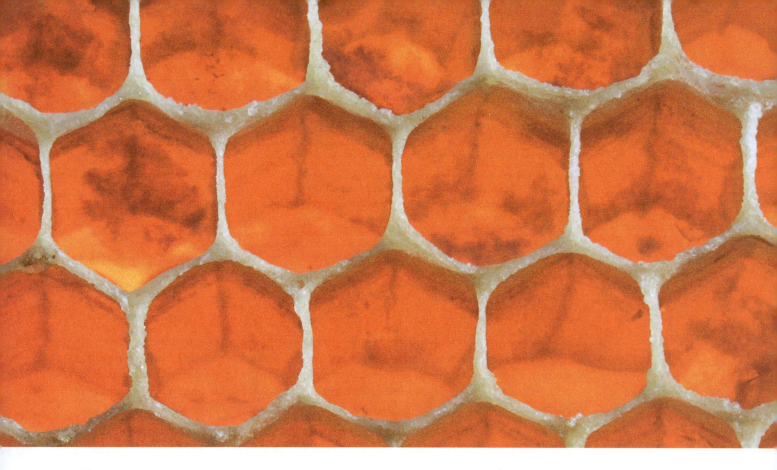

Chapter 19
Conclusion

Ed Rose and Michael Butler

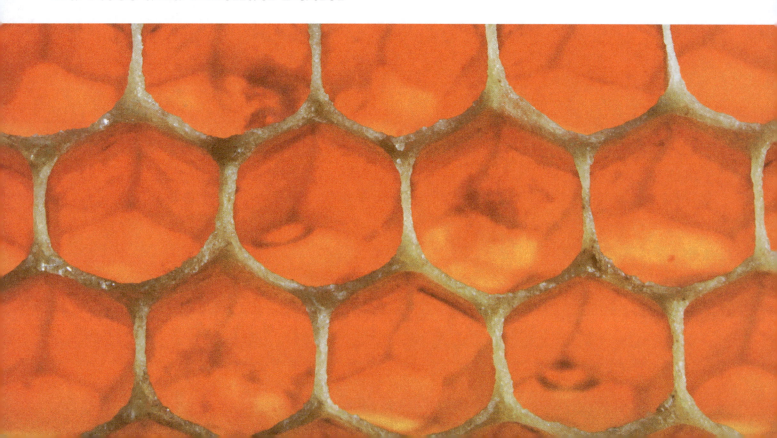

The purpose of this short conclusion is to reinforce the approach and features of the book in relation to what it sets out to accomplish. We then go on to identify briefly some of the main contemporary and emerging issues and trends which have been alluded to in many of the book's contributory chapters. It should be borne in mind that the book is an 'introduction to organisational behaviour', and as such, no prior knowledge of organisational behaviour on the part of the student is required. In common with the majority of organisational behaviour texts currently on the market, the book is structured in terms of levels of analysis that progresses from the individual to groups and then to the organisation and finally through to society. Nevertheless, it could be argued that in many respects these are 'artificial' levels of analysis because the impression gained is one of separation into discrete units or levels which bear no relation to the complexity of organisational life. We attempt to overcome this by the various devices within each chapter which have been described and which emphasise that all employees and workers, managerial and non-managerial are not discrete units but are entrenched within the structures and processes that operate within the larger society.

A RÉSUMÉ OF THE MAIN FEATURES OF THE BOOK

First of all, the book attempts to provide a balance between the approaches to work and organisations taken by managers (the so-called 'top-down' managerialist perspective) and 'bottom-up' employee perspectives. In other words, the book aims to be both prescriptive and critical. Both approaches are subject to critical evaluation – that is to say, a weighing up of the strengths and weaknesses of the approaches and how they might privilege certain world views which should not necessarily be taken for granted. One example is how the managerialist approach might disenfranchise certain social groups – for instance, women senior managers – as Chapter 12 illustrates. A further example would relate to conflict perceived by both employer and worker, as exemplified in Chapter 8. There are managerial prescriptions for the many topics covered in the book. For example, with regard to motivation and satisfaction (Chapter 5), one of the prescriptive assumptions concerns the extent to which employees can be motivated in order to become more efficient and productive. This assumption suggests not only that 'a motivated employee is a more productive employee,' but also that a more productive worker will contribute more effort to secure the economic well-being of the organisation (usually but not exclusively a private sector organisation). However, management prescriptions often belie the reality of organisational and working life experienced by non-managerial employees. It is therefore important to highlight the conflicts of ideology and expectations which often arise between managers, particularly senior managers and other employees. For example, both Chapters 8 and 13 consider how employees react to what they perceive as unfair treatment either individually or collectively, and both chapters provide an effective counterbalance to the overly prescriptive nature of much organisational behaviour literature.

A second feature of the book is that it provides many instances of an international focus within a globalised context, including examples drawn from both developed and developing countries. As we have demonstrated throughout the chapters of this book, many organisations are transnational or multinational and have to be sensitive to the economic, ecological and ethical issues in whatever country they invest in. Globalising tendencies have consequences not only for people working in those organisations but also for indigenous workers in developing countries making products such as clothing destined for developed economies. A third feature of the book is that it is intimately and inevitably concerned with the 'world of work' and emphasises the practicalities of participating in organisational activities. Each of the main chapters therefore contains at the outset Practitioner insight case study boxes which relate to a variety of organisations and their practitioners who have experienced specific challenges that directly relate to the organisational behaviour topic of the chapter. Practitioners are drawn from any function, any level and any interactive parties within and between organisations, including customers, service users or people browsing the websites of organisations they might buy from. Examples of practitioners range from the chief executive of a large local authority to section heads within small private or not-for-profit organisations. The inclusion of best and worst practice examples help the reader to be critical of organisations that engage in sub-optimal practice and, additionally, theory-to-practice examples help the reader to appreciate the relevance of theory to a range of practice.

Finally, we attempt to encourage the student reader to engage with their own experience of organisations, which is partly achieved by website activities and by providing examples of companies, products and brands which are familiar to students and to which they can relate. The underlying philosophy of the book is not only to encourage student engagement with organisational reality but also for the student to be aware and alive to employability issues concerning the development of future managers and leaders who can manage people effectively and empathically. To this end we also identify key skills required of managers which are appropriate to each chapter and which students can relate to and act out in workshops, tutorials and online activities.

AN OVERVIEW OF IMPORTANT CONTEMPORARY AND EMERGENT TRENDS

Many of the contemporary and emergent issues and trends which impact upon organisational behaviour have been dealt with in the majority of the chapters of this book. We here identify a few of the most important of such issues and trends. These are labour market trends and the changing workforce, emerging employment relationships within and outside organisations, and workplace values and ethics.

Labour market trends

Labour market trends are important in relation to organisational behaviour. The evidence indicates that there has been a growth of non-standard employment as typified by the secondary labour market described below. To what extent this influences the prescriptive material concerning, for example, motivation, leadership and teamworking is debatable. The recent period of recession would suggest that the trends concerning the growth of the secondary labour market are and will be drastically accelerated, and will give credence to the argument that labour in certain sectors of the economy is inherently dispensable. The so-called 'flexible' labour market where organisations require relatively unskilled labour of a temporary or seasonal nature in order to meet cyclical or daily fluctuations in demands for products or services has been on the increase in the UK and USA for a number of years and shows no signs of abating in the foreseeable future.

The labour force in the UK comprises all those aged 16 and over in civilian jobs who are either in work or seeking work. Women are projected to make up 46.1% of the total labour force in 2011, compared with 45.9% in 2002. The gender composition of the labour force has changed considerably over the past 50 years. While the number of men in employment has been fairly stable on average, the number of women in employment has increased year on year. There has also been an overall shift from full-time employment to part-time employment – this trend being much more marked with women than with men. In 2006, for example, 77.6% of all people of working age who worked part-time were women, and around 42.4% of women in employment worked part-time, up from 42% in 1988. The proportion of men working part-time is small but rising, and rose from 5% in 1988 to nearly 12% in 2009 (Gregg and Wadsworth, 2010).

The changes identified above have prompted considerable discussion concerning the state of the labour market in the 1990s and 2000s. It has been argued that the contemporary labour market is characterised by a dualism which on the one hand exposes workers to the variations of the laws of supply and demand, and on the other protects workers from these competitive pressures – the effective division of an economy into two parts: typically, a prosperous and stable 'core' sector of enterprises and jobs, and a peripheral sector which is relatively and systematically disadvantaged.

The first part is known as the primary sector and the second as the secondary sector. In the primary sector, work is characterised by relatively good working conditions and pay levels, opportunities for advancement; fair treatment at work, and stability of employment. In the secondary sector, workers are worse off in all the respects identified for the primary sector and their work is associated with considerable instability of employment, usually of a part-time nature, together with a high labour turnover rate. They tend to be people who are easily dispensed with, possess clearly visible social differences, are little interested in training or gaining high economic reward, and tend not to organise themselves into trade unions.

Given these features and the social and cultural characteristics of the wider society, we tend to find recruitment to the secondary labour force drawing to a disproportionate extent on women, blacks, immigrants, unqualified teenagers, students seeking part-time work and disabled persons. Within the secondary sector such as cleaning services, hotels and catering, retail, non-teaching education and health services, women and ethnic minorities tend to be over-represented. On the other hand, much of the increase in labour market participation over the last decade has been concentrated among women with higher qualifications and in professional and managerial occupations where women are traditionally under-represented.

Emerging employment relationships

One main issue here is employability, and another issue concerns the use of information technology. Recent trends suggest that employees increasingly perform a variety of work activities rather than hold specific jobs, and are expected to constantly learn skills that will keep them employed. This is a major concern for employees who work on a full-time basis because it may affect security of employment. On the other hand, motivation, group and leadership theories suggest that the intensity of training and development of employees involving the acquisition of new skills may result in an increased commitment to their organisation. Another issue that is related to the secondary labour market is, as noted above, the increased proportion of mainly (but not exclusively) part-time workers, those workers on short-term contracts and those workers who are employed by an agency and who are not employees of the organisation they work for (Kersley *et al*, 2006). This is a trend which has continued throughout the 1990s and 2000s and has been exacerbated by the recent recession. Other trends which involve the use of increasingly sophisticated information technology software include the rising numbers of employees and self-employed workers who work from home using computer facilities. Another development which is becoming more prevalent concerns the creation of 'virtual teams' that operate across space, time, and organisational boundaries whereby team members communicate mainly through electronic technologies. Additionally, information technology on a global scale allows small businesses in developing countries to compete in the global marketplace, and can lead to the creation of 'network organisations' which comprise alliances of several organisations for the purpose of creating products and/or serving clients and customers on a global scale.

Ethics and workplace values

Ethical concerns and issues are becoming increasingly relevant to most organisations with growing pressure upon organisations to engage in ethical practices. As was argued in Chapter 18, the rise of globalisation and globalising tendencies, the impact of organisations upon the local community and the ethical consequences of corrupt practices all have implications for organisational behaviour and the management of employees.

Glossary

Chapter 2

Agency the capacity of an individual to act and have an impact on their surroundings (as opposed to merely being affected by their surroundings)

Contingency theory theory that argues that there is no 'one best way' to organise because the optimal solution is contingent on the context, and thus the appropriate mode of organising is that which aligns most effectively with these contingent factors

Deconstruction form of analysis that seeks the meaning of a text and in doing so demonstrates that the 'foundations' of the text are irreducibly complex and unstable (and thus unknowable). It demonstrates that there isn't a meaning of text, but meanings which are irreconcilable and often contradictory. Text therefore has more than one interpretation, and interpretation of text can only go so far but never grasp the 'true' meaning

Discourse term typically used to refer to 1) text, 2) the spoken word, or 3) a formal discussion regarding a topic (often governed by rules and conventions). Discourse, particularly of the formal, governed kind, can be related to ideas of ideology. Discourse is both the means of expression, but also the way in which subjectivity is produced. Its ability to produce subjectivity through formal discourse demonstrates its link with power

Division of labour the specialisation and co-ordination of work activity in order to achieve economic advantage. The tasks are divided to make the process of work more efficient

Embodied describing the way in which the mind is affected by the body. Embodiment has particular relevance for understanding how people's experiences of their body and how they relate to their body shapes the way they think and live. It is often used by those working in gender studies to demonstrate the differences sex/gender makes in the experience of organisation/s

False consciousness term – often related to the writing of Marx – used to describe a mindset in which people who are disadvantaged by the relations in society nonetheless participate in them willingly. It refers to the fact that people are misled and do not perceive the real state of affairs, and thus participate unwittingly. It is closely linked to the idea of power

Feminist theory theory that seeks to understand the nature of gender inequality through understanding women's experiences and role in society. It seeks to expose the systematic nature of discrimination and promote women's rights and interests

Globalisation the way in which economies and societies worldwide have become integrated. The driver for this is primarily economic (international trade, cross-border investment, worker migration) but there are also cultural, political, technological drivers, amongst others. Changes in patterns and ease of communication have assisted in the pace of globalisation

Grand narratives Lyotard's expression for narratives that reflect a legitimised knowledge that becomes dominant. The Enlightenment project of modernism argued that reason would produce universal knowledge

Identity a person's conception and expression of himself or herself – of both his/her individuality, and also his/her affiliations (such as gender identity, cultural identity, and so on). Identity reflects and affects how you see yourself and your relations to others

Ideology form of thought, often dominant in society, that is often treated as if it is 'real' rather than illusory. Marxist research employs the notion of ideology to demonstrate the dominance of the ruling class in setting the world view which neglected the needs of the working class

Intersubjectivity subjectivity refers to a person's (subject's) perspective which is influenced by their experiences, attitudes, and so on. Intersubjectivity refers to this experience as it is shared by more than one subject

Legitimised/ legitimated description of actions, processes or ways of thinking that concur with or are recognised as the 'norm' in a society. Legitimacy also has authority. It is hard to resist or contradict that which is legitimised/legitimated because in doing so you go against that which is recognised as the norm

Managerial/managerialism where managers are perceived as having excusive power to define goals of the organisation and manage accordingly

Modernism linked to the Enlightenment project where reliance on myths and superstition were challenged with science and reason, modernists believed in the value of science and reason in achieving progress in society. For postmodernism, this narrative of progress was a discourse rather than a reality

Objectification process by which a socially constructed, abstract concept created is treated as if it is a concrete thing

Objective/Objectivity said to be approximated when something is considered to exist independent of one's thinking of it (such as a scientific 'fact'). Its existence is contested as it is also argued that things can only exist in the way we perceive them

Postcolonialism body of work or perspective that seeks to analyse and critique the effects of colonialism, thus not only looking at the period after colonial power but also the process of (European) colonialism and the impact on local cultures. Postcolonial theory draws on *postmodernism* for its theoretical discourse, and its political concerns typically focus on the way in which those who have been colonised are at the periphery of global society, while Westerners (and their approaches) are at the 'centre' and dominant in shaping global discourse. Said's *Orientalism* (1978) is often argued to be one of the founding texts of this field

Postmodernism best understood in contrast to modernism, postmodernism is related to novelty, anti-elitism, and playfulness. It challenges the 'grand narratives' in society that are based on rationality and reason. Postmodernism challenges the restriction of rationalism in favour of pluralism. Critics argue that it undermines values, and promotes irrationalism (where 'anything goes')

Reductionist describing an approach to understanding the nature of complex things that involves simplifying or reducing the thing to the interactions of its parts, as if it is merely the sum of its parts (reducing it to accounts of individual components)

Scientific management form of methodological (mechanistic) working relating to the ideas of Frederick Taylor, which attempted a 'scientific' analysis of working practice that sought to calculate and implement the most efficient working patterns. It is also often criticised for dehumanising the workplace

Sense-making the way in which we make sense of – assign meaning to – our experiences. This process occurs individually and collectively, through which we create a shared awareness and understanding

Socio-technical theory (or socio-technical system) approach to work design that integrates the social systems of people in society with the technical systems of organisations and seeks their joint optimisation

Chapter 3

Behaviourism theoretical perspective suggesting that all human behaviours are simple responses to environmental stimuli

Big Five model largely agreed framework of personality traits, comprising extraversion, agreeableness, conscientiousness, emotional stability, and openness/intellect

Cognitive ability/intelligence general mental capability that reflects people's capability for comprehending their surroundings, making sense of things and figuring out how to solve problems

Contextual performance see *Organizational citizenship behaviour*

Holland's RIASEC model practical, influential framework for representing occupational interests, classifying them into six types (realistic, investigative, artistic, social, enterprising, conventional)

Implicit personality theory layperson's understanding of personality and individual behaviour

Individual differences (or differential psychology) study of differences between individuals that lead to differences in behaviour or life outcomes. Major areas of interest are individual differences in personality, cognitive ability, and emotion

Job analysis systematic process of determining the tasks and person requirements of a particular job

Job satisfaction attitudes held by a person about their job, which may be general or targeted towards specific aspects of employment

Meta-analysis technique by which the results of multiple studies can be combined statistically to give an overall result, corrected for the effects of statistical artifacts such as unreliability and sampling error. Highly influential in research because it allows conclusions to be drawn from accumulated published studies

Organisational citizenship behaviour behaviour or performance that extends beyond task performance, comprising co-operation and support for other people, for the organisation, and conscientious initiative for improving work and learning

Organisational commitment extent to which a person feels an emotional tie, or obligation, towards their organisation, or an *inability* to leave the organisation

Personality patterns of behaviour, thought and emotion, combined with mechanisms and processes that determine those patterns, all belonging to and characteristic of one individual

Personality inventory/questionnaire survey or questionnaire containing items seeking to learn the way that people feel, think, or behave

Personality traits regularities or patterns in behaviour, thoughts, and emotions

Personality type theory alternative, and flawed, conceptualisation of individual differences in personality that suggests that people can be classified into discrete 'types'. Often associated with Jungian theory and the use of the Myers-Briggs Type Indicator

Recruitment and selection process of attracting people to apply for jobs in an organisation, followed by the systematic identification of the most suitable individual(s) to employ

Reinforcement intervention to control or shape behaviour, delivered immediately after behaviour has taken place. Reinforcement may be positive (to promote behaviour) or negative (to inhibit or prevent it)

Self-efficacy self-belief that behaviour will lead to a positive or successful outcome

Social learning theory that suggests that human behaviour is the product of observed, learned, and rehearsed responses to environmental stimuli

Task performance performance or behaviour at work that is related to the technical core of jobs or the organisation more broadly

Trait theory theory that proposes that human behaviour can be predicted and understood by stable personality traits. There is disagreement about whether traits should be conceptualised as *explaining* (ie causing) or merely *describing* regularities in behaviour, thought and emotion

Vocational interests interests and preferences for specific kinds of job tasks or occupations

Chapter 4

Antecedent-focused emotion regulation ability to think differently of, or in, a situation in order to manage *emotions*. This form of emotion management does not require work to be carried out on the individual's emotions directly but on the way they perceive the situation more generally

Antipathetic emotional labour emotion management technique that involves inducing negative *emotions* such as fear, anger and sadness. Typically associated with the work of debt collectors and bouncers

Attribution bias tendency to externalise failings and internalise successes

Bureaucracy hierarchical organisation in which tasks are controlled and co-ordinated by those who hold official positions of authority. Bureaucracies are designed rationally to provide the most appropriate and efficient pursuit of organisational goals

Deep acting emotion management technique through which individuals begin to believe that the emotion they are performing is how they really feel. It requires individuals not only to pretend to others but also to pretend to themselves

Dramaturgy term used in sociology to make sense of the way individuals 'present' themselves in society, in the same way as an actor plays a part in a play

Emotions outward manifestation(s) of feelings, that are open to management, manipulation and commodification. Emotions are made sense of through an understanding of culture and society

Emotion management umbrella term describing the ability to induce and/or suppress one's own *emotions* in an attempt to induce a required emotional response in others

Emotion work form of emotion management by which an individual personally chooses to manage his/her *emotions* in a particular way to induce a particular emotion in others. This is usually characterised by having *use value* and being performed in a private context for non-compensated benefit

Emotional intelligence ability to understand and manage both one's own and the emotions of others. Emotional intelligence is regarded as a desirable skill by many organisations, sometimes even more important than traditional intelligence

Emotional labour ability to 'induce or suppress feelings in order to sustain the outward countenance that produces the proper state of mind in others…'. This is usually characterised by having *exchange value*, being performed in a work context in return for a wage, and follows organisationally prescribed display and feeling rules

Empathetic emotional labour emotion management technique that involves inducing positive *emotions* such as happiness and security. Typically associated with the work of the caring professions such as nurses and other front-line customer service roles

Exchange value financial value of goods, a service, or an emotion, that can be traded in a free market because people are willing and able to pay for it

False consciousness inability to perceive things, particularly as they relate to social relations and relations of power and exploitation

Feeling rules rules for managing the way we should or should not feel. Feeling rules are determined by our social membership and the social and occupational roles we occupy. Different roles are associated with a different set of feeling rules

Feelings sensations aroused by internal psychological states

Halo effect *perception* that occurs when a single positive characteristic, trait or action biases the perceiver's assessment of the whole individual

Labour process theory study of how, why and at what cost labour power is commodified and manipulated within a capitalist system to extract surplus value

Modern organisation organisation run in the spirit of 'modernism', in which operations were usually guided by the principles of rationality according to which control and reason were applied to human behaviour

Perception complex set of processes relating to the active project of *sense-making*

Post-industrial describing the structure of society in a time when industrial forms of production no longer dominate employment and the economy. The term also refers to the way society is organised and understood beyond the key principles of modernity

Principles of rationality as defined by Max Weber, organisational operations characterised by calculability, control, predictability and efficiency. Weber argued that these principles would not be used to run organisations but they would come to shape the rest of society

Projection attributing one's own thoughts, preferences and emotions to others

Response-focused emotion regulation direct management of displayed emotions. This form of emotion management is like wearing a mask to disguise true feelings

Rusty halo or devil effect *perception* that occurs when a a single negative characteristic, trait or action biases the assessment of the whole individual

Selective perception interpretation of events solely according to an individual's own interests, experiences and background

Self-fulfilling prophecy what happens when *perceptions* and actions shape processes and events so that initial predictions come true

Senses physiological components of *perception* based around seeing, hearing, feeling, touching, tasting

Sense-making daily mental processes by which we come to a conclusion about what is real and what is illusory

Stereotyping assumption that some apparent features or characteristics apply to every individual member of a group

Surface acting emotion management technique involving outward impressions. We pretend to feel a certain way despite knowing that this is not how we really feel on the inside

Use value according to Marx, something has use value if it is possible to gain pleasure or use from it. However, it does not have to be worth anything in the free market. An example of something that may be considered to hold use value would be a warm summer's day. In general, things that possess use value cannot be traded

Chapter 5

Content theories sometimes described as universal theories of *motivation* because they can be applied in the same way to all individuals regardless of culture

Equity theory theory that suggests individuals will compare the effort that they make against the efforts of those around them and if there is a perceived difference will endeavour to redress the balance

Expectancy theory theory developed by Vroom which suggests that *motivation* is driven by the expectation of the preferred outcome and the strength of the attractiveness of the outcome to the individual

Extrinsic motivation *motivation* concerned with 'real, tangible' rewards that can be achieved by an individual

Goal-setting theory theory underpinned by the notion that individuals' goals or intentions affect the individual's behaviour because they influence the amount of effort, persistence and direction afforded by the individual

Hierarchy of needs hierarchy developed by Maslow that suggests people have instinctual basic needs and desire those needs to be met. Maslow suggests an order to these needs, with physiological needs at the bottom and self-actualisation at the top

Intrinsic motivation *motivation* that comes from within and is therefore 'psychological' in nature, such as feelings of recognition, appreciation and satisfaction

Job redesign process of making jobs more enriching, traditionally through methods such as enlargement (adding tasks) and enrichment (increasing responsibility)

Job satisfaction hybrid concept stemming from psychology and sociology that relates to the attitude or feelings individuals have about their work

Motivation feelings within a person that encourage movement, intensity and persistence for him/her to achieve a personal need, goal or expectation

Motivational interviewing (MI) client-centred directive method for enhancing *intrinsic motivation* and causing change by exploring and resolving ambivalence

Process theories theories that focus on multiple factors of *motivation* which work in different ways and in different contexts over time

Two-factor theory theory developed by Herzberg which suggests that outcomes of satisfaction and dissatisfaction are independent states and are affected by different factors

Chapter 6

360-degree feedback or multi-rater feedback tool that gives an employee an opportunity to seek professional evaluation from various individuals who have direct or indirect contact with the employee, such as peers, superiors and subordinates, and/or who can benefit from his/her services, such as customers and suppliers, based on a framework of competencies

Action learning group process of learning which aims to develop a group of people with different levels of responsibilities, skills and experience by focusing on dealing with an actual work problem within their professional environments, and to develop an action plan

Behaviourist theories of learning theories based on the principle of 'stimulus-response', according to which behaviour is caused by an external stimulus and does not require an internal mental state or consciousness. Principal contributors to behaviourism are Pavlov and Skinner

Coaching method of training individuals that focuses on development/issues at work. It helps another person to improve awareness, to set and achieve goals in order to improve a particular behavioural performance

Cognitive theories theories interested in how people process and understand material

Counselling method of problem-solving for individuals that focuses on providing support (perhaps through pastoral care and/or a series of workplace workshops) regarding employees' personal concerns such as motivation and self-confidence

Development centres (sometimes known as assessment centres) learning/training events that focus on developing a holistic evaluation of employees' potential and development needs by exploring their personality, intellectual capability, behaviour and life values

Distance learning paper-based learning materials delivered through the post that in time may lead to a professional or academic qualification

E-learning the use of computers to deliver training, often through corporate intranets

Evaluation traditionally the final stage in a systematic approach aiming to improve performance through formative evaluation or making an assessment about value added and effectiveness (summative evaluation)

Formal training training given in the form of various courses and/or workshops, particularly when it comes to first management jobs and as a precursor to promotion

Goal-based model model of an evaluation process that focuses on the purpose of the evaluation, which might range from purely technical to strategic

Humanist theories theories which assume that learners have a natural desire to learn and that teachers need to facilitate their learning process. These theories are particularly associated with Rogers and Maslow

Informal learning what people learn while at work, without involving targeted training.

Learning knowledge-developing process through experience

Management competencies or capabilities specific abilities that are useful in carrying out specific managerial functions; when formally listed, they are seen as a way of aligning the organisational objectives with performance management, as identified in the selection process, in appraisal and for rewards, training and development

Management development the entire structured process by which managers learn and improve their skills for the benefit of their employing organisations and themselves

Mentoring method of problem-solving for individuals that focuses on the career and personal development of employees. Sharing an individual's beliefs and values helps in a positive way. Mentoring is often a longer-term career supervisory relationship by someone who has 'done it before'

Performance and development review process that seeks to relate individual contribution and career aspirations to the achievement of the business vision, aims and objectives

Project working development process consisting of procedures and methods that guide teams in working effectively throughout an assigned project involving different functions

Secondment temporary move of one employee to another position and role within the same organisation or in another organisation, for a year or two

Socio-cultural theories of learning theories that focus on learning in a social context – ie people learn from each other by observation, imitation and modelling. An important contributor to socio-cultural theories is Vygotsky

Succession planning process by which one or more individuals (successors) are identified for future key jobs within the organisation

Systems approach methodology concerned with the context, the current situation and the identified planning, design and implementation of a programme, as well as the measurement of the results

Training needs analysis process to identify gaps in the skills of an organisation and specify appropriate training to cover any such gap

Chapter 7

Constructive controversy process whereby team members openly question their assumptions and consider different approaches, ask each other to elaborate their perspectives, thus allowing the team to engage in effective questioning

Group polarisation tendency for teams to make more radical, risky, controversial or extreme decisions than the average decision made by any one team member individually

Groupthink tendency for a group of people who are involved in working together closely to settle for the first outcome that has unanimous agreement and over-riding consensus, rather than to critically appraise multiple alternative courses of action

Multi-disciplinary team (also referred to as inter-professional team) team comprising team members from a diverse range of professional backgrounds who come together to work collaboratively towards a shared goal

Participative safety (also referred to as psychological safety) aspect of team climate in which team members feel safe to speak openly and honestly about their thoughts and opinions, without fearing negative consequences such as embarrassment or rejection

Production blocking tendency for individuals to come up with fewer ideas (which are typically of lower quality) when working in a group setting than they would have done working on the same task alone

Pseudo team team characterised by incomplete characteristics – eg a group of people that call themselves a 'team' even though they do not have a common goal and a degree of task interdependence

Reflexivity extent to which team members communicate together to reflect upon their current objectives, processes and strategies, and change them according to new or anticipated events within their task environment

Social loafing tendency for individuals to contribute less effort and commitment to a task when it is not possible to decipher and evaluate each team member's unique contribution

Team (real team) group of people working together in an organisation who are recognised as a team, who are committed to achieving clear team-level objectives upon which they agree, who have to work closely and interdependently in order to achieve these objectives, whose members are clear about their roles within the team and have the necessary autonomy to decide how to carry out team tasks, and who communicate regularly as a team in order to reflect upon the team's effectiveness and how it could be improved

Team-based working approach to organisational design where the basic units of work are performed by teams working together in a multi-team system

Team effectiveness extent to which a team works together collaboratively and efficiently in order to successfully achieve its intended objectives, while also enjoying an enriching working environment in which the members have the opportunity for learning, growth and satisfaction

Team innovation degree to which a team introduces new ways of doing things when carrying out processes or delivering products or services in the workplace

Team potency the shared belief within a team that it can be effective

Team viability preference and capability of a team to remain working together in the future

Chapter 8

Affective conflict conflict of a personal and emotional nature which occurs within teams and results in animosity which, in turn, has a negative or detrimental effect on decision-making and performance

Arbitration form of third-party intervention which involves an independent person or agency assisting the parties in a dispute to reach a settlement in a prescriptive manner by imposing a remedy

Cognitive conflict healthy or positive conflict which emanates from task-related discussion and debate among team members over differing perspectives, which results in enhanced decision-making

Conciliation form of third-party intervention which involves an independent person or agency assisting the parties in a dispute to reach a settlement in a manner which is neither proactive nor prescriptive

Conflict coaching form of conflict resolution involving a professional coach who works with an individual to increase his/her understanding of conflict and to develop his/her interpersonal skills and management style in order to deal with conflict situations

Disputes procedure formal procedure, often part of a collective agreement with a trade union, which establishes a set method for dealing with disputes/conflict and which defines the stages and parties involved

Distress specific term to describe the negative stress that an individual might experience when engaged in challenging activities perceived to be beyond his/her capability

Dysfunctional conflict conflict that is considered in negative terms and seen as harmful to the organisation; such as industrial action

Equity theory process theory of motivation which is concerned with people's perceptions of how fairly they are treated in comparison with others

Eustress term to describe the positive stress that an individual might experience when engaging in challenging activities that are perceived to be within their capability

Fall-back position negotiating term used to describe the least that each party will accept from the other in a settlement and beyond which confrontation is the preferred option

Final-offer arbitration form of third-party intervention (also referred to as 'last offer', 'flip-flop' or 'pendulum' arbitration) in which the arbitrator imposes a solution that is the final offer of one side

Functional conflict conflict consistent with organisational goals and seen as positive – for example, between individuals or groups who explore and debate alternative ways of achieving the goals or tasks set

Grievance-handling formal internal system involving a set number of stages through which employee grievances/complaints are progressed to resolution

Ideology set of ideas or beliefs to which an individual or a group subscribes that forms the basis of their adopted viewpoint and their consequent actions

Inter-group conflict conflict between two or more groups – in many cases, management and trade union, or perhaps between different trade unions in the same organisation

Interpersonal conflict conflict between individuals in an organisation – this might be between a manager and a subordinate or between two co-workers

Intra-group conflict conflict that arises within a group between the various members – for example, a conflict within a team of management negotiators which must be resolved prior to meeting the trade union's negotiating team

Mediation form of third-party intervention which involves an independent person or agency assisting the parties in a dispute to reach a settlement in a

manner that is more proactive than conciliation but that is still non-prescriptive

Moral dilemma situation in which an individual is torn between two morally right courses of action, but cannot do both, and is thereby condemned to failure in one

Most favoured position negotiating term used to describe the most a party can realistically expect to gain from bargaining

Negotiation interactive process through which the parties involved in conflict engage in a discussion with the aim of resolving their differences and reach a mutually agreeable settlement

Organisational justice perceptions facet of motivation theory concerned with people's perception of fairness regarding the distribution of rewards (distributive justice), the process for deciding how rewards are distributed (procedural justice), or the way that people are treated when policies and procedures are implemented (interactional justice)

Personal conflict conflict which is internal to the individual, possibly created by divided loyalties or a *moral dilemma*

Person-organisation fit degree of compatibility between the individual and the organisation based on the fundamental characteristics of individuals and the values they subscribe to

Role ambiguity irresolute situation at work that arises when an individual is uncertain of the nature of his/her job, his/her duties and responsibilities, or the amount of authority he/she has

Role conflict term used to describe the conflict created when an individual is torn between conflicting demands of a role or where an individual occupies two roles and places more emphasis on one to the detriment of the other

Stress general term used to express a tense state of mind. It develops as a result of excessive or prolonged pressure and may lead to physical and/or psychological illness

Third-party intervention action taken by an independent person or agency (third party) to assist the parties in a dispute to reach a settlement – for example, arbitration, coaching conciliation or mediation

Whistle-blowing revelation of an organisational wrongdoing, either internally to a superior or externally to a regulatory body or the authorities, by an employee who is concerned about organisational impropriety, which may be of an ethical, financial or environmental nature

Work–life balance potentially satisfactory balance between the demands of work and those of personal life

Chapter 9

Decoding by decoding a message, a receiver – who needs to analyse the message for its content and meaning – ideally interprets the meaning intended by the sender

Encoding a message has to go through an encoding process before it can be transmitted by the sender to the receiver. It is therefore put into words or symbols that, ideally, carry the same meaning for the receiver

Gossip unverified, context-specific facts about people. Gossip must be tackled early on by management to minimise detrimental effects to the organisation

Information richness the amount of information contained in a message. The more stimuli such as words, symbols, body language, that can be transmitted through a communication medium, the higher is its information richness

Non-verbal communication any type of communication that is not in the form of spoken words – such as behavioural cues, clothes or facial expressions. Non-verbal communication is a significant part of face-to-face communication because it carries information that may either support or conflict with the spoken message

Receiver person receiving and decoding a transmitted message. The receiver will analyse the message for its content, symbols, words and, ideally, transform it into personally meaningful information

Rumours unverified facts about events such as organisational changes or politics. Rumours must be clarified early on in order to avoid negative effects on the organisation

Sender person sending and encoding a transmitted message. The sender needs to keep the *receiver* in mind, in order to transmit the message through media that are appropriate and use symbols and words that are grounded on mutual understanding

Transmission process by which a message travels from sender to receiver. Transmission processes are often interrupted through noise or differences in individual perceptions such as different understandings of words

Verbal communication communication in the form of spoken words. Often occurs face-to-face or over the telephone. It carries a high level of *information richness* and should be used in complex situations

Chapter 10

Charismatic leadership describing an individual and unique appeal which somebody has, enabling him/her to reach followers on a fundamental and emotional basis to inspire, motivate and follow his/her example

Contingency approach supposition that leadership effectiveness depends on various situational factors, such as follower- or task-related variables, and not only on the leader

Culturally endorsed implicit leadership theories (CLTs) theories that describe abilities, personal characteristics and skills perceived by members of the same culture as promoting or as inhibiting leadership effectiveness

Ethical leadership the leader's showing integrity and adherence to generally accepted moral principles and core values for the common good of society. These principles are reflected in everything a leader does to guide and command subordinates at all times

Fiedler's contingency model supposition that leadership effectiveness is dependent on leader-member relations, position power and task structure. For each combination of these factors a specific leadership style (people- or task-oriented) is recommended for the leader in order to be most effective

Leader development training of individuals to enhance their knowledge, skills and abilities in order to make them better leaders and foster intrapersonal competencies

Leader-member exchange theory (LMX) theory which is concerned with the quality of relationships and group processes taking place between the leader and the followers. It builds on the notion that leaders develop individual and mutually reciprocated relationships with subordinates

Leadership ability of an individual to influence, motivate and enable others to contribute towards the effectiveness and success of the organisations of which they are members

Leadership development building interpersonal and social qualities (eg empathy, team orientation, conflict management) within the organisation through spanning personal networks, promoting co-operation and resource exchange

Neutralisers of leadership factors that negate the leader's influence in all regards. They counteract leadership behaviours and thereby decrease leadership effectiveness

Path-goal theory theory which proposes that leaders should motivate and support their subordinates, enabling them to achieve set goals. This is done by guiding the followers, removing obstacles and providing incentives along the way

Philosophical approach to ethical leadership general set of principles about morals, what should be valued, how to behave, what is good and what is bad, regarded as precepts by a leader

Romance of leadership tendency for people to attribute organisational performance to the leader rather than to other factors that might have had a greater effect on organisational operations

Situational leadership theory (SLT) theory which proposes that the type of leadership should be adjusted to the contextual situation which depends upon subordinates' developmental stage, encompassing their motivation and their abilities to do the task

Social scientific approach to ethical leadership approach to leadership that promotes the actual application of educational scientific knowledge about ethical behaviours and manifested ethical principles

Style approach approach to leadership concerned with the kind of behaviours leaders display towards their followers. Leader behaviours are categorised either as task- or people-oriented

Substitutes for leadership factors that replace the functions and the purpose of leadership. The leader's ability to improve or impair subordinate performance is not needed anymore since everything relevant is provided by the subordinates themselves or given through task or organisational characteristics

Trait approach supposition that leaders are born with a specific set of personal characteristics, making them particularly suitable for leadership positions

Transactional leadership type of leadership that encompasses motivation and direction of subordinates mainly through appealing to their own self-interests – for example, by giving out appropriate rewards

Transformational leadership type of leadership that occurs when a leader appeals to subordinates' higher-order needs (eg self-esteem or self-actualisation) by broadening their viewpoints and interests beyond what is required by the task, for the good of themselves but more so for the group and the organisation as a whole

Chapter 11

Age of reason definitions vary, but the time period covered includes the seventeenth and eighteenth centuries. This was a period when some philosophers, particularly influential in France, England and Scotland, began to ask whether it was right to unquestioningly believe in and obey religious rulings. There began to be more respect for logical reasoning and scientific thinking. Importantly, people in the West began to believe that they could significantly change things

Bounded rationality the practical real-life 'boundaries' that prevent people from making decisions in a purely rational, logical, manner. Boundaries include time constraints. Rationality is also affected by the complexity and quality of information, disagreement, error, perception and politics. March and Simon (1958) were among the pioneers researching this area

Consensus unanimous agreement that everyone can accept and support. Alternatives include individual or majority vote decisions. Compared to these, consensus takes better account of a variety of ideas, and leads to improved support for a decision. A downside of obtaining consensus is that the negotiations required can make it time-consuming. Consensus is more commonly sought in Eastern than Western cultures

Creativity process with a set of specific characteristics (creative thinking skills, expertise and motivation) which require practical application. Many people associate creativity with a moment of inspiration bringing a new idea. However, such moments generally rely on prior preparation and related expertise, and they are only really useful if subsequently acted upon. Creativity involves the whole process, not just the eureka moment

Decision traps things that cause us to make incorrect decisions, particularly mental short-cuts (heuristics) and generalisations. A great deal of research has been done on these traps. This chapter lists some common traps, and discusses how to avoid them

Drawing of lots method of random selection widely used throughout history. A common form in previous centuries in the UK was the drawing of straws, where people picked straws from a collection of apparently the same length until one person pulled out the short straw and was selected. More controversially, lots could also be used as a way of discerning divine will or of deciding upon guilt

Evolutionary psychology form of psychology that attempts to explain psychological traits as products of natural selection or sexual selection. From this view, human behaviour is generated by psychological adaptations that evolved to solve recurrent problems in human ancestral environments. Evolutionary psychologists would see the biases in recruitment and selection as nearly universal and that are as such more likely to reflect evolved adaptations – a view which runs contrary to the idea that human brain processes are learning mechanisms

Forming, storming, norming and performing four stages of a team development model devised by Bruce Tuckman in the 1960s and adapted by Tuckman and others since. The idea is that all teams need to pass through all four stages in the right order (from forming to performing), although they may get stuck or fail part way through. People have proposed an additional stage or stages for the completion of a task and for the break-up of a team

Groupthink what can happen in groups where the desire to achieve consensus and maintain cohesiveness is taken too far, so that it impacts on the group's ability to perceive or examine alternative ideas, and reduces its creativity

Heuristics mental short cuts to help people quickly reach decisions. These short cuts are normally very useful, but can lead us astray (see *decision traps*). Some short cuts have evolved (see *evolutionary psychology*) whereas others are learned

Industrial Revolution revolution in manufacturing technology that led to further revolutions in workplace and eventually even social systems. The Industrial Revolution started in the United Kingdom in the early eighteenth century, spread to Europe and America, then the rest of the world. Inventions, mechanisation, improved transport and communications, drastically changed society

Intrinsic motivation motivation that comes from within, and is directly related to a task, in comparison with extrinsic motivation, which connects motivation to external rewards or punishments. In reality people may have mixed motivations

Rational decision-making supposition that decision-making should be logical and reasonable, following sensible thought processes and judgements rather than emotion, prejudice or chance. Various people have defined processes, or steps, to help achieve rational decision-making. It is still the default ideal for most people in the West

Reflexivity two-way process by which thinking about or investigating a subject also affects that subject and changes it in the process. One type of reflexivity is a self-fulfilling prophecy. More positive forms of reflexivity can be individually or group driven. In the context of decision-making, one example of reflexivity would be to learn about *decision traps*, to reflect whether they have affected past decisions, and because of that knowledge, to change individual or group behaviours to minimise the re-occurrence of the traps

Service blueprinting diagrammatically representing processes from a customer point of view, mapping out customer interactions and understanding their experiences. This enables improvements that enhance that experience, and hence customer satisfaction and repeat business

Synergy where the combined performance is greater than the sum of the parts. Co-operation, trust and openness all help in achieving this, so it may be harder to achieve for new teams than established ones. A team achieving synergy is likely to value diversity and use it to develop new ideas

Chapter 12

Diversity valued uniqueness of individuals and difference between people, and the consequent recognition of the value that workers, irrespective of gender, race and ethnicity, disability, age, religion and sexual orientation, can provide for their organisation

Equality sameness – and an understanding of the sameness – of all people, leading to treating people equally and providing equal opportunities for all

Ethnicity cultural practices and outlooks of a specific community of people that set them apart from others – that is, make them culturally distinct from other groups in society

Ethnocentrism suspicion of outsiders combined with a tendency to evaluate the culture of others in terms of one's own culture

Gender bias favouritism shown towards one gender over the other

Gender identity how a person perceives his or her *gender role*

Gender role attitudes and behaviour that are considered appropriate for each sex and learned through the socialisation process

Gender socialisation accepted gender patterns relating to a particular society

Glass ceiling restriction of employment opportunities for top managerial and administrative posts (particularly in relation to women)

Group closure process whereby groups maintain boundaries separating themselves from others

Mainstreaming ensuring the integration of diversity practices within all areas and activities of the organisation

Patriarchal describing a hierarchical system of social organisation in which cultural, political and economic structures are dominated by men

Scapegoating blaming people (and particularly individuals or small groups) for things/events which are not necessarily their fault or even their responsibility

Sexual division of labour see *Gender socialisation*

Sexual harassment unwelcome conduct of a sexual nature that detrimentally affects the work environment or leads to adverse job-related consequences for its victims

Sexual orientation pattern of emotional, romantic, and/or sexual attraction to men, women, both genders or neither gender

Sociobiological describing the view that gender differences can be explained through biological and physical attributes

Stereotyping thinking in terms of fixed and inflexible categories

Sticky floor pattern of employment opportunities that disproportionately concentrates certain social groups at lower-level jobs

Chapter 13

Authority power which is seen by all as legitimate and acceptable. Formal authority is vested in the status of all employees and 'acted out' as part of an employee role, according to the contract of employment. Authority also means that subordinates may be given the right to make decisions on behalf of managers

Bureaucracy type of organisational structure common to most large organisations, based upon the formal hierarchy of an organisation (formal authority), specialisation of tasks, formal decision-making, formal rules and regulations, and impersonal relationships

Control system and process whereby employees are monitored and supervised by managers and/or by the technology employees work with. Control is linked to performance and targets, and as such may motivate good performance or 'punish' poor performance

Empowerment the granting to employees of greater freedom, autonomy and control over work, together with greater responsibility for decision-making

Glass ceiling phenomenon associated with rising and senior female managers who perceive that they are prevented from progressing their careers within the organisation

Hegemonic despotism authoritarian control structure and power relationships within a context of continuous surveillance

Info-normative control characteristic of service workflows and in which IT-generated information forms the basis for control. The normative element is provided by facilitative and supportive supervision on the part of team leaders

Information power power measured by the extent to which managers need access to information and become dependent upon those who hold such information

Latent power *manifest power* is the tip of the iceberg, latent power is the iceberg itself – it is 'hidden power' and 'potential power'. For example, a large organisation has the latent power to close one or all of its UK or US call centres and relocate them to India for reasons of economy

Manifest power power which is obvious to and observable by all. In most organisations, power resides at the top where the trappings of power may be observable

Output-procedural control methodology typical of sales workflows, where 'output measurement based on customer decisions (to apply and qualify for loans, for example) is complemented mainly by enforcement of company procedures'

Panopticon metaphor popularised by Michel Foucault, the French sociologist, for all-embracing control and the ability to be all-seeing. Originally, the panopticon, designed by Bentham in the eighteenth century, was an architectural structure located centrally in penal institutions such as prisons which enabled total surveillance and in which those under surveillance could not tell they were being observed but were aware that they might be always under surveillance

Personal power power which resides in the individual irrespective of the position held by that individual. This type of power is often associated with personal charisma and French and Ravens' referent and expert power bases

Position power power linked to authority by virtue of status, rank or level, and often regarded as being synonymous with it. Normally equated with French and Ravens' reward, coercive and legitimate power bases

Post-bureaucracy flatter organisational structure than the bureaucratic form, characterised by fewer levels and positions of authority, more informal relationships and less specialisation of tasks

Process power power characterised by control over methods of production. For example, an organisation may appoint a financial auditor to examine and report back upon the efficiency of a production process

Service and sales workflow type of front-line work that interfaces with customers – often, but not exclusively, within call centres

Socio-normative control form of control that exists in the relatively highly skilled contexts of knowledge workflows where management and peers (or co-workers) influence the work process simultaneously and where peer or co-worker influence is expected to be the main characteristic of this type of control

Span of control the number of subordinates who report directly to a manager or supervisor

Sweatshop view metaphor applicable to call centre workers to describe the intense nature of call centre work under constant surveillance

Technology means by which an organisation transforms its inputs into outputs

Chapter 14

Adhocracy form of *organic* structure identified by Mintzberg (1980), which has low centralised control and tends to be organised on a project or *matrix* basis

Alienation term first used by Karl Marx to describe the estrangement of people from themselves as human beings under capitalism. Particularly associated with industrial methods of work such as *Fordism* and *scientific management* that critics believe are dehumanising

Bureaucracy complex and hierarchical form of organisational design based on Weber's notion of the 'rational-legal' authority of rules, laws and procedures. Associated with clear division of labour between offices/departments and clear demarcation of where one department's authority ends and another begins

Bureaucratic personality term coined by Merton (1957) to describe the impersonal, officious and sometimes even aloof characteristics of bureaucrats

Contingency theory approach whereby an organisation's design is dependent upon its environment and particular needs and strengths

Co-operatives autonomous organisations jointly owned by their employees or those who use their services

Craftwork traditional form of work where workers had control over their work and work methods, typically conducted individually or in small organisations. Seen by Braverman as the antithesis of *deskilling*

Deskilling thesis idea of Harry Braverman (1974) that work was becoming ubiquitously less skilled because of mass industrial organisation and the simplification and fragmentation of work through the *micro-division of labour, scientific management* and *Fordism*

Differentiated organisational structure form of MNC structure where operations are localised – for example, on a national basis

Division of labour manner in which work tasks are divided between workers

Divisional organisational structures organisational form designed around product or service divisions each having its own functions (see *functional organisational structures*). Tend to allow workers the chance to work in a number of areas of the business

Employee stock ownership plans (ESOPs) schemes that allow employees to purchase a stake in their organisation through purchasing shares

Flexible specialisation form of industrial organisation that challenged Fordism and relied upon economies of scope and the ability to change quickly from one product line to another and vary output in response to market demands

Fordism method of management first used by Henry Ford, reliant on automated production lines and the *micro-division of labour* to mass-produce standardised products

Functional organisational structures *mechanistic* organisational form designed around functional specialisms (such as HR, accounting, marketing etc). Tend to be tall, hierarchical and generally *bureaucratic*

Japanisation management technique based upon models developed by Japanese car manufacturers. The system sought to eliminate waste and improve efficiency through *JIT* systems and some employee involvement schemes such as quality circles

Just in Time Management (JIT) management system associated with *Japanisation* where components are delivered to production lines just when they are needed, to eliminate waste and storage costs

Knowledge economy economy in which competition is based upon the knowledge and creativity of highly skilled individuals (see also *upskilling thesis*)

Lean production – see *Japanisation* and *JIT management*

McDonaldisation thesis as devised by Ritzer (2004), thesis that describes the increasing use of organisational principles associated with McDonald's across numerous contexts globally. The thesis highlights a high degree of continuity in principles associated with *scientific management, Fordism* and to a lesser extent *bureaucracy*

Mechanistic organisations as identified by Burns and Stalker (1961), traditionally designed organisations following an inflexible *bureaucratic* or similar structure

Micro-division of labour extension of the *division of labour* to break tasks down into their smallest discrete elements. Associated particularly with *scientific management, Fordism* and *McDonaldisation*

Multinational corporations (MNCs) large organisations that operate in a number of countries

Offshoring process of organisations moving parts of their operations (generally those that do not directly create profit) overseas to lower-cost economies

Organic organisations contrasted with *mechanistic* organisations by Burns and Stalker (1961). Such organisations take more *post-Fordist* forms and allow greater discretion for individuals and groups over their work, alongside a higher level of worker democracy

Portfolio people term coined by Handy (2002). Multi-skilled knowledge workers who sell their specialised services to clients on a project-based freelance basis

Post-Fordist organisations organisations that eschew traditional *mechanistic* or *bureaucratic* designs and operate with flatter and less hierarchical *organic* structures. Often associated with project-based organisation and teamworking. Includes structures such as *adhocracies, matrix organisations* and the *shamrock organisation*

Post-industrial organisations – see *Post-Fordist organisations*

Scientific management method of management devised by F. W. Taylor relying on time and motion studies, the *micro-division of labour* and strict managerial prescriptions as to exactly how and when tasks should be done. Its aim was to increase efficiency and output in a 'rational' system

Shamrock organisation form of flexible organisation popularised by Handy (2002) which has a small core of career-minded workers, complemented by a professional contractual fringe of knowledge workers and a flexible labour force of transient lower-skilled workers

Siloing phenomena most common in *functional organisational structures* where employees have narrow organisational experience and serve the purposes of their function rather than the wider organisation

Soldiering tactic used by shopfloor workers to limit production in order to preserve piece-rates. Particularly associated with F. W. Taylor and *scientific management*

Starbucks economy economy characterised by high amounts of consumer choice and a wide range of unstandardised products

Taylorism see *Scientific management*

Teleworking method of working in which workers use ICT to work away from a fixed workplace. Associated also with freelancing, *portfolio people, virtual organisations* and the *shamrock organisation*

Trained incapacity term first coined by Merton (1957) to describe how the highly specialised training and skills of those working in a *bureaucracy* may become their weaknesses, especially when encountering change or uncertainty

Upskilling thesis associated with the work of Daniel Bell (1976), refers to a general increase in the skills, education and qualifications of workers across the developed world

Virtual organisations networked organisations reliant on ICT, in which employees and contractors are almost always widely dispersed geographically

Chapter 15

Artifacts most superficial level in Schein's model. Consists of visible manifestations of an organisation's culture

Basic assumptions deepest level in Schein's model. They are at the core of the organisational culture and are implicit, deeply rooted and often unconscious. Basic assumptions are generally concerned with broad beliefs about nature and humanity, and guide members' perceptions, feelings and thoughts

Differentiation perspective as defined by Martin, it emphasises differences and diversity. It acknowledges the existence of a highly differentiated vision of culture where subcultures exist within a dominant culture, sometimes in harmony, sometimes in conflict

Emergent change approach approach that views change as dynamic, contested, unpredictable and unplanned. Change is a collaborative process within the organisation and can be implemented as a bottom-up process, not only as top-down

Employee branding processes by which workers are encouraged to buy into symbolic representations of organisational values by consuming the companies' products and 'living the brand' away from the workplace

Ethnography research method based on observation and full participation, traditionally used in anthropology to study all forms of cultures. It is also used in organisational research and is considered the most appropriate method to study organisational culture

Fragmentation perspective as defined by Martin, a perspective that considers the confusions, paradoxes and unknowns encountered every day in organisational lives. Ambiguity is seen as the essence of any cultural description and is a permanent and a continuous state. Culture is considered a metaphor for organisational life rather than a variable to manipulate

Integrationist perspective as defined by Martin, an approach that views culture as manifested in a company's values and sees it as a mechanism that integrates and holds together different individuals and groups

Normative control the systems of organisational norms, regulations and expectations which provide the basis for the employee's desired behaviour and his/her identification with the company

Organisational development (OD) planned, organisation-wide effort to increase an organisation's effectiveness as response to a change. The approach has been developed on the basis of Kurt Lewin's work on group dynamics, change and action research

Organisational justice viewpoint that is concerned with the perceptions people form about their work outcomes and the procedure by which these outcomes are allocated

Planned change approach approach that highlights the fact that organisational changes are planned by management and that in the realisation of the intended change outcomes management go through a list of steps

Psychological contract perceptions of mutual obligations held by the two parties in the employment relationship: the employer and the employee

Theory Z term used by William Ouchi referring to a distinctive type of organisational culture which represents a US adaptation of the Japanese management style also known as 'hierarchical clan' culture

Values and behavioural norms medium level in Schein's model, located between *artifacts* and the *basic assumptions*. They refer to the principles, standards and expected behaviours held by an organisation and are linked to the moral and ethical codes

Chapter 16

Change agent roles roles fulfilled by a change agent to achieve successful information systems implementation through designing and planning in the traditional role, building a coalition in the advocate role, and creating shared meaning in the facilitator role

Collaborative technology technology which, via a platform, applications and functionalities, facilitates the interaction, communication and collective accomplishing of tasks, mostly in the form of team and/or project work, by people within or across organisations

Enterprise system *information system* in the form of a vendor-released commercial package that integrates the information flows within the organisation based on industry best practices, and that always requires some degree of customisation to the organisation

Functional information system *information system* used to support employees in the execution of a specific functionally demarcated task

Information system technology-enabled system that supports the sharing of information and communication between both digital media and humans

Management information system *information system* that provides integrated and higher-level information to support managerial decision-making

Managing by results managers' use of performance information – derived from measures related to managerial goal-setting – to support their decision-making towards reaching desired outcomes and to keep stakeholders informed

Offshoring relocation of work overseas from high-wage countries to lower-wage countries, mostly found in the Far East

Social media user-driven online services that rely on user interaction and collaboration via social behaviour enabling technological channels or platforms

Transactional processing system *information system* that provides all the information needed in accordance with legislation and organisational policies to keep business processes running both within and across functional areas

Chapter 17

Individualism personal and professional outlook in which emphasis is placed on individual rather than collective interests

Unitarism managerial perspective based on the notion that everyone in an organisation is a member of a team with a common purpose

References

Chapter 1

BIS (Department for Business, Innovation and Skills) (2009) *Higher Ambitions – The future of universities in a knowledge economy.* London: BIS.

Boyer, E. L. (1997) *Scholarship Reconsidered: Priorities of the professoriate.* San Francisco: Jossey-Bass/Carnegie Foundation for the Advancement of Teaching.

Butler, M. J. R. (2008) 'Inquiring how a lecturer keeps learning about their teaching – a personal case history on reflective imagination', *International Journal of Quality and Standards*, Vol.2, No.1: 1–39.

Butler, M. J. R. (2010) 'Innovative management education through work-based assessment – the case of "strategy for future leaders"', *Learning and Teaching in Higher Education*, Special issue on work-based learning.

Butler, M. J. R. and Reddy, P. (2010) 'Developing critical understanding in HRM students – innovative teaching methods encourage deep approaches to study', *Journal of European Industrial Training*, Vol.34, No.8-9: 772–89.

Cassidy, S. (2006) 'Developing employability skills: peer assessment in higher education', *Education and Training*, Vol.48, No.7: 508–17.

Coffield, F. (2000) 'Introduction: a critical analysis of the concept of a learning society', in Coffield, F. (ed.) *Different Visions of a Learning Society*, Volume 1. Bristol: Policy Press.

Connor, H. and Shaw, S. (2008) 'Graduate training and development: current trends and issues', *Education and Training*, Vol.50, No.5: 357–65.

Cotton, K. (2001) *Developing Employability Skills.* Portland: Northwest Regional Educational Research Laboratory.

Entwistle, N. P. (1990) 'Teaching and the quality of learning in higher education', in Entwistle, N. P. (ed.) *Handbook of Educational Ideas and Practices.* London: Routledge.

Farnham, D. and Smith, P. (2005) *People Management and Development.* Revision Guide. London: CIPD.

Frand, J. L. (2000) 'The information age mindset: changes in students and implications for higher education', *Education Review*, Vol.35, No.5: 14–24.

Hurtado, S. (2009) 'How diversity affects teaching and learning. A climate of inclusion has a positive effect on learning outcomes', available online at: http://www.diversityweb.org/ research_and_trends/research_evaluation_impact/benefits_of_diversity/sylvia_hurtado.cfm [accessed 28 October 2009].

Malcolm, M. (2009) 'Nurturing critical minds', *Times Higher Education*, No. 1918, 15–21 October, 24.

Lord Mandelson (2009) 'Individual and national success demands one path to higher skills', *Times Higher Education*, No.1918, 15–21 October: 24–5.

Martin, F. and Saljo, R. (1976) 'On qualitative differences in learning: 1 – Outcome and process', *British Journal of Educational Psychology*, Vol.46: 4–11.

Mintzberg, H. and Gosling, J. (2002) 'Educating managers beyond borders', *Academy of Management Learning and Education*, Vol.1, No.1: 64–76.

Prensky, M. (2001) 'Digital natives, digital immigrants', *NCB University Press*, Vol.9, No.5: 1–6.

Romanovitch, S. (2009) 'Human resources', Letters to the Editor, *The Times*, 16 October: 39.

Senior, C., Butler, M. J. R., Wood, J. and Reddy, P. (2009) 'The virtual pedagogy initiative', in Higson, H. (ed.) *Good Practice Guide in Learning and Teaching* – Volume 6, Quality Unit, Aston Business School. Birmingham: Aston University.

Wilson, R. (1998) 'Research-university presidents dispute Carnegie report on undergraduate education', *Chronicle of Higher Education*, Vol.44, No.36: 10–13.

Wilton, N. (2008) 'Business graduates and management jobs: an employability match made in heaven?', *Journal of Education and Work*, Vol.21, No.2: 143–58.

Chapter 2

Abrahamson, E. (1996) 'Management fashion, academic fashion and enduring truths', *Academy of Management Review*, Vol.21, No.1: 254–85.

Acker, J. and Van Houten, D. (1974) 'Differential recruitment and control: the sex structuring of organizations', *Administrative Science Quarterly*, Vol.19: 152–63.

Ackroyd, S. and Thompson, P. (1999) *Organizational Misbehaviour*. London: Sage.

Alvesson, M. (2004) *Knowledge Work and Knowledge-Intensive Firms*. Oxford: Oxford University Press.

Alvesson, M. and Willmott, H. (1991) 'On the idea of emancipation in management and organization studies', *Academy of Management Review*, Vol.17, No.3: 432–64.

Alvesson, M. and Willmott, H. (2003) *Studying Management Critically*. London: Sage.

Barnard, C. (1938) *The Functions of the Executive*. Cambridge, MA: Harvard University Press.

Bauman, Z. (1989) *Modernity and the Holocaust*. Cambridge: Polity.

Bendix, R. (1956) *Work and Authority in Industry*. London: Chapman & Hall.

Berger, P. L. and Luckmann, T. (1966) *The Social Construction of Reality: A treatise in the sociology of knowledge*. New York: Doubleday.

Bertalanffy, L. von (1968) *General Systems Theory: Foundations, development, applications*. New York: George Braziller.

Blumer, H. (1969) *Symbolic Interactionism: Perspective and method*. Englewood Cliffs, New Jersey: Prentice Hall.

Bottomore, T. and Rubel, M. (1963) *Karl Marx: Selected writings in sociology and social philosophy*. Harmondsworth: Penguin.

Burrell, G. and Morgan, G. (1979) *Sociological Paradigms and Organizational Analysis*. London: Heinemann.

Chia, R. and Morgan, S. (1996) 'Educating the philosopher manager', *Management Learning*, Vol.27, No.1: 37–64.

Clegg, S. and Palmer, G. (1996) *The Politics of Management Knowledge*. London: Sage.

Cooper, R. and Burrell, G. (1988) 'Modernism, post-modernism and organizational analysis: an introduction', *Organization Studies*, Vol.9, No.1: 91–122.

De Cock, C. and Jeanes, E. L. (2006) 'Questioning consensus, cultivating conflict', *Journal of Management Inquiry*, Vol.15, No.1: 18–30.

Deetz, S. (2003) 'Disciplinary power, conflict suppression and human resources management', in M. Alvesson and H. Willmott (eds) *Studying Management Critically*. London: Sage.

Derrida, J. (1976) *Of Grammatology*. Baltimore, MD: John Hopkins University Press.

Du Gay, P. (2000) *In Praise of Bureaucracy*. London: Sage.

Edwards, R. (1979) *Contested Terrain: The transformation of the workplace in the twentieth century*. New York: Basic Books.

Fayol, H. (1949) *General and Industrial Management*. London: Pitman.

Follett, M. P. (1924) *Creative Experience*. New York: Longmans, Green.

Foucault, M. (1980) *Power/Knowledge*. London: Tavistock.

Gabriel, Y. (2008) *Organizing Words*. Oxford: Oxford University Press.

Gergen, K. J. and Gergen, M. M. (1991) 'Toward reflexive methodologies', in F. Steier (ed.) *Research and Reflexivity*. London: Sage.

Giddens, A. (1984) *The Constitution of Society. Outline of the theory of structuration*. Cambridge: Polity.

Grey, C. (2005) *A Very Short, Fairly Interesting and Reasonably Cheap Book about Studying Organizations*. London: Sage.

Hardt, M. and Negri, A. (2001) *Empire*. Cambridge, MA: Harvard University Press.

Hatch, M. J. and Cunliffe, A. L. (2006) *Organization Theory*. Oxford: Oxford University Press.

Jackson, N. and Carter, P. (2000) *Rethinking Organisational Behaviour*. Harlow: Pearson Education.

Jacques, R. (1996) *Manufacturing the Employee: Management knowledge from the 19th to 21st centuries*. Thousand Oaks, CA: Sage Publications.

Jeanes, E. L. and Muhr, S. L. (2010) 'The impossibility of guidance – a Levinasian critique of business ethics', in *Ethics and Organizational Practice – Questioning the Moral Foundations of Management*. Cheltenham: Edward Elgar.

Kilduff, M. (1993) 'Deconstructing organizations', *Academy of Management Review*, Vol.18: 13–31.

Landsberger, H. A. (1958) *Hawthorne Revisited*. New York: Cornell University Press.

Levinas, E. (1969) *Totality and Infinity: An essay on exteriority*. Pittsburgh, PA: Duquesne University Press.

Linstead, S. (1993) 'Deconstruction in the study of organizations', in J. Hassard and M. Parker (eds) *Postmodernism and Organizations*. London: Sage.

Linstead, S. (2004) 'Introduction: Opening up paths to a passionate postmodernism', in *Organization Theory and Postmodern Thought*. London: Sage.

Lyotard, J.-F. (1979) *The Postmodern Condition: A report on knowledge*. Minneapolis: Minnesota University Press.

Mead, G. H. (1934) *Mind, Self and Society*. Chicago: University of Chicago Press.

Morgan, G. (1997) *Images of Organization*. London: Sage.

Noon, M. and Blyton, P. (2007) *The Realities of Work*. Houndsmill: Palgrave Macmillan.

O'Connor, E. S. (1996) 'Lines of authority: readings of foundational texts on the profession of management', *Journal of Management History*, Vol.2, No.3: 26–49.

Parker, M. (2000) 'Postmodernizing organizational behaviour: new organizations or new organization theory?', in J. Barry, J. Chandler, H. Clark, R. Johnston and D. Needle (eds) *Organization and Management: A critical text*. London: Thomson Learning.

Parker, M. (2002) *Against Management*. Oxford: Polity.

Peters, T. and Waterman, R. H. (1982) *In Search of Excellence*. New York: Harper & Row.

Pfeffer, J. (1993) 'Barriers to the advancement of organization science', *Academy of Management Review*, Vol.18: 599–620.

Prasad, A. (2003) *Postcolonial Theory and Organizational Aanalysis: A critical engagement*. New York: Palgrave.

Pugh, D. S., Hickson, D. J., Hinings, C. R. and Turner, C. (1969) 'The context of organization structures', *Administrative Science Quarterly*, Vol.14, No.1: 91–114.

Ritzer, G. (1996) *The McDonaldization of Society*. London: Pine Forge Press.

Roethlisberger, F. J. and Dickson, W. J. (1939) *Management and the Worker*. Cambridge, MA: Harvard University Press.

Smith, A. (1776) *An Inquiry into the Nature and Causes of the Wealth of Nations*. London: W. Strahan and T. Cadell.

Taylor, F. W. (1911) *The Principles of Scientific Management*. New York: Harper.

Thompson, P. (1995) 'Postmodernism: fatal distraction', in J. Hassard and M. Parker (eds) *Postmodernism and Organization*. London: Sage.

Townley, B. (1993) 'Foucault, power/knowledge, and its relevance for human resource management', *Academy of Management Review*, Vol.18: 518–45.

Trist, E. L. and Bamforth, K. W. (1951) 'Some social and psychological consequences of the longwall method of coal getting', *Human Relations*, Vol.4: 3–38.

Van Maanen, J. (1995) 'Style as theory', *Organization Science*, Vol.7, No.4: 641–52.

Weber, M. (1978) *Economy and Society*. Berkeley, CA: University of California Press.

Weick, K. E. (1969) *The Social Psychology of Organizing*. Reading, MA: Addison-Wesley.

Weick, K. E. (1995) *Sensemaking in Organizations*. London: Sage.

Wilson, F. M. (2010) *Organizational Behaviour and Work*. Oxford: Oxford University Press.

Woodward, J. (1965) *Industrial Organization: Theory and practice*. Oxford: Oxford University Press.

Chapter 3

Ackerman, P. L. and Heggestad, E. D. (1997) Intelligence, personality and interests: evidence for overlapping traits. *Psychological Bulletin*, 121, 219–45.

Allen, N. J. and Meyer, J. P. (1990) The measurement and antecedents of affective, continuance and normative commitment to the organization. *Journal of Occupational Psychology*, 63, 11–18.

Anderson, C. R. and Schneider, C. E. (1978) Locus of control, leader behaviors and leader performance among management students. *Academy of Management Journal*, 21, 690–8.

Ashton, M. C., Jackson, D. N., Paunonen, S. V., Helmes, E. and Rothstein, M. G. (1995) The criterion validity of broad factor scales versus specific facet scales. *Journal of Research in Personality*, 29, 432–42.

Bandura, A. (1978) The self-system in reciprocal determinism. *American Psychologist*, 33, 344–58.

Barrick, M. R. and Mount, M. K. (1991) The Big Five personality dimensions and job performance: A meta-analysis. *Personnel Psychology*, 44, 1–26.

Barrick, M. R. and Mount, M. K. (1994, April) Do specific components of conscientiousness predict better than the overall construct? in Page, R. (Chair) Personality and Job Performance: Big Five versus specific traits. Symposium conducted at the annual meeting of the Society for Industrial and Organisational Psychology, Nashville, TN.

Barrick, M. R. and Mount, M. K. (2005) Yes, personality matters: Moving on to more important matters. *Human Performance*, 18(4), 359–72.

Barrick, M. R., Mount, M. K. and Judge, T. A. (2001) Personality and performance at the beginning of the new millennium: What do we know and where do we go next? *International Journal of Selection and Assessment*, 9, 9–30.

Barrick, M. R., Stewart, G. L., Neubert, M. J. and Mount, M. K. (1998) Relating member ability and personality to work-team processes and team effectiveness. *Journal of Applied Psychology*, 83(3), 377–91.

Bell, S. T. (2007) Deep-level composition variables as predictors of team performance: A meta-analysis. *Journal of Applied Psychology*, 92(3), 595–615.

Blanchard, K. H. and Johnson, S. (1983) *The One Minute Manager*. New York: Blanchard Family Partnership and Candle Communications Corporation.

Bono, J. E. and Judge, T. A. (2004) Personality and transformational leadership: A meta-analysis. *Journal of Applied Psychology*, 89(5), 901–10.

Borgatta, E. F. (1964) The structure of personality characteristics. *Behavioural Science*, 9, 8–17.

Borges, N. J. and Savickas, M. L. (2002) Personality and medical specialty choice: A literature review and integration. *Journal of Career Assessment*, 10(3), 362–80.

Borman, W. C. and Motowidlo, S. J. (1997) Task performance and contextual performance: The meaning for personnel selection research. *Human Performance*, 10(2), 99–109.

Borman, W. C., Penner, L. A., Allen, T. D. and Motowidlo, S. J. (2001) Personality predictors of citizenship performance. *International Journal of Selection and Assessment*, 9, 52–69.

Bouchard, T. J. Jr (1994) Gene, environment and personality. *Science*, 264, 1700–1.

Caldwell, D. F. and Burger, J. M. (1998) Personality characteristics of job applicants and success in screening interviews. *Personnel Psychology*, 51, 119–36.

Caspi, A. and Roberts, B. W. (1999) Personality continuity and change across the life course. In L. Pervin and O. P. John (eds) *Handbook of Personality Psychology: Theory and Research*. (2nd ed). New York: Guilford Press.

Costa, P. T. Jr and McCrae, R. R. (1992) *NEO-PIR Professional Manual*. Odessa, FL: Psychological Assessment Resources.

De Fruyt, F. and Mervielde, I. (1999) RAISEC types and big five traits as predictors of employment status and nature of employment. *Personnel Psychology*, 52, 701–27.

Dudley, N. M., Orvis, K. A., Lebiecki, J. E. and Cortina, J. M. (2006) A meta-analytic investigation of conscientiousness in the prediction of job performance: Examining the intercorrelations and the incremental validity of narrow traits. *Journal of Applied Psychology*, 91, 40–57.

Epstein, S. (1980) The stability of behaviour: Implications for psychological research. *American Psychologist*, 35, 790–806.

Erdheim, J., Wang, M. and Zickar, M. J. (2006) Linking the Big Five personality constructs to organizational commitment. *Personality and Individual Differences*, 41, 959–70.

Fabio, A. and Palazzeschi, L. (2009) Emotional intelligence, personality traits and career decision difficulties. *International Journal of Education and Vocational Guidance*, 9, 135–46.

Funder, D. C. (2001) Personality. *Annual Review of Psychology*, 52, 197–221.

George, J. M. and Zhou, J. (2001) When openness to experience and conscientiousness are related to creative behaviour: An interactive approach. *Journal of Applied Psychology*, 86, 513–24.

Goldberg, L. R. (1990) An alternative "description of personality": the Big Five factor structure *Journal of Personality and Social Psychology*, 59, 1216–29.

Guion, R. M. and Gottier, R. F. (1965) Validity of personality measures in personnel selection. *Personnel Psychology*, 18, 135–64.

Hampson, S. E. (1988) *The Construction of Personality: An introduction*. London: Routledge.

Hampson, S. E. (1999) State of the art: personality. *The Psychologist*, 12, 284–8.

Hastings, S. E. and O'Neill, T. A. (2009) Predicting workplace deviance using broad versus narrow personality variable. *Personality and Individual Difference*, 47, 289–93.

Hofstede, G. (1980) *Cultures and Organisations: Software of the mind*. London: McGraw-Hill.

Hofstee, W. K. B. (1984) What's in a trait: reflections about the inevitability of traits, their measurement, and taxonomy, in Bonarius, H., Van Heck, G. L. and Smid, N. (eds) *Personality Psychology in Europe: Theoretical and empirical developments*. Lisse: Swets & Zeitlinger.

Hogan, R., Curphy, G. J. and Hogan, J. (1994) What we know about leadership: effectiveness and personality. *American Psychologist*, 49, 493–504.

Hogan, J. and Holland, B. (2003) Using theory to evaluate personality and job performance relations: a socioanalytic perspective. *Journal of Applied Psychology*, 88, 100–12.

Hough, L. M. and Oswold, F. L.(2000) Personal selection: looking toward the future –remembering the past. *Annual Review of Psychology*, 51, 631–64.

House, R. J. and Aditya, R. N. (1997) The social scientific study of leadership: Quo vadis? *Journal of Management*, 23, 409–73.

Hurtz, G. M. and Donovan, J. J. (2000) Personality and job performance: the Big Five revisited. *Journal of Applied Psychology*, 85, 869–79.

Jorm, A. F., MacKinnon, A. J., Christensen, H., Henderson, S., Scott, R. and Korten, A. (1993) Cognitive functioning and neuroticism in an elderly community sample. *Personality and Individual Differences*, 1(6), 721–3.

Judge, T. A., Bono, J. E., Ilies, R. and Gerhardt, M. W. (2002) Personality and leadership: a qualitative and quantitative review. *Journal of Applied Psychology*, 87(4), 765–80.

Judge, T. A., Heller, D. and Mount, M. K. (2002) Five-factor model of personality and job satisfaction: a meta-analysis. *Journal of Applied Psychology*, 87, 530–41.

Judge, T. A., Higgins, C. A., Thoresen, C. J. and Barrick, M. R. (1999) The Big Five personality traits, general mental ability, and career success across the life span. *Personnel Psychology*, 52, 621–52.

Judge, T. A. and Ilies, R. (2002) Relationship of personality to performance motivation: a meta-analytic review. *Journal of Applied Psychology*, 87(4), 797–807.

Judge, T. A., Klinger, R., Simon, L. S. and Yang, W. F. (2008) The contributions of personality to organizational behaviour and psychology: findings, criticisms, and future research directions. *Social and Personality Compass*, 2/5, 1982–2000.

Judge, T. A., Thoresen, C. J., Bono, J. E. and Patton, G. K. (2001) The job satisfaction-job performance relationship: a qualitative and quantitative review. *Psychological Bulletin*, 127, 376–407.

Levine, J. M. and Moreland, R. L. (1990) Progress in small group research. *Annual Review of Psychology*, 41, 585–634.

Locke, E. A. (1976) The nature and causes of job satisfaction, in Dunnette, M. D. (ed.) *Handbook of Industrial and Organizational Psychology*. Chicago, IL: Rand McNally.

Locke, E. A., Shaw, K. N., Saari, L. M. and Latham, G. P. (1981) Goal setting and task performance, 1968–1980. *Psychological Bulletin*, 90, 125–52.

Lounsbury, J. W., Hutchens, T. and Loveland, J. M. (2005) An investigation of big five personality traits and career decidedness among early and middle adolescents. *Journal of Career Assessment*, 13(1), 25–39.

McClelland, D. C. (1967) *Motivational Trends in Society*. Morristown, NJ: General Learning Press.

McCrae, R. R. and Costa, P. T., Jr (1995) Trait explanations in personality psychology. *European Journal of Personality*, 9, 231–52.

Mischel. W. (1968) *Personality and Assessment*. New York: Wiley.

Mol, S. T., Born, M. P. H., Willemsen, M. E. and van der Molen, H. T. (2005) Predicting expatriate job performance for selection purposes: a quantitative review. *Journal of Cross-Cultural Psychology*, 36, 620.

Mowday, R., Steers, R. and Porter, L. (1979) The measurement of organizational commitment. *Journal of Vocational Behaviour*, 14, 224–47.

Neuman, G. A. and Wright, J. (1999) Team effectiveness: beyond skills and cognitive ability. *Journal of Applied Psychology*, 84(3), 376–89.

Norman, W. T. (1963) Toward an adequate taxonomy of personality attributes: Replicated factor structure in peer nomination personality ratings. *Journal of Abnormal and Social Psychology*, 66, 574–83.

Ones, D. S., Dilchert, S., Viswesvaran, C. and Judge, T. A. (2007) In support of personality assessment in organisational settings, *Personnel Psychology*, 60, 995–1027.

Ones, D. S. and Viswesvaran, C. (1996) Bandwidth-fidelity dilemma in personality measurement for personnel selection. *Journal of Organisational Behaviour*, 17(6), 609–26.

Ones, D. S. and Viswesvaran, C. (1997) Personality determinants in the prediction of aspects of expatriate job success, in Z. Aycan (ed.) *Expatriate Management: Theory and research*. London: JAI Press.

Organ, D. W. and Ryan, K. (1995) A meta-analysis review of attitudinal and dispositional predictors of organizational citizenship behaviour. *Personnel Psychology*, 48, 775–802.

Parks, L. and Guay, R. P. (2009) Personality, values, and motivation. *Personality and Individual Differences*, 47, 675–84.

Pearson, P. R. (1993) Cognitive functioning and neuroticism in elderly psychiatric patients. *Personality and Individual Differences*, 14(1), 265–266.

Pervin, L. A. (1980) *Personality: Theory, assessment and research*. New York: Wiley.

Plomin, R. (1994) *Genetics and Experience: The interplay between nature and nurture*. Thousand Oaks, CA: Sage.

Robbins, S. P. and Judge, T. A. (2009) *Organizational Behavior* (Pearson International Edition). London: Pearson/Prentice-Hall.

Salgado, J. F. (1997) The five factor model of personality and job performance in the European Community. *Journal of Applied Psychology*, 82, 30–43.

Salgado, J. F. (2003) Predicting job performance using FFM and non-FFM personality measures. *Journal of Occupational and Organisational Psychology*, 76, 323–46.

Saucier, G., Hampson, S. E. and Goldberg, L. R. (2000) Cross-language studies of lexical personality factors, in S. E. Hampson (ed.) *Advances in Personality Psychology: Volume 1*. Hove, E. Sussex: Psychology Press.

Tokar, D., Fischer, A. and Subich, L. M. (1998) Personality and vocational behavior: a selective review of the literature, 1993–1997. *Journal of Vocational Behavior*, 53, 147–79.

Tokar, D. M. and Swanson, J. L. (1995) More on RIASEC and the five-factor model of personality: Direct assessment of Prediger's (1982) and Hogan's (1983) dimensions. *Journal of Vocational Behaviour*, 52, 246–59.

Tupes, E. C. and Cristal, R. E. (1961) *Recurrent Personality Factors Based on Trait Ratings* (ASD-TR-61-97). Lackland Air Force Base, TX: Aero-nautical Systems Division, Personnel Laboratory.

Viswesvaran, C. and Ones, D. S. (2000) Perspectives on models of job performance. *International Journal of Selection and Assessment*, 8, 216–26.

Wanous, J. P., Reichers, A. E. and Malik, S. D. (1984) Organisational specialisation and group development: towards an integrated perspective. *Academy of Management Review*, 9(4), 670–83.

Watson, J. B. and Rayner, R. (1920) Conditioned emotional reactions. *Journal of Experimental Psychology*, 3, 1–14.

Woods, S. A. and Hampson, S. E. (2005) Measuring the Big Five with single items using a bipolar response scale. *European Journal of Personality*, 19(5), 373–90.

Woods, S. A. and Hampson, S. E. (2010) 'Predicting adult occupational environments from gender and childhood personality traits', *Journal of Applied Psychology*, 95: 1045–1057.

Chapter 4

Ashforth, R. and Humphrey, B. (1993) 'Emotional labour in service roles: the influence of identity', *Academy of Management Review*, 18/1: 88–118.

Baxter, L. F. and Ritchie, J. M (2004) 'The sensation of smell in researching a bakery: from the yummy to the abject', Standing Conference on Organisation Symbolism, Halifax, Nova Scotia.

Brotheridge, C. and Grandey, A. (2002) 'Emotional labour and burnout: comparing two perspectives of people work', *Journal of Vocational Behaviour*, 60: 17–39.

Callahan, J. L. and McCollum, E. E. (2002) 'Obscured variability: the distinction between emotion work and emotional labour', in N. J. Ashkanasy, W. J. Zerbe and C. E. J. Hartel (eds) *Managing Emotions in the Workplace*. New York: M. E. Sharpe.

Cochrane, K. (2005) 'Are all men rapists after all?' *New Statesman*, 26 Sept.

Colville, I. (2008) 'Sensemaking', in R. Thorpe, and R. Holt (eds) *The Sage Dictionary of Qualitative Management Research* (London: Sage).

Cooper, R. and Sawaf, A. (1997) *Executive EQ* (London: Orion Business).

Craib, I. (1995) 'Some comments on the sociology of the emotions'. *Sociology*, 29: 151–58.

Douglas, M. (1966) *Purity and Danger* (London: Routledge & Kegan Paul).

Fineman, S. (2000) *Emotions in Organizations* (London: Sage Publications).

Fineman, S. (2004) 'Getting the measure of emotion – and the cautionary tale of emotional intelligence', *Human Relations*, 57/6: 719–40.

Frost, P. (2003) *Toxic Emotions at Work* (Boston: Harvard Business School Press).

Gibson, D. E. (2006) 'Emotional episodes at work: an experiential exercise in feeling and expressing emotions', *Journal of Management Education*, 30/3: 477–500.

Goffman, E. (1959) *The Presentation of Self in Everyday Life* (London: Penguin Books).

Goleman, D. (1996) *Emotional Intelligence: Why it can matter more than IQ* (London: Bloomsbury).

Grandey, A. (2000) 'Emotion regulation in the workplace: a new way to conceptualise emotional labour', *Journal of Occupational Health Psychology*, 5/1: 95–110.

Hancock, P. and Tyler, M. (2001) *Work, Postmodernism and Organization: A critical introduction* (London: Sage Publications).

Hernes, T. (2007) *Understanding Organization as Process: Theory for a tangled world* (Abingdon: Routledge).

Hochschild, A. R. (1979) 'Emotion Work, Feeling Rules, and Social Structure', *The American Journal of Sociology*, 85/3: 551–75.

Hochschild, A. R. (1983) *The Managed Heart: Commercialization of human feeling* (London: University of California).

Hofstede, G. (2001) *Culture's Consequences: Comparing values, behaviors, institutions, and organizations across nations* (2nd ed.) Thousand Oaks, CA: Sage Publications.

Hughes, J. (2005) 'Bringing emotion to work: emotional intelligence, employee resistance and the reinvention of character', *Work Employment & Society*, 19/3: 603–25.

Korczynski, M. (2002) *Human Resource Management in Service Work* (Basingstoke: Palgrave).

Korczynski, M. and Ott, U. (2004) 'When production and consumption meet: cultural contradictions and the enchanting myth of consumer sovereignty', *Journal of Management Studies*, 41/4: 575–99.

Linstead, S. and Linstead, A. (2005) 'Managing change', in S. Linstead., L. Fulop. and S. Lilley, *Management and Organization: a critical text* (Hampshire: Palgrave Macmillan).

Lukacs, G. (1923/1971) *History and Class Consciousness: Studies in Marxist dialectics*. London: The Merlin Press.

Marx, K. (1976) *Capital: Critique of political economy* Vol.1. (London: Penguin).

Merton, R. (1957) *Social Theory and Social Structure* (Glenco, NY: Free Press).

Plato (1974) *The Republic* (2nd edition) (London: Penguin).

Raz, A. E. (2002) *Emotions at Work: Normative control, organizations, and culture in Japan and America* (Cambridge, MA: Harvard University Press).

Ritzer, G. (1996) *The McDonaldization of Society: An investigation into the changing character of contemporary social life* (Rev. ed.), (Thousand Oaks: CA, Pine Forge Press).

The Economist (2010) 'Female power', 2–8 January: 49–51.

Thompson, P. and McHugh, D. (2009) *Work Organisations* (Hampshire: Palgrave Macmillan).

Ward, J. (2009) *Managing Emotions*. PhD thesis. York: University of York Management School.

Weber, M. (1948) *Essays in Sociology* (London: Routledge).

Weick, K. (1979) *The Social Psychology of Organizing* (New York: Random House).

Weick, K. (1995) *Sense Making in Organisations* (Thousand Oaks, CA: Sage Publications).

Weick, K. (1996) 'Drop your tools: an allegory for organizational studies' *Administrative Science Quarterly*, 41/2: 301–13.

Whitehead, A. N. (1929/1957) *The Aims of Education, and other essays*. (New York: Free Press).

Chapter 5

Adams, J. S. (1963) Toward an understanding of inequity. *Journal of Abnormal and Social Psychology*, 67, 422–36.

Aldag, R. J., Barr, S. and Brief, A. (1981) Measurement of perceived task characteristics. *Psychological Bulletin*, 90, 415–31.

Alderfer, C. P. (1972) *Existence, Relatedness and Growth*. London: Collier Macmillan.

Aram, J. D. and Piraino, T. G. (1978) 'The Hierarchy of Needs Theory: An evaluation in Chile', *Interamerican Journal of Psychology*, 12, 179–88.

Argyle, M. (1974) *The Social Psychology of Work*. Harmondsworth: Penguin.

Arnolds, C. A. and Boshoff, C. (2002) 'Compensation, esteem valence and job performance: an empirical assessment of Alderfer's ERG theory', *Human Resource Management*, 13, 697–719.

Binswanger, H. (1991) Volition as cognitive self regulation, *Organisational Behaviour and Human Decision Processes*, 50, 154–78.

Blauner, R. (1964) *Alienation and Freedom*. Chicago, IL: University of Chicago Press.

Briscoe, D. R. and Schuler, R. (2004) *International Human Resource Management*. Oxford: Routledge.

Campolo, T. (2009) *Choose Love NOT Power*. California: Regal.

Chinoy, E. (1955) *Automobile Workers and the American Dream*. Garden City: Doubleday.

Clark, A. E. (1996) 'Job satisfaction in Britain', *British Journal of Industrial Relations*, 34, 189–217.

Cooper, R. (1973) How jobs motivate. *Personnel Review*, 2, 4–12.

Fan, J., Meng, H., Billings, R. S., Litchfield, R. C. and Kaplan, I. (2008) On the role of goal orientation traits and self-efficacy in the goal setting process: distinctions that make a difference. *Human Performance*, 21, 354–82.

Frankl, V. F. (1978) *The Unheard Cry For Meaning*. New York: Simon & Schuster.

Frankl, V. F. (2004) Psychodynamic influences, in Freeman, A., Mahoney, M., Devito, P. and Martin, D. (eds) *Cognition and Psychotherapy*, 2nd ed. New York: Springer Publishing.

Freeman, R. B. (1978) 'Job satisfaction as an economic variable'. Ninetieth Annual Meeting of the American Economic Association. The *American Economic Review*.

Fried, Y. and Ferris, G. (1987) The validity of the job characteristics model: a review and meta-analysis. *Personnel Psychology*, 40, 287–322.

Goldberg, R. (1998) p28, cited in Vick, D. (1999) *A Study of the Action Learning Process*. Unpublished PhD thesis. Revans Action Learning & Research Institute.

Goldthorpe, J., Lockwood, D., Bechhoffer, F. and Platt, J. (1968) *The Affluent Worker: Industrial attitudes and behaviour*, Cambridge: Cambridge University Press.

Grant, A. (2008) Designing jobs to do good: dimensions and psychological consequences of prosocial job characteristics. *The Journal of Positive Psychology*, 3, 19–39.

Griffin, R. W. and Bateman, T. S. (1986) 'Job satisfaction and organisational commitment', *International Review of Industrial and Organizational Psychology*, 157–88.

Hackman, R. J. and Lawler, E. E. (1971) Employee reactions to job characteristics. *Journal of Applied Psychology Monography*, 55, 259–286.

Hackman, R. J. and Oldham, G. R. (1975) Development of the job diagnostic survey. *Journal of Applied Psychology* 60, 159–170.

Hackman, R. J. and Oldham, G. R. (1979) *Work Redesign.* Reading, MA: Addison-Wesley.

Hamermesh, D. S. (2001) The changing distribution of job satisfaction. *The Journal of Human Resources*, 36, 1–30.

Harrison, P. (2006) Questioning in action learning: rhetoric or reality? *International Journal of Management Education*, 5, 15–20.

Harrison, P. (2007) Knowledge sharing. *People Management*, 13, 64.

Herzberg, F. (1968) *Work and the Nature of Man.* St. Albans: Staples Press.

Herzberg, F. (2003) 'One more time: how do you motivate employees?', *Harvard Business Review*, 81, 86–96.

Herzberg, F., Mausner, B. and Snyderman, B. B. (1959) *Motivation to Work.* London: John Wiley & Sons.

Holman, D. and Fernie, S. (2000) 'Can I help you? Call centres and job satisfaction', *Centrepiece.* London: LSE.

Iaffaldano, M. T. and Muchinsky, P. M. (1985) 'Job satisfaction and job performance: a metaanalysis', *Psychological Bulletin*, 97, 251–73.

Kelly, J. (1992) Does job re-design explain job re-design outcomes? *Human Relations*, 45, 753–74.

Korman, A. K., Greenhause, J. H. and Badin, I. J. (1977) Personnel attitudes and motivation. *Annual Review Psychology*, 28, 175–96.

Lawler, E. E. I. (1973) *Motivation in Work Organisations.* Monterey, CA:, Brooks/Cole.

Levin, J. (2010) 'Mind of a killer', *Sunday Times*, 6 June.

Locke, E. A. (1968) Toward a theory of task motivation and incentives. *Organisational Behaviour and Human Performance*, 157–89.

Locke, E. A. (1976) 'The nature and causes of job satisfaction', in Dunnette, M. D. (ed.) *Handbook of Industrial and Organisational Psychology.* Chicago: Rand-McNally.

Locke, E. A., Alvi, M. and Wagner, J. (1997) 'Participation in decision-making: an information exchange perspective', in FERRIS, G. (ed.) *Research in Personnel and Human Resource Management.* Greenwich, CT: JAI Press.

Locke, E. A. and Latham, G. P. (2002) Building a practically useful theory of goal setting and task motivation. *American Psychologist*, 57, 705–17.

Lowry, R. (1998) 'Forward', in Maslow, A. H. (ed.) *Toward a Psychology of Being*, 3rd ed. New York: John Wiley & Sons.

Luthans, F. (1998) *Organisational Behaviour.* Singapore: McGraw-Hill.

Marshall, L. and Rowland, F. (1998) *A Guide to Learning Independently.* Buckingham: Open University Press.

Maslow, A. H. (1998) *Toward a Psychology of Being.* New York: John Wiley & Sons.

Mills, C. W. (1956) *White Collar.* Oxford: Oxford University Press.

Mitchell, T. R. (1974) Expectancy models of job satisfaction, occupational preference and effort. *Psychological Bulletin*, 81, 1053–77.

Mottaz, C. J. (1985) The relative importance of intrinsic and extrinsic rewards as determinant of work satisfaction. *The Sociological Quarterly*, 26, 365–85.

Mumford, A. (1995) Managers developing others through action learning. *Industrial and Commercial Training*, 27, 19.

Muraven, M., Rosman, H. and Gagne, M. (2007) Lack of autonomy and self-control: performance contingent rewards lead to greater depletion. *Motive Emot*, 31, 322–30.

Penn, R., Rose, M. and Rubery, J. (1994) 'The SCELI skill findings', in M. R. Rose, R. Penn and J. Rubery (eds) *Skill and Occupational Change.* Oxford: Oxford University Press.

Porter, L. W. and Lawler, E. E. (1968) *Managerial Attitudes and Performance.* Homewood, IL: Dorsey Press.

Rauschenberger, J., Schmitt, N. and Hunter, J. (1980) A test of the need hierarchy concept by a Markov model of change in need strength. *Administrative Science Quarterly*, 654–70.

Revans, R. W. (1983) *ABC of Action Learning.* Middlesex: Chartwell-Bratt Ltd.

Roethlisberger, F. J. and Dickson, W. J. (1964) *Management and the Worker.* Cambridge, MA: Harvard University Press.

Rollnick, S., Miller, W. R. and Butler, C. (2008) *Motivational Interviewing in Health Care – Helping Patients Change Behaviour.* London: Guildford Press.

Rose, M. (1994) 'Job satisfaction, job skills and personal skills', in Penn, R., Rose, M. and Rubery, J. (eds) *Skill and Occupational Change.* Oxford: Oxford University Press.

Rose, M. (2000) 'How far can I trust it? The job satisfaction data in the WERS Employee Survey', *Workplace Employee Relations Survey 98* Users' One-Day Conference. Working Paper 4, Work Centrality and Careers Projected. London: National Institute of Economic and Social Research.

Shackle, S. (2010) Maslow motion. *New Statesman,* 15 March.

Smerek, R. E. and Peterson, M. (2007) Examining Herzberg's theory: improving job satisfaction among non-academic employees at a university. *Research in Higher Education,* 48.

Thompson, P. and Mchugh, D. (2002) *Work Organisations.* Houndsmills: Palgrave.

Vogt, E. and Brown, J. (2004) *The Art of Powerful Questions: Catalyzing insight, innovation and action.* London: Whole Systems Associates.

Vogt, E., Brown, J. and Isaacs, D. (2003) *The Art of Powerful Questions: Catalyzing insight, innovation and action.* Mill Valley, CA: Whole Systems Associates.

Vroom, V. (1964) *Work and Motivation.* New York: John Wiley & Sons.

Watson, T. J. (2004) *Sociology, Work and Industry.* London: Routledge.

Weir, M. (1976) *Job Satisfaction Challenge and Response in Modern Britain.* Glasgow: Williams Collins.

Woods, R. (2010) 'Behind the smile', *Sunday Times,* 6 June.

Chapter 6

Allinson, C. W. and Hayes, J. (1990) 'Validity of the Learning Styles Questionnaire', *Psychological Reports,* 67: 859–66.

Allinson, C. W. and Hayes, J. (1994) 'Cognitive style and its relevance for management practice', *British Journal of Management,* 5/1: 53–72.

Armstrong, M. (2010) *Armstrong's Handbook of Human Resource Management Practice,* 11th ed. (London: Kogan Page).

Bandura, A. (1977) *Social Learning Theory.* (Englewood Cliffs, NJ: Prentice Hall).

Bandura, A. and Huston, C. (1961) 'Identification as a process of incidental learning', *Journal of Abnormal Social Psychology,* 63: 311–18.

Bryman, A. and Bell, E. (2003) *Business Research Methods.* (Oxford: Oxford University Press).

Bushnell, D. S. (March, 1990) Input, process, output: a model for evaluating training. *Training and Development Journal,* 44/3: 41–3.

Carnevale, A. P. and Schulz, E. R. (July, 1990) Return on investment: accounting for training. *Training and Development Journal,* 44/7: 1–32.

Coffield, F., Moseley, D., Hall, E. and Ecclestone, K. (2004) *Learning Styles and Pedagogy in Post-16 Learning: A systematic and critical review.* (London: Learning and Skills Research Centre).

Curry, L. (1983) *Learning Styles in Continuing Medical Education.* (Ottowa: Canadian Medical Association).

Dixon, N. M. (1996) New routes to evaluation. *Training and Development,* 50/5: 82–6.

Duffy, A. and Duffy, T. (2002) 'Psychometric properties of Honey and Mumford's Learning Styles Questionnaire (LSQ)', *Personality and Individual Differences,* 33: 147–63.

Eseryel, D. (2002) Approaches to evaluation of training: theory and practice, *Educational Technology and Society,* 5/2.

Fitz-Enz, J. (July, 1994) Yes…you can weigh training's value. *Training,* 31/7: 54–8.

Gordon, J. (1991) Measuring the "goodness" of training. *Training,* 28/8, August: 19–25.

Gustafson, K. L. and Branch, R. B. (1997) *Survey of Instructional Development Models,* 3rd ed. (Syracuse, NY: ERIC Clearinghouse on Information and Technology).

Hackett, P. (2003) *Training Practice*. (London: CIPD).

Harrison, R. (2009) *Learning and Development*, 5th ed. (London: CIPD).

Hicks, C. and Hennessy, D. (1997) 'Identifying training objectives: the role of negotiation', *Journal of Nursing Management*, 5/5: 263–5.

Holbeche, L. (1999) *Aligning Human Resources and Business Strategy*. (Oxford: Butterworth-Heinemann).

Honey, P. and Mumford, A. (1982) *The Manual of Learning Styles*. (Maidenhead: P. Honey).

Honey, P. and Mumford, A. (1996) *Managing the Learning Environment*. (Maidenhead: P. Honey).

Jung, C. (1923) *Psychological Types*. (London: Pantheon Books).

Lucy Kellaway (2005) the *Financial Times* management columnist.

Kirkpatrick, D. L. (1959) Techniques for evaluating training programs. *Journal of the American Society of Training Directors*, 13: 3–26.

Kirkpatrick, D. L and Kirkpatrick, J. D. (2009) *Evaluating Training Programs: The four levels*, 3rd ed. (San Francisco, CA: Berrett-Koehler Publishers).

Knowles, M. (1973) *The Adult Learner: A neglected species*. (Houston, TX: Gulf Publishing).

Kohler, W. (1925) *The Mentality of Apes*. Translated by Winter, E. (London: Routledge & Kegan Paul).

Kolb, D. A. (1976) 'Management and the learning process', *California Management Review*, 18/3: 21–31.

Kolb, D. A. (1984) *Experiential Learning: Experience as the source of learning and development*. (Englewood Cliffs, NJ: Prentice Hall).

Kolb, D. A. (2000) *Facilitator's Guide to Learning*. (Boston, MA: Hay/McBer).

Lewin, K. (1923) *A Dynamic Theory of Personality*. (New York: McGraw-Hill).

Lewin, K. (1948) *Resolving Social Conflicts: Selected papers on group dynamics*. (New York: Harper & Row).

Marchington, M. and Wilkinson, A. (1996) *Core Personnel and Development*. (London: LSC).

Maslow, A. (1954) *Motivation and Personality*. (New York: Harper & Row).

Mayo, A. and Lank, E. (1994) *The Power of Learning*. (London: Institute of Personnel Management).

McGehee, W. and Thayer, P. W. (1961) *Training in Business and Industry*. (New York: John Wiley & Sons).

Mumford, A. (1997) *How to Choose the Right Development Method* (Maidenhead: P. Honey).

Mumford, A. and Gold, J. (2004) *Management Development: Strategies for action.*3rd ed. London: CIPD.

Myers, I. B. (1962) *Manual: The Myers-Briggs Type Indicator*. (Palo Alto, CA: Consulting Psychologists Press).

Pavlov, I. P. (1927) *Conditioned Reflexes: An investigation of the physiological activity of the cerebral cortex*, transl. and ed. G. Anrep. (Oxford: Oxford University Press).

Phillips, J. J. (1991) *Handbook of Training Evaluation and Measurement Methods*, 2nd ed. (Houston, TX: Gulf Publishing).

Phillips, J. J. (1997) A rational approach to evaluating training programs including calculating ROI. *Journal of Lending and Credit Risk Management*, 79/11, July: 43–50.

Pollard, E. and Hillage, J. (2001) *Exploring E-Learning*, Report 376 (Brighton: Institute of Employment Studies).

Riding, R. and Rayner, S. (2002) *Cognitive Styles and Learning Strategies: Understanding style differences in learning and behaviour*, 5th ed. (London, David Fulton).

Rogers, C. R. (1969) *Freedom to Learn*. (Columbus, OH: Merrill).

Sadler-Smith, E. (2006) *Learning and Development for Managers*. (Oxford: Blackwell).

Shury, J., Winterbotham, M, Davies, B., Oldfield, K., Spilsbury, M. and Constable, S. (2010) *UK Commission for Employment and Skills: National Employer Skills Survey for England 2009: Key findings report*.

Skinner, B. F. (1953) *Science and Human Behavior*. (New York: Macmillan).

Sloman, M. (2005) *Training to Learning*, Change agenda. (London: CIPD).

Stern, E. and Sommerlad, E. (1999) *Workplace Learning, Culture and Performance*. (London: IPD).

Stewart, J. (2010) 'E-learning', in Gold, J. *et al.*(eds) *Human Resource Development Theory and Practice*. (London: Palgrave).

Stewart, J. and Winter, R. (1994) 'Open and distance learning', in S. Truelove (ed.) *Handbook of Training and Development*, 2nd ed. (Oxford: Blackwell).

Vygotsky, L. S. (1978) *Mind in Society*. (Cambridge, MA: Harvard University Press).

Witkin, H. A. and Goodenough, D. R. (1981) *Cognitive Styles—Essence and Origins: Field dependence and field independence*. New York: International Universities.

Wood, D., Bruner, J. S. and Ross, G. (1976) 'The role of tutoring in problem solving'. *Journal of Child Psychology and Psychiatry and Allied Disciplines*, 17, 89–100.

Worthen, B. R. and Sanders, J. R. (1987) *Educational Evaluation*. (New York: Longman).

Chapter 7

Alderfer, C. P. (1977) 'Group and intergroup relations', in J. R. Hackman and J. L. Suttle (eds) *Improving Life at Work*. Santa Monica, CA: Goodyear.

Appelbaum, E. and Batt, R. (1994) *The New American Workplace*. Ithaca, NY: ILR Press.

Bakker, A. B., van Emmerik, H. and Euwema, M. C. (2006) 'Crossover of burnout and engagement in work teams', *Work and Occupations*, 33: 464–89.

Barrick, M. R., Bradley, B. H., Kristof-Bown, A. L. and Colbert, A. E. (2007) 'The moderating role of top management team interdependence: implications for real teams and working groups', *Academy of Management Journal*, Vol.50, No.3: 544–57.

Batt, R. (2004) 'Who benefits from teams? Comparing workers, supervisors, and managers', *Industrial Relations*, 43: 183–212.

Batt, R. and Appelbaum, E. (1995) 'Worker participation in diverse settings: does the form affect the outcome, and if so, who benefits?', *British Journal of Industrial Relations*, 33: 353–78.

Baumeister, R. F. and Leary, M. R. (1995) 'The need to belong: desire for interpersonal attachments as a fundamental human motivation', *Psychological Bulletin*, 117/3: 497–529.

Belbin, R. M. (1993) *Team Roles at Work*. Oxford: Butterworth-Heinemann.

Boning, B., Ichniowski, C. and Shaw, K. (2001) 'Opportunity Counts: Teams and the Effectiveness of Production Incentives', NBER Working Paper No. 8306. Cambridge, MA: National Bureau of Economic Research.

Bourgeois, L. J. (1980) 'Performance and consensus', *Strategic Management Journal*, 1: 227–48.

Brown, R. (2000) *Group Processes*, 2nd ed. Oxford: Blackwell.

Campion, M. A., Medsker, G. J. and Higgs, C. A. (1993) 'Relations between work group characteristics and effectiveness: implications for designing effective work groups', *Personnel Psychology*, 46/4: 823–50.

Carter, S. M. and West, M. A. (1998) 'Reflexivity, effectiveness and mental health in BBC-TV Production Teams', *Small Group Research*, 5: 583–601.

Cohen, S. G. and Bailey, D. E. (1997) 'What makes teams work: group effectiveness research from the shop floor to the executive suite', *Journal of Management*, 23: 239–90.

Cohen, S. G., Ledford, G. E. and Spreitzer, G. M. (1996) 'A predictive model of self-managing work team effectiveness', *Human Relations*, 49, 643–76.

Cooke, W. N. (1994) 'Employee participation programs, group-based incentives, and company performance: a union-nonunion comparison', *Industrial and Labour Relations Review*, 47: 594–609.

Dawson, J. F., Yan, X. and West, M. A. (2008) 'Positive and negative effects of team working in healthcare: real and pseudo-teams and their impact on safety', Birmingham: Aston University Working Paper Series.

De Dreu, C. K. W. (2007) 'Cooperative outcome interdependence, task reflexivity and team effectiveness: a motivated information processing approach', *Journal of Applied Psychology*, 92: 628–38.

De Dreu, C. and Weingart, L. (2003) 'Task versus relationship conflict, team performance and team member satisfaction: a meta-analysis', *Journal of Applied Psychology*, 88: 741–9.

Delarue, A., Van Hootegem, G., Huys, R. and Gryp, S. (2004) *Dossier: Werkt teamwerk? De PASO resultaten rond arbeidsorganisatie doorgelicht*. Leuven: Hoger Instituut voor de Arbeid, Departement TEW, Departement Sociologie.

Delarue, A., Van Hootegem, G., Procter, S. and Burridge, M. (2008) 'Teamworking and organisational performance: a review of survey-based research', *International Journal of Management Reviews*, 10/2: 127–48.

Devine, D. J. (2002) 'A review and integration of classification systems relevant to teams in organisations', *Group Dynamics: Theory, Research, and Practice*, 6/4: 291–310.

Diehl, M. and Stroebe, W. (1987) 'Productivity loss in brainstorming groups: towards the solution of a riddle', *Journal of Personality and Social Psychology*, 53: 497–509.

Edmondson, A. C. (1996) 'Learning from mistakes is easier said than done: group and organisational influences on the detection and correction of human error', *Journal of Applied Behavioural Science*, 32: 5–28.

Eisenhardt, K. and Schoonhoven, C. (1990) 'Organisational growth: linking founding team, strategy, environment, and growth among U.S. semiconductor ventures, 1978–1988', *Administrative Science Quarterly*, 35: 504–29.

Elmuti, D. (1997) 'The perceived impact of teambased management systems on organisational effectiveness', *Team Performance Management*, 3/3: 179–92.

French, J. R. P., Jr. and Raven, B. H. (1959) 'The bases of social power', in D. Cartwright (ed.), *Studies in social power*. Ann Arbor, MI: Institute for Social Research.

Furnham, A. and Gunter, B. (1993) 'Corporate culture: diagnosis and change', in C. L. Cooper and I. T. Robertson (eds) *International Review of Industrial and Organisational Psychology*, Vol 8. Chichester: John Wiley.

Galagan, P. (1986) 'Work teams that work', *Training and Development Journal*, 11: 33–5.

George, J. M. (1990) 'Personality, affect, and behavior in groups', *Journal of Applied Psychology*, 75: 107–16.

Gladstein, D. L. (1984) 'Groups in context: a model of task group effectiveness', *Administrative Science Quarterly*, 29: 499–517.

Glassop, L. I. (2002) 'The organisational benefits of teams', *Human Relations*, 55: 225–49.

Godard, J. (2001) 'High performance *and* the transformation of work? The implications of alternative work practices for the experience and outcomes of work', *Industrial and Labour Relations Review*, 54: 776–805.

Guzzo, R. and Dickson, M. (1996) 'Teams in organisations: recent research on performance and effectiveness', *Annual Review of Psychology*, 47: 307–38.

Guzzo, R. and Salas, E. (eds) (1995) *Team Effectiveness and Decision Making in Organisations*. San Francisco, CA: Jossey-Bass.

Guzzo, R. A., Yost, P. R., Gampbell, R. J. and Shea, G. P. (1993) 'Potency in groups: articulating a construct', *British Journal of Social Psychology*, 32: 87–106.

Hackman, J. R. (1986) 'The psychology of self-management in organisations', in M. S. Pallak and R. Perloff (eds) *Psychology and Work*. Washington DC: American Psychological Association.

Hackman, J. R. (1987) 'The design of work teams', in Lorsch, J. (ed.) *Handbook of Organisational Behavior*. Englewood Cliffs, NJ: Prentice-Hall.

Hackman, J. R. (2002) *Leading Teams. Setting the stage for great performances*. Boston: Harvard Business School Press.

Hackman J. R. and Oldham G. R. (1976) 'Motivation through the design of work: test of a theory', *Organisational Behavior and Human Performance*, 16: 250–79.

Harris, C. L. and Beyerlein, M. M. (2003) 'Team-based organisation: creating an environment for team success', in M. A. West, C. Tjosvold, and K. G. Smith (eds) *International Handbook of Organisational Teamwork and Cooperative Working*. Hoboken, NJ: John Wiley.

Heaphy, E. D. and Dutton, J. E. (2008) 'Positive social interactions and the human body at work: linking organisations and physiology', *Academy of Management Review*, 33/1: 137–62.

Hollenbeck, J. R., Ilgen, D. R., Sego, D. J., Hedlund, J., Major, D. A. and Phillips, J. (1995) 'Multilevel theory of team decision making: decision performance in teams incorporating distributed expertise', *Journal of Applied Psychology*, 80/2: 292–316.

Janis, I. L. (1982) *Groupthink*, 2nd ed. Boston: Houghton Mifflin.

Jehn, K. A. (1995) 'A multimethod examination of the benefits and detriments of intragroup conflict', *Administrative Science Quarterly*, 40/2: 256–82.

Karau, S. J. and Williams, K. D. (1993) 'Social loafing: a meta-analytic review and theoretical integration', *Journal of Personality and Social Psychology*, 65: 681–706.

Katzenbach, J. R. (1997) *Teams at Top: Unleashing the potential of both teams and individual leaders*. Boston, MA: Harvard Business School Press.

Katzenbach, J. R. and Smith, D. K. (1998) *The Wisdom of Teams*. Berkshire: McGraw-Hill.

Kozlowski, S. W. J. and Bell, B. S. (2003) 'Work groups and teams in organisations', in W. C. Borman, D. R. Ilgen and R. Klimoski (eds) *Industrial/Organisational Psychology*, Vol. XII. Chichester: John Wiley & Sons.

Kozlowski, S. W. J., Gully, S. M., Nason, E. R. and Smith, E. M. (1999) 'Developing adaptive teams: a theory of compilation and performance across levels and time', in D. R. Ilgen and E. D. Pulakos (eds) *The Changing Nature of Work Performance: Implications for staffing, personnel actions and development*. San Francisco: Jossey Bass.

Kozlowski, S. W. J. and Ilgen, D. R. (2006) 'Enhancing the effectiveness of work groups and teams', *Psychological Science in the Public Interest*, 7: 77–124.

Learmonth, M. (2009) 'Girls' working together without teams: how to avoid the colonization of management language', *Human Relations*, 62/12: 1887–1906.

Levine, J. M. and D'Andrea-Tyson, L. (1990) 'Participation, productivity and the firm's environment', in A. S. Blinder (ed.) *Paying for Productivity*. Washington, DC: Brokkings Institution.

Lickel, B., Hamilton, D. L. and Sherman, S. J. (2001) 'Elements of a lay theory of groups: types of groups, relational styles, and the perception of group entitativity', *Personality and Social Psychology Review*, 5/2: 129–40.

Macy, B. A. and Izumi, H. (1993) 'Organisational change, design and work innovation: a meta-analysis of 131 North American field studies, 1961–1991', *Research in Organisational Change and Design*, Vol. 7. Greenwich, CT: JAI Press.

Marks, M. A., DeChurch, L. A., Mathieu, J. E., Panzer, F. J. and Alonso, A. (2005) 'Teamwork in multiteam systems', *Journal of Applied Psychology*, 90/5: 964–71.

Martz, W. B. Jr, Vogel, R. R. and Nunamaker, J. F. Jr (1992) 'Electronic meeting systems: results from the field', *Decision Support Systems*, 8: 141–58.

Mathieu, J., Maynard, T. M., Rapp, T. and Gilson, L. (2008) 'Team effectiveness 1997–2007: a review of recent advancements and a glimpse into the future', *Journal of Management*, 34: 410–76.

Mayo, E. (1993) *The Human Problems of an Industrialized Civilization*. London: Macmillan.

McGrath, J. E. (1964) *Social Psychology: A brief introduction*. New York: Holt Rinehart & Winston.

Mickan, M. S. and Rodger, S. A. (2005) 'Effective health care teams: a model of six characteristics developed from shared perceptions', *Journal of Interprofessional Care*, 19/4: 358–70.

Mount, M. K., Barrick, M. R. and Stewart, G. L. (1998) 'Five-factor model of personality and performance in jobs involving interpersonal interactions', *Human Performance*, 11: 145–65.

Muthusamy, S. K., Wheeler, J. V. and Simmons, B. L. (2005) 'Self-managing work teams: enhancing organisational effectiveness', *Organisation Development Journal*, 23: 53–66.

Nieva, V. F., Fleishman, E. A. and Reick, A. (1985) *Team Dimensions: Their identity, their measurement, and their relationships*. Research Note 85–12. Washington, DC: U.S. Army, Research Institute for the Behavioral and Social Sciences.

Paris, C. R., Salas, E. and Cannon-Bowers, J. A. (2000) 'Teamwork in multi-person systems: a review and analysis', *Ergonomics*, 43/8: 1052–75.

Richardson, J. and West, M. A. (2010) 'Dream teams: a positive psychology of team working', in A. Linley, S. Harrington and N. Garcea (eds) *Oxford Handbook of Positive Psychology and Work*. New York: Oxford University Press.

Richardson, J., West, M. A. and Dawson, J. F. (2008) 'But what is a team?' Paper presented at 12th International Workshop on Team Working. Birmingham: Aston Business School.

Rousseau, V., Aubé, C. and Savoie, A. (2006) 'Teamwork behaviours: a review and an integration of frameworks', *Small Group Research*, 37: 540–70.

Scharf, A. (1989) 'How to change seven rowdy people', *Industrial Management*, 31: 20–2.

Schneider, B. (1990) 'The climate for service: an application of the climate construct', in B. Schneider (ed.) *Organisational Climate and Culture*. San Francisco: Jossey Bass.

Schwenk, C. and Cosier, R. (1993) Effects of consensus and devil's advocacy on strategic decision-making, *Journal of Applied Social Psychology*, 23: 126–39.

Spreitzer, G. M. (1995) 'Psychological empowerment in the workplace: dimensions, measurement and validation', *Academy of Management Journal*, 38/5: 1442–65.

Stewart, G. L. and Barrick, M. R. (2000) 'Team structure and performance: assessing the mediating role of intrateam process and the moderating role of task type', *Academy of Management Journal*, 43: 135–48.

Straus, S. G. and McGrath, J. E. (1994) 'Does the medium matter? The interaction of task type and technology on group performance and member reactions', *Journal of Applied Psychology*, 79/1: 87–97.

Sundstrom, E., De Meuse, K. P. and Futrell, D. (1990) 'Work teams: applications and effectiveness', *American Psychologist*, 45: 120–33.

Sundstrom, E., McIntyre, M., Halfhill, T. and Richards, H. (2000) 'Work groups: from Hawthorne studies to work teams of the 1990s and beyond', *Group Dynamics: Theory, Research, and Practice*, 4/1: 44–67.

Tata, J. and Prasad, S. (2004) 'Team self-management, organisational structure, and judgements of team effectiveness', *Journal of Managerial Issues*, 16: 248–65.

Thoms, P., Pinto, J. K., Parente, D. H. and Druskat, V. U. (2002) 'Adaptation to self-managing work teams', *Small Group Research*, 33: 3–31.

Tjosvold, D. (1998) 'Cooperative and competitive goal approaches to conflict: Accomplishments and challenges', *Applied Psychology: An International Review*, 47: 285–342.

Tjosvold, D., Tang, M. M. L. and West, M. (2004) 'Reflexivity for team innovation in China: the contribution of goal interdependence', *Group and Organization Management*, 29/5: 540–59.

Van Knippenburg, D. and Schippers, M. C. (2007) 'Work group diversity', *Annual Review of Psychology*, 58: 515–41.

Wageman, R., Hackman, J. R. and Lehman, E. (2005) 'Team diagnostic survey. Development of an instrument', *Journal of Applied Behavioural Science*, 41/4: 373–98.

Walker, T. G. and Main, E. C. (1973) 'Choice shifts in political decision making: federal judges and civil liberties cases', *Journal of Applied Social Psychology*, 3: 39–48.

Weldon, E. and Weingart, L. R. (1993) 'Group goals and group performance', *British Journal of Psychology*, 61: 555–69.

West, M. A. (2000) 'Reflexivity, revolution and innovation in work teams', in M. Beyerlein (ed.) *Product Development Teams: Advances in interdisciplinary studies of work teams*. Greenwich, CT: JAI Press.

West, M. A. (2002) 'Sparkling fountains or stagnant ponds: an integrative model of creativity and innovation implementation in work groups', *Applied Psychology: An International Review*, 51: 355–87.

West, M. A. (2004) *Effective Teamwork: Practical lessons from organisational research*. Oxford: Blackwell/British Psychological Society.

West, M. A., Borrill, C. S. and Unsworth, K. L. (1998) 'Team effectiveness in organisations', in C. L. Cooper and I. T. Robertson (eds) *International Review of Industrial and Organisational Psychology*, Vol.13. Chichester: Wiley.

West, M. A. and Markiewicz, L. (2004) *Building Team-Based Working. A practical guide to organisational transformation*. Oxford: Blackwell/British Psychological Society.

West, M. A., Tjosvold, D. and Smith, K. G. (eds) (2003) *International Handbook of Organisational Teamwork and Cooperative Working*. Chichester: John Wiley & Sons.

Zwick, T. (2004) 'Employee participation and productivity', *Labour Economics*, 11: 715–40.

Chapter 8

ACAS (2009a) *Discipline and Grievances at work* (London: ACAS). Online version also available at: http://www.acas.org.uk [accessed 13 January 2010].

ACAS (2009b) *Managing Conflict at Work* (London: ACAS). Online version also available at: http://www.acas.org.uk [accessed 13 January 2010].

Adams, J. S. (1965) 'Inequity in social exchange', in L. Berkowitz, (ed.), *Advances in Experimental Psychology 2*. San Diego, CA: Academic Press.

Alternative Dispute Resolution Committee (2009) Report: *Energy Law Review*, 30/2: 195–9.

Amason, A. C. (1996) 'Distinguishing the Effects of Functional and Dysfunctional Conflict on Strategic Decision Making: Resolving a Paradox of Top Management Teams, *Academy of Management Journal*, 39: 123–48.

Analoui, F. and Kakabadse, A. (2000) *Sabotage: How to Recognize and Manage Employee Defiance*. London: Management Books.

Ariss S. (2002) 'Computer monitoring: benefits and pitfalls facing management', *Information and Management*, 39/7: 553–8.

Bal, V., Campbell, M. and McDowell-Larsen, S. (2009) 'Good versus bad stress', *Personal Excellence*, January, 14/1: 10.

Baron, R. A. (1991) 'Positive effects of conflict: a cognitive perspective', *Employee Responsibilities and Rights Journal*, 4/1: 25–36.

Beauregarde, T. A. and Henry, L. C. (2009) 'Making the link between work-life balance practices and organizational performance', *Human Resource Management Review*; 19/1: 9–22.

Bird, F. B. and Waters, J. A. (1989) 'The moral muteness of managers', *California Management Review*, 32: 73–88.

Bolger, N., DeLongis, A., Kessler, R. C. and Schilling, E. A. (1989) 'Effects of daily stress on negative mood', *Journal of Personal and Social Psychology*, 57: 808–18.

Bolton, G. E. and Katok, E. (1998) 'Reinterpreting arbitration's narcotic effect: an experimental study of learning in repeated bargaining', *Games and Economic Behavior*, 25/1: 1–33.

Braverman, H. (1974) *Labor and Monopoly Capital: The degradation of work in the twentieth century.* New York: Monthly Review Press.

Brett, J. M., Barsness, Z. I. and Goldberg, S. B. (1996) 'The effectiveness of mediation: an independent analysis of cases handled by four major service providers', *Negotiation Journal*, 12/3: 259–69.

Brinkert, R. (2006) Conflict coaching: advancing the conflict resolution field by developing an individual disputant process', *Conflict Resolution Quarterly*, 23/4: 517–28.

Burawoy, M. (1985) *The Politics of Production.* London: Verso.

Carmichael, M. (2009) 'Who says stress is bad for you?', *Newsweek online*, Feb 14. Online version also available at: http://www.newsweek.com/id/184154 [accessed 17 January 2010].

CIPD (2009a) *Stress at Work.* Factsheet. (London: CIPD). Online version also available at: http://www.cipd.co.uk/subjects/health/stress/stress.htm [accessed 15 January 2010].

CIPD (2009b) *Line Managers Behaviour and Stress at Work: Refined Framework for Line Managers* (London: CIPD). Online version also available at: http://www.cipd.co.uk/subjects/health/stress/_strwkcmptn.htm [accessed 22 January 2010].

Cooper, C. L., Dewe, P. J. and O'Driscoll, M. P. (2001) *Organizational Stress: A Review and Critique of Theory, Research and Applications.* Thousand Oaks, CA: Sage Publications.

Cosier, R. A., Dalton, D. R. and Taylor, L. A. (1991) 'Positive effects of cognitive conflict and employee voice', *Employee Responsibilities and Rights Journal*, 4/1: 7–11.

Crossman, A. and McIlwee, T. (1995) *Signalling Discontent: A study of the 1994 signal workers dispute.* Wrexham: Limelight.

Culbertson, S. S., Huffman, A. H. and Alden-Anderson, R. (2010) 'Leader-member exchange and work-family interactions: the mediating role of self-reported challenge- and hindrance-related stress', *Journal of Psychology*, 144/1: 15–36.

Deluga, R. J. (1989) 'Employee-influence strategies as possible stress-coping mechanisms for role conflict and role ambiguity', *Basic and Applied Social Psychology*, 10/4: 329–35.

Dijkstra, M. T. M., van Dierendonck, D. and Evers, A. (2005) 'Responding to conflict at work and individual well-being: the mediating role of flight behaviour and feelings of helplessness', *European Journal of Work and Organizational Psychology*, 14/4: 119–35.

Dunlop, J. T. (1993) *Industrial Relations Systems*, Revised edition. Boston, MA: Harvard Business School Press.

Fells, R. E. (1998) 'Overcoming the dilemmas in Walton and McKersie's mixed bargaining strategy', *Relations Industrielles/Industrial Relations*, 53/2: 1–27.

Fink, S. L., Beak, J. and Taddeo, K. (1971) 'Organizational crisis and change', *Journal of Applied Behavioural Science*, 7/1: 15–37.

Fox, A. (1966) *Industrial sociology and industrial relations.* Research Paper No.3. London: Royal Commission on Trade Unions and Employers' Associations.

Fox, A. (1973) 'Industrial relations: a social critique of pluralist ideology', in J. Child (ed.) *Man and Organization.* London: Allen & Unwin.

Fox, S. and Stallworth, L. E. (2009) 'Building a framework for two internal organizational approaches to resolving and preventing workplace bullying: alternative dispute resolution and training', *Consulting Psychology Journal: Practice and Research*, 61/3: 220–41.

French, J. R. P. and Caplan, R. D. (1970) 'Psychosocial factors in coronary heart disease', *Industrial Medicine*, 39: 383–97.

Friedman, M. and Rosenman, R. (1974) *Type A Behaviour and Your Heart*. New York: Knopf.

Gerzon, M. (2006) *Leadership Through Conflict: How successful leaders transform differences into opportunities*. Boston, MA: Harvard Business School Press.

Glazer, M. (1983) 'Ten whistle-blowers and how they fared', *Hastings Centre Report* (December): 33–41.

Goodrich, C. L. (1975) *The Frontier of Control: A study in British workshop politics*. London: Pluto Press.

Greenberg, J. (1990) 'Organizational justice: yesterday, today, and tomorrow', *Journal of Management*, 16/2: 399–432.

Gundlach, M. J., Martinko, M. J. and Douglas, S. C. (2008) 'A new approach to examining whistle-blowing: the influence of cognitions and anger', *SAM Advanced Management Journal*, Autumn: 40–50.

Hale, D. (2009) 'Labour disputes in 2008', *Economic & Labour Market Review*, 3/6, June: 26–38.

HSE (2004) *Management Standards for Work-Related Stress*. London: Health and Safety Executive.

HSE (2009a) *Stress-related and Psychological Disorders: Overall scale*. London: Health and Safety Executive. Online version available at: http://www.hse.gov.uk/statistics/causdis/stress/ scale.htm [accessed 15 January 2010].

HSE (2009b) *What is Stress: Definition of stress*. London: Health and Safety Executive. Online version available at: http://www.hse.gov.uk/stress/furtheradvice/whatisstress.htm [accessed 15 January 2010].

Hirschman, A. O. (1970) *Exit, Voice, and Loyalty: Responses to decline in firms, organizations, and states*. Cambridge, MA: Harvard University Press.

Ilies, R., Schwind, K. M., Wagner, D. T., Johnson, M. D., DeRue, D. S. and Ilgen, D. R. (2007) 'When can employees have a family life? The effects of daily workload and effect on work-family conflict and social behaviours at home', *Journal of Applied Psychology*, 92/5: 1368–79.

Jacques, E. (1970) *Work, Creativity and Social Justice*. London: Heinemann.

Jameson, J. K. (2001) 'Employee perceptions of the availability and use of interest-based, right-based, and power-based conflict management strategies', *Conflict Resolution Quarterly*, 19/2: 163–96.

Janis, I. L. (1972) *Victims of Groupthink: A psychological study of foreign policy decisions and fiascos*. Boston, MA: Houghton Mifflin.

Jehn, K. A. (1995) 'A multi-method examination of the benefits and detriments of intergroup conflict', *Administrative Science Quarterly*, 40: 256–82.

Kanter, R. M. (1977) *Work and Family Life in the United States: A critical review of agenda for research and policy*. New York: Russell Sage Foundation.

Keashly, L. and Newberry, J. (1995) 'Preference for the fairness of intervention: influence of third-party control, third-party status and conflict setting', *Journal of Social and Personal Relationships*, 12/2: 277–93.

Koch, J. (1999) 'Employee sabotage: don't be a target', *Workforce*, 78/7: 32–43. Available at: http://www.workforce.com/archive/feature/22/20/88/index.php [accessed 9 January 2010].

Lazarus, R. S. (1966) *Psychological Stress and the Coping Process*. New York: McGraw-Hill.

Lipsky, D. B. and Seeber, R. L. (2000) 'Resolving workplace disputes in the United States: the growth of alternative dispute resolution in employment relations', *Journal of Alternative Dispute Resolution in Employment*, 2/3: 37–49.

Lobel, O. (2009) 'Citizenship, organizational citizenship, and the laws of overlapping obligations', *California Law Review*, 97: 433–99.

McKenna, E. (2006) *Business Psychology and Organisational Behaviour*. Hove: Psychology Press.

Menzel, D. C. (1993) 'Ethics induced stress in the local government workplace', *Public Personnel Management*, 22/4, 523–36.

Mooney, A. C: Holahan, P. J. and Amason, A. C. (2007) 'Don't take it personally: cognitive conflict as a mediator of affective conflict', *Journal of Management Studies*, 44/5: 733–58.

Motowidlo, S. J., Packard, J. S. and Manning, M. R. (1986) 'occupational stress: its causes and consequences for job performance', *Journal of Applied Psychology*, 71(4): 618–29.

Osborne, A. (2009) 'British Airways cabin crews pour vintage wine down sink in protest at changes', *Daily Telegraph*, 12 January: B1.

Parkes, K. R. (1989) 'Personal control in an occupational context', in A. Steptoe and A. Appels (eds) *Stress, Personal Control and Health*. Chichester: Wiley.

Poneman, L. A. (1994) 'Whistle-blowing as an internal control mechanism: individual and organizational considerations', *Auditing: A Journal of Practice and Theory*, 13/2: 118–30.

Quinn, R. E. (1988) *Beyond Rational Management: Managing the paradoxes and competing demands of high performance*. San Francisco: Jossey-Bass.

Schuler, R. S. (1984) 'Organisational stress and coping: a model and overview', in A. S. Sethi and R. S. Schuler (eds) *Handbook of Organizational Stress Coping Strategies*. Cambridge, MA: Ballinger.

Selye, H. (1946) 'The general adaptation syndrome and the diseases of adaptation', *Journal of Clinical Endocrynology*, 6: 117–231.

Selye, H. (1977) *Citation Classics: Classic commentaries: 1977*. Philadelphia, PA: University of Pennsylvania. Online version also available at: http://www.garfield.library.upenn.edu/ classics1977/classics1977.html [accessed 16 Jan 2010].

Sosik, I. J. and Godschalk, V. W. (2000) 'Leadership styles, mentoring functions received and job-related stress: a conceptual model and preliminary study', *Journal of Organizational Behaviour*, 21: 365–90.

Storey, J. (1992) 'HRM in action: the truth is out at last', *Personnel Management*, 24/4: 28–31.

Taylor, H., Fieldman, G. and Altman, Y. (2008) 'E-mail at work: a cause for concern? The implications of the new communication technologies for health, wellbeing and productivity at work', *Journal of Organisational Transformation and Social Change*, 5/2: 159–173.

Thomas, K. W. (1992) 'Conflict and conflict management', in M. D. Dunnett (ed.) *Handbook of Industrial and Organizational Psychology*, 2nd ed. Chicago, IL: Rand McNally.

Thomson, A. W. J. and Murray, V. V. (1976) *Grievance Procedures*. Farnborough: Saxon House.

Tjosvold, D. (2008) 'The conflict-positive organization', *Journal of Organizational Behavior*, 29: 19–28.

Townsend, R. (1985) *Further Up the Organisation*. Philadelphia, PA: Coronet Books.

Tuckman, B. W. (1965) 'Development sequence in small groups', *Psychological Bulletin*, 63: 384–99.

Vandekerckhove, M. and Commers, M. S. R. (2004) 'Whistle blowing and rational loyalty', *Journal of Business Ethics*, 53: 225–33.

Vartia, M. (2001) 'Consequences of workplace bullying with respect to the well-being of its targets and the observers of bullying', *Scandinavian Journal of Work Environment and Health*, 27/1: 63–9.

Wagner, J. A. III and Hollenbeck, J. R. (2010) *Organizational Behavior: Securing competitive advantage*. New York: Routledge.

Walton, R. and McKersie, R. (1965) *A Behavioral Theory of Labor Negotiations*. New York: McGraw-Hill.

Weick, K. E. (1995) *Sensemaking in Organizations*. Thousand Oaks, CA: Sage Publications.

Weick, K. E. (2001) *Making Sense of the Organization*. Malden, MA: Blackwell.

Wharton, A. S. (1996) 'The affective consequences of service work: managing emotions on the job', *Work and Occupations*, 20: 205–32.

Wirtz, W. (1963) Address before national academy of arbitrators. *Daily Labor Report*, 23, 1–4.

Wood, J. (1985) 'Last offer arbitration', *British Journal of Industrial Relations*, 23/3: 415–24.

Chapter 9

Adams, D. A., Todd, P. A. and Nelson, R. (1993) 'A comparative evaluation of the impact of electronic and voice mail on organizational communication', *Information and Management*, 24: 9–21.

Allen, T. J. (1977) *Managing the Flow of Technology*. Cambridge, MA: MIT Press.

Alsop, R. J. (2004) 'Corporate reputation: anything but superficial – the deep but fragile nature of corporate reputation', *Journal of Business Strategy*, 25/6: 21–9.

Bordia, P. (1997) 'Face-to-face versus computer-mediated communication: a synthesis of the experimental literature', *Journal of Business Communication*, 34/1: 99–120.

Bordia, P., Jones, E., Gallois, C., Callan, V. J. and Difonzo, N. (2006) 'Management are aliens', *Group and Organization Management*, 31/5: 601–21.

Cataldo, M. and Herbsleb, J. D. (2008) 'Communication networks in geographically distributed software development', *Proceedings of the ACM 2008 Conference.* San Diego, California.

Clark, H. H. and Wilkes-Gibbs, D. (1986) 'Referring as a collaborative process', *Cognition*, 22: 1–39.

Cranefield, J. and Yoong, P., (2007) 'Interorganisational knowledge transfer: the role of the gatekeeper', *International Journal of Knowledge and Learning*, 3/1: 121–38.

Daft, R. L., Lengel, R. H. and Trevino, L. K. (1987) 'Message equivocality, media selection, and manager performance: implications for information systems', *MIS Quarterly*, 11/3: 355–66.

Finholt, T. and Sproull, L. (1990) 'Electronic groups at work', *Organizational Science*, 1/1: 41–64.

Fornell, C. and Westbrook, R. A. (1984) 'The vicious circle of consumer complaints', *Journal of Marketing*, 48/Summer: 68–73.

Fussell, S. R. and Krauss, R. M. (1992) 'Coordination of knowledge in communication: effects of speaker's assumptions about what others know', *Journal of Personality and Social Psychology*, 6/3: 378–91.

Gibson, C. B. and Gibbs, J. L. (2006) 'Unpacking the concept of virtuality: the effects of geographic dispersion, electronic dependence, dynamic structure, and national diversity on team innovation', *Administrative Science Quarterly*, 51/3: 451–95.

House, R. J. and Aditya, R. N. (1997) 'The social scientific study of leadership: quo vadis?', *Journal of Management*, 23/3: 409–73.

Huber, G. P. and Daft, R. L. (1987) 'The information environments of organizations', in F. M. Jablin, L. L. Putnam, K. H. Roberts and L. W. Porter (eds) *Handbook of Organizational Communication: An interdisciplinary perspective.* Newbury Park, CA: Sage Publications.

Isaacs, E. A. and Clark, H. H. (1987) 'References in conversation between experts and novices', *Journal of Experimental Psychology*: General, 116/1: 26–37.

Lurey, J. S. and Raisinghani, M. S. (2001) 'An empirical study of best practices in virtual teams', *Information & Management*, 38: 523–44.

Markus, M. L. (1992) 'Asynchronous tools in small face-to-face groups', *Information Technology and People*, 6/1: 29–48.

Markus, M. L. (1994) 'Electronic mail as the medium of managerial choice', *Organization Science*, 5/4: 502–27.

McCarthy, G. (2005) 'Leadership practices in German and UK organisations', *Journal of European Industrial Training*, 29/2: 217–34.

Mohr, J. and Nevin, J. R. (1990) 'Communication strategies in marketing channels: a theoretical perspective', *Journal of Marketing*, 54/4: 36–51.

Peppers, D. and Rogers, M. (1993) *The One to One Future: Building relationships one customer at a time.* New York: Doubleday.

Reich, R. (1991) *The Work of Nations: Preparing ourselves for 21st century capitalism.* New York: Knopf.

Rosnow, R. L. (2001) 'Rumor and gossip in interpersonal interaction and beyond: A social exchange perspective', in R. M. Kowalski (ed.) *Behaving Badly: Aversive behaviors in interpersonal relationships.* Washington, D.C.: American Psychological Association.

Schramm, W. (1973) *Men, Messages, and Media: A look at human communication.* New York: Harper & Row.

Townsend, A. M., DeMarie, S. M. and Hendrickson, A. R. (1998) 'Virtual teams: technology and the workplace of the future', *Academy of Management Executive*, 12/3: 17–29.

Trevino, L. K., Lengel, R. H. and Daft, R. L. (1987) 'Media symbolism, media richness, and media choice in organizations: a symbolic interactionist perspective,' *Communication Research*, 14/5: 553–74.

Tushman, M. L. and Katz, R. (1980) 'External communication and project performance: an investigation into the role of gatekeepers', *Management Science*, 26/11: 1071–85.

van der Kleij, R., Lijkwan, J. T. E., Raskera, P. C. and De Dreuc, C. K. W. (2009) 'Effects of time pressure and communication environment on team processes and outcomes in dyadic planning', *International Journal of Human-Computer Studies*, 67/5: 411–23.

Verona, G. (1999) 'A resource-based view of product development', *Academy of Management Review*, 24/1: 132–42.

Windahl, S. and Signitzer, B. (1992) *Using Communication Theory.* London: Sage.

Yu, H. C. and Miller, P. (2005) 'Leadership style: the X generation and baby boomers compared in different cultural contexts', *Leadership and Organization Development Journal*, 26/1: 35–50.

Chapter 10

Barling, J., Weber, T. and Kelloway, E. K. (1996) Effects of transformational leadership training on attitudinal and financial outcomes: a field experiment. *Journal of Applied Psychology*, 81, 827–32.

Bass, B. M. (1985) *Leadership and Performance Beyond Expectations*. New York: Free Press.

Bass, B. M. (1990) From transactional to transformational leadership: learning to share the vision. *Organizational Dynamics*, 18, 19–31.

Bass, B. M. (1997) Does the transactional-transformational leadership paradigm transcend organizational and national boundaries? *American Psychologist*, 52, 130–9.

Blake, R. R. and Mouton, J. S. (1964) *The Managerial Grid*. Houston, TX: Gulf Publishing.

Brown, M. and Treviño, L. (2006) Ethical leadership: a review and future directions. *The Leadership Quarterly*, 17, 595–616.

Collins, D. and Holton, E. (2004) The effectiveness of managerial leadership development programs. *Human Resource Development Quarterly*, 15, 217–48.

Conger, J. A. and Kanungo, R. N. (1987) Toward a behavioral theory of charismatic leadership in organizational settings. *Academy of Management Review*, 12, 637–47.

Dalton, M. A. and Ernst, C. T. (2004) Developing leaders for global roles, in C. D. McCauley and E. Van Velsor (eds) *The Center for Creative Leadership Handbook of Leadership Development*, 2nd ed. San Francisco, California: Jossey-Bass.

Day, D. V. (2000) Leadership development: a review in context. *Leadership Quarterly*, 11, 581–613.

Day, D. V. and Lord, R. G. (1988) Executive leadership and organizational performance: suggestions for a new theory and methodology. *Journal of Management*, 14, 453–64.

DeGroot, T., Kiker, D. S. and Cross, T. C. (2000) A meta-analysis to review organizational outcomes related to charismatic leadership. *Canadian Journal of Administrative Sciences*, 17, 356–71.

Dienesch, R. M. and Liden, R. C. (1986) Leader-member exchange model of leadership: a critique and further development. *Academy of Management Review*, 11, 618–34.

Dvir, T., Eden, D., Avolio, B. J. and Shamir, B. (2002) Impact of transformational leadership on follower development and performance: a field experiment. *Academy of Management Journal*, 735–44.

Fiedler, F. E. (1964) A contingency model of leadership effectiveness, in L. Berkowitz (ed.) *Advances in Experimental Social Psychology*. New York: Academic Press.

Fiedler, F. E. (1967) *A Theory of Leadership Effectiveness*. New York: McGraw-Hill.

Fleishman, E. A. (1953) The description of supervisory behavior. *Personnel Psychology*, 37, 1–6.

Gerstner, C. R. and Day, D. V. (1997) Meta-analytic review of leader-member exchange theory: correlates and construct issues. *Journal of Applied Psychology*, 82, 827–43.

Graeff, C. L. (1997) Evolution of situational leadership theory: a critical review. *Leadership Quarterly*, 8, 153–70.

Graen, G. B. and Scandura, T. A. (1987) Toward a psychology of dyadic organizing. *Research in Organizational Behavior*, 9, 175–208.

Grojean, M., Resick, C., Dickson, M. and Brent Smith, D. (2004) Leaders, values, and organizational climate: examining leadership strategies for establishing an organizational climate regarding ethics. *Journal of Business Ethics*, 55, 223–41.

Groves, K. (2007) Integrating leadership development and succession planning best practices. *Journal of Management Development*, 26, 239–60.

Hackman, J. R. and Wageman, R. (2005) A theory of team coaching. *Academy of Management Review*, 30, 269–87.

Hersey, P. and Blanchard, K. H. (1969) *Management of Organizational Behavior: Utilizing human resources*. Englewood Cliffs, NJ: Prentice Hall.

House, R. J. (1971) A path-goal theory of leader effectiveness. *Administrative Science Quarterly*, 16, 321–39.

House, R. J. (1977) A 1976 theory of charismatic leadership, in J. G. Hunt and L. L. Larson (eds) *Leadership: The cutting edge*. Carbondale: Southern Illinois University Press.

House, R., Javidan, M., Hanges, P. and Dorfman, P. (2002) Understanding cultures and implicit leadership theories across the globe: an introduction to project GLOBE. *Journal of World Business*, 37, 3–10.

House, R. J. and Mitchell T. R. (1974) Path-goal theory of leadership. *Journal of Contemporary Business*, 3, 81–98.

House, R. J., Hanges, P. J., Javidan, M., Dorfman, P. W. and Gupta, N. (eds) (2004) *Culture, Leadership, and Organizations: The GLOBE study of 62 societies*. Thousand Oaks, CA: Sage Publications.

Howell, J. M. and Frost, P. J. (1989) A laboratory study of charismatic leadership. *Organizational Behavior and Human Decision Processes*, 43, 243–69.

IBE (2007) Business ethics committees. *Business Ethics Briefing*, 1–2.

Ilies, R., Nahrgang, J. D. and Morgeson, F. P. (2007) Leader-member exchange and citizenship behaviors: a meta-analysis. *Journal of Applied Psychology*, 92, 269–77.

Judge, T. A. and Bono, J. E. (2000) Five-factor model of personality and transformational leadership. *Journal of Applied Psychology*, 85, 751–65.

Judge, T. A., Bono, J. E., Ilies, R. and Gerhardt, M. W. (2002) Personality and leadership: a qualitative and quantitative review. *Journal of Applied Psychology*, 87, 765–79.

Judge, T. A., Colbert, A. E. and Ilies, R. (2004a) Intelligence and leadership: a quantitative review and test of theoretical propositions. *Journal of Applied Psychology*, 89, 542–52.

Judge, T. A. and Piccolo, R. F. (2004) Transformational and transactional leadership: a meta-analytic test of their relative validity. *Journal of Applied Psychology*, 89, 755–67.

Judge, T. A., Piccolo, R. F. and Ilies, R. (2004b) The forgotten ones? The validity of consideration and initiating structure in leadership research. *Journal of Applied Psychology*, 89, 36–50.

Kark, R., Shamir, B. and Chen, G. (2003) The two faces of transformational leadership: empowerment and dependency. *Journal of Applied Psychology*, 88, 246–54.

Katz, D., Maccoby, N. and Morse, N. (1950) *Productivity, Supervision, and Morale in an Office Situation*. Ann Arbor, MI: Institute for Social Research.

Kerr, S. and Jermier, J. (1978) Substitutes for leadership: their meaning and measurement. *Organizational Behavior and Human Performance*, 22, 375–403.

Kohlberg, L. (1984) *The Psychology of Moral Development: The nature and validity of moral stages*. New York: Harper & Row.

Kotter, J. P. (1990) *A Force for Change: How leadership differs from management*. New York: Free Press.

Liden, R. C., Sparrowe, R. T. and Wayne, S. J. (1997) Leader-member exchange theory: the past and potential for the future. *Research in Personnel and Human Resources Management*, 15, 47–120.

McCauley, C., Drath, W., Palus, C., O'Connor, P. and Baker, B. (2006) The use of constructive-developmental theory to advance the understanding of leadership. *Leadership Quarterly*, 17, 634–53.

McCrae, R. R. and Costa, P. T. (1987) Validation of the five-factor model of personality across instruments and observers. *Journal of Personality and Social Psychology*, 52, 81–90.

Meindl, J. R., Ehrlich, S. B. and Dukerich, J. M. (1985) The romance of leadership. *Administrative Science Quarterly*, 78–102.

Peters, H. L., Hartke, D. D. and Pohlmann, J. T. (1985) Fiedler's contingency theory of leadership: an application of the meta-analysis procedures of Schmidt and Hunter. *Psychological Bulletin*, 97, 274–85.

Pillai, R. and Meindl, J. R. (1998) Context and charisma: a meso-level examination of the relationship of organic structure, collectivism, and crisis to charismatic leadership. *Journal of Management*, 24, 643.

Podsakoff, P. M., MacKenzie, S. B., Ahearne, M. and Bommer, W. H. (1999) Searching for a needle in a haystack: trying to identify the illusive moderators of leadership behaviors. *Journal of Management*, 21, 422–70.

Scandura, T. A. and Graen, G. B. (1984) Moderating effects of initial leader-member exchange status on the effects of a leadership intervention. *Journal of Applied Psychology*, 69, 428–36.

Schriesheim, C. A., Tepper, B. J. and Tetrault, L. A. (1994) Least preferred co-worker score, situational control, and leadership effectiveness: a meta-analysis of contingency model performance predictions. *Journal of Applied Psychology*, 79, 561–73.

Shamir, B., House, R. J. and Arthur, M. B. (1993) The motivational effects of charismatic leadership: a self-concept based theory. *Organization Science*, 577–94.

Stogdill, R. M. (1948) Personal factors associated with leadership: a survey of the literature. *Journal of Psychology*, 25, 35–71.

Stogdill, R. M. (1974) *Handbook of Leadership: A survey of the literature*. New York: Free Press.

Strube, M. J. and Garcia, J. E. (1981) A meta-analytical investigation of Fiedler's contingency model of leadership effectiveness. *Psychological Bulletin*, 90, 307–21.

Weber, M. (1947) *The Theory of Social and Economic Organization* (trans. A. M. Henderson and T. Parsons). New York: Oxford University Press.

Wofford, J. C. and Liska, L. Z. (1993) Path-goal theories of leadership: a meta-analysis. *Journal of Management*, 19, 857–76.

Chapter 11

Adair, J. (2001) *Decision-Making and Problem Solving*. London: Chartered Institute of Personnel and Development.

Adler, N. (2006) 'The arts and leadership: Now that we can do anything, what will we do?', *Academy of Management and Education*, 5/4: 486–99.

Amabile, T. M. (1998) 'How to kill creativity', *Harvard Business Review*, 76/5: 76–87.

Balogun, J. and Hope-Hailey, V. (2004) *Exploring Strategic Change*, 2nd ed. Harlow: *Financial Times*/Prentice Hall.

Bazerman, M. H. and Chugh, D. (2006) 'Decisions without blinders', *Harvard Business Review*, January, 88–97.

Bazerman, M. H., Tenbrunsel, A. E. and Wade-Benzoni, K. (1998) 'Negotiating with yourself and losing: making decisions with competing internal preferences', *Academy of Management Review*, 23/2: 225–41.

Bitner, M. J., Ostrom, A. L. and Morgan, F. N. (2008) 'Service blueprinting: a practical technique for service innovation', *California Management Review*, 50/3: 66–94.

Butler, M. J. R. and Allen, P. (2008) 'Understanding policy implementation processes as self-organizing systems', *Public Management Review*, 10/3: 421–40.

Butler, M. J. R., Sweeney, M. and Crundwell, D. (2009) 'Facility closure management – the case of Vauxhall Motors, Luton', *International Journal of Operations and Production Management*, 29/7: 670–91.

Butler, M. J. R., Wilkinson, J. and Allen, P. (2010) 'Exploring innovation in policy-making within central government: the case of the UK's Highways Agency', *Public Policy and Administration*, 25/2: 137–55.

Davis, J. and Devinney, T. (1997) *The Essence of Corporate Strategy – Theory for Modern Decision-Making*. Australia: Allen & Unwin.

Hammond, J. S., Keeney, R. L. and Raiffa, H. (2006) 'The hidden traps in decision making', *Harvard Business Review*, January, 118–26.

Handy, C. (1993) *Understanding Organizations*, 2nd ed. London: Penguin Books.

Hatch, M. J. (1997) *Organization Theory – Modern Symbolic and Postmodern Perspectives*. Oxford: Oxford University Press.

Hersey, P. and Blanchard, K. H. (2007) *Management of Organizational Behaviour: Utilizing human resources*, 9th ed. London: Prentice Hall.

Janis, I. L. (1982) *Victims of Groupthink*, 2nd ed. Boston, MA: Houghton Mifflin.

Kahneman, D. and Tversky, A. (eds) (2002) *Choices, Values, and Frames*. Cambridge: Cambridge University Press.

Keegan, A. and Turner, J. R. (2002) 'The management of innovation in project-based firms', *Long Range Planning*, 35/4: 367–88.

Lehrer, J. (2009) *The Decisive Moment – How the Brain Makes Up Its Mind*. Edinburgh: Canongate.

Longman New Universal Dictionary (1982) Dictionary. Harlow: Longman Group.

March, J. G. and Simon, H. A. (1958) *Organisations*. New York: John Wiley.

Miller, S. J. and Wilson, D. C. (2006) 'Perspectives on organizational decision making', in S. R. Clegg, C. Hardy, T. B. Lawrence and W. R. Nord (eds) *The Sage Handbook of Organization Studies*. London: Sage.

Mintzberg, H. (1994) *The Rise and Fall of Strategic Planning*. Harlow: *Financial Times*/ Prentice Hall.

Mintzberg, H. and Westley, F. (2001) 'Decision making: it's not what you think', *MIT Sloan Management Review*, 42/3: 89–93.

Mumford, M., Connelly, S., Gaddis, B. and Strange, J. (2002) 'Leading creative people: orchestrating expertise and relationships', *Leadership Quarterly*, 13: 705–50.

Neale, M. A., Tenbrunsel, A. E., Galvin, T. and Bazerman, M. H. (2006) 'A decision perspective on organizations: social cognition, behavioural decision theory and the psychological links to micro- and macro-organizational behaviour', in S. R. Clegg, C. Hardy, T. B. Lawrence, and W. R. Nord (eds) *The Sage Handbook of Organization Studies*. London: Sage.

Russell, P. and Evans, R. (1992) *The Creative Manager – Finding Inner Vision and Wisdom in Uncertain Times*. New York: Jossey-Bass Incorporated.

Sahlin-Andersson, K. and Söderholm, A. (eds) (2002) *Beyond Project Management*. Copenhagen: Liber.

Senior, C. and Butler, M. J. R. (eds) (2007) *The Social Cognitive Neuroscience of Organizations*. Boston: Blackwell.

Senior, C., Lau, A. and Butler, M. J. R. (2007) 'The effects of the menstrual cycle on social decision-making', *International Journal of Psychophysiology*, 63/2: 186–91.

Snowden, D. J. (2002) 'Complex acts of knowing: paradox and descriptive self-awareness', *Journal of Knowledge Management*, Special Edition 6/2: 1–14.

Sydow, J., Lindkvist, L. and DeFillippi, R. (2004) 'Project-based organizations, embeddedness and repositories of knowledge: editorial', *Organization Studies*, 26/9: 1475–89.

Chapter 12

Adorno, T. W., Frenkel-Bruswick, E., Levinson, D. J. and Sanford, R. N. (1950) *The Authoritarian Personality*. New York: Harper & Row.

Allard, M. J. (2002) 'Theoretical underpinnings of diversity' in C. P. Harvey and M. J. Harvey (eds) *Understanding and Managing Diversity: Readings, cases and exercises*, 2nd ed. Harlow: Prentice Hall.

Beechey, V. (1983) 'The sexual division of labour and the labour process: a critical assessment of Braverman', in S. Wood (ed.) *The Degradation of Work: Skill, deskilling and the labour process*. London: Hutchinson.

Brooks, E. (2002) 'The ideal sweatshop? Gender and transnational protest', *International Labour and Working Class History*, 61: 91–111.

Broughton, A. and Strebler, M. (2008) 'Reaping benefits from diversity', *Strategic Human Resource Review*, 7/5: 5–10.

Carr-Ruffino, N. (2007) *Managing Diversity*, 8th ed. Harlow: Pearson.

Chubb, L. and Phillips, L. (2007) 'Commissioner urges employers to take a broader view of diversity', *People Management*, 3/22: 9.

CIPD (2008) *Diversity: An overview*. Available online at http://www.cipd.co.uk/subjects/ dvsequl/general/ divover.htm.

Clifford, D. and Royce, M. (2007) 'Equality, diversity, ethics and management in social work education', *Social Work Education: The International Journal*, Vol.27, No.1: 3–18.

Cornelius, N. (2002) *Building Workplace Equality: Ethics, diversity and inclusion*. London: Thomson.

Cornelius, N., Gooch, L. and Todd, S. (2000) 'Managers leading diversity for business excellence', *Journal of General Management*, 25/3: 67–8.

Cox, T. (1991) 'The multicultural organisation', *Academy of Management Executive*, 5/2: 34–7.

Cox, T. and Blake, S. (1991) 'Managing cultural diversity: implications for organisational competitiveness', *Academy of Management Executive*, 5/3: 45–56.

CRE (2007) *Annual Report 2007*. London: CRE.

Dass, P. and Parker, B. (1999) 'Strategies for managing human resource diversity. From resistance to learning', *Academy of Management Executive*, 13/2: 68–80.

De Cieri, H. and Olekalns, M. (2001) 'Workforce diversity in Australia: challenges and strategies for diversity management'. Working paper. Monash University, Caulfield East, Victoria, Australia.

De Lowernthal, E. (2003) 'Preparing teachers for practicing equal opportunities: a study of leaders of programmes for university teachers with particular reference to race', *Race, Ethnicity and Education*, 6/4: 134–50.

Dibben, P., James, P. and Cunningham, I. (2001) 'Senior management commitment to disability: the influence of legal compulsion and best practice', *Personnel Review*, Vol.30, No.4: 454–67.

Doeringer, P. and Piore, M. (1971) *Internal Labour Markets and Manpower Analysis*. Lexington, Mass: D. C. Heath.

EOC (2006) *Facts about Women and Men*. Manchester: EOC.

EHRC (2008) *Sex and Power*. Available online at http://www.equalityhumanrights.com/uploaded_files/sex_and_power_2008_pdf.pdf.

Gardiner, C. (1992) *Gender and Substitution Theory*. Cambridge: Polity Press.

Giddens, A. (1998) *Sociology*. Cambridge: Polity Press.

Gurr, B. (2009) 'Equality and Human Rights Commission slammed for rehiring staff', *Times* Online. Available at http://www.timesonline.co.uk/tol/news/uk/article/6720688.ece [accessed 20 July 2009].

Hicks-Clarke, D. and Iles, P. (2000) 'Climate for diversity and its effects on career and organisational attitudes and perceptions', *Personnel Review*, 29/3: 324–45.

Iles, P. and Hayers, P. K. (1997) 'Managing diversity in transnational project teams: a tentative model and case study', *Journal of Managerial Psychology*, 12/2: 95–117.

Jackson, C. (2006) 'Feminism spoken here: epistemologies for interdisciplinary development research', *Development and Change*, 37/3: 525–547.

Jackson, S. (1992) 'Consequences of group composition for the interpersonal dynamics of strategic issue processing', in P. Shrivastava, A. Huff and J. Dutton (eds) *Advances in Strategic Management*. Greenwich, CT: JAI Press.

Jewson, N. and Mason, D. (1992) 'The theory and practice of equal opportunities policies: liberal and radical approaches', in P. Braham, A. Rattansi and R. Skellington, (eds), *Racism and Antiracism*. London: Sage, 124–41.

Kandola, R. and Fullerton, J. (1998) *Diversity in Action*, 2nd ed. London: CIPD.

Kirton, G. and Greene, A. (2000) *The Dynamics of Managing Diversity: A critical approach*. London: Butterworth Heinemann.

Kirton, G., Greene, A. and Dean, D. (2007) 'British diversity professionals as change agents – radicals, tempered radicals or liberal reformers?', *International Journal of Human Resource Management*, 18/1: 1979–94.

Knouse, S. B. and Stewart, J. B. (2003) '"Hard" measures that support the business case for diversity: a balanced scorecard approach', *Diversity Factor*, 11/4: 5–6.

Lawrence, E. (2000) 'Equal opportunities officers and managing equality changes', *Personnel Review*, 29/3: 381–401.

Lorbiecki, A. (2001) 'The openings and burdens for women and minority ethnics being vanguards of diversity management'. Paper presented at the Rethinking Gender, Work and Organization Conference, 27–29 June 2001, Keele University.

MacPherson, W. (1999) *The Stephen Lawrence Inquiry: The report of an inquiry*. London: HMSO.

McCloud, P. and Lobel, S. (1992) 'The effects of ethnic diversity on idea generation in small groups'. Paper presented to the Annual Meeting of the Academy of Management, Las Vegas. Cited in Richard, O. (2000) 'Racial diversity, business strategy and firm performance: a resource-based view', *Academy of Management Journal*, 43/2: 164–77.

Modood, T., Berthoud, R., Lakey, J., Nazroo, J., Smith, P., Virdee, S. and Beishon, S. (1997) *Ethnic Minorities in Britain*. London: Policy Studies Institute.

Morrison, A. M. (1992) *The New Leaders: Guidelines on leadership diversity in America*. San Francisco: Jossey-Bass.

Neal, S. (1998) *The Making of Equal Opportunities Policies in Universities*. Buckingham: Open University Press.

Ngo, H., Foley, S., Wong, A. and Loi, R. (2003) 'Who gets more of the pile? Predictors of perceived gender inequity at work', *Journal of Business Ethics*, 45/3: 227–41.

Niven, B. (2008) 'The EHRC: transformational, progressively incremental or a disappointment?', *The Political Quarterly*, 79/ 1: 17–26.

Oakley, A. (1981) *Subject Women*. Oxford: Martin Robertson.

Parker, S., Naylor P. and Warmington, P. (2004) 'Widening participation in higher education: what we can learn from the ideologies and practices of committed practitioners', *Journal of Access and Policy and Practice*, 2/2: 140–160.

Parsons, E. (2008) 'Right on!', *Community Care*, 1729: 30.

Price, A. (2004) *Human Resource Management in a Business Context*, 2nd ed. London: Thomson.

Patrickson, M. and O'Brien, P. (2001) *ManagingDiversity: An Asian and Pacific focus*. Brisbane: John Wiley.

Pfeffer, J. (1994) *Competitive Advantage through People*. Boston: Harvard University Press.

Rees, T. (1999) *Women and Work: 25 years of gender equality in Wales*. Cardiff: University of Wales Press.

Richard, O. (2000) 'Racial diversity, business strategy and firm performance: a resource-based view', *Academy of Management Journal*, 43/2: 164–77.

Ross, R. and Schneider, R. (1992) *From Equality to Diversity*. London: Pitman.

Rossett, A. and Bickham, T. (1994) 'Diversity training: hope, faith and cynicism', *Training*, 31/1: 41–6.

Saunderson, W. (2002) 'Women, academia and identity: constructions of equal opportunities in the 'new managerialism' – a case of lipstick on the gorilla', *Higher Education Quarterly*, 56/4: 376–406.

Spencer, S. (2008) 'Equality and the Human Rights Commission: a decade in the making', *The Political Quarterly*, 79/2: 6–16.

Thompson, P. and McHugh, D. (2002) *Work Organisations*, 3rd ed. Houndmills: Palgrave.

Torrington, D., Hall, L. and Taylor, S. (2007) *Human Resource Management*. 7th ed. Harlow: Financial Times/ Prentice Hall.

Townsend, S. and Wilner, T. (2009) 'Equality body considers revamp' *http://www.britannica.com/bps/ additionalcontent/18/43878545/Equality-body-considers-revamp*.

Warner, D. and Crosthwaite, E. (1993) 'Human resource management in higher education', *Current Business Research*, Vol.1, No.3: 48–70.

Walsh, V. (2002) 'Equal opportunities without 'equality': redeeming the irredeemable', in G. Howie and A. Tauchert (eds), *Gender, Teaching and Research in Higher Education: Challenges for the 21st Century*. Aldershot: Ashgate.

Chapter 13

Argyris, C. (2006) *Reasons and Rationalizations: The limits to organizational knowledge*. Oxford: Oxford University Press.

Baldry, C., Bain, P. and Taylor, P. (1998) 'Bright satanic offices: intensification, control, and team Taylorism', in P. Thompson and C. Warhurst (eds) *Workplaces of the Future*. London: Macmillan.

Blauner, R. (1964) *Alienation and Freedom*. Chicago: University of Chicago Press.

Bowen, D. E. and Lawler, E. E. (1992) 'Theempowerment of service workers: what, why, how, and when', *Sloan Management Review*, 33/3: 31–39.

Brooks, I. (2009) *Organisational Behaviour: individuals, groups and organisation*. 4th ed. Harlow: FT Prentice Hall.

Buchanan, D. and Badham, R. (2008) *Power, Politics and Organizational Change: Winning the turf game*. London: Sage.

Burawoy, M. (1979) *Manufacturing Consent: Changes in the labour process under monopoly capitalism*. Chicago: University of Chicago Press.

Callaghan, G. and Thompson, P. (2001) 'Edwards revisited: technical control and call centres', *Economic and Industrial Democracy*, 22/1: 13–37.

Child, J. (1984) *Organisation: A guide to problems and practice*. London: Harper and Row.

Child, J. and Faulkner, D. (1998) *Strategies of Co-operation: Managing alliances, networks and joint ventures*. Oxford: Oxford University Press.

Clegg, S. R., Courpasson, D. and Philips, N. (2006) *Power and Organisations*. London: Sage.

Clegg, S., Kornberger, M. and Pitsis, T. (2008) *Managing and Organisations*. London: Sage.

Conger, J. A. and Pearce, C. L. (2009) 'Using empowerment to motivate people to engage in effective self- and shared leadership' in E. A. Locke (ed.) *Handbook of Principles of Organizational Behaviour*. 2nd ed. Chichester: Wiley.

Datamonitor (2009) *2010 Trends to Watch: Customer relationship outsourcing.* Manchester: Datamonitor.

Deery, S., Iverson, R. and Walsh, J. (2004) 'The effect of customer service encounters on job satisfaction and emotional exhaustion', in S. Deery and N. Kinnie (eds) *Call Centres and Human Resource Management: A cross national perspective.* Houndmills: Palgrave.

Edwards, R. (1979) *Contested Terrain: The transformation of the workplace in the twentieth century.* London: Heinemann.

Fayol, H. (1949) *General and Industrial Management.* London: Pitman.

Fernie, S. and Metcalf, D. (1998) *Not Hanging on the Telephone: Payment systems in the new sweatshops.* London: Centre for Economic Performance, LSE.

Foucault, M. (1979) *Discipline and Punish: The birth of the prison.* London: Penguin.

French, J. P. and Raven, B. (1986) 'The bases of social power', in D. Cartwright and A. E. Zander (eds) *Group Dynamics: Research and theory.* New York: Harper and Row.

French, R., Rayner, C., Rees, G. and Rumbles, S. (2009) *Organisational Behaviour.* Chichester: John Wiley.

Frenkel, S., Korczynski, M., Shire, K. and Tam, M. (1999) *On the Front Line: Organisation of work in the information economy.* Ithaca, NY: ILR.

Frenkel, S., Tam, M., Korczynski, M. and Shire, K. (1998) 'Beyond bureaucracy? Work organisation in call centres', *International Journal of Human Resource Management*, 9/6: 958–979.

Gerth, H. and Mills, C. W. (1976) 'Power and authority', in L. A. Coser and B. Rosenberg (eds) *Sociological Theory: A book of readings.* pp148–150. London: Collier Macmillan.

Gerth, H. and Mills, C. W. (2009) *From Max Weber: Essays in sociology.* London: Routledge.

Goldsmith, A., Nickson, D., Sloan, D. and Wood, R. C. (2002) *Human Resource Management for Hospitality Services.* London: Thomson Learning.

Hales, C. and Kildas, A. (1998) 'Empowerment in five-star hotels: choice, voice or rhetoric?', *International Journal of Contemporary Hospitality Management*, 10/3: 88–95.

Hardy, C. (2005) 'Understanding power: bringing about strategic change', *British Journal of Management*, 17/1: 3–16.

Hicks, H. G. and Gullett, C. R. (1977) *The Management of Organisations.* 3rd ed. Irwin, CA: McGraw Hill.

Hill, S. (1981) *Competition and Control at Work.* London: Heinemann.

Hochschild, A. R. (1983) *The Managed Heart: The commercialisation of human feeling.* Berkeley: University of California Press.

Hollinshead, G., Nicholls, P. and Tailby, S. (2003) *Employee Relations.* 2nd ed. Harlow: FT Prentice Hall.

Houghton, J. D., Neck, C. P. and Manz, C. C. (2003) 'Self-leadership and super leadership: the heart and art of creating shared leadership in teams', in C. L. Pearce and J. A. Conger (eds) *Shared Leadership: Reframing the hows and whys of leadership.* Thousand Oaks, CA: Sage Publications.

Hyman, J. and Mason, B. (1995) *Managing Employee Involvement and Participation.* London: Sage.

Lashley, C. (2001) *Empowerment: HR strategies for service excellence.* Oxford: Butterworth Heinemann.

Longhi, S. and Platt, L. (2008) *Pay Gaps across Equalities Areas.* London: Equality and Human Rights Commission.

Luthans, F. (2006) *Organisational Behaviour.* 11th ed. Irwin, CA: McGraw-Hill.

Mayes, B. T. and Allen, R. W. (1977) 'Towards a definition of organisational politics', *Academy of Management Review*, 2/4: 674–678.

Morgan, G. (1996) *Images of Organisation.* Newbury Park, CA: Sage.

Mullins, L. (2006) *Essentials of Organisational Behaviour.* Harlow: FT Prentice Hall.

Owen, J. (2007) *Power at Work: The art of making things happen.* Harlow: Pearson.

Pearce, C. L. and Conger, J. A. (2003) *Shared Leadership: Reframing the hows and whys of leadership.* Thousand Oaks, CA: Sage.

Pettigrew, A. (2002) 'Strategy formulation as a political process', in S. R. Clegg (ed.) *Central Currents in Organisation Studies.* London: Sage.

Pfeffer, J. (1992) *Managing with Power: Politics and influence in organisations.* Boston, MA: Harvard Business School Press.

Rose, E. (2002) 'The labour process and union commitment within a banking services call centre', *The Journal of Industrial Relations*, 44/1: 40–62.

Rose, E. (2008) *Employment Relations*. 3rd ed. Harlow: FT Prentice Hall.

Rose, E. (2009) *Control, Alienation, Commitment and Satisfaction Amongst Call Centre Workers*. Unpublished doctoral thesis. Liverpool: Liverpool J.M. University.

Rose, E. and Wright, G. (2005) 'Satisfaction and dimensions of control among call centre customer service representatives', *International Journal of Human Resource Management*, 16/1: 139–163.

Russell, B. (2008) 'Call centres: a decade of research', *International Journal of Management Reviews*, 10/3: 195–219.

Spreitzer, G. M. (1995) 'Individual empowerment in the workplace: dimensions, measurement, and validation', *Academy of Management Journal*, 38/3: 1442–1465.

Tawney, R. H. (1931) *Equality*. London: Allen and Unwin.

Taylor, P. and Bain, P. (2007) 'Reflections on the call centre – a reply to Glucksman', *Work, Employment and Society*, 21/ 2: 349–362.

Thompson, P. and McHugh, D. (2002) *Work Organisations*. 3rd ed. Houndmills: Palgrave.

Weber, M. (1947) *The Theory of Social and Economic Organisation*. New York: Oxford University Press.

Wilkinson, A. (1998) 'Empowerment: theory and practice', *Personnel Review*, 27/ 1: 40–56.

Wright, E. O. (1976) 'Class boundaries in advanced capitalist societies,' *New Left Review*, 1/ 98: 23–31.

Yukl, G. l. and Falbe, C. M. (1992) 'Consequences for managers of using single influence tactics and combinations of tactics', *Academy of Management Journal*, 35/3: 638–652.

Chapter 14

Albrow, M. (1994) 'Accounting for organisational feeling', in L. Ray and M. Reed (eds) *Organizing Modernity*. London: Routledge.

Albrow, M. (1997) *Do Organisations have Feeling?* London: Routledge.

Atkinson, J. (1984) 'Manpower strategies for flexible organisations', *Personnel Management*, August.

Baldry, C., Bain, P. and Taylor, P. (1998) 'Bright satanic offices: intensification, control and team Taylorism', in P. Thompson and C. Warhurst (eds) *Workplaces of the Future*. Basingstoke: Macmillan.

Baldry, C., Bain, P., Taylor, P., Hyman, J., Scholarios, D., Marks, A., Watson, A., Gilbert, K., Gall, G. and Bunzel, D. (2007) *The Meaning of Work in the New Economy*. Basingstoke: Palgrave Macmillan.

Bell, D. (1976) *The Coming of Post Industrial Society: A venture in social forecasting*, 2nd ed. London: Penguin.

Beynon, H. (1975) *Working for Ford*. Wakefield: E. P. Publishing.

Blauner, R. (1964) *Alienation and Freedom: The factory worker and his industry*. Chicago: University of Chicago Press.

Bolton, S. (2005) *Emotion Management in the Workplace*. Basingstoke: Palgrave Macmillan.

Boreham, P. (1992) 'The myth of post-Fordist management: work organisation and employee discretion in seven countries', *Employee Relations*, 14/2: 13–24.

Boxall, P. and Purcell, J. (2003) *Strategy and Human Resource Management*. Basingstoke: Palgrave Macmillan.

Bradley, H., Erickson, M., Stephenson, C. and Williams, S. (2000) *Myths at Work*. Cambridge: Polity Press.

Braverman, H. (1974) *Labor and Monopoly Capital: The degradation of work in the twentieth century*. New York: Monthly Review Press.

Burawoy, M. (1985) *The Politics of Production*. London: New Left Books.

Burnes, B. (2004) *Managing Change*, 4th ed. Harlow: FT/Prentice Hall.

Burns, T. and Stalker, G. M. (1961) *The Management of Innovation*. London: Tavistock.

Chandler, A. D. (1962) *Strategy and Structure: Chapters in the history of the industrial enterprise*. Cambridge, MA: MIT Press.

Cocco, M. (2008) 'The Starbucks culture', *Washington Post*, 24 July.

Coriat, B. (1992) 'The revitalization of mass consumption in the computer age', in M. Storper and A. J. Scott (eds) *Pathways to Industrialization and Regional Development*. New York: Routledge.

Cornforth, C., Thomas, A., Lewis, J. and Spear, R. (1988) *Developing Successful Worker Cooperatives*. London: Sage.

Crouch, C., Finegold, D. and Sako, M. (1999) *Are Skills the Answer? The political economy of skill creation in advanced industrial countries*. Oxford: Oxford University Press.

De Sanctis, G. and Monge, P. (1999) 'Introduction to the Special Issue: Communication processes for virtual organizations', *Organization Science*, 10/6: 693–703.

Despres, C. and Hiltrop, J. (1995) 'Human resource management in the information age: current practices and perspectives on the future', *Employee Relations*, 17/1: 9–23.

Du Gay, P. (2000) *In Praise of Bureaucracy: Weber-Organization-Ethics*. London: Sage.

Edgell, S. (2006) *The Sociology of Work*. London: Sage.

Felstead, A., Gallie, D., Green, F. and Zhou, Y. (2007) *Skills at Work 1986–2006*. Oxford: Economic and Social Research Council.

Fineman, S. (ed.) (2000) *Emotions in Organizations*, 2nd ed. London: Sage.

Fineman, S. (2003) *Understanding Emotions at Work*. London: Sage.

Flecker, J. and Hofbauer, J. (1998) 'Capitalising on subjectivity: the new 'model worker' and the importance of being useful', in P. Thompson and C. Warhurst (eds) *Workplaces of the Future*. Basingstoke: Macmillan.

Fontaine, C. W. (2007) *Organizational Structure: A critical factor for organizational effectiveness and employee satisfaction*. Boston, MA: Northeastern University.

General Motors (2010) *Company Profile*. Available online at http://www.gm.com/corporate/ about/company.jsp.

Ghoshal, S. and Noria, N. (1993) 'Horses for courses: organizational forms for multinational corporations', *Sloan Management Review*, 34/2: 23–35.

Gilmore, S. and Williams, S. (2009) *Human Resource Management*. Oxford: Oxford University Press.

Goos, M. and Manning, A. (2003) 'McJobs and MacJobs: the growing polarisation of jobs in the UK', in R. Dickens, P. Gregg and J. Wadsworth (eds) *The Labour Market Under New Labour*. Basingstoke: Palgrave.

Goos, M. and Manning, A. (2007) 'Lovely and lousy jobs: the rising polarisation of work in Britain', *Review of Economics and Statistics*, 89/1: 118–33.

Gouldner, A. W. (1954) *Wildcat Strike*. New York: Harper & Row.

Gouldner, A. W. (1954a) *Patterns of Industrial Bureaucracy*. New York: Free Press.

Green, F. (2006) *Demanding Work: The paradox of job quality in the affluent economy*. Princeton, NJ: Princeton University Press.

Grey, C. (2009) *A Very Short, Fairly Interesting and Reasonably Cheap Book About Studying Organizations*, 2nd ed. London: Sage.

Handy, C. (2002) *The Age of Unreason*, New ed. London: Random House.

Hochschild, A. R. (1983) *The Managed Heart: Commercialisation of human feelings*. Berkeley, CA: University of California Press.

Hofstede, G. (1993) 'Cultural constraints in management theories', *Academy of Management Executive*, 7/1: 81–94.

Huczynski, A. (2004) *Influencing Within Organisations*, 2nd ed. London: Routledge.

Hurrell, S. A. (2009) *Soft Skills Deficits in Scotland: Their patterns, determinants and employer responses*. Unpublished Doctoral Thesis. Glasgow: University of Strathclyde.

International Co-operative Alliance (2004) *The Present Application of the Rochdale Principles of Co-Operation (1937)*. Available online at http://www.ica.coop/coop/1937-02.html.

Jenkins, S., Delbridge, R. and Roberts, A. (2010) 'Emotional management in a mass customized call-centre: examining skill and knowledgeability in interactive service work', *Work, Employment and Society*, 24/3: 546–64.

Kalleberg, A. L. (2000) 'Nonstandard employment relations: part-time, temporary and contract work', *Annual Review of Sociology*, 26: 341–65.

Kanigel, R. (1997) *The One Best Way: Frederick Winslow Taylor and the enigma of efficiency*. New York: Penguin.

Kelly, J. and Kelly, C. (1991) '"Them and us": social psychology and the new industrial relations', *British Journal of Industrial Relations*, 34/4: 515–38.

Kersley, B., Alpin, C., Forth, J., Bryson, A., Bewley, H., Dix, G. and Oxenbridge, S. (2006) *Inside the Workplace: Findings from the 2004 Workplace Employment Relations Survey*. London: Routledge.

Korczynski, M. (2002) *Human Resource Management in Service Work*. Basingstoke: Palgrave.

Lambert, D. M., Stock, J. R. and Elram, L. M. (1998) *Fundamentals of Logistics Management*. Boston, MA: McGraw-Hill.

Legge, K. (2007) 'Networked organisations and the negation of HRM?', in J. Storey (ed.) *Human Resource Management: A critical text*, 3rd ed. London: Thomson.

Leidner, R. (1993) *Fast Food, Fast Talk*. Berkeley, CA: University of California Press.

Marx, K. and Engels, F. (2004) *The Communist Manifesto*, first published 1848. London: Penguin.

Merton, R. (1957) *Social Theory and Social Structure*. Glencoe, IL: Free Press.

Mintzberg, H. (1980) 'Structure in 5's: a synthesis of the research on organization design', *Management Science*, 6/3: 322–41.

Noon, M. and Blyton, P. (2007) *The Realities of Work*, 3rd ed. Basingstoke: Palgrave Macmillan.

Ouchi, W. D. and Dowling, J. B. (1974) 'Defining the span of control', *Administrative Science Quarterly*, 193: 357–65.

Parsons, T. (1947) 'The author and his career', in T. Parsons (ed.) *Max Weber: The theory of social and economic organisation*. New York: Free Press.

Penn, M. J. and Zalesne, E. K. (2007) *Microtrends: Surprising tales of the way we live today*. New York: Penguin.

Piore, M. J. (1986) 'Perspectives on labour market flexibility', *Industrial Relations Journal*, 25/2: 146–66.

Piore, M. J. and Sabel, C. F. (1984) *The Second Industrial Divide: Possibilities for prosperity*. New York: Basic Books.

Reich, R. (1992) *The Work of Nations: Preparing ourselves for 21st century capitalism*. New York: Vintage Books.

Ritzer, G. (2004) *The McDonaldization of Society*, Revised new century edition. Thousand Oaks, CA: Pine Forge Press.

Robinson, A. and Perotic, V. (1997) 'Is profit sharing the answer?', *New Economy*, 4: 112–16.

Rollinson, D. (2001) 'Globalisation and the cross-national organisation', in D. Rollinson and A. Broadfield (eds) *Organisational Behaviour and Analysis: An integrated approach*, 2nd ed. London: FT/Prentice Hall.

Scarbrough, H. (1996) *The Management of Expertise*. Basingstoke: Macmillan.

Smith, A. (1776) *An Inquiry into the Nature and Causes of the Wealth of Nations*. London: Strahan & Caddell.

Statistical Indicators Benchmarking, the Information Society (SIBIS) (2003) *Work, Employment and Skills*: Topic Report No.5. Bonn: Empirica.

Stewart, P., Richardson, M., Danford, A., Richardson, T. and Wass, V. (2009) *We Sell Our Time No More: Workers' struggles against lean production in the British car industry*. London: Pluto Press.

Taylor, F. W. (1947) *Scientific Management*. New York: Harper & Row.

Taylor, P. and Bain, P. (1999) '"An assembly-line in the head": work and employee relations in the call centre', *Industrial Relations Journal*, 30/2: 101–17.

Taylor, P. and Bain, P. (2000) 'Entrapped by the electronic panopticon? Worker resistance in the call centre', *New Technology Work and Employment*, 15/1: 2–18.

Warhurst, C. and Thompson, P. (1998) 'Hands, hearts and minds: changing work and workers at the end of the century', in P. Thompson and C. Warhurst (eds) *Workplaces of the Future*. Basingstoke: Macmillan.

Weber, M. (1947) 'The types of authority and imperative co-ordination', in T. Parsons (ed.) *Max Weber: The theory of social and economic organisation*. New York: Free Press.

Wilson, F. (2010) *Organizational Behaviour and Work: A critical introduction*, 3rd ed. Oxford: Oxford University Press.

Wood, G., Szamosi, L. T. and Psychogios, A. (2009) 'International HRM', in T. Redman and A. Wilkinson *Contemporary Human Resource Management*, 3rd ed. Harlow: FT/Prentice Hall.

Womack, J. and Jones, D. (1996) *Lean Thinking*. New York: Simon & Schuster.

67

Chapter 15

Ackroyd, S. and Crowdy, P. A. (1990) Can culture be managed? Working with 'raw' material: the case of English slaughtermen, *Personnel Review*, 19(5), 3–13.

Agence France-Presse (AFP) (2009) Jaguar Land Rover workers accept four-day week and pay freeze to avoid job cuts. *Daily Telegraph*, 5 March.

Anderson, N. and Ostroff, C. (1997) 'Selection as socialisation', in N. Anderson and P. Herriot, *The International Handbook of Selection and Assessment*. Chichester: John Wiley & Sons.

Barclays Plc (2010) *Our Vision and Strategy*. http://group.barclays.com/About-us/Who-we-are-and-what-we-do/Our-vision-and-strategy [accessed 5 May 2010].

Bligh, M. C. (2006) Surviving post-merger 'culture clash'. Can cultural leadership lessen the casualties? *Leadership*, 2(4), 395–426.

Brannan, M. J., Parsons, E. and Priola, V. (2011) *Branded Lives: Identity and work in the era of the brand*. Cheltenham: Edward Elgar.

Brannan, M. J. and Priola, V. (2009) 'Girls who do boys like they're girls'? Exploring the role of gender in the junior management of contemporary service work, *Gender, Work and Organization*, December.

Brown, A. (1998) *Organizational Culture*, 2nd ed. Harlow: FT/Prentice Hall.

Burke, R. J. and Cooper, C. L. (2000) The new organizational reality: transition and renewal, in R. J. Burke and C. L. Cooper (eds) *The Organization in Crisis: Downsizing, restructuring and privatization*. Oxford: Blackwell.

Burnes, B. (2004) *Managing Change*, 4th ed. London: FT/Prentice Hall.

Bygren, M. and Kumlin, J. (2005) Mechanisms of organizational sex segregation, *Work and Occupations*, 32(1), 39–65.

Carnall, C. A. (2003) 'Managing complexity', in *Managing Change in Organizations*, 4th ed. London: FT/Prentice Hall.

Child, J. (1997) Strategic choice in the analysis of action, structure, organizations and environment: retrospect and prospect, *Organization Studies*, 18(1), 43–76.

Cropanzano, R. and Prehar, C. A. (2001) 'Emerging justice concerns in an era of changing psychological contracts', in R. Cropanzano (ed.) *Justice in the Workplace: From theory to practice*, Vol.2. London: Lawrence Erlbaum Associates.

Cummings, T. G. and Worley, C. G. (2005) 'The organizational development practitioner', in *Organization Development and Change*, 8th ed. Mason, OH: South-Western.

Deal, T. and Kennedy, A. (1982) Culture: a new look through old lenses, *Journal of Applied Behavioural Science*, 19(4), 497–507.

De Tienne, K. B. and Lewis, L. W. (2005) The pragmatic and ethical barriers to corporate social responsibility disclosure: the Nike case, *Journal of Business Ethics*, 60, 359–76.

Drennan, D. (1992) *Transforming Company Culture*. London: McGraw-Hill.

European Foundation for the Improvement of Living and Working Conditions (EFILWC) (2009) *Social Dialogue and the Recession*. Dublin: EFILWC.

Fox, A. (1974) *Beyond Contract: Work power and trust relations*. London: Faber.

Gatrell, C. J. and Swan S. E. (2008) *Gender and Diversity in Management: A concise introduction*. London: Sage.

Guest, D. E. and Conway, N. (2002) Communicating the psychological contract: an employer perspective. *Human Resource Management Journal*, 12(2), 22–38.

Guidroz, A. M., Kotrba, L. M. and Denison, D. R. (2009) Workplace diversity. Is national or organizational culture predominant? Linkageinc.com – Denison Consulting, LLC, http://www.linkageinc.com/thinking/linkageleader/Documents/Denison_Consulting_Workplace_Diversity_Is_National_or_Organizational_Culture_Predominant.pdf [accessed 10 May 2010].

Hamel, G. and Prahalad, C. K. (1994) Competing for the future. *Harvard Business Review*, Jul/Aug, 122–8.

Hampden-Turner, C. and Trompenaars, A. (1993) *The Seven Cultures of Capitalism*. New York: Currency Doubleday.

Hatch, M. J. (2006) *Organization Theory: Modern, symbolic, and postmodern perspectives*, 2nd ed. Oxford: Oxford University Press.

Herriot, P. and Pemberton, S. (1997) Facilitating new deals. *Journal of Human Resource Management*, 7(1), 45–56.

Hofstede, G. (1980) *Cultures Consequences: International differences in work related values*. Beverly Hills, CA: Sage Publications.

Hofstede, G. (1990) 'The cultural relativity of organisational practices and theories', in R. Wilson and R. Rosenfeld (eds) *Managing Organizations: Texts, readings and cases*. Maidenhead: McGraw-Hill.

Hofstede, G. (1993) Cultural constraints in management theories. *Academy of Management Executive*, 7/1: 81–94.

Hofstede, G. (2002) Dimensions do not exist: a reply to Brendan McSweeney. *Human Relations*, 55/11: 1–7.

Hopfl, H. (1992) The challenges of change: the theory and practice of organisational transformation. Paper presented to the Employment Research Unit Annual Conference, Cardiff University, September.

Hughes, M. (2006) *Change Management: A critical perspective*. London: CIPD.

Hurley, R. F., Church, A. H., Burke, W. W. and Van Eynde, D. F. (1992) Tension, change and values in OD. *OD Practitioner*, 29(3), 1–5.

Janssens, M. and Zanoni, P. (2005) Many diversities for many services. Theorising diversity (management) in service companies. *Human Relations*, 58(3), 311–40.

Kanter, R. M., Stein, B. A. and Jick, T. D. (1992) *The Challenge of Organisational Culture*. New York: Free Press.

Kersley, B., Alpin, C., Forth, J., Bryson, A., Bewley, H., Dix, G. and Oxenbridge, S. (2006) *Inside the Workplace: Findings from the 2004 Workplace Employment Relations Survey*. London: Routledge.

Kieser, A. (1993) Review of Geert Hofstede, 'Culture and organizations: software of the mind'. *Organization Studies*, 14(1), 85–8.

Kotter, J. P. and Heskett, J. L. (1992) *Corporate Culture and Performance*. New York: Free Press.

Kübler-Ross, E. (1973) *On Death and Dying*. New York: Macmillan Routledge.

Legge, K. (1994) 'Managing culture: fact or fiction', in K. Sisson (ed.) *Personnel Management: A comprehensive guide to theory and practice in Britain*. Oxford: Blackwell.

Lewin, K. (1947) 'Frontiers in group dynamics', in D. Cartwright (ed.) (1952) *Field Theory in Social Science*. London: Social Science Paperbacks.

Linstead, S., Fulop, L. and Lilley, S. (2009) *Management and Organization. A critical text*, 2nd ed. London: Palgrave Macmillan.

Louis, M. R. (1980) 'Organizations as culture-bearing milieux', in Pondy, L. R., Frost, P. J., Morgan, G. and Dandridge, T. C. (eds) *Organizational Symbolism*. Greenwich, CT: JAI Press.

Martin, J. (1992) *Cultures in Organizations. Three perspectives*. Oxford: Oxford University Press.

Maume, D. J. (1999) Glass ceiling and glass escalators. *Work and Occupations*, 26(4), 483–509.

Miles, S. J. and Mangold, W. G. (2004) 'A conceptualization of the employee branding process', *Journal of Relationship Marketing*, 3(2/3), 65–87.

Miles, R. E. and Snow, C. C. (1978) *Organizational Strategy, Structure and Process*. New York: McGraw-Hill.

Morgan, D. E. and Zeffane, R. (2003) Employee involvement, organizational change and trust in management. *International Journal of Human Resource Management*, 14(1), 55–75.

Morgan, G. (1986) *Images of Organization*. London: Sage.

Muzio, D., Ackroyd, S. and Chanlat, J.-F. (2007) 'Redirections in the study of expert labour: lawyers, doctors and business consultants', in D. Muzio, S. Ackroyd and J.-F. Chanlat, *Redirections in the Study of Expert Labour: Established professions and new expert occupations*. Basingstoke: Palgrave Macmillan.

National Audit Office (NAO) (2008) *Increasing Employment Rates for Ethnic Minorities*. London: The Stationery Office.

Ogbonna, E. and Wilkinson, B. (1990) Corporate strategy and corporate culture: the view from the checkout. *Personnel Review*, 19(4), 9–15.

Ouchi, W. G. (1981) *Theory Z*. Reading, Mass.: Addison-Wesley.

Parker, M. (2000) *Organizational Culture and Identity. Unity and Division at Work*. London: Sage.

Pascale, R. T. (1985) The paradox of "corporate culture": reconciling ourselves to socialization. *California Management Review*, 27(2), 26–41.

Peters, T. and Waterman. R. (1982) *In Search of Excellence*. New York: Warner Communications.

Priola, V. (2009) 'Masculinity and femininity', in Mills, A., Durepos, G. and Wiebe, E. (eds) *Sage Encyclopedia of Case Study Research*. London: Sage.

Priola, V. and Brannan, M. J. (2009) Between a rock and a hard place: exploring women's experiences of participation and progress in managerial careers. *Equal Opportunities International*, 28(5), 378–97.

Ray, C. A. (1986) Corporate culture: the last frontier of control? *Journal of Management Studies*, 23(3), 287–97.

Rogers, C. R. (1967) *On Becoming a Person: A therapist's view of psychotherapy*. London: Constable.

Rollinson, D. (2005) 'Organisational change and development', in D. Rollinson, *Organisational Behaviour and Analysis*: *An integrated approach*, 3rd ed. London: FT/Prentice Hall.

Schein, E. H. (1985) *Organizational Culture and Leadership: A dynamic view*. San Francisco: Jossey-Bass.

Schein, E. (1990) 'Organizational culture', *American Psychologist*, 45(2), 109–119.

Schein, E. H. (1996) Kurt Lewin's change theory in the field and in the classroom: notes towards a model of management learning. *Systems Practice*, 9(1), 27–47.

Schwarts, H. and Davies, S. M. (1981) Matching corporate culture and business strategy. *Organizational Dynamics*, 10, 30–48.

Senge, P. (1990) *The Fifth Discipline: The art and practice of the learning organisation*. London: Random House.

Siehl, C. and Martin, J. (1984) 'The role of symbolic management: how can managers effectively transmit organizational culture?', in J. Hunt, D. Hosking, C. Schreisheim, and R. Stewart (eds) *Leaders and Managers: International perspectives on managerial behavior and leadership*. New York: Pergamon Press.

Sinclair, A. (1991) After excellence: models of organisational culture for the public sector. *Australian Journal of Public Administration*, 50(3), 321–32.

Smircich, L. (1983) Concepts of culture and organizational analysis. *Administrative Science Quarterly*, 28(3), 339–58.

Smith, P. R. (1999) *Strategic Marketing Communication. New ways to build and integrate communication*. London: Kogan Page

Søndergaard, M. (1994) Hofstede's 'Consequences': a study of reviews, citations and replications. *Organization Studies*, 15(3), 447–56.

Spencer, S. and Adams, A. (1990) *Life Changes: Growing through personal transitions*. New York: Paraview.

Stiles, P., Gratton, L., Truss, C., Hope-Hailey, V. and McGovern, P. (1997) Performance management and the psychological contract. *Journal of Human Resource Management*, 7(1), 57–66.

Stuart, R. (1995) Experiencing organisational change: triggers, processes and outcomes of change journeys. *Personnel Review*, 24(2), 3–87.

Tannenbaum, R. and Hanna, R. W. (1985) 'Holding on, letting go, and moving on: understanding a neglected perspective on change', in R. Tannenbaum, N. Margulies and F. Massarik (eds) *Human Systems Development*. San Francisco: Jossey-Bass.

Thompson, P. and McHugh, D. (2002) *Work Organisations*, 3rd ed. Basingstoke: Palgrave Macmillan.

Unite (2009) Jaguar job cuts underline urgency of support for the industry. Press release: available online at http://www.unitetheunion.com/news__events/latest_news/ jaguar_job_cuts_underline_urge.aspx

Weber, M. (1947) 'The types of authority and imperative co-ordination', in A. M. Henderson and T. Parsons (eds) *The Theory of Social and Economic Organisation*. New York: Free Press.

Weick, K. (1987) Organizational culture as a source of high reliability. *California Management Review*, 39(2), 112–27.

Weiss, J. W. (2001) *Organizational Behavior and Change: Managing diversity, cross-cultural diversity and ethics*. Cincinnati: Thomson Learning.

Williams, A., Dobson, P. and Walters, M. (1989) *Changing Culture*. London: IPM.

Wilmott, H. (2000) The place of culture in organization theory: introducing the morphogenetic approach. *Organization*, 7(1), 95–128.

Wilson, F. (2010) *Organizational Behaviour and Work. A critical introduction*, 3rd ed. Oxford: Oxford University Press.

Wilson, F. and Nutley, S. (2003) A critical look at staff appraisal: the case of women in Scottish universities. *Gender, Work and Organization*, 10(3), 301–19.

Wilson-Kovacs, M. D., Ryan, M. K. and Haslam, S. A. (2006) The glass-cliff: women's career paths in the UK private IT sector. *Equal Opportunities International*, 25(8), 674–87.

Wood, G., Szamosi, L. T. and Psychogios, A. (2009) 'International HRM', in T. Redman and A. Wilkinson, *Contemporary Human Resource Management*, 3rd ed. Harlow: FT/Prentice Hall.

Woodward, S. and Hendry, C. (2004) Leading and coping with change. *Journal of Change Management*, 4(3), 155–83.

Chapter 16

Axelrod, R. M. (1976) *The Structure of Decision: Cognitive maps of political elites*. Princeton, NJ: Princeton University Press.

Bajwa, D. S., Lewis, L. F., Pervan, G., Lai, V. S., Munkvold, B. E. and Schwabe, G. (2008) 'Factors in the global assimilation of collaborative information technologies: an exploratory investigation in five regions', *Journal of Management Information Systems*, 25/1: 131–166.

Barrett, M. I. (1999) Challenges of EDI adoption for electronic trading in the London insurance market, *European Journal of Information Systems*, 8, 1–15.

Bartunek, J. M. and Moch, M. K. (1994) Third-order organizational change and the Western mystical tradition, *Journal of Organizational Change Management*, 7(1), 24–41.

Bartunek, J. M. and Ringuest, J. L. (1989) Enacting new perspectives through work activities during organizational transformation, *Journal of Management Studies*, 26(6), 541–60.

Beer, M. and Nohria, N. (2000) Cracking the code of change. *Harvard Business Review*, 78(3), 133–41.

Bondarouk, T. V. (2004) *Using Group Learning to Enhance the Implementation of Information Technology: The results of discourse analysis*. Enschede: University of Twente, Enschede.

Bougon, M., Weick, K, and Binkhorst, D. (1977) Cognition in organizations: an analysis of the Utrecht Jazz Orchestra, *Administrative Science Quarterly*, 26, 606–39.

Constantinides, E. (2010) 'Connecting small and medium enterprises to the new consumer: The Web 2.0 as marketing tool', in P. Bharati, I. Lee and A. Chaudhury (eds) *Global Perspectives on Small and Medium Enterprises and Strategic Information Systems: International approaches*. Hershey, PA: IGI Group.

Dale, T. (1994) 'The evolution of interpersonal computing', in P. Lloyd (ed.) *Groupware in the 21st century. Computer supported cooperative working toward the millenium*. London: Adamantine Press.

Davenport, T. H. (1998) Putting the enterprise into the enterprise system, *Harvard Business Review*, 76(4), 121–31.

Davidson, E. (2002) Technology frames and framing: a socio-cognitive investigation of requirements determination, *MIS Quarterly*, 26, 329–58.

Deming (1986) *Out of the Crisis*. Cambridge, MA: MIT Center for Advanced Engineering Study.

Drucker, P. F. (1964) *Managing for Results: Economic tasks and risk-taking decisions*. New York: Harper & Row.

Dutton, J. E., Ashford, S. J., O'Neill, R. M. and Lawrence, K. A. (2001) Moves that matter: issue selling and organizational change, *Academy of Management Journal*, 44(4), 716–36.

Dutton, J. E. and Jackson, S. E. (1987) Categorizing strategic issues: links to organizational action, *Academy of Management Review*, 12(1), 76–90.

Ehrenhard (2009) *The Structuring of Managing by Results: A perspective on the practices of middle managers in the Dutch Central Government*. Enschede, the Netherlands: University of Twente.

Ellis, C. and Wainer, J. (1994) 'A conceptual model of groupware', in *Proceedings ACM 1994 Conference on Computer Supported Cooperative Work* (CSCW'94) 22–26 October. Chapel Hill, NC: ACM Press.

Fiol, C. M. (1993) Consensus, diversity, and learning in organizations. Working paper. University of Colorado at Denver.

Floyd, S. W. and Wooldridge, B. (1992) Managing strategic consensus: the foundation of effective implementation, *Academy of Management Executive*, 6, 27–39.

Fligstein, N. (1991) 'The structural transformation of American industry: an institutional account of the causes of diversification in the largest firms, 1919–1979', in W. W. Powell and P. J. DiMaggio (eds) *The New Institutionalism in Organizational Analysis*. Chicago, IL: University of Chicago Press.

Geertz, C. (1973) *The Interpretation of Cultures*. London: Fontana.

Giddens, A. (1986) *The Constitution of Society: Outline of the theory of structuration*. Berkeley: University of California Press.

Giles, J. (2005) Special report: Internet encyclopaedias go head to head, *Nature*, 438, 900–1.

Gioia, D. A., Donnellon, A. and Sims, H. P. (1989) Communication and cognition in appraisal: a tale of two paradigms, *Organization Studies*, 10(4), 503–30.

Goodhew, G. W., Cammock, P. A. and Hamilton, R. T. (2004) Managers' cognitive maps and intra-organizational performance differences, *Journal of Managerial Psychology*, 20(2), 124–36.

Greenwood R. and Hinings, C. R. (1996) Understanding radical organizational change: bringing together the old and the new institutionalism, *Academy of Management Review*, 21(4), 1022–54.

Hodgkinson, G. P. (1997) The cognitive analysis of competitive structures: a review and critique, *Human Relations*, 50, 625–54.

Hodgkinson, G. P. and Johnson, G. (1994) Exploring the mental models of competitive strategists: the case for a processual approach, *Journal of Management Studies*, 31(4), 525–51.

Hodgkinson, G. P. and Sparrow, P. R. (2006) *The Competent Organization: A psychological analysis of the strategic management process*. Buckingham: Open University Press.

Iivari, N. and Abrahamsson, P. (2002) The interaction between organizational subcultures and user-centred design – a case study of an implementation effort, *Proceedings of the 35th Hawaii International Conference on System Sciences*, 5–8 January 2002. Los Alamitos, CA: IEEE, HCIEG02.

Jenkins, M. and Johnson, G. (1997) Linking managerial cognition and organizational performance: a preliminary investigation using causal maps, *British Journal of Management*, 8, 577–90.

Kohli, R. and Kettinger, W. J. (2004) Informing the clan: controlling physicians' costs and outcomes, *MIS Quarterly*, 28(3), 363–94.

Kukafka, R., Johnson, S. B., Linfante, A. and Allegrante, J. (2003) Grounding a new information technology implementation framework in behavioral science: a systematic analysis of the literature on IT use, *Journal of Biomedical Informatics*, 36, 218–27.

Kumar, K. and Van Hillegersberg, J. (2000) ERP: experiences and evolution, *Communications of the ACM*, 43(4), 23–6.

Laukkanen, M. (1994) Comparative cause mapping of organizational cognitions, *Organization Science*, 5(3), 322–43.

Li, J. P. and Kishore, R. (2006) How robust is the UTAUT instrument? A multigroup invariance analysis in the context of acceptance and use of online community weblog systems. *Proceedings of the 2006 ACM SIGMIS CPR Conference*, 2006, 183–9.

Liker, J. K., Haddad, C. J. and Karlin, J. (1999) Perspectives on technology and work organization, *Annual Review of Sociology*, 25: 575–96.

Lord, R. G. and Maher, K. J. (1991) 'Cognitive theory in industrial and organizational psychology', in M. D. Dunnette and M. H. Leatta (eds) *Handbook of Industrial and Organizational Psychology 2*. Palo Alto, CA: Consulting Psychologists Press.

Mark, G. and Wulf, V. (1999) Changing interpersonal communication through groupware use, *Behaviour and Information Technology*, 18(5), 385–95.

Markus, M. L. and Benjamin, R. I. (1996) Change agentry: the next IS frontier, *MIS Quarterly*, 20(4), 385–407.

Markus, M. L. and Tanis, C. (2000) 'The enterprise systems experience: from adoption to success', in R. W. Zmud (ed.) *Framing the Domains of IT Research: Glimpsing the future through the past*. Cincinnati, OH: Pinnaflex Educational Resources.

McKinsey (2007) How businesses are using Web 2.0: a McKinsey global survey. *McKinsey Quarterly*, March.

McKinsey (2009) How companies are benefiting from Web 2.0: McKinsey global survey results. *McKinsey Quarterly*, September.

Orlikowski, W. J. and Gash, D. C. (1994) Technological frames: making sense of information technology in organizations, *ACM Transactions on Information Systems*, 2(2), 174–207.

Pfeffer, J. and Salancik, G. R. (1974) Organizational decision making as a political process: the case of a university budget, *Administrative Science Quarterly*, 19(2), 135–51.

Rao, H. (2009) *Market Rebels: How activitsts make or break radical innovations*. Princeton, NJ: Princeton University Press.

Simon, H. A. (1997) *Administrative Behavior: A study of decision-making processes in administrative organizations*, 4th ed. New York: Free Press.

Thomas, J. B., Clark, S. M. and Gioia, D. A. (1993) Strategic sensemaking and organizational performance: linkages among scanning, interpretation, action, and outcomes, *Academy of Management Journal*, 36(2), 239–70.

Venkatesh,V., Morris, M. G., Davis, G. B. and Davis, F. D. (2003) User acceptance of information technology: towards a unified view, *MIS Quarterly*, 27(3), 425–78.

Walsham, G. (1993) Reading the organization: metaphors and information management, *Journal of Information Systems*, 3, 33–46.

Yen, D. C., Wen, H. J., Lin, B. and Chou, D. C. (1999) Groupware: a strategic analysis and implementation, *Industrial Management and Data Systems*, 99(2), 64–70.

Young, G. O. (2009) *Can Enterprise Web 2.0 Survive the Recession? What vendor strategists should expect during the downturn*. Cambridge, MA: Forrester Research.

Chapter 17

Bach, S. (ed.) (2005) *Managing Human Resources: Personnel management in transition*. 4th ed. Oxford: Blackwell.

Barney, J. B. (1991) 'Firm resources and sustained competitive advantage', *Journal of Management*, 17: 99–120.

Barney, J. B. and Hesterly, W. (2007) *Strategic Management and Competitive Advantage: Concepts and cases*. Harlow: Prentice Hall/Pearson Education.

Becker, B. and Gerhart, B. (1996) 'The impact of human resource management on organizational performance: progress and prospects', *Academy of Management Journal*, 39/4: 77–801.

Beer, M., Lawrence, P., Mills, D. Q. and Walton, R. (1984) *Managing Human Assets*. New York: Free Press.

Boxall, P. and Purcell, J. (2003) *Strategy and Human Resource Management*. London: Palgrave Macmillan.

CIPD. (2009a) *Performance Management*. Survey report. London: CIPD.

CIPD. (2009b) *Recruitment, Retention and Turnover*. Annual survey report. London: CIPD.

Donnelly, R. (forthcoming a) 'The coalescence between synergies and conflicts of interest in a top consultancy firm: an analysis of the implications for consultants' attitudes and behaviours'.

Donnelly, R. (forthcoming b) 'Ambiguities and tensions over the creation and capture of value from consultancy services: an insight into the views of fee-earning HR consultants in a leading consultancy firm'.

Fombrun, C., Tichy, N. and Devanna, M. (eds) (1984) *Strategic Human Resource Management*. New York: Wiley.

Francis, H. and Keegan, A. (2006) 'The changing face of HRM: in search of balance', *Human Resource Management Journal*, 16/3: 231–249.

Galbreath, J. and Galvin, P. (2004) 'Which resources matter? A fine-grained test of the resource-based view of the firm', *Academy of Management Proceedings*, pL1-L6, 6p; (AN 13863763).

Gelade, G. and Ivery, M. (2003) 'The impact of human resource management and work climate on organizational performance', *Personnel Psychology*, 56: 383–404.

Guest, D. (1987) 'Human resource management and industrial relations', *Journal of Management Studies*, 24/5: 503–521.

Hendry, C. and Pettigrew, A. (1986) 'The practice of strategic human resource management', *Personnel Review*, 15: 3–8.

Kaufman, B. (2008) 'The development of HRM in historical and international perspective', in P. Boxall, J. Purcell and P. Wright (eds) *The Oxford Handbook of Human Resource Management*. Oxford: Oxford University Press.

Legge, K. (1995/2005) *Human Resource Management: Rhetorics and realities*. London: Palgrave Macmillan.

Lepak, D. and Snell, S. A. (2008) 'Employment subsystems and the HR architecture', in P. Boxall, J. Purcell and P. Wright (eds) *The Oxford Handbook of Human Resource Management*. Oxford: Oxford University Press.

Miles, R. E. and Snow, C. C. (1984) 'Organisation strategy, structure and process', *Academy of Management Review*, 2: 546–562.

Newell, S. (2005) 'Recruitment and selection', in S. Bach (ed.) *Managing Human Resources*. 4th ed. Oxford: Blackwell.

Paauwe, J. (2004) *HRM and Business Performance: Achieving long-term viability*. Oxford: Oxford University Press.

Peters, T. and Waterman, R. H. (1982) *In Search of Excellence*. New York: Harper & Row Publishers Inc.

Pfeffer, J. (1994) *Competitive Advantage through People*. Boston: Harvard Business School Press.

Porter, M. (1980) *Competitive Strategy*. New York: Free Press.

Purcell, J. (1995) 'Ideology and the end of institutional industrial relations', in C. Crouch and F. Traxler (eds) *Organized Industrial Relations in Europe: What future?* Aldershot: Avebury.

Schuler, R. S. and Jackson, S. E. (1987) 'Linking competitive strategies with human resource management practices', *Academy of Management Executive*, No. 3 (August).

Searle, R. (2003) *Selection and Recruitment: A critical text*. Milton Keynes: Open University Press.

Spence, J. R. and Keeping, L. M. (forthcoming) 'The impact of non-performance information on ratings of job performance: A policy-capturing approach', *Journal of Organizational Behavior*.

Storey, J. (1989) *New Perspectives on Human Resource Management*. London: Routledge.

Storey, J. (1995) *Human Resource Management: A critical text*. London: Routledge.

Storey, J. (ed.) (2007) *Human resource management: A critical text*. 3rd ed. London: Thompson.

Strauss, G. (2001) 'HRM in the United States: correcting some British impressions', *International Journal of Human Resource Management*, 12: 873–97.

Ulrich, D., Allen, J., Brockbank, W., Younger, J. and Nyman, M. (2009) *HR Transformation: Building human resources from the outside in*. New York: McGraw-Hill.

Chapter 18

Baron, D. P. (2006) *Business and Its Environment*. 5th ed. New Jersey: Pearson/Prentice Hall.

Bentham, J. (1789) *An Introduction to the Principles of Morals and Legislation*. Oxford: Clarendon Press.

Clegg, S., Kornberger, M. and Pitsis, T. (2008) *Managing and Organisations*. London: Sage.

French, R., Rayner, C., Rees, G. and Rumbles, S. (2009) *Organisational Behaviour*. Chichester: John Wiley.

Hamilton, V. L. and Kelman, H. C. (1990) *Crimes of Obedience: Towards a social psychology of authority and responsibility*. London: Yale University Press.

Hinrich, T. K. (2007) 'Follower propensity to commit crimes of obedience: the role of leadership beliefs', *Journal of Leadership and Organisational Studies*, No,14, August: 69–76.

Johnson, G., Scholes, K. and Whittington, R. (2008) *Exploring Corporate Strategy: Text and cases*, 8th edition. Harlow: *Financial Times*/Prentice Hall.

Milgram, S. (2005) *Obedience to Authority*. London: Pinter & Martin.

Mill, J. S. (1861) 'Utilitarianism', in J. S. Mill, J. Bentham and A. Ryan (eds) (1987) *Utilitarianism and Other Essays*. London: Penguin.

Rawls, J. (1971) *A Theory of Justice*. Cambridge, MA: Belknap Press.

Velasquez, M. G. (1998) *Business Ethics: Concepts and cases*. 4th ed. Englewood Cliffs, NJ: Prentice-Hall.

Velasquez, M. G., Moberg, D. J. and Cavanagh, G. F. (1983) 'Organisational statesmanship and dirty politics: ethical guidelines for the organisational politician', *Organisational Dynamics,* 11/3: 73–85.

Chapter 19

Gregg, P. and Wadsworth, J. (2010) 'Unemployment and inactivity in the 2008/2009 recession', *Economic and Labour Market Review*, Vol.4, No.8: 44–50. Available online at http://www.statistics.gov.uk/elmr/08_10/downloads/ELMR_Aug10.pdf.

Kersley, B., Alpin, C., Forth, J., Bryson, A., Bewley, H., Dix, G. and Oxenbridge, S. (2006) *Inside the Workplace: Findings from the 2004 Workplace Employment Relations Survey*. London: Routledge.

Index